AF685553

WITHDRAWN FROM
Business Library
Golden Gate University
536 Mission St.
San Francisco, CA 94105

# CURBING CORRUPTION IN ASIAN COUNTRIES: AN IMPOSSIBLE DREAM?

# RESEARCH IN PUBLIC POLICY ANALYSIS AND MANAGEMENT

## Series Editor: Lawrence R. Jones

Recent Volumes:

| | |
|---|---|
| Volume 1–9: | Research in Public Policy Analysis and Management |
| Volume 10: | Public Management: Institutional Renewal for the Twenty-First Century – Edited by Lawrence R. Jones and Fred Thompson |
| Volume 11A & B: | Learning from International Public Management Reform – Edited by Lawrence R. Jones, James Guthrie and Peter Steane |
| Volume 12: | The Transformative Power of Dialogue – Edited by Nancy C. Roberts |
| Volume 13: | Strategies for Public Management Reform – Edited by Lawrence R. Jones, Kuno Schedler and Riccardo Mussari |
| Volume 14: | Public Ethics and Governance: Standards and Practices in Comparative Perspective – Edited by Denis Saint-Martin and Fred Thompson |
| Volume 15: | Comparative Public Administration: The Essential Readings – Edited by Eric E. Otenyo and Nancy S. Lind |
| Volume 16: | Cultural Aspects of Public Management Reform – Edited by Kuno Schedler and Isabella Proeller |
| Volume 17: | Comparative Governance Reform in Asia: Democracy, Corruption, and Government Trust – Edited by Clay Wescott and Bidhya Bowornwathana |
| Volume 18: | The Many Faces of Public Management Reform in the Asia-Pacific Region – Edited by Clay Wescott, Bidhya Bowornwathana and L.R. Jones |
| Volume 19: | Public Administration Singapore Style – By Jon S. T. Quah |

RESEARCH IN PUBLIC POLICY ANALYSIS AND MANAGEMENT VOLUME 20

# CURBING CORRUPTION IN ASIAN COUNTRIES: AN IMPOSSIBLE DREAM?

BY

**JON S. T. QUAH**

*Anti-Corruption Consultant, Singapore*
*Vice-President*
*Asian Association for Public Administration*

UNIVERSITY LIBRARY
GOLDEN GATE UNIVERSITY
536 Mission Street
San Francisco, CA 94105-2968

Emerald

United Kingdom – North America – Japan
India – Malaysia – China

Emerald Group Publishing Limited
Howard House, Wagon Lane, Bingley BD16 1WA, UK

First edition 2011

Copyright © 2011 Emerald Group Publishing Limited

**Reprints and permission service**
Contact: booksandseries@emeraldinsight.com

No part of this book may be reproduced, stored in a retrieval system, transmitted in any form or by any means electronic, mechanical, photocopying, recording or otherwise without either the prior written permission of the publisher or a licence permitting restricted copying issued in the UK by The Copyright Licensing Agency and in the USA by The Copyright Clearance Center. No responsibility is accepted for the accuracy of information contained in the text, illustrations or advertisements. The opinions expressed in these chapters are not necessarily those of the Editor or the publisher.

**British Library Cataloguing in Publication Data**
A catalogue record for this book is available from the British Library

ISBN: 978-0-85724-819-0
ISSN: 0732-1317 (Series)

ISOQAR ENVIRONMENTAL SYSTEM ISO 14001 UKAS ENVIRONMENTAL MANAGEMENT 026 Certificate number 1985

Emerald Group Publishing Limited, Howard House, Environmental Management System has been certified by ISOQAR to ISO 14001:2004 standards

ISOQAR QUALITY ASSURED ISO 9001 UKAS QUALITY MANAGEMENT 026 Certificate number 1985

Awarded in recognition of Emerald's production department's adherence to quality systems and processes when preparing scholarly journals for print

INVESTOR IN PEOPLE

*For Stella*

# CONTENTS

# LIST OF TABLES

# LIST OF BOXES

# ABBREVIATIONS

| | |
|---|---|
| ACA | Anti-Corruption Agency |
| ACAC | Anti-Corruption Advisory Committee (Singapore) |
| ACB | Anti-Corruption Branch (Singapore) |
| | Anti-Corruption Bureau (India) |
| ACC | Anti-Corruption Committee (Thailand) |
| ACD | Anti-Corruption Department (Taiwan) |
| ACL | Anti-Corruption Law, 2006 (Mongolia) |
| ACO | Anti-Corruption Office (Hong Kong) |
| ACRC | Anti-Corruption Review Committee (Singapore) |
| | Anti-Corruption Civil Rights Commission (South Korea) |
| ADB | Asian Development Bank |
| AGO | Attorney-General's Office (Indonesia) |
| ANA | All Nippon Airways (Japan) |
| AVD | Administrative Vigilance Division (India) |
| BAI | Board of Audit and Inspection (South Korea) |
| BAPENAS | National Development Planning Agency (Indonesia) |
| BBC | British Broadcasting Corporation |
| BI | Bureau of Immigration (Philippines) |
| BIFGO | Board of Inspection and Follow-up of Government Operations (Thailand) |
| BIR | Bureau of Internal Revenue (Philippines) |
| BJP | Bharatiya Janata Party (India) |
| BMA | British Military Administration (Singapore) |
| BOA | Board of Audit (Japan) |
| BPK | State Auditing Agency (Indonesia) |
| CACS | Center of Anti-Corruption Studies (Hong Kong) |
| CAD | Commercial Affairs Department (Singapore) |
| CBI | Central Bureau of Investigation (India) |
| CCA | Counter-Corruption Act (Thailand) |
| CCC | Counter Corruption Commission (Thailand) |
| CCP | Chinese Communist Party (China) |
| CDA | Constitution Drafting Assembly (Thailand) |

| | |
|---|---|
| CDIC | Central Disciplinary Inspection Committee (China) |
| CDRM | Council for Democratic Reform under Constitutional Monarchy (Thailand) |
| CED | Corruption Elimination Department (Taiwan) |
| CEO | Chief Executive Officer |
| CET | Corruption Eradication Team (Indonesia) |
| CGA | Customs General Administration (Mongolia) |
| CID | Criminal Investigation Department (Singapore and Hong Kong) |
| CIO | Complaints and Investigations Office (Philippines) |
| CMEA | Council for Mutual Economic Assistance (Mongolia) |
| COA | Commission of Audit (Philippines) |
| CPA | Central Personnel Administration (Taiwan) |
| CPC | Commission for the Prevention of Corruption (South Korea) |
| CPCICP | Crime Prevention Center for International Crime Prevention |
| CPD | Corruption Prevention Department (Hong Kong)<br>Criminal Police Department (Mongolia) |
| CPI | Corruption Perceptions Index |
| CPIB | Corrupt Practices Investigation Bureau (Singapore) |
| CPIU | Corrupt Practices Inspection Unit (South Korea) |
| CRD | Community Relations Department (Hong Kong) |
| CSC | Civil Service Commission (Philippines and Thailand) |
| CVC | Central Vigilance Commission (India) |
| CVO | Central Vigilance Officer (India) |
| DECS | Department of Education, Culture and Sports (Philippines) |
| DENR | Department of Environment and Natural Resources (Philippines) |
| DepEd | Department of Education (Philippines) |
| DGEE | Department of Government Employee Ethics (Taiwan) |
| DJP | Democratic Justice Party (South Korea) |
| DPP | Democratic Progressive Party (Taiwan) |
| DPR | *Dewan Perwakilan Rakyat* (House of Representatives) (Indonesia) |
| DPWH | Department of Public Works and Highways (Philippines) |
| DSPE | Delhi Special Police Establishment (India) |
| ECD | Economic Crime Division (Mongolia) |
| ECPC | Economic Crime Prevention Center (Taiwan) |
| EDB | Economic Development Board (Singapore) |
| FEER | *Far Eastern Economic Review* |
| GAC | Governance Advisory Council (Philippines) |

| | |
|---|---|
| GDP | Gross Domestic Product |
| GDS | Governance and Decentralization Survey (Indonesia) |
| GIO | Government Information Office (Taiwan) |
| GPA | Government Procurement Act (Taiwan) |
| GPO | General Prosecutor's Office (Mongolia) |
| HKEDC | Hong Kong Ethics Development Center |
| HPO | High Prosecutors Office (Taiwan) |
| IAAC | Independent Authority against Corruption |
| IACC | Inter-Agency Anti-Graft Coordinating Council (Philippines) |
| IAS | Indian Administrative Service |
| ICAC | Independent Commission against Corruption (Hong Kong) |
| ICS | Indian Civil Service |
| ID | Investigation Department (Mongolia) |
| JHPC | Japan Highway Public Corporation |
| JMC | Jeverps Manufacturing Corporation (Philippines) |
| JPSPC | Japan Postal Services Public Corporation |
| KICAC | Korea Independent Commission against Corruption (South Korea) |
| KKN | *Korupsi, Kolusi dan Nepotisme* (Corruption, Collusion and Nepotism) |
| KMT | Koumintang (Taiwan) |
| KPK | *Komisi Pemberantasan Korupsi* (Corruption Eradication Commission) (Indonesia) |
| LAC | Law on Anti-Corruption, 1996 (Mongolia) |
| LDP | Liberal Democratic Party (Japan) |
| LTO | Land Transportation Office (Philippines) |
| MDU | Mongolian Democratic Union |
| MHA | Ministry of Home Affairs (India, Japan, and Singapore) |
| MJIB | Ministry of Justice Investigation Bureau (Taiwan) |
| MOD | Ministry of Defense (India, Mongolia, South Korea, and Thailand) |
| MOJ | Ministry of Justice (Taiwan) |
| MOS | Ministry of Supervision (China) |
| MP | Member of Parliament |
| MPO | Misdemeanors Punishment Ordinance (Hong Kong) |
| MPP | Mongolian People's Party |
| MPR | *Majelis Permusyawaratan Rakyat* (People's Consultative Assembly) (Indonesia) |
| MPRP | Mongolian People's Revolutionary Party |

| | |
|---|---|
| NACC | National Anti-Corruption Commission (Thailand) |
| NCCC | National Counter Corruption Commission (Thailand) |
| NCPB | National Corruption Prevention Bureau (China) |
| NDA | National Democratic Alliance (India) |
| NDP | National Democratic Party (Mongolia) |
| NPA | National Police Administration (Taiwan)<br>National Police Agency (Japan and South Korea) |
| NPSEA | National Public Service Ethics Act (Japan) |
| NSB | National Security Bureau (Taiwan) |
| NSCB | National Statistical Coordination Board (Philippines) |
| OCD | Organized Crime Division (Mongolia) |
| OECD | Organization for Economic Cooperation and Development |
| OMB | Office of the Ombudsman (Philippines) |
| ONCCC | Office of the National Counter Corruption Commission (Thailand) |
| OPEN | Online Procedure Enhancement for Civil Applications (South Korea) |
| PAD | People's Alliance for Democracy (Thailand) |
| PAGC | Presidential Anti-Graft Commission (Philippines)<br>Presidential Anti-Graft Committee (Philippines) |
| PAGCOM | Presidential Anti-Graft Committee (Philippines) |
| PAP | People's Action Party (Singapore) |
| PARGO | Presidential Agency on Reforms and Government Operations (Philippines) |
| PCAC | Presidential Complaints and Action Commission (Philippines) |
| PCAGC | Presidential Commission against Graft and Corruption (Philippines) |
| PCAO | Presidential Complaints and Action Office (Philippines) |
| PCAPE | Presidential Committee on Administrative Performance Efficiency (Philippines) |
| PCGG | Presidential Commission on Good Government (Philippines) |
| PCPEA | Presidential Committee on Public Ethics and Accountability (Philippines) |
| PD | Presidential Decree (Philippines) |
| PERC | Political Economic Risk Consultancy (Hong Kong) |
| PFCL | Political Funds Control Law (Japan) |
| PFFC | Presidential Fact-Finding Committee (Philippines) |
| PMO | Prime Minister's Office (Singapore and Thailand) |
| POBO | Prevention of Bribery Ordinance (Hong Kong) |

| | |
|---|---|
| POCA | Prevention of Corruption Act (India, Singapore) |
| POCO | Prevention of Corruption Ordinance (Singapore, Hong Kong) |
| PPO | Policy Planning Office (South Korea)<br>Public Prosecutors' Office (Japan, South Korea, and Taiwan) |
| PPP | People's Power Party (Thailand) |
| PRC | People's Republic of China |
| PRCB | Public Relations and Cooperation Bureau (South Korea) |
| PS21 | Public Service for the 21st Century (Singapore) |
| PSC | Public Service Commission (Singapore) |
| PSD | Public Service Division (Singapore) |
| PSPD | People's Solidarity for Participatory Democracy (South Korea) |
| PUB | Public Utilities Board (Singapore) |
| RHKPF | Royal Hong Kong Police Force |
| RIB | Report Inspection Bureau (South Korea) |
| SACs | Social Audit Committees (Afghanistan) |
| SADS | Secret Auto Destruct System (India) |
| SCS | Singapore Civil Service |
| SDP | Social Democratic Party (Mongolia) |
| SIA | Singapore Airlines |
| SID | Special Investigation Department (Japan) |
| SMD | Single Member District |
| SNTV | Single Nontransferable Vote |
| SPF | Singapore Police Force |
| SPO | Supreme Prosecutors Office (Taiwan) |
| SPP | Supreme People's Procuratorate (China) |
| SVC | State Vigilance Commission (India) |
| SWS | Social Weather Stations (Philippines) |
| TAN | Transparency and Accountability Network (Philippines) |
| TDB | Trade Development Board (Singapore) |
| TDP | Textbook Delivery Program (Philippines) |
| TDPO | Taipei District Prosecutors Office (Taiwan) |
| TGPTPK | Joint Team for the Eradication of Corruption (Indonesia) |
| TI | Transparency International (Berlin) |
| TRT | *Thai Rak Thai* (Thailand) |
| UNCAC | United Nations Convention against Corruption |
| UNDP | United Nations Development Programme |
| UNODC | United Nations Office for Drug Control |

# ABOUT THE AUTHOR

*Jon S. T. Quah, Ph.D.*, was a professor of Political Science at the National University of Singapore (NUS) and co-editor of the *Asian Journal of Political Science* until his retirement in June 2007. He is now an anti-corruption consultant based in Singapore, and a vice-president of the Asian Association for Public Administration. He was a Vice-Dean of the Faculty of Arts and Social Sciences at NUS (July 1990 to June 1991), Head of the Department of Political Science (1992–1998), and Coordinator of the European Studies Program (1990–1998). He was Acting Director of the Institute of Policy Studies in Singapore from January 1989 to June 1990.

He received his B.Soc.Sc. (Honors) and M.Soc.Sc. in Political Science from the University of Singapore in June 1969 and March 1971, respectively. He was a Fulbright-Hays scholar at the Department of Government, Florida State University, where he received his Ph.D. in Political Science majoring in Public Administration in June 1975. His visiting appointments include: the East-West Center in Honolulu, Hawaii; the Harvard-Yenching Institute and Harvard Institute of International Development; the Institute of Governmental Studies, University of California at Berkeley; the Stanford Program in International Legal Studies and the Asia-Pacific Research Center at Stanford University; the National Center for Development Studies, Australian National University; and the Department of Public Policy and Management, Shih Hsin University, in Taipei, Taiwan.

He has published widely on anticorruption strategies and civil service reform in Asian countries and on public administration in Singapore. His major publications include: *Government and Politics of Singapore* (co-editor with Chan Heng Chee and Seah Chee Meow) (Singapore: Oxford University Press, 1985 and 1987); *Friends in Blue: The Police and the Public in Singapore* (co-author with Stella R. Quah) (Singapore: Oxford University Press, 1987); *In Search of Singapore's National Values* (editor) (Singapore: Times Academic Press, 1990 and 1999); *Curbing Corruption in Asia: A Comparative Study of Six Countries* (Singapore: Eastern Universities Press, 2003); *Combating Corruption Singapore-Style: Lessons for Other Asian Countries*

(Baltimore: School of Law, University of Maryland, 2007); *Public Administration Singapore-Style* (Bingley, UK: Emerald Group Publishing, 2010) and *Taiwan's Anti-Corruption Strategy: Suggestions for Reform* (Baltimore: School of Law, University of Maryland, 2010). Details of his other publications are available from his website at http://www.jonstquah.com.

# FOREWORD

Just a generation ago few scholars, and even fewer international policy makers, had much to say about corruption. It was no secret; indeed, in all too many places corrupt dealings were the rule rather than the exception, practiced all too often in an atmosphere of impunity, intimidation, and at times violence. Yet because of resignation or fear at the grassroots, and vested interests at higher levels, analysis and action was rare. Those who brought up the "C-word" were seen as naïve or, worse, as troublemakers – best ignored, or silenced.

## A MOVEMENT COMES OF AGE

The view from 2011 is strikingly different. Corruption problems figure prominently not only in news reports of political and economic transformations but also as concerns in international development policy, foreign assistance, business strategy, and democratization. Once corruption was seen as a distraction, or indeed as a "functional" influence on developing societies; now, a strong consensus holds that it is bad for growth and democratization. Reform efforts are regularly launched around the world, often with great fanfare. Annual country rankings are eagerly anticipated in many quarters and viewed with apprehension in others. An immense policy and scholarly literature has sprung up on corruption, reform, and ways of dealing with and assessing both. An anticorruption movement that began in various places, and reflected disparate agendas, at the end of the Cold War has now matured into a significant international policy and advocacy force – one that arguably has reshaped basic ideas about development, accountability, and justice.

And yet, virtually all the claims about the state of corruption 20 years ago can still be made today. Indeed, in some societies problems have become far worse, with relatively tightly controlled dealings and clear-cut formal rules giving way to unstructured scrambles for wealth, influence, and the power to make the rules. Links between corruption and violence have become all too commonplace, and we now have an awareness of its connections to terror and trafficking groups in some very dangerous parts of the world. Perhaps most discouraging is the fact that anticorruption success stories remain few and far between. The accomplishments of Hong Kong and Singapore are well known, but transferring their examples to larger and more liberal societies has proved a challenge. Botswana gives us reasons for careful optimism, but some of its African neighbors are caught in heartbreaking spirals of poverty, official theft and exploitation. To the extent that corruption rankings are any indication, Japan and Belgium have improved their governance over time, but those are affluent societies that have long had relatively strong frameworks of institutions.

The agenda has changed, smart and courageous people have worked tirelessly, and we have learned a great deal. Why, after such momentous changes, does it seem that the reform task is still just beginning?

## THE VIEW FROM ASIA

To answer that question we need to comprehend breadth and depth – both a range of diverse cases and a wealth of detail. In this book Jon S. T. Quah provides that kind of account, based on years of study of 10 societies in Asia. Asia presents a challenging setting for analysis, yet an essential one. It is home to a third, or more, of humanity. The region presents both notable success stories and some of the most entrenched corrupt regimes. It includes societies that are small and unified, and others of staggering scale and complexity. Some Asian societies seem to have reconciled pervasive corruption with rapid growth, and even with democratization, seemingly in defiance of what we think we know about such things, while in others the detrimental effects of illicit connections between wealth and power are on display for all to see. All manner of aspirations and apprehensions are in play in Asia, with much of the future of the world economy and its modes of government at stake.

Better than any other region, then, Asia offers the opportunity to examine a limited number of cases in depth and detail, including at the same time critical variations and contrasts. The same can be said for anti-corruption strategies: Quah lays out three major approaches to corruption control – relying on laws alone; supplementing laws with several Anti-Corruption Agencies (ACAs); and delegating the enforcement of laws to a single, independent, and impartial ACA – and then tracks their origins and consequences across ten nations.

The results, as we might expect, diverge in important ways. More to the point, they are critically dependent on *policy context* – another way for saying that segments of government and the economy with corruption problems cannot somehow be extracted, "fixed," and put back into place. Institutions, processes of influence and accountability, incentive systems, and expectations – to name just a few contextual factors – shape the success or failure of the three anticorruption strategies, just as they do other kinds of policy and implementation. Solutions must be based on a detailed knowledge of that context, and of how it is evolving. Moreover, they will require resources, sustained support, and a considerable amount of time.

## THE GENERATION TO COME

There is no single such entity as "Asian corruption," any more than there is "Asian reform." Experiences in the region will need considerable adaptation when and if we seek to transplant them elsewhere. Quah's analysis yields no "cookbook" for reformers, nor was it intended to do so. Instead, it is an introduction to the sheer level of detail and the breadth of analysis, we will need to bring corruption under control anywhere. That sort of understanding will be essential for the next generation of reformers, who will have to deal not only with a certain amount of "anti-corruption fatigue" but also with an ever-more-integrated world economy in which people, money, and illicit commodities move at blinding speed. The processes, and perpetrators, of the next two decades' corruption problems may seem to operate everywhere, yet be based nowhere.

Still, the nation-state, its government apparatus, and its citizens and economic actors will be the foundation stones of whatever control strategies we choose or evolve. How they are likely to work, how we can assess their effects – and indeed, what we need to know just to ask those questions in intelligent ways – are all issues Jon Quah addresses in this book. The outcomes of the next generation of reform remain difficult to predict, but we may well conclude that while the anticorruption movement began in many places, it encountered its sternest tests, had many of its greatest successes, and learned some of its most sobering lessons in the societies and economies of Asia.

Michael Johnston
March 2011

# PREFACE

My interest in doing research on corruption in Asian countries can be traced to my participation in the "Bureaucratic Behavior in Asia" project initiated by the late Dr Raul P. de Guzman, Dean of the College of Public Administration of the University of the Philippines, in 1977 with funding from the International Development Research Center of Canada. I am grateful to Raul for inviting me and my former colleague, the late Dr David Seah Chee Meow, to be the two members of the Singapore research team in the seven country comparative study, which included also scholars from Hong Kong, Malaysia, Nepal, the Philippines, South Korea, and Thailand (Carino, 1986b).

After this initial foray in analyzing the anticorruption measures and police corruption in Singapore, I extended my research focus to a comparative analysis of the anticorruption measures in Indonesia, Malaysia, the Philippines, Singapore, and Thailand in 1982, and a comparative study of Hong Kong and Singapore in 1995 (Quah, 1978b, 1979, 1982a, 1982b, 1995, 2003d). I added South Korea and Taiwan when I was invited by Dr Larry Diamond of Stanford University to present a paper comparing the anticorruption agencies in these two countries and Thailand at the conference on "Institutionalizing Horizontal Accountability: How Democracies can fight Corruption and Abuse of Power" in Vienna, Austria on June 26–29, 1997 (Quah, 1997, 1999b, 1999d). Mongolia was added to the list when I was invited by Ms Pauline Tamesis of the United Nations Development Programme (UNDP) in New York to be the lead consultant for a UNDP mission to Ulaanbataar to prepare a national anticorruption plan for the Government of Mongolia in September and October 1998 (Quah, 1998, 1999a, 2003a).

I was invited to present a paper on "Anti-Corruption Strategies in Asian Countries: Some Lessons for India" at the India States' Reform Forum organized by the World Bank in New Delhi, India, on November 23–25, 2000. The preparation of this paper enhanced my interest and resulted in further research on corruption in India (Quah, 2003a, 2003c, 2008). My research on corruption in Indonesia was developed further in 2002 when I was invited by Sarwar Lateef of the World Bank to prepare a background paper on bureaucratic corruption in Indonesia (World Bank, 2004; Quah, 2002).

I spent my final sabbatical leave from the National University of Singapore (NUS) as a Visiting Scholar at the Asia-Pacific Research Center at Stanford University from January to June 2006 under the joint sponsorship of Dr Larry Diamond and Dr Donald Emmerson. My six months at Stanford were devoted to an analysis of corruption Japanese-style as I wanted to account for the paradoxical coexistence of a high level of grand corruption with a low level of petty corruption in Japan. Chapter 2 on Japan is the result of the research I did at Stanford.

In December 2008, I visited the Department of Government Employee Ethics (DGEE) in Taipei and the Taipei City Government's Department of Civil Service Ethics to learn about their anticorruption efforts. These visits enhanced my knowledge of anticorruption measures in Taiwan and resulted in the publication of a monograph on Taiwan's anticorruption strategy (Quah, 2010d).

This book is the result of many years of teaching and research on the anticorruption strategies in Asian countries, particularly of these 10 countries: Hong Kong SAR, India, Indonesia, Japan, Mongolia, the Philippines, Singapore, South Korea, Taiwan, and Thailand. I taught a module PS3246 Corruption and Governance in Asia for six years at the Department of Political Science at NUS. I have visited all these countries and studied their anticorruption measures during the past 34 years. In writing this book, I have received a great deal of help from many persons to whom I am very grateful. I would like to take this opportunity to acknowledge their kind assistance.

First, I would like to thank Dr Michael Johnston, the Charles A. Dana Professor of Political Science at Colgate University, for kindly agreeing to write the Foreword for this book despite his many commitments. I first met Michael when we both attended the Sixth International Anti-Corruption Conference in Cancun, Mexico, on November 22–25, 1993. Since that initial meeting, I have met Michael at many international conferences and have been inspired by and learnt a great deal from his numerous publications on corruption (Johnston, 1982, 1996, 1999, 2005a, 2005b, 2010a, 2010b).

Second, I am very grateful to many good friends for reading the draft chapters of the book. For the chapter on Japan, I would like to thank Minoru O'uchi, Director of Transparency International Japan and Visiting Professor, Advanced School, Institute of Developing Economies (Ajiken) in Tokyo, for providing me with the data on political scandals in Japan from 1948 to 2008, and for his useful comments on the chapter. The chapter on India benefited greatly from the comments provided by Dr Krishna K. Tummala, Professor of Public Administration at Kansas State University. Dr Thomas J. Bellows, Professor of Political Science at the University of Texas at San Antonio provided constructive feedback on the chapters on Singapore and Taiwan. I would also like to acknowledge my gratitude to Mr Soh Kee Hian, the former Director of the Corrupt Practices Investigation Bureau in Singapore, for commenting on my research papers on corruption in Singapore and for sharing two of his conference papers with me (Soh, 2008a, 2008b).

I would like to thank Dr Sonny Lo Shiu Hing, Professor and Associate Dean (Research and Postgraduate Education), Faculty of Arts and Sciences, Hong Kong Institute of Education, for his incisive comments on the chapter on Hong Kong SAR. Dr Likhit Dhiravegin, former Professor of Political Science at Thammasat University in Bangkok was kind enough to review the chapter on Thailand and shared with me his extensive knowledge of Thai politics. Similarly, Dr Jon S. Jun, Professor Emeritus of Public Administration at California State University East Bay, provided insightful comments on the chapter on South Korea. I am also very grateful to my former colleague, Dr Leo Suryadinata, Professor and Director of the Chinese Heritage Center at Nanyang Technological University in Singapore for his detailed and helpful comments on the chapter on Indonesia.

For the onerous and sometimes difficult task of collecting relevant data on the anticorruption measures in the 10 Asian countries, I am very grateful to the various anticorruption agencies that provided useful and comprehensive information on their websites. As the English website of Mongolia's Independent Authority Against Corruption (IAAC) did not provide the required information on the IAAC's budget and personnel and the salaries of the political leaders and civil servants, I wrote to Mr. Batzorig Badam, Head of the Research and Analysis Division of the IAAC for these data. I would like to thank him for sending me the required data that enabled me to update my analysis in the chapter on Mongolia.

I would like to acknowledge my gratitude to Dr Yu-Ying Kuo, Professor and Chair, Department of Public Policy and Management, Shih Hsin University in Taipei, Taiwan, for contacting the Ministry of Justice Investigation Bureau (MJIB) and the DGEE and sending me the data on their budget and personnel from 2008 to 2010. I am grateful to Ms Ming-Huei Cheng, Director of Social Marketing, Transparency International Chinese Taipei for extracting the MJIB's budget for its anticorruption activities from the MJIB's Chinese website for me. I would also like to thank Ms Lin Ya-Feng, Minister without Portfolio in the Examination Yuan in Taipei for giving me a copy of the Ministry of Justice's *Government*

*Employee Ethics White Paper 2009*. Thanks are also due to my former student, Mr Paul Lim, and his fiancée, Ms Jasmine Goh, for translating some documents in Chinese into English for the chapter on Taiwan.

For the chapter on Thailand, I am thankful to Mr Nitiphan Prachuabmoh of the National Anti-Corruption Commission (NACC) in Bangkok for facilitating my access to his colleague, Mr Ryan Keeratitha-nachaiyos, Communication Specialist at the NACC, who sent me the data on the personnel of the NACC and its predecessor, the National Counter Corruption Commission (NCCC) from 1999 to 2009. Finally, I am grateful to my former colleague, Dr Kilkon Ko, for providing me with current information on civil servants' salaries in South Korea.

Apart from Professor Michael Johnston's works, I have also benefited from the publications of two close friends, Dr Leslie Palmier, former Reader in Sociology and Director of the Center for Development Studies at the University of Bath, and Dr Gerald E. Caiden, Professor of Public Administration at the University of Southern California. My favorite book on corruption in Asian countries is Leslie's pioneering comparative study of the anticorruption measures in Hong Kong, India, and Indonesia (Palmier, 1985). I have also learnt a great deal from Gerald's many publications on corruption (Caiden & Caiden, 1977; Caiden, 1988, 1997, 2001; Caiden, Dwivedi, & Jabbra, 2001).

In conducting the research for this book, I have relied on the excellent collection of books and journal articles on corruption in Asian countries in the NUS Central Library. I would like to acknowledge the assistance and support provided by Mr Tim Yap Fuan, Principal Librarian, Special Collections, and Mr Patrick Lye Siew Kuan, Principal Librarian, Loans and Membership Department. My research has also been greatly facilitated by Transparency International's *Daily Corruption News*, which provides the latest press reports on corruption scandals around the world five times a week.

I owe a special debt of gratitude to Dr Lawrence R. Jones, George F.A. Wagner Chair Professor of Public Management at the Naval Postgraduate School in Monterey, California, and Series Editor of the Research in Public Policy and Management (RPPAM) for accepting this book for publication as Volume 20 of the RPPAM. It has been a great pleasure working with Larry again. I have benefited tremendously from his careful reading of all the chapters and his constructive and wise feedback. I would also like to thank Ms Stephanie Hull, Development Editor, Emerald Group Publishing, for her kind advice and professional assistance in facilitating the publication of this book.

Last, but certainly not least, I wish to record my appreciation to my family for their support and encouragement of my academic pursuits. I am grateful to my late father, Quah Wee Khiam, my mother, Chew Chye Guat, my sister, Jill, my brothers Jan and Jeffrey, and my wife, Stella, for their love and support. Above all, I am indebted to Stella, who was a Professor of Sociology at NUS, for patiently reading and commenting on my research on corruption in Asian countries and other topics during our 40 years of marriage. Even though we have not co-authored a book since 1988, this book could not have been written without her constant support and encouragement. This explains why I am also dedicating this book to her.

Jon S. T. Quah
Singapore
March 2011

# CHAPTER 1

# CORRUPTION IN ASIAN COUNTRIES: CAUSES, CONSEQUENCES AND CONTROL PATTERNS

> Corruption has many damaging effects: weakened national institutions, inequitable social services, and blatant injustice in the courts – along with widespread economic inefficiency and unchecked environmental exploitation. And it hits hardest at the poor – who often depend heavily on public services and the natural environment and are least able to pay bribes for essential services that should be theirs by right.
>
> – UNDP (2008, p. 1)

> We need to reinforce the notion that there is nothing "tenuous" about the link between corruption and death. It is predictable that one will lead to the other whenever a government official is performing a health, safety, or security function. Millions of government employees perform these functions. Corruption kills.
>
> – W. K. Black (2007, p. 453)

## THE PROBLEM OF CORRUPTION

The above quotations highlight the adverse consequences of corruption in many countries around the world today. Indeed, the research taboo on corruption, which Gunnar Myrdal identified in 1968, no longer exists, and the silence on the "C" word (corruption) in the World Bank was broken by James Wolfensohn in his famous October 1996 speech, which focused on the negative consequences of the "cancer of corruption" on the World Bank's aid programs.

Corruption is a serious problem in many Asian countries today, judging from the many press reports and exposes of corruption scandals in these countries in recent years. In its cover story on "Corruption: The Asian Lubricant" in September 1974, the *Far Eastern Economic Review* (FEER) observed: "With pathetically few exceptions, the countries in this region are so riddled with corruption that the paying of 'tea money' has become almost a way of life." More than two decades later, in another cover story on "Corruption: Reform's Dark Side" in the 20 March 1997 issue of the FEER, Aparisim Ghosh (1997, p. 18) observed that "from Pakistan to Japan, corruption was the year's biggest story" in 1996.

Beginning from 1995, the Berlin-based nongovernmental organization, Transparency International (TI), has published an annual Corruption Perceptions Index (CPI) that is based on at least three independent surveys of the perceptions of selected groups of businessmen, risk analysts, and the general public, on the extent of corruption in many countries (Lambsdorff, 2008). The sample size of TI's CPI has increased from 41 countries in 1995 to 178 countries in 2010. While the CPI has enhanced the public awareness of corruption around the world, it is not perfect and has several limitations.[1] Table 1.1 shows the ranking and scores of various Asian countries on the CPI from 1995 to 2010. From Table 1.1, Singapore is perceived as the least corrupt country and Indonesia is perceived as the most corrupt country in Asia (in 1995, 1997–2000), followed by Bangladesh (in 1996, 2001–2002), Myanmar (in 2003–2008), and Afghanistan (in 2009). In 2010, Singapore was ranked joint first with Denmark and New Zealand with a score of 9.3 among the 178 countries surveyed.

Table 1.2 shows the Political and Economic Risk Consultancy's (PERC) ranking of 12–13 Asian countries. The number of countries was increased to 16 in the 2009 and 2010 PERC surveys with the inclusion of Australia, Cambodia, and the United States. PERC's ranking generally confirms the CPI's ranking as Singapore is also ranked as the least corrupt Asian country and Indonesia is ranked as the most corrupt Asian country except in 1996, 2001, 2007, and 2008.

## FROM RESEARCH TABOO TO GROWTH INDUSTRY

Ronald Wraith and Edgar Simpkins published their pioneering book, *Corruption in Developing Countries* in 1963, when it was quite difficult to do research on such a sensitive topic. Despite the book's title, they confined their analysis to Britain and Nigeria because of their familiarity with these countries (Wraith & Simpkins, 1963, p. 9). However, their "moralizing approach" of viewing corruption as an immoral activity with negative consequences for those individuals involved and the society is not useful as

***Table 1.1.*** Performance of Asian Countries on the Corruption Perceptions Index, 1995–2010.

| Country | 1995 | 1996 | 1997 | 1998 | 1999 | 2000 | 2001 | 2002 |
|---|---|---|---|---|---|---|---|---|
| Singapore | **3** (9.26) | **7** (8.80) | **9** (8.66) | **7** (9.1) | **7** (9.1) | **6** (9.1) | **4** (9.2) | **5** (9.3) |
| Hong Kong | **17** (7.12) | **18** (7.01) | **18** (7.28) | **16** (7.8) | **15** (7.7) | **15** (7.7) | **14** (7.9) | **14** (8.2) |
| Japan | **20** (6.72) | **17** (7.05) | **21** (6.57) | **25** (5.8) | **25** (6.0) | **23** (6.4) | **21** (7.1) | **20** (7.1) |
| Taiwan | **25** (5.08) | **29** (4.98) | **31** (5.02) | **29** (5.3) | **28** (5.6) | **28** (5.5) | **27** (5.9) | **29** (5.6) |
| Malaysia | **23** (5.28) | **26** (5.32) | **32** (5.01) | **29** (5.3) | **32** (5.1) | **36** (4.8) | **36** (5.0) | **33** (4.9) |
| Mongolia | NA | NA | NA | NA | **43** (4.3) | NA | NA | NA |
| South Korea | **27** (4.29) | **27** (5.02) | **34** (4.29) | **43** (4.2) | **50** (3.8) | **48** (4.0) | **42** (4.2) | **40** (4.5) |
| Sri Lanka | NA | NA | NA | NA | NA | NA | NA | **52** (3.7) |
| Thailand | **34** (2.79) | **37** (3.33) | **39** (3.06) | **61** (3.0) | **68** (3.2) | **60** (3.2) | **61** (3.2) | **64** (3.2) |
| Philippines | **36** (2.77) | **44** (2.69) | **40** (3.05) | **55** (3.3) | **54** (3.6) | **69** (2.8) | **65** (2.9) | **77** (2.6) |
| China | **40** (2.16) | **50** (2.43) | **41** (2.88) | **52** (3.5) | **58** (3.4) | **63** (3.1) | **57** (3.5) | **59** (3.5) |
| India | **35** (2.78) | **46** (2.63) | **45** (2.75) | **66** (2.9) | **72** (2.9) | **69** (2.8) | **71** (2.7) | **71** (2.7) |
| Pakistan | **39** (2.25) | **53** (1.00) | **48** (2.53) | **71** (2.7) | **87** (2.2) | NA | **79** (2.3) | **77** (2.6) |
| Vietnam | NA | NA | **43** (2.79) | **74** (2.5) | **75** (2.6) | **76** (2.5) | **75** (2.6) | **85** (2.4) |
| Indonesia | **41** (1.94) | **45** (2.65) | **46** (2.72) | **80** (2.0) | **96** (1.7) | **85** (1.7) | **88** (1.9) | **96** (1.9) |
| Bangladesh | NA | **51** (2.29) | NA | NA | NA | NA | **91** (0.4) | **102** (1.2) |
| Sample size | 41 | 54 | 52 | 85 | 99 | 90 | 91 | 102 |

| Country | 2003 | 2004 | 2005 | 2006 | 2007 | 2008 | 2009 | 2010 |
|---|---|---|---|---|---|---|---|---|
| Singapore | **5** (9.4) | **5** (9.3) | **5** (9.4) | **5** (9.4) | **4** (9.3) | **4** (9.2) | **3** (9.2) | **1** (9.3) |
| Hong Kong | **14** (8.0) | **16** (8.0) | **15** (8.3) | **15** (8.3) | **14** (8.3) | **12** (8.1) | **12** (8.2) | **13** (8.4) |
| Japan | **21** (7.0) | **24** (6.9) | **21** (7.3) | **17** (7.6) | **17** (7.5) | **18** (7.3) | **17** (7.7) | **17** (7.8) |
| Macao | NA | NA | NA | **26** (6.6) | **34** (5.70 | **43** (5.4) | **43** (5.3) | **46** (5.0) |
| Taiwan | **30** (5.7) | **35** (5.6) | **32** (5.9) | **34** (5.9) | **34** (5.7) | **39** (5.7) | **37** (5.6) | **33** (5.8) |
| Malaysia | **37** (5.2) | **39** (5.0) | **39** (5.1) | **44** (5.0) | **43** (5.1) | **47** (5.1) | **56** (4.5) | **56** (4.4) |
| South Korea | **50** (4.3) | **47** (4.5) | **40** (5.0) | **42** (5.1) | **43** (5.1) | **40** (5.6) | **39** (5.5) | **39** (5.4) |

*Table 1.1.* (*Continued*)

| Country | 2003 | 2004 | 2005 | 2006 | 2007 | 2008 | 2009 | 2010 |
|---|---|---|---|---|---|---|---|---|
| Bhutan | NA | NA | NA | **32** (6.0) | **46** (5.0) | **45** (5.2) | **49** (5.0) | **36** (5.7 |
| China | **66** (3.4) | **71** (3.4) | **78** (3.2) | **70** (3.3) | **72** (3.5) | **72** (3.6) | **79** (3.6) | **78** (3.5) |
| India | **83** (2.8) | **90** (2.8) | **88** (2.9) | **70** (3.3) | **72** (3.5) | **85** (3.4) | **84** (3.4) | **87** (3.3) |
| Thailand | **70** (3.3) | **64** (3.6) | **59** (3.8) | **63** (3.6) | **84** (3.3) | **80** (3.5) | **84** (3.4) | **78** (3.5) |
| Sri Lanka | **66** (3.4) | **67** (3.5) | **78** (3.2) | **84** (3.1) | **94** (3.2) | **92** (3.2) | **97** (3.1) | **91** (3.2) |
| Mongolia | NA | **85** (3.0) | **85** (3.0) | **99** (2.8) | **99** (3.0) | **102** (3.0) | **120** (2.7) | **116** (2.7) |
| Vietnam | **100** (2.4) | **102** (2.6) | **107** (2.6) | **111** (2.6) | **123** (2.6) | **121** (2.7) | **120** (2.7) | **116** (2.7) |
| Nepal | NA | **90** (2.8) | **117** (2.5) | **121** (2.5) | **131** (2.5) | **121** (2.7) | **143** (2.3) | **146** (2.2) |
| Philippines | **92** (2.5) | **102** (2.6) | **117** (2.5) | **121** (2.5) | **131** (2.5) | **141** (2.3) | **139** (2.4) | **134** (2.4) |
| Pakistan | **92** (2.5) | **129** (2.1) | **144** (2.1) | **142** (2.2) | **138** (2.4) | **134** (2.5) | **139** (2.4) | **143** (2.3) |
| Indonesia | **122** (1.9) | **133** (2.0) | **137** (2.2) | **130** (2.4) | **143** (2.3) | **126** (2.6) | **111** (2.8) | **110** (2.8) |
| Bangladesh | **133** (1.3) | **145** (1.5) | **158** (1.7) | **156** (2.0) | **162** (2.0) | **147** (2.1) | **139** (2.4) | **134** (2.4) |
| Cambodia | NA | NA | **130** (2.3) | **151** (2.1) | **162** (2.0) | **166** (1.8) | **158** (2.0) | **154** (2.1) |
| Laos | NA | NA | **77** (3.3) | **111** (2.6) | **168** (1.9) | **151** (2.0) | **158** (2.0) | **154** (2.1) |
| Afghanistan | NA | NA | **117** (2.5) | NA | **172** (1.8) | **176** (1.5) | **179** (1.3) | **176** (1.4) |
| Myanmar | **129** (1.6) | **142** (1.7) | **155** (1.8) | **160** (1.9) | **179** (1.4) | **178** (1.3) | **178** (1.4) | **176** (1.4) |
| Sample size | 133 | 146 | 159 | 163 | 180 | 180 | 180 | 178 |

*Source*: Compiled from Transparency International's Corruption Perceptions Index from 1995–2010, available at http://www.transparency.org.

*Notes*: The scores are indicated within brackets and range from 0 (most corrupt) to 10 (least corrupt). NA refers to not available. **Bold** refers to indicate the CPI rank.

**Table 1.2.** Performance of Selected Asian Countries on the PERC Surveys on Corruption, 1995–2010.

| Country | 1995 | 1996 | 1997 | 1998 | 1999 | 2000 | 2001 | 2002 |
|---|---|---|---|---|---|---|---|---|
| Singapore | **1** (1.20) | **1** (1.09) | **1** (1.05) | **1** (1.43) | **1** (1.55) | **1** (0.71) | **1** (0.83) | **1** (0.90) |
| Hong Kong | **3** (2.80) | **3** (2.79) | **2** (3.03) | **2** (2.74) | **2** (4.06) | **2** (2.49) | **3** (3.77) | **3** (3.33) |
| Japan | **2** (2.00) | **2** (1.93) | **3** (4.60) | **3** (5.00) | **3** (4.25) | **3** (3.90) | **2** (2.50) | **2** (3.25) |
| Malaysia | **6** (4.60) | **4** (5.00) | **4** (5.80) | **5** (5.38) | **6** (7.50) | **4** (5.50) | **4** (6.00) | **4** (5.71) |
| Taiwan | **5** (4.20) | **6** (5.53) | **5** (5.96) | **4** (5.20) | **5** (6.92) | **5** (6.89) | **4** (6.00) | **6** (5.83) |
| South Korea | **4** (4.00) | **5** (5.16) | **8** (7.71) | **7** (7.12) | **8** (8.20) | **7** (8.33) | **6** (7.00) | **5** (5.75) |
| Philippines | **8** (6.60) | **9** (6.95) | **6** (6.50) | **8** (7.17) | **4** (6.71) | **8** (8.67) | **9** (9.00) | **8** (8.00) |
| Thailand | **7** (5.90) | **7** (6.55) | **7** (7.49) | **11** (8.29) | **7** (7.57) | **6** (8.20) | **8** (8.55) | **10** (8.89) |
| China | **10** (7.3) | **12** (8.0) | **10** (8.06) | **6** (6.97) | **10** (9.0) | **9** (9.11) | **7** (7.88) | **7** (7.00) |
| Vietnam | NA | **11** (7.78) | **9** (8.00) | **10** (8.25) | **9** (8.50) | **10** (9.20) | **12** (9.75) | **9** (8.25) |
| India | **9** (7.00) | **8** (6.86) | **11** (8.20) | **9** (7.40) | **11** (9.17) | **11** (9.50) | **11** (9.67) | **11** (9.17) |
| Indonesia | **10** (7.30) | **10** (7.69) | **12** (8.67) | **12** (8.95) | **12** (9.91) | **12** (9.88) | **11** (9.67) | **12** (9.92) |
| Sample size | 11 | 12 | 12 | 12 | 12 | 12 | 12 | 12 |

| Country | 2003 | 2004 | 2005 | 2006 | 2007 | 2008 | 2009 | 2010 |
|---|---|---|---|---|---|---|---|---|
| Singapore | **1** (0.38) | **1** (0.50) | **1** (0.65) | **1** (1.30) | **1** (1.20) | **1** (1.13) | **1** (1.07) | **1** (1.42) |
| Hong Kong | **2** (3.61) | **3** (3.60) | **3** (3.50) | **3** (3.13) | **2** (1.87) | **2** (1.80) | **2** (1.89) | **3** (2.67) |
| Australia | NA | NA | NA | NA | NA | NA | **3** (2.40) | **2** (2.28) |
| USA | NA | NA | NA | NA | NA | NA | **4** (2.89) | **4** (3.42) |
| Japan | **3** (4.50) | **2** (3.00) | **2** (3.46) | **2** (3.01) | **3** (2.10) | **3** (2.25) | **5** (3.99) | **5** (3.49) |
| Macao | NA | NA | NA | **4** (4.78) | **4** (5.18) | **4** (3.30) | **7** (5.84) | **6** (4.96) |
| South Korea | **4** (5.50) | **5** (6.67) | **6** (6.50) | **5** (5.44) | **8** (6.3) | **5** (5.65) | **6** (4.64) | **7** (5.98) |
| Malaysia | **5** (6.00) | **6** (7.33) | **7** (6.80) | **7** (6.13) | **6** (6.25) | **6** (6.37) | **10** (6.7) | **9** (6.47) |
| Taiwan | **6** (6.33) | **4** (6.10) | **4** (6.15) | **6** (5.91) | **5** (6.23) | **7** (6.55) | **9** (6.47) | **8** (6.28) |
| Philippines | **7** (7.67) | **9** (8.33) | **12** (8.80) | **11** (7.80) | **13** (9.40) | **13** (9.00) | **11** (7.0) | **13** (8.06) |
| China | **8** (8.33) | **7** (7.48) | **9** (7.68) | **9** (7.58) | **7** (6.29) | **10** (7.98) | **8** (6.16) | **10** (6.52) |
| Thailand | **9** (8.75) | **8** (7.80) | **8** (7.20) | **10** (7.64) | **11** (8.03) | **12** (8.00) | **15** (7.63) | **12** (7.60) |

***Table 1.2.*** *(Continued)*

| Country | 2003 | 2004 | 2005 | 2006 | 2007 | 2008 | 2009 | 2010 |
|---|---|---|---|---|---|---|---|---|
| Vietnam | **10** (8.83) | **10** (8.71) | **11** (8.65) | **12** (7.91) | **10** (7.54) | **9** (7.75) | **12** (7.11) | **14** (8.07) |
| India | **11** (9.30) | **11** (8.90) | **10** (8.63) | **8** (6.76) | **9** (6.67) | **8** (7.25) | **13** (7.21) | **11** (7.18) |
| Cambodia | NA | NA | NA | NA | NA | NA | **14** (7.25) | **15** (9.10) |
| Indonesia | **12** (9.33) | **12** (9.25) | **13** (9.10) | **13** (8.16) | **11** (8.03) | **11** (7.98) | **16** (8.32) | **16** (9.27) |
| Sample size | 12 | 12 | 13 | 13 | 13 | 13 | 16 | 16 |

*Sources*: PERC (2001, 2008, p. 7); Hussain (2009, p. B5); and *Straits Times* (2010a).
*Notes*: The scores are indicated within brackets and range from 0 (least corrupt) to 10 (most corrupt). NA refers to not available. **Bold** refers to indicate the CPI rank.

their approach is subjective, and they have not provided relevant evidence for the negative effects of corruption. Colin Leys (1989, p. 53) has aptly pointed out that the subject of corruption deserves "a more systematic and open-minded approach" than that adopted by Wraith and Simpkins.

In 1968, the Swedish economist, Gunnar Myrdal, observed that corruption was "almost taboo as a research topic" and was "rarely mentioned in scholarly discussions of the problems of government and planning." He attributed the research taboo on corruption to "diplomacy in research," which avoided such embarrassing questions as corruption by "ignoring the problems of attitudes and institutions." He illustrated how the taboo could be broken by discussing the "folklore," causes and anticorruption campaigns in South Asian countries (Myrdal, 1968, pp. 938–939).

As indicated in the Preface, I began doing research on corruption in Singapore in 1977 through my participation in a seven-country project on "Negative Bureaucratic Behavior in Asian Countries," which was funded by the International Development Research Center (IDRC) of Canada. The purpose of this project was to analyze "the causes, structural patterns and consequences of graft and corruption" in Hong Kong, Malaysia, Nepal, Philippines, Singapore, South Korea, and Thailand (de Guzman, 1986, p. iv). However, as it was not politically correct to use the term "corruption" at that time, the project team replaced it with "negative bureaucratic behavior" in its application for research funding from the IDRC.

In his farewell presentation at the World Bank on December 9, 2008, Daniel Kauffman (2008) described the period 1980–1995 as the "Corruption Prohibition" era in the World Bank because the corruption taboo was only lifted during the mid-to-late 1990s. The World Bank's silence on corruption was only broken by its then president, James Wolfensohn, in his famous October 1996 address at the Annual Meeting of the World Bank Group, when he identified the negative consequences of the "cancer of corruption" on the World Bank's aid programs.

However, the World Bank did not address the impact of corruption on its lending operations. Indeed, "the 'C word' did not appear in official Bank reports prior to the Wolfensohn initiative; nor was there an accepted strategy for dealing with corruption in lending operations" (Volcker et al., 2007, p. 7; Mauro, 2007, p. 68). Wolfensohn revealed that:

> When I came to the World Bank, I was told that there was one word I could not use, which was the "C" word, the "C" word being "corruption". Corruption, you see, was identified with politics, and if I got into that I would have a terrible time with my Board. (quoted in Krastev, 2000, p. 31)

Accordingly, the World Bank had to depoliticize corruption first before it could address the problem. Wolfensohn visited several countries and redefined the "C" word in 1996 as a socioeconomic issue rather than a political issue (Krastev, 2000, p. 32). In September 1997, the World Bank's Board of Executive Directors endorsed a broad anticorruption strategy and the Department of Institutional Integrity was only established in 2001 (Volcker et al., 2007, p. 7).

Fortunately, this research taboo on corruption in Asian countries no longer exists because of the great deal of research conducted since the 1980s and the 1990s. In contrast to the dearth of such research in the 1960s, research on Asian corruption has mushroomed into a growth industry since the 1990s as can be seen from the studies cited in this book. Indeed, the global anticorruption industry has channeled "hundreds of millions of dollars in anti-corruption assistance projects" in more than 100 countries (Sampson, 2009, p. 170). Moreover, since the end of the Cold War, the number of news stories on corruption in the *Economist,* the *Financial Times* and the *New York Times* "quadrupled between 1984 and 1995" (Leiken, 1996/1997, p. 58). According to Ivan Krastev (2000, p. 25):

> Between 1982 and 1987 the word "corruption" appeared on average 229 times a year on the pages of *The Economist* and the *Financial Times*. In the period between 1989 and 1992 "corruption" appeared on average 502 times a year. In 1993 the word was mentioned 1,076 times in the two most respected European publications on politics and finance. In 1994 corruption was mentioned 1,099 times, and in 1995 a total of 1,246 times.

This "global corruption epidemic" is the result of two trends: (1) the end of the Cold War and the emergence of civil societies have contributed to the disclosure of corruption scandals in many countries, and (2) the trend toward democracy and markets, which has paradoxically "increased both the opportunities for graft and the likelihood of exposure" (Leiken, 1996/1997, p. 58). In addition to these trends, Hess and Dunfee (2000, p. 9) contend that the high-profile corruption scandals in South Korea, Italy, Brazil, Venezuela, Mexico, Spain, and Ecuador in the 1990s also "increased the attention placed on corruption."

## WHAT IS CORRUPTION?

It is necessary to define "corruption" given the plethora of definitions and the various meanings given to it.[2] For example, Gerald E. Caiden (1988, p. 5) has identified the 20 "most commonly recognized" forms of corruption. Similarly, L. Michael Hager (1973, pp. 200–201) has described the "great variety of sins" of corruption in his analysis of corruption in India by referring to the 34 types of corrupt practices reported by the Central Vigilance Commission (CVC) from 1964 to 1966. Hence, it is not surprising that Michael Johnston (1991, p. 48) has described "studying corruption" as "a tricky business" because "definitions are controversial, and solid evidence is often elusive."

Perhaps the most useful way of classifying the many contemporary social science definitions of corruption is Arnold J. Heidenheimer's threefold classification of public-office-centered, market-centered, and public-interest-centered definitions (Heidenheimer, Johnston, & LeVine, 1989, pp. 8–11). Public-office-centered definitions of corruption focus on the concept of the public office and describe corruption in terms of the deviations from the norms binding upon its incumbents. An example of a public-office-centered definition is that provided by Joseph S. Nye (1967, p. 419), who defines corruption as

> behavior which deviates from the normal duties of a public role because of private-regarding (family, close private clique), pecuniary or status gains; or violates rules against the exercise of certain types of private-regarding influence. This includes such behavior as bribery (use of reward to pervert the judgement of a person in a position of trust); nepotism (bestowal or patronage by reason of ascriptive relationship rather than merit); and misappropriation (illegal appropriation of public resources for private-regarding influence.

While Nye's definition is useful, it should be noted that in those countries where corruption is a way of life, corrupt behavior is not viewed as deviant as it is practised by the majority of the population. Indeed, in these countries those who are incorrupt are considered to be deviant as they constitute the minority.

In contrast, market-centered definitions of corruption shift the emphasis from the public office to the market. Jacob van Klaveren (1989, p. 26) has provided the following market-centered definition of corruption:

> A corrupt civil servant who regards his public office as a business, the income of which he will ... seek to maximize. The office then becomes a "maximizing unit." The size of his income depends ... upon the market situation and his talents for finding the point of maximal gain on the public's demand curve.

The third type of definition views corruption as an erosion of the public interest. Rejecting the public-office-centered definitions as being too narrow and the market-centered definitions as being too broad, Carl Friedrich recommended the use of public-interest-centered definitions instead. He has defined corruption thus:

> The pattern of corruption can be said to exist whenever a powerholder who is charged with doing certain things, i.e., who is a responsible functionary or officeholder, is by monetary or other rewards not legally provided for, induced to take actions which favor whoever provides the rewards and thereby does damage to the public and its interests. (Friedrich, 1989, p. 15)

However, the problem with the above definition is that the concept of public interest is itself vague and has not been defined at all.

For this book, a public-office-centered definition of corruption is preferred because it is more relevant and useful than the market-centered and public-interest-centered definitions. The United Nations Development Programme (UNDP) has defined corruption as "the misuse of public power, office or authority for private benefit – through bribery, extortion, influence peddling, nepotism, fraud, speed money or embezzlement" (UNDP, 1999, p. 7). This definition identifies the major forms of corruption and focuses on the public sector. However, as corruption also occurs in the private sector in many Asian countries, this book adopts the UNDP definition of corruption with a minor addition of the two words "or private" thus: "the misuse of public *or private* power, office or authority for private benefit." The advantage of this modified UNDP definition of corruption is its applicability to both the public and the private sectors in the 10 Asian countries discussed in this book.

Bearing in mind the revised UNDP's definition of corruption, there are two important distinctions that must be noted. First, is corruption a fact of life or a way of life? (Caiden, 1981, pp. 58–62). Corruption is a fact of life in a country when cases of corruption are the exception rather than the rule, and are examples of individual rather than systemic corruption. Conversely, corruption is a way of life in a country when it is rampant, occurs at all levels, and is the norm rather than the exception. In similar vein, David W. Lovell (2005, p. 79) distinguishes between incidental and endemic corruption and argues that this distinction is useful for analyzing corruption in postcommunist states like those of the former Soviet Union. According to him, "incidental corruption takes place against a background of established rational-legal authority" while "endemic corruption takes place where rational-legal authority is not yet predominant."

Second, is corruption grand or petty in nature? Grand corruption refers to corruption by political leaders and senior civil servants and usually involves "large, international bribes and 'hidden' overseas bank accounts" (Pope, 2000, p. xix). George Moody-Stuart (1997, p. 2) has defined grand corruption as "the misuse of public power by heads of state, ministers and top officials for private, pecuniary profit." On the contrary, petty or "survival" corruption is practiced by underpaid junior civil servants who demand bribes from the people to expedite their applications or perform other favors. For example, as mentioned in Chapter 4, many civil servants in the Philippines are paid "starvation" wages and resort to petty corruption to supplement their meager incomes.

While grand corruption causes more damage than petty corruption, this does not mean that nothing should be done to minimize petty corruption. The UNDP (2008, p. 2) contends that petty corruption is a "misnomer" because it affects "the daily lives of a very large number of people" especially the poor. In the same vein, William K. Black (2007, p. 440) recommends that the term "petty corruption" should be abandoned because it is "a dangerously inaccurate rhetorical device." Thus, an anticorruption strategy is only effective if it is able to curb *both* grand and petty corruption simultaneously in the country.

## REPORTING THE EXTENT OF CORRUPTION

According to Inge Amundsen (1999, p. 28), the "illicit or immoral nature" of political corruption makes it "even more inaccessible to scientific investigation than most other human behavior." The "concealed, under-communicated and illegal nature" of corruption "indicates the feebleness of statistical methods in assessing [its] quantitative aspects." It is difficult if not impossible to measure the actual extent of corruption in a country for four reasons. First, it is difficult to collect data on bureaucratic corruption in government agencies as corrupt bureaucrats usually conceal their activities because they would be arrested if they were discovered.

Second, given the sensitive and secretive nature of bureaucratic corruption, survey research methods cannot be employed to obtain direct measures of corrupt behavior as corrupt officials would not risk losing their jobs by admitting that they were corrupt. Azfar and Murrell (2007, p. 352) found that many respondents in Romanian corruption surveys were "reticent" and preferred to give "incomplete or non-truthful responses." Similarly, Hwang (1996, pp. 142, 235) reported that South Korean respondents were reluctant to answer questions on the number of times they had offered bribes to civil servants, the number of times they had received a bribe when performing their duties, and their reaction if they had received bribes.

Accordingly, scholars doing research on corruption usually obtain their data indirectly by asking members of the public or other groups whether civil servants are corrupt or not. However, such data are based on the respondents' perceptions of the extent of bureaucratic corruption and not on the actual extent of corruption. As corruption is a consensual crime conducted in secrecy and is not legally and/or socially condoned, it is impossible to ascertain the actual extent of corruption in a country.

This means that scholars must rely instead on the reported extent of bureaucratic corruption and the accuracy of the estimate depends on the sources employed. For example, John C. Meyer Jr. (1973) relied on data on police corruption collected by a north-eastern police department in the United States for his analysis. His data consisted of allegations of police corruption made by citizens and police officers in the same north-eastern city in the United States. Meyer's caution regarding the incompleteness of his data should be noted:

> It must therefore be remembered that these data do not represent the true picture of corruption. They do show the nature and extent of corruption as reported by the various complaints. As such, the data show the picture of corruption as was available to the police chief and his staff. They do not show if, in fact, there was more corruption than was actually reported. (Meyer, 1973, p. 39)

Similarly, Quah (1979, p. 17) has relied on the reported cases of police corruption in the major English language newspaper, the *Straits Times*, during 1845–1921 and 1965–1977 to ascertain the reported extent of police corruption in Singapore during the British colonial period and the first 12 years after independence. Kim (1994, pp. 101–129) and Hwang (1996, pp. 179–182) also relied on the reported cases of bureaucratic corruption in two major newspapers, *Hankuk Ilbo* and *Dong-A Ilbo*, to estimate the extent of bureaucratic corruption in South Korea from 1960–1979 and 1993–1994, respectively.

However, the limitation of this source is the uneven quality of data provided in the newspapers as the ethnic group and rank of the policemen involved in corruption in Singapore are not always recorded in the newspaper reports. In the same vein, the reports on bureaucratic corruption in the South Korean newspapers also do not include the rank or position of the corrupt officials. Furthermore, echoing Meyer's caution, Kim (1994, p. 112), who had compiled reports of bureaucratic corruption in the *Hankuk Ilbo* and *Dong-A Ilbo* for six years, has warned his readers that:

> the reported incidents do not necessarily reflect the reality of corruption phenomena in [South] Korea, since the dark or hidden area of bureaucratic corruption (i.e., unreported and unknown incidents) might be in existence behind the reported incidents.

The distinction between the actual and the reported extent of bureaucratic corruption in a country is important, as regardless of the method of data collection employed, it is impossible to ascertain the actual extent of corruption. In his study of *Criminal Behavior*, Herschel Prins (1982, p. 20) has employed the analogy of an iceberg to distinguish between three types of crime: "detected and prosecuted crime," "crimes known to the police but neither prosecuted nor cleared up," and "the dark or hidden area of crime (unreported and unknown)." Estimates by criminologists on the extent of unknown and unreported criminal offenses range from "a minimum of twice and a maximum of four and a half times the number shown in the criminal statistics" to "about 50 per cent overall" in the United States (Prins, 1982, p. 21).

Following Prins, the iceberg analogy can also be used to distinguish between detected and prosecuted corrupt offenses, corrupt offenses that are not prosecuted or cleared up, and the unreported and unknown corrupt offenses. Hence, researchers have to be satisfied with the reported extent of bureaucratic and political corruption and the limitations of such data, otherwise no research can be done.

Third, the problem of gathering evidence on corruption is particularly difficult in communist countries or former communist countries like Mongolia. This problem still exists today even though corruption is no longer as sensitive a topic as it was in the 1960s. According to Maria Los (1988, p. 150), whose study of corruption in Poland was based on reports of corruption in several weekly magazines and daily newspapers, these reports "paint a bleak, deeply disturbing picture of a country plagued by injustice, corruption and exploitation," but she cautioned that such reports "present a rather cautious diagnosis, more likely understated than overstated" because of censorship and other constraints in a totalitarian country.

Similarly, in the case of Cuba, Sergio Diaz-Briquets and Jorge Perez-Lopez (2006, p. 124) contend that "official reporting underestimates corruption and is not a reliable indicator of the nature and extent of corruption on the island." Accordingly, their assessment of the extent of corruption in contemporary Cuba is based on "examples of corrupt acts from the literature (official documents, the work of independent journalists residing on the island, the international press, defector tales, and academic studies) and by examining Cuba's performance in international measures of corruption, governance, and economic freedom developed by reputable organizations" (Diaz-Briquets & Perez-Lopez, 2006, pp. 126–127).

Finally, Hager (1973, pp. 201–202) contends that "it is impossible to gauge the extent of bureaucratic corruption" because "records showing the number of complaints, investigations, and proceedings may measure more accurately the vigor of law enforcement than the gravity of the corruption problem." Consequently, scholars conducting research on corruption in India and elsewhere are "left with impressionistic reports, indirect evidence, and vigilance records" (Hager, 1973, p. 202).

## CAUSES OF CORRUPTION

Under what conditions does corruption thrive? What are the factors that induce civil servants or political leaders to commit corrupt acts? Conversely, what prevents or discourages individuals from being corrupt? An individual is more likely to commit a corrupt act if he or she (1) is paid a low or inadequate salary; (2) is exposed to ample opportunities for corruption; and (3) perceives corruption to be a low-risk, high-reward activity. In other words, corruption thrives when the individuals concerned receive meager salaries, have ample opportunities to be corrupt, and are unlikely to be caught and not severely punished even if they are caught.

In his comparative study of the control of bureaucratic corruption in Hong Kong, India, and Indonesia, Leslie Palmier (1985, p. 271) identifies these three factors as important causes of corruption: *opportunities* (which depended on the extent of involvement of civil servants in the administration or control of lucrative activities), *salaries*, and *policing* (the probability of detection and punishment). Palmier (1985, p. 272) hypothesized thus:

> bureaucratic corruption seems to depend not on any one of the [three] factors identified, but rather on the *balance* between them. At one extreme, *with few opportunities, good salaries, and effective policing, corruption will be minimal;* at the other, *with many opportunities, poor salaries, and weak policing, it will be considerable* (emphasis added).

Thus, following Palmier's hypothesis, an effective anticorruption strategy should reduce or remove the opportunities for corruption, raise the salaries of civil servants and political leaders, and ensure a high degree of policing.

### *Low Salaries*

According to Hedrick Smith (1976, pp. 116–117), there is a saying in Odessa, Ukraine, that "if you get really mad at another person, you put a curse on him – 'let him live on his salary.' It's a terrible fate. No one can imagine it." Palmier (1985, p. 2) has identified low salaries as an important cause of corruption: "If the official is not to be tempted into corruption and disaffection, clearly there is an obligation on the government to provide or at least allow such benefits as will ensure his loyalty; one might call it an implicit contract." Consequently, "adequate pay" is "an essential ingredient in reform" (Palmier, 1985, p. 6). Similarly, Mauro (1997, p. 5) contends that "when civil service pay is too low, civil servants may be obliged to use their positions to collect bribes as a way of making ends meet, particularly when the expected cost of being caught is low."

In 1969, Theodore M. Smith (1971, pp. 28–29) conducted a survey of regional civil servants in Indonesia and found that there was "not a single official who can live by his government income alone" as the "official income amounts to approximately half of [his] essential monthly needs." A more recent survey on corruption in Indonesia of 2,300 respondents (650 public officials, 1,250 households and 400 business enterprises) found that low salaries were identified as the most important cause of corruption by 51.4 percent of the public officials, 36.5 percent of the business enterprises, and 35.5 percent of the households (Partnership for Governance Reform, 2001, p. 39).

Mongolia is another country where the low salaries of its civil servants and political leaders contribute to corruption. As shown in Chapter 11, while the monthly salary of the President has risen by more than 10 times from US$71 in 1998 to US$761 in 2010, his salary is still low by international standards. Similarly, in 1998, Mongolian judges earned between US$33 to US$51 per month and one-third of them in the countryside were homeless. While the monthly salaries of judges have increased to between US$421 and US$491 (see Table 11.7), their salaries are also modest by world standards and barely sufficient to meet the rising cost of living in Mongolia.

In South Korea, some scholars have recommended that civil service salaries, which constitute only 70 percent of private sector wages, should be raised to reduce corruption. For example, Jun and Yoon (1996, p. 107) have suggested that it is unrealistic to expect South Korean civil servants "to show dedication without providing adequate remuneration and changing the administrative culture."

In the case of Thailand, Kasem Suwanagul (1962, pp. 79–80) found that the low salaries of civil servants during the postwar period contributed to more bureaucratic corruption as their low salaries were insufficient to meet inflation and below those offered in the private sector. Similarly, in his analysis of the consequences of low salaries on the prestige of the Philippine Civil Service, Padilla (1995, pp. 195–202, 206) found that civil servants supplemented their low wages by vending within the office, holding a second job, teaching part-time, practicing their profession after office hours, engaging in research and consultancy projects, and resorting to petty corrupt practices.

In Singapore, the most important cause of police corruption during the colonial period was the low salaries of the members of the Singapore Police Force (SPF), especially those in the lower ranks. This factor was also blamed for the SPF's inefficiency and its inability to recruit suitably qualified personnel (Quah, 1979, p. 28). Given the poor salaries of the policemen, it was not surprising that the *Straits Times* commented on October 4, 1887, that "the native constables and the European police of the Inspector class are so underpaid that scandals are unavoidable" (quoted in Quah, 1979, p. 29).

In short, "if bureaucrats are paid a high enough wage, even a small chance of losing their jobs would discourage them from being corrupt." On the contrary, if the real salary of civil servants decreases drastically, "even the most rigidly honest bureaucrats will be tempted to go beyond the law to preserve their standard of living" (Banerjee, 1996, p. 110).

### *Opportunities for Corruption and Red Tape*

The scope of public administration has grown and the role of the public bureaucracy in national development has become more important with the advent of the modern administrative state (Caiden, 1971, pp. 23–24). The expanding role of the public bureaucracy in national development has increased the opportunities for administrative discretion and corruption as "regulations governing access to goods and services can be exploited by civil servants in extracting 'rents' from groups vying for access to such goods and services" (Gould & Amaro-Reyes, 1983, p. 17). A good example is provided by Hong Kong, where "the necessity for the government to regulate, control and prohibit certain activities" increased the opportunities for corruption in the "areas of construction, import and export, health, hygiene, safety, prostitution, gambling, drugs, markets and stalls, immigration and emigration" (de Speville, 1997, p. 14).

In Indonesia, Donald P. Warwick (1987, p. 43) introduced the interesting distinction made by civil servants between "wet" and "dry" agencies, depending on their budget and access to the public. "Wet" agencies like the customs, immigration, internal revenue, and police will provide more opportunities for corruption than "dry" agencies like research and administrative departments, which do not interact directly with the public. Indeed, as "dry" agencies have reduced opportunities for corruption, "being posted to a dry position is about the worst fate any official could fear" (Loveard, 1999, p. 111).

*The Knapp Commission Report on Police Corruption* identified three factors that influenced the opportunities for corruption among police officers in New York City. First, the branch of the department to which an officer was assigned is important as a plainclothesman would have more and different opportunities than a uniformed policeman. Second, the area to which an officer was assigned influenced not only the opportunities for corrupt behavior but also the major sources of corruption payments. For example, in New York City, some precincts in Harlem provided more opportunities for corruption than Central Park. Finally, the officer's assignment determined the amount and type of graft available to him as an officer in a patrol car would have more opportunities to be corrupt than his counterpart on guard duty (Knapp, 1972, pp. 67–68).

The Corruption Prevention Department (CPD) of Hong Kong's Independent Commission Against Corruption (ICAC) identified four "more pernicious and prevalent" factors that increased opportunities for corruption. The first factor is delay, which "provides both the opportunity to extort a bribe and the incentive to offer one, and is also an inevitable consequence of bureaucratic processes." Second, insufficient publicity "leads the public to believe that individual public servants have the authority to decide whether a particular law shall be enforced or who shall benefit from a public service, so creating a situation ripe for exploitation." The third factor providing opportunities for corruption is excessive discretion, which often results from "a well-intended delegation of authority in order to expedite business." The fourth and most important factor was the lack of supervision or accountability, especially of junior officers who operate away from an office. As supervisors are usually preoccupied with other administrative duties that require their presence in their comfortable offices, they are reluctant to visit their junior officers in the field and resort to supervision through correspondence. To minimize the lack of supervision or accountability of junior officers, the CPD recommended that "all supervisory officers should spend sufficient time with their staff and in the field, to gain their own insight into the problems within their area of responsibility and conditions on the ground" (Palmier, 1985, pp. 179–181).

Red tape refers to "bureaucratic procedures characterized by mechanical adherence to regulations, excessive formality and attention to routine, and the compilation of large amounts of extraneous information resulting in prolonged delay or inaction" (Chandler & Plano, 1988, p. 233). In his classic book, *Red Tape: Its Origins, Uses, and Abuses*, Herbert Kaufman (1977, p. 5) observed that "when people rail against red tape, they mean that they are subjected to too many constraints, that many of these constraints seem pointless, and that agencies seem to take forever to act." He further argued that civil servants are tempted "by opportunities to sell their official discretion and information" and "by the opportunities to extort payments" as "permits can be delayed, licenses held up, deliberations protracted, proceedings prolonged, unless rewards are offered" (Kaufman, 1977, pp. 51–53).

Red tape and cumbersome administrative procedures provide civil servants with the excuse to extort bribes from those members of the public who are prepared to pay "speed money" to "cut" red tape and reduce delay by expediting their applications for permits or licenses (Quah, 2009b, pp. 820–821). For example, red tape in South Korea (44 documents must be submitted for a permit to build a factory) resulted in delay and increased the costs in time and money for business firms, which resorted to bribing civil servants to reduce delay by expediting their applications for permits or licenses (Kim, 1997, pp. 261–262).

### *Low Risk of Detection and Punishment*

As corruption is an illegal activity in all countries, those individuals found guilty of corrupt offenses should be punished accordingly. However, in reality, the probability of detection and punishment of corrupt offenses varies in the different Asian countries. Corruption thrives in those Asian countries where the public perceives it to be a "low risk, high reward" activity as corrupt offenders are unlikely to be detected and punished. On the contrary, corruption is not a serious problem in those Asian countries where corruption is perceived as a "high risk, low reward" activity because those involved in corrupt behavior are likely to be caught and severely punished.

An important cause of the pervasive corruption in the former Soviet Union before its collapse was the lack of fear of punishment among the corrupt officials. Indeed, cases of high-level corruption in the Soviet Union were seldom punished because the regime was "permissive towards its ruling elite." Syed Hussein Alatas (1991, p. 121) contends that the "involvement of the highest leadership in turn causes permissiveness towards corruption," which is "the greatest cause of its perpetuation."

Similarly, even though bribery exceeding 100,000 yuan (US$12,000) is a capital offense in China, the death penalty has not been imposed until recently on senior party officials found guilty of accepting bribes exceeding this amount. For example, the former Beijing party chief, Chen Xitong, became the highest ranking Chinese Communist Party (CCP) member to be jailed for corruption when he was sentenced to 16 years imprisonment for graft of 555,000 yuan and dereliction of duty on July 31, 1998. Chen's sentence was lenient as more junior party cadres were given life imprisonment or the death penalty for corruption involving smaller sums of over 100,000 yuan (*Straits Times*, 1998, p. 14). In other words, senior party officials can "short-circuit corruption investigations by appealing to their protectors in the party hierarchy" (Root, 1996b, p. 752).

However, Premier Zhu Rongji initiated a crusade against corrupt officials and on March 5, 2000, he informed party delegates at the National People's Congress that: "All major cases, no matter which department or who is involved, must be thoroughly investigated, and corrupt officials must be brought to justice" (*Straits Times*, 2000a, p. 23). To reinforce Zhu's message, Hu Changqing, Deputy Governor of Jiangxi province, was the highest ranking public official to be executed three days later on March 8 for corruption involving 5.44 million yuan between May 1995 and August 1999 (*Straits Times*, 2000b, p. 30). Similarly, Li Chenglong, Deputy Mayor of Guigang City, was executed on April 23 2000 for taking US$478,500 worth of bribes (*Straits Times*, 2000c, p. 2). Zhu's commitment to minimizing corruption among senior party officials improved China's ranking on TI's CPI. Table 1.1 shows that China's CPI score has improved from 2.16 in 1995 to 3.5 in 2010.

The final example is provided by Bangladesh, which was ranked the most corrupt country in the world on the CPI from 2001 to 2005. This is not surprising as corruption has been institutionalized in the public service in Bangladesh from the early 1970s (Khan, 1998, p. 35). According to Mohammad Mohabbat Khan (1998, p. 36), Bangladesh's high level of corruption can be attributed to these four factors:

> First, bureaucrats involved in corrupt practices in most cases do not lose their jobs. Very rarely they are dismissed from service on charges pertaining to corruption. Still rarely they are sent to prison for misusing public funds. They have never been compelled to return to the state their ill-gotten wealth. Second, the law-enforcing officials including police personnel are extremely corrupt. They are happy to share the booty with other corrupt bureaucrats. Third, the people have a tendency not only to tolerate corruption

> but to show respect to those bureaucrats who made fortune through dubious means.... Fourth, it is easier for a citizen to get quick service because he has already "paid" the bureaucrat rather than wait for his turn.

For the population in a country to perceive corruption as a "high risk, low reward" activity, the incumbent government must publicize through the mass media the detection of corrupt behavior among civil servants and politicians and their punishment according to the law if they are found guilty. Accordingly, Leslie Palmier (1985, p. 279) has stressed the crucial role of the communications media, which reduces corruption by exposing it because corruption "thrives in secrecy, and withers in the light."

If the media emphasizes the harmful effects of corruption and publicizes the punishment of public officials for their corrupt offenses, such negative publicity can serve as an effective deterrent against corruption. In this connection, Lee Kuan Yew, Singapore's former prime minister, contended in 1987 that "the strongest deterrent is in a public opinion which censures and condemns corrupt persons, in other words, in attitudes which make corruption so unacceptable that the stigma of corruption cannot be washed away by serving a prison sentence" (*Straits Times*, 1987a, p. 11). On the contrary, the governments of Indonesia under President Soeharto and India during the Emergency of the 1970s, which "shackle the media," had the opposite effect of "encouraging the corrupt" (Palmier, 1985, p. 279).

In short, Palmier argues that corruption thrives in those Asian countries that (1) pay its civil servants and political leaders low salaries; (2) expose them to ample opportunities for corruption; and (3) are unlikely to detect and punish those public officials involved in corrupt behavior. However, Palmier's analysis is not exhaustive as he has ignored the importance of two additional factors namely, cultural factors and the lack of political will in curbing corruption.

### *Cultural Factors*

In his insightful review of Palmier's book, Peter B. Harris (1987, p. 91) observed that there was no "discussion of whether cultural factors promote or inhibit corruption." In 1951, Clyde Kluckhohn reviewed various definitions of culture and defined "culture" generally as a community's "design for living" and specifically as:

> patterned ways of thinking, feeling, and reacting, acquired and transmitted mainly by symbols, constituting the distinctive achievements of human groups, including their embodiments in artifacts;... traditional (i.e., historically derived and selected) ideas and especially their attached values. (Kluckhohn, 1951, p. 86)

Culture contributes to corruption in a country when cultural practices like gift-giving and family ties influence individuals to give or receive bribes. Gift-giving is common in many Asian countries. As shown in Chapter 2, it is difficult to distinguish between a gift and a bribe in Japan because gift-giving is an accepted social tradition. Similarly, the tradition of gift-giving in Mongolia means that a person receiving a gift has to reciprocate by returning a small token instead of an empty container. Apart from promoting reciprocity in social relations, gift-giving also encourages bribery among civil servants, who accept gifts provided by those wishing to cut red tape or to obtain licenses or permits improperly.

In South Korea, the tradition of gift-giving takes the corrupt form of expensive offerings to political leaders or civil servants in return for favors. Gift-giving in South Korea has gradually evolved from a way of showing respect and reciprocity, into a means of "obtaining business, political election, favors" and "degenerating into bribery and graft." Bribery is ingrained among South Korean large business firms that bribe civil servants to avoid paying taxes or to gain lucrative contracts (Genzberger, 1994, p. 23).

In Thailand, as mentioned in Chapter 9, Likhit Dhiravegin (1978, pp. 98–99) found that qualified civil servants are only promoted if they provide gifts and services to their superiors including golf-bags, Buddha statues, or honey for the supervisor's wife. Furthermore, giving gifts to officials in Thailand for services rendered is not considered as bribery but as *sin nam jai* or gifts of goodwill. Thais also do not view bribes as a form of corruption as long as no one is hurt. Indeed, the Thai population's tolerance of corruption is reflected in their acceptance of the corrupt practices of the civil servants, military leaders, and politicians.

Edward Banfield coined the concept of "amoral familism" from his study of a small village in southern Italy. In his view, "in a society of amoral familists, no one will further the interest of the group or community except as it is to his private advantage to do so" (Banfield, 1958, pp. 83–84). Furthermore, amoral familists who are office-holders will take bribes when they can get away with it (Banfield, 1958, p. 92). In other words, amoral familism encourages corruption and deviance from universalistic norms and merit because "anything goes that advances the interests of one's self and family" (Lipset & Lenz, 2000, p. 120). Hence, it is not surprising that, as shown in Chapter 4, corruption thrives in the Philippines because of the importance of family ties that are reinforced by the *compadre* system and the cultural value of *utang na loob*.

### *Lack of Political Will*

Perhaps the most important cause of corruption is the lack of political will or commitment to curb corruption in a country. If a country's political leaders are not committed to fighting corruption this lack of commitment will be reflected in the absence of comprehensive anticorruption legislation, and the anticorruption agencies' inadequate budget and personnel. According to Ian Senior (2006, pp. 184, 187):

> The principal people who can change a culture of corruption if they wish to do so are politicians. This is because they make the laws and allocate the funds that enable the laws to be enforced. If, however, politicians at the top of the hierarchy have routinely worked their way up by accepting bribes to fund their parties and themselves, there is little prospect that they will wish to cleanse their colleagues or their nation of corruption. ... The very people who are the greatest beneficiaries of corruption have the greatest power and use the corrupt nature of government to maintain that power.

In other words, if the government is committed to curbing corruption in a country, it should demonstrate its political will by providing the anti-corruption agency (ACA) or agencies with adequate personnel and budget to enforce the anticorruption laws impartially. However, as Ian Senior (2006, p. 187) has aptly observed, corrupt political leaders are unlikely to be committed to curbing corruption because they will not "kill the goose that lays the golden eggs."

## CONSEQUENCES OF CORRUPTION

Nathaniel H. Leff (1964, pp. 8–14) argued that bureaucratic corruption had positive effects because it encouraged a government to promote economic growth, provided an incentive for mobilizing the bureaucracy, enhanced foreign investment, stimulated economic innovation, and increased competition among entrepreneurs. However, Leff's argument that bureaucratic corruption is beneficial for economic development is not valid for two reasons. First, Leff failed to substantiate his thesis because he did not provide the required empirical evidence. Second, and more importantly, subsequent research by other scholars has demonstrated that corruption has toxic rather than tonic consequences for a country's development.

In her comprehensive analysis of the consequences of corruption in Hong Kong, Malaysia, Nepal, Philippines, Singapore, South Korea, and

Thailand, Ledivina V. Carino (1986a) rejected Leff's claim that corruption is beneficial for economic development. Corruption only benefits those who are corrupt by providing them with more money, power, and social mobility at the expense of those who are not corrupt in the country. However, corruption increases administrative costs through overpayment of supplies and materials and losses in government revenue. Corruption also increases administrative inefficiency by undermining the formal hierarchy of authority. Policies can be distorted by corruption through the imposition of unauthorized controls or fees on the population or changing the target beneficiaries. Above all, corruption weakens the political system and undermines political stability (Carino, 1986b, pp. 170–190). Carino (1986b, p. 192) concluded that corruption has "largely toxic consequences to the organization and the society."

In the same vein, *Human Development in South Asia 1999: The Crisis of Governance* began its chapter on "The Corruption Menace" by identifying these negative consequences of corruption:

> Corruption is one of the most damaging consequences of poor governance. It undermines investment and economic growth, decreases the resources available for human development goals, deepens the extent of poverty, subverts the judicial system, and undermines the legitimacy of the state. In fact, when corruption becomes entrenched, it can devastate the entire economic, political, and social fabric of a country.... Corruption breeds corruption – and a failure to combat it effectively can lead to an era of entrenched corruption. (Haq, 1999, pp. 96, 105)

Mark Bannister (2003, pp. 323, 325) has described corruption as a "killing virus" because it kills the potential for development by "scaring off investors, causing international marginalization, curtailing growth, increasing economic transaction costs, misallocating public funds, undermining public policy and weakening governance." Agreeing with this analysis, Mansoor Ahmad (2009) has argued that corruption in Pakistan "could eat up all development funds." He wrote:

> Corruption [in Pakistan] has plagued every aspect of society and caused substantial damage to the economy, leading to calls for prudent measures to stop misuse of public office or public assets for private gains. Governance experts have pointed out that all development funds would go down the drain if this menace is not controlled.... They regret Pakistan is facing both top and low level corruption.... The existence of corruption ... is indeed symptomatic of weak governance and, more importantly, weak institutions. ... While corruption damages a country's development ... it is highly regressive and inequitable ... for the poor.... They say in a corrupt environment, government spending tends to be diverted from social expenditures (such as health and

> education, which benefit the poor) to heavy infrastructure projects. Evidence has shown that in a corrupt environment, actions of ministers and civil servants focus heavily on transactions rather than on policies. Competition for "juicy government ministries" increases because these have large procurement budgets each year. (Ahmad, 2009)

Perhaps the most serious consequence of corruption is that it kills when lives are lost from the actions or inactions of corrupt individuals, organizations, or governments. According to William K. Black (2007, p. 440):

> Corruption causes millions of unnecessary deaths by keeping nations poor and incompetently managed. Millions die and are maimed unnecessarily from drinking bad water, from being infected as a result of inadequate sewerage disposal, and from wars that corrupt regimes engage in as an opportunity for profit.

Nicholas Ambraseys and Roger Bilham (2011, pp. 153–155) have found that 83 percent of all deaths caused by the collapse of buildings during earthquakes during the past 30 years occurred in those countries where corruption is widespread and worse than expected. They also estimate that 550,000 people around the world have died in shoddy buildings during earthquakes (Munro, 2011).

Press reports on the recent crisis in Zimbabwe illustrate vividly Black's argument that corruption kills. In her article, "Physicians: Corruption killing people in Zimbabwe," Michelle Faul (2009) wrote:

> An international physicians' group said Tuesday that corruption is killing Zimbabweans and President Mugabe should be investigated by the International Criminal Court for possible crimes against humanity.
>
> "Government hospitals have shut down, after operating for months without running water or sufficient medical supplies, in large part because doctors and nurses do not earn enough to pay for transport to work and amid hyperinflation" according to the World Health Organization. David Sanders, a Zimbabwean doctor and Professor of Public Health at South Africa's University of the Western Cape, said that officials of Mugabe's party had "plundered $7.3 million of $11 million from the Global Fund for Aids that was only returned in November amid international outrage."

The plight of desperate women and children fleeing from Zimbabwe is described by Barry Bearak (2009) thus:

> With their nation in a prolonged sequence of crises, more unaccompanied children and women than ever are joining the rush of desperate Zimbabweans illegally crossing the frontier at the Limpopo River, according to the police, local officials and aid workers.

> What they are escaping is a broken country where half the people are going hungry, most schools and hospitals are closed or dysfunctional and a cholera epidemic has taken a toll in the thousands.
>
> For those in the know, crossing the border can be a simple chore, a bribe paid on one side and a second bribe on the other.

In sum, corruption has negative consequences for a country's development, and its most serious consequence is the unnecessary loss of lives resulting from the activities of corrupt individuals, organizations, or governments.

## PATTERNS OF CORRUPTION CONTROL IN ASIAN COUNTRIES

There are three patterns of corruption control in Asian countries depending on the anticorruption measures employed (Table 1.3). The first pattern relies on anticorruption laws, but there is no ACA to implement these laws. An example of pattern 1 can be found in Mongolia, which had the Law on Anti-Corruption and three provisions restricting bribery in the Criminal Code. However, there was no special ACA before December 2006 as the task of curbing corruption was shared between the police, the General Prosecutor's Office (GPO), and the courts. Perhaps the best example of this first pattern of corruption control is exhibited in Japan, which does not have an ACA as it relies on the Public Prosecutor's Office (PPO) to investigate corruption cases.

The second pattern of corruption control involves the combination of anticorruption laws and multiple ACAs. This strategy can be found in both democratic and communist countries. In the case of India, the Prevention of Corruption Act (POCA) is implemented by the Central Bureau of Investigation (CBI), the CVC, the state anticorruption bureaus (ACBs), and the state vigilance commissions (SVCs). The Philippines has the most anticorruption measures in Asia as it has 7 laws and 19 anticorruption agencies since the 1950s. Taiwan relies on the Ministry of Justice Investigation Bureau (MJIB), the Department of Government Employee Ethics (DGEE), and the Public Prosecutors' Offices to combat corruption.

In China, the anticorruption laws are implemented by three agencies, depending on the sector. The Supreme People's Procuratorate (SPP) was re-established in 1978 to combat corruption in the judicial sector. The SPP formed the Procuratorial Division of Graft and Bribery in 1989 after the Tiananmen anticorruption and democracy movement. Below the SPP, the Bureau for Embezzlement and Bribery of the People's Procuratorate is

***Table 1.3.*** Patterns of Corruption Control in 10 Asian Countries.

| Pattern and Country | Anti-Corruption Laws | Anti-Corruption Agencies |
|---|---|---|
| Pattern 1: Japan | Penal Code 1908 (Art 193–198); Political Funds Control Law 1948; National Public Service Ethics Act 1999; Bidding Correction Law 2000; *Dango* Prevention Law 2002 | Special Investigation Departments, Public Prosecutors Offices in Tokyo, Osaka, and Nagoya |
| Pattern 2: India | Prevention of Corruption Act, 1988 | Central Bureau of Investigation, Central Vigilance Commission, State anti-corruption bureaus, State vigilance organizations |
| Pattern 2: | Philippines | Republic Act of 1960 and Presidential Decrees |
| Special Anti-Graft Court, Office of the | Ombudsman, Presidential Commission on Good Government, Inter-Agency Anti-Graft Coordinating Council, Presidential Committee on Effective Governance, Presidential Anti-Graft Commission, Governance Advisory Council | |
| Pattern 2: Taiwan | Anti-Corruption Statute, 1963; Government Procurement Act, 1998; Criminal Code, Articles 142–148; Presidential and Vice Presidential Election and Recall Law; Public Officials Election and Recall Law | Ministry of Justice Investigation Bureau, Department of Government Employee Ethics and all Government Ethics Units, Public Prosecutors' Offices |
| Pattern 3: Singapore | Prevention of Corruption Act, 1960; Corruption, Drug Trafficking and Other Serious Crimes (Confiscation of Benefits) Act, Chapter 65A, 1999 | Corrupt Practices Investigation Bureau |
| Pattern 3: Hong Kong, SAR | ICAC Ordinance of 1974<br>Prevention of Bribery Ordinance, 1971 | Independent Commission Against Corruption |
| Pattern 3: Thailand | Organic Act on Counter Corruption, 1999 and 2001 | National Counter Corruption Commission (until 14 July 2008); National Anti-Corruption Commission (from 15 July 2008) |
| Pattern 3: South Korea | Anti-Corruption Act, 2001 | Korea Independent Commission Against Corruption (until 28 February 2008)<br>Anti-Corruption Civil Rights Commission (from 29 February 2008) |
| Pattern 3: Indonesia | Law No. 30 of 2002 | Corruption Eradication Commission (*Komisi Pemberantasan Korupsi*) |
| Pattern 3: Mongolia | Anti-Corruption Law, 2006 | Independent Authority Against Corruption |

*Source*: Compiled by author.

responsible for handling and preventing cases of embezzlement and bribery. As China is a large country, it is not surprising that there are 3,563 agencies for embezzlement and bribery (Luo, Miao, & Guo, n.d., p. 3).

For the administrative sector, the Ministry of Supervision (MOS) was reestablished in 1986 to curb corruption in the civil service. The Central Disciplinary Inspection Committee (CDIC) was formed in 1978 to check corruption among the members of the CCP (Chan, 1999, pp. 300–301). Even though the MOS had received more than 700,000 reports in 1993, both the CDIC and the MOS failed to reduce corruption because the "authorities appear[ed] to lack the political will to handle corruption cases among more senior party members" (Burns, 1994, pp. 57–58).

The National Corruption Prevention Bureau (NCPB) was established on September 13, 2007, with Ma Wen, the minister of supervision, the CDIC deputy secretary, and a Central Committee party member, as its head. Unlike the SPP, MOS, and CDIC that focus on prosecution, the NCPB is concerned with "implementing preventive measures, monitoring the transfer of assets across organizations, facilitating and promoting information sharing between agencies, and policing corrupt practices" among private enterprises, social organizations, and nongovernmental organizations (Becker, 2008, pp. 287–288, 291).

Cambodia and Vietnam also rely on multiple ACAs to curb corruption. In Cambodia, the six agencies are: the Anti-Corruption Unit, Complaints and Investigating Department, Department of Conflict Resolution, Department of Inspection, Department of Inspection Relations with Ministries and Institutions, and Department of Monitoring Law Enforcement. Similarly, Vietnam's six agencies are: Anti-Corruption Department (ACD), Prime Minister's Office (PMO); Central Inspection Commission of the Communist Party of Vietnam; Government Inspectorate; National Anti-Corruption Steering Committee; People's Procuracy; and State Audit (Quah, 2007a, pp. 4–5).

The third pattern of corruption control involves the impartial implementation of comprehensive anticorruption laws by a single ACA. In Singapore, the POCA is implemented by the Corrupt Practices Investigation Bureau (CPIB), which was formed in October 1952 to take over the function of corruption control from the Anti-Corruption Branch in the SPF. Similarly, in Hong Kong, the Independent Commission against Corruption (ICAC) was established in February 1974 to implement the ICAC Ordinance and Prevention of Bribery Ordinance (POBO).

Malaysia, Thailand, South Korea, Indonesia, and Mongolia have also adopted the third pattern of corruption control, but these countries have been less effective than Singapore and Hong Kong. In Malaysia, the ACA was established on October 1, 1967, with three major functions: (1) to investigate and prosecute offenses under the POCA of 1961, (2) to introduce preventive measures against corruption in the civil service and statutory boards, and (3) to investigate disciplinary complaints against civil servants (Marican, 1979, pp. 601, 603).

The ACA was initially staffed with seconded police officers who were not trained to investigate corruption offenses. Furthermore, these police officers were reluctant to investigate corrupt practices in the police force and other departments where they might be posted to in future (Quah, 1982a, p. 170). These initial teething problems were resolved by its reorganization in 1968. However, more recently, the ACA was criticized for not investigating corruption cases involving "big fish" impartially as the November 1998 to April 1999 corruption trial and conviction of former Deputy Prime Minister Anwar Ibrahim showed that other "big fish" were not similarly targeted, and the ACA, which was not known for its swift action in investigating "big fish," had "acted with alacrity in pursuing corruption allegations against Anwar Ibrahim" (Painter, 2001, p. 131). The ACA was replaced by the Malaysian Anti-Corruption Commission in January 2009.

In Thailand, the Counter Corruption Commission (CCC) was created in February 1975 with the enactment of the Counter Corruption Act (CCA) (Quah, 1982a, p. 172). However, the CCC was ineffective for three reasons. First, the CCC's task of curbing corruption was handicapped by the tolerant Thai attitude toward corruption, which was not viewed to be against the public interest (Mulder, 1996, pp. 173–174). Second, the CCC encountered difficulty in performing its role because of the constant conflict between the Cabinet and the bureaucracy (Dalpino, 1991, p. 66). Finally, and most importantly, the CCC was viewed by its critics as a "paper tiger" without real teeth, as "it could only send reports to the prime minister and Cabinet" since it lacked "direct authority to punish public officials" (Amara, 1992, p. 240). The promulgation of the "People's Constitution" on October 11, 1997, led to the replacement of the ineffective CCC by the National Counter Corruption Commission (NCCC) in November 1999. The NCCC was renamed the National Anti-Corruption Commission (NACC) on July 15, 2008.

In South Korea, the Anti-Corruption Act was enacted on July 24, 2001, and the Korea Independent Commission against Corruption (KICAC) was established in January 2002. President Park Chung-Hee created the Board of Audit and Inspection (BAI) in 1963 to provide a check on the economic bureaucracy, and its functions included the investigation of corrupt offenses by civil servants. In March 1975, Park initiated the *Seojungshaeshin* (General Administration Reform) Movement to curb corruption in the civil service. However, the BAI remained unchanged until President Kim Young-Sam strengthened it in 1993 and formed the Commission for the Prevention of Corruption (CPC) to assist the BAI's chairman. South Korea's anticorruption strategy was further strengthened by the comprehensive anticorruption reforms introduced by President Kim Dae-Jung in 1999, which culminated in the introduction of the Anti-Corruption Act and the formation of the KICAC. In short, the evolution of South Korea's anticorruption strategy shows that it has changed from pattern 1 (1963–2001) to pattern 3 from 2002.

Finally, Indonesia established the Corruption Eradication Commission (CEC) or *Komisi Pemberantasan Korupsi* (KPK) in December 2003, and Mongolia formed the Independent Authority against Corruption (IAAC) in December 2006. Table 1.3 provides details of the anticorruption laws and ACAs in the 10 Asian countries according to the three patterns of corruption control.

## POLICY CONTEXTS OF 10 ASIAN COUNTRIES

In 1947, John Merriman Gaus (1947, p. 6) contended that "the study of public administration must include its ecology." He elaborated on the importance of the ecological approach in public administration thus:

> An ecological approach to public administration builds, then, quite literally from the ground up; from the elements of a place – soils, climate, location, for example – to the people who live there – their numbers and ages and knowledge, and the ways of physical and social technology by which from the place and in relationships with one another, they get their living. It is within this setting that their instruments and practices of public housekeeping should be studied so that they may better understand what they are doing, and appraise reasonably how they are doing it. (Gaus, 1947, pp. 8–9)

In his more recent analysis of health care policy in Germany, Great Britain, the Soviet Union, and Japan, Howard M. Leichter (1979, p. 39) recommended the accounting scheme or "an inventory of those factors that influence the making of public policy." More specifically, Leichter's accounting scheme consists of situational, structural, cultural, and environmental factors (Leichter, 1979, pp. 41–42). Similarly, Donald P. Warwick (1979, pp. 296–320) focused on the "remote and proximate environment" in his comparative study of the formulation and implementation of population programs in Egypt, Kenya, Mexico, and the Philippines. A final example is provided by Robert C. Williamson's comparative analysis of Latin American cultures that focused on the geographical, anthropological, historical, and sociological bases of these cultures (Williamson, 2006, chaps. 2–4).

The policy context refers to the geographical, historical, economic, demographic, and political aspects of a country's environment that influence the nature and style of public policy formulation and implementation (Quah, 1984, p. 109). A country's policy context can promote or hinder its incumbent government's anticorruption efforts depending on whether the contextual factors are conducive or hostile to the implementation of public policies.

More specifically, these four aspects can assist or hinder an incumbent government in the implementation of its anticorruption measures:

1. *Size of the country*: A large country or archipelago would encounter more difficulties in enforcing the anticorruption measures in the provinces or outer islands than a small country or city-state.
2. *GDP per capita*: A poor country would have more difficulty than a rich one in implementing anticorruption measures if it does not receive

***Table 1.4.*** Policy Contexts of 10 Asian Countries.

| Country | Land Area (sq km) | Population (million) 2009 | Population Density per sq km | GDP per Capita 2009 | 2010 CPI score | Political System |
|---|---|---|---|---|---|---|
| Hong Kong SAR | 1,075 | 7.0 | 6,511.6 | US$29,826 | 8.4 | SAR of China |
| India | 3,287,263 | 1,198.0 | 364.4 | US$1,031 | 3.3 | Federal Parliamentary Democracy |
| Indonesia | 1,904,443 | 230.0 | 120.7 | US$2,329 | 2.8 | Presidential Democracy |
| Japan | 377,727 | 127.2 | 336.7 | US$39,731 | 7.8 | Constitutional Monarchy |
| Mongolia | 1,565,000 | 2.7 | 1.7 | US$1,560 | 2.7 | Presidential Democracy |
| Philippines | 300,000 | 92.0 | 306.6 | US$1,746 | 2.4 | Presidential Democracy |
| Singapore | 710 | 4.9 | 7,022 | US$37,293 | 9.3 | Parliamentary Democracy |
| South Korea | 99,274 | 48.3 | 486.5 | US$17,074 | 5.4 | Presidential Democracy |
| Taiwan | 36,179 | 23.1 | 638.4 | US$16,392 | 5.8 | Presidential Democracy |
| Thailand | 513,115 | 67.8 | 132.1 | US$3,940 | 3.5 | Constitutional Monarchy |

*Sources*: *Economist* (2010a); Schwab (2010, pp. 361–362); Department of Statistics (2010, p. 9); http://www.transparency.org/policy_research/surveys_indices/cpi/2010/results

financial and technical assistance from donor organizations and countries.

3. *Nature and size of the population*: A country with a small and homogeneous population would have less difficulty than a country with a large and heterogeneous population in implementing anticorruption measures.
4. *Nature of the political system*: Is the political system democratic or authoritarian? What is the role of the military in politics? Are elections held freely and at regular intervals? Are the political leaders accountable for their actions? Is corruption a fact of life or a way of life? (Quah, 2006a, p. 2).

Table 1.4 provides a summary of the policy contexts in the 10 Asian countries analyzed in this book. These 10 countries are selected for three reasons. The first reason is the availability of published research in English on corruption in these countries. Second, the author is also more familiar with these countries as he has visited and conducted research on corruption there. Finally, the 10 countries selected reflect the three patterns of corruption control with Japan employing the first pattern, India, the Philippines and Taiwan practicing the second pattern, and Singapore, Hong Kong SAR, Thailand, South Korea, Indonesia, and Mongolia relying on the third pattern.

## AIM OF THE BOOK

During 1993–1997, corruption was "transformed from a predominantly national or regional preoccupation to an issue of global revolutionary force." Indeed, corruption has emerged in the 1990s as "a truly global political issue eliciting a global political response" (Glynn, Kobrin, & Naim, 1997, p. 7). Consequently, many international organizations like the Asian Development Bank, the Institute for International Economics, the Organization for Economic Co-operation and Development, Transparency International, the United Nations, and the World Bank have organized conferences, symposia, and workshops on the causes, consequences, and control of corruption in various countries to enable the participants from many countries to share and learn the best practices in fighting corruption round the world. Some of these conference proceedings have been published during 1997–2000 (Elliot, 1997; Kpundeh & Hors, 1998; Stapenhurst & Kpundeh, 1999; ADB, 2000).

With the globalization of corruption and the harmful effects of corruption, it is important to account for the different levels of corruption in Asian countries. Why is corruption a serious problem in India, Indonesia, Japan, Mongolia, the Philippines, South Korea, Taiwan, and Thailand? On the contrary, why have Singapore and Hong Kong SAR been able to minimize corruption? Is minimizing corruption in India, Indonesia, Japan, Mongolia, the Philippines, South Korea, Taiwan, and Thailand an impossible dream? The aim of this book is to answer these questions by comparing how these 10 Asian countries have dealt with the problem of corruption.

## PREVIEW OF THE CHAPTERS

More specifically, this book analyzes the three patterns of corruption control in Hong Kong SAR, India, Indonesia, Japan, Mongolia, the Philippines, Singapore, South Korea, Taiwan, and Thailand. These countries are selected for analysis because of the author's knowledge of their anticorruption measures. Chapter 2 analyzes Japan's weak anticorruption measures as an example of the first pattern of corruption control. Chapters 3–5 describe and evaluate respectively the anticorruption measures in India, Philippines, and Taiwan, to illustrate the second pattern of corruption control.

The third pattern of corruption control is best illustrated by the anticorruption measures of Singapore and Hong Kong SAR, which are also the least corrupt countries in Asia. The experiences of these city-states in curbing corruption are examined in Chapters 6 and 7 respectively. The case of Thailand is analyzed in Chapter 8, which traces the evolution of anticorruption agencies from the formation of the Board of Inspection and Follow-up of Government Operations in September 1972 to the establishment of the NCCC in November 1999.

Chapter 9 focuses on South Korea, which adopted the third pattern of corruption control in January 2002 with the creation of the KICAC. Chapter 10 traces the evolution of anticorruption measures in Indonesia from the *Kopkamtib* to the KPK in December 2003. With the formation of the IAAC in December 2006, Mongolia became one of the most recent Asian countries to adopt the third pattern of corruption. The transformation of Mongolia's pattern of corruption control is dealt with in Chapter 11.

The patterns of corruption control in these 10 countries are analyzed using a common framework to facilitate comparative analysis. Each of the 10 country chapters begins with a short description of an important corruption scandal in the country, followed by a discussion of these salient aspects of the country's policy context namely, its geography, history, economy, demography, and political system. The perceived extent of corruption in the country is ascertained, including the identification of the major causes of corruption. Following this, the anticorruption measures in the country are described and evaluated in terms of their effectiveness in curbing corruption.

Chapter 12 concludes the book by comparing the effectiveness of the 10 Asian countries in curbing corruption according to five indicators. While pattern 3 is more effective than patterns 1 and 2, not all the countries that have adopted pattern 3 have been equally successful in minimizing corruption. Of the six countries that have employed a single ACA to curb corruption, only Singapore and Hong Kong SAR have been effective because of the political will of their governments and their favorable policy contexts. Finally, the features of an effective anticorruption strategy are identified and the question of whether such a strategy can be transferred to other Asian countries is also considered.

## NOTES

1. For example, Fredrik Galtung (2006, pp. 109–123) has identified these "seven failings" of the CPI: (1) it is one-sided and focuses only on the major bribe-takers; (2) its coverage of countries is "irregular and uncontrolled"; (3) it is culturally biased because its sample is private-sector oriented, male, and rich; (4) its sources are imprecise and "sometimes ignorant"; (5) its definition of corruption is narrow and imprecise; (6) it does not measure trends and cannot reward genuine reformers; and (7) aid donors have relied on the CPI as a criterion for granting aid to developing countries.
2. For three excellent discussions of the genesis and difficulties in defining and measuring corruption, see Johnston (1996), Heller (2009), and Underkuffler (2009).

# CHAPTER 2

# JAPAN

> Corruption in Japan is in a sense legitimized by its systematic perpetration. It is so highly organized, and has become so much a part of the extra-legal ways of the Japanese System on so many levels, that most citizens and foreign residents do not recognize it for what it is, but accept it as 'part of the system.' The press calls it 'structural corruption,' implicitly acknowledging that it is a necessary aspect of the System in its present condition.
>
> – Karel van Wolferen (1993, p. 179)

> When there is government scandal involving bribery, buying influence, or using power for anything other than the public advantage, the Japanese call it black mist, for it hangs over the political landscape like smog over a city … . In the meantime the public can only hope that a strong breeze will come along and blow the smog of corruption away. In recent years, the public has been constantly disappointed; not only does the atmosphere not clear, but political scandals seem to occur ever more frequently.
>
> – Marshall E. Dimock (1968, p. 84)

## THE LOCKHEED SCANDAL

The Lockheed scandal was exposed during the 4 February 1976 hearings of the Sub-Committee on Multinational Corporations of the United States Senate Committee on Foreign Relations. These hearings revealed that Lockheed Aircraft Corporation paid illegal payments in several countries including Japan to promote the sale of its planes to prevent bankruptcy. The Securities Exchange Commission obtained documents showing that Lockheed paid more than US$10 million to Yoshio Kodama, a "fixer" and Lockheed's secret representative, and the Marubeni Corporation, which was Lockheed's agent in Japan since 1959. During the same hearings on 6 February, A. Carl Kotchian, vice president of Lockheed, informed the committee that a senior Japanese government official received US$2 million from Marubeni and that his company relied on Kenji Osano, a close associate of former Prime Minister Kakuei Tanaka, as an intermediary in its efforts to sell 21 Lockheed's L-1001 Tristar airbuses to All Nippon Airways (ANA) (Macdougall, 1988, pp. 193–195).

The US Senate hearings on the Lockheed scandal led to a joint investigation by the Tokyo District's Public Prosecutor's Office (PPO), the Metropolitan Police Headquarters, and the Tokyo office of the National Tax Bureau. The PPO indicted Kodama on 13 March 1976 for tax evasion for not declaring the US$6,274,000 in commissions that he received from Lockheed (Macdougall, 1988, p. 196). More than three months later, the PPO and the Tokyo Metropolitan Police arrested four persons including Toshiharu Okubo of Marubeni and Yuji Sawa of ANA.

On 27 July 1976, Tanaka was arrested by the PPO, and on 16 August, he was indicted for violating the Foreign Exchange Control Law and for receiving bribes of ¥500 million (US$2.1 million). He was released the next day after payment of ¥200 million bail. Tanaka was convicted after a lengthy trial on 12 October 1983 and sentenced by the Tokyo District Court to four years imprisonment and a fine of ¥500 million (Macdougall, 1988, pp. 197–198). He filed an appeal, and two months later, he was reelected to the Diet by an overwhelming majority of voters in his constituency of Niigata (Allen, 1990, pp. 160–161). On 29 July 1987, the Tokyo High Court upheld the 1983 district court ruling and sentenced Tanaka to four years and a ¥500 million fine (Shiratori, 1994, p. 189). Tanaka appealed against the high court decision, and the appeals process lasted for a decade and only ended with his death on 16 December 1993 (Mabrey, 2007, p. 176).

The Japanese government indicted a total of 16 persons including politicians and officials from the Marubeni Corporation and ANA (Macdougall, 1988, pp. 197–198). However, the biggest culprit, Tanaka, was not punished for his bribery because he appealed several times against his sentence until his death in December 1993. In January 1995, the *Yomiuri Shimbun* conducted an opinion poll to ask ordinary Japanese to rank "those people who have done the most to help Japan succeed since the Second World War." Tanaka was ranked first, followed by three other prime ministers (Yoshida Shigeru, Sato Eisaku, and Ikeda Hayato) who were also corrupt (Bowen, 2003, pp. 5–6).

According to Nakamura and Dairokuno (2003, pp. 106–107), "even now, Tanaka still commands a great deal of respect from both fellow politicians and his hometown constituency" because

> The majority of Tanaka's followers do not regard his conduct as a serious crime. In their opinion, certainly, Tanaka took the bribes; however, they argue that he did not use them for his personal benefit. Instead his supporters contend, he dispensed all the bribe monies to his followers for their various political activities. In the view of his allies, Tanaka was a 'caring man', who epitomized the role model of a Japanese leader, because he tried the best he could to look after his supporters.

Roger Bowen (2003, p. 6) attributes the Japanese public's contradictory high regard for Tanaka in spite of their declining confidence in its government to the "absence of the sort of democratic disposition that is unforgiving of political corruption." However, in his biography of Tanaka, James Babb (2000, pp. 95–96) contends that the Lockheed scandal "dogged Tanaka for the rest of his political career and limited his future as a politician to a greater extent than he was willing to acknowledge." Finally, Chalmers Johnson (1995, p. 211) astutely observes that "whatever Tanaka may have achieved, he did not make Japanese politics accountable to the people."

## AIM OF THE CHAPTER

Bull and Newell (2003, p. vi) describe Japan as a "somewhat corrupt" country in their book on corruption in 13 contemporary democracies. Among the various Asian countries included in Transparency International's annual Corruption Perceptions Index (CPI) since 1995, Japan has been consistently perceived to be the third least corrupt Asian country after Singapore and Hong Kong Special Administrative Region (SAR). Rothacher (2003, p. 106) refers to this paradox regarding corruption Japanese style: while "there is virtually no petty corruption" there is, however, grand corruption because "corruption is a structural component of Japan's power structure" and "is endemic in a system run by an oligarchy operating in a gift culture."

In his 1983 inaugural lecture at Oxford University, Stockwin (1983, pp. 10–11) has identified the serious problem of "structural corruption" as one of the features of contemporary Japan, which merited criticism. Similarly, as indicated in the opening quotation of this chapter, Karel van Wolferen (1993, p. 179) describes the "structural corruption" in Japan as being "legitimized by its systematic perpetration," and "so highly organized, and has become so much a part of the extralegal ways of the Japanese System." On the contrary, the absence of petty corruption means that the Japanese are fortunate that they do not need to pay civil servants bribes to obtain basic services. However, juxtaposed with the low level of petty corruption is the extensive grand corruption, which is reflected in the many bribery scandals during the postwar period (Ziemba & Schwartz, 1992, p. 279).

Although research has been done on corruption in Japan,[1] Babb (2005, pp. 177–178) contends that corruption in Japan has not been identified as a research focus because it was not discussed in major works such as Ramseyer and Rosenbluth (1997) and Kohno (1997). Curtis (1999, p. 73) has observed that "political corruption is an old story in Japan" because of the prevalence of corruption scandals during the prewar and postwar periods. However, there has been no attempt to systematically explain this paradox of corruption Japanese style, namely, the coexistence of a high level of grand corruption with a low level of petty corruption. At first glance, the absence of petty corruption in the Japanese Civil Service (JCS) is all the more remarkable as the salaries of Japanese civil servants are adequate but much lower than those of their counterparts in the private sector. Indeed, as will be discussed later, the prevalence of gift-giving in Japan and the difficulty in distinguishing between a gift and a bribe helps to explain its low level of petty corruption.

In short, the situation in Japan is unique as petty corruption is a fact of life, but grand corruption is a way of life. The aim of this chapter is twofold. First, to explain this puzzle: why does a low level of petty corruption coexist with a high level of grand corruption in Japan? The second aim of this chapter is to explain why the Japanese government has not been committed to curbing corruption. This chapter contends that the prevalence of grand corruption in Japan is a reflection of the lack of political will of its government in curbing corruption. It begins by describing the policy context in Japan, ascertaining the perceived extent of Japanese corruption and identifying its major causes before proceeding to analyze and evaluate the government's anticorruption measures.

## JAPAN'S POLICY CONTEXT

### *Geography*

Japan has a land area of 377,727 sq km (Economist, 2010a, p. 170) and is an archipelago consisting of four main islands – Honshu, Hokkaido, Shikoku, and Kyushu – and 6,800 smaller islands (Statistics Bureau of Japan, 2008, p. 2). Honshu is the largest of the four main islands and also the most visited by tourists because of its historical and cultural importance. In contrast, Hokkaido, is the second largest island and is considered as Japan's last frontier. Kyushu served as a gateway to China and Korea because of its proximity to these countries. Shikoku is the smallest and least developed of the four islands (Reiber & Spencer, 1996, pp. 7–8).

Nearly two-thirds (66.4 percent) of the country is mountainous, and only 12.6 percent is farmland (Statistics Bureau of Japan, 2008, p. 4). As most of the mountains are volcanic in origin, with 60 active volcanoes, it is not surprising

**Box 2.1.** Japan's Policy Context

| | |
|---|---|
| Land area | 377,727 sq km |
| Arable land | 12% |
| GDP | US$4,911 billion (2008) |
| GDP per capita | US$38,460 (2008) |
| Unemployment rate | 4.0% |
| Population | 127.9 million (2008) |
| Population density | 339.2 persons per sq km |
| Urban population | 66.8% |
| Adult literacy rate | 99% |
| Political system | Constitutional monarchy |
| "Colonial" rule | Allied Occupation (1945–1952) |
| 2010 CPI rank and score | 17/178 and 7.8/10 |
| 2010 PERC rank and score | 5/16 and 3.49/10 |

*Sources*: Economist (2010a, p. 170); http://www.transparency.org/policy_research/surveys_indices/cpi/2010/results; *Straits Times* (2010a).

that Japan is plagued by earthquakes throughout the centuries (Sakaguchi, 1980, p. 4). In addition to earthquakes, Japan has also been adversely affected during summer and autumn by typhoons as "80 percent of the disasters due to storm and heavy rains are caused by typhoons" (Maejima, 1980, p. 70). The mountainous nature of the country has resulted in the concentration of the population in only 10 percent of Japan's land area, with the rest of the area devoted to agriculture (Reiber & Spencer, 1996, p. 8).

The well-developed infrastructure of roads and highways and the excellent public transport system of bus, mass rapid transit, and railways have enabled the population to travel easily and speedily across the four main islands. The ease of travel throughout the country and its advanced communications system have enabled the government to respond swiftly to natural disasters such as earthquakes and typhoons. In other words, geography is not an obstacle to the enforcement of the anticorruption laws in Japan.

### *History*

Bribery in traditional Japan was illegal and viewed as immoral by Confucianists. Nevertheless, according to Richard H. Mitchell (1996, p. iv), bribery was ubiquitous in traditional Japan in spite of "moral restraints, anti-bribery laws, and occasional harsh punishments" because of the low salaries of officials and the custom of gift-giving. Bribery was widespread in the Tokugawa bureaucracy, and merchants gave "gifts in anticipation" to magistrates when submitting bids for work. After receiving the contracts, the merchants sent "thank-offerings" to the magistrates who selected them (Mitchell, 1996, p. 4).

The Tokugawa Shogunate (1603–1867) was replaced in 1868 by the Meiji state. However, in spite of "official exhortations and new anti-bribery laws," the previous pattern of corruption continued because of the "Tokugawa legacy of ignoring anti-bribery regulations coupled with the arrogance of a victorious elite." In the mid-1880s, it was reported that the Mitsubishi Company initiated a special fund of ¥400,000 for bribing government officials. Even though bribery was made a criminal offense in Article 91 of the Election Law of 11 February 1889, bribery was widespread in the first national election of July 1890 as small bribes were given to many voters as gifts and larger bribes were given by the candidates to buy specific votes (Mitchell, 1996, pp. 10–13). This pattern of politicians providing money and gifts to voters became institutionalized in subsequent elections during the following decades.

Unlike other scholars, Mitchell (1996, p. xvi) contends that the origin of the Japan's structural corruption can be traced to the prewar period because the Teijin incident of the 1930s illustrates clearly the "inside workings of the system of structural corruption."[2] Bribery was also rampant during the Allied Occupation as reflected in Showa Electric Company scandal, which resulted in the resignation of the Ashida Hitoshi cabinet.

Thus, corruption in contemporary Japan will be a difficult problem to eradicate because of the long history of widespread bribery during the Tokugawa Shogunate, the Meiji state, the prewar period, and the Allied Occupation.

### *Economy*

In 2008, Japan's gross domestic product (GDP) of US$4,911 billion made it the second largest economy in the world after the United States. Its GDP per capita of US$38,460 makes it one of the richest Asian countries too. Japan's economic affluence is also reflected in these statistics: there are 99.0 color television sets per 100 households; 38 telephone lines per 100 population; 86.7 mobile telephone subscribers per 100 population; and 422.7 Internet hosts per 1,000 of population (Economist, 2010a, pp. 170–171).

Craig Freedman (2007, pp. 26–38) divides the evolution of the postwar Japanese economy into four periods. During the first period of the "miracle economy" (1945–1973), the government's commitment to industrialization and research and development resulted in its "double-digit growth." The economy remained dominant during the second period (1973–1992), and it performed better than other economies with "higher growth, lower inflation and lower unemployment" in spite of the 1973 and 1978 oil shocks. However, the Japanese economy was described as "anorexic" and "almost narcoleptic" during the third period (1992–2003) because its average annual growth rate was only 1 percent. The economy began to recover during 2003, and by 2005, domestic consumption increased and unemployment was reduced to 4.2 percent.

Even though the economy has contracted by 3.3 percent during the final quarter of 2008 because of "a collapse in overseas demand compounded by a strong yen" (Economist, 2009b), the fact remains that the Japanese government can afford to allocate the required resources to curb corruption effectively. However, as will be shown later in this chapter, the government has not done so, not because it cannot afford to do so, but because it lacks the political will to curb corruption.

## *Demography*

Japan's population of 127.9 million persons in 2008 is the 10th largest in the world and the 6th largest in Asia (Economist, 2010a, p. 14). Its population density is 339.2 persons per sq km and 66.8 percent of the population live in the urban areas (Economist, 2010a, p. 170). The population is homogeneous as 99 percent are Japanese. The homogeneity in language and culture of the population is an important advantage for the government's efforts in spreading the anticorruption message among all Japanese.

On the contrary, the cultural tradition of gift-giving and the practice of *amakudari* (descent from heaven) hinder anticorruption efforts for two reasons. First, the socially accepted custom of gift-giving in Japan makes it difficult for prosecutors to distinguish between gifts and bribes. Second, *amakudari* or the practice of rewarding senior civil servants with lucrative jobs in the private sector after their retirement encourages collusion and corrupt behavior among retiring bureaucrats and businessmen. These two practices will be analyzed in greater detail later as they constitute two important causes of corruption in Japan.

### *Political System*

Japan has a constitutional monarchy with the emperor as the head of state. However, executive power resides in the Cabinet and the Prime Minister. There is a bicameral legislature consisting of the House of Representatives, which has 480 members elected for a 4-year term, and the 242-member House of Councilors (O'uchi et al., 2006, p. 18). Even though there are eight political parties, Japan has a one-party dominant system because the Liberal Democratic Party (LDP) had the majority of seats in the Diet from 1955 to 1993 (Hrebenar, 2000, p. 9).

The Japanese political system is vulnerable to corruption for three reasons. First, it is extremely expensive to get elected in Japan even though the government has subsidized the cost of election campaigns and prohibited certain types of campaign activities. The cost of being elected to the House of Councilors has increased from ¥500 million (US$1.7 million) in 1974 to ¥700 million in 1980. In contrast, election to the House of Representatives was less expensive as ¥40 million was needed by an incumbent to retain his or her seat before 1996. Most of the candidates had to spend ¥100 million, and new candidates needed to spend ¥200 million to get elected. In the 1990 lower house elections, the LDP candidates spent more than ¥200 billion (US$1.3 billion) on campaigning (Hrebenar, 2000, pp. 66–68).

Secondly, a member of the Diet in Japan receives an annual compensation from the government of US$170,000 and an additional US$10,000 in expenses for transportation and communications (O'uchi et al., 2006, pp. 18–19). However, this official income is inadequate for a Diet member to meet his or her social obligations, which include the attendance of weddings, funerals, and parties. A survey found that the average LDP Diet member has attended an average of over 30 ceremonies, receptions, or funerals each month. It becomes very expensive for Diet members to attend these events as they are expected to provide a gift of ¥10,000 (US$119 on 11 December 2010) for a funeral, and ¥30,000 (US$357) for a wedding. It has been estimated that the average LDP Diet member spends about ¥100 million (US$1,191,000) per year to meet his or her social obligations (Hrebenar, 2000, p. 67).

As their compensation cannot cover all their expenses, Diet members have to rely on various financial sources. The increase in election expenses favored those candidates with strong ties with the business community (Richardson & Flanagan, 1984, p. 23). A 1989 survey conducted by the *Asahi Shimbun* found that corporate contributions accounted for 39 percent of the funds required by Diet members, followed by fund-raising parties (17 percent), individual contributions (15 percent), government salaries or subsidies (12 percent), member's factional leader (9 percent), and loans (8 percent) (Hrebenar, 2000, pp. 67–68).

The third weakness of the Japanese political system is the "rotten triangle" or collusion between the politicians, businessmen, and bureaucrats. Politicians collude with businessmen by receiving donations from them for intervening on their behalf with administrative agencies to favor a specific business enterprise or sector. The collusion between bureaucrats and businessmen is manifested in the practices of *amakudari* (descent by parachute) and *kansei-dango* (bureaucrat-led bid rigging) (O'uchi et al., 2006, pp. 35–36).

## PERCEIVED EXTENT OF CORRUPTION

Richard H. Mitchell (1996, p. xiii) observes that many writers have speculated on "the amount of political bribery" in Japan. For example, Edwin Reischauer (1988, pp. 283, 285) has noted that political corruption is less widespread in Japan, and major corruption cases are rare. However, William Chapman (1991, p. 155) contends that based on the "frequency of scandals, the prominence of those involved, and the amounts of money changing hands, it would seem that Japan's politics is the world's most corrupt." Whose assessment is correct?

In his perceptive book on Japan, Marshall E. Dimock (1968, p. 84) refers to "black mist," which is used by the Japanese to describe a "government scandal involving bribery, buying influence, or using power for anything other than the public advantage." According to him, "scarcely a day passes when the press in Japan does not contain articles or editorials on the money-in-elections issue and its direct relation to corruption in government and the loss of the voters' confidence." However, in recent years, the public has been constantly disappointed because "not only does the atmosphere not clear, but political scandals seem to occur ever more frequently" (Dimock, 1968, pp. 76, 84).

Rothacher (2003, p. 111) has classified the corruption scandals in Japan into three categories: (1) political corruption arising from the insatiable funding needs of the politicians; (2) bureaucratic corruption involving public officials; and (3) collusion between organized crime (*Yakuza*) and big business, LDP politicians, some ministries and the police. Table 2.1 shows that 52 corruption scandals have occurred in Japan from 1948 to 2008.

*Table 2.1.* Number of Corruption Scandals in Japan, 1948–2008.

| Year | Number | Name of Scandal |
|---|---|---|
| 1948 | 2 | Shoden (Showa Denko), Tankan |
| 1949 | 1 | Japan Silk |
| 1950 | 1 | Fertilizer Corporation |
| 1952 | 1 | Dentsu |
| 1953 | 1 | Sato (Sugar Dealers) |
| 1954 | 2 | Zosen, Hozen Keizaikai |
| 1955 | 1 | Tokyo Metropolitan Government |
| 1956 | 2 | Den-Den Kaihatsu (Imported Rice), Zen-Ko-Ren |
| 1957 | 1 | Prostitution |
| 1958 | 1 | Graman Lockheed |
| 1961 | 1 | Bushu Railway |
| 1966 | 1 | Shinano River Basin |
| 1966–1967 | 1 | Kyowa Seito |
| 1967 | 1 | Osaka Taxi |
| 1968 | 1 | Nittsu (Nihon Tsuun) |
| 1976 | 2 | Lockheed; Fukushima, Chiba, Gifu Prefecture Governors |
| 1979 | 4 | Fictitious business trips (Postal Service, Environment Agency, Cabinet Secretariat)<br>Crime of Soliciting and Accepting Bribes<br>(Miyazaki Prefecture Governor) |
| 1985 | 1 | Nihon Nenshi-Ko-ren |
| 1988 | 2 | Jarisen (Gravel Ship), Recruit |
| 1989 | 1 | Labor & Education Vice-Ministers arrested |
| 1991–1993 | 1 | Zenecon (General Construction) |
| 1992 | 1 | Kyowa |
| 1993 | 2 | Zenecon (Hazama); Tokyo Sagawa Kyubin |
| 1995 | 1 | Two Credit Associations |
| 1996 | 1 | Fictitious business trips (Hokkaido Government officials) |
| 1997 | 1 | Orange Kyosai Kumiai |
| 1998 | 2 | Nissho Securities; Defense Agency |
| 2000 | 2 | Construction; KDS |
| 2001 | 2 | P.O. Managers; Foreign Ministry |
| 2002 | 1 | Suppression of Mitsui whistle-blowing |
| 2004 | 1 | Niigata public works bidding |
| 2005 | 2 | Japan Dental Association;<br>Japan Highway Public Corporation |
| 2006 | 2 | Dango 3 Prefecture Governors<br>Defense Facilities Agency |
| 2007 | 2 | Nagoya subway expansion bidding<br>Green Resources Organization |
| 2008 | 3 | Ohita Prefecture teacher recruitment<br>Defense Vice-Minister Moriya<br>PCI |
| Total | 52 | – |

*Sources*: Compiled from information provided by Professor Minoru O'uchi, and from Ziemba and Schwartz (1992, p. 279), Babb (2005, p. 179), and O'uchi et al. (2006, p. 12).

In their 2006 country study report on Japan's national integrity system, Minoru O'uchi et al. focus on five major types of corruption. First, administrative corruption involving junior civil servants and private individuals has declined from several thousand cases yearly after World War II to an average of 1,000 persons arrested annually from 1960 to 1970. The average number of those arrested for bribery and embezzlement has decreased from 768 in the 1970s to 549 in the 1980s and to 263 in the 1990s. However, from 2000 to 2004, the average number of arrests has risen to 369 persons per year. In terms of sector, those arrested came from construction and public works, licensing and sanctioning, and examination and inspection. More importantly, it should be noted that 80 percent of those arrested for administrative corruption are local government officials, with the remaining 20 percent equally divided between national government officials and private individuals (O'uchi et al., 2006, p. 12).

In 2004, it was reported that 80 percent of Japanese civil servants who were dismissed for disciplinary reasons came from the Japan Postal Services Public Corporation (JPSPC). On 12 August 2004, the JPSPC's auditing unit in Osaka dismissed a postmaster for embezzling ¥8 million in cash held in a lockbox. The Osaka Public Prosecution Office found that the post office had spent ¥79 million without indicating the purpose and that the postmaster had used part of the money for buying a Mercedes Benz and race horses. *Shukan Post* obtained documents that identified 60 cases of embezzlement in the JPSPC, which was much higher than the number of embezzlement cases in banks (*Japan Today*, 2004).

Corruption is a serious problem at the local government level as "there have been countless cases of bribery of town mayors and other officials" involving the granting of contracts for public works or providing services. Many charges and arrests have been made for massive vote buying or gift-giving in Chiba, Niigata and Kofu Prefectures, including six governors (Woronoff, 1986, pp. 314–315). The number of corruption cases involving local governments and public corporations in Japan increased from 135 in 1999 to 139 in 2000. The total number of local government or public corporation heads and employees implicated in these corruption scandals rose from 167 to 175 during 1999–2000 (*Japan Today*, 2001).

The bankruptcy of Yubari City, Hokkaido, a prosperous mining town, in June 2006, has highlighted the financial problems faced by local governments in Japan. Apart from its aging population (40 percent are over 65 years old), the other important reason for Yubari City's bankruptcy is "the lack of transparent fiscal management and, possibly, corruption." Indeed, "corrupt management is rampant throughout Japanese municipalities" and is manifested in examples such as "unnecessary foreign travel by members of local assemblies; public investment in unwanted roads and bridges; off-the-books money for wining and dining officials; and a lack of discipline" for guarantees to "third-sector companies" (Umeda, Yamazahi, & O'uchi, 2008, p. 200).

The second type of corruption is individual political corruption where senior civil servants, politicians, and businessmen are involved in "secret collusion" with illegal donations and collusive bidding. For example, the Japan Dental Association was indicted in 2005 for illegally donating ¥100 million in 2001 to the LDP without being formally registered as required by law. Similarly, the Japan Highway Public Corporation (JHPC) was indicted in July 2005 for initiating and arranging collusive bidding in favor of those construction companies that had agreed to employ retired JHPC officials (O'uchi et al., 2006, p. 12).

Third, there is also institutionalized or systemic corruption that involves the manipulation of state organs by politicians and businessmen in their own interest through their close relationships with senior civil servants. In 2006, senior officials of the Defense Facilities Administration Agency were arrested for collusive bidding with the suppliers of goods, services, and facilities in return for accepting its retired officials for jobs and provision of bribes (O'uchi et al., 2006, p. 12).

Private sector corruption, the fourth type of corruption in Japan, usually takes the form of bid-rigging or *dango* between a supplier and a receiver who collude to induce and share illicit profits at the expense of their trusting partners. Private sector firms have been found guilty of defrauding their consumers, shareholders, or regulators. Commodities can also be disguised illegally with the deceptive reporting of imported beef or pork and defective diesel particulate filters. The fifth type of corruption is international or externally induced corruption by "politicians, businessmen and their agents in collusion with government officials from both donor and recipient countries" (O'uchi et al., 2006, pp. 12–13).

The bureaucracy has not been immune from corruption with the most prevalent form being accounting irregularities involving the padding of bills, namely:

> overtime which had not been worked was listed, official trips with related travel, meals and accommodation were reported although they had never been taken, wages were entered as paid out to non-existent workers, or there were indications of fictitious purchases (along with the corresponding vouchers). (Woronoff, 1986, pp. 315–316)

The rationale for the padding of these bills is twofold. First, those bureaucrats who padded their overtime or travel expenses are illegally increasing their earnings to supplement their income. Second, the additional income is channeled into slush funds to pay for the lavish entertainment of politicians and bureaucrats whose favors are being sought (Woronoff, 1986, p. 316). More than five decades ago, Chitoshi Yanaga (1956, pp. 317–318) observed that

> Expensive banquets and receptions have come to be regarded by the bureaucrats as an indispensable part of the official procedure. Resort to padding payrolls is made to increase entertainment funds while entertainment money and even travel funds are frequently if not regularly used as bonuses for the staff members ... Even in government public works, 15 percent of the total amount appropriated is spent for the entertainment of local bigwigs and those involved in the contract.

Japanese politicians spend a great deal of money for entertainment at expensive restaurants and golf courses. In 1988, elite LDP politicians spent ¥686 million on wining and dining. During the same year, Prime Minister Toshiki Kaifu's political group spent ¥17.5 million on 92 visits to a restaurant in Akasaka, whereas the deputy head of the National Land Agency, Shozaburo Jimi, and his colleagues spent ¥5.7 million on 38 occasions at a Ginza club. As golf helps to "keep the political wheels greased," 12 prominent Diet members and other LDP politicians spent ¥24 million on golfing excursions in 1988 (*Mainichi Daily News*, 1989, p. 12).

Hence it is not surprising that political parties are perceived to be the most corrupt institution in Japan. TI's Global Corruption Barometer confirms that political parties are consistently perceived to be the most corrupt sector in Japan from 2004 to 2010. Table 2.2 shows that the highest score has been attained by political parties in Japan throughout the four years, ranging from 4.0 in 2006 to 4.2 in 2005 and 2010 and to 4.3 in 2004, 2007, and 2009. Table 2.2 also notes that the police are perceived to be the second most corrupt sector in Japan in 2004 and 2005, the third most corrupt sector in 2006 and 2007, and the fifth most corrupt sector in 2010.

From September 1999 to March 2000, there were 166 cases of police misconduct in Japan, which resulted in the arrest of 113 police officers and the dismissal or pay cuts for 434 of them (Johnson, 2003b, p. 23). In December 2003, the Tokyo Metropolitan Police Department punished 42 police officers for corruption as they allowed themselves "to be wined and dined, treated to rounds of golf and entertained at sex industry establishments" (*Kyodo News Service*, 2003). The spate of scandals has resulted in "unprecedented criticism" of the Japanese police and a loss of public trust

*Table 2.2.* Perceived Level of Corruption in Japan by Sector, 2004–2010[a].

| Sector | 2004 | 2005 | 2006 | 2007 | 2009 | 2010 |
|---|---|---|---|---|---|---|
| Political parties | 4.3 | 4.2 | 4.0 | 4.3 | 4.3 | 4.2 |
| Parliament | 3.7 | 3.7 | 3.7 | 3.8 | 3.9 | 3.8 |
| Legal system/judiciary | 3.1 | 3.0 | 3.0 | 3.0 | 3.2 | 3.1 |
| Police | 3.9 | 3.8 | 3.6 | 3.7 | NA | 3.7 |
| Public officials/civil servants | NA | NA | NA | NA | 4.3 | 3.9 |
| Business sector | 3.3 | 3.3 | 3.6 | 3.6 | 3.8 | 3.7 |
| Tax revenue | 3.4 | 3.5 | 3.2 | 3.3 | NA | NA |
| Customs | 3.0 | 2.9 | NA | NA | NA | NA |
| Media | 3.3 | 3.4 | 3.4 | 3.5 | 3.6 | 3.5 |
| Medical services | 3.7 | 3.6 | 3.6 | 3.6 | NA | NA |
| Education | 3.1 | 3.1 | 3.1 | 3.3 | NA | 3.6 |
| Registry and permit services | 2.6 | 2.7 | 2.7 | 2.7 | NA | NA |
| Utilities | 3.0 | 3.2 | 3.0 | 3.1 | NA | NA |
| Military | 3.0 | 3.0 | 3.1 | 3.2 | NA | 3.3 |
| NGOs | 2.9 | 3.0 | 3.0 | 3.1 | NA | 3.1 |
| Religious bodies | 3.6 | 3.8 | 3.7 | 3.7 | NA | 4.0 |

*Sources*: Compiled from Transparency International (2004, p. 18; 2005, p. 18; 2006, p. 21; 2007, p. 22; 2009, p. 28; 2010, p. 43).
[a]The score ranges from 1 (not at all corrupt) to 5 (extremely corrupt); NA, not available.

(Johnson, 2003b, p. 25). A nationwide survey conducted by *Yomiuri Shimbun* in January 2000 found that only 52 percent of the respondents trusted the police, a significant decline from the 74 percent who indicated their trust of the police in a similar survey conducted by the same newspaper in December 1998 (Takeshi, 2000, p. 41).

David Johnson (2003b, pp. 26–33) contends that police corruption is a serious problem because the mechanisms for exposing misconduct are undeveloped in Japan. Indeed, there are three important manifestations of this problem: the embezzlement of money from police slush funds; the opportunities for corruption from the police control of the *pachinko* industry; and police tolerance of organized crime by the *yakuza*. Police corruption in Japan results in these adverse consequences: "it reinforces a culture of secrecy and deceit that is itself a breeding ground for other abuses of authority, and it prevents police from properly enforcing laws against other wrongdoers." Johnson is pessimistic about police reform in Japan because police corruption is not restricted to "a few rotten apples" but is symptomatic of "a failed organization."

## THE CULTURE OF GIFT-GIVING

Why is petty corruption not a serious problem in Japan? The answer is that gift-giving is an important Japanese tradition, and it is "not unusual for a Japanese family to spend over 100,000 yen (1,000 U.S. dollars) a year on presents" (Parry, 1998, p. 27). There are two major seasons for giving gifts in Japan: midsummer and the end of the year. The midsummer gift or *ochugen* resulted from a combination of a Chinese Taoist ceremony and Japan's Buddhist bon festival. Indeed, "the custom of making offerings to ancestors during the bon festival has been extended to giving presents to customers, supervisors, and others of higher rank, or to persons who have provided special favors in the past." In the same way, the *oseibo* or December gifts began with offerings to the returning spirits of ancestors and gods at the new year. Accordingly, Japanese companies pay their employees summer and winter bonuses during these gift-giving seasons (Parry, 1998, p. 28). Indeed, for politicians, "election time is the most expensive gift season" because they have to provide cash gifts for their supporters and pay for their trips to Tokyo (Rothacher, 2003, p. 108).

In addition to seasonal gifts, Japanese also provide souvenir gifts for their family, friends, and colleagues when they return from a trip. This practice originated from those making pilgrimages to the main Shinto shrine in central Japan. As it was expensive to go on a pilgrimage, a village would help to pay for one of them to make the trip on their behalf. Consequently, the pilgrims would return with *omamori* or good luck charms and other gifts for their sponsors. The average Japanese makes 1.5 domestic trips per year and spends more than 65,000 yen (US$65) on souvenir gifts for each trip (Parry, 1998, pp. 28–29).

The importance of gift-giving in Japan is also manifested in rites of passage such as weddings and funerals, which are "occasions for the most elaborate forms of gift-giving." Wedding guests are expected to give cash gifts to the couple, and "the amount given depends on the wealth and status of the giver and where the wedding and reception take place" (Parry, 1998, pp. 29–30). Those attending funerals express their condolences by donating about 3,000 yen each (US$30), and they receive a small gift in return when they leave. Befu has identified 37 occasions when Japanese give ceremonial gifts (Davies & Ikeno, 2002, p. 235). The frequency of gift-giving occasions in Japan facilitates the passing of bribes from "businessman to politician or from politician to voter" (Reed, 1996, pp. 396–397).

Whether gifts are seasonal, souvenir, or ceremonial, gift-giving in Japan is related to status and form in social relationships by strengthening mutual ties and obligations between givers and recipients. According to Parry (1998, pp. 30–31),

> The giving of presents indicates status. Giving *omiyage* indicates that you have enough money and knowledge to travel; your seasonal gifts of beer and soap wrapped in expensive gift-wrap marked with the logo of a famous department store demonstrate that you can afford to shop there and that you know the rules of the game.

Finally, gift-giving reinforces mutual ties between companies, between employers and employees, businesses and customers, and among colleagues (Parry, 1998, p. 31).

On the basis of his fieldwork conducted in 1969, Harumi Befu (1971, p. 3) found that "a large proportion of households in Japan are practically daily giving or receiving one kind of gift or another with their neighbors, friends, relatives, children's playmates, and husband's workmates and business associates." For example, the family of a 38-year-old man working for a bus company received an average of 25 gifts and gave an average of 16 gifts during a nine-month period.

Furthermore, the "protocol of gift-giving in Japan requires the receiver to go through the motion of refusing the gift, knowing full well that he is going to accept it in the last analysis." In other words, "adamant and absolute refusal of the gift" is not acceptable as it "flusters the giver, if he perceives that the refusal is genuine and not ritual." To avoid losing face and to discourage the receiver from refusing the gift, the giver will threaten to terminate future relationships. In other words, "in this game of gift offering the receiver has little choice but to accept" the gift (Befu, 1971, pp. 5–7).

Befu has also noted that "the only possible situation in which one can refuse a gift is when there are specific institutional regulations against receiving a gift." For example, some companies have informed their employees to refrain from giving gifts to their superiors. Similarly, "government officials are instructed not to receive gifts which might be construed as bribes." However, in reality, civil servants might find it difficult to refuse gifts because "all these regulations are counter to cultural norms, expectations of the society which approve, encourage and often require gift-giving." Befu (1971, pp. 7–8) explains why it will be difficult for civil servants to refuse gifts under such circumstances:

> One must act as if he is in a predicament of wanting to receive the gift in accordance with the cultural norm but cannot because of the regulations. The giver, upon being informed of the regulations, still might insist on giving, after all did he not say that the gift was a trifle nothing anyway? And by offering the gift is no longer his, he would be quite embarrassed to take back what once he gave up. Thus, even when one is truly

determined not to receive a gift because of institutional regulations, one might still succumb to the giver's forceful insistence and end up accepting it. In such a case, the give and take goes beyond the expected ritual and the receiver is no longer playing a game; he truly feels his right to refuse based on proclaimed regulations was infringed upon and that he had no choice in the matter.

"What motivates the Japanese to give gifts, and to give so insistently?" Befu has provided four reasons for the Japanese penchant for gift-giving. First, gifts are given because it is customary to do so on occasions such as the end of the year and at weddings and funerals. Second, those receiving gifts at weddings or funerals are expected to reciprocate by providing gifts to the givers on future occasions. Third, gifts are "an expression of thanks for a favor done in the past" by the receiver for the giver. For example, a student gives a gift (*seibo*) at the end of the year to his teacher or former teacher to express his gratitude. However, such gifts are tokens of appreciation and "do not cancel the debt incurred by the favor done by another." More importantly, a person who does not reciprocate with a favor or gift is chastised for being "unmindful of social norms." Finally, gifts are given as "an advanced appreciation of an anticipated favor (*sewa*)." In short, gift-giving in Japan is "a social lubricant" as it "smoothes over human relations" as a gift "obligates the receiver at least to act in a more civil manner toward the giver than without the gift" (Befu, 1971, pp. 9–10, 13–14).

The regulations prohibiting gift-giving among employees of business companies and civil servants provide "relief to those who prefer a lighter load of social obligations." Befu (1971, pp. 14–15) contends that "taking Japanese society as a whole, however, such relief is only slight" because "formal organization is often ignored and regulations blatantly violated when such organization and rules interfere with achievement of a goal, in so far as an informal substructure operates to overlook organizational obstacles and to smooth over these rough spots."

As the social norms in Japan "encourage, compel and prescribe gift-giving," the government and company regulations prohibiting gift-giving are ineffective because they contradict all the traditional norms. Indeed, a person who observes these regulations is expected to justify his behavior and would be considered by many Japanese to be "a bit odd" for not accepting gifts. In contrast, those violating the regulations regarding gift-giving are not ostracized, but their behavior is reinforced by the social norms (Befu, 1971, p. 15).

The new forms of corruption that were introduced after World War II included "the sending of gifts or presents to officials at their arrival and departure and on occasions like the birth of a child, *mah jong* parties at which officials were made to win large sums of money by those seeking favors, and providing lavish geisha entertainment" (Yanaga, 1956, p. 318). Prime Minister Tanaka employed the custom of gift-giving to disburse funds. During the summer of 1974, the press reported that Tanaka had given summer gifts (*o-chugen*) of ¥3 to ¥5 million to every Diet member and many bureau chiefs in the ministries (Johnson, 1995, p. 193).

In Japan, bribery is defined legally as "an act of receiving or giving any compensation, outside the legally specified salary, for the execution of public duties." There are three forms of bribery: acceptance of compensation with a request to execute an irregular act (*seitaku shuwai*), execution of an irregular act for compensation, and receiving compensation to use his official capacity to influence another official to execute an irregular act (*assen shuwai*) (Befu, 1971, p. 22). To complicate matters, the regulations concerning bribery do not apply to the same occupations in both the public and the private sectors.

For example, "a physician of a private hospital … is not subject to bribery regulations, whereas a professor of a national medical school, who performs the same duties as a private physician, is." Thus, a private physician can accept gifts from grateful patients without breaking the law. However, "if a gift is given to a professor of a medical school of a national university by a patient he has treated at the affiliated hospital, the act is clearly and unmistakably bribery." Nevertheless, this has not prevented patients from giving gifts to professors as such gift-giving is more prevalent at the national medical schools (because of the expertise of their staff and better facilities) than at private hospitals. Even though such "bribery is a daily affair, it has been years and years since a doctor of a national university hospital has been indicted with a bribery charge" (Befu, 1971, pp. 23–25).

Given the importance of gift-giving in Japan, is it possible to distinguish a bribe from a gift? Kaplan and Dubro (2003, p. 153) notes that "the concept of bribery in Japan is a muddy one" because of the widespread and institutionalized custom of gift-giving. Furthermore, gift-giving and *giri* or obligation not only contribute to bribery but also make the Japanese "particularly vulnerable to blackmail, intimidation, and a host of related acts" (Kaplan & Dubro, 2003, p. 157).

However, Befu (1971, pp. 27–28) provides four indicators for distinguishing between a gift and a bribe. First, a gift constitutes a bribe "when money is given to a person to whom one would not customarily give money." A second indicator that gift-giving is bribery occurs when "giving cash on non-appropriate [*sic*] occasions in an inappropriate manner, without wrapping, giving dirty used bills, or giving cash to one's social superior are telltale signs of bribery." Accordingly, this explains "why Japanese would try to disguise a bribe as a genuine gift by giving clean bills placed in a money envelope, or, better yet, they would give gift-certificates purchased at department stores, since a gift-certificate is more versatile, and appropriate for more occasions, and therefore less subject to interpretation as bribery." In other words, the Japanese emphasize the formal aspects of gift-giving to provide a "thin veil of propriety" for a bribe so that it can be viewed as a gift instead.

Thirdly, in court hearings of bribery cases in Japan, the prosecutor focuses on the manner of giving the bribes to distinguish "customary" gift-giving from bribery. More specifically, details such as the use of wrinkled money or the absence of gift-money envelope are used as evidence to substantiate the prosecutor's claim that the money offered was a bribe and not a gift. Indeed, Befu (1971, p. 29) acknowledges that the court's task of determining what constitutes customary gift-giving is extremely difficult because it has to acknowledge and accept the cultural practices and norms regarding gift-giving in Japan.

The final indicator of distinguishing a bribe from a gift is the past relationship between the giver and the receiver. According to Befu (1971, p. 30),

> If they have long been friends or associates and have been in a gift-giving relationship and the gift involved in a bribery case was not too out of ordinary in comparison with the past gifts they have exchanged, then the prosecutor would have a hard time convincing the judge that the gift constitutes a bribe. Thus for each case the court must determine whether or not the gift given was customarily appropriate.

Thus, it is difficult to distinguish a bribe from a gift, especially when all the formal features of proper gift-giving have been observed. This explains why the court has ignored the "borderline" cases and focused on the clear-cut cases of bribery instead. It also means that very few bribery cases are tried in court as many other cases have not been considered.

Hence, it is not surprising that B. C. Koh found that the number of bribery cases involving Japanese civil servants from 1960 to 1985 has declined from 80 in 1960 to 12 in 1985 as noted in Table 2.3. A total of 465 civil servants were disciplined for bribery, and of these, only 149 (32 percent) were dismissed. In contrast, 1,275 civil servants were disciplined for embezzlement, and 890 (70 percent) of them were dismissed (Koh, 1989, p. 228). Table 2.4 reports that there were 762 bribery cases involving public

***Table 2.3.*** Bribery Cases Involving Civil Servants in Japan, 1960–1985.

| Year | No. of Bribery Cases | Total as Percentage of all Civil Servants |
|---|---|---|
| 1960 | 80 | 0.01000 |
| 1965 | 228 | 0.02000 |
| 1970 | 85 | 0.01000 |
| 1975 | 39 | 0.00458 |
| 1980 | 21 | 0.00245 |
| 1985 | 12 | 0.00142 |
| Total | 465 | – |

*Source*: Compiled from Koh (1989, p. 228).

***Table 2.4.*** Bribery Cases Involving Public Officials in Japan, 1990–1999.

| Type of Public Official | 1990–1994 | 1995–1999 | Total |
|---|---|---|---|
| Local public officials | 196 | 185 | 381 (50.0%) |
| Members of local assemblies | 135 | 156 | 291 (38.2%) |
| National public officials | 17 | 18 | 35 (4.6%) |
| Officials of public corporations | 5 | 4 | 9 (1.2%) |
| Others | 15 | 31 | 46 (6.0%) |
| Total | 368 | 394 | 762 (100%) |

*Source*: National Police Agency quoted in Tachi (2001, p. 12).

officials during 1990–1999. Half of these bribery cases were committed by local public officials, whereas the members of local assemblies were responsible for 38.2 percent of the cases. It is significant that only 35 national public officials (4.6 percent) and 9 officials of public corporations (1.2 percent) were involved in bribery cases.

The number of bribery cases among national government officials remains small in 2005–2006, but the number of embezzlement cases has increased. Table 2.5 notes that the number of bribery cases has declined from 32 in 2005 to 20 in 2006, but the number of embezzlement cases has increased from 179 to 257 during the same period. Table 2.6 indicates that the number of bribery cases among local government officials has decreased marginally from 50 in 2004 to 47 in 2005. Similarly, the number of local government officials punished for embezzlement has also declined from 103 to 92 during 2004–2005.

***Table 2.5.*** Punishment for National Government Officials for Corruption Offenses, 2005–2006.

| Type of Punishment | 2005 | | 2006 | |
|---|---|---|---|---|
| | Bribery | Embezzlement | Bribery | Embezzlement |
| Disciplinary dismissal | 7 | 107 | 6 | 114 |
| Suspension from duty | 1 | 10 | 0 | 2 |
| Wage cut | 13 | 26 | 3 | 59 |
| Reprimand | 11 | 36 | 11 | 82 |
| Total | 32 | 179 | 20 | 257 |

*Source*: Adapted from Table 12.1 in Akio (2010, p. 259).

***Table 2.6.*** Punishment for Local Government Officials for Corruption Offenses, 2004–2005.

| Type of Punishment | 2004 | | 2005 | |
|---|---|---|---|---|
| | Bribery | Embezzlement | Bribery | Embezzlement |
| Disciplinary dismissal | 32 | 79 | 30 | 87 |
| Suspension from duty | 11 | 6 | 1 | 3 |
| Wage cut | 4 | 11 | 10 | 1 |
| Reprimand | 3 | 7 | 6 | 1 |
| Total | 50 | 103 | 47 | 92 |

*Source*: Adapted from Table 12.2 in Akio (2010, p. 259).

## *AMAKUDARI* (DESCENT FROM HEAVEN)

In addition to the socially accepted tradition of gift-giving, which is a major cause of corruption in Japan, a second contributory factor is *amakudari*, which refers to "the re-employment of top-level bureaucrats in high-level positions in private and public corporations as well as their movement to national political office" after their retirement. Indeed, *amakudari* is responsible for the "alliance of top bureaucrats, leading LDP politicians and corporate elites," which ensures the stability of the power structure in Japan (Colignon & Usui, 2003, p. 2). According to Edward Trimnell (2008, p. 11), "the metaphor behind the term *amakudari* is the idea that newborn executives have 'descended from the heaven' of government administration to the more earthly realm of private enterprise." Similarly, Boye Lafayette de Mente (1997, p. 34) explains that *amakudari* connotes that "life for a top-level bureaucrat is both safe and soft, and leaving such a position for the hurly-burly of the commercial world is like coming down from the clouds."

Referring to *amakudari* as the Japanese version of the "old boys club," Andrew Sheng (2009, pp. 57–58) has observed that, unlike their British counterparts, successful Japanese civil servants felt responsible for finding "a job for those in his cohort who had to drop out because top posts became scarce as one moved higher up the hierarchy." *Amakudari* becomes an "unofficial channel of government influence on the business sector" because the new employers of the retired bureaucrats have access to the senior officials through this unofficial channel. Thus, the personnel section of a ministry fosters informal networks by assigning prestigious positions in the private or quasi-private sector to retired senior civil servants through *amakudari* (Choi, 2007, p. 934).

The number of persons involved in *amakudari* annually is small as among the 3,000 senior bureaucrats who retired in their 50s, 1,700 (57 percent) join private firms, public or semipublic corporations, local political offices, or industrial associations, or run for national political office, with the remaining 1,300 (43 percent) taking positions at research institutes and public universities (Trimnell, 2008, p. 10). In fact, from 2007 to 2009, 1,757 active and former senior bureaucrats were employed through *amakudari* by organizations and companies that had received subsidies or business contracts from the government (*Japan Times*, 2010).

There are four forms of *amakudari*. The first form of *amakudari* involves the movement of bureaucrats from ministries or agencies to profit-making enterprises, which is subject to legal restrictions. The second form is known as *yokosuberi* or sideslip when bureaucrats move into public corporations or special legal entities without legal restrictions. Thirdly, bureaucrats are described as *wataridori* or migratory birds when they have serial retirements in the public or private sectors. Finally, retired bureaucrats from important national or regional agencies become politicians, and this movement to political office is referred to as *seikai tensin* (Trimnell, 2008, p. 11).

Chalmers Johnson (1995, p. 151) contends that *amakudari* does not contribute to "flagrant corruption because the individual official does not normally seek his own post-retirement job." The usual procedure is that the political and administrative leaders in a ministry find jobs for their retiring bureaucrats. However, he cautions that over time, the continued practice of *amakudari* has contributed to corruption as manifested in the bribery and bid-rigging scandals in the construction industry in 1993, when former officials of the Ministry of Construction were employed by general contractors and local governments to participate in the bidding on public works projects.

Mark Beeson (2003, p. 30) has suggested two ways of assessing *amakudari*. On the positive side, *amakudari* can be viewed as a "legitimate recompense for both the modest nature of public service compensation and the likelihood that only a small number of any bureaucratic cohort would achieve the highest offices." On the contrary, *amakudari* also reflects the cronyism and collusion between senior public servants and private sector executives, which are "a recipe for encouraging corruption." Indeed, Sheng (2009, pp. 58–59) has identified these adverse consequences of *amakudari* when the *yakuza* are involved as in the real estate sector:

> *Amakudari* was dangerous precisely because the downward integration of officials into the financial sector intersected with the upward integration of Japanese gangsters or *yakuza* into the real estate business ... [where they] ... became strong arm men for property developers to get rid of squatters and inconvenient tenants for property development. They soon found that property developers depended on bankers to fund their projects and once property deals became gangster ridden, it was almost impossible for government officials to take action against problem banks, where the senior bank officials may have been former colleagues through the *amakudari* connection.

*Amakudari* is also dysfunctional because strong ministry-business ties contribute to bureaucratic corruption in the construction industry in the form of the *dango* (or secret bid-rigging) system, which is illegal. The *dango* system allows construction firms to predetermine both the winner of the bidding and the price the winner will bid. The Ministry of Construction allocates public works projects to the firms belonging to the officially recognized cartels. Firms participate in contract bidding and receive contracts without market competition. Two important features should be highlighted. First, the final bidding prices include commissions of 1–3 percent of the total construction costs to maintain the network relationship. Second, the successful firms provide *amakudari* positions for the ministry and assist in political campaigns. Hence, it is not surprising that the Ministry of Construction has a large number of *amakudari* positions for its retired senior bureaucrats in the construction and real estate sectors (Choi, 2007, pp. 934–935).

Junichiro Koizumi, who was prime minister from 2001 to 2006, stopped the practice in 2002, in response to the adverse public opinion on *amakudari* as a source of corruption (Sheng, 2009, p. 58). Even though there are regulations concerning *amakudari*, Stockwin (2003, p. 10) observes that these regulations are "lightly policed" and "every year several hundred senior officials of the national government 'descend from heaven' in this way." However, *amakudari* has "not died out, despite the intense criticism to which it has been subjected." O'uchi et al. (2006, p. 9) have recommended that the practice of early retirement of senior career officials should be abolished and the power of the National Personnel Authority to scrutinize *amakudari* should be enhanced because "by nature *amakudari* is tantamount to bribery with promises of reemployment in return for favorable treatment of their corporation." However, it is difficult, if not impossible, to eradicate *amakudari* because of the tremendous benefits for retiring senior civil servants, who will receive much higher salaries in their new postretirement jobs to compensate for their relatively low pay as bureaucrats. Indeed, "the more politically powerful a ministry is and the more instrumental role a civil servant plays in it, the better his or her chances are for a lucrative *amakudari* position" (Choi, 2007, p. 934). In short, *amakudari* enables the ministries in Japan to ensure a second career for their retiring senior employees.

## STRUCTURAL CORRUPTION

The third and most important cause of corruption in Japan is structural. In other words, corruption results from the prevalence of money politics in the Japanese political system. Rosenbluth and Thies (2010, p. 69) view Japan as "a democracy flawed by corruption." Similarly, Roger Bowen (2003, p. 3) describes Japan's democracy as "real" but is afflicted by the following defects: "personalism, graft, cronyism, favoritism, bribery, money politics, factionalism, and collusion – all elements of what the Japanese refer to as 'structural corruption' (*kozo oshoku*)." According to him, corruption in Japan is "structural" because

> it is built into the way politics works. It endures in part because Japan's politicians who engage in acts of corruption are nearly always reelected and consequently have little reason to change their behavior or practices. (Bowen, 2003, p. 3)

As mentioned earlier, Japan's political system is vulnerable to corruption for three reasons: (1) the high cost of being elected; (2) the official income of a Diet member is inadequate to meet his or her social obligations; and (3) the collusion between politicians, bureaucrats and businessmen. These three factors will be analyzed further later because they account for the structural corruption in Japan.

According to Potter (2000, p. 183), corruption occurs in Japanese electoral politics because of "violations of campaign finance laws and related bribery and tax laws." He contends that the nature of the Japanese electoral system and the inadequacy of the electoral laws are responsible for corruption in the electoral campaigns. He wrote,

> The combination of multimember constituencies and restrictive campaign laws generates demand by elected officials for large amounts of money to maintain expensive campaign organizations outside the parties and the formal requirements of electoral laws. Lax enforcement of electoral and bribery laws, and public expectations of political behavior, do not provide sufficiently powerful negative sanctions to correct the temptation toward abuse. (Potter, 2000, pp. 183–184)

Elections are very expensive affairs in Japan. Yanaga (1968, p. 80) estimated that party leaders had publicly reported only one-fifth to one-third of their total contributions in the 1960s. In 1992, the amount of political funds declared by all national political groups to the Ministry of Home Affairs was "a staggering 1.74 trillion yen." In 1993, the National Tax Agency indicated that the amount that was unreported for "political donations, bribes and hush money" by the top 500 corporations was $53 million (Potter, 2000, p. 184).

Bouissou (1997, pp. 133–134) describes Japan as "the most expensive political system" because "Japanese political personnel represent an annual expenditure of over ¥900 billion a year on average (roughly £6.5 billion)." As the salaries of the Diet members "barely allow them more than a comfortable living wage," it is not surprising that most of "their entire expenditure on political activity comes from fund-raising from firms, associations and individuals" (Bouissou, 1997, p. 134).

In spite of the strict election rules and various restrictions on election campaigns, Japanese elections are the "most expensive among industrial democracies" because of the nature of the electoral constituencies and the structure of the political parties (Potter, 2000, pp. 184–185). Before the 1994 electoral reforms, the Diet elections in postwar Japan were conducted in multimember constituencies and voters were given a single nontransferable vote (SNTV). This meant that the members of the LDP had to compete among themselves for seats by allying themselves with a faction leader to obtain campaign funds or by relying on campaign organizations loyal to them (Potter, 2000, p. 185).

The faction bosses in the LDP procure and distribute money to their members to help them in their reelection efforts. The *Far Eastern Economic Review* estimated in 1990 that a faction with 91 members needed about US$7.5 million annually to maintain their members' loyalty. The LDP could not guarantee funding to its candidates because the existence of multimember constituencies meant that different factions supported their own candidates. Gerald L. Curtis (1988, p. 177) attributes the high cost of campaigning in Japan to the necessity for every LDP politician to build and maintain his own political machine by employing staff in his district and in Tokyo for handling his constituents' requests and for fund-raising.

Consequently, candidates have to rely on their supporters' clubs or *koenkai* to retain the loyalty of their voters during the "non-campaign" period by "attending weddings and other social events, sponsoring clubs, organizing trips for key constituents to tourist spots, and holding political discussion meetings" (Potter, 2000, p. 186). These "non-campaigning" activities are expensive as indicated by Bouissou (1997, p. 137):

> For every socially recognized occasion, money is directly forthcoming. In the case of a marriage, a deputy may go up to ¥50,000 (£350) there may be half that amount for a funeral; the annual bill may well go beyond ¥10 million. Equally costly in an election year are 'travel expenses' (*o-kuruma dai*), distributed by the secretaries quite openly at meetings although the law forbids this.

A *koenkai* consists of clubs that represent city districts or small rural communities, with "20 to 30 individuals led by a local worthy, to cover the area." A strong *koenkai* has several hundred of these small groups with different interests. For example, former Prime Minister Kakuei Tanaka's *koenkai* had 100,000 members. By performing various functions "ranging from mutual aid to collusion between small business people," a *koenkai* becomes "a machine for distributing money and freebies" among its members (Bouissou, 1997, pp. 136–137).

Where does the money for the candidates come from? There are two major sources of political funds in Japan. The largest contributor of political funds is "big business" because business federations prefer to keep conservative and pro-business parties such as the LDP in power. Consequently, LDP politicians have provided the corporate world with a channel of access to the bureaucracy by acting as "brokers between the business community and the powerful state bureaucracy" (Potter, 2000, p. 187).

The construction industry in Japan is the second important source of illegal campaign funding for the LDP as it provided between two-thirds to three quarters of corporate "undisclosed funds" from the late 1980s to the early 1990s (Potter, 2000, p. 188). Bribery, bid fixing, and kickbacks are endemic in the construction industry, which are dependent on public work contracts (Woodall, 1996). Wilkinson (1993, p. 5) has described the symbiotic relationship between the politicians and the construction firms; thus, "the politicians cannot be elected without money but are able to attract projects; the construction firms cannot survive without being contracted for projects, but have money."

In sum, political corruption in Japan is "an essential glue and lubricant in the country's power triad consisting of big business, the central ministries and the governing party." Elaborating further, Rothacher (2003, p. 117) contends that corruption in Japan "derives from the use and abuse of personal connections driven to epidemic proportions in the context of an over-affluent ossified power elite ruling a largely pre-modern centralized political system."

## ANTICORRUPTION MEASURES

The most important reason for the structural corruption in Japan is the lack of political will to change the status quo, which ensures its continued existence. Indeed, there is no incentive for Japanese politicians to undermine the system that maintains them in power. The absence of political will is clearly manifested in Japan's adoption of pattern 1 of corruption control, namely, the reliance on many anticorruption laws without a single independent ACA to enforce these laws.

### *Anticorruption Laws*

The most important anticorruption legislation in Japan is found in the Penal Code of 1907, in Chapter 25, "Crimes of Corruption," which consists of Articles 193–198.[3] The various offenses covered by Articles 193–198 and the corresponding penalties are summarized in Table 2.7. Corruption is not defined explicitly, but Articles 193–196 focus on the abuse of authority by public officers, whereas Articles 197–198 deal with bribery. Article 7 defines a public officer as "a national or local government official, a member of an assembly or committee, or other employees engaged in the performance of public duties in accordance with laws and regulations."

Article 197 (1) states that "a public officer or arbitrator who accepts, solicits or promises to accept a bribe in connection with his/her duties shall be punished by imprisonment with work for not more than five years." The phrase "in connection with his/her duties" is important because it distinguishes between the "normal acceptance of some presents from his/her friends etc. and illegal acceptance of a bribe" (Tachi, 2001, p. 6). As discussed earlier, this explains why it is difficult to distinguish between a gift

***Table 2.7.*** Offenses and Penalties in Chapter 25, Articles 193–198, of the Penal Code.

| Article | Offense | Penalty |
|---|---|---|
| 193 | Abuse of authority by public officers | Imprisonment with or without work for two years |
| 194 | Abuse of authority by public officers performing judicial, prosecutorial, or police duties | Imprisonment with or without work for 6–10 months |
| 195 | Assault and cruelty by public officers performing judicial, prosecutorial, or police duties | Imprisonment with or without work for seven years |
| 196 | Abuse of authority causing death or injury by public officers performing judicial, prosecutorial, or police duties | Imprisonment with or without work for seven years |
| 197 | Acceptance of bribes: acceptance upon request; acceptance in advance of assumption of office | Imprisonment with work for between five to seven years |
| 197-2 | Passing of bribes to a third party | Imprisonment with work for five years |
| 197-3 | Aggravated acceptance; acceptance after resignation of office | Imprisonment with work for one to five years |
| 197-4 | Acceptance for exertion of influence | Imprisonment with work for five years |
| 197-5 | Confiscation and collection of a sum of equivalent value | Offender has to repay the amount of the bribe accepted |
| 198 | Giving of bribes | Imprisonment with work for three years and a fine of 2,500,000 yen |

*Source*: Compiled by the author from Chapter 25 of the Penal Code of 1907.

and a bribe. It is interesting to note that the penalty imposed on those found guilty of giving bribes in Article 198 is three-year imprisonment with work and a fine of 2,500,00 yen (US$29,777),[4] which is shorter than the five- to seven-year imprisonment with work for those found guilty of accepting bribes.

Apart from Articles 197 and 198 in the Penal Code, there are also provisions for bribery in laws such as the Horse Racing Law, the Cycle Racing Law, the Bankruptcy Law, and the Corporate Reorganization Law, to mention four examples. For example, the Horse Racing Law has a provision prohibiting a jockey, horse trainer, or his/her assistant from receiving bribes in connection with horse racing. Those found guilty of this offense will be imprisoned with work for three years (Tachi, 2001, pp. 7–8).

The National Public Service Ethics Act (NPSEA) of 1999 ensures the public's trust of their public officials by regulating conflicts of interest among them by requiring those with the rank of assistant director or higher to report on a quarterly basis gifts, hospitality, or compensation worth more than ¥5,000 that they receive to their heads of ministries or agencies. Those very senior officials with the rank of deputy director general or higher are required to submit quarterly reports to their superiors their annual exchange of stocks and bonds and their annual incomes (Government of Japan, 1999, pp. 6–8). The National Public Service Ethics Board is formed within the National Personnel Authority by Article 10 of the NPSEA to monitor matters concerning conflicts of interest among public officials by conducting on-site investigations or to request witnesses to submit reports or relevant materials (Government of Japan, 1999, pp. 6–8, 9–10; Smith, 2008, p. 19).

Article 3 of the NPSEA identifies the three ethical principles that public officials should observe in performing their duties, namely, no discrimination toward citizens, no abuse of their positions for private interests, and no receipt of gifts from those persons under their authority. Bearing in mind these ethical principles, Article 5 defines the National Public Service Ethics Code as a cabinet order, which includes,

> the matters which the officials should observe concerning the prevention of acts that may bring about suspicion and distrust from the citizens such as contacting with those who have interests with the duties of the officials such as the prohibitions and restrictions of receiving gifts, etc. from those who have interests in the duties of the officials. (Government of Japan, 1999, p. 6)

The Political Funds Control Law (PFCL), which was enacted in 1948, regulates political contributions and financing of political parties and political organizations by requiring these organizations to submit a report of their revenues and expenditures to the Minister of Public Management and Home Affairs or to a prefectural election control committee. However, the Recruit scandal of 1988 and the Tokyo Sagawa Kyubin scandal of 1993 led to the revision of the PFCL in 1994 by the Hosokawa administration. The revised PFCL reduces the disclosure limit from ¥1 million to ¥50,000 and requires that the names of individual or corporate donors whose contributions exceed ¥50,000 be made public (Umeda, 2004, p. 2).

Finally, there are many laws regulating public bidding and public procurement in Japan. For example, the Bidding Correction Law of 2000 regulates the bidding and contacts for public works by the central government, state corporations, and local governments. Other relevant laws include the Law to Prevent Delay in Payment for Government

Contracts, the Ecological or Green Procurement Law, the *Dango* Prevention Law, and the World Trade Organization's Government Procurement Agreement (O'uchi et al., 2006, p. 27).

### *Law Enforcement Agencies*

Unlike the other nine Asian countries discussed in this book, Japan does not rely on an ACA to enforce the many anticorruption laws. As corruption is viewed as a crime, the police and the public prosecutors are responsible for enforcing the anticorruption laws (OECD, 2000, p. 210). Although the police are responsible for investigating more than 99 percent of criminal cases, public prosecutors conduct supplementary investigations of criminal cases referred to them by police officers. The public prosecutors and police officers usually cooperate with one another in their investigations. When police officers conduct the criminal investigation in those bribery cases exposed by them, they are supervised by public prosecutors to prevent incomplete interpretation of the law and evaluation of physical evidence. Furthermore, public prosecutors and police officers usually meet to discuss a particular case before an identified suspect is transferred from the police station to the public prosecutor's office (PPO) (Hasegawa, 2000, p. 470).

Police officers in Japan usually question more suspects than the public prosecutors. For example, the police questioned 150 suspects compared to the 20 suspects interrogated by the public prosecutors in 1997. Even though the number of suspects investigated by the public prosecutors is small, they are responsible for exposing most of the bribery offenses committed by public officials (Hasegawa, 2000, p. 471). Public prosecutors are empowered to investigate and prosecute misconduct and corruption in the civil service (OECD, 2000, p. 210). They initiate and complete independent investigations without police assistance in bribery or large-scale financial crimes involving politicians, senior government officials, or executives of large corporations (Tachi, 2002, pp. 119–120). The PPOs are independent because public prosecutors are protected by the Public Prosecutor's Office Law from removal and direct interference in their criminal investigations by the Minister of Justice.

The Special Investigation Departments (SIDs) of the PPOs in Tokyo, Osaka, and Nagoya are responsible for initiating investigations in cases concerning bribery, breach of trust, tax evasion, securities exchange violations, and the noncompliance with laws governing the prohibition of private monopolies and the maintenance of free trade. For example, the Tokyo SID was responsible for investigating the 1976 Lockheed scandal, the 1988 Recruit scandal, and the 1991 Kyowa scandal (Tachi, 2002, pp. 120–121).

In 1999, the Tokyo SID had 125 legal officials, consisting of 40 public prosecutors and 85 public prosecutor's assistant officers. The three SIDs rely on three investigative techniques to detect a bribe in progress. First, the public prosecutors review newspapers, magazines, question and answer proceedings in the Diet or local government assembly sessions, or conduct interviews and background investigations. Second, the PPOs receive complaints or accusations from complainants or accusers for corruption offenses. Each SID has a public prosecutor who is responsible for accepting written complaints or accusations and letters from the informants. These complaints and accusations are investigated by the SID and constitute a major source of information for detecting leads for ongoing bribery cases. Third, public prosecutors are on the lookout for signs of suspicious activities in their investigation of corruption offenses (Hasegawa, 2000, p. 472).

The SID initiates the investigation of bribery cases with a thorough search for physical items of evidence such as account books and business diaries in the offices of the accused persons to prove the alleged offense of corruption. The investigators analyze the account books seized in the raids to identify the source of funds as bribes and how these funds are used. The public prosecutors also question suspects or witnesses to obtain their statements regarding the offenses that are presented as evidence in court. Bribery investigations are lengthy, exhaustive, and highly complex and require a lot of manpower. As the Tokyo SID has only 40 public prosecutors, it relies on public prosecutors from other District Prosecutors Offices throughout Japan to assist it in complex bribery and large-scale economic cases (Hasegawa, 2000, pp. 472–474).

In addition to the police and public prosecutors, the Board of Audit (BOA) audits the accounts of public corporations and government agencies. If it discovers evidence of corruption during an audit, the BOA has to inform the PPO, which may conduct further investigation. However, in practice, such notice to the PPO is seldom given (Smith, 2008, p. 19). Indeed, the BOA stops inspection after identifying budget irregularities and does not take action against organized corruption except in some individual cases of bribery (O'uchi et al., 2006, p. 17).

## EVALUATION OF ANTICORRUPTION MEASURES

How effective are the anticorruption measures in Japan? These five indicators are employed to assess the perceived extent of corruption in Japan: (1) TI's CPI from 1995 to 2010 covering 178 countries; (2) PERC's annual survey of corruption in 16 Asia-Pacific countries from 1995 to 2010; (3) World Bank's control of corruption governance indicator from 1996 to 2009 covering 213 countries; (4) the ease of doing business rank in the World Bank's *Doing Business Survey* from 2007 to 2011; and (5) the *Global Competitiveness Report's* indicator on the public trust of politicians in 139 countries from 1999 to 2010–2011.

First, Table 2.8 indicates that Japan's performance on the CPI has improved from 20th position with a score of 6.72 in 1995 to 17th position with a score of 7.8 in 2010. Japan's CPI score ranges from 5.8 in 1998 to 7.8 in 2010. Second, Japan's rank on PERC has fluctuated between second and third position behind Singapore and Hong Kong SAR from 1995 to 2008, with its score ranging from 1.93 to 5.00 during the same period. However,

***Table 2.8.*** Japan's Performance on CPI, PERC, and Control of Corruption 1995–2010.

| Year | CPI Rank and Score[a] | PERC Rank and Score[b] | Control of Corruption Percentile Rank |
|---|---|---|---|
| 1995 | 20th (6.72) | 2nd (2.00) | NA |
| 1996 | 17th (7.05) | 2nd (1.93) | 80.1 |
| 1997 | 21st (6.57) | 3rd (4.60) | NA |
| 1998 | 25th (5.8) | 3rd (5.00) | 85.4 |
| 1999 | 25th (6.0) | 3rd (4.25) | NA |
| 2000 | 23rd (6.4) | 3rd (3.90) | 86.9 |
| 2001 | 21st (7.1) | 2nd (2.50) | NA |
| 2002 | 20th (7.1) | 2nd (3.25) | 82.5 |
| 2003 | 21st (7.0) | 3rd (4.50) | 85.9 |
| 2004 | 24th (6.9) | 2nd (3.00) | 86.9 |
| 2005 | 21st (7.3) | 2nd (3.46) | 85.0 |
| 2006 | 17th (7.6) | 2nd (3.01) | 90.3 |
| 2007 | 17th (7.5) | 3rd (2.10) | 85.5 |
| 2008 | 18th (7.3) | 3rd (2.25) | 85.5 |
| 2009 | 17th (7.7) | 5th (3.99) | 87.1 |
| 2010 | 17th (7.8) | 5th (3.49) | NA |

*Sources*: Compiled from http://www.transparency.org; PERC (2001, 2008, p. 7); Hussain (2009, p. B5); *Straits Times* (2010a); and http://info.worldbank.org/governance/wgi/sc_chart.asp
[a]The CPI score ranges from 0 (most corrupt) to 10 (least corrupt).
[b]The PERC score ranges from 0 (least corrupt) to 10 (most corrupt).

Japan's rank has dropped to fifth position during 2009 and 2010, and its scores have increased to 3.99 and 3.49, respectively. Third, Japan's percentile rank on the control of corruption indicator has increased from 80.1 in 1996 to 90.3 in 2006. It has consistently been ranked third behind Singapore and Hong Kong SAR from 1996 to 2009.

Table 2.9 confirms that red tape is still a problem in Japan even though it is ranked between 11th among the 175 economies in 2007 and 18th among the 183 economies in 2011. In terms of starting a business, Japan's rank has also declined from 18 to 98 from 2007 to 2011. Similarly, the time required to get a construction permit has increased from 96 days in 2007 to 187 days in 2011, and the longer time taken is reflected in the deterioration of its rank from 2nd to 44th position. Finally, Japan's rank in registering a property has also decreased from 39th position in 2007 to 59th position in 2011. In sum, the existence of red tape indicates that corruption remains a problem in Japan.

Table 2.10 notes that the public trust of politicians in Japan is low and ranges from 31st position among 59 countries in 1999 to 58th position among 139 countries in 2010–2011. It is not surprising that the Japanese public do not trust their politicians in view of the many corruption scandals in Japan during the postwar period. Japan's score has increased from 2.0 in 2002–2003 to 3.4 in 2007–2008. In 2010–2011, Japan's score of 3.1 places it

***Table 2.9.*** Ease of Doing Business in Japan, 2007–2011.

| Indicator | 2007 ($N=175$) | 2008 ($N=178$) | 2009 ($N=181$) | 2010 ($N=183$) | 2011 ($N=183$) |
|---|---|---|---|---|---|
| Ease of doing business (rank) | 11 | 12 | 12 | 15 | 18 |
| Starting a business (rank) | 18 | 44 | 64 | 91 | 98 |
| No. of procedures | 8 | 8 | 8 | 8 | 8 |
| Time (days) | 23 | 23 | 23 | 23 | 23 |
| Cost (% of income per capita) | 7.5 | 7.5 | 7.5 | 7.5 | 7.5 |
| Dealing with construction permits or licenses (rank) | 2 | 32 | 39 | 45 | 44 |
| No. of procedures | 11 | 15 | 15 | 15 | 15 |
| Time (days) | 96 | 177 | 187 | 187 | 187 |
| Cost (% of income per capita) | 19.8 | 17.8 | 19.1 | 19.3 | 20.8 |
| Registering property (rank) | 39 | 48 | 51 | 54 | 59 |
| No. of procedures | 6 | 6 | 6 | 6 | 6 |
| Time (days) | 14 | 14 | 14 | 14 | 14 |
| Cost (% of property value) | 4.1 | 5.0 | 5.0 | 5.0 | 5.5 |
| CPI Rank and Score | 17th (7.5) | 18th (7.3) | 17th (7.7) | 17th (7.8) | NA |

*Sources*: World Bank (2006b, p. 120, 2007, p. 129, 2008, p. 112, 2009, p. 130, 2010a, p. 172) and http://www.transparency.org

***Table 2.10.*** Public Trust of Politicians in Japan, 1999 to 2010–2011.

| Year | Rank | Score[a] | No. of Countries |
|---|---|---|---|
| 1999 | 31st | 2.89 | 59 |
| 2000 | 34th | 2.90 | 59 |
| 2001–2002 | 40th | 2.60 | 75 |
| 2002–2003 | 50th | 2.00 | 80 |
| 2003–2004 | 51st | 2.30 | 102 |
| 2007–2008 | 33rd | 3.40 | 131 |
| 2008–2009 | 45th | 3.30 | 134 |
| 2009–2010 | 54th | 3.10 | 133 |
| 2010–2011 | 58th | 3.10 | 139 |
| Average | 44th | 2.84 | – |

*Sources*: Compiled from Schwab, Porter, Sachs, Warner, and Levinson (1999, p. 327), Porter et al. (2000, p. 253), Schwab, Porter, Sachs, Cornelius, and McArthur (2002, p. 408), Cornelius (2003, p. 619), Sala-i-Martin (2004, p. 499), Schwab and Porter (2007, p. 379), Schwab and Porter (2008, p. 367), Schwab (2009, p. 349), and Schwab (2010, p. 369).

[a]The score ranges from 1 (very low) to 7 (very high) for the respondents' answers to this statement: "How would you rate the level of public trust in the ethical standards of politicians in your country."

in 11th position among the 20 Asian countries included in the survey after Singapore, Hong Kong SAR, Brunei, China, Vietnam, Malaysia, Taiwan, Cambodia, Indonesia and Timor-Leste (Schwab, 2010, p. 369).

In sum, while Table 2.8 shows that Japan's performance on the CPI, PERC and control of corruption, is consistently third behind Singapore and Hong Kong SAR, these three indicators do not reflect the structural corruption inherent in the Japanese political system because the Japanese public and foreign businessmen and journalists interviewed for these surveys are not directly affected by the "rotten triangle" of politicians, businessmen, and bureaucrats. Rather, Japan's third ranking on the three indicators is a reflection of its low level of petty corruption. On the contrary, Table 2.9 notes that red tape remains a problem in Japan, and Table 2.10 demonstrates that the Japanese do not trust their politicians because of the frequent corruption scandals during the past six decades.

Susan J. Pharr (2000, p. 194–199) has compiled an Asahi Corruption Report Database of over 15,000 items from the reports on corruption in the *Asahi Shimbun*, a major Japanese daily newspaper, from 1948 to 1996. She found that there was a strong relationship between reports of officials' misconduct and levels of citizen satisfaction with politics and concluded that

> The more numerous the media reports of leaders' misconduct in office – as measured by the number of corruption stories between 1978 and 1996 in one of Japan's leading newspaper – the lower the public's confidence in government. (Pharr, 2000, p. 199)

Unlike the other nine countries discussed in this book, Japan has enacted many anticorruption laws that are not enforced by an independent ACA, but by the police and the PPOs. The absence of a comprehensive anticorruption strategy indicates that the various governments in Japan after World War II lack the political will to curb corruption. This is not surprising because those in power do not want to undermine the status quo by curbing corruption effectively.

Apart from not establishing an independent ACA to enforce the anticorruption laws, all the postwar governments in Japan have responded reactively to the many corruption scandals by requesting the SIDs to investigate a corruption scandal whenever it is exposed. As there are only three SIDs in Tokyo, Osaka and Nagoya, to investigate the many corruption scandals in Japan, they cope with their lack of manpower by assisting each other in complex bribery investigations.

Michael Johnston (2005b, pp. 82–83) has observed that the Japanese public prosecutors usually treat corruption allegations involving politicians and senior public officials cautiously. The weak anticorruption responses in Japan can be attributed to its elite political culture, which favors harmony and deference as well as tolerance for corruption. Furthermore, it is difficult to convict politicians for bribery if they claim that they have received campaign contributions and not bribes, or if they can show that they cannot provide the expected benefits.

In his comparative study of the effectiveness of prosecutors in dealing with corruption cases in Italy and Japan, David Johnson (2003a, p. 257) found that the Italian prosecutors were "insulated from the world of electoral politics" and were more independent than their Japanese counterparts, who had "limited independence" from outside political influence. An analysis of the shipbuilding scandal of 1954, the Lockheed scandal of 1976, and the Recruit and Sagawa Kyubin scandals of 1988 confirms that "prosecutors in Japan operate in an institutional environment that leaves them susceptible to outside political control." Indeed, since 1955, LDP leaders have manipulated "the institutional structure of prosecution in order to exert political control over prosecutors and thereby protect party members and their cronies from indictment" (Johnson, 2003a, p. 273).

The prevalence of police corruption in Japan makes it difficult for the police to enforce the anticorruption laws impartially. For example, the

Kanagawa Prefectural Police initiated disciplinary action against those policemen involved in scandals in 1999 but did not publicize these scandals or conduct proper investigation of their misconduct (Sugita, 1999, p. 1). Keisuke Sugita (1999, pp. 2–4) provides five reasons for the Japanese police's lack of self-cleansing power:

1. Crimes committed by police officers are not investigated properly or promptly.
2. The investigation system within the police is dysfunctional because the inspector stationed at each prefectural police headquarters is responsible for investigating crimes or scandals involving policemen and recommending appropriate disciplinary action to the chief. However, in the case of the police scandals in Kanagawa, the inspector's office covered up the crimes committed by the policemen.
3. The National Police Agency is supervised by the National Public Safety Commission, and the Prefectural Police headquarters are supervised by the Prefectural Public Safety Commissions. However, these commissions are ineffective because of their limited authority and the lack of independence of their personnel and structure from the police system.
4. The problem of police secrecy has been aggravated by the inadequate system of public information on the police.
5. Japanese policemen are not allowed to form trade unions by law, and their right to organize has been suppressed.

Finally, Sugita (1999, p. 4) concludes that "the nature and structure of the Japanese police provide a hotbed for corruption" because the prefectural governors and prefectural public safety commissions have limited power over the prefectural units, which constitute the basis for the Japanese police system.

As mentioned in the previous section, there are many anticorruption laws in Japan. However, the absence of a comprehensive anticorruption law and a single independent ACA to enforce it impartially are two major weaknesses affecting anticorruption efforts in Japan. For example, even though the PFCL exists in Japan, there is no specific agency to control political financing (Umeda, 2004, p. 2). Furthermore, Masami Ito (2007, pp. 1–3) points out that the PFCL is not effective because "wily politicians" have undermined it by exploiting its loopholes by breaking down their expenditures into payments below ¥50,000 to avoid attaching receipts. Another loophole is to use dummy political action groups as a channel for transferring money to politicians. Indeed, every time the PFCL is amended, the loopholes are left intact and many scandals involving politicians and their secretaries are exposed subsequently (*Japan Press Weekly*, 2009).

In spite of the many laws enacted to curb *dango*, it remains "the most popular form of price cartel in the public procurement market" and is rampant throughout Japan because of the "weakness of the political will to quench corruption and the lack of development of law enforcement mechanisms." Consequently, the existing anti-*dango* measures should be reviewed and strengthened, including the enhancement of penalties for offenders (O'uchi, et al., 2006, pp. 9, 27–28).

The final weakness of Japan's incremental and reactive anticorruption strategy is its emphasis on investigating corruption scandals *after* their occurrence and not before. This emphasis on post hoc corruption investigations at the expense of corruption prevention and education is the Achilles' heel of Japan's anticorruption strategy and confirms the government's disinterest in curbing corruption effectively. As discussed earlier, the SIDs in Tokyo, Osaka and Nagoya are responsible for investigating bribery cases. However, as there is no independent ACA, there is no agency responsible for preventing corruption or for educating the population on the adverse consequences of corruption on society.

## CONCLUSION

Japan is unique among the 10 Asian countries discussed in this book because of the coexistence of a high level of grand corruption with a low level of petty corruption. Corruption is a structural problem in Japan because the high cost of getting elected and remaining in power makes it one of the most expensive political systems in the world. On the contrary, petty corruption is not a serious problem in Japan because the widely accepted social tradition of gift-giving makes it difficult to distinguish between gifts and bribes, and civil servants are also paid adequate salaries that are, however, lower than those of their private sector counterparts. Tables 2.3 and 2.4 have shown that the number of bribery cases involving public officials in Japan is relatively low.

Corruption is endemic in the Japanese political system because it is extremely expensive for politicians to get elected and to perform their duties after their election. As discussed earlier, the costs of getting elected to both Houses of the Diet have increased greatly in recent years. Furthermore, the official incomes received by Diet members are insufficient to cover their expenses and social obligations. Consequently, politicians rely on their parties, *koenkai*, business federations, and construction companies for additional sources of income.

The symbiotic relationships between Japanese politicians, bureaucrats, and businessmen, described pejoratively as the "rotten triangle," are likely to endure and reinforce the practices of *amakudari* and *kansei-dango*. As these three groups benefit and thrive from the structural corruption, there is no incentive for them to undermine the status quo and their predominance in the political system, especially when corrupt offenders are not always punished severely. According to Rothacher (2003, p. 118),

> The corruption purges of 1992–2000 hit roughly 10 percent of the Japanese power elite consisting of some 3,000 individuals in national politics, big business and the top players of the central ministries. For some this meant imprisonment or death by suicide .... However, for most, especially if they were young and resourceful enough, it meant only a temporary setback and a shameful episode that could be overcome within a few years.

In short, the lack of political will to curb corruption in Japan makes sense because the existing system of structural corruption favors the "rotten triangle" of politicians, bureaucrats, and businessmen. Hence, it is unlikely that the members of this triumvirate would want to undermine the structural basis for their dominance in the political system. This explains not only why structural corruption persists in Japan but also why the government continues to rely on many ineffective anticorruption laws and on the three inadequately staffed SIDs to investigate corruption scandals when they are exposed instead of an independent ACA. Indeed, the focus on investigating corruption scandals after their occurrence at the expense of corruption prevention and education reaffirms the Japanese government's lack of commitment in minimizing corruption.

## NOTES

1. For examples of such research, see Babb (2005), Bowen (2003), Dairokuno (2000), Dixon (1977), Kearns (1990), Mitchell (1996), Reed (1996), Schlesinger (1999), Woodall (1996), and Yayama (1990).
2. For a comprehensive analysis of the Teijin scandal, see Mitchell (2002).
3. The English translation of the Penal Code (Act No. 45 of 1907) of Japan is available at http://www.cas.go.jp/jp/seisaku/hourei/data/PC.pdf, accessed on 9 December 2010. The text of Chapter 25, Articles 193–198 can be found on pp. 40–42.
4. This is based on the exchange rate of US$1 = 83.9564 Japanese Yen on 9 December 2010.

# CHAPTER 3

# INDIA

> Corruption is the largest single element to be found most in India. All roads, from the maternity hospital to the crematorium, smell of corruption. No individual is free from it, no area can be found where corruption is not a ritual.
>
> – C. Kohli (1975, p. 67)

> India's biggest growth industry isn't outsourcing, pharmaceu-tical or auto manufacturing – I believe it's political corruption.
>
> – P. Agrawal (2010)

## THE TEHELKA SCANDAL

During a press conference at the Imperial Hotel in Delhi on 13 March 2001, the Internet news site, Tehelka.com, showed secret video footage of senior politicians, bureaucrats, and army officers accepting money in a fake defense deal. Two journalists from Tehelka, Anirudha Bahal and Mathew Samuel, posed as arms dealers from a fictitious arms company called West End International to sell nonexistent handheld thermal cameras to senior officials of the Ministry of Defense (MOD) in India. Bahal and Samuel paid bribes to politicians, civil servants, and army officers to procure government contracts. The journalists used three hidden cameras to videotape the corrupt politicians and officials accepting the bribes, with the most dramatic video clip showing the Bharatiya Janata Party (BJP) President, Bangaru Laxman, accepting a wad of currency notes from them. Laxman later claimed that he was not guilty of wrongdoing for accepting Rs. 100,000 (US$2,170) as a donation for the BJP. Describing the episode as "concocted," he added that he had given the donation to the BJP's treasurer (BBC News, 2001a).

Tehelka initiated "Operation West End" to expose the culture of bribery at the MOD. In addition to bribery, the army officers were also shown on tape drinking whisky and partying with the prostitutes provided by the journalists. A total of 16 individuals had accepted money from the journalists, who had secretly taped their meetings for four months, from September to December 2000 (Trehan, 2009, pp. 1–2). The public outcry that resulted from the exposure of the scandal led to the resignation of the Defense Minister, George

Fernandes (who was reinstated seven months later), Laxman's resignation as the BJP's President, and the suspension of four senior MOD officials. Larry Kilman (2005, p. 4), Director of Communications of the World Association of Newspapers, observed that "Tehelka was praised by the public and media for exposing corruption in the highest places of the Indian administration" because they had viewed "Operation West End" as "the proper use of the tools available to journalists to expose a serious problem."

In contrast, the government reacted by accusing Tehelka of working for "opposition parties, or Pakistani and European intelligence agencies, or even for Indian organized crime." Furthermore, Tehelka was investigated by the tax authorities and the enforcement directorate of the intelligence bureau. Tehelka's investors were also investigated by the customs, police, and the tax authorities. More importantly, the government committee appointed to investigate Tehelka's findings devoted its efforts to criticizing Tehelka's journalistic methods instead of focusing on corruption (Kilman, 2005, p. 4). Tarun Tejpal, the Editor-in-Chief of Tehelka, admitted that he had underestimated the government's response:

> The Secret Auto Destruct System's (SADS) wheels started turning smoothly. The government's core wringing team, just cranked the machine and squeezed them, utilizing every department, every agency that could search and destroy, then simply moved on to the next crisis that needed spinning and doctoring and forgot about Tehelka .... The government appointed a Commission of Inquiry and launched the SADS from all sides. The government transformed Tarun, Aniruddha, and even the concept of Tehelka into a quick, tiny hiccup in the public's perception of national developments. For editors, Tehelka became an old story, no longer worth covering. (Trehan, 2009, pp. 569–570)

Unfortunately, the major victims of the Tehelka scandal were the journalists and Tarun Tejpal and not those corrupt individuals who accepted the bribes, whisky, and sexual services. Indeed, Tejpal was shocked by the government's "brazenness" in stonewalling the investigation into the irregularities uncovered by his colleagues (Laskar, 2002). He was charged with "immoral trafficking" in September 2001 for offering prostitutes to the MOD officials during the sting operation. Tehelka's major financial sponsor, Shanker Sharma, was imprisoned without charge. Consequently, the number of Tehelka's employees was reduced from 120 to only 4 employees in January 2003. By then, the company was practically ruined as there were only "a few dusty chairs, three computers and a forlorn air-conditioning unit" left in Tehelka's office in suburban south Delhi (Harding, 2003).

When Kavin Gulati, Tehelka's lawyer, asked Tarun Tejpal this question: "What has been the fall-out of this investigation on Tehelka as a result of this expose?" his answer was most revealing:

> Today the only casualty of our expose in corruption is not an individual or political party but Tehelka.com itself. For the last one and a half years, we have been harassed by all kinds of agencies in the government. The angel investors of the company have been destroyed, their business shut down … . Thanks to all that, Tehelka.com has not received even a single rupee of investment since we broke the story. Today, of course, it is true that we have not paid salary for five months, there are people who have not received it for eight months and Tehelka is one-fifteenth of the size it was when we broke the story. Every department from the Enforcement Directorate, Income Tax, CBI, we have been harassed by every agency and the kind of harassment has to be seen to be believed. (Trehan, 2009, p. 570)

In short, by exposing corruption in the MOD, Tehelka and its journalists paid the price for being the whistle-blowers. Instead of being rewarded for whistle-blowing, the company and its reporters were punished. On the contrary, the corrupt offenders were not punished except for some army officers. Vir Sanghvi (2004) has referred to this paradox: "the targets of Tehelka flourish while Tehelka itself has closed down." According to him,

> When the scandal broke, Tarun Tejpal was a hero and Bagaru Laxman, George Fernandes and Jaya Jaitly [a close aide of Fernandes] were in disgrace … . In fact, the opposite has happened [two years later]. Tejpal may still be a hero … .but he is a hero who is deeply in debt. Of his targets, George Fernandes is back as Defense Minister and acts as though Tehelka never happened … . The NDA [National Democratic Alliance] government was not fatally wounded even though most of us wrote it off in the immediate aftermath of Tehelka … . On the other hand, Tehelka itself has closed down … . Everybody in politics (though not the service officers who have been court-martialed) indicted by Tehelka has flourished, but Tehelka and its backers have been finished. (Sanghvi, 2004)

## AIM OF THE CHAPTER

In his 1953 assessment of the state of public administration in India, Paul A. Appleby (1953, pp. 51–54) devoted Section VI of his report to "Irregularity and Corruption." He was impressed with the low level of corruption in India and the honesty of its government and people. He wrote:

> In view of structural and procedural defects and the very low rates of pay for most subordinate employees, the general situation appears to be surprisingly good. This would indicate that the shortcomings are not attributable to any low state of personal integrity. On the contrary, my impression is that the people here are rather more than ordinarily honest … . All in all, I believe that the general judgment I have expressed about the quality of the government of India applies in respect of honesty. This is to say that India is one of the dozen or so governments in which honesty has been carried to its highest levels. (Appleby, 1953, pp. 53–54)

However, in his insightful assessment of Appleby's contribution to Indian public administration, Krishna K. Tummala (2004, p. 222) observes that

Appleby "would have been surprised, even amazed at the current situation" regarding corruption in India.

In stark contrast, S. R. Maheshwari (2005, pp. 232–233) has painted this negative picture of the civil service and civil servants in India:

> The civil servant has forsaken his truly professional traits and is increasingly inclined to seek personal favors … . Today, a civil servant has become a seeker of favors … . The civil servants are perceived by society to be arrogant, self-opinionated, inaccessible, career-minded, and power-hungry … . The civil service presently suffers from over-staffing, wastefulness, corruption, politicization, and excessive generalism. It must be made accountable, ethical and sensitive to the citizens.

Similarly, Satya Prakash Garg (2006, p. v), a former senior civil servant in India with 35 years experience, has also criticized the Indian bureaucracy for being

> accountability-free, unapproachable, backward looking and obstructs development. The complaints of the citizens are not heeded – a citizen never gets a reply to his complaints. The citizens and the government remain on the opposite side of the fence rather than being friendly and helpful to each other. Corruption is rife and persons in high positions in the government embezzle crores of rupees while those lower down steal lakhs. Fake stamp papers, currency notes, passports, driving licenses and caste certificates proliferate.

What has happened in India during the past 57 years that has resulted in a more negative perception of the civil service and the perceived extent of corruption among its civil servants? This chapter addresses this question by first describing the policy context in India before discussing the perceived extent of corruption and identifying its causes, followed by a review of the various anticorruption measures employed by the government since 1941, when the Delhi Special Police Establishment (DSPE) was formed as the first Anti-Corruption Agency (ACA). The seventh section of this chapter evaluates the effectiveness of the anticorruption measures adopted in India and explains why these measures are ineffective. The final section concludes the chapter by arguing that curbing corruption in India is an impossible dream because the government lacks the political will to minimize corruption for the foreseeable future.

## INDIA'S POLICY CONTEXT

### *Geography*

India is a huge country with a total land area of 3,287,263 sq km. It is the seventh largest country in the world and has a land frontier of

***Box 3.1.*** India's Policy Context

| | |
|---|---|
| Land area | 3,287,263 sq km |
| Arable land | 53% |
| GDP | US$1,159 billion (2008) |
| GDP per capita | US$1,020 (2008) |
| Population | 1,186.2 million (2008) |
| Population density | 360.8 persons per sq km |
| Urban population | 30% |
| Adult literacy rate | 62.8% |
| Political system | Parliamentary democracy |
| Colonial rule | British colonial rule (1858–1947) |
| 2010 CPI rank & score | 87/178 and 3.3/10 |
| 2010 PERC rank & score | 11/16 and 7.18/10 |

*Sources*: Economist (2010a, p. 158); http://www.transparency.org./policy_research/surveys_indices/cpi/2010/results; and *Straits Times* (2010a).

15,200 kilometers and a coastline of 7,516 kilometers. India shares its borders with these six countries: Pakistan, China, Nepal, Bhutan, Bangladesh, and Myanmar. Given its vast territory, India has a federal system with 28 states and 6 union territories administered by the central government. Accordingly, there are four layers of administration at the central, state, local, and district levels.

Indeed, India's complex administrative structure provides many opportunities for corruption, and its large size and diversity makes the enforcement of the anticorruption laws difficult, especially at the state, local, and district levels. N. Vittal and S. Mahalingam (2000, p. 271) have astutely referred to the difficulties posed by India's geography thus:

> In terms of geographical space India may be one country but when it comes to time India is a country which is spread over a few centuries. India is like a snake whose head is in the twentieth century and the tail is in the seventeenth century. Geographically, India may be in one place but chronologically it occupies different time zones.

## *History*

India was a British colony for 89 years from 1 September 1858, when the East India Company was dissolved and its powers were transferred to the

British Crown, until independence was achieved on 15 August 1947. The legacy of British rule was generally positive as it created a centralized administration in the form of the Indian Administrative Service (IAS); introduced meritocracy in recruitment to the IAS; constructed an extensive network of roads, railways, and telecommunications; and promoted the rule of law, respect for personal liberty, and equality.

In his excellent study of bureaucrats in India, Richard P. Taub (1969, pp. 153–161) observed that the British had maintained control over India by means of three methods. First, the British created several levels of administration with the Indian Civil Service (ICS) and the district and local administration. Second, rules were created to ensure control over the decision-making powers of the Indian subordinate officials. However, these rules cause delay and confusion today and provide ample opportunities for corruption. The third method was the centralization of decision-making, which required junior civil servants to obtain approval from their superior officers for their decisions. Thus, the British method of creating rules to maintain control over the decision-making powers of the Indian subordinate civil servants had caused delay and confusion and provided many opportunities for corruption. Indeed, Palmier (1985, pp. 83–99) has argued that delays in investigations, prosecutions, and the courts in India have further increased the opportunities for corruption as "delay breeds corruption."

### *Economy*

India's economy is the third largest in Asia after Japan and China as its GDP in 2008 was US$1,159 billion and its GDP per capita was US$1,020 (Economist, 2010a, pp. 24, 158). India is rich in natural resources such as rubber, timber, chromium, coal, iron, manganese, copper ore, bauxite, mica salt, limestone, and gypsum. It also has reserves of coal, gas, and oil, but India remains a net importer of crude oil as domestic generation cannot meet the demand (Dunung, 1998, p. 339).

The percentage of arable area is 53 percent and agriculture contributes to 17 percent of the country's GDP (Economist, 2010a, p. 158). The major crops produced are rice, wheat, pulses, sugar cane, cotton, jute, oilseeds, tea, coffee, and tobacco. India has a diversified manufacturing base, and the major manufacturing industries are cotton and jute textiles; iron, steel, and other basic metals; petrochemicals; electrical machinery and appliances; transport equipment; chemicals; cement; fertilizers; medicines and pharmaceuticals; and food products (Dunung, 1998, p. 339).

In spite of its abundant natural resources, there is a great deal of poverty in India, and this is reflected in the following indicators of consumer goods ownership in 2008: there are 31.7 color television sets per 100 households; 3.2 telephone lines per 100 population; 29.4 mobile telephone subscribers per 100 population; 3.3 computers per 100 population; and 3.8 Internet hosts per 1,000 population (Economist, 2010a, p. 159). According to Michael P. Todaro and Stephen C. Smith (2003, p. 243), India "epitomizes the problem of absolute poverty" as it has "one of the highest poverty rates in the world (44.2 percent in 1996) and by far the greatest number of people living on less that $1 a day (509 million, compared to China's 274 million)." A more recent estimate by UNICEF (2010) indicates that the percentage of population below the international poverty line of US$1.25 per day from 1992 to 2007 is 42 percent. Hence, it is not surprising that Steven D. Levitt and Stephen J. Dubner (2010, p. 3) contend that India would not be a wise choice if one could select his or her birthplace anywhere in the world today because

> Despite its vaunted progress as a major player in the global economy, the country as a whole remains excruciatingly poor. Life expectancy and literacy rates are low; pollution and corruption are high. In the rural areas where more than two-thirds of Indians live, barely half of the households have electricity and only one in four homes has a toilet.

India's absolute poverty and its low GDP per capita of US$1,020 are responsible for the low wages of civil servants and political leaders, which is a major cause of the rampant corruption in the country.

### *Demography*

India's population in 2008 was 1,186.2 million, which is the second largest in the world after China with a population density of 360.8 persons per sq km (Economist, 2010a, p. 158). The population is heterogeneous in terms of ethnicity and religion. The population consists of 72 percent Indo-Aryans, 25 percent Dravidians, and 3 percent Mongoloid. There are three major religious groups: 83 percent Hindu, 11 percent Muslim, and 3 percent Christian (Andrews, 2002, p. 79). There is also a great deal of linguistic diversity as apart from Hindi, the official language, English, the language of administration, commerce, and higher education, there are 17 other major Indian languages (Desai, 1999, pp. 93–94) and 1,652 dialects (Tummala, 2002, pp. 44–45). In addition to its diversity, the literacy rate of the population is 62.8 percent, and the proportion of the urban population is 30 percent in 2008 (Economist, 2010a, p. 158). This means that 70 percent of the population live in rural India and "remains traditional and provincial with strict beliefs and practices that have changed very little throughout the centuries" (Dunung, 1998, p. 341).

As 83 percent of the population is Hindu, it is necessary to discuss the cultural dimension of Hinduism and the implications for fighting corruption. Krishna K. Tummala (2002, pp. 46–47) has astutely identified two aspects of Hinduism, which might hinder anticorruption efforts. First, Hinduism's forgiving nature and the tendency to show leniency toward offenders might undermine the enforcement of the anticorruption measures. Second, "deviance in personal and material life is accepted and forgiven when the search is for a supposedly higher truth" and "apparently contradictory, but not necessarily conflicting behavior patterns are manifest and tolerated in India."

Finally, because of the influence of Hinduism, many Indians are fatalistic and believe that there are limits to what an individual can do to change his or her life (Dunung, 1998, p. 343). This fatalistic attitude of most Indians is not conducive for fighting corruption as they believe that they cannot change the status quo, that is, to minimize the problem of corruption.

### *Political System*

Perhaps the most enduring legacy of British colonial rule is the adoption of parliamentary democracy in India, which has a Council of States or *Rajya Sabha* consisting of 245 members elected for six years, and the House of the People or *Lok Sabha* with 543 members elected for five years and two appointed. To accommodate the country's diversity, India adopted a federal system of government and has 28 states and 7 union territories (Andrews, 2002, pp. 72, 79).

During the first 20 years of independence, the Congress Party was the dominant party in India. In 1967, the Congress Party lost its predominant position at both the national and the state levels. The defeat of the Congress Party in the 1977 general election resulted in a split within the party and the emergence of the Congress (I) Party. After the defeat of the Congress (I) Party in the 1989 election, there have been six general elections in 20 years, with 9 governments, all of which were coalition governments. The growing importance of coalition governments in Indian politics in recent years and the resulting lack of political continuity make it more difficult for the incumbent governments to combat corruption effectively.

## PERCEIVED EXTENT OF CORRUPTION

Corruption in India is a way of life, and both grand and petty forms of corruption are pervasive. On 6 September 1974, the *Far Eastern Economic Review* devoted its cover story to a survey of corruption in Asian countries. In his unfavorable assessment of the situation in India, A. Hariharan (1974, p. 25) wrote:

> The prevailing feeling is that corruption in Indian public life is all pervasive. Not only the President and the Prime Minister but lesser dignitaries, businessmen, bureaucrats, contractors, journalists, vice-chancellors, teachers, doctors and nurses all come under suspicion .... Elections undoubtedly involve corruption, with black money and clandestine expenses for campaigns.

In 1997, three separate evaluations confirm that corruption is a way of life in India. First, Madhav Godbole (1997, p. 61), a former senior civil servant, observed that the ICS is not "a paragon of virtue" and is "marked by corruption, subservience, venality, misuse of power and position, nepotism and favoritism." This observation is not surprising because "corruption has permeated the administration at all levels in the local self-government institutions, State governments and the Centre" (Godbole, 1997, p. 60). During the colonial period, the ICS was described as the "steel frame" because it was responsible for maintaining British colonial rule in India (Roy, 1967, p. 40). However, the pervasiveness of corruption in postindependent India has resulted instead in the description of the civil service today as the "steal frame."

The second assessment is by Gurharpal Singh (1997, p. 211), who contended that political corruption in India was a serious problem in the 1980s and 1990s because "scams, scandals, charges and counter-charges of corruption have become the daily diet of Indian political life." He referred to a recent poll that found that most of the respondents were "no longer surprised by reports of corruption in politics" and that nearly half of them felt that "one has to be corrupt to survive in politics today." The 1996 index of corruption ranking of 49 countries compiled by the World Economic Forum ranked India 45th in terms of the honesty of government officials, 46th in the ability of corporate directors to ensure honesty, and 40th in terms of corporate and individual willingness to pay tax. Consequently, on 30 November 1996, *India Today* commented on these findings by observing that it was not surprising that India was perceived as "one of the more corrupt nations in the world, with corporate ethics in short supply and the shareholders' interests usually getting sacrificed."

The third assessment is provided by S. Guhan (1997, pp. 15–16) who argues that corruption in India in the 1980s and 1990s has assumed critical proportions when compared with the situation in the 1950s and 1960s. Corruption is "a cancer endangering India's society, polity and economy" as reflected in (1) the increase in the number and amounts of corrupt transactions involving defense contracts, telecommunication contracts, commodity imports, privatization, housing allotments, the financial sector, and violations of the Foreign Exchange Regulation and Income Tax Acts; (2) the resignations of 14 ministers in the Union Cabinet and 3 governors of states in the P. V. Narasimha Rao government (1991–1996) because of their alleged involvement in irregular financial transactions; (3) the involvement of chief ministers and ministers in some states in major corruption scams concerning liquor regulations, real estate approvals, large government contracts, allocation of scarce materials, and transfers of public servants; and (4) petty corruption is rampant in the administration of welfare schemes, the public distribution system, the police, revenue, and irrigation departments (Guhan, 1997, pp. 16–17).

In their study, *The Citizen and the Administrator in a Developing Democracy*, Eldersveld, Jagannadham, and Barnabas (1968) conducted interviews with citizens and civil servants in Delhi in India from January to May 1964 to collect data, among other things, on the public perceptions and evaluations of the Indian administrative system. They found that the attitudes of the Indian citizens toward the civil servants and public agencies differed according to their place of residence and social status because the rural public "was consistently more supportive than the urban public, less alienated, more confident about how to act in relationship to officials, possessed of more 'instrumental knowledge' about the administrative process." Furthermore, high-status groups were also "more critical of government, more sceptical of the worthwhileness of government," and "more self-confident about their relationships with bureaucrats" (Eldersveld et al., 1968, p. 52). More importantly, 59 percent of the urban sample and 57 percent of the rural sample perceived that at least half of the civil servants were corrupt. Accordingly, Eldersveld et al. observed that "the expectation of dishonesty and corruption in government is high in India and, paradoxically, for the same people who see government service as prestigeful." Thus, government service in India is viewed as both "corrupt and prestigeful" (Eldersveld et al., 1968, p. 30).

A more recent survey of corruption in five South Asian countries involving 16,525 respondents conducted by TI between November 2001 and May 2002 found that the police was identified as the most corrupt sector in

Bangladesh, India, Pakistan, and Sri Lanka and the third most corrupt sector after land administration and customs in Nepal (Thampi, 2002, pp. 9–10, 12). In India, it was reported that:

> 53 percent of respondents reported that political intervention was the main form of corruption they faced in their interactions with the police department; 14 percent said that money was demanded for making an FRI (First Information Report). 50 percent of all those who interacted with the police admitted paying bribes. The police officer on duty was seen by 54 percent as the chief beneficiary. (Thampi, 2002, p. 14)

The above finding on the extensive police corruption in India is not surprising as it was also observed previously by other scholars. For example, David H. Bayley (1969, pp. 283–284) found that "corruption in the police has become a byword in India, as indeed it has for government servants generally." Indeed, 55.1 percent of the urban respondents in Kanpur and 33.2 percent of respondents in Bangalore thought that there was a "great deal" of police corruption (Bayley, 1969, pp. 284–285). Bayley (1969, pp. 286–288) concluded that:

> In sum, the Indian public not only believes that there is a good deal of corruption in the police ... but about one out of five has seen it and a similar proportion has taken the lesson to heart and would take money with them in their dealings with the police in order to secure action ... . Indians have no illusions about the morality of their policemen. Dishonesty is readily associated with the police and colors their image of the police in striking hues.

The *Global Corruption Barometer 2010*, conducted by Transparency International (2010, p. 43) has again confirmed that the police are the second most corrupt institution in India after political parties. Among the 22 Asia-Pacific countries included in the survey, the police in India are ranked joint third with Malaysia, with a score of 4.1 after Pakistan (4.5) and Bangladesh (4.4).

The studies conducted by the Public Affairs Center in Bangalore provide empirical evidence for the extensive "retail" corruption in Ahmedabad, Bangalore, Calcutta, Madras, and Pune. Even the poor are not spared as Table 3.1 notes that the percentage of the urban poor who paid bribes was the highest in Bangalore, followed by Madras, Ahmedabad, Calcutta, and Pune. Not surprisingly, Samuel Paul and Manubhai Shah (1997, pp. 151–152) have concluded that "corruption is a pervasive phenomenon in India's public services."

Samuel Paul (2002, p. 33) initiated the use of a report card to provide public feedback on the public services provided in Bangalore and found that there was widespread "retail" corruption. Table 3.2 notes that all the households interviewed had paid bribes to many public agencies with about a third of the respondents paying an average bribe of Rs. 648 (US$21.60) to

*Table 3.1.* The Speed Money Phenomenon in Five Indian Cities.

| City | Percentage of Poor Paying Bribes (%) | Amount of Bribe |
|---|---|---|
| Ahmedabad | 20 | Rs. 500 |
| Bangalore | 33 | Rs. 850 |
| Calcutta | 12 | NA |
| Madras | 26 | NA |
| Pune | 6 | Rs. 350 |

*Source*: Paul and Shah (1997, pp. 151–152).

*Table 3.2.* The Speed Money Phenomenon in Bangalore.

| Public Agency | Proportion in Sample Who Have Paid a Bribe (%) | Average Payment Per Transaction (in Rs.)[a] |
|---|---|---|
| Karnataka Electricity Board | 11 | 206 (US$6.87) |
| Bangalore Water Supply and Sewerage Board | 12 | 275 (US$9.12) |
| Bangalore City Corporation | 21 | 656 (US$21.87) |
| Public hospitals | 17 | 396 (US$13.20) |
| Regional Transport Office | 33 | 648 (US$21.60) |
| Bangalore Telecom | 4 | 110 (US$3.67) |
| Average | 14 | 857 (US$28.57) |

*Source*: Paul (2002, p. 45).
[a]US$1 = Rs. 30 (in 1994).

the Regional Transport Office. However, the highest amount of Rs. 656 (US$21.87) per transaction was paid by 21 percent of the sample to the Bangalore City Corporation. Only 4 percent of the respondents paid an average bribe of Rs. 110 (US$3.67) to the Bangalore Telecom.

Paul (2002, p. 47) found that "extortion by officials was the dominant feature of corruption in Bangalore's public agencies, with bribery also playing a significant, but secondary role" because "many customers believe that if they did not bribe, they would not receive the benefits they were seeking." For the poor households in Bangalore, 32 percent reported that they had to pay bribes to solve their problems, but 40 percent of them complained that they did not get satisfactory results, even after paying bribes. In contrast, only 14 percent of the middle-class households had to pay bribes. In other words, "the lower the income level of a household, the greater the chances of extortion" (Paul, 2002, p. 50).

In their analysis of corruption in the electricity sector, Mohinder Gulati and M. Y. Rao (2007, p. 120) confirm that "usually it is the poor who bear the brunt of corruption" because "they have low rates of access to the power grid, and power sector subsidies crowd out expenditures on other public services that primarily benefit the poor." This was illustrated in a 2001 World Bank study on the supply of free power to the farmers in two states in India, which found that only a small proportion of the farmers had benefited from the scheme.

In the wake of the Tehelka scandal, Prem Kumar (2001) contends that small-scale corruption is "ugly and costly" too because it "touches the common man the most." His explanation is:

> The bribe he has to give for a telephone, electricity or water connection, the money he has to pay the lineman to keep his telephone working or for uninterrupted supply of electricity, the tip he has to pay the postman or even a sanitation karamchari for their services, they are all small amounts but paid with a lot of difficulty.

He concludes that huge corruption scandals are exposed, debated, and tackled at the expense of small-scale corruption, which should not be ignored because it is widespread and "all small amounts could together run into a mind-boggling sum indeed" (Kumar, 2001).

In November 2003, Ron Moreau and Sudip Mazumdar (2003) observe that Indians are suffering from "corruption fatigue" because "almost daily they seem to be bombarded with yet another official scandal." Furthermore, the "most recent scandals involve increasingly large sums of money, encompass officials from coast to coast and seem to be occurring with greater frequency." However, instead of admitting that corruption is a national problem, the major political parties are "unabashed" by the reports of corruption and blame "their rivals of either fabricating the scandal or of being even more corrupt."

In similar vein, Kamala Prasad (2006, p. 310) laments that "legal remedies in the last fifty years have neither created a climate of greater compliance nor succeeded in punishing the really guilty and giving protection and assurance to the honest." Consequently, the level of corruption has reached "intolerable levels." The replacement of the "license-permit raj" with the "tender raj" has "merely privatized corruption." While the "floodgates of corruption in high places became wide open during the regime of Indira Gandhi and her successors," political corruption only became "a household story" from the late 1980s (Prasad, 2006, p. 312).

The allegations of "corruption, nepotism, incompetence and sheer negligence" during the preparations for the Commonwealth Games in

October 2010 confirm that corruption is a serious problem in India (Tandon, 2010). The problems reported include "corruption scandals, huge cost overruns, shoddy construction that means completed facilities with leaky roofs or subsiding floors" (Burke, 2010). Furthermore, there are also "ticketing and transportation problems, security concerns, fears of a dengue fever outbreak and the collapse of a pedestrian bridge at the main stadium" (VOA News, 2010). Investigations by Indian newspapers reveal that the Delhi Organizing Committee has agreed "to pay more than [US]$23,000 in transport and hire costs for each treadmill rented for the Games period – and almost [US]$400 for rolls of toilet paper" (Hodge, 2010). *India Today* released "internal documents which showed organizers spent [US]$80 on one roll of toilet paper, [US]$125 on a first-aid kit and [US]$61 on a soap dispenser which retails in India for only [US]$2."

Hence, it is not surprising that the Delhi Commonwealth Games have become the most expensive in the event's history because the Indian government has spent about US$5 billion instead of the original estimated budget of US$500 million (Tandon, 2010). Chetan Baghat, India's best-selling author, describes the recent Commonwealth Games as a "lootfest" because it is "by far, the biggest and most blatant exercise in corruption in independent India's history." He further adds, "Not only have they stolen public money, they've made a mess of the job at hand" (Burke, 2010).

Finally, the most scathing but credible assessment of the perceived extent of corruption in India is voiced by Pratyush Sinha, when he retired as the Central Vigilance Commissioner in early September 2010. According to Sinha:

> When we were growing up, I remember if somebody was corrupt, he was generally looked down upon. There was at least some social stigma attached to it. That is gone. So there is greater social acceptance .... 20 percent of Indians are honest, regardless of the temptations, because this is how they are. They have a conscience. There would be around 30 percent who would be utterly corrupt. But the rest [50 percent] are the people who are on the borderline. (*Straits Times*, 2010b, p. A19)

## CAUSES OF CORRUPTION

In their analysis of corruption in the public services in India, Samuel Paul and Manubhai Shah (1997, pp. 147–149) have identified five major causes. First, the government's monopoly in the supply of public goods and services has reduced competition and created opportunities for corruption by restricting supply either deliberately or through inefficiency. A second related cause is that the discretion of public agencies in decision-making provides opportunities and incentives for corruption among those involved. Third, corruption exists because of the relative lack of accountability of the service providers to the citizens. Fourth, information barriers also contribute to corruption when service providers have information not available to citizens. Finally, as the average citizen is exposed to corruption in the public sector on an episodic and not daily basis, "it is unlikely that he will invest his time and resources in a systemic reform," and this explains "why it is difficult to organize effective collective action against corruption in public services." However, this analysis of the causes of corruption by Paul and Shah is not exhaustive because they have excluded several other important causes.

### *Low Salaries*

As discussed in Chapter 1, Leslie Palmier (1985, pp. 271–272) has identified ample opportunities, low salaries, and poor policing as the three important causes of corruption in his comparative analysis of how bureaucratic corruption is curbed in Hong Kong, India, and Indonesia. His analysis applies to India also because its pervasive corruption can be attributed to the low salaries of the civil servants, their ample opportunities for corruption, and ineffective policing.

The Third Pay Commission (1970–1973) in India stresses the link between low salaries and corruption thus:

> While it is not argued that the payment of high salaries by itself is a guarantee for the honesty and integrity of the public service, it can be confidently stated that the payment of a salary which does not satisfy the minimum reasonable needs of a government servant is a direct invitation to corruption. (quoted in Das, 2001, p. 105)

More recently, the Chief Justice, K. G. Balakrishnan (2009) contends that "the considerable disparity between the pay-scales offered in the public and private sectors" is a major cause of corruption in India.

TI's survey of corruption in five South Asian countries found that the low salaries of employees in various sectors were identified by the respondents as an important cause of corruption. In India, 12 percent of the respondents identified low salaries as a cause of corruption in the education sector, 8 percent of them blamed poor wages for the corruption in the power sector, and 6 percent attributed police corruption to their low salaries (Thampi, 2002, pp. 20, 26, 34).

In his survey of civil service pay in South Asia, David C. E. Chew (1992, p. 78) found that "despite salary revisions and dearness allowances, the

***Table 3.3.*** Comparative Analysis of Monthly Salaries of Political Leaders in Four Asian Countries in 1996.

| Country | Monthly Salary of Prime Minister | Monthly Salary of Minister | Monthly Salary of Member of Parliament |
|---|---|---|---|
| Singapore | US$67,738 | US$47,873 | US$5,431[a] |
| Japan | US$32,921 | US$24,026 | US$19,615 |
| Thailand | US$4,533 | US$4,135 | US$3,062 |
| India | US$417 | US$405 | US$381 |

*Sources*: Compiled from data provided in *Straits Times*, 24 February 1996 and Srivastava (2001, pp. 91–93).
[a]This is a tax-free allowance as Members of Parliament in Singapore who are not members of the government have their own careers.

starting basic salaries of the five kinds of civil servants in South Asia remained very low in December 1987 by international standards.'' Table 3.3 summarizes the comparison by C. P. Srivastava (2001, p. 91) of the monthly salaries of the prime ministers in 1996 in India, Japan, Singapore, and Thailand. He found that the monthly salary of Singapore's prime minister (US$67,738) was 162 times higher than that of the Indian prime minister (US$417). Similarly, a cabinet minister in Singapore earns 118 times more each month than his Indian counterpart. In contrast, the monthly salary of the Japanese Member of Parliament (MP) is 51 times higher than that of the Indian MP. The monthly allowance of Singapore's MPs is 14 times more than the monthly salary of their Indian counterparts. The Thai MP also earns eight times as much per month as an Indian MP. In short, ''the salaries paid to India's prime minister, ministers and MPs are extremely low compared to the salaries paid to their peers in other developing countries'' (Srivastava, 2001, p. 94).

On 20 August 2010, the Indian government increased the monthly salary of MPs by three times to Rs. 50,000. Their office and constituency allowances were also increased from Rs. 40,000 to Rs. 45,000 per month. However, the MPs were unhappy that the government had not met their demands that their monthly salary should be increased to Rs. 80,001 (US$1,717) and for an increase in nontaxable benefits such as travel, office, and constituency allowances. Opposition MP, Lalu Prasad, complained in Parliament that:

> We have to give people thousands of cups of tea and feed them, the houses allotted to us are like hotels, we have to give constituents money for medical treatment, write letters for them and pay for their rail tickets back home. We are on duty 24 hours. (Chakraborty, 2010)

## Red Tape

The best evidence that red tape is a serious problem is provided by the World Bank's *Doing Business Surveys* from 2007 to 2011. Table 3.4 reports that India was ranked 134th among 175 economies for the ease of doing business in 2007. Its rank for the ease in doing business improved to 120th among 178 economies in 2008 and to 122nd among 181 economies in 2009. However, its rank in the ease of doing business deteriorated to 133rd and 134th, respectively, among the 183 economies in 2010 and 2011. More importantly, India's rank for starting a business has declined from 88th position in 2007 to 165th position in 2011. Similarly, for construction permits and licenses, India's rank has worsened from 155th position in 2007 to 177th position in 2011. Even the number of procedures for obtaining such permits and licenses has nearly doubled from 20 to 37 during the same period; the time taken has been reduced from 270 days to 195 days. However, the cost (percentage of income per capita) has spiraled from 606 percent to 2,143.7 percent from 2007 to 2011. On the contrary, in terms of registering property, the improvement of India's rank from 110th position to 94th position is reflected in the reduction of six to five procedures, the

***Table 3.4.*** Ease of Doing Business in India, 2007–2011.

| Indicator | 2007 ($N=175$) | 2008 ($N=178$) | 2009 ($N=181$) | 2010 ($N=183$) | 2011 ($N=183$) |
|---|---|---|---|---|---|
| Ease of doing business (rank) | 134 | 120 | 122 | 133 | 134 |
| Starting a business (rank) | 88 | 111 | 121 | 169 | 165 |
| No. of procedures | 11 | 13 | 13 | 13 | 12 |
| Time (days) | 35 | 33 | 30 | 30 | 29 |
| Cost (% of income per capita) | 73.7 | 74.6 | 70.1 | 66.1 | 56.5 |
| Dealing with construction permits or licenses (rank) | 155 | 134 | 136 | 175 | 177 |
| No. of procedures | 20 | 20 | 20 | 37 | 37 |
| Time (days) | 270 | 224 | 224 | 195 | 195 |
| Cost (% of income per capita) | 606.0 | 519.4 | 414.7 | 2,394.9 | 2,143.7 |
| Registering property (rank) | 110 | 112 | 105 | 95 | 94 |
| No. of procedures | 6 | 6 | 6 | 5 | 5 |
| Time (days) | 62 | 62 | 45 | 44 | 44 |
| Cost (% of property value) | 7.8 | 7.7 | 7.5 | 7.4 | 7.4 |
| CPI rank and score | 72nd (3.5) | 85th (3.4) | 84th (3.4) | 87th (3.3) | NA |

*Sources*: World Bank (2006b, p. 118, 2007, p. 126, 2008, p. 110, 2009, p. 127, 2010a, p. 169) and http://www.transparency.org

number of days taken from 62 days to 44 days, and the cost (percentage of property value) from 7.8 percent to 7.4 percent.

### *Low Probability of Detection and Punishment*

Another important cause of corruption in India is the insufficient policing devoted to curbing corruption (Palmier, 1985, p. 280). In other words, as the probability of detecting and punishing corrupt behavior is not high in India, the public perceives corruption as a low risk, high reward activity as those involved in corrupt practices are unlikely to be detected and punished.

In his analysis of corruption in the ICS, P. C. Alexander (1995, p. 79) has identified as a major cause of corruption, "the ease with which corrupt officials are able to get away without punishment [that is] commensurate with their offense." According to him:

> The constitution has justly given the guarantee to all officials that they cannot be dismissed, removed or reduced in rank except after an enquiry for which they will be given a reasonable opportunity of being heard. However the procedures involved in such enquiries have become so complicated and dilatory that the protection intended for the honest official has also become the loophole for the corrupt to escape .... When punishments are not prompt and deterrent, they cease to be disincentives for the dishonest. (Alexander, 1995, p. 80)

Ahmad and Brookins (2004, p. 29) observe that in Bangladesh, India, and Sri Lanka, "official punitive action has seldom been taken against corrupt officials" in spite of the large number of corruption reports. On the basis of the large number of corruption reports in the *Bangladesh Observer* in Dhaka, the *Times of India* in Mumbai, and the *Daily News* in Colombo, from November to December 1996, they identify a total of 119 cases in India, 91 cases in Sri Lanka, and 77 cases in Bangladesh. However, only 18 cases (15 percent) in India have resulted in official punitive action, followed by eight cases (10 percent) in Bangladesh and four cases (4 percent) in Sri Lanka (Ahmad & Brookins, 2004, p. 24). Consequently, Ahmad and Brookins (2004, p. 29) conclude that:

> The general leniency may well contribute to the continued levels of corruption and could serve to lead to its spreading into areas heretofore unmarked by corruption. Genuine reform may not be had until there is greater effort to make corrupt persons accountable for their actions.

Finally, the fear of conviction is an important factor deterring corrupt behavior. However, the combined effect of "poor evidence and judicial delays" makes corruption a low-risk activity in India. For example, in Orissa, as only 70 (or 35 percent) of the 200 cases handled annually are disposed by the courts, it would take them decades to clear the backlog. According to Vikram Menon (2006, p. 345), 12 percent of the defendants in Orissa "die before their case comes to trial; the evidence base collapses and memories blur, making prosecution an impossible task."

### *Societal Tolerance of Corruption*

Tummala (2002, p. 64) has attributed the extensive corruption in India to the society's attitude toward corruption as "no amount of legal restrictions would help combat corruption in India so long as the society itself in general is lenient and tolerant." Indeed, the Santhanam Committee (Santhanam, 1964, p. 101) had noted that "in the long run, the fight against corruption will succeed only to the extent to which a favorable social climate is created." As Hindus constitute 83 percent of the population in India, Tummala (2002, pp. 45–46, 64) contends that "the Hindu system of life, as being not only absorbing but also forgiving in itself appears to be a hurdle" in combating corruption as "a corrupt official can always count on the benevolence of a superior authority." According to Tummala (2002, pp. 46–47):

> An errant individual can always go to the superior (religious or otherwise) and fall on his/her feet, literally and unashamedly, and the chances are that leniency is shown almost immediately regardless of the fact the culprit may or may not have repented for good.

Robert Wade (1985, p. 487) observes that Indians "vote for whom they think can give *them* most favors in a particularist way." Consequently, "most voters do not see an issue of corruption" but that "they themselves have not been successful enough in corrupting." However, Gurharpal Singh (1997, p. 222) notes that in various opinion polls, "voters perceive politicians as corrupt" regardless of their caste, ethnicity, gender, or region. What is most troubling is the finding of one opinion poll that most voters prefer "a leader who is corrupt but efficient to one who is honest but inefficient."

Finally, the fatalism of Indians, according to V. Raghunathan (2006, pp. 44–45), also contributes to corruption:

> Will the country's corruption rating on Transparency International get any better if I stop greasing a palm? … This is how we usually reason. This fatalism, ingrained as it is in our psyche, is visible in our day-to-day actions. … The opposite phenomenon – 'But everybody else is doing it' – is equally common, and leads to the same behavior. Everybody is being corrupt, so why shouldn't I accept that bribe? … These dual attitudes reflect the extent of our fatalism, our mute acceptance of circumstances … .

Indeed, Raghunathan (2006, p. 46) concludes pessimistically that Indians' "fatalism becomes a self-fulfilling prophecy" because they have become so fatalistic that they "no longer even seem to suffer a guilty conscience" when they give or take bribes.

### *Lack of Political Will*

The most important cause of corruption in India is the lack of commitment of its political leaders, many of whom, according to Palmier (1985, p. 112) "are themselves corrupt, and are in no position to cast stones at officials." As will be shown later, this lack of political will is also reflected in the government's unwillingness to provide adequate resources for the CBI and the CVC. Palmier (1985, p. 113) elaborated on this deficiency thus:

> The notion is simply ludicrous that one Central Vigilance Commissioner can effectively consider the files of all gazetted officers charged with corruption, or that their cases can be properly investigated by a handful of Commissioners for Departmental Inquiries. True priorities are shown by the allocation of resources more than by any rhetoric; on that score the control of corruption cannot be said to be very high on the list of preferences of thc Government of India. The Central Vigilance Commission and the Central Bureau of Investigation appear to have been given just enough powers and resources to permit some activity, *but not enough to make them effective.* (emphasis added)

Apart from not allocating adequate manpower and resources to the CBI and CVC to enable them to perform their functions effectively, the political leaders have continued to rely on these ACAs even though they have been ineffective for the past 47 years. Furthermore, as will be discussed in more detail later, the CBI has not been viewed by the public in India as an independent agency but rather as a tool of the incumbent government. Indeed, instead of enforcing the anticorruption laws impartially, the CBI has focused its efforts on catching the "small fish" at the expense of convicting the "big fish."

## ANTICORRUPTION MEASURES

In 1860, corruption was defined in the Indian Penal Code as "acceptance by public servants of any gratification, other than legal remuneration, in exchange for an official act" (Shunglu, 2000, p. 13). Section 161 specified that the punishment for corruption was imprisonment for three years and/or a fine (Hager, 1973, p. 205). However, India only initiated her struggle against corruption in 1941, when the DSPE was established to "investigate cases of bribery and corruption in transactions" involving the War and Supply Departments because the tremendous increase in expenditure during the early stages of World War II provided many opportunities for corruption. In December 1942, the DSPE's activities were expanded to include corruption cases in railways, which were responsible for the movement and supply of war materials (CBI, 2010a, p. 2). The DSPE's officers were empowered in 1943 by Ordinance No. 22 to investigate corruption cases involving central government departments in India. This Ordinance was replaced in September 1946 by the DSPE Act, 1946, which transferred control of the DSPE to the Home Department, which is now known as the Ministry of Home Affairs (MHA) (Palmier, 1985, p. 30).

The Indian government announced its anticorruption policy in the first Five-Year Plan thus:

> The influence of corruption is insidious. It not only inflicts wrongs which are difficult to redress, but it undermines the structure of administration and the confidence of the public in administration. There must, therefore, be a continuous war against every species of corruption within the administration as well as in public life generally and the methods to root out this evil should be constantly reviewed. (quoted in Hager, 1973, p. 203)

## *Prevention of Corruption Act*

In March 1947, the POCA incorporated relevant sections of the Indian Penal Code and became law. Its objective was the "more effective prevention of bribery and corruption" and was directed against the acceptance of gifts, bribery, embezzlement, and nepotism. Hager (1973, p. 205) noted that the POCA's "first major accomplishment" was to narrow the "proof of motive" requirement in Section 5(1), which specified the four instances when a public servant was guilty of criminal misconduct in discharging his duty. Second, the POCA increased the penalty for corruption offenses to imprisonment from one to seven years and/or a fine.

In 1948, the DSPE was placed under the charge of the Inspector General of Police (CBI, 2010a, p. 2). In 1949, the government formed a committee chaired by Baksi Tek Chand to review the POCA's operation and to evaluate the DSPE's effectiveness in curbing corruption. Three years later, the Chand Committee recommended that the DSPE's activities should be expanded. The government accepted this recommendation, and an enforcement wing was added to the DSPE in 1953 to handle offenses involving violation of import and export regulations at Bombay, Calcutta, and Madras. In 1955, an Administrative Vigilance Division (AVD) was established within the MHA to coordinate anticorruption measures within the central government (Palmier, 1985, pp. 13, 31).

In June 1962, the Santhanam Committee was appointed "to review the existing instruments for checking corruption in the Central Services" and to provide advice on the "practical steps that should be taken to make anti-corruption measures more effective." The Santhanam Report made three important recommendations. First, it had recommended the formation of a CVC to "investigate any complaint or suspicion of improper behavior" against a civil servant. The second recommendation was the appointment of a Chief Vigilance Officer (CVO) in each ministry or department to supervise its vigilance staff. The Santhanam Report's final recommendation was the amendment of the POCA to include the provision that "the possession by a public servant of assets disproportionate to income, and for which a satisfactory explanation could not be made, was itself criminal misconduct" (Palmier, 1985, p. 14).

The POCA 1947 was replaced by the POCA 1988, which was passed by the Parliament of India on 9 September 1988. The rationale for the POCA 1988 was to curb the "uncontrollable" corruption and bribery during 1967–1988, which resulted from the absence of speedy trials and the limited prosecution of public servants in corruption cases (Abidi, 1998, p. v). The POCA 1988 incorporated the provisions of the Indian Penal Code (Sections 161–165A), the POCA 1947, and the Criminal Law Amendment Act 1952 in a single statute. The raison d'etre of the POCA 1988 was to tackle corruption among public servants by incorporating provisions of Chapter IX of the Indian Penal Code. More importantly, it expanded the definition of public servants to include those persons employed by the government for performing any public duty who were not covered by the POCA 1947, which had adopted the Indian Penal Code's definition in Section 21 (Jain, 2000; Transparency International India, 2002).

### *Central Bureau of Investigation*

In April 1963, the government created the CBI by incorporating the DSPE as one of its six divisions, namely, the Investigation & Anti-Corruption Division. The other five divisions were Technical Division; Crime Records and Statistics Division; Research Division; Legal and General Division; and Administration Division. The rationale for creating the CBI was explained thus:

> A growing need was felt for a Central Police Agency at the disposal of the Central Government, which could investigate not only cases of bribery and corruption, but also violation of Central fiscal laws, major frauds relating to Government of India

> Departments, Public Joint Stock Companies, Passport Frauds, crimes on the High Seas, crimes on the Airlines and serious crimes committed by organized gangs and professional criminals. (CBI, 2010a, p. 2)

In 1964, the CBI was strengthened with the addition of an Economic Offenses Wing to deal with cases of violation of fiscal laws in February and a Food Offenses Wing in September to gather intelligence on hoarding, black marketing, smuggling, and profiteering in food grains. These two wings were merged to form the Economic Offenses Wing in 1968. The CBI's increased workload led to the formation in 1987 of the Anti-Corruption Division and the Special Crimes Division, which was responsible for dealing with conventional crimes and economic offenses (CBI, 2010a, pp. 3–4).

The liberalization of India's economy contributed to the vast increase in securities scam cases and economic offenses. Consequently, the Economic Crimes Division was created in 1994 to deal with bank and financial fraud cases; import export and foreign exchange violations; and smuggling of narcotics, antiques, cultural property, and other contraband items. The Special Crimes Division was responsible for dealing with terrorism cases, bomb blasts, homicides, kidnapping, and organized crime (CBI, 2010a, p. 4).

Thus, the CBI today is divided into the following seven divisions: Anti-Corruption Division; Economic Offenses Division; Special Crimes Division; Policy and International Police Cooperation Division; Administration Division; Directorate of Prosecution; and Central Forensic Science Laboratory. The Director of CBI, as the Inspector General of Police, DSPE, is responsible for the administration of the CBI (CBI, 2010a, p. 5).

Table 3.5 reports that the CBI's actual staff strength has increased by 241 from 4,908 personnel in 2002 to 5,149 personnel in 2010. However, its establishment has not been filled as the number of vacancies has increased from 1,012 positions to 1,353 positions during 2002–2010.

In contrast to the modest growth in the CBI's actual staff strength from 2002 to 2010, the CBI's budget has grown by nearly three times from US$30,252,939 in 2005 to US$82,005,141 in 2009. More specifically, Table 3.6 notes that the CBI's budget has increased significantly by US$40,788,939 to US$52,122,368 from 2007 to 2008 and by US$29,882,773 from 2008 to 2009.

Among the nine aspects highlighted in the CBI's vision, the following three represent its core functions:

1. Combating corruption in public life, curb economic and violent crimes through meticulous investigation and prosecution.

**Table 3.5.** Personnel of CBI, 2002–2010.

| Year | Establishment | Actual Strength | Vacancies |
|---|---|---|---|
| 2002 | 5,920 (100%) | 4,908 (82.9%) | 1,012 (17.1%) |
| 2003 | 5,886 (100%) | 4,938 (83.9%) | 948 (16.1%) |
| 2004 | 5,891 (100%) | 4,811 (81.7%) | 1,080 (18.3%) |
| 2005 | 5,891 (100%) | 4,711 (80.0%) | 1,180 (20.0%) |
| 2006 | 5,959 (100%) | 4,652 (78.1%) | 1,307 (21.9%) |
| 2007 | 5,959 (100%) | 4,623 (77.6%) | 1,336 (22.4%) |
| 2008 | 5,960 (100%) | 4,874 (81.8%) | 1,086 (18.2%) |
| 2009 | 5,961 (100%) | 5,242 (87.9%) | 719 (12.1%) |
| 2010[a] | 6,502 (100%) | 5,149 (79.2%) | 1,353 (20.8%) |

*Source*: CBI (2005, p. 29, 2006, p. 38, 2008, p. 45, 2010a, p. 56, 2010b).
[a]Figures provided are for 1 November 2010.

**Table 3.6.** Budget of CBI, 2005–2009 (in Rupees).

| Budget Item | 2005 | 2007 | 2008 | 2009 |
|---|---|---|---|---|
| Plan (revenue) | 10,000,000 | 170,000,000 | 41,400,000 | 40,000,000 |
| Plan (capital) | 200,000,000 | 110,000,000 | 260,000,000 | 1,459,000,000 |
| Non-plan (revenue) | 1,152,800,000 | 1,327,800,000 | 2,224,350,000 | 2,329,000,000 |
| Capital (Non-plan) | 700,000 | 100,000 | 100,000 | 0 |
| Total[a] | 1,363,500,000 (US$30,252,939) | 1,607,900,000 (US$40,788,939) | 2,525,850,000 (US$52,122,368) | 3,828,000,000 (US$82,005,141) |

*Sources*: CBI (2006, p. 44, 2008, p. 50, 2009, p. 65, 2010a, p. 63).
[a]The conversion of the total budget from Rs. to US$ is based on these exchange rates: US$1 = 45.07 Rs (2005); US$1 = 39.42 Rs (2007); US$1 = 48.46 Rs (2008); and US$1 = 46.68 Rs (2009) provided in the Economist (2006, p. 156, 2008, p. 158, 2009c, p. 158, 2010a, p. 158).

2. Help fight cyber and high-technology crime.
3. Play a lead role in the war against national and transnational organized crime (CBI, 2010a, p. iv).

This means that apart from combating public sector corruption, the CBI is also responsible for tackling economic and violent crimes, cyber and high-technology crime, as well as organized crime.

As the CBI's role is to investigate crimes handled by the DSPE, the DSPE Act of 1946 remains in force and provides the legal sanction and authority for investigations by the CBI, which does not have any statutory basis itself. Thus, the MHA, through its AVD, assumed control of the CBI's work and provided for its budget. Arising from the recommendations of the Administrative Reforms Commission of 1966, the CBI and AVD were transferred from the MHA to the new Department of Personnel, Cabinet Secretariat in 1970 (Palmier, 1985, pp. 31–32).

The CBI derives its investigating powers from the DSPE Act of 1946 as its section 5 states that the central government can empower it to investigate the notified offenses in any state, but such empowerment is only possible with the consent of the government of that state. The Constitution of India states that law and order come under the jurisdiction of the states. Accordingly, the CBI, as a police organization of the central government, cannot operate in the states without the permission of the state concerned because of this constitutional provision.

C. V. Narasimhan, a former CBI director, observed that the CBI did not encounter any problem within the states when the Congress Party was in power in the states and center during the postindependent period. However, the situation changed drastically when different political parties assumed power in the states because some state governments had withdrawn the consent given by their predecessors "whenever they felt that an investigation taken up by the CBI was politically embarrassing or uncomfortable for them." In other words, the CBI's status as an investigating agency in the states depends on their governments' mercy. Narasimhan (1997, pp. 255–256) has identified this CBI's weakness as "a serious handicap in planning any nation-wide network of investigating units for anti-corruption inquiries."

The CBI has 16 zones and 60 branches. This means that each state has at least a branch or unit of the CBI at the state capital or at a major city (CBI, 2010a, p. 6). The 28 states in India have their own SVCs or ACBs for dealing, respectively, with vigilance and anticorruption work, but these ACBs derive their powers of investigation from the Police Act as they are regular police units. The SVCs are patterned after the CVC and are assisted by the special police establishments in conducting investigations. Their role is advisory in nature, and their jurisdiction covers matters within the executive power of the states but excludes cases of political corruption. The SVCs investigate those transactions where public servants are suspected or alleged to be involved in corrupt behavior (Sharma & Sharma, 2009, pp. 437–438).

If there is public pressure for an inquiry into the misconduct of a minister, the central or state government concerned will form a commission to inquire into the specific allegations against the minister. The Commission of Inquiry will present its report on the facts ascertained during the inquiry to the government concerned, which will refer the matter to the CBI or state ACB for investigation if a person is to be prosecuted. However, the investigation process and the ensuing trial are time-consuming and do not result in swift punishment of the guilty persons (Narasimhan, 1997, pp. 257–258). Narasimhan (1997, p. 258) laments that "not a single CBI case involving ministers has ended in a firm conviction in the court during the last 40 years."

### *Central Vigilance Commission*

Following the recommendation of the Santhanam Committee, the CVC was formed in February 1964 to perform the following four functions:

1. To investigate any transaction in which a public servant is alleged to act for an improper purpose.
2. To examine any complaint that a public servant had exercised his powers for improper or corrupt purposes and any complaint of corruption, misconduct, lack of integrity. or other malpractices by a public servant, including members of the All India Services.
3. To request reports from ministries, departments. and public enterprises to enable it to check and supervise their vigilance and anticorruption work.
4. To request the CBI to investigate a case or to entrust the complaint, information, or case for inquiry to the CBI or the ministry, department, or public enterprise concerned (Narasimhan, 1997, pp. 264–265).

During 1964–1998, the CVC was headed by a Commissioner, who was appointed by the President on the recommendation of the Prime Minister for five years. In September 1997, an independent review committee appointed by the Central Government recommended conferring statutory status on the CVC (CVC, 2009, p. 1). The Supreme Court of India found that the CBI did not follow proper procedure in investigating the Hawala scandal because the alleged offenders were powerful persons.[1] Accordingly, it directed on 18 December 1997, among other things, that the supervision of the CBI should be transferred from the Central Government to the CVC, which should be given a statutory status. On 8 April 1998, the Government asked the Law Commission for its advice. The Law Commission submitted its report and a draft of the CVC Bill to the Government on 13 August 1998 (Joshi, 2003, p. 1).

The CVC Ordinance was enacted on 25 August 1998 to comply with the directions of the Supreme Court. The Central Government promulgated another Ordinance on 8 January 1999, and the CVC functioned under the Resolution of 4 April 1999 until the CVC Act 2003 was passed in Parliament on 11 September 2003 and transformed the CVC into a statutory body to supervise the operations of the CBI (CVC, 2009, p. 1). The CVC consists of a Central Vigilance Commissioner as Chairperson and two Vigilance Commissioners, who are appointed for four years by the President on the recommendation of a Committee consisting of the Prime Minister, the Minister of Home Affairs, and the Leader of the Opposition in the House of the People (Sections 3 [1], 4 [1]).

The three commissioners are assisted by a Secretariat of 23 members, the Chief Technical Examiners' Unit consisting of 16 engineers and support staff, and 14 Commissioners for Departmental Inquiries (CVC, 2009, p. 6). Even though the CVC's sanctioned strength has increased marginally from 285 to 288 during 2004–2008, its actual strength has decreased from 251 to 230 over the same period because the number of vacant positions has increased from 34 to 58 (CVC, 2005, p. 86; 2009, p. 57).

The CVC's first function is to supervise the CBI's investigation of offenses committed under the POCA 1988 by holding monthly meetings with the Director of the CBI to review the progress and quality of the cases investigated by the CBI. Its second function is to provide advice to the disciplinary and other agencies in disciplinary cases involving vigilance at the investigation and inquiry stages. Thirdly, the CVC supervises the vigilance and anticorruption work in ministries and departments of the Central Government. The Chief Vigilance Officers (CVOs) in the ministries and departments provide advice relating to vigilance administration and the establishment of effective systems and procedures to plug systemic failures or loopholes. The CVOs submit monthly and annual reports to the CVC, which holds annual zonal meetings to review and monitor their performance (CVC, 2009, pp. 2, 6).

## EVALUATION OF THE ANTICORRUPTION MEASURES

As discussed earlier, India began its fight against corruption in 1941 and has relied on the CBI, CVC, and the state ACBs to curb corruption. S. S. Gill (1998, pp. 237–238), a former senior civil servant, wrote, "Looking to the number of agencies created to tackle corruption, it would appear that the government was in dead earnest to eradicate this malady." However, "this elaborate and multi-layered apparatus to control administrative corruption has hardly made a dent on the situation."

Indeed, the fact that corruption is a way of life in India is clearly a manifestation of the failure of its anticorruption measures. Gill (1998, pp. 125–127) argues that:

> One cannot think of any sphere of public administration which is not infested with corruption … . Corruption in the countryside is mostly a petty, retail phenomenon, though practiced on a vast scale. It is the urban corruption where large sums are involved and the operational modalities are much more sophisticated … . Corruption, unlike a headache, is not confined only to the top; it infects the whole system. Every level devises its own methods of extortion.

The ineffectiveness of India's anticorruption measures is also reflected in its low ranking and scores on these four indicators: TI's CPI from 1995 to 2010; PERC's annual surveys on corruption, 1995–2010; World Bank's Control of Corruption from 1996 to 2009; and the *Global Competitiveness Report's* indicator on the public trust of politicians from 1999 to 2010–2011.

First, Table 3.7 notes that even though India's CPI score has improved from 2.78 in 1995 to 3.5 in 2007, its relatively low score is also reflected in the fact that it was ranked 87th position with a score of 3.3 among the 178 countries included in the 2010 CPI. India is ranked 12th position among the

***Table 3.7.*** India's Performance on CPI, PERC, and Control of Corruption, 1995–2010.

| Year | CPI Rank and Score | PERC Rank and Score | Control of Corruption Percentile Rank |
|---|---|---|---|
| 1995 | 35th (2.78) | 9th (7.00) | NA |
| 1996 | 46th (2.63) | 8th (6.86) | 36.4 |
| 1997 | 45th (2.75) | 11th (8.20) | NA |
| 1998 | 66th (2.9) | 9th (7.40) | 43.7 |
| 1999 | 72nd (2.9) | 11th (9.17) | NA |
| 2000 | 69th (2.8) | 11th (9.50) | 41.3 |
| 2001 | 71st (2.7) | 11th (9.67) | NA |
| 2002 | 71st (2.7) | 11th (9.17) | 39.3 |
| 2003 | 83rd (2.8) | 11th (9.30) | 44.7 |
| 2004 | 90th (2.8) | 11th (8.90) | 45.1 |
| 2005 | 88th (2.9) | 10th (8.63) | 43.2 |
| 2006 | 70th (3.3) | 8th (6.76) | 50.0 |
| 2007 | 72nd (3.5) | 9th (6.67) | 44.4 |
| 2008 | 85th (3.4) | 8th (7.25) | 44.4 |
| 2009 | 84th (3.4) | 13th (7.21) | 46.7 |
| 2010 | 87th (3.3) | 11th (7.18) | NA |

*Sources*: Compiled from http://wwwtransparency.org; PERC (2001, 2008, p. 7); Hussain (2009, p. B5); and *Straits Times* (2010a).

24 Asian countries in the 2010 CPI. Second, India's rank on PERC's annual surveys on corruption among the 11–16 countries varies between 8th position (in 1996, 2006, and 2008) and 13th position (in 2009). Third, the World Bank's control of corruption indicator also confirms India's low score, which ranges from 36.4 percentile rank in 1996 to 50 percentile rank in 2006. In 2009, India is ranked 11th among the 25 Asian countries for control of corruption with a percentile rank of 46.7.

Fourth, Table 3.8 notes that the level of Indians' public trust of politicians is low because India is ranked 82nd among 102 countries in 2003–2004 with a score of 1.70. Its rank improved slightly to 79th position among 133 countries, and its score increased to 2.40 in 2009–2010. However, India is ranked 14th among the 20 Asian countries included in the 2010–2011 survey. In other words, the low level of public trust of politicians is a reflection of the rampant corruption in India.

## *Evaluation of the CBI*

The first criticism of the CBI is the public perception that it is "a pliable tool of the ruling party, and its investigations tend to become cover-up operations for the misdeeds of ministers" (Gill, 1998, p. 238). Madhav

***Table 3.8.*** Public Trust of Politicians in India, 1999 to 2010–2011.

| Year | Rank | Score[a] | No. of Countries |
|---|---|---|---|
| 1999 | 53rd | 1.85 | 59 |
| 2000 | 53rd | 1.90 | 59 |
| 2001–2002 | 49th | 2.10 | 75 |
| 2002–2003 | 57th | 1.90 | 80 |
| 2003–2004 | 82nd | 1.70 | 102 |
| 2007–2008 | 83rd | 2.20 | 131 |
| 2008–2009 | 84th | 2.30 | 134 |
| 2009–2010 | 79th | 2.40 | 133 |
| 2010–2011 | 88th | 2.30 | 139 |
| Average | 70th | 2.07 | – |

*Sources*: Compiled from Schwab et al. (1999, p. 327), Porter et al. (2000, p. 253), Schwab et al. (2002, p. 408), Cornelius (2003, p. 619), Sala-i-Martin (2004, p. 499), Schwab and Porter (2007, p. 379), Schwab and Porter (2008, p. 367), Schwab (2009, p. 349), and Schwab (2010, p. 369).
[a]The score ranges from 1 (very low) to 7 (very high) for the respondents' answers to this statement: "How would you rate the level of public trust in the ethical standards of politicians in your country."

Godbole (2000, p. 88), a former senior civil servant, has also criticized the CBI's poor performance thus:

> The CBI was also found to have been used by the then Prime Minister Indira Gandhi, as an instrument of persecution … . The record of the CBI in respect of investigation of cases involving the high, the mighty and the powerful is, to put it very mildly, disgraceful.

Table 3.9 provides details of the CBI's output according to four indicators from 2003 to 2009. The number of cases registered has increased from 1,068 in 2003 to 1,119 in 2009, with a peak of 1,267 cases in 2005. Second, the number of investigation cases finalized during each year has also increased from 1,112 to 1,127 during the same period. Third, the number of cases under investigation at the end of the year has decreased from 1,435 to 988 from 2003 to 2009. Fourth, the CBI's output in terms of the number of two-year-old cases under investigation at the end of the year has been reduced from 208 in 2003 to 89 in 2009. Fifth, the CBI's per capita output in finalizing investigation cases ranges from 0.21 in 2009 to 0.27 in 2004.

The CBI's conviction rate has increased from 65.6 percent in 2005 to 72.9 percent in 2006 (CBI, 2006, p. 29; CVC, 2009, p. 54). However, it declined from 67.7 percent in 2007 to 64.4 percent in 2009 (CBI, 2009, p. 36; 2010a, p. 30). On the contrary, S. S. Gill (1998, p. 238) expresses skepticism regarding the CBI's high conviction rates, which are deceptive because

> If there are thirty cases of heinous crimes and seventy of minor thefts, and you get conviction in sixty cases of theft, it would be sheer deceit to claim a sixty percent rate of success.

***Table 3.9.*** CBI's Output, 2003–2009.

| Indicator | 2003 | 2004 | 2005 | 2006 | 2007 | 2008 | 2009 | Total |
|---|---|---|---|---|---|---|---|---|
| Cases registered | 1,068 | 1,193 | 1,267 | 1,156 | 940 | 991 | 1,119 | 7,734 |
| Investigation cases finalized (a) | 1,112 | 1,282 | 1,231 | 1,143 | 1,216 | 1,127 | 1,127 | 8,238 |
| Cases under investigation at the end of year | 1,435 | 1,354 | 1,402 | 1,417 | 1,143 | 1,005 | 988 | 8,744 |
| Two-year-old cases under investigation at the end of year | 208 | 158 | 137 | 139 | 135 | 116 | 89 | 982 |
| CBI's staff strength (b) | 4,938 | 4,811 | 4,711 | 4,652 | 4,623 | 4,874 | 5,242 | – |
| Per capita output in finalizing investigation cases (a/b) | 0.23 | 0.27 | 0.26 | 0.25 | 0.26 | 0.23 | 0.21 | – |

*Sources*: CBI (2006, pp. 8, 24–25, 2008, pp. 6, 19–20, 2009, pp. 6, 24–26, 2010a, pp. 8, 20–21).

Furthermore, Gill (1998, p. 238) has also accused the CBI of going "only after the small fry" as only one gazetted officer was dismissed in 1972 and two officers in 1992. Indeed, the CBI's ineffectiveness is also reflected in its "dismal" record in investigating the various mega scams such as the Bofors scandal, Jain Hawala scandal, securities scam, sugar import scam, Sukh Ram's telecom scandal, Indian Bank scam, and the fodder scandal, because "not a single conviction has been secured so far by the CBI" (Gill, 1998, p. 238).

Table 3.5 notes that while the establishment of the CBI has increased from 5,920 personnel in 2002 to 6,502 in 2010, its actual strength has only grown from 4,908 to 5,149 personnel during the same period. This means that the number of vacancies in the CBI has also risen from 1,012 (17.1 percent) in 2002 to 1,353 (20.8 percent) in 2010. The CBI's large number of vacancies explains why B. R. Lall (2007, p. 230), a former CBI joint director, has described it as "a very small organization as compared to the quantum of crimes committed in the country." Accordingly, he has recommended the expansion of the CBI's staff by 20 percent annually for the next decade until the CBI has 6,000 investigators (Lall, 2007, p. 231).

Apart from being understaffed, Table 3.10 notes that the CBI's staff–population ratio of 1:243,373 is less favorable than those of the CPIB in Singapore and the ICAC in Hong Kong even though the CBI has more personnel than the CPIB and ICAC. Similarly, the CBI's annual budget of US$52.1 million for 2008 is higher than the CPIB's budget of US$11.2 million, but lower than the ICAC's budget of US$97.7 million. However, the CBI's per capita expenditure of US$0.04 is much lower than the CPIB's per capita expenditure of US$2.32 and the ICAC's per capita expenditure of US$13.40. The CBI's inadequate personnel and budget is a clear manifestation of the Indian government's lack of political will in curbing corruption.

***Table 3.10.*** Comparative Analysis of the Personnel and Budget of the CBI, CPIB and ICAC in 2008.

| Item | CBI | CPIB | ICAC |
|---|---|---|---|
| Personnel | 4,874 | 86 | 1,263 |
| Budget | US$52.1 million | US$11.2 million | US$97.7 million |
| Population of country | 1,186.2 million | 4.83 million | 7.3 million |
| Staff–population ratio | 1: 243,373 | 1: 56,163 | 1: 5,780 |
| Per capita expenditure | US$0.04 | US$2.32 | US$13.40 |

*Sources*: CBI (2009, pp. 60, 65); Republic of Singapore (2010, p. 382); ICAC (2009, pp. 28, 81); and Economist (2010a, pp. 154, 158, 208).

There are two other weaknesses of the CBI, which have adversely affected its effectiveness in curbing corruption. First, unlike the CPIB and ICAC, the CBI has maintained the traditional British method of relying on the police to curb corruption since 1963 even though this method has been shown to be ineffective. In Chapters 6 and 7, the experiences of the CPIB and ICAC have shown the folly of relying on the police to curb corruption when the police are corrupt. Singapore's experience in combating corruption, which is analyzed in Chapter 6, shows that from 1937 to 1951, the Anti-Corruption Branch (ACB) within the Criminal Investigation Department (CID) of the SPF was ineffective because of its limited resources and the prevalence of police corruption. The discovery by the British colonial government in October 1951 of the involvement of some senior police officers and detectives in the robbery of S$400,000 worth of opium (known as the Opium Hijacking scandal) made it realize the necessity of removing the task of corruption control from the police. Consequently, the CPIB was formed as an independent ACA in October 1952.

Similarly, as explained in Chapter 7, the British colonial government employed the same method of corruption control used in Singapore in Hong Kong also by forming the ACB in 1948 as a special unit of the CID of the Royal Hong Kong Police Force (RHKPF) to deal with the investigation and prosecution of corruption cases. The ACB was separated from the CID in 1952, but it still remained within the RHKPF. As the ACB was ineffective, it was upgraded into an Anti-Corruption Office (ACO) with the enactment of the Prevention of Bribery Ordinance (POBO) in May 1971. Even though the ACO was given more manpower, its lack of independence from the RHKPF remained a serious obstacle. The ACO's credibility was undermined on 8 June 1973, when a corruption suspect, Chief Superintendent Peter F. Godber, escaped to Britain while he was under investigation. Godber's escape angered the public, and the government responded by appointing the Blair-Kerr Commission of Inquiry to investigate the circumstances leading to his escape. Consequently, the Governor, Sir Murray MacLehose, was forced by public criticism to accept the Blair-Kerr Commission's recommendation to establish an independent agency, separate from the RHKPF, to fight corruption. In October 1973, he informed the Legislative Council of his decision, and four months later, the ICAC was established on 15 February 1974.

In short, Singapore's and Hong Kong's success in curbing corruption can be attributed to their rejection of the British colonial government's method of relying on the police to curb corruption and their reliance instead on the CPIB and ICAC, respectively. Singapore has taken 15 years (1937–1952), whereas Hong Kong has taken 26 years (1948–1974) to learn this important lesson: do not rely on the police to curb corruption especially when police corruption is pervasive (Quah, 2004, pp. 1–2). India has not learnt this lesson yet because it still relies on a police agency – the CBI – to fight corruption in the midst of rampant police corruption in the country.

In view of the prevalence of police corruption in India, it is surprising that the government has continued to rely for the past 47 years on the CBI to curb corruption even though this traditional British method of relying on the police for corruption control has been shown to be ineffective. The CBI's second weakness is that it is a police agency and is not concerned with fighting corruption only as it has three major areas of operation: anticorruption, economic crimes, and special crimes (including organized crime and terrorism). Given the current international emphasis on combating terrorism and especially after the 26 November 2008 terrorist attack in Mumbai, it will be difficult for the CBI to focus exclusively on its anticorruption activities in view of the competing demands on its limited resources.

Accordingly, to improve the CBI's effectiveness, the following reforms, which require political will, must be introduced: (1) the CBI must be removed from police control and be transformed into an independent ACA and (2) the CBI's powers must be increased by amending the Constitution so that it does not have to obtain permission from the state governments to investigate corruption cases in the states.

### *Evaluation of the CVC*

Table 3.11 provides details of the CVC's output in terms of the receipt and disposal of vigilance cases. The number of vigilance cases received by the CVC has increased from 3,929 cases in 1995 to 6,993 cases in 2003. The number of vigilance cases disposed by the CVC has also increased from 2,456 cases (62.5 percent) to 8,042 cases (115 percent) during the same period. The CVC's most productive year was 1997, when it disposed all the 4,304 cases received and the 1,443 cases brought forward from previous years. In contrast, the number of cases received by the CVC during 1985–1992 was lower, as there were 28,317 cases during this period, or an average of 3,540 cases per year (Das, 2001, p. 144). Das (2001, p. 143) contends that the number of cases received by the

*Table 3.11.* CVC's Output, 1995–2008.

| Year | No. of Cases Received (a) | No. of Cases Disposed (b) | Percentage of (b)/(a) (%) |
|---|---|---|---|
| 1995 | 3,929 | 2,456 | 62.5 |
| 1996 | 4,263 | 4,246 | 99.6 |
| 1997 | 4,304 | 5,747[a] | 133.5 |
| 1998 | 5,076 | 5,064 | 99.8 |
| 1999 | 6,141 | 5,168 | 84.2 |
| 2000 | 6,285 | 6,538[a] | 104.0 |
| 2001 | 6,774 | 6,612 | 97.6 |
| 2002 | 6,465 | 6,626[a] | 102.5 |
| 2003 | 6,993 | 8,042[a] | 115.0 |
| 2004 | 5,987 | 6,134[a] | 102.5 |
| 2005 | 5,394 | 5,314 | 98.5 |
| 2006 | 4,798 | 4,683 | 97.6 |
| 2007 | 4,941 | 4,672 | 94.6 |
| 2008 | 4,721 | 4,238 | 89.8 |

*Sources*: CVC (2005, pp. 13–14; 2009, p. 16).
[a]Includes cases brought forward from previous years.

CVC during 1985–1992 constitutes "a very small percentage of the total number of civil servants working in the central government, public sector undertakings and autonomous organizations, and this is so in the context of a country where corruption is admittedly rampant." Finally, it should be noted that the number of cases received by the CVC has deceased significantly from 6,993 in 2003 to 4,721 in 2008 even though corruption remains a serious problem in India.

As mentioned earlier, the CVC advises other public agencies in disciplinary cases involving vigilance at the investigation and inquiry stages. Table 3.12 provides information on the number of public officials prosecuted and punished by these agencies during 2000–2008 arising from the advice provided by the CVC. Although the number of public officials prosecuted has increased from 51 in 2000 to 192 in 2007, the proportion of such officials remains low, ranging from 1.4 percent in 2002 to 7.1 percent in 2007. Indeed, only 1,023 public officials (3.8 percent) were prosecuted during 2000–2008. Table 3.12 also notes that major penalties were awarded to almost 40 percent of public officials, minor penalties were imposed on 37.2 percent of public officials, and 19.5 percent of public officials were punished by administrative action from 2000 to 2008.

The CVC's Achilles' heel is that it is an advisory body that has to rely on other public agencies to investigate the complaints of misconduct by civil

***Table 3.12.*** Prosecution Sanctioned and Punishment Awarded by Public Agencies following the CVC's Advice, 2000–2008.

| Year | Prosecution Sanctioned | Punishment Awarded | | | |
|---|---|---|---|---|---|
| | | Major penalty | Minor penalty | Administrative action | Total |
| 2000 | 51 (2.0%) | 1,116 (43.8%) | 876 (34.4%) | 507 (19.9%) | 2,550 (100%) |
| 2001 | 53 (2.0%) | 1,067 (40.4%) | 861 (32.6%) | 661 (25.0%) | 2,642 (100%) |
| 2002 | 51 (1.4%) | 1,162 (32.9%) | 957 (27.1%) | 1,360 (38.5%) | 3,530 (100%) |
| 2003 | 127 (3.6%) | 1,432 (40.9%) | 1,372 (39.2%) | 568 (16.2%) | 3,499 (100%) |
| 2004 | 120 (2.8%) | 1,951 (45.4%) | 1,616 (37.6%) | 611 (14.2%) | 4,298 (100%) |
| 2005 | 141 (5.0%) | 1,084 (38.4%) | 1,136 (40.2%) | 462 (16.4%) | 2,823 (100%) |
| 2006 | 150 (6.1%) | 1,024 (41.9%) | 936 (38.3%) | 332 (13.6%) | 2,442 (100%) |
| 2007 | 192 (7.1%) | 1,002 (36.9%) | 1,164 (42.8%) | 360 (13.2%) | 2,718 (100%) |
| 2008 | 138 (5.2%) | 909 (34.3%) | 1,173 (44.3%) | 429 (16.2%) | 2,649 (100%) |
| Total | 1,023 (3.8%) | 10,747 (39.6%) | 10,091 (37.2%) | 5,290 (19.5%) | 27,151 (100%) |

*Sources*: CVC (2005, pp. 16–17, 2009, p. 19).

servants that it receives. Vikram Menon (2006, p. 339) elaborates on this limitation of the CVC:

> The Central Vigilance Commission is not meant to undertake direct investigation into complaints of serious irregularities by government servants or in government departments, and while the commission has decided to exercise powers conferred on it under the 2003 Act to summon records and look directly into serious complaints, given its human and financial resources this can only be exceptional. The commission will have to continue to rely on vigilance divisions in government organizations and public sector units, which remain weak.

However, the internal vigilance machinery in the ministries and government departments is ineffective because of the lack of manpower as reflected in the absence of full-time CVOs in many public sector agencies. The posts of CVOs are filled instead by public servants who are seconded for a short period from other public agencies. This arrangement is unsatisfactory because these seconded officers cannot "develop the insights and continuous focus needed for locating and tackling corruption" in the public agencies. On the contrary, for those public organizations with a large vigilance setup such as the railways, the CVOs might not be objective or independent in their assessments as they are employees appointed to these positions from the same organization (Menon, 2006, p. 339). Another limitation is that vigilance work is perceived by civil servants to be "an additional and non-serious task," and the "very low level of convictions and enormous delay" also reflect their "tolerant attitude towards bureaucratic corruption" (Menon, 2006, pp. 339–340). Prasad (2006, p. 324) describes the vigilance machinery as "dysfunctional" because it is "clogged with too many complaints" and there is also a tendency to pass the buck to another agency to avoid pressure.

It is not surprising that corruption in service delivery is prevalent in many states because their anticorruption agencies and administrative agencies to check corruption are "weak and under-funded and open to political interference." Indeed, the major structural weakness is the "multiplicity of agencies responsible for tackling corruption including the Vigilance Commissions, *Lok Ayuktas* and police agencies like Anti-Corruption Bureaus." The Administrative Reforms Commission had recommended the establishment of an ombudsman or *Lok Pal* in 1967 to redress citizens' grievances and eradicate corruption. However, the non-passage of the *Lok Pal* bill, which was introduced in 1968, on eight occasions is "a clear case of the absence of political will and political consensus in India to tackle corruption" (Menon, 2006, p. 340).

Apart from the lack of political will that is reflected in the CBI's ineffectiveness and the CVC's limitations, India's anticorruption strategy has also been hindered by the country's unfavorable policy context. Gill (1998, p. 251) has astutely observed that "God seems to have taken special care to make India ungovernable. Her extreme diversities and disparities make the emergence of large common denominators almost impossible." As discussed earlier, the policy context is not conducive for the implementation of the anticorruption measures because India is the seventh largest country with the second largest population in the world. Furthermore, its complex administrative structure with its four layers of administration at the central, state, local, and district levels provides many opportunities for corruption, and its large size and diversity make the enforcement of the anticorruption laws difficult, especially at the state, local, and district levels.

Even though India has the third largest economy in Asia and has abundant natural resources, there is still a great deal of poverty, which together with its low GDP per capita are responsible for the low wages of civil servants and political leaders. As the majority of the population is Hindu, Hinduism's forgiving nature and its tendency to show leniency toward offenders have undermined the enforcement of the anticorruption measures. Furthermore, as Hindus, many Indians are also fatalistic and do not believe that they can change the status quo to minimize the problem of corruption. Thus, the low public sector salaries and the fatalism of the Indian population are two important causes of the rampant corruption in India.

Finally, as mentioned earlier, the legacy of British colonial rule was generally positive with the creation of the IAS; the introduction of meritocracy; the development of an extensive infrastructure of roads, railways, and telecommunications; and the promotion of the rule of law, respect for personal liberty, and equality. However, the defeat of the Congress Party in the 1977 general election and the Congress (I) Party in the 1989 general election led to political instability and the growing importance of coalition governments in India. The lack of political continuity during the past three decades makes it more difficult for the incumbent government to curb corruption effectively.

## CONCLUSION

Is curbing corruption in India an impossible dream? The answer, frankly, is yes as the government has so far not demonstrated strong political will in combating corruption as reflected in the ineffectiveness of the CBI, the limitations of the CVC, and the unfavorable policy context, which has hindered the implementation of the anti-corruption measures.

Prashant Agrawal (2010) recently described political corruption as India's "biggest growth industry" after the resignation of the Communications and Information Technology Minister, Andimuthu Raja, former Maharashtra Chief Minister Ashok Chavan, and former Congress Party Secretary Suresh Kalmadi during the first two weeks of November 2010 for three different scandals (Thoppil and Sharma, 2010). Agrawal (2010) admits that "it's too much to ask for an end to corruption in one fell swoop" but he warns that "the government needs to end the astronomical scaling-up" of corruption to prevent the occurrence of the "biggest Indian scandal" involving "the sum of a truly unfathomable [US]$1 trillion."

On the contrary, in his analysis of the strategies employed to combat corruption in India, Lall (2007, pp. 284–285) observes that:

> We have continued to skirt the biggest problem [of corruption] that the country has been facing during the past six decades since independence. The excuses advanced from time to time for not sorting out the problem [of corruption] are of no consequence … . The present mess, if allowed to continue, threatens the very integrity of our nation … . It is possible to retrieve the situation, to prevent corruption and to stop the drain of resources of the nation. However, it can be [done] neither through slogan shouting, nor by displaying boards and hoardings, but by strict and equitable laws and their firm enforcement without fear or regard for any one's status or position. It is strong unwavering action against corruption and the corrupt which really will make the difference and change the mindset.

Lall (2007, p. 287) concludes his book on an optimistic note with the following prescription:

> A strong and determined Prime Minister can make all the difference, liberate these agencies and give their souls to them. Very few persons are required for the task of cleansing the rot and there is no dearth of such people in this country. Only they have to be placed in right positions .... All we require is a straightforward, effective, honest, firm, bold and a well-meaning Prime Minister for a few years at least.

Similarly, Tummala (2010, p. 92) contends that change is only possible if political parties in India are disciplined and "led by honorable and just party leaders" who will follow Mahatma Gandhi's advice not to indulge in "politics without principle."

Who is right and what is the likely scenario in India in terms of combating corruption in the foreseeable future? In my view, India's anticorruption strategy appears to be "hopeless" because its political leaders have so far not demonstrated the political will required to improve its ineffective anti-corruption measures, especially the CBI and CVC, which appear to have been designed to fail. My answer to the question: "Is curbing corruption in India an impossible dream?" is in the affirmative because the Indian political leaders have not taken the critical first step of demonstrating their sincere commitment to curbing corruption in their country. In other words, curbing corruption in India remains an impossible dream so long as its political leaders are unwilling to impartially implement an effective anticorruption strategy.

Finally, the hopeless situation in India in terms of curbing corruption is best captured in the following joke entitled: "God's Response to Corruption":

> Perturbed by [the] annual CPI rankings, many prime ministers and presidents of corrupt countries approached God for help in eliminating corruption. God's response was that it might not happen in their lifetime. It was a shock to them and all of them wept bitterly on God's shoulder. [The] Indian prime minister also sought God's help and advice so that he could also eliminate corruption from India. The response of God was "NOT IN MY LIFE TIME" and God commenced shedding tears. However, God did say that corruption could be eliminated provided people are educated and empowered about this evil. (Transparency International India, 2002)

## NOTE

1. For more details of the Hawala scandal, see Singh (1999, pp. 162–177).

# CHAPTER 4

# THE PHILIPPINES

> Don't steal. The government hates competition.
> Bumper sticker spotted on a Manila street
>
> – (quoted in Stuart Grudgings, 2003)

> The Philippines does not need a foreign invader to destroy it. The officials in government are already doing a good job in causing the nation our heroes fought for so dearly to ultimately perish.
>
> – R. J. A. Olaguer (2006, p. 88)

## IMELDA MARCOS' 3,000 PAIRS OF SHOES

In his March 1986 article in *Newsweek*, Russell Watson exposed "Queen Imelda" Marcos's life of indulgence as the Philippines' First Lady in the opening paragraph:

> Three thousand pairs of shoes, size eight and a half. Five shelves of unused Gucci handbags, still stuffed with paper, price tags still attached. Five hundred bras, mostly black, and a trunk full of girdles, 40 and 42 inches around the hips. Huge bottles of perfume, vats of Christian Dior wrinkle cream, a walk-in-safe littered with dozens of empty jewelry cases. When the palace of Ferdinand and Imelda Marcos was opened to the public as a museum last week, foreigners and Filipinos alike gawked at what the former First Lady had left behind. "It was the worst case of conspicuous consumption I have ever seen," said an American visitor, Rep. Stephen Solarz. "Compared to her, Marie Antoinette was a bag lady." (Watson, 1986, p. 14)

Imelda was described as a "world class shopper" because she spent enormous sums of money during her shopping sprees around the world. According to Craig Wolff (1990):

> One day on a trip to Moscow in 1982, Imelda Marcos spent $7,842.31 on scarves and chocolates. On another day she spent$1,332 on macadamia nuts, and she apparently lost $1,000 in an airborne poker game. On a single day in September of that year, she spent almost $190,000 on jewellery and $62,000 on artwork in Manhattan. And on July 25. 1983, she made a $1 million down-payment on a Michelangelo painting.

It was also reported that during a shopping trip to New York, Copenhagen, and Rome, Imelda spent more than £3 million. Furthermore, "wherever she stayed, there was a standing order that the hotel would furnish her suite with £500 worth of flowers" (Cawthorne, 1999, p. 132).

During her trial in New York in March 1990, Imelda was accused by the prosecution for "systematically looting the country." Oscar Carino, the manager of the Philippine National Bank's branch in New York, testified as a prosecution witness that

> when Imelda was in town, she used the National Bank like her own 'personal piggy bank.' He regularly delivered up to $100,000 cash to her hotel room as loose change for her shopping sprees. When state investigators examined the books, they found unreimbursed withdrawals totalling over $22 million. (Cawthorne, 1999, p. 134)

The former archbishop, the late Cardinal Jaime Sin, was once reported to be in a car with Ferdinand and Imelda Marcos. As the road was bad and the driver was worse, Cardinal Sin began praying. Imelda asked him, "What are you praying for?". Cardinal Sin answered:, "To not die like Jesus between two thieves" (Hilton, 2000). This anecdote illustrates the late Cardinal Sin's disgust for the Marcos's corrupt behavior. Unfortunately, both of them have not been punished for plundering their country's wealth. Ferdinand Marcos died in exile in Honolulu on 28 September 1989. Imelda Marcos was acquitted on 10 March 2008 by Judge Silvino Pampilo in a 17-year-old case involving 32 counts of dollar salting of US$863 million in Swiss bank accounts (CBC News, 2008).

## AIM OF THE CHAPTER

The Philippines attained its independence from the United States on 4 July 1946. John Andrews (2002, p. 152) describes the Philippines as "a country which fell from grace" from being "one of Asia's richest countries in the 1950s" to "become one of the poorest" countries in the 1980s. In the same vein, Alasdair Bowie and Danny Unger (1997, p. 98) refer to the Philippines as "the East Asian capitalist laggard" because "its economic performance after the 1950s, and particularly after the early 1980s, was considerably less impressive than that of the other commodity-rich economies of Southeast Asia." There are many reasons for the decline in economic performance in the Philippines. This chapter focuses on one of the major reasons for the Philippines' economic decline, namely, the rampant corruption in the country.

Corruption is a serious problem in the Philippines according to Transparency International's 2010 Corruption Perceptions Index (CPI), the

PERC's 2010 survey of corruption in Asian countries, and the World Bank's 2009 data on the control of corruption indicator. Why is corruption rampant in the Philippines? What measures have been taken by the various governments to combat corruption in the Philippines? How effective are the anticorruption measures that have been introduced since the 1950s, when the fight against corruption began? Is curbing corruption in the Philippines an impossible dream? This chapter addresses these questions and contends that the major obstacle to curbing corruption in the Philippines is the lack of political will of the various governments since the attainment of independence from the United States in July 1946.

This chapter is divided into six sections. The following section describes the policy context in the Philippines in terms of its geography, history, economy, demography, and political system. The second section documents the perceived extent of corruption in the Philippines by examining various sources. The third section identifies the causes of corruption in the Philippines. The fourth section analyzes the anticorruption measures initiated by various governments since the establishment of the first ACA in May 1950. The fifth section evaluates the effectiveness of the anticorruption measures. The concluding section contends that without political will, curbing corruption in the Philippines will remain an impossible dream.

***Box 4.1.*** The Philippines' Policy Context

| | |
|---|---|
| Land area | 300,000 sq km |
| GDP | US$167 billion (2008) |
| GDP per capita | US$1,850 (2008) |
| Population | 89.7 million (2008) |
| Population density | 299 persons per sq km |
| Urban population | 48.9% |
| Adult literacy rate | 93.6% |
| Political system | Presidential democracy |
| Colonial rule | Spanish colonial rule (1565–1898)<br>American colonial rule (1898–1913) |
| 2010 CPI rank and score | 134/178 and 2.4/10 |
| 2010 PERC rank and score | 13/16 and 8.06/10 |

*Sources*: Economist (2010a, p. 196); http://www.transparency.org/policy_research/surveys_indices/cpi/2010/results; and *ABS-CBN News* (2010).

## THE PHILIPPINES' POLICY CONTEXT

### *Geography*

The Philippines is an archipelago of 7,107 islands, comprising a total land area of 300,000 sq km, approximately the same size as Italy. However, only 1,000 islands are populated, and the 11 largest islands constitute 94 percent of the total land mass (Steinberg, 1982, p. 8; Andrews, 2002, p. 152). The Philippines is "a highly fragmented country" as its islands are "scattered over some 1,295,000 sq km of oceanic waters," its beaches are stretched "along its length of 1,851 sq km and breadth of 1,107 sq km," and "the boundaries of water and mountain make internal travel and communication difficult" (Carino, 1988, pp. 4–5).

Although its archipelagic nature has resulted in "considerable fragmentation," the relative ease of water transportation in the Philippines has "facilitated inter-island commerce and migration" particularly in the central Visayan region. On the contrary, "the mountainous nature" of the country has made "intra-island interaction more difficult," especially in Mindanao. Indeed, "geography and linguistics overlap to divide the Philippines into three regions," namely, Luzon island, the Visayan islands, and Mindanao island (Timberman, 1991, p. 4). The two islands of Luzon (105,708 sq km) and Mindanao (92,586 sq km) constitute 65 percent of the total land area and are inhabited by 60 percent of the population (Woods, 2006, p. 2).

Although "the boundaries of water and mountain make internal travel and communication difficult" in the Philippines, these boundaries "make more uneconomical and unbalanced the exploitation and utilization of resources," "hinder governance and administration," and "cultivated parochial loyalties and given rise to internecine conflicts which inhibit nationalism and unified development" (Carino, 1988, p. 5). A final source of diversity is the tremendous difference between urban and rural life. Almost 63 percent of the population live in the urban areas, which are "more exposed to Western values." In contrast, the rural Filipinos are "more traditional, more conservative, and less politically active than city dwellers" (Timberman, 1991, p. 6).

The location of the Philippines makes it vulnerable to earthquakes as 10 percent of the 220 volcanoes are still active. There were 2,126 recorded earthquakes in the Philippines during 1950–1975 (Bankoff, 2005, p. 165). In addition to earthquakes, the Philippines also experience an average of more than 20 typhoons a year. Greg Bankoff contends that the vulnerability of the Philippines to these natural disasters provides ample opportunities for corruption among politicians and those involved in disaster management and relief. According to him:

> More than simply making political capital out of disasters in the Philippines, however, some among the political elite and those with family or social ties to them actually make a profit from these emergency situations through corruption, fraud, and graft. Specifically, they are able to consolidate and even enhance their financial and political position in society directly through the misappropriation of public money designated for relief and rehabilitation programmes or, more circuitously, through the patronage that control over such funds confers upon them. (Bankoff, 2005, p. 173)

As the Philippines is divided into 16 regions, 79 provinces, 113 cities, and 1,496 municipalities (Woods, 2006, p. 3), the archipelagic and fragmented nature of the Philippines has made the task of fighting corruption more arduous, especially in the provinces and rural areas.

## *History*

The Philippines was colonized by the Spanish for 333 years from 1565 to 1898, and the Americans for 48 years from 1898 to 1946. The Spanish colonial administration was concerned not only with commercial profit but also with spreading their religion. The conversion of the local population to Roman Catholicism contributed to the emergence of the church and its own bureaucracy. A second feature of Spanish colonial rule was the discrimination against the native Filipinos who, as a result, had lower salaries and occupied more junior positions than their Spanish counterparts who were the principal bureaucrats of the central government in Manila and their petty functionaries (Quah, 1978a, p. 413).

Corruption was introduced to the Philippines by the Spanish as the "low salaries and poor working conditions of the bureaucrats and the many opportunities available for corrupt behavior contributed to the widespread corruption in the colonial bureaucracy" (Quah, 1982a, p. 158). For example, the *gobernadorcillo* or petty governor was paid a miserable salary of two pesos a month, which was not commensurate with the extensive duties he had to perform including, among other things, being the village mayor, justice of the peace, and supervisor of tribute and tax collections (Corpuz, 1957, pp. 111–112). A public office was viewed as a grant or favor from the king during the Spanish colonial period and "many bureaucrats actually treated the transaction as a business – selling an office at a profit and buying a more lucrative one" (Endriga, 1979, pp. 247–249). Corpuz (1957, p.129) contended that the most serious weakness of the Spanish colonial bureaucracy was the "internal moral corruption of its members."

Damon L. Woods (2006, pp. 156–157) traced the roots of political corruption in the Philippines to the Spanish system of governance. The King of Spain appointed a friend or supporter as the governor-general to represent him in the Philippines. As the governor-general and his officials were "not always qualified or dedicated," they had also expected to "profit, through graft and corruption, from 'service.'" Similarly, the petty officials also made their fortunes through bribery and neglecting the instructions from the central government in Manila. Accordingly, public service was viewed by the population as a means of obtaining financial benefits for their own families. In short, individuals were expected to advance their personal and family's interests at the expense of the community's interests.

The Spanish colonial period ended in 1898 with the defeat of Spain by the United States in the Spanish–American War. In contrast to the Spanish, the Americans adopted a secular colonial policy that provided Filipinos with more opportunities for participating in the affairs of their country. This was reflected in the establishment of a modern civil service by the Americans and their efforts to localize it. The First Philippine Commission recommended the creation of an efficient and nonpartisan civil service in 1899. On 19 September 1900, the Second Philippine Commission passed an act for the establishment and maintenance of an efficient and honest civil service in the Philippines (Corpuz, 1957, p. 191). Thus, an important legacy of American colonial rule is the introduction of meritocracy in the Philippines.

During the American colonial period (1898–1913), there were two groups of corrupt bureaucrats: civilians and discharged soldiers appointed without examination by the previous military government; and the justices of the peace who were also appointed without examination and did not receive salaries, but they could collect fees for their judicial services (Corpuz, 1957, p. 169). Scandals involving the police, the Bureau of Public Works, and the Philippine General Hospital were also reported during the administration of Governor-General W. Cameron Forbes (1909–1913) (Gleeck, 1998, pp. 152–153). However, the bureaucracy as a whole was quite clean during the American colonial period for two reasons: the bureaucrats received higher salaries and corrupt officials were promptly prosecuted. Thus, the two major causes of corruption responsible for the rampant corruption during the Spanish colonial period – low salaries and ineffective legal measures – were removed in the American colonial bureaucracy, and this explains why it was less corrupt than the Spanish colonial bureaucracy (Endriga, 1979, p. 254).

In short, the origins of corruption in the Philippines can be traced to the Spanish colonial period when civil servants were poorly paid, public offices were sold for a profit, and the governor-general and his officials were appointed by the King of Spain on the basis of patronage and not merit. However, corruption declined during the American colonial period because the bureaucrats were better paid and those who were guilty of corruption were punished.

## *Economy*

With abundant natural resources such as timber, coconuts, sugar, bananas, rubber, and minerals, it was not surprising that the Philippines had a very high economic growth rate in Asia in the 1950s. However, as a result of incorrect economic policies, the Philippines economy has declined from the 1960s. According to John Andrews (2001, pp. 158–159):

> In the 1950s industrialization concentrated on import substitution, but in the 1960s there was no attempt to build export-oriented industries based on the import-substituting factories. By the end of the 1960s the Philippines was the slowest growing economy in non-communist South-East Asia. It compounded its problems by erecting high tariffs to protect its industries (and the profits of their owners) from foreign competition. The consequence was a country living beyond its means.

The Philippines "slipped behind other countries in the region" when President Ferdinand Marcos was in power during 1965–1986 (Bowie & Unger, 1997, p. 99). He appointed his relatives and close friends as directors of government agencies, corporations, and development projects in the sugar and coconut industries, hotels and resorts, and the construction sector. Their "mismanagement and agenda of personal gain" resulted in adverse consequences as the country's foreign debt increased from US$16.98 billion to US$26 billion from 1982 to 1985 because the government had to bail out Marcos' cronies (Rebullida, 2006, p. 170).

The average Filipino also suffered from the corruption, cronyism, and economic mismanagement of the Marcos' era as there was a serious decline in incomes and living standards during 1970–1980. A University of the Philippines study found that the

> real earnings of salaried employees in 1980 were only 93 percent of their 1972 earnings and the real earnings of wage workers were only 87 percent of their 1972 level … . Census figures show that the poorest 60 percent of all Filipino households received 25 percent of the nation's total income in 1971. By 1979 their share of national income had shrunk to only 22.5 percent. The rich were in fact becoming richer while the poor were becoming poorer. (Timberman, 1991, p. 113)

As agriculture provides employment for 37 percent of the population (Economist, 2010a, p. 196), it is not surprising that "rural life focuses around the production of four main crops: rice, corn, coconut and sugar." Rice and corn are produced for local consumption, whereas coconut and sugar are exported. In spite of the government's Green Revolution of 1969–1971, the production of rice was the lowest in Asia in the early 1970s. Wurfel (1988, p. 53) contends that "low agricultural production is a root cause of rural poverty in the Philippines."

In 2008, the Philippines had a GDP of US$167 billion and a GDP per capita of US$1,850 (Economist, 2010a, p. 196). However, according to the National Statistical Coordination Board (NSCB), the extent of poverty in the Philippines has increased from 23.8 million (30 percent of the population) in 2003 to 27.6 million (32.9 percent) in 2006. The percentage of poor families has increased from 24.4 percent to 26.9 percent during the same period (NSCB, 2008). The high level of poverty in the Philippines and the government's inability to raise civil service salaries increase the incentive for corruption and also make it more difficult for the incumbent government to minimize corruption in the country.

### *Demography*

The Philippines has a population of 89.7 million and a population density of 299 persons per sq km in 2008 (Economist, 2010a, p. 196). The heterogeneity of the population in the Philippines is reflected in the fact that there are 111 different cultural and racial groups, who speak 70 different languages (Andrews, 2001, p. 158). In terms of ethnic composition, the Malays form the majority with 91.5 percent, followed by the aborigines (6 percent) and the Chinese (1.5 percent). However, "the potential divisiveness of these ethnic differences" was mitigated by "a widespread acceptance of mixed marriages in the Philippines" (Timberman, 1991, p. 5).

As a result of the Spanish colonial government's religious conversion of the population, most Filipinos today are Christians with 83 percent being Roman Catholics and 9 percent Protestants, and only 5 percent who are Muslims. Consequently, the Philippines' higher crude birth rate of 25 births per 1,000 population can be attributed to the Catholic Church's opposition to birth control (Economist, 2010a, p. 196).

In the Philippines, the family plays an important role because it is responsible for socializing the young and provides emotional and financial support for its members. According to David Timberman (1991, p. 16), the family's primacy is reinforced by custom, the teachings of the Catholic Church, and the Constitution. Indeed, Article 2, section 12 of the Philippine Constitution of 1986, states that "the State recognizes the sanctity of family life and shall protect and strengthen the family as a basic autonomous social institution" (McCoy, 1994, p. 7). The importance of the family and the cultural value of *utang na loob* (debt of gratitude) among Filipinos account for their tolerant attitude toward corruption.

## *Political System*

The Philippines has a presidential system of government, which is a legacy of American colonial rule. President Ferdinand Marcos' declaration of martial law on 22 September 1972 resulted in "the immediate, dramatic, and unprecedented curtailment of civil liberties" and nearly 13 years of authoritarian rule (Timberman, 1991, pp. 76, 81). However, the initial benefits of the Marcos regime could not be sustained and "favoritism and venality became rampant," and the economy was adversely affected by "mounting corruption and mismanagement" (Timberman, 1991, pp. 91–92). The magnitude of corruption increased exponentially as "graft and corruption reached its all time high" during Marcos' martial law regime as both "had permeated almost all aspects of bureaucratic life and institutions which saw the start of the systematic plunder of the country" (Varela, 1995, p. 174).

To prevent the dictatorship of the Marcos era from occurring again, the 1987 Constitution limited the president to a single six-year term. Furthermore, the president cannot overrule a two-thirds vote by Congress or abolish Congress, and he can only impose martial law for a maximum of 60 days. The legislature is bicameral with a 24-member Senate, directly elected for six years, and a 208-member House of Representatives elected by constituency for a three-year term.

The political system in the Philippines is highly unstable with frequent changes in political leadership. This is confirmed by the decrease in percentile rank for political stability in the Philippines from 25.5 in 1996 to 10.8 in 2009 (World Bank, 2010b). In other words, the percentile rank for political stability has declined by 14.7 during 1996–2009. In her insightful analysis of policy implementation in the Philippines, Linda K. Richter (1987, p. 74) concluded that, unlike developed countries such as Japan and the United States, "the Philippine bureaucracy faces obstacles without the safety margins for error and the slack provided by prosperity, political stability, and secure and long-established political institutions." Indeed, the lack of political continuity and political stability in the Philippines has adversely affected the capacity of the incumbent government in policy formulation and implementation.

## PERCEIVED EXTENT OF CORRUPTION

After World War II, the bureaucracy in the Philippines suffered from "low prestige, incompetence, meager resources, and a large measure of cynical corruption" (Corpuz, 1957, pp. 222–223). The colonial bureaucracy's low prestige was the result of its low salaries and the corrupt behavior of its members. Bureaucratic corruption became a serious problem during the 1950s, especially during the administration of President Elpidio Quirino (1948–1953) because corruption "permeated the entire gamut of the Philippine bureaucracy, extending from the lowest level of the civil service to the top, excepting the President himself" (Alfiler, 1979, p. 323).

In January 1959, President Carlos Garcia highlighted the problem of graft and corruption in his State-of-the-Nation address to Congress:

> In our essay at making our social and economic objectives a fact accomplished, we are hampered by a cancer gnawing at our national entrails. Graft and corruption ... is ... a national problem. The problem of graft and corruption is not peculiar to our administration in this country. Nor is it a new one. It has plagued all administrations before us. Nevertheless, I do not condone nor minimize the significance of this blight. (quoted in Iglesias, 1963, p. 20)

In 1969, the Philippine Ethnic Group Attitude Surveys found, among other things, that 66 percent of the 1,381 Filipinos interviewed believed that graft and corruption were prevalent and constituted a major problem. When the respondents were asked, "Which officials are corrupt?", 38 percent identified politicians as corrupt, 36 percent viewed government employees as corrupt, and 22 percent considered local politicians as corrupt. Finally, the respondents from Manila viewed politicians and government employees as corrupt unlike the Ilocano, Muslim, Pampangan, and lower-income respondents (Averech, Koehler, & Denton, 1971, pp. 31–33).

In their analysis of the bureaucracy in the Philippines, Raul P. de Guzman, Alex B. Brillantes, Jr., and Arturo G. Pacho (1988, pp. 197–198) identified a total of 13 problems facing the bureaucracy, including the problem of graft and corruption. They also referred to a study on corruption and red tape conducted by the College of Public Administration, University of the

Philippines, which confirmed "the existence of the systemic form of corruption in many agencies."

Similarly, David Timberman (1991, p. 25) pointed out that corruption was not only endemic to Philippine politics, but the more serious problem was "the widespread assumption that corruption is unavoidable." Consequently, "few Filipino politicians have left office without having significantly increased their wealth" because "money is needed to acquire and hold public office, particularly national office." He further observed that the magnitude of corruption had increased exponentially during the Marcos administration, which was described as a "kleptocracy" by the U.S. Congressman, Stephen Solarz (Timberman, 1991, p. 104).

Corruption in the Philippines reached its highest level during the 21 years of Marcos' rule (1965–1986). According to Amelia P. Varela (1995, pp. 173–174):

> Graft and corruption reached its all time high during the martial law regime under Marcos … . Graft and corruption under Marcos had permeated almost all aspects of bureaucratic life and institutions which saw the start of the systematic plunder of the country.

In the same vein, Joel Rocamora (1998, pp. 22–23) observed that Marcos "perfected … 'a vacuum cleaner approach' to corruption" as he and his relatives "picked the government clean, siphoned large chunks of the tens of billions of dollar loans which flowed liberally in the 1970s." Grand corruption under the Marcos regime "ranged from theft of foreign and military aid to the domestic system of crony capitalism" and required "an extensive use of money laundering devices" (Chaikin & Sharman, 2009, p. 153).

The most comprehensive study of corruption in Philippines during Marcos' rule was conducted by Belinda A. Aquino. She described the "politics of plunder" perpetrated by Marcos and his relatives and cronies in the following words:

> His declaration of martial law in 1972 under false pretexts not only protected the fortune he had already acquired, most illicitly over the past two decades. It also served to accelerate the amassing of even more power and wealth for several more years … . He lorded it [the economy] over a rapacious team of trusted friends and associates whom he had given lucrative fiefdoms in the economy. Together they stole high and low, from both rich and poor. They treated the Philippine treasury as if it were their personal checking account. The consuming preoccupation with wealth accumulation was abetted by multi-million international loans and massive U.S. foreign assistance packages that were meant for economic development. These resources provided easy opportunities for massive graft. As long as they were available, the stealing by Marcos and his cronies went unabated … . In the end, the Philippines had been bled of billions of dollars and had become the 'basket case of Asia' by the late 1970s. (Aquino, 1999, pp. 120–121)

Carmen Navarro Pedrosa (1987, p. 222) estimated that Marcos had amassed "a staggering $15 billion," which was more than half of the country's national debt. The Marcoses used the government banks as "piggy banks" and diverted US$27 million of Philippine National Bank funds for their own use (Chaikin & Sharman, 2009, p. 160). Among the 10 most corrupt political leaders identified by TI in 2004, Marcos was ranked second after President Soeharto of Indonesia as Marcos was estimated to have embezzled between US$5 and US$10 billion. Joseph Estrada, who was ranked as the 10th most corrupt political leader, had embezzled between US$78 million and US$80 million when he was President of the Philippines from 1998 to 2001 (Hodess, Inowlocki, Rodriguez, & Wolfe, 2004, p. 13).

The Marcos regime was described as "sultanistic" by Mark Thompson (1998, p. 216) as it was based on personalism, and loyalty to Marcos was motivated by a mixture of fear and rewards to his collaborators. President Marcos had appointed his relatives and close friends as directors of government agencies, corporations, and development projects in the sugar and coconut industries, hotels and resorts, and the construction sector. The Marcos kleptocracy was characterized by the provision of "behest loans" to members of his family, cronies, or political supporters by the government-owned financial institutions.[1] Needless to say, their "mismanagement and agenda of personal gain" had adverse consequences as the government was deprived of "positive returns on investments and profitable use of foreign loans." More importantly, the government had to bear the deficits and losses and incurred heavy foreign debts, which increased from US$16.98 billion to US$26 billion from 1982 to 1985, for bailing out Marcos' cronies (Rebullida, 2006, p. 170).

The annual surveys of business enterprises on corruption conducted by the Social Weather Stations (SWS) from 2000 to 2007 have shown that, on the average, nearly two-thirds of the managers interviewed said that there was "a lot" of corruption in the public sector in the Philippines. Table 4.1

***Table 4.1.*** Managers' Perception of Extent of Public Sector Corruption in the Philippines, 2000–2007.

| Extent | 2000 (%) | 2001 (%) | 2002/03 (%) | 2003/04 (%) | 2005 (%) | 2006 (%) | 2007 (%) | Average (%) |
|---|---|---|---|---|---|---|---|---|
| A lot | 63 | 77 | 60 | 66 | 66 | 67 | 61 | 65.7 |
| Some | 25 | 19 | 29 | 26 | 28 | 28 | 33 | 26.9 |
| A little | 10 | 4 | 10 | 6 | 5 | 5 | 5 | 6.4 |
| None | 2 | 0 | 1 | 2 | 1 | 1 | 0.3 | 1.0 |

*Source*: Guerrero, Mangahas, and Laroza (2007, p. 7).

notes that while the proportion of managers indicating that there was "a lot" of public sector corruption has declined from 77 percent in 2001 to 61 percent in 2007, the average percentage for 2000–2007 is 65.7 percent. The percentage of managers who perceived that there was "a lot" of public sector corruption increased to 64 percent in 2008 and 2009 (Guerrero, Mangahas, & Laroza, 2010, p. 5). Consequently, it is not surprising that J. D. R. Obejas (2009, p. 97) has observed that

> The network of corruption in the Philippines comprehends such a wide range of civic and legal necessities and requisites that Filipinos are left with little or no choice but to live with it … . Truth to tell, it is widely perceived that corruption has footprints on the floors of every public office in the Philippines, including the Presidential Palace.

The managers were also asked to identify those government agencies or corporations with a "bad reputation due to corruption." Table 4.2 notes that the seven most corrupt government agencies in the Philippines identified by the managers were the Bureau of Customs, Bureau of Internal Revenue (BIR), Department of Public Works and Highways (DPWH), Philippine National Police (PNP), Land Transportation Office (LTO), Department of Environment and Natural Resources (DENR), and Department of Education (DepEd).

In the 2009 SWS Surveys of Enterprises on Corruption, the respondents were asked to rate the sincerity or insincerity of government agencies in fighting corruption. Table 4.3 reports that the Bureau of Customs, DPWH, and BIR were perceived by the managers to be the least sincere in combating corruption. It should be noted that the Office of the President was ranked fifth with its net sincere rating of −37 percent. The three ACAs were also viewed negatively by the managers with the Office of the Ombudsman

***Table 4.2.*** Managers' Perception of Most Corrupt Government Agencies in the Philippines, 2000–2007.

| Agency | 2000 (%) | 2001 (%) | 2002/03 (%) | 2003/04 (%) | 2005 (%) | 2006 (%) | 2007 (%) | Average (%) |
|---|---|---|---|---|---|---|---|---|
| Customs | 74 | 65 | 66 | 70 | 65 | 61 | 60 | 65.9 |
| BIR | 72 | 67 | 68 | 68 | 64 | 51 | 46 | 62.3 |
| DPWH | 57 | 38 | 49 | 49 | 46 | 37 | 35 | 44.4 |
| PNP | 16 | 32 | 29 | 28 | 19 | 11 | 11 | 20.9 |
| LTO | 4 | 5 | 20 | 21 | 17 | 13 | 15 | 13.6 |
| DENR | 5 | 10 | 14 | 10 | 17 | 12 | 7 | 10.7 |
| DepEd | 22 | 7 | 8 | 8 | 9 | 7 | 7 | 9.7 |

*Source*: Guerrero et al. (2007, p. 16).

*Table 4.3.* Net Sincere Rating of Government Agencies in Fighting Corruption in 2009.

| Agency | Sincere Rating (a) (%) | Insincere Rating (b) (%) | Net Sincere Rating (a–b) (%) |
|---|---|---|---|
| Bureau of Customs | 9 | 78 | −69 |
| DPWH | 10 | 75 | −65 |
| BIR | 14 | 71 | −57 |
| LTO | 21 | 60 | −39 |
| Office of President | 24 | 61 | −37 |
| House of Representatives | 20 | 54 | −34 |
| DENR | 23 | 57 | −34 |
| PAGC | 16 | 49 | −33 |
| DOTC | 21 | 50 | −29 |
| PCGG | 19 | 47 | −28 |
| DILG | 24 | 49 | −25 |
| DA | 27 | 46 | −19 |
| PNP | 27 | 44 | −17 |
| DBM | 27 | 44 | −17 |
| Ombudsman | 32 | 40 | −8 |
| COMELEC | 33 | 41 | −8 |
| GSIS | 33 | 39 | −6 |
| DOJ | 36 | 41 | −5 |
| DOF | 34 | 38 | −4 |
| Senate | 35 | 37 | −2 |

*Source*: Guerrero et al. (2010, p. 7).

(OMB) receiving a net sincere rating of −8 percent, followed by −28 percent for the Presidential Commission on Good Government (PCGG), and −33 percent for the Presidential Anti-Graft Commission (PAGC).

Surprisingly, the Bureau of Immigration (BI) was not identified among the most corrupt government agencies in Table 4.2 even though it was riddled with corruption. According to retired Colonel Salvador Rodolfo, a former intelligence consultant of the BI:

> The Bureau of Immigration is the worst agency in the Philippine republic enmeshed in graft and corruption, and the only language spoken from commissioners down to clerks and janitors is money, money, dirty money. (quoted in Chua & Rimban, 1998, p. 153)

Corruption in the BI was systemic and permeated "every rung in the bureau's hierarchy" because of the "discretion given to immigration officials to determine the lives and destinies of both aliens living in the Philippines and Filipinos leaving for abroad, the opportunities for payoffs abound" (Chua & Rimban, 1998, pp. 153–154).

The DPWH was identified in Table 4.2 as the third most corrupt government agency and in Table 4.3 as the second least sincere government agency in fighting corruption in 2009. The DPWH had "earned a reputation as a bastion of graft" because it encouraged the payment of commissions and bribes and discouraged honesty because "honest employees and whistle-blowers risk ostracism by their colleagues." As the DPWH dealt with huge infrastructure projects involving vast sums of expenditure, bribes were usually paid in cash and commissions were given after winning the contracts. Consequently, the DPWH became known as "a den of corrupt practices" because there were ample opportunities for corruption among its employees and external vested interests (Vitug, 1998, p. 188).

Similarly, Yvonne T. Chua's excellent case study of the Philippines' Department of Education, Culture and Sports (DECS) demonstrates graphically "an education bureaucracy so ridden with graft that it is barely able to deliver the most basic educational services to the country's 15 million public school students" (Chua, 1999, p. 1). She contends that corruption has become systemic at the DECS and has permeated all levels of the public educational system. Corruption in the DECS has assumed many forms, from petty or survival corruption to top-level corruption, with procurement and recruitment being the areas most vulnerable to corruption. According to Chua (1999, p. 3):

> Money changes hands at nearly every stage of procurement, from the accreditation to the payment of suppliers. Money is also given out from the time a teacher applies for a job up to the time she requests for a change in assignment or works for a promotion. In some cases, expensive gifts replace money in cash-less transactions that take place in the education bureaucracy.

Furthermore, embezzlement, nepotism, influence peddling, fraud, and other types of corruption also flourish at the DECS. Indeed, corruption has been institutionalized in the DECS because "payoffs have become the lubricant that makes the bureaucracy run smoothly" (Chua, 1999, p. 3). Finally, Chua (1999, p. 1) lamented that "one of the greatest tragedies of corruption in the public school system is when teachers pass on their warped values to students. In some schools, teachers teach young schoolchildren to cheat in tests because it is on the basis of these tests that the school's performance is assessed."

Unfortunately, Chua's expose of the rampant corruption in the DECS did not result in the introduction of policy reforms by the government in the DECS to reduce the opportunities for corruption. A more recent study of the Textbook Delivery Program (TDP) in the DepEd has confirmed that "documented corruption linkages in the TDP are alarmingly high" with corrupt practices taking the form of "(i) falsification of records to obtain substantial money transactions; (ii) delivery of substandard textbooks, delay in actual deliveries and insufficient amounts; and (iii) the misuse and diversion of resources to unauthorised uses" (Reyes, 2007, p. 121). Vicente Chua Reyes (2009, pp. 218–219) has attributed the TDP's vulnerability to corruption to the following five factors: (1) insubordination and ambiguity in sanction control among the key actors; (2) TDP operating procedures were in disarray; (3) TDP implementers, especially the school-based supply officers, were incapable of performing their jobs efficiently; (4) discordance and lack of coordination among the TDP implementers at different levels; and (5) the exercise of abusive discretionary authority.

In May 2009, DepEd officials suspended Jeverps Manufacturing Corporation (JMC) for supplying overpriced and substandard noodles to schools involved in the 427 million pesos food aid program to improve the nutritional needs of school children in 13 food-poor provinces. This program provided meals for 373,440 preschool and first-grade school children for 104 days to keep them in school. JMC won the contract to supply 19 million packs of supposedly vitamin-fortified noodles to schools participating in the program in 2009. The winning tender of 22 pesos per packet of noodles with higher nutritional content was almost three times more expensive than those sold in shops. JMC was investigated for corruption, and the food-aid program was reviewed by independent experts to ascertain the nutritional contents of the noodles and the program's cost-effectiveness (*Daily Tribune*, 2009).

In short, the preceding analysis confirms the prevalence of corruption in the Philippines. Rachel Caoili (2005, p. 9) contends that, in spite of its commitment to liberal democratic values, a culture of corruption persists in the Philippines. In the same vein, Eric C. Batalla (2001, p. 50) argues that the most serious consequence of "institutionalized corruption" in the Philippines is that "it damages the national psyche" because "it mis-educates and tells people that there is nothing wrong in being corrupt" as "corrupt people have not been punished even if the public knows them."

Corruption is, perhaps, the most serious weakness of the Philippine polity because it "prevents national progress and perpetuates inequality and poverty thereby seriously undermining the legitimacy of the government and democracy (Caoili, 2005, p. 9). Poverty in the Philippines is at an "unacceptable" level as "one in three Filipinos survived on $1 a day or less" in 2006 (Cerojano, 2009). This high level of poverty means that corruption in the Philippines "hits the poor hardest" because of their inability to "pay bribes for services that should be theirs by right" (UNDP, 2008, p. 17). Accordingly, the UNDP has urged governments in the Asia-Pacific region to reduce "the forms of corruption that hit the poor the hardest" because "the poor will benefit more from efforts to eliminate the corruption that plagues their everyday lives" (UNDP, 2008, p. 152).

## CAUSES OF CORRUPTION

### *Low Salaries*

Why is corruption such a serious problem today in the Philippines? The first factor responsible for corruption in the contemporary Philippines is the low salaries of the political leaders and civil servants. For example, employees of the Bureau of Immigration are under-qualified and paid "starvation wages." Consequently, they find it "difficult to survive without accepting bribes, one way or the other, because nearly everyone is doing it" (Chua & Rimban, 1998, p. 154). The monthly salary of the most junior civil servant (salary grade 1, step 1) in 1976 was 286 pesos (US$36), and the monthly salary of the most senior civil servant (salary grade 28, step 8) was 5,935 pesos (US$747) (Fernandez, 1980, p. 422). According to Perfecto L. Padilla (1995, p. 187), "the grossly low compensation is an unchallenged fact in Philippine government administration" because salary revisions cannot keep pace with the rising cost of living, and civil service salaries are not as "attractive and competitive as those offered by private companies, multinational corporations, and regional/international organizations."

In a survey of public attitudes toward corruption in the Philippines conducted in September 1998, the problem of low salaries was cited most often as the major cause of corruption (Beschel, 1999, p. 9). Table 4.4 notes that the monthly salary of the President of the Philippines is 57,750 pesos (US$1,321), whereas the Vice President, Speaker of the House of Representatives, and Chief Justice of the Supreme Court earn between 46,200 and 54,917 pesos (between US$1,056 and US$1,256) per month. The monthly salaries of senators, members of the House of Representatives, associate justices of the Supreme Court, and chairman of the Constitutional Commission range from 40,425 to 48,052 pesos (from US$924 to US$1,099). The Commissioner of the Constitutional Commission, who is on salary grade 30, earns between 28,875 and 34,323 pesos (between US$660 and US$785) per month. In contrast, most of the civil servants earn salaries that are "74 percent below comparable jobs in the private sector, [thus]

***Table 4.4.*** Salary Grades and Salaries of Constitutional Officials in the Philippines.

| Position | Salary Grade | Monthly Salary[a] | Annual Salary |
|---|---|---|---|
| President of the Philippines | 33 | 57,750 PHP (US$1,321) | 693,000 PHP (US$15,847) |
| Vice President of the Philippines, President of the Senate, Speaker of the House of Representatives, Chief Justice of the Supreme Court | 32 | 46,200 to 54,917 PHP (US$1,056 to 1,256) | 554,400 to 659,004 PHP (US$12,678 to 15,070) |
| Senator Member of the House of Representatives Associate Justices of the Supreme Court Chairman, Constitutional Commission | 31 | 40,425 to 48,052 PHP (US$924 to 1,099) | 485,100 to 576,624 PHP (US$11,093 to 13,186) |
| Commissioner Constitutional Commission | 30 | 28,875 to 34,323 PHP (US$660 to 785) | 346,500 to 411,876 PHP (US$7,924 to 9,419) |

*Source*: Brillantes and Sonco (2010, pp. 221–222).

[a]Except for salary grade 33, salary grades 30, 31, and 32 have eight steps each. The monthly salary indicated for each position is the range from step 1 to step 8. The conversion of pesos to US$ is based on the exchange rate of US$1 = 43.73 pesos on 26 February 2011.

encouraging corruption in all levels of the bureaucracy" (*Reuters India*, 2009). Consequently, these poorly paid civil servants "augment their meager incomes" by resorting to practices such as selling goods to their colleagues in the office, "moonlighting," part-time teaching, private professional practice after office hours, research and consultancy projects, and petty corrupt practices (Padilla, 1995, pp. 195–206).

Recently, 11,000 Filipino doctors retrained themselves as nurses to emigrate to other countries such as the United States because "it is much harder for a Philippine-trained doctor to pass medical board exams in a foreign country than for a Filipino nurse to be certified abroad" (Harden, 2008, pp. A13–A14). The health care brain drain of physicians in the Philippines to other countries to work as nurses has strangled rural hospitals across the country. The motivation for this change in career is financial as in the United States, "a nurse can make 10 times the [US]$4,700 annual salary" of a government doctor in the Philippines. The exodus of doctors from the provinces has resulted in a shortage of them in the poor rural areas. Rey Melchor F. Santos, the President of the Philippine Medical Association, has revealed that "there are rural hospitals that are no longer operating because they have no medical manpower" (Harden, 2008, p. A14).

### *Red Tape*

Second, the excessive red tape and inefficiency of the Philippine Civil Service provide ample opportunities for corruption. Indeed, papers in the government are processed in an unsystematic and time-consuming manner. Furthermore, the cumbersome and complicated procedures also slow down paper processing. The filing systems are disorganized, and there is no disposal policy for files accumulated for many years. In other words, "there is much room for simplifying procedures in the bureaucracy" (de Guzman, Brillantes, & Pacho, 1988, p. 199). Excessive regulations coupled with increased bureaucratic discretion provide opportunities and incentives for corruption as regulations governing access to goods and services are exploited by civil servants to extract "rents" from groups vying for access to these goods and services (Gould & Amaro-Reyes, 1983, p. 17). Accordingly, businessmen in the Philippines resort to paying "speed money" (bribes) to expedite the processing of their applications for licenses or permits from the relevant government agency (de Guzman et al., p. 198).

The *Doing Business Surveys 2007–2011* conducted by the World Bank show that red tape is a serious problem in the Philippines as reflected in its consistently poor ranking for the ease of doing business: 126th position among 175 economies in 2007; 133rd position among 178 economies in 2008; 140th position among 181 economies in 2009; 144th position among 183 economies in 2010; and 148th position among 183 economies in 2011. Furthermore, Table 4.5 notes that the Philippines' rank for starting a business deteriorated from 108th position in 2007 to 156th in 2011 because the number of procedures increased from 11 to 15; the length of time was reduced from 48 to 38 days; and the cost rose from 18.7 percent to 29.7 percent.

### *Low Risk of Detection and Punishment*

Third, corruption has flourished in the Philippines because of the low risk of detection of corrupt offenses and the low probability of punishment for

***Table 4.5.*** Ease of Doing Business in the Philippines, 2007–2011.

| Indicator | 2007 ($N=175$) | 2008 ($N=178$) | 2009 ($N=181$) | 2010 ($N=183$) | 2011 ($N=183$) |
|---|---|---|---|---|---|
| Ease of doing business (rank) | 126 | 133 | 140 | 144 | 148 |
| Starting a business (rank) | 108 | 144 | 155 | 162 | 156 |
| No. of procedures | 11 | 15 | 15 | 15 | 15 |
| Time (days) | 48 | 58 | 52 | 52 | 38 |
| Cost (% of income per capita) | 18.7 | 26.8 | 29.8 | 28.2 | 29.7 |
| Dealing with construction permits or licenses (rank) | 113 | 77 | 105 | 111 | 156 |
| No. of procedures | 23 | 21 | 24 | 24 | 26 |
| Time (days) | 197 | 177 | 203 | 203 | 169 |
| Cost (% of income per capita) | 113.4 | 75.9 | 90.1 | 81.7 | 778.5 |
| Registering property (rank) | 98 | 86 | 97 | 102 | 102 |
| No. of procedures | 8 | 8 | 8 | 8 | 8 |
| Time (days) | 33 | 33 | 33 | 33 | 33 |
| Cost (% of property value) | 5.7 | 4.2 | 4.3 | 4.3 | 4.3 |
| CPI rank and score | 131st (2.5) | 141st (2.3) | 139th (2.4) | 134th (2.4) | NA |

*Sources*: World Bank (2006b, p. 135; 2007, p. 144; 2008, p. 128; 2009, p. 145; 2010a, p. 187) and http://www.transparency.org

corrupt offenders. Leslie Palmier (1985, p. 271) uses the term "policing" to refer to "the probability of detection and punishment." Corruption thrives in a country where the public perceives it to be a "low risk, high reward" activity as corrupt offenders are unlikely to be detected and punished (Quah 2003a, p. 13).

In his memoirs, Senior Minister Lee Kuan Yew of Singapore has attributed the lack of punishment of Marcos, his family, and cronies for their corrupt activities to the "soft, forgiving culture" of the Philippines. He observed:

> Only in the Philippines could a leader like Ferdinand Marcos, who pillaged his country for over 20 years, still be considered for a national burial. Insignificant amounts of the loot have been recovered, yet his wife and children were allowed to return and engage in politics .... General Fabian Ver, Marcos's commander-in-chief ... had fled the Philippines together with Marcos in 1986. When he died in Bangkok, the Estrada government gave the general military honours at his burial. (Lee, 2000, pp. 342–343)

Robert P. Beschel (1999, p. 8) observed that sanctions were imposed inconsistently in the Philippines, "with draconian punishment being meted out for relatively minor infractions and major crimes receiving lenient treatment – particularly when they are committed by the rich, the powerful and the politically well-connected." In his comparative analysis of successful prosecution of corrupt offenders in Hong Kong and the Philippines, Beschel (1999, p. 8) found that a person committing a corrupt offense in Hong Kong was 33 times more likely to be detected and punished than his counterpart in the Philippines. More specifically, he found that Hong Kong's ICAC successfully prosecuted approximately 8.24 cases per 10,000 civil servants for corruption in 1997. On the contrary, the comparable figure in the Philippines was less than 0.25 per 10,000. The lower probability of being convicted for corruption in the Philippines was confirmed by the former Ombudsman, Simeon V. Marcelo (2004, p. 37), who revealed that the Office of the Special Prosecutor's conviction rate at the *Sandiganbayan* (the Anti-Graft Court) was "a dismal 6 percent," which means that "a high-ranking government official accused of graft and corruption has a 94 percent chance of walking away scot-free."

### *Cultural Factors*

Fourth, the importance of the family and the cultural value of *utang na loob* among Filipinos have made them more tolerant of corruption. According to Jean Grossholz (1964, pp. 86–87), the family in the Philippines is "the strongest unit of society, demanding the deepest loyalties of the individual and coloring all social activity with its own set of demands," but its "communal values" are "often in conflict with the impersonal values of the institutions of the larger society."

Another characteristic of the Filipino family is that kinship ties extend bilaterally to include the families of both spouses. It is further extended through the "*compadre* system, in which a prominent man in the community" is chosen as "the child's godfather and the *compadre* of the parent." This explains why Ferdinand Marcos was reported to have been godfather to thousands of godchildren when he was president. The godfather or godmother acts as an intermediary in dealings with the government, and he/she receives in return "gifts or free labor services in election campaigns and other political situations." In other words, the *compadre* system encourages the Filipinos to work through an intermediary whenever possible (Langston, 1991, p. 71).

Gaudioso C. Sosmena (1995, p. 13) has attributed the culture of patronage in the Philippines to the Filipino's reverence for the family because "whenever one holds a seat of administrative and political power," the members of this person's family and immediate relatives "use the power and influence" of the position "as a bridge in getting preferential government employment." More recently, Balanga Bishop Socrates Villegas has described corruption in the Philippines as "family-based" thus:

> The singular trademark of graft and corruption in the Philippines ... is that our type of corruption is family-based .... The "corruption syndicate" is either husband and wife partnership or a father and son connivance or a whole family in cahoots. Corruption is done through the family, with the family and in the family .... Families are no longer just corruptible but have become blatantly corrupt and corrupting. (quoted in Acuna, 2009)

Another contributing factor to the culture of patronage is the importance of the cultural value of *utang na loob* or "debt of gratitude," which is incurred when one receives a favor, service, or goods, and it also implies a deep sense of obligation to reciprocate when the appropriate moment comes (Langston, 1991, pp. 78–79). Indeed, *utang na loob* reinforces the strength of the network of strong inter-family groups as it demands that "all favors be returned in like or greater value." These favors "encourage patronage between superiors and subordinates and perpetuate the domination of elite groups deriving their power from the extensiveness of their networks" (Kharas, 1997, p. 471).

Consequently, it is not surprising that nepotism is prevalent in the Philippines as public officials readily perform favors for their relatives including the appointment of unqualified persons. For example, in the case of education, many people "unfit for the teaching profession end up teaching in and running public schools," and they "pay P3,000 to P5,000 in 'bribes' to ensure their admission and give up one to three months' pay to recompense their *utang na loob* (debt of gratitude) to their superiors when their initial paychecks arrive" (Chua, 1999, p. 10). A more recent example of nepotism is the appointment by Constancia de Guzman, Chairperson of the PAGC, of her son, nephew, and her son's girlfriend to sensitive positions in the PAGC. However, she claimed that they were exempted from the law against nepotism because they were qualified and appointed to positions of trust and confidence (*ABS-CBN News*, 2009b).

With the introduction of meritocracy in the Philippines during the American colonial period, it is not surprising that "civil service regulations demand merit-based recruitment and promotion." However, in practice, recruitment and promotion in the contemporary Philippine bureaucracy is based on *utang na loob* than on merit as "those with power to select or influence the selection of employees often are tempted to select friends or relatives as a way of reciprocating their help or of securing close allies."

Although this practice is tolerated by those in authority if they obtain "their share of discretionary appointments," Linda K. Richter (1987, p. 60) has pointed out that the reliance on *utang na loob* hinders policy implementation when the "casual" employees hired do not perform their duties effectively.

### *Lack of Political Will*

Finally, the lack of political will is responsible for the rampant corruption in the Philippines. Defining "political will" as "the use of the power one has to effect changes desired by the society," Ledivina V. Carino (1994, pp. 115–118) identified six reasons for the lack of political will in curbing corruption in the Philippines. First, the decentralization of power was not accompanied by regular monitoring and evaluation of the subordinates' performance. Second, the inability of the political elite and senior civil servants to distinguish between public needs and private interests resulted in many conflicts of interest. Third, officials were not punished for their failure to perform their duties. Fourth, political will was lacking as there was unequal or selective enforcement of the laws. Fifth, political will did not exist as pronouncements were not followed by action. Sixth, political will was absent as adequate manpower and funds were not provided for the implementation of the anticorruption measures.

In short, the rampant corruption in the Philippines is the combined result of several causes. The following paragraph by Co, Lim, Lao, and Juan (2007, pp. 35, 37) provides a good summary of the preceding analysis on the causes of corruption in the Philippines:

> Bribery proliferates and is sustained among agencies that do not address the need for efficiency for procedures and effectiveness of service delivery. Bribery is sustained in a system where personnel get meager pay from government employment … . The culture of corruption is sustained by a sub-culture … of gift giving, reciprocity, 'clientelism,' the so-called 'dark side of social capital,' fixing, facilitation used in a negative way, dualism, and the expansive yet discretionary use of bureaucratic power.

## ANTICORRUPTION MEASURES

The fight against corruption began in May 1950, when President Quirino created the Integrity Board consisting of five members to investigate complaints of graft and corruption against civil servants. However, this first

ACA was short-lived as the lack of public support led to its dissolution five months later (Quah, 1982a, p. 159).

After winning the 1953 presidential election, Ramon Magsaysay established the Presidential Complaints and Action Commission (PCAC) to reduce inefficiency and dishonesty in the civil service. He also issued Administrative Order No. 1 to prevent public officials from participating in certain types of official transactions with their real or imaginary relatives. The first anticorruption law was the Forfeiture Law of 1955, which authorized "the state to forfeit in its favor any property found to have been unlawfully acquired by any public officer or employer" (Alfiler, 1979, pp. 324–325). Unfortunately, this law was ineffective as there were no conviction even after four years of its passage.

President Magsaysay's untimely death in an air crash in 1957 led to the emergence of the Garcia administration (1957–1962), which abolished the PCAC and replaced it with the Presidential Committee on Administrative Performance Efficiency (PCAPE) and the Presidential Fact-Finding Committee (PFFC) in 1958 to implement the government's anti-graft campaign. In February 1960, President Garcia formed a third agency known as the Presidential Anti-Graft Committee (PAGC) (Alfiler, 1979, pp. 331–337). Two months later, the second anticorruption law, the Republic Act (RA) No. 3019, entitled the Anti-Graft and Corrupt Practices Act, was passed.[2] RA No. 3019 identified 11 types of corrupt acts among public officials and required them to file every two years a detailed and sworn statement of their assets and liabilities.

President Garcia was succeeded by President Diosdado Macapagal, who served from 1962 to 1965. Macapagal created the Presidential Anti-Graft Committee (PAGCOM). In 1965, Ferdinand Marcos replaced Macapagal as President and abolished PAGCOM and formed in its place the Presidential Agency on Reforms and Government Operations (PARGO) in January 1966. Three other agencies were created to assist PARGO to fight corruption: the Presidential Complaints and Action Office (PCAO), the Complaints and Investigations Office (CIO), and the Special Cabinet Committee in Backsliding (Alfiler, 1979, pp. 339–346). The third anticorruption law, RA No. 6028, which provided for the formation of the Office of the Citizens' Counsellor, was passed in August 1969, but was not implemented.

President Marcos declared martial law on 22 September 1972 and "ended over a quarter century of robust, if often irresponsible and elitist, democratic politics" (Timberman, 1991, p. 75). The remaining anticorruption laws were the four Presidential Decrees (PD) issued by President Marcos after the establishment of martial law. PD No. 6 identified 29 administrative offenses and empowered heads of departments to dismiss guilty officials immediately. This resulted in the sacking of nearly 8,000 public officials. Two months later, PD No. 46 prevented public officials from receiving and private individuals from giving gifts on any occasion including Christmas. Finally, PD No. 677 and PD No. 749 are amendments to RA No. 3019, requiring all government employees to submit statements of their assets and liabilities every year, instead of every other year, and providing immunity from prosecution for those willing to testify against public officials or citizens accused of corruption (Alfiler, 1979, pp. 326–327).

However, these purges were ineffective as "many of those who were fired were already retired or dead, while others were exonerated and the charges were dropped. Ten months later, many implicated officials were still at their posts." Moreover, the criteria for these purges were random and "encouraged fear and indifference rather than excellence." Most importantly, the Marcos regime's efforts in curbing corruption lacked credibility among the public as there was "growing suspicion that the worst offenders were sitting in the president's palace" (Root, 1996a, p. 116). By 1976, corruption had become rampant as grand corruption by Marcos and his cabinet encouraged the spread of petty corruption.

The Philippines is the Asian country with the most anticorruption measures as it has relied on 7 laws and 19 presidential ACAs since it began its fight against corruption in the 1950s. Table 4.6 provides details of the 19 presidential ACAs. The proliferation of ACAs is the result of the frequent changes in political leadership as these agencies are either created or abolished by the President. From May 1950 to January 1966, five ACAs were formed and dissolved as there were five changes in political leadership during that period. Similarly, President Marcos created another five ACAs during his 21 years in power because the first three agencies were ineffective and lasted between eight months and two years (Quah, 1982a, pp. 168–169). In July 1979, President Marcos formed the *Sandiganbayan* (Special Anti-Graft Court) and the *Tanodbayan* (Ombudsman) by issuing PD No. 1606 and PD No. 1603 respectively.

President Aquino assumed office in February 1986, and "there was high expectation that the end of the culture of graft and corruption was near" (Varela, 1995, p. 174). She established the PCGG to identify and retrieve the money stolen by the Marcos family and its cronies. Unfortunately, Aquino's "avowed anti-graft and corruption" stance was viewed cynically by the public as two of her Cabinet members and her relatives (referred to derisively by her critics as "rela-thieves") were accused of corruption. The PCGG had many enemies and was also a target for charges of corruption,

***Table 4.6.*** Presidential Anticorruption Agencies in the Philippines (1950 to Present).

| Anticorruption Agency | President | Period |
|---|---|---|
| Integrity Board | Quirino | May to November 1950 |
| Presidential Complaints and Action Committee | Magsaysay | December 1953 to July 1958 |
| Presidential Committee on Administrative Performance Efficiency | Garcia | July 1958 to December 1961 |
| Presidential Anti-Graft Committee | Garcia | February 1960 to December 1961 |
| Presidential Anti-Graft Committee | Macapagal | January 1962 to January 1966 |
| Presidential Agency on Reforms and Government Operations | Marcos | January to September 1966 |
| Presidential Complaints and Action Office | Marcos | September 1966 to October 1967 |
| Presidential Agency on Reforms and Government Operations | Marcos | October 1967 to February 1970 |
| Complaints and Investigations Office | Marcos | February 1970 to February 1986 |
| Special Cabinet Committee in Backsliding | Marcos | October 1973 to February 1986 |
| *Tanodbayan* (Office of the Ombudsman) | Marcos | July 1979 to April 1988 |
| | Aquino | Reorganized in May 1988 |
| Presidential Commission on Good Government | Aquino | February 1986 to present |
| Presidential Committee on Ethics and Accountability | Aquino | February 1986 to 1988 |
| Presidential Commission Against Graft and Corruption | Ramos | February 1994 to June 2000 |
| Inter-Agency Anti-Graft Coordinating Council | Estrada | August 1999 to present |
| Presidential Committee on Effective Governance | Estrada | October 1999 to present |
| National Anti-Corruption Commission | Estrada | July 2000 to April 2001 |
| Presidential Anti-Graft Commission | Arroyo | April 2001 to November 2010 |
| Governance Advisory Council | Arroyo | July 2001 to present |

*Sources*: Compiled from Alfiler (1979, p. 347), Batalla (2001, p. 47), and Oyamada (2005, pp. 100–101).

favoritism, and incompetence. Quintin S. Doromal, who was the PCGG Commissioner from 2 April 1986 to 16 October 1987, was charged for violating the Anti-Graft and Corrupt Practices Act (Republic Act No. 3019) on 25 January 1988. PCGG Commissioners Ramon A. Diaz and Mary Concepcion Bautista were also charged in 1989 for the same offense (AISS, 2003, pp. 143, 465). Furthermore, 5 of its agents also faced graft charges and 13 more were being investigated (Quah, 1999c, p. 81).

In May 1987, Aquino created the Presidential Committee on Public Ethics and Accountability (PCPEA) to respond to increasing public criticism. However, the PCPEA was also ineffective as it lacked personnel and funds. In other words, Aquino's "honesty has not been matched by the political will to punish the corrupt" (Timberman, 1991, p. 235). In November 1987, Archbishop Cardinal Jaime Sin criticized the "continued graft in government despite the ouster of former president Ferdinand Marcos." He lamented that "Ali Baba [Marcos] is gone, but the 40 thieves [corrupt officials] remain" (*Straits Times*, 1987c, p. 44).

Aquino's ineffectiveness in curbing corruption was manifested in the declining proportion of those citizens who were satisfied with the performance of her administration in tackling corruption from 72 percent in March 1987 to 26 percent in July 1989. In short, Aquino herself had "shared the people's exasperation and despair that she could not achieve the very thing that she wanted to leave as a legacy: a clean and accountable government" (Carino, 1994, p. 113). According to Reid and Guerrero (1995, p. 2), Aquino "left behind a mixed legacy" as the "democratic institutions she struggled to rebuild remained flawed and weak. Corruption prevailed, and Filipinos were increasingly cynical about the state of their nation."

The *Tanodbayan* or Office of the Ombudsman (OMB) was "reborn" in 1988 during Aquino's term of office and she appointed Conrado Vasquez for the position. However, the Ombudsman "failed to attract much public scrutiny" during 1988–1995 as the "limelight" was "hogged by the more high-profile *Sandiganbayan*." Thus, instead of "inspiring confidence in the judicial system," the OMB elicited "only disappointment–if not contempt–among many of those seeking redress for the wrong done them by public officials" as it had taken a long time to process the complaints received by it (Balgos, 1998, pp. 247–248).

A more serious weakness was caused by the quota system introduced by Vasquez as it encouraged inefficiency as investigators "finished the easier cases first to fulfil their quota" and left the more complex ones "untouched for months, or even years." Consequently, by December 1994, the OMB had accumulated a backlog of 14,652 cases or 65 percent of its total workload. Nearly three years later, in August 1997, the OMB still had pending cases dating back to 1979. The *Sandiganbayan's* record was worse than the Ombudsman as it completed only 13 percent of its total caseload in 1996 (Balgos, 1998, pp. 250–251).

In May 1992, Fidel Ramos was elected president for a six-year term. Even though the major focus of his administration was the recovery of the economy, he established the Presidential Commission Against Graft and Corruption (PCAGC) in 1994 to investigate violations of the anti-graft laws by presidential appointees and appointed Eufemio Domingo as its chairman. After serving for three years, Domingo lamented that "the system is not working" because "we are not making it work" for the following reasons:

> We have all the laws, rules and regulations and especially institutions not only to curb, but to eliminate, corruption. The problem is that these laws, rules and regulations are not being faithfully implemented .... I am afraid that many people are accepting [corruption] as another part of our way of life. Big-time grafters are lionized in society. They are invited to all sorts of social events, elected and re-elected to government offices. It is considered an honor – in fact a social distinction – to have them as guests in family and community affairs. (quoted in Balgos, 1998, pp. 267–268)

Joseph Estrada succeeded Ramos as president and in his State of the Nation Address on 28 July 1998, Estrada identified the struggle against graft and corruption as his major priority. In early 1999, he requested the World Bank to make recommendations to help his government strengthen its fight against corruption in the Philippines. The World Bank submitted its preliminary findings in December 1999 and recommended "a national strategy for fighting corruption" in the Philippines by "reducing opportunities and motivation for corruption" and making "corruption a high-risk, low-reward activity" (Bhargava, 1999, p. 1, 5).

The *Financial Times* reported in June 2000 that "perceived corruption in the Philippines reached its highest levels in two decades in 1998 and 1999, the first two years of the Estrada administration" (Lande, 2001, p. 92). Four months later, on 5 October 2000, the Senate Minority Leader, Teofisto Guingona, accused President Estrada of receiving "large cash payouts from *jueteng*, an illegal numbers game." On 9 October 2000, one of Estrada's cronies, Governor Luis Singson, "claimed that he had given the president 400 million pesos (US$10 million) from *jueteng* collections nationwide" (Lande, 2001, p. 92). Singson's "revelations triggered a major political earthquake" (Magno, 2001, p. 259).

Lande contends that "it was Estrada's mismanagement of the economy that most decisively turned the upper and middle classes against him." Moreover, the business community did not accept cronyism, and its members were disturbed by the preferential treatment given to Estrada's friends. However, "the last straw was the revelation that he himself was brazenly corrupt" (Lande, 2001, p. 92). The minority members of the House of Representatives initiated impeachment proceedings against the president. During the impeachment trial, Clarissa Ocampo, senior vice president of PCI-Equitable Bank, informed the court that Estrada, "under a false identity, was the true owner of several bank accounts holding hundred of millions of pesos" (Magno, 2001, p. 251).

The impeachment trial was covered live by the mass media from 6 December 2000 to 16 January 2001, and it "broke all audience records" because it was "a telenovela that outclassed all the others simply because it was real." This trial became "the single most important educational event on civics and the rule of law in Philippine political history" as it was "a large classroom where the weaknesses of institutions were exposed and the innermost secrets of political corruption revealed" (Magno, 2001, p. 260, 262).

On 16 January 2001, two pro-Estrada senators prevented "damning evidence" from being revealed in the trial and their action "provoked a firestorm of public outrage." The House prosecutors left in disgust and the Senate president Pimentel resigned. "Civil society exploded in non-violent anger and, acting where the Senate had failed to act, moved over five days of massive demonstrations to force the president from office" (Lande, 2001, p. 94).

On 20 January 2001, Gloria Macapagal-Arroyo was sworn in as the president by the chief justice after Estrada agreed to resign when the military withdrew its support. In her inaugural speech, President Arroyo emphasized that one of the four core beliefs was to "improve moral standards in government and society, in order to provide a strong foundation for good governance." However, Sheila S. Coronel, Executive Director of the Philippine Center for Investigative Journalism, astutely observed that Arroyo's government was unlikely to be "reformist" as "I was at her headquarters and I could see the old faces coming out, people who have been accused of corruption in the past" (Sheehan, 2001, p. 17). Nevertheless, three months after her inauguration as president, Arroyo formed the Presidential Anti-Graft Commission (PAGC) in April 2001, followed three months later by the establishment of the Governance Advisory Council (GAC) in July 2001.

During the second anniversary of her assumption of office, President Arroyo launched a war against corruption and announced that US$55 million would be allocated for her anticorruption crusade against "entrenched vested interests" or the "corruption of the powerful." As she had initially announced that she would not be standing for reelection in 2004, she claimed that she would be more effective in curbing corruption as "a President without the baggage of re-election can move faster, hit harder and work to greater effect." However, President Arroyo's anticorruption efforts were not supported by all Filipinos as some opposition politicians had filed an impeachment complaint in Congress against her for alleged graft and other offenses (Channel News Asia, 2003).

In October 2002, the Arroyo administration introduced "lifestyle checks" on all government officials, including the police and military. These lifestyle checks focus on the following four areas: "behavioral (such as leisure habits); asset value; relatives checks (means checking relatives who could have gained employment through the official's influence); and conflict of interest" (Oyamada, 2005, p. 106). In March 2003, the Inter-Agency Anti-Graft Coordinating Council (IACC) released a "lifestyle checklist" that identified the "tell-tale signs that a public official or bureaucrat has amassed wealth 'disproportionate' to his declared sources of income—wealth probably stolen from government coffers" (*Straits Times*, 2003, p. A15). The 11 indicators of a corrupt civil servant in the Philippines are identified in Box 4.2.

***Box 4.2.*** Tell-Tale Signs of a Corrupt Bureaucrat in the Philippines

How to tell if a public official or bureaucrat has amassed wealth "disproportionate" to his declared sources of income:

- Has multiple families or mistresses
- Frequently gambles in casinos and cock-fighting pits
- Maintains high-cost vices such as taking illegal drugs
- Goes on frequent foreign trips
- Owns country club shares
- Patronizes expensive restaurants or nightclubs
- Send children to exclusive schools with expensive tuition
- Buys additional houses or other real estate
- Owns a large number of stocks
- Has huge bank deposits
- Has a big collection of jewelry, antiques, or paintings

*Source*: *Straits Times* (2003, p. A15).

## EVALUATION OF ANTICORRUPTION MEASURES

How effective are the various anticorruption measures in the Philippines? In its editorial on 21 October 2008, the *Philippine Daily Inquirer* astutely observed that:

> But who cares if programs to combat corruption fail? The crooks in government are happiest to see anti-corruption drives falter, because they can continue their corrupt ways without fear of being caught and punished. And there are many of them in high and low places.

The fact that corruption is a way of life in the Philippines is a clear manifestation of the ineffectiveness of the various anticorruption measures employed by the various administrations since the 1950s. The systemic and rampant nature of corruption in the Philippines is further corroborated by its consistently low ranking on TI's CPI from 1995 to 2010. Table 4.7 notes that the ranking of the Philippines on the CPI has declined from 36th position in 1995 to 134th position in 2010. More importantly, its CPI score rose from 2.77 in 1995 to a peak of 3.6 in 1999. Since 2000, the Philippines' CPI score has further declined from 2.8 to 2.4 from 2005 to 2009 and 2010.

***Table 4.7.*** Philippines' Performance on the CPI, 1995–2010.

| Year | Ranking | Score[a] | No. of Countries |
|---|---|---|---|
| 1995 | 36th | 2.77 | 41 |
| 1996 | 44th | 2.69 | 54 |
| 1997 | 40th | 3.05 | 52 |
| 1998 | 55th | 3.3 | 85 |
| 1999 | 54th | 3.6 | 99 |
| 2000 | 69th | 2.8 | 90 |
| 2001 | 65th | 2.9 | 91 |
| 2002 | 77th | 2.6 | 102 |
| 2003 | 92nd | 2.5 | 133 |
| 2004 | 102nd | 2.6 | 146 |
| 2005 | 117th | 2.5 | 159 |
| 2006 | 121st | 2.5 | 163 |
| 2007 | 131st | 2.5 | 180 |
| 2008 | 141st | 2.3 | 180 |
| 2009 | 139th | 2.4 | 180 |
| 2010 | 134th | 2.4 | 178 |
| Average | 89th | 2.7 | – |

*Source*: http://www.transparency.org

[a]The score ranges from 0 (most corrupt) to 10 (least corrupt).

Its average rank from 1995 to 2010 is 89th position and its average CPI score is 2.7.

Similarly, Table 4.8 notes that the Philippines' ranking and scores on PERC's annual surveys from 1995 to 2010 have consistently been low throughout this period. The Philippines' best performance was in 1999, when it was ranked fourth among the 12 Asian countries with its best score of 6.71. It was ranked last among the 13 Asian countries surveyed for 2007–2008 because its score had increased to 9.40 and 9.00, respectively. In 2009, the Philippines was ranked 11th with an improved score of 7.00. However, its rank dropped to 13th position in 2010 and its score also decreased to 8.06.

The World Bank's governance indicator on the control of corruption from 1996 to 2009 also confirms the Philippines' inability to curb corruption effectively. Table 4.9 notes that the Philippines' percentile rank in controlling corruption has declined from 52.9 in 1996 to 27.1 in 2009. Its governance score also decreased from −0.23 to −0.71 for the same period. Among the 25 Asian countries included in the 2009 survey, the Philippines was ranked 16th for control of corruption with a percentile rank of 27.1.

***Table 4.8.*** Philippines' Performance on PERC Surveys on Corruption, 1995–2010.

| Year | Ranking | Score[a] | No. of Countries |
|---|---|---|---|
| 1995 | 8th | 6.60 | 11 |
| 1996 | 9th | 6.95 | 12 |
| 1997 | 6th | 6.50 | 12 |
| 1998 | 8th | 7.17 | 12 |
| 1999 | 4th | 6.71 | 12 |
| 2000 | 8th | 8.67 | 12 |
| 2001 | 9th | 9.00 | 12 |
| 2002 | 8th | 8.00 | 12 |
| 2003 | 7th | 7.67 | 13 |
| 2004 | 9th | 8.33 | 13 |
| 2005 | 12th | 8.80 | 13 |
| 2006 | 11th | 7.80 | 13 |
| 2007 | 13th | 9.40 | 13 |
| 2008 | 13th | 9.00 | 13 |
| 2009 | 11th | 7.00 | 16 |
| 2010 | 13th | 8.06 | 16 |
| Average | 9th | 7.84 | – |

*Sources*: Compiled from PERC (2001, 2008, p. 7), Hussain (2009, p. B5), and *ABS-CBN News* (2010).

[a]The score ranges from 0 (least corrupt) to 10 (most corrupt).

***Table 4.9.*** Philippines' Performance on Control of Corruption, 1996-2009.

| Year | Percentile Rank (1–100) | Governance Score (+2.5 to −2.5) |
|---|---|---|
| 1996 | 52.9 | −0.23 |
| 1998 | 48.1 | −0.23 |
| 2000 | 39.3 | −0.46 |
| 2002 | 41.3 | −0.41 |
| 2003 | 41.3 | −0.43 |
| 2004 | 36.4 | −0.53 |
| 2005 | 36.9 | −0.55 |
| 2006 | 26.2 | −0.72 |
| 2007 | 29.0 | −0.66 |
| 2008 | 30.9 | −0.67 |
| 2009 | 27.1 | −0.71 |

*Source*: Compiled from http://info.worldbank.org/governance/wgi/sc_chart.asp.

***Table 4.10.*** Public Trust of Politicians in the Philippines, 1999 to 2010–2011.

| Year | Rank | Score[a] | No. of Countries |
|---|---|---|---|
| 1999 | 49th | 2.02 | 59 |
| 2000 | 51st | 2.00 | 59 |
| 2001–2002 | 52nd | 2.10 | 75 |
| 2002–2003 | 69th | 1.50 | 80 |
| 2003–2004 | 94th | 1.40 | 102 |
| 2007–2008 | 119th | 1.70 | 131 |
| 2008–2009 | 123rd | 1.50 | 134 |
| 2009–2010 | 130th | 1.60 | 133 |
| 2010–2011 | 134th | 1.60 | 139 |
| Average | 91st | 1.71 | – |

*Sources*: Compiled from Schwab et al. (1999, p. 327), Porter et al. (2000, p. 253), Schwab et al. (2002, p. 408), Cornelius (2003, p. 619), Sala-i-Martin (2004, p. 499), Schwab and Porter (2007, p. 379), Schwab and Porter (2008, p. 367); Schwab (2009, p. 349), and Schwab (2010, p. 369).
[a]The score ranges from 1 (very low) to 7 (very high) for the respondents' answers to this statement: "How would you rate the level of public trust in the ethical standards of politicians in your country."

The previous three indicators provide data on the perceived extent of corruption in the Philippines. Table 4.10 provides data on the Philippines' rankings and scores on the *Global Competitiveness Report's* indicator on public trust of politicians. The Philippines' declining rank from 49th position among 59 countries in 1999 to 134th position among 139 countries in 2010–2011 and the corresponding decrease in its score from 2.02 to 1.60 during the same period for this indicator is a clear reflection of the Filipino citizens' negative reaction to the corrupt behavior of their politicians.

Why has the Philippines been ineffective in curbing corruption even though it has relied on 7 laws and 19 ACAs? According to Edna Co et al. (2007, p. 11):

> If laws and policies were to be the bases of the state of corruption in a country, the Philippines would be ranked among the most corrupt-free. Numerous laws and policies are legislated and programs are in place all across the public sector. However, the enormous constraint lies in the enforcement of these laws and policies.

Indeed, as indicated earlier, the anticorruption laws have not been enforced impartially because of the lack of political will, which is the most important reason for the ineffectiveness of the Philippines' anticorruption measures as the government has not allocated sufficient personnel and budget to the various ACAs to enable them to perform their duties effectively. For example, the OMB, which is the lead ACA, is understaffed, and according to a former Ombudsman, Simeon V. Marcelo (2005, p. 1), it is "designed to fail because of its crippling lack of resources."

To demonstrate the OMB's "severe" lack of resources, Marcelo (2005, p. 3) compared the personnel and budget of the OMB with those of Hong Kong's ICAC. Table 4.11 shows vividly how understaffed and under-resourced the OMB is compared to the ICAC. The OMB's field investigator-bureaucracy ratio of 1:17,045 compares unfavorably with the ICAC's ratio of 1: 208. The

***Table 4.11.*** Comparison of the Personnel and Budgets of the OMB and ICAC in 2004.

| Item | Office of the Ombudsman | Independent Commission Against Corruption |
|---|---|---|
| No. of field investigators | 88 | 837 |
| Total no. of staff | 1,141 | 1,326 |
| Size of bureaucracy | 1,500,000 | 174,175 |
| Field investigator-bureaucracy ratio | 1: 17,045 | 1: 208 |
| Budget | 480 million pesos | 4.94 billion pesos |
| Population of country | 81.4 million | 7.1 million |
| Per capita expenditure | 6 pesos | 696 pesos |
| Staff–population ratio | 1: 71,340 | 1: 5,354 |

*Sources*: Marcelo (2005, p. 3) and *Economist* (2006, pp. 152, 194).

OMB's staff–population of 1: 71,340 is much higher than the ICAC's ratio of 1: 5,354. In terms of per capita expenditure, the ICAC's figure of 696 pesos exceeds that of the OMB's 6 pesos by 116 times. Marcelo (2005, p. 4) captures the essence of the OMB's powerlessness by describing it as "a hunter hunting for crocodiles with only a flyswatter in hand" because "there is no way it can kill its prey, i.e., the corrupt public officials." Even before Marcelo became the Ombudsman, Eric Batalla (2001, p. 73) had recommended the expansion of the OMB's capacity and the improvement of its capability to enhance its effectiveness. More recently, Raymundo Julio A. Olaguer (2006, p. 79) has recommended that the OMB's budget be increased "to solve the problem of overworked and underpaid prosecutors and investigators" and to provide the OMB with "modern and state-of-the-art equipment for surveillance and evidence-gathering."

Secondly, even though the OMB is the lead ACA in the Philippines, it performs these five functions: investigation of inefficiency and anomalies; prosecution of graft cases in the *Sandiganbayan*; disciplinary control over all elective and appointed officials (except members of Congress and Judiciary and impeachable officials); public assistance; and graft prevention.[3] In other words, apart from its lack of resources, the OMB is not a specialized ACA dedicated solely to combating corruption, as it is also responsible for disciplinary control and public assistance. This means that the OMB does not enjoy the two advantages of specialized ACAs, namely, the "centralization of all necessary information and intelligence about corruption" and the "resolution of coordination problems among multiple agencies through vertical integration" (Meagher, 2005, p. 80).

Another limitation of the OMB is that it only has jurisdiction over public officials and not those employed in private companies (Quah, 2009a, p. 774). The OMB has been "tainted with allegations of wrongdoing" as impeachment complaints were filed three times against Ombudsman Aniano Desierto during his seven-year term. However, the charges against him were dismissed by the Congress. The OMB has also been accused of not taking action or dismissing cases "despite overwhelming evidence against suspected offenders" (Dizon, 2007, p. 117).

Thirdly, the reliance on multiple ACAs has not benefited the Philippines as the proliferation of these agencies has led to "duplication, layering and turf wars" (Quimson, 2006, p. 30). There is also no coordination or cooperation among the various ACAs, which compete for recognition, staff, and resources because they are understaffed and poorly funded. Even though their basic mandates are defined, these ACAs have overlapping jurisdiction, which diffuses anticorruption efforts, and results in "poor coordination in policy and program implementation, weak management and wastage of resources" (Oyamada, 2005, p. 99).

Edna Co et al. (2007, p. 21) have questioned why new ACAs are created by a new administration without evaluating the effectiveness of the existing ones thus:

> Each administration created flagship programs and projects, sending the message that the political leadership was doing something against graft and corruption. However, the creation of such commissions and bodies may have been redundant and costly for the government. Although this may not be an efficient way of doing things ... the creation of these bodies itself should be examined to ascertain whether or not they contribute to the commission of corruption in the public administrative system. An attendant question one could raise is why a new program needs to be created each time a new administration steps in instead of merely building upon past efforts.

The IACC is a voluntary alliance of the OMB, the Civil Service Commission (CSC), the Commission of Audit (COA), the Presidential Anti-Graft Commission (PAGC), the Department of Justice, and the National Bureau of Investigation (NBI). It was formed in June 1997 to enhance coordination among these six agencies, to conduct interagency skills training programs, and to promote interagency conferences (Ursal, 2006, pp. 222–223). The IACC's role is to improve coordination among these agencies, but "in reality, it is not active" (Oyamada, 2005, p. 99). The IACC met twice, and the "slow progress in its revitalization" reflects the inability of these six agencies to collaborate effectively among themselves (Holmes, 2007, p. 181).

Unlike the previous Ombudsman, Simeon Marcelo, the current Ombudsman, Ma. Merceditas N. Gutierrez, "deactivated" the IACC by not convening it. Thus, instead of cooperating with the CSC, the OMB competed with it by also implementing the Oplan Red Plate program, which the OMB, COA, and CSC had earlier agreed under the Solana Covenant to be the CSC's responsibility (TAN, 2009, p. 5). Apart from not convening the IACC, Gutierrez has also been criticized for devoting the OMB's limited resources on investigating petty corruption instead of continuing her predecessor's exposure of "corruption in high places." Consequently, the OMB has been described as "the Street Ombudsman" because of its emphasis on petty corruption (*Newsbreak Online*, 2006). The Transparency and Accountability Network (TAN) has attributed the OMB's "disappointing performance" to the following factors:

> From the looks of it, the apparent weakness of the Ombudsman as an institution ... is the doing of poor leadership. The low conviction rate is explained by a highly centralized system, a weakened Office of the Special Prosecutor, and a demoralized staff. This and bad relations with other anticorruption organizations contribute to the bad image of the Ombudsman and thus its growing unpopularity. (TAN, 2009, p. 5)

The PAGC was created by President Arroyo in 2001 to perform the following three functions: (1) the investigation or hearing of administrative complaints against presidential appointees; (2) the investigation of administrative cases against non-presidential appointees conspiring with presidential appointees alleged to have performed irregular acts; and (3) providing assistance to the president in the campaign against graft and corruption. However, it lacks fiscal autonomy and depends solely on the Office of the President for its budget, which is "a fraction of what [the] OMB receives." The PAGC has been ineffective in securing convictions as it dealt with 1,004 cases since its inception in 2001, but only 9 percent of these cases had punitive recommendations because 40 percent were dismissed for lack of jurisdiction, and 59 percent were dismissed for insufficient evidence. Indeed, the PAGC is not viewed as a credible ACA because of its lack of organizational and financial independence and its organizational proximity to the President (Quimson, 2006, pp. 29–30).

According to a critic, there have been 14 versions of the PAGC because it was first created in the 1950s. Unfortunately, "like its predecessors, the present PAGC has had a negligible impact in the fight against corruption" (Dizon, 2007, p. 117). The PAGC conducted a total of 287 lifestyle checks on government officials from 2003 to 2005 (Ursal, 2006, p. 202). However, according to Romulo Pagulayan (2007, p. 112), these lifestyle checks are "selective and ineffective" as "no secretaries, presidential assistants, general managers of government-owned or government-controlled corporations" were subjected to lifestyle checks. Unlike the President who has declared that she was open to a lifestyle check, the spokesperson for her husband, the First Gentleman, "insisted that he is a private person" and is therefore not subject to a lifestyle check. Furthermore, "the hype generated by the lifestyle check diverts the people's attention from the more massive and systemic graft, even plunder committed by political appointees, top bureaucrats and the President's relatives and cronies." In short, like the other anticorruption measures, the lifestyle check is ineffective because it focuses on "the lowly government workers [who] have become convenient scapegoats and easy prey" and ignores the "fat cats of government" (Pagulayan, 2007, pp. 112–113).

President Arroyo introduced anticorruption measures such as the PAGC, the GAC, and the "lifestyle checks" as discussed earlier. However, she could not focus all her attention on fighting corruption because she was also concerned with improving the economy and dealing with terrorism. After her reelection in May 2004, she promised to continue the fight against corruption, but her credibility was severely eroded by the revelation that she had tried to influence an election commissioner during the 2004 presidential election. The revelation of the "Hello Garci" tapes sent a clear message throughout the Philippines that

> the fight against corruption cannot truly be won since the highest government official, no less than the President, is tainted by corruption. Any Filipino, be he a simpleton in the streets or a scholar would indubitably arrive at the conclusion that corruption, if committed in high places, may go unpunished. This brings the efforts of the anti-corruption campaign to naught. (Olaguer, 2006, p. 35)

President Arroyo's expression of her confidence in May 2005 that "her government's campaign against corruption would bear fruit in six to seven years at the end of her term" (Oyamada, 2005, p. 103) appears to be premature and misplaced as there is no evidence that her anticorruption measures have been effective. On 11 September 2007, former President Joseph Estrada was found guilty by the *Sandiganbayan* of receiving payoffs and kickbacks before his ouster from office and sentenced to a maximum of 40 years imprisonment (Conde, 2007, p. 3). On 25 October 2007, President Arroyo pardoned Estrada six weeks after his conviction even though anticorruption advocates and state prosecutors have urged her not to do so (*Deutsche Presse-Agentur*, 2007). The *Economist* (2007a) criticized Arroyo's pardon of Estrada because it renews "concerns in many quarters that the rich and powerful remain immune from punishment" and fails "to dispel concerns about entrenched corruption in the Philippines."

More importantly, President Arroyo's pardoning of Estrada's conviction for plunder has also undermined the rule of law and the credibility of her anticorruption efforts. According to the *South China Morning Post* (2007, p. 14):

> Philippine President Gloria Macapagal-Arroyo claims to be dedicated to ridding her country of its biggest scourge, corruption. Her predecessor Joseph Estrada was convicted last month of a worse crime, plunder. Granting him a pardon and dangling a government job for him shows she is interested not in the national well-being but in political survival .... Mrs Arroyo has done the Philippines a disservice. She has undermined the rule of law and told officials that graft and corruption are not serious crimes. It is hardly surprising that growing numbers of Filipinos want her out of office.

Hence it is not surprising that a nationwide Pulse Asia survey conducted from 20 to 31 October 2007 found that 42 percent of the respondents believed that President Arroyo was the most corrupt president among the last five presidents. Table 4.12 notes that the ranking of the other four presidents was Marcos (35 percent); Estrada (16 percent); Ramos (5 percent); and Aquino (1 percent) (GMA News.TV, 2007).

***Table 4.12.*** Perceived Level of Corruption of Presidents in the Philippines, 2007.

| President | Percentage Believing that the President was Corrupt (%) |
|---|---|
| Gloria Macapagal-Arroyo (2001 to present) | 42 |
| Ferdinand E. Marcos (1972–1986) | 35 |
| Joseph E. Estrada (1998–2001) | 16 |
| Fidel V. Ramos (1992–1998) | 5 |
| Corazon C. Aquino (1986–1992) | 1 |

*Source*: GMA News.TV (2007).

In its editorial on 21 October 2008, the *Philippine Daily Inquirer* (2008) lamented that:

> People who keep hoping for clean and honest government that uses taxpayers' money wisely and well will have to wait for another administration. The President thinks corruption is not a problem or at least not the serious problem businessmen and other observers take it to be. Nothing, not even neutral surveys and studies, will change her mind. It would be pointless and futile to look up to her for a solution.

In sum, President Arroyo's commitment to curbing corruption in the Philippines was eroded after nine years in office. In a survey conducted by Pulse Asia from 1 to 11 July 2010, after she stepped down from office, 26 percent of the 1,200 Filipinos interviewed nationwide believed that corruption was Arroyo's biggest mistake. The survey also showed that 67 percent of the respondents distrusted Arroyo, and 62 percent of them were dissatisfied with her performance during her last three months in office (Dizon, 2010).

## CONCLUSION

Corruption will remain a serious problem in the Philippines as long as the five causes identified in an earlier section are not eliminated. The salaries of the civil servants and political leaders are unlikely to be increased substantially because the government would not be able to afford such an expensive strategy without sustained economic growth. Furthermore, Singapore's experience shows that "salary revision is a necessary but insufficient condition for curbing corruption if other reforms are not undertaken also"

(Quah, 2007b, p. 43). Although the opportunities for corruption can be minimized by reducing red tape and improving the efficiency of the civil service by streamlining the cumbersome and complicated administrative procedures, such opportunities will remain as long as low salaries or "starvation wages" reinforce the need for civil servants to accept "speed money" for expediting the approval of applications for permits. As discussed earlier, the population's tolerance for corruption is reinforced by the importance of the family and particularistic values such as *utang na loob* in Philippine society.

In the final analysis, the key factor responsible for combating corruption effectively in the Philippines is the political will or commitment of its political leadership. In other words, without political will, the probability of detection and punishment for corrupt offenses cannot be enhanced, and the resources required for a comprehensive anticorruption strategy will not be allocated by the incumbent government.

In May 2005, Tony Kwok, the former Deputy Commissioner of the ICAC in Hong Kong, was appointed by President Arroyo as her special advisor on anticorruption. Soon after his appointment, he informed a group of businessmen in Manila that "Corruption can be eradicated. We did it in Hong Kong. It can be done in the Philippines" (Conde, 2005). A few days later, President Arroyo confidently declared that:

> Tony [Kwok] says, with our political will and working together, what Hong Kong was able to do in seven years, we could perhaps be able to do in three years. We shall win this war against corruption. (Conde, 2005)

Three months later, Kwok reinforced President Arroyo's optimistic assessment when he asserted that "nothing is impossible" because "there is no shortage of political will to fight corruption here in the Philippines" (Vanzi, 2005).

Unfortunately, contrary to the expectations of President Arroyo and Tony Kwok, corruption in the Philippines has not improved during the past five years as they had predicted. On the contrary, corruption in the Philippines has worsened according to TI's CPI and PERC's annual survey of corruption from 2005 to 2010, and the World Bank's control of corruption indicator from 2005 to 2009. As corruption is a way of life in the Philippines, it is unrealistic to expect corruption to be eradicated within three years as promised by Tony Kwok. Apart from the significant contextual differences between Hong Kong, which is a city-state of 1,075 sq km with 7.3 million people and a GDP per capita of US$30,860 and the Philippines, which is an archipelago of 7,017 islands covering a vast area of 300,000 sq km with a population of 89.7 million and a GDP per capita of

US$1,850 (Economist, 2010a, pp. 154, 196), the critical difference is the lack of political will in fighting corruption in the Philippines.

Thus, curbing corruption in the Philippines remains an impossible dream for the foreseeable future until its political leaders can demonstrate that they have the political will to do so. So far, the political leaders in the Philippines are "either incompetent or corrupt" and have "failed to lead the battle against corruption" (Co et al., 2007, p. 33). This pessimistic conclusion is based on the fact that none of the presidents who have governed the Philippines since its attainment of independence in July 1946 have modified or improved their anticorruption strategies even though the plethora of ACAs and anticorruption laws has been ineffective in curbing corruption. Instead, each president has created new ACAs without evaluating or learning from the mistakes of his or her predecessor.

In other words, political leaders in the Philippines are unlikely to succeed in curbing corruption unless they replace their modus operandi of relying on ineffective multiple, overlapping, uncoordinated, and poorly staffed and funded ACAs with the establishment of a single independent, powerful, adequately funded, and staffed ACA such as the CPIB in Singapore or Hong Kong's ICAC. Although a single ACA is not a magic bullet that can eradicate corruption overnight in the Philippines, the success of the CPIB and ICAC in curbing corruption shows that if there is political will, the establishment of a single independent ACA will be an asset and a powerful weapon against corrupt politicians, civil servants, and business persons. However, if political will is lacking, the ACA's extensive powers can be abused by a corrupt government to victimize its political foes instead (Quah, 2010a, p. 51).

Benigno S. Aquino III, who was inaugurated on 30 June 2010 as the 15th President of the Philippines, has promised to curb corruption. Earl Parreno of the Institute for Political and Electoral Reforms contends that President Aquino has to demonstrate his commitment in his anticorruption campaign by "mobilizing resources and manpower to weed out deeply rooted corruption" in government cost centers and revenue agencies (Mogato, 2010). On 15 November 2010, President Aquino signed Executive Order 13, which abolished the PAGC as part of the administration's "policy of streamlining the government bureaucracy to promote economy and efficiency in government" (Cheng, 2010). The PAGC has been dissolved because its functions are already performed by the OMB. Hopefully, President Aquino will learn from the mistakes of his predecessors and avoid taking the same path taken by them by establishing an independent, adequately staffed, and funded ACA to replace the existing ineffective multiple ACAs.

## NOTES

1. According to Chaikin and Sharman (2009, pp. 164–165), "Behest loans are insider loans that are granted or executed on uneconomic terms and that are diverted for uses contrary to their original purposes."

2. For an account of how this law was passed, see Iglesias (1963, pp. 17–68).

3. See the OMB's web site at http://www.ombudsman.gov.ph/index.php?opt = 1&about=6

# CHAPTER 5

# TAIWAN

> Taiwan is a vigorous democracy, and has made extraordinary strides toward political openness and freedom. But its democracy is also seriously blighted by corruption, vote buying, political favoritism, and the penetration of organized crime into politics. It is a disgrace that known organized crime figures sit in parliament.
>
> – Larry Diamond (2000, p. 10)

> In my analysis, Taiwan faces at this point one very deadly problem.... The gravest threat to our democratic nation is the widespread presence of organized crime in politics. As long as organized crime remains a major influence, the various reform projects that are put forward are doomed to fail.
>
> – Brian Kennedy (2000, p. 8)

## CHEN SHUI-BIAN'S CORRUPTION SCANDAL

In his autobiography, Chen Shui-bian (1999, p. 40) condemned the Koumintang's (KMT's) corruption and praised the Democratic Progressive Party (DPP) for being free from money politics and corruption. The DPP fought the 1992 Legislative Yuan election campaign effectively on an anticorruption platform and used the same strategy in subsequent elections. If Chen Shui-bian had criticized the KMT for its involvement with "black gold" politics and had won the 2000 presidential election on his anticorruption platform, why was he and his family found guilty of corruption after his second term of office? The short answer is that even though he had promised to curb corruption, President Chen himself had succumbed to corruption after assuming office. In June 2002, *Keesing's Contemporary Archives* cited a poll in Taiwan that indicated that more respondents had perceived the DPP to be more corrupt than the KMT (Copper, 2006, p. 14).

During the campaign for the 2004 presidential election, Chen Yu-hao, former chairman of Tuntex Group, revealed that he had "secretly given Chen Shui-bian money in 2000" and "funneled" NT$20 million into the DPP-affiliated Formosa Foundation. Indeed, the DPP was viewed as a corrupt party and Chen Shui-bian's administration seen as "venal and dishonest" after the 2004 presidential election because of the increase in corrupt activities. The DPP and President Chen had expected to lose the

2004 presidential election, and therefore, he and his colleagues "wanted to cash in before leaving" office (Copper, 2009a, p. 12).

There were also numerous media reports on the first lady's lavish spending habits and speculation on her involvement in insider trading in Taiwan's stock market. In May 2006, she was shown on television spending the gift certificates she had received for assisting in the takeover bid of Taipei's SOGO Department Store. Shih Ming-teh, a former DPP chairman, launched an anticorruption movement in August 2006 to pressure President Chen to resign from office. The movement was called the "one million persons movement against corruption" because Shih's aim was to raise NT$100 million by asking one million Taiwanese citizens to contribute NT$100 each. The target of one million donors was attained ahead of schedule (Copper, 2006, pp. 15, 21).

In November 2006, the first lady, Wu Shu-chen, was indicted for stealing NT$14.8 million (US$450,000) in government funds, forgery, and perjury. Prosecutors also revealed that she had spent US$1.5 million on diamond rings and other luxury items (Copper, 2008, p. 29; *China Post*, 2006). After collapsing at the beginning of her trial, she failed to show up in court for 18 times during the next two years (AFP, 2008b). She finally pleaded guilty on February 10, 2009, to money laundering and admitted to wiring US$2.2 million abroad from a political donation and not a bribe. She also admitted to forging documents in another case involving embezzled public funds, but denied using the money for personal gain (AFP, 2009).

Other corruption scandals involving DPP officials tainted the DPP's image and contributed to the defeat of the DPP candidate, Frank Hsieh, in the 2008 presidential election. After losing his immunity from prosecution on leaving office in May 2008, Chen Shui-bian was accused of embezzlement, taking bribes, and money laundering. He was arrested on November 11, 2008, on suspicion of corruption (CNN.com, 2008a). Chen and his wife, Wu Shu-chen, were accused of embezzling NT104 million (US$3.12 million) from a special presidential fund, and received bribes of US$9 million in connection with a government land procurement deal. Wu was also accused of accepting a bribe of US$2.73 million from a government construction project (Associated Press, 2008). Chen was released on bail one month later on December 13, 2008, while the prosecutors were still preparing their case against him on several corruption charges (CNN.com, 2008b). However, on December 30, 2008, Chen was jailed again because he was considered a flight risk (CNN.com, 2008c).

On September 11, 2009, the Taipei District Court sentenced Chen and his wife to life imprisonment after finding them and 11 co-defendants guilty.

Chen was imprisoned for life and fined NT$200 million (US$6.1 million) for violating the Punishment of Corruption Act, Money Laundering Control Act, and the Criminal Code. The court also found Chen and his wife guilty of embezzlement and taking bribes amounting to NT$800 million. His wife was also given a life sentence and fined NT$300 million. Both of them were also found guilty of accepting NT$10 million in bribes from Diana Chen, former Taipei Financial Center Corporation Chairperson, and for receiving NT$300 million in political donations from Jeffrey Koo Jr., former vice chairman of Chinatrust Financial Holding Company. Chen's son, Chen Chih-chung, was imprisoned for two and a half years and fined NT$150 million on money laundering charges. Chen's daughter-in-law, Huang Jui-ching, was given a sentence of 20 months and fined NT$150 million on money laundering charges (Huang, 2009, p. 1).

On June 8, 2010, the Taipei District Court acquitted Chen Shui-bian in a case of embezzlement involving US$330,000 in secret diplomatic funds because the evidence provided by the prosecutors did not prove that Chen had embezzled diplomatic funds (Chang, 2010a, p. 1). Three days later, the Taiwan High Court reduced Chen's life sentence to 20 years imprisonment and the NT$200 million fine to NT$170 million because it was found that the amount embezzled was less than previously found by a lower court. The High Court also reduced the life sentence of Chen's wife, Wu Shu-chen to 20 years and the NT$300 million fine to NT$200 million. Similarly, the 30-month sentence and NT$150 million fine imposed on Chen's son, Chen Chi-chung, was reduced to 14 months and a fine of NT$30 million; and the 20-month sentence and NT$150 million fine imposed on Chen's daughter-in-law, Huang Jui-ching, was reduced to a year and a fine of NT$30 million (Chao, 2010a, p. 1).

On November 11, 2010, the Supreme Court sentenced Chen Shui-bian to 11 years imprisonment for accepting bribes in a land deal and another sentence of eight years jail in another bribery case when he was president. On December 6, 2010, the Taiwan High Court decided that Chen should be imprisoned for 17.5 years instead of the combined 19-year sentence and fined a total of NT$154 million (US$5.05 million). Chen's wife, Wu Shu-chen was also sentenced to 11 years imprisonment for taking bribes in a land deal and another 8.5 years jail for money-laundering (Chao, 2010c, p. 1).

## AIM OF THE CHAPTER

In April 2009, the Hong Kong-based Political Economic Risk Consultancy (PERC) reported in its annual survey of corruption in Asian countries that

Taiwan was ranked 9th with a score of 6.47, behind China, which was ranked 8th with a score of 6.16 (*ABS-CBN News*, 2009a). President Ma Ying-jeou rejected this finding and ordered the anti-corruption agencies (ACAs) in Taiwan to "produce a review report on major corruption cases and work out a plan to improve the situation within three months" (Low, 2009). On the contrary, as will be shown later, Taiwan's rank and score on TI's 2009 and 2010 CPI are higher than those of China's. Similarly, PERC's 2010 survey ranked Taiwan 8th with a score of 6.28, ahead of China, which was ranked 10th with a score of 6.52 (*Straits Times*, 2010a).

How serious is the problem of corruption in Taiwan? What are the causes of corruption in Taiwan? How does Taiwan combat corruption and how effective are its anticorruption measures? What can be done to improve these measures? This chapter addresses these questions by providing a comprehensive analysis of the anticorruption measures adopted by the various governments in Taiwan since the relocation of the KMT government in December 1949 from mainland China to Taiwan after its defeat by the Chinese Communist Party (CCP). While some research has been done on corruption in Taiwan, this chapter hopes to rectify the significant research gap on the causes of corruption in Taiwan and how it combats corruption.

## TAIWAN'S POLICY CONTEXT

### *Geography*

Taiwan is an island separated from the southeastern coast of mainland China by the narrow Taiwan Strait.[1] It is 394 km long and 144 km wide, and has a land area of 36,179 sq km and a coastline of 1,566.3 km (GIO, 2010, chap. 1). Eastern Taiwan is mountainous, and consequently, 90 percent of the population lives in the flat plains in the west. Taiwan has a marine climate in the northern part and mountainous areas but the south has a tropical climate and is warm and humid throughout the year. The rainy season lasts from May to June and from July to October, and Taiwan is vulnerable to typhoons, with an average of four typhoons per year.

As 55 percent of the island is forest, only 24 percent of the total land is arable. The natural resources in Taiwan include small deposits of asbestos, coal, copper, gold, natural gas, and marble. In addition to typhoons, Taiwan is also vulnerable to earthquakes because of its location along the seismic belt and its mountainous nature. With 42 active faults on the island, it is not surprising that Taiwan experienced about 20,000 earthquakes

***Box 5.1.*** Taiwan's Policy Context

| | |
|---|---|
| Land Area | 36,179 sq km |
| GDP | US$403 billion (2008) |
| GDP per capita | US$17,050 (2008) |
| Population | 23,069,000 (2009) |
| Population Density | 638 persons per sq km |
| Adult Literacy Rate | 96.1% |
| Political System | Presidential Democracy |
| Colonial Rule | Japanese colonial rule (1895–1945) |
| 2010 CPI Rank and Score | 33/178 and 5.8/10 |
| 2010 PERC Rank and Score | 8/16 and 6.28/10 |

*Sources*: *Economist* (2010a, p. 224); GIO (2010, chap. 2); http://www.transparency.org./policy_research/surveys_indices/cpi/2010/results; and *Straits Times* (2010a).

during 1994–2008. Taiwan has a well-developed transportation network of 40,000 km of roads and a public railway system that provides services between more than 200 stations and covering 1,100 kilometers in length.[2] It also provides advanced telecommunications services. Taiwan's advanced transportation and telecommunications infrastructure is an important asset in fighting corruption as the various ACAs would have no difficulty in enforcing the anticorruption laws throughout the country.

However, Taiwan's susceptibility to natural disasters like earthquakes and typhoons means that there will be opportunities for corruption during the postcrisis periods when government agencies and international relief agencies provide humanitarian assistance to those affected by the disasters. This means that the ACAs in Taiwan must be vigilant during such periods to detect and take action against corrupt behavior.

## *History*

There are two important historical experiences that have influenced Taiwan's anticorruption strategy today. The first is the five decades of Japanese colonial rule from 1895, when the First Sino-Japanese War resulted in the ceding of Taiwan to Japan, until the surrender of the Japanese forces in Nanjing on September 9, 1945. The second important historical experience is the conflict between the KMT government and the CCP, which resulted in the formation of the People's Republic of China on the mainland and the relocation of the KMT government in Taiwan in December 1949 after its defeat by the CCP.

Japanese colonial rule has influenced Taiwan's anticorruption strategy in two ways. First, as a Japanese colony, Taiwan adopted Japan's voting system where "local factions are in fact connected to national factions" (Bosco, 1992, p. 164). During the Japanese colonial period, the landlords and peasants were involved in a landlord patronage system where the peasants were dependent on the landlords for physical protection and economic aid. The landlords had special access to the Japanese state, and they used their personal resources to maintain patron–client ties. The prewar landlord patronage system has been replaced today by faction machine patronage, where "faction leaders offer a channel to state resources" but "do not generally offer goods and services of their own" (Bosco, 1992, p. 167). Second, and as a consequence of adopting the Japanese voting system, Taiwan like Japan, is also vulnerable to vote-buying, which will be discussed in subsequent sections.

The CCP's defeat of the KMT forces under the leadership of Generalissimo Chiang Kai-shek is also significant because the rampant corruption in China under KMT rule was a major cause of the CCP's victory and the KMT's defeat. Keith Maguire (1998, p. 29) has identified significant differences between the CCP-controlled and KMT-controlled areas:

> In the red base areas, the communists paid for the food that they took and were strictly indoctrinated into being polite and friendly to the peasants. Education and health care were encouraged and there was a sound control of public finance. The administration of the KMT areas was a very different story. Looting was widespread and the troops were often poorly paid and low morale was the norm. Corruption was endemic with the result that the population had no particular sympathy for the KMT.

When the US Marines reached north China in late September 1945, they were appalled by the "filthy, poverty stricken, [and] unhealthy sanitary conditions." Graft and corruption prevailed in China, and "it was common for individuals to take advantage of their official position first to occupy a building and then to manipulate things in such a way as to have the building sold to them." An investigating committee found that "officials down to the soldiers are using the resources of the country as their personal property." The KMT officials believed that "as public functionaries they had suffered so much hardship and privation in the interior during the seven years of war that they had a right to indulge themselves." An Office of Strategic Services officer lamented that "graft and corruption prevail and the only winners are the

Communists" (Spector, 2007, pp. 56, 59–61). Hence, it was not surprising that "the web of corruption that had spread through Nationalist China eroded the regime's ability to defend itself" (Maguire, 1997, p. 76).

In short, the prevalence of corruption in Taiwan during the Japanese colonial period and after the Japanese surrender in September 1945 means that corruption is not a problem that can be easily resolved overnight.

### *Economy*

Taiwan's transformation from a poor country after the World War II to its economic affluence today is the result of its success in promoting economic growth and the effectiveness and stability of its financial sector. In 2008, Taiwan was the 22nd largest trading nation in the world, the 26th largest economy, and 7th in terms of official reserves held. Its GDP was US$403 billion, and its GDP per capita was US$17,050 in 2008. The services sector accounted for 71 percent of the GDP and employed 59 percent of the labor force. The goods-producing industries constituted 25 percent of the GDP and employed 37 percent of the work force. In contrast, agriculture contributed only 2 percent of the GDP and provided employment for 5 percent of the population (*Economist*, 2010a, pp. 24, 32, 36, 224).

Taiwan's economic affluence is also reflected in these communications data: there are 99.4 color television sets per 100 households; 62 telephone lines per 100 population; 110.3 mobile telephone subscribers per 100 population; and 272 Internet hosts per 1,000 population (*Economist*, 2010a, p. 225). More importantly, Taiwan's economic affluence means that the government has no difficulty in allocating sufficient personnel and financial resources to various ACAs to enable them to perform their anticorruption functions effectively. Thus, unlike other poorer developing countries, the Taiwanese government can afford to provide the multiple ACAs with adequate budgets and personnel to enforce the anticorruption laws impartially if it is committed to fighting corruption.

### *Demography*

Taiwan has a homogeneous population consisting of over 95 percent of Han Chinese and the remainder consisting of Austronesian (Malayo-Polynesian) peoples and recent immigrants. Its population in June 2009 was 23,069,000, with the 14 indigenous groups constituting 499,500. With the declining birth rate in the 1970s, Taiwan is now an aging society as the proportion of those aged 65 and older has increased from 2.5 percent in 1949 to 10.4 percent in 2008 (GIO, 2010, chap. 2).

As a predominantly Chinese society, Taiwan's major religions are Buddhism and Taoism (GIO, 2010, chap. 21). More importantly, there are two important aspects of Chinese culture that have important implications for Taiwan's efforts in curbing corruption. First, as will be discussed later, the concept of *guanxi* influences vote-buying and encourages corrupt behavior among the population. Second, gift-giving, which is an important social tradition among the Taiwanese, combined with the importance of *guanxi* not only encourages corruption but also makes it difficult for the ACAs to distinguish between gifts and bribes.

In other words, the social importance of *guanxi* and gift-giving for the Taiwanese not only makes them vulnerable to corruption and vote-buying but also makes it difficult for the ACAs to enforce the anticorruption laws impartially.

### *Political System*

Taiwan's political system has been transformed from an authoritarian system into a democracy in 2000, with the election of President Chen Shui-bian of the opposition DPP. The KMT's defeat by the CCP in October 1949 led to the relocation two months later of the KMT government under Chiang Kai-shek's leadership to Taiwan, which came under martial law and de facto one-party rule until July 1987, when President Chiang Ching-kuo ended nearly four decades of martial law. To maintain its power in mainland China, the KMT made alliances with the Shanghai Triad societies and some warlord cliques. The alliance with the Triad societies resulted in "an ethos of corruption in Chinese society that became endemic and entrenched over time" (Maguire, 1998, p. 5). Furthermore, the KMT leaders retained the allegiance of the regional warlords through bribery because it lacked the military resources to defeat them. The corrupt and repressive nature of the state resulted in "little popular loyalty to the state or the KMT," which "in turn became associated with corruption and repression" (Maguire, 1997, pp. 74–75). Indeed, the KMT had alienated the local population through its corruption and brutality (Maguire, 1998, p. 32).

The transformation of Taiwan's political system from authoritarianism to democracy after 51 years has two important implications for its anti-corruption strategy.[3] First, Taiwan's democratization is an important asset in the country's fight against corruption as it ensures that the political leaders are accountable for their actions. On the contrary, after four decades of authoritarian rule, the KMT had "accumulated problematic baggage: self-complacency, corruption, abuse of power, and arrogance" (Kau, 1996, p. 292). Apart from being "entrapped by its own historical baggage," the KMT had to deal with "the new problems of factionalism, money politics, and gangster influence" that accompanied the process of democratization (Kau, 1996, p. 301). Indeed, according to Bruce J. Dickson (2001, p. 128), a "hard lesson" to be learnt from Taiwan's democratization is that: "Democratization itself does not cure corruption, though it can make it more visible and easier to address."

## PERCEIVED EXTENT OF CORRUPTION

### *Bureaucratic Corruption*

The KMT initiated the reorganization of the civil service and conducted examinations from 1929 for the recruitment of civil servants. However, these examinations were ineffective in recruiting qualified candidates. Consequently, the civil service failed to meet the demand for competent officials because "the overwhelming majority of public servants gained their positions through other means that were less objective and impartial" (Ch'i, 1982, pp. 136–137). The civil service was ineffective as the low salaries of the junior civil servants made them vulnerable to corruption. In 1934, Chiang Kai-shek launched the New Life Movement to encourage the promotion of more traditional moral virtues "to fight against entrenched attitudes of graft and corruption" (Maguire, 1998, p. 23). The KMT's reorganization began with the purging of the C.C. clique, which was led by the two brothers, Chen Guo-fu and Chen Li-fu, because they were blamed for the KMT's endemic corruption (Maguire, 1998, p. 32).

Corruption was a serious problem during the KMT's rule on mainland China. The KMT government's ability to collect taxes was hindered not only by the war but also by "poor laws and improper management." Businessmen evaded the payment of taxes by concealing or falsifying their income records, and the tax administrators were corrupt and inexperienced. Consequently, the proportion of direct taxes decreased from 12 percent of the government's cash budgetary receipts in 1943 to 5 percent in 1944. Furthermore, the budgetary procedure was plagued by these weaknesses: haphazard preparation of budget requests by lower agencies; there was no system of priorities; faulty or nonexistent screening process; allocations were not based on merit but on personal and factional grounds; and, most important of all, "a very ineffective and often corrupt system of accounting to check on performance" (Ch'i, 1982, pp. 167, 169).

After the surrender of Japanese troops to the Allied command in Taiwan on October 25, 1945, Taiwan was transferred from Japan to the sovereignty of the Republic of China. Chiang Kai-shek appointed Chen Yi, the former governor of Fukien province, to head the executive team to administer Taiwan. Chen was not corrupt himself, but his subordinates were "opportunists and carpetbaggers who polluted the administrative core of the transitional government" (McBeath, 1998, p. 23). Indeed, he had replaced "the foreign, but efficient, Japanese colonial government with a regime preoccupied with mainland affairs and riddled with corruption" (Rigger, 1999, p. 56). Consequently, "bureaucratic corruption was rife, with payoffs to most KMT officials expected, expensive permits required for virtually every transaction, and mountains of time-consuming and expensive government red tape" (McBeath, 1998, p. 23). In other words, the KMT had "brought with it to Taiwan the epidemic of corruption that was sapping its strength on the mainland" as the *Min Pao* newspaper had reported six incidents of corruption over a 10-day period in early 1946 (Rigger, 1999, p. 57).

Some senior KMT members were corrupt, and corruption was also rampant in the army. Many senior generals in the Central Army had "taken advantage of their power in ways that involved unethical or illegal misuse of funds" (Taylor, 2009, p. 221). Apart from abuses of power by the senior officers, the Central Army was also afflicted by graft and nepotism (Taylor, 2009, p. 163). Corruption was also prevalent in the civil service because the civil servants' low salaries (Maguire, 1997, p. 81). Chiang Kai-shek acknowledged the problem of corruption in the KMT in his speech at the KMT's Party Congress in 1952 and initiated reforms in the KMT by excluding some senior leaders (Maguire, 1997, p. 77). He ordered banks to provide all individual and company account statements to the tax authorities and increased the salaries of the police and common soldiers but not for military officers (Taylor, 2009, pp. 487–488). The KMT and the army were purged and reorganized. To curb corruption in the civil service, the salaries and working conditions of civil servants were improved, the disciplinary code for corruption offenses was enhanced, and the "best of Taiwan's academic elite" were recruited (Maguire, 1997, pp. 81–82). However, in 1964, corruption "began creeping into what had been a comparatively honest bureaucracy" because civil service salaries had not kept up with inflation, thus forcing teachers and military officers to accept bribes to maintain their standards of living (Taylor, 2009, p. 525).

Perhaps the best way to gauge the extent of bureaucratic corruption in Taiwan is to analyze the data on corruption cases provided in the *Anti-Corruption Yearbooks* published by the Ministry of Justice Investigation Bureau (MJIB) from 1993 to 2009. Table 5.1 indicates that there were 6,350 corruption cases and 30,795 suspects during 1989–2009. Table 5.2 identifies the six common forms of corrupt practices in Taiwan during 1989–2002 with illicit gains (33.6 percent) being the most common practice, followed by malfeasance and other types (19.3 percent), bribery (17.7 percent), misappropriation of public funds (16.4 percent), and graft (13 percent).

Table 5.3 shows that civil servants constitute 47.6 percent of the 30,795 suspects from 1989–2009. It should be noted that during this 20-year period, civil servants constitute the majority during 11 years: from 1989 to 1998 and 2001. In contrast, the majority of the suspects are noncivil servants from 1999 to 2000 and from 2002 to 2009. Table 5.4 indicates that the four major types of

***Table 5.1.*** Corruption Cases and Suspects in Taiwan, 1989–2009.

| Year | No. of Cases | No. of Suspects |
|---|---|---|
| 1989 | 315 | 1,187 |
| 1990 | 480 | 1,586 |
| 1991 | 413 | 1,241 |
| 1992 | 272 | 703 |
| 1993 | 276 | 878 |
| 1994 | 299 | 913 |
| 1995 | 269 | 908 |
| 1996 | 272 | 1,022 |
| 1997 | 260 | 977 |
| 1998 | 239 | 752 |
| 1999 | 256 | 931 |
| 2000 | 247 | 946 |
| 2001 | 315 | 1,544 |
| 2002 | 264 | 932 |
| 2003 | 334 | 2,142 |
| 2004 | 309 | 2,233 |
| 2005 | 273 | 1,643 |
| 2006 | 254 | 2,056 |
| 2007 | 395 | 3,190 |
| 2008 | 301 | 2,753 |
| 2009 | 307 | 2,258 |
| Total | 6,350 | 30,795 |

*Sources*: Republic of China (1995–2003) and Republic of China (2009, pp. 219, 244, 2010, pp. 218, 220).

***Table 5.2.*** Types of Corrupt Practices in Taiwan, 1989–2002.

| Year | Illicit Gains | Malfeasance and Others | Bribery | Misappropriation of Public Funds | Graft | Total No. of Cases |
|---|---|---|---|---|---|---|
| 1989 | 149 | 7 | 73 | 56 | 30 | 315 |
| 1990 | 176 | 61 | 108 | 81 | 54 | 480 |
| 1991 | 157 | 52 | 74 | 82 | 48 | 413 |
| 1992 | 100 | 27 | 37 | 74 | 34 | 272 |
| 1993 | 112 | 33 | 56 | 41 | 34 | 276 |
| 1994 | 128 | 39 | 38 | 51 | 43 | 299 |
| 1995 | 85 | 54 | 47 | 46 | 37 | 269 |
| 1996 | 89 | 38 | 66 | 37 | 42 | 272 |
| 1997 | 70 | 65 | 46 | 36 | 43 | 260 |
| 1998 | 80 | 47 | 41 | 44 | 27 | 239 |
| 1999 | 79 | 72 | 31 | 35 | 39 | 256 |
| 2000 | 58 | 99 | 28 | 35 | 27 | 247 |
| 2001 | 70 | 114 | 52 | 36 | 43 | 315 |
| 2002 | 50 | 98 | 44 | 32 | 40 | 264 |
| Total | 1403 (33.6%) | 806 (19.3%) | 741 (17.7%) | 686 (16.4%) | 541 (13%) | 4177 (100%) |

*Source*: Republic of China (1995–2003).

corruption investigated by the MJIB from 1992 to 2002 are: public office election bribery (938 cases); public works construction (739 cases); judicial fraud (376 cases); and 195 cases of police corruption from 1995 to 2002 as data from 1992 to 1994 are not available.

Police corruption is the fourth most common type of corruption in Taiwan from 1995 to 2002 as Table 5.4 shows that there are 195 cases during this period. The police force in Taiwan is "marred by corruption, incompetence, and low morale." Indeed, police corruption is a serious problem in Taiwan because many local police officers are "closely affiliated with, and take bribes from, gangsters, politicians, and business owners within their jurisdictions" (Chin, 2003, p. 185). Apart from disciplinary problems, the police in Taiwan are plagued by many scandals. For example, in July 2006, the promotion of a corrupt police officer in Kaohsiung undermined police morale until a whistleblower revealed that the officer had received bribes. Three months later, four immigration police officers were arrested for accepting NT$5 million in bribes from a human smuggling syndicate that arranged the fraudulent marriages of 80 mainland Chinese women with Taiwanese men. In November 2006, nine police officers were prosecuted for accepting bribes from vice establishments and illegal casinos and mahjong parlors (Lo, 2008, pp. 72–73).

***Table 5.3.*** Corruption Suspects in Taiwan by Type, 1989–2009.

| Year | Civil Servants | Noncivil Servants | Total Suspects |
|---|---|---|---|
| 1989 | 678 (57.1%) | 509 (42.9%) | 1,187 (100%) |
| 1990 | 1,027 (64.8%) | 559 (35.2%) | 1,586 (100%) |
| 1991 | 817 (65.8%) | 424 (34.2%) | 1,241 (100%) |
| 1992 | 465 (66.1%) | 238 (33.9%) | 703 (100%) |
| 1993 | 531 (60.5%) | 347 (39.5%) | 878 (100%) |
| 1994 | 574 (62.9%) | 339 (37.1%) | 913 (100%) |
| 1995 | 599 (66.0%) | 309 (34.0%) | 908 (100%) |
| 1996 | 657 (64.3%) | 365 (35.7%) | 1,022 (100%) |
| 1997 | 513 (52.5%) | 464 (47.5%) | 977 (100%) |
| 1998 | 449 (59.7%) | 303 (40.3%) | 752 (100%) |
| 1999 | 431 (46.3%) | 500 (53.7%) | 931 (100%) |
| 2000 | 378 (40.0%) | 568 (60.0%) | 946 (100%) |
| 2001 | 874 (56.6%) | 670 (43.4%) | 1,544 (100%) |
| 2002 | 428 (46.0%) | 504 (54.0%) | 932 (100%) |
| 2003 | 746 (34.8%) | 1,396 (65.2%) | 2,142 (100%) |
| 2004 | 955 (42.8%) | 1,278 (57.2%) | 2,233 (100%) |
| 2005 | 689 (41.9%) | 954 (58.1%) | 1,643 (100%) |
| 2006 | 733 (35.7%) | 1,323 (64.3%) | 2,056 (100%) |
| 2007 | 1,234 (38.7%) | 1,956 (61.3%) | 3,190 (100%) |
| 2008 | 1,058 (38.4%) | 1,695 (61.6%) | 2,753 (100%) |
| 2009 | 808 (35.8%) | 1,450 (64.2%) | 2,258 (100%) |
| Total | 14,644 (47.6%) | 16,151 (52.4%) | 30,795 (100%) |

*Source*: As in Table 5.1.

The police force in Taiwan is closely linked with the underworld as more than 70 percent of its officers are from the counties of Changhua, Yunlin, Chiayi, and Pingtung, where most gangsters come from. This explains why the police and criminals "get along so well" since they originate from the same counties. Hence, it is not surprising that the police in Taiwan are "corruptible and act in ways that are not in the public interest but designed to protect their public image" (Chin, 2003, p. 185).

### *Vote-buying in Elections*

Vote-buying is defined as "the exchange of money or gifts for a vote" between candidates or their agents (vote brokers) and voters during an election campaign with the aim of winning the election (Wu and Huang, 2004, p. 757). Joseph Bosco (1992, p. 169) identifies two types of vote-buying

***Table 5.4.*** Cases Investigated by Major Types of Corruption, 1992–2002.

| Year | Public Office Election Bribery | Public Works Construction | Judicial Fraud | Police Corruption |
|---|---|---|---|---|
| 1992 | 21 | 47 | 62 | NA |
| 1993 | 13 | 49 | 51 | NA |
| 1994 | 128 | 46 | 43 | NA |
| 1995 | 70 | 42 | 35 | 31 |
| 1996 | 66 | 55 | 33 | 29 |
| 1997 | 10 | 106 | 40 | 29 |
| 1998 | 89 | 89 | 26 | 15 |
| 1999 | 39 | 56 | 25 | 20 |
| 2000 | 10 | 86 | 25 | 13 |
| 2001 | 67 | 88 | 23 | 23 |
| 2002 | 425 | 75 | 13 | 35 |
| Total | 938 | 739 | 376 | 195 |

*Sources*: Republic of China (1996, pp. 50–51, 2000a, p. 69, 2002, p. 66, 2003, p. 37).

in Taiwan. First, in most cases of vote-buying, the gift is usually money. In addition to money, many candidates give soap, towels, or china, and the KMT gives such gifts as pens, paperweights, and watches. Other gifts provided by candidates to influence voting include election banquets, transfer of loans, increasing employees' salaries, and payment of voters' tax bills (Wu and Huang, 2004, p. 757). For example, of the 91 cases of electoral corruption in 2007, 46 cases were vote-buying with money, 16 cases involved vote-buying with gifts, and 11 cases concerned vote-buying with meals. The most common gifts in vote-buying were tea, imported liquor, cigarettes, clothing and pots. For vote-buying with meals, the candidates paid for fund-raising parties, year-end parties, community parties, or company parties, and solicited votes from those attending these parties (Republic of China, 2008, pp. 31–32).

For vote-buying involving money, the amount was less than the value of a day's work. For example, voters in Wandan received between NT$200 (US$7.70) and NT$300 (US$11.50) for the township executive and NT$200 for County Assembly representative in January 1990. It should be noted that for this first type of vote-buying, "money does not buy votes but firms up the loyalty of supporters." Furthermore, the voters are obligated to accept the money offered because they know the donors and consider the money as a gift and not a purchase (Bosco, 1992, pp. 169–170).

Second, true vote-buying occurs when candidates have to spend more money per vote and to solicit in those areas where they would not receive support. In January 1990 Xinyuan Township election, votes were sold for between NT$500 and NT$600 (US$19 and US$23) each (Bosco, 1992, p. 170). However, the amount has increased to between NT$500 and NT$1,000 per vote for legislators, county or city counselors, or neighborhood heads in 2007. For the election of chairperson and vice-chairperson of township or town representative assemblies, the cost of a vote has increased to NT$500,000 (Republic of China, 2008, p. 31).

Faction leaders and candidates rely on *tiau-a-ka* or vote brokers to influence voters to vote for them. Accordingly, candidates reward *tiau-a-ka* with money and gifts and entertain them with banquets and trips during election campaigns. Candidates in a Taipei City election paid these amounts to their vote brokers: NT$10,000 to NT$20,000 (US$400 to US$800) and such gifts as cassette recorders, calculators, tea pot sets etc. to ward leaders; NT$10,000 (US$400) to subdistrict committee chairpersons; NT$5,000 (US$200) to subdistrict committee secretariats and ward administrators; and NT$2,000 (US$80) to neighborhood leaders (Rigger, 1999, pp. 87, 92).

Furthermore, vote-buying also depends on the target. For the direct elections of the president, city mayor, county magistrate, township mayor, village chief and other elected public representatives, the target of vote-buying is a citizen who has the right to vote. However, for the election of speaker and deputy assembly speaker, those public representatives who can vote for these positions are the targets of vote-buying. Generally, the targets of vote-buying in local elections are easier to monitor, and vote-buying is more effective in such elections because of the smaller electoral districts with fewer voters (Wu and Huang, 2004, p. 757).

There are two functions of vote-buying. The first function of vote-buying is the redistribution of wealth where "the poor voter exchanges the political 'power' of his vote for money while the wealthy politician exchanges his wealth for power." In Taiwan, this function of vote-buying is secondary because "each vote is worth about one-third of a day's wages" in contrast to the Philippines where each vote is equivalent to a month's income (Jacobs, 2008, pp. 176–177). However, in Taiwan, the second function of vote-buying is to make the voters aware of the candidates competing in the election. This function is more important because it makes the voters aware of the campaign and encourages them to vote. Thus, vote-buying increases popular participation and the voters' awareness of the political process.

During 1994–1995, seven local elections were held in Taiwan involving 14 million voters, who elected more than 13,000 people's representatives and

***Table 5.5.*** Prosecuted Vote-Buying Cases Investigated by MJIB, 1993–2009.

| Year | No. of Vote-buying Cases Investigated |
|---|---|
| 1993 | 13 |
| 1994 | 121 |
| 1995 | 35 |
| 1996 | 54 |
| 1997 | 52 |
| 1998 | 92 |
| 1999 | 39 |
| 2000 | 11 |
| 2001 | 155 |
| 2002 | 435 |
| 2003 | 81 |
| 2004 | 32 |
| 2005 | 369 |
| 2006 | 497 |
| 2007 | 91 |
| 2008 | 148 |
| 2009 | 102 |
| Total | 2,327 |

*Source*: Republic of China (2010, p. 234).

heads of provincial, county, city, township, and village governments. However, the emergence of money politics prompted the government to initiate large-scale investigations, searches, seizures, and arrests on vote-buying in many parts of Taiwan during and after the elections in 1994. The government found that there was vote-buying in 18 of 23 cities and counties, and 341 councilmen (or 39 percent of all the 883 councilmen) were indicted (Ma, 1995, p. 1). On November 30, 2001, the Justice Minister Chen Ding-nan revealed that 3,509 vote captains were arrested for their involvement in bribery cases related to the December 2001 legislative election (Chuang, 2001, p. 1). Table 5.5 shows that 2,327 prosecuted vote-buying cases were investigated by the MJIB from 1993 to 2009.

### *Heijin or "Black Gold" Politics*

In Taiwan, the literal meaning of *heijin* is "black gold" as *hei* or black refers to gangsters or the underworld, and *jin* means money or rich businessmen

(Clark, 2002, p. 148). More specifically, Ko-lin Chin (2003, pp. 5, 8) has defined "black gold" politics as "the penetration into politics of violent underworld figures and greedy business tycoons and the inevitable subsequent social ills such as vote buying, political violence, insider trading, bid rigging, and official (and unofficial) corruption." A related term, *heidao*, means "the black way" and refers to the underworld in Taiwan.

The abolition of martial law in Taiwan had the unintended consequence of escalating gang violence because of the availability of handguns and the release of those criminals who were arrested during "Operation Clean-sweep" in October 1984. Some of these criminals transformed themselves into businessmen and politicians and called themselves *dongshizhang* (chairmen of the board) and *mindai* (elected representatives), respectively. Consequently, "Operation Thunderbolt" was launched in 1990 to destroy the Celestial Alliance, which was formed in prisons by those crime bosses who were arrested in 1984 (Chin, 2003, p. 7).

As Taiwan became more democratic in the early 1990s with the emergence of many political parties, many gangsters realized that they had to become politicians to protect themselves from future crackdowns. The increased involvement of gangsters in politics and business resulted in "Operation Chih-ping" in 1996, which targeted gangsters who were local politicians (Baum, 1996, pp. 18–20). Ma Ying-jeou, who was the Minister of Justice from 1993–1996, led "Operation Chih-ping," which resulted in the arrest of 100 gangsters, including some politicians (White, 2009, p. 334). However, in spite of these crackdowns, the crime rate in Taiwan increased by nearly three times during 1961–1997 (Chin, 2003, pp. 168–179).

How serious is the problem of "black gold" politics in Taiwan? In 1994, the MJIB's director-general, Wu Tung-ming, revealed that 62 councilors had *heidao* (underworld) backgrounds. During the same year, the National Police Agency's (NPA's) Hoodlum Division indicated that there were 28 hoodlums, 29 gangsters, and 150 individuals with *heidao* connections among 883 city and county councilors. Intelligence reports in 1995 estimated that 37.8 percent of town representatives had *heidao* backgrounds, followed by 26.5 percent of county and city councilors, and 3 percent of the national representatives. In his November 16, 1996, speech to the business community, the Minister of Justice, Liao Cheng-hao, informed his audience that 286 councilors or one-third of the 858 city and county councilors had links to the underworld. He added that 25 percent of the Provincial Assembly members and 5 percent of the legislators and National Assembly deputies had *heidao* backgrounds. In 1997, the NPA Commissioner declared that almost all the chairpersons and members of the Law and Order Committees of the elected bodies had *heidao* affiliations.

Finally, the president of Academia Sinica, Lee Yuan-tseh, claimed that half of the elected deputies had *heidao* backgrounds (Chin, 2003, p. 15).

The term "black gold" evokes the nexus between bribery and gangsters, and the Taiwanese people are aware that it is a serious problem through their knowledge of vote-buying in local and national elections and the collusion between civil servants, politicians, and gangsters in bid rigging. In their view, *heijin* is "linked with the $6 billion in assets on which the KMT reportedly draws to buy votes" (Cheng, 2000, p. 24). Indeed, the KMT has been blamed for the development of "black gold" politics because it has cultivated the support of gangsters and *jiaotou* (local crime groups) figures to ensure that its candidates win elections (Chin, 2003, pp. 14–15).

However, it is more accurate to attribute the development of "black gold" politics in Taiwan to the symbiosis or convergence of interests between the three stakeholders: businessmen, gangsters, and politicians. First, businessmen prefer to be associated with politicians because those enterprises that are closely related with powerful politicians are more likely to get government contracts and receive government aid when they are in financial distress and also "less likely to be targeted by law enforcement authorities for irregular business practices" (Chin, 2003, p. 16). Businessmen also like to be associated with gangsters to provide protection against gang victimization and help them settle business disputes in private. Businessmen who run for public office also rely on gangsters in their election campaigns.

Second, gangsters benefit from the protection provided by politicians from law enforcement authorities. Elected deputies usually visit police stations to ensure the quick release of their constituents if they are arrested. Politicians also help gang members from being harassed by police raids on their vice businesses. Similarly, businessmen provide gangsters with many opportunities for making money and help them by patronizing their gambling operations (Chin, 2003, pp. 17–18).

Third, politicians rely on businessmen to provide them with campaign funds. They also associate with gangsters because gang members are good vote captains. In other words, "money from businessmen can help politicians buy votes, and intimidation from the gangs can ensure the efficiency of vote buying" (Chin, 2003, p. 16).

Unlike the problem of mob penetration into business and politics in other countries, Ko-lin Chin (2003, p. 19) contends that "black gold" politics in Taiwan is "qualitatively different" because the integration of the upperworld and underworld has contributed to the "development of a morally confusing society where politicians are talking and acting like gangsters and gangsters are talking and acting like politicians."

## CAUSES OF CORRUPTION

### *Low salaries*

Surveys conducted in many Asian countries confirm the significance of low salaries as this has been identified as an important cause of corruption by the respondents. As civil service salaries in Taiwan have improved with the country's economic growth, the salary differential between the public and the private sectors today is a more important cause of corruption than low salaries, which was a key factor in the past.

Historically, the best example of using high salaries to prevent corruption in Taiwan was reflected in the honesty of the Japanese judicial officials during the colonial period. While the judiciary was criticized by many Taiwanese antigovernment political organizations during the Japanese colonial period, there was no doubt that the Japanese judges and procurators were honest because of their high rank, high salaries, and high social status. On the contrary, the magistrates during Ch'ing imperial rule (1683–1895) were corrupt because their official salaries were "so low that they could neither support their families and private legal staff nor make 'presents' to their superiors. It was only natural that they accepted bribes from litigants" (Wang, 2000, p. 86).

As discussed earlier, low salaries was an important reason for the civil service's ineffectiveness in Taiwan during the 1930s. Keith Maguire (1998, p. 23) observed that "the salary levels of the lower echelons of the bureaucracy were so bad that corruption became necessary in order for those officials to survive." He had attributed the endemic corruption in the civil service to the "poor" salaries of civil servants (Maguire, 1997, p. 81). Furthermore, the KMT government's "irresponsible fiscal policy" resulted in inflation as the "incomes of salaried workers had increased only 31 times over the 1937 level, but the cost of living had increased 183 times" by December 1943. Consequently, many qualified persons did not join the civil service because "they could not make ends meet with their official salaries." Some civil servants "had to hold several jobs at the same time in order to draw several salaries concurrently, or to pursue sideline businesses to supplement their official incomes." However, many civil servants "simply threw their scruples to the winds and indulged in reckless corruption" (Ch'i, 1982, p. 175).

Accordingly, salaries and working conditions in the civil service were improved to attract the "best and brightest" Taiwanese to become civil servants (Maguire, 1997, pp. 81–82). However, by 1964, corruption was rearing its ugly head again because civil service salaries failed to keep up with the rising inflation and teachers and army officers were forced to accept bribes to maintain their living standards (Taylor, 2009, p. 525). To prevent corruption in the Customs Department in the late 1950s and early 1960s, the customs officials were paid higher salaries that were double those of other civil servants. Furthermore, the harsh penalties imposed for corruption also discouraged customs staff from engaging in corrupt practices. Thus, apart from minimizing corruption, the higher salaries also enabled the Customs Department to attract many talented graduates (Jenkins, Kuo and Sun, 2003, p. 186).

The salaries of the political leaders in Taiwan are lower than the salaries of their counterparts in Singapore, Hong Kong, Japan, and South Korea.[4] The president of Taiwan has an annual salary of US$180,000, followed by the prime minister, who earns US$121,500 yearly, and ministers with annual salaries of US$72,000. These salaries are higher than the salaries of political leaders in Malaysia, Thailand, Philippines, Indonesia, Vietnam, and Cambodia (Backman, 2004, pp. 26–28). Similarly, the salaries of Taiwanese civil servants are also lower than the salaries of their counterparts in Singapore, Hong Kong, Japan, and South Korea, but higher than the salaries of civil servants in Malaysia, Thailand, Philippines, Indonesia, Vietnam, and Cambodia. Tables 5.6 and 5.7 provide details of the monthly salaries of administrative officers and civil servants respectively in Taiwan.

While Taiwanese civil servants are not poorly paid when compared to their counterparts in such Asian countries as Malaysia, Thailand, Philippines, Indonesia, Vietnam, or Cambodia, what is perhaps more important is the salary gap between the public and the private sectors in Taiwan. This salary gap was first highlighted by Robert Wade (1990, p. 219) two decades ago:

***Table 5.6.*** Monthly Salaries of Administrative Officers.

| Job Title | Monthly Salary |
|---|---|
| Five Academy Department Head, Office of the Premier | NT$314,080 (US$10,557) |
| Five Academy Deputy Department Head, Office of Premier | NT$208,080 (US$6,994) |
| Various Ministers | NT$184,960 (US$6,217) |
| Various Deputy Ministers | NT$161,020 (US$5,413) |

*Source*: Data provided by the Central Personnel Administration in Taipei.
*Note*: The exchange rate was US$1 = NT$29.75 on February 25, 2011.

*Table 5.7.* Monthly Salaries of Civil Servants.

| Job Title | Monthly Salary |
|---|---|
| 14th Grade Permanent Secretary | NT$140,920 (US$4,736) |
| Director of the 13th Grade | NT$113,490 (US$3,814) |
| Division Director of the 12th Grade | NT$108,280 (US$3,639) |
| Deputy Division Director of the 11th Grade | NT$92,725 (US$3,116) |
| Director of the 10th Grade | NT$83,560 (US$2,808) |
| Chief of the 9th Grade | NT$68,780 (US$2,311) |
| Section Chief of the 8th Grade | NT$62,945 (US$2,115) |
| Chief of the 7th Grade | NT$56,545 (US$1,900) |
| Section Officer of the 6th Grade | NT$48,725 (US$1,638) |
| Section Officer of the 5th Grade | NT$42,050 (US$1,413) |
| Office Worker of the 4th Grade | NT$39,295 (US$1,321) |
| Office Worker of the 3rd Grade | NT$37,780 (US$1,270) |
| Clerk of the 2nd Grade | NT$34,490 (US$1,159) |
| Clerk of the 1st Grade | NT$28,470 (US$957) |

*Source*: Data provided by the Central Personnel Administration in Taipei.
*Note*: The exchange rate was US$1 = NT$29.75 on February 25, 2011.

> Salary differentials are large – commonly 30 to 50 percent lower in the government than in the large-scale private sector. For example, a thirty-seven year-old deputy division chief, in a division of about twenty people, with thirteen years' experience in IDB [Industrial Development Bureau], gets NT$30,000 a month plus an extra month's bonus, before tax. Private firms have offered her twice as much for starters. Her boss, forty-three years old, makes NT$33,000, and could easily double his salary in the private sector. Yet they stay, and fairly happily.

Wade contends that the gap between civil service salaries and private sector salaries makes civil servants vulnerable to bribes from businessmen. He wrote:

> Personal connections may be sweetened with money.... Taiwan businesspeople know the techniques of negotiating bribe money with officialdom as a fine art. They listen for what the official says about the cost of living, what he says about his hobbies. They may bring him a cookie box full of money, present it to him as a gift for his children, and wait to see if he returns the box and contents. Or they may simply leave him with a 'red envelope,' as it is called, full of 'gift' money. Such special persuasion is concentrated in the expected places: in offices of public works, taxes, urban planning, customs, duty rebates, and traffic police. (Wade, 1990, pp. 286–287)

While civil servants earn lower salaries than their private sector counterparts, it should be recognized that their salaries are also more stable, and they enjoy more benefits including a generous retirement package (Wang, 1995, pp. 6–7). In February 2009, the president of the Examination Yuan, John

Kuan, explained why Taiwan would not follow Singapore's decision to reduce the salaries of senior civil servants and ministers by 19 percent because of the economic recession:

> Singapore's situation was different from Taiwan's, in that senior civil servants there are offered very high salaries and a percentage of their annual salary is linked to GDP growth, while Taiwan's civil servants are not particularly highly paid and their salaries are fixed. The financial crisis should not affect the salaries of civil servants in Taiwan because government expenditure for personnel is less than 1 percent of GDP. (*Taipei Times*, 2009, p. 3)

Four months later, the Central Personnel Administration (CPA) confirmed that Taiwan would not follow what Hong Kong, Singapore, and South Korea did because it was "evidently improper" to cut the salaries of senior civil servants in Taiwan, which have remained the same for four years after an increase of 3 percent in 2005. According to the CPA:

> The new monthly salary for a ministerial-level official in Hong Kong would be NT$1.3 million (US$39,900), seven times higher than the monthly payment of NT$185,000 for a ministerial-level in Taiwan, while a Singaporean minister's annual income is NT$20 million, much higher than the NT$2.5 million of their counterparts in Taiwan. (Executive Yuan, 2009)

### *Red Tape*

Table 5.8 shows that, according to the World Bank's *Doing Business Surveys* from 2007 to 2011, red tape is still a problem in Taiwan as it is ranked 47th for the ease of doing business among the 175 economies surveyed in 2007. The problem deteriorated during the next two years as Taiwan's rank for the ease of doing business has declined further to 50th position in 2008, and to 61st position in 2009 among the 178–181 economies in the two surveys. However, the trend is reversed in 2010 because Taiwan's rank has improved to 46th position with a further improvement to 33rd position in 2011.

Table 5.8 also confirms the prevalence of red tape in Taiwan as it is ranked 94th for starting a business in 2007 because it requires eight procedures, takes 48 days and costs 4.6 percent of the income per capita. Taiwan is ranked 148th during the same year for dealing with construction permits, which requires 32 procedures, takes 206 days, and costs 231.9 percent of the income per capita. However, in terms of registering property, Taiwan is ranked 24th in 2007 requiring three procedures and five days and costing 6.2 percent of the property value. Taiwan's improvement in the ease

***Table 5.8.*** Ease of Doing Business in Taiwan, 2007–2011.

| Indicator | 2007 (*N* = 175) | 2008 (*N* = 178) | 2009 (*N* = 181) | 2010 (*N* = 183) | 2011 (*N* = 183) |
|---|---|---|---|---|---|
| Ease of doing business (rank) | 47 | 50 | 61 | 46 | 33 |
| Starting a business (rank) | 94 | 103 | 119 | 29 | 24 |
| No. of procedures | 8 | 8 | 8 | 6 | 6 |
| Time (days) | 48 | 48 | 42 | 23 | 15 |
| Cost (% of income per capita) | 4.6 | 4.1 | 4.1 | 3.9 | 4.1 |
| Dealing with construction permits or licenses (rank) | 148 | 128 | 127 | 97 | 95 |
| No. of procedures | 32 | 30 | 29 | 28 | 28 |
| Time (days) | 206 | 198 | 193 | 142 | 142 |
| Cost (% of income per capita) | 231.9 | 206.9 | 123.6 | 96.2 | 100.9 |
| Registering property (rank) | 24 | 24 | 26 | 30 | 32 |
| No. of procedures | 3 | 3 | 3 | 3 | 3 |
| Time (days) | 5 | 5 | 5 | 5 | 5 |
| Cost (% of property value) | 6.2 | 6.2 | 6.2 | 6.2 | 6.2 |
| CPI Rank and Score | 34 (5.7) | 39 (5.7) | 37 (5.6) | 33 (5.8) | NA |

*Sources*: World Bank (2006b, p. 145, 2007, p. 154, 2008, p. 138, 2009, p. 156, 2010a, p. 198).

of doing business to 33rd position in 2011 is also reflected in starting a business and dealing with construction permits or licenses. In terms of starting a business, Taiwan's rank has improved tremendously from 94th to 24th position during 2007–2011 with the reduction of time taken from 48 to 15 days. Similarly, the time required to obtain a construction permit has been reduced from 206 to 142 days with an improvement of its ranking from 148th to 95th position during the same period.

Taiwan has made progress in making it easier to do business by reducing red tape as manifested in its improved rankings on the World Bank's *Doing Business Surveys* from 2007 to 2011. In his analysis of government reforms in Taiwan from 1990 to 2006, Jay N. Shih (2007, pp. 306, 311–312) observed that both the KMT and the DPP governments had introduced the single-stop window, simplification of functions, relaxation of regulations, and e-Government to improve efficiency. However, with the exception of e-Government, which has been the "greatest achievement," Taiwan's efforts to improve its national competitiveness have been hindered by its "poor performance in promoting government efficiency." Indeed, there is still "too much red-tape and too many personnel management rigidities" that hinder the government's efforts to promote flexibility, innovation and productivity. As red tape remains a problem, the *Taipei Times* has recommended the reduction of red tape to curb corruption in Taiwan thus:

> More muddled regulations mean more administration [*sic*] discretion, which in turn means more opportunities for corruption. Administrative regulations, such as business licensing rules, should be clear and transparent. They also need to be implemented efficiently. Taiwan's many bristling, muddled regulations allow for bribery between government officials and businesses. Simple, transparent rules and efficient administration are the most important tools for preventing corruption. (*Taipei Times*, 2001, p. 8)

### *Low Probability of Detection and Punishment for Corrupt Offenders*

What is the punishment for corrupt offenses in Taiwan? As will be discussed in the section on Taiwan's anticorruption measures, Article 4 of the Anti-Corruption Statute of 1963 states that those found guilty of the five corruption offenses will be imprisoned from 10 years to life and fined a maximum amount of NT$100 million. The penalty for accepting donations from foreign groups or foreigners is five years imprisonment. However, the penalty for accepting other donations is reduced to one year of imprisonment, detention, or a fine of NT$30,000. The penalty for election bribery is imprisonment of five years, detention, or a fine of NT$150,000. Article 142 of the Criminal Code states that a person who interferes with another person's right to vote will be punished by a prison term of five years. Article 143 indicates that voters demanding or accepting bribes to vote for certain candidates in elections will be imprisoned for three years and fined NT$5,000. Finally, according to Article 144, those persons who promise, offer, or give bribes to qualified voters to influence them to vote for particular candidates will be punished with imprisonment of five years and a fine of NT$7,000 (Republic of China, 1995, p. 314).

Articles 89 and 90-1 of the Public Officials Election and Recall Law of 1980 have increased the penalty for election bribery. Article 89 indicates that the punishment for a person who bribes a candidate to withdraw from the election is imprisonment of five years and a fine of between NT$600,000 to NT$6 million. Article 90-1 states that a person who bribes a qualified voter "from exercising his/her right to vote" will be imprisoned for five years and fined between NT$400,000 and NT$4 million.[5]

How likely are offenders in Taiwan punished if they are caught for committing corrupt acts or election bribery? Table 5.9 shows first that the

***Table 5.9.*** Judicial Results of Corruption Cases in Taiwan, 1991–2002.

| Year | Not Prosecuted | Not Guilty First Trial Verdict | Verdict Upheld by Supreme Court | Total |
|---|---|---|---|---|
| 1991 | 56 (60.2%) | 29 (31.2%) | 8 (8.6%) | 93 (100%) |
| 1992 | 26 (48.2%) | 18 (33.3%) | 10 (18.5%) | 54 (100%) |
| 1993 | 25 (67.6%) | 4 (10.8%) | 8 (21.6%) | 37 (100%) |
| 1994 | 15 (42.8%) | 10 (28.6%) | 10 (28.6%) | 35 (100%) |
| 1995 | 33 (36.3%) | 26 (28.6%) | 32 (35.1%) | 91 (100%) |
| 1996 | 47 (53.4%) | 17 (19.3%) | 24 (27.3%) | 88 (100%) |
| 1997 | 34 (36.2%) | 26 (27.6%) | 34 (36.2%) | 94 (100%) |
| 1998 | 59 (59.6%) | 20 (20.2%) | 20 (20.2%) | 99 (100%) |
| 1999 | 54 (62.8%) | 15 (17.4%) | 17 (19.8%) | 86 (100%) |
| 2000 | 35 (54.7%) | 12 (18.7%) | 17 (26.6%) | 64 (100%) |
| 2001 | 27 (56.2%) | 6 (12.5%) | 15 (31.3%) | 48 (100%) |
| 2002 | 34 (65.4%) | 4 (7.7%) | 14 (26.9%) | 52 (100%) |
| Total | 445 (52.9%) | 187 (22.2%) | 209 (24.9%) | 841 (100%) |

*Sources*: Republic of China (1996, p. 33, 1998, pp. 44–46, 2000, pp. 44–49, 2002, pp. 44–47, 2003, pp. 91–94).

proportion of corruption cases that are not prosecuted ranges from 36.2 percent in 1997 to 67.6 percent in 1993. Second, the proportion of corruption cases that are found not guilty varies from 10.8 percent in 1993 to 33.3 percent in 1992. Third, the proportion of those corruption cases found guilty ranges from 8.6 percent in 1991 to 36.2 percent in 1997. Fourth, and perhaps most importantly, more than half (52.9 percent) of the corruption cases from 1991 to 2002 are not prosecuted, almost one-quarter (24.9 percent) of the corruption cases are found guilty, with the remaining 22.2 percent of the corruption cases found not guilty. In short, the probability of being convicted for corruption cases in Taiwan is not high as only 209 or 24.9 percent of the 841 corruption cases investigated during 1991–2002 are found guilty.

Larry Diamond (2001, p. 10) has identified an important reason for the low probability of punishment of corrupt public officials in Taiwan. According to him, while the Control Yuan can impeach corrupt public officials, their punishment is decided by a committee of the Judicial Yuan. Consequently, "many impeached officials never get seriously punished, giving the Control Yuan the image of a toothless tiger."

Cheng-tian Kuo (2000, pp. 99–100) has criticized the judiciary system in Taiwan for not being politically neutral. He substantiated his argument by referring to the charging of 434 local representatives in 1994 by the state attorney's office for their involvement in bribery cases involving the election of local assembly speakers and deputy-speakers. The lower courts found 381 of the representatives guilty, but the higher courts, "famous for their institutional corruption," upheld only 37 of the guilty verdicts and "sent the others free or imposed probation only." In other words, 87.8 percent of the 434 local representatives arrested by the state attorney's office were found guilty by the lower courts, but only 37 guilty verdicts (9.7 percent) were upheld by the higher courts. The judges exonerated the politicians because vote-buying was viewed as part of Taiwan's electoral culture and "a pseudo norm for politicians." Similarly, a 1997 Ministry of Justice (MOJ) survey found that from 1993 to 1996 the punishment for those found guilty of vote-buying was not severe as 82 percent were sentenced to imprisonment for less than a year, and 67 percent were sentenced to probation only.

Weng Yu-jung (1996, pp. 388–389), a judge with 25 years experience has given two reasons for the low conviction rate for corruption and malfeasance cases in Taiwan. First, if direct evidence is lacking in these cases, it is difficult to obtain an admission of guilt from the suspect "if there is any oversight in tracking down evidence, or during the trial, if an unethical lawyer makes trouble, the result is that some of the evidence gained through great difficulty falls a bit short of the mark and the case is not tried, or the suspect is found not guilty." Second, according to Weng, "the gap between reasonable suspicion and compelling evidence is another primary reason that a not guilty verdict is handed down after charges are pressed." Similarly, Yen Da-ho, the director of the MOJ's Department of Prosecutorial Affairs, has observed that it is difficult to track the act of election bribery because "vote-buying often takes the form of oral agreements, without any written records" and "the bribe money can easily be disguised as personal loans" (Lin, 2000a, p. 4).

In short, even though vote-buying is illegal in Taiwan, it is seldom reported. Furthermore, even when vote-buying is reported, it is rarely investigated, and such investigations usually do not lead to convictions because of insufficient evidence.

### Guanxi, *Gift-giving, and Vote-buying*

Cultural factors like *guanxi* and the tradition of gift-giving constitute a fourth important cause of corruption in Taiwan because these factors encourage vote-buying. Yadong Luo (2007, p. 2) defines *guanxi* as "the concept of drawing on connections in order to secure favors in personal relations" and "includes reciprocal obligations to respond to requests for assistance." Gift-giving is a common tradition in many Asian countries, including Taiwan. Vote-buying is important in local elections in Taiwan because it cements the connection between *guanxi* and gift-giving. On the one hand, most of the votes in rural elections in Taiwan are "bought, sold and cast on the basis of *guanxi*" as candidates cannot buy votes unless they have a close *guanxi* with the voters (Jacobs, 2008, p. 177). As gift-giving is an important social tradition in Taiwan, the voters do not object to vote-buying because they have a close *guanxi* with the candidates and therefore view the money offered as a gift and not as a bribe for their votes. Vote-buying is acceptable to most voters because they consider it as "a form of gift-giving intended to demonstrate a candidate's compassion, good will or respect" (Schaffer, 2004, p. 84). Nevertheless, the reality is that gifts reinforce the personal relationships between the candidates and voters, and cast "the shadow of corruption over elections" in Taiwan (Rigger, 1999, p. 88).

Elections have been held at the local level after the relocation of the KMT government from mainland China to Taiwan in December 1949. However, elections at the national level have only been held since 1969. Two types of voting systems are used for both local and national elections in Taiwan: the single-member district (SMD) plurality system for the election of administrative officers such as county magistrates and city mayors; and the single nontransferable vote (SNTV) system for the election of the members of the legislative bodies at various levels (Hsieh, 1996, p. 195). The most serious weakness of the SNTV system is that it encourages vote-buying and corruption because its candidates rely "heavily on personal connections, money, or physical force" that "pollutes the electoral process" (Hsieh, 1996, p. 209).

In short, an important cause of corruption in Taiwan is the powerful combination of *guanxi*, gift-giving, and vote-buying, which has been sustained by the SNTV system for local elections and until 2005, for national elections. However, it remains to be seen whether the introduction of the mixed-member system has reduced vote-buying in the 2008 Legislative Yuan election.

### *Lack of Political Will*

The best way to demonstrate the importance of political will in curbing corruption in Taiwan is to examine how Chiang Kai-shek and his successors have dealt with the problem of corruption. Among the five presidents who have governed Taiwan during the past six decades, only Chiang Ching-kuo and Ma Ying-jeou have demonstrated their commitment to fighting corruption.

In December 1925, Chiang Kai-shek announced that a major goal in preparing for the Northern Expedition was to curb corruption in the military. Accordingly, he ordered the military supply bureau to provide funds directly to the divisions and did not allow any military unit to manage its money. However, most of his army commanders "simply rejected his proposal to centralize military financial matters," and Chiang was forced to "give the fight against corruption much lower priority" to maintain cohesion and loyalty among his civilian and military allies (Taylor, 2009, pp. 50–51).

After re-locating his government to Taiwan, Chiang Kai-shek served as president from March 1950 until his death in April 1975. Chiang set an example by maintaining a "notably modest or ascetic" lifestyle himself and believed that KMT officers and officials should uphold high professional standards and private morals. However, he failed to centralize financial arrangements and curb corruption in the military because he was compelled to give lower priority to fighting corruption than promoting cohesion and loyalty among his civilian and military supporters. Thus, Chiang tolerated corruption, which was of secondary importance because it was not rampant, and he believed that it should only be dealt with after the restoration of peace and unity (Taylor, 2009, pp. 222, 330).

Unlike his father, Chiang Ching-kuo was concerned about curbing corruption in Shanghai in the late 1940s and was aware of the damage that corruption had caused to the KMT on the mainland (Maguire, 1997, p. 78). After his appointment as vice premier in June 1969, Ching-kuo launched an anticorruption drive that exposed the "pervasive graft in the banana business" (Taylor, 2009, p. 541). On June 10, 1972, he issued to all civil servants the "Ten Rules of Reform" and "Ten Taboos," which did not permit them to patronize "girlie restaurants," "black coffee shops," or karaoke bars, or to host large wedding and funeral banquets. These rules were enforced by police officers who visited the proscribed establishments and checked the identity cards of the customers. Consequently, some officials were fired for hosting extravagant weddings (Taylor, 2009, p. 580, 2000, p. 310).

He also initiated a crackdown on bribe-taking and abuse of office that resulted in the arrests of 50 officers in the Garrison Command by the Investigation Bureau. The director-general of the Government Personnel Bureau, Wang Cheng-yi, was charged with taking a large bribe from a building contractor. Ching-kuo personally approved Wang's arrest and life sentence even though Wang was his cousin (Taylor, 2000, pp. 310–311). The vice director of the Tax Bureau, who was also found guilty of corruption, was sentenced to death (Taylor, 2009, p. 580). During his term of office, the government and provincial bureaucracy did not tolerate political corruption and punished those found guilty of such behavior. Consequently, his officials did not want to associate with prominent business persons (Myers, Chao and Kuo, 2002, p. 81).

Chiang Ching-kuo died in January 1988 and was succeeded by the vice president, Lee Teng-hui, who continued Ching-kuo's program to democratize Taiwan's political system. However, unlike his predecessor, Lee was not committed to curbing political and bureaucratic corruption during his term of office. Lee's personal friendships with business tycoons encouraged them to use their friendship with him to obtain political favors. As Lee had cultivated them when he was governor of Taiwan, he asked them to finance his electoral campaigns during the democratic era (Moody, 2002, p. 35). Consequently, with the broadening of elections after 1990, the scale and cost of vote-buying increased because many KMT candidates believed that they could only be elected if they resorted to vote-buying with local political factions. Furthermore, the Lee administration did not punish KMT candidates who had engaged in vote-buying (Myers et al., 2002, p. 81).

Ya-li Lu (2002, p. 65) contends that Lee Teng-hui has "worsened" the problem of corruption in two ways. First, in competing with his political rivals, he usually requested the support of the local politicians and tolerated their misconduct in return for their support. Second, among Lee's close friends, there were many leading businessmen who relied on their connections with senior government officials to obtain favors such as huge loans from public banks.

Taiwan became a liberal democracy under Lee Teng-hui's leadership, but he was also responsible for the "rampant spread" of "black gold" politics (*Taipei Times*, 2000, p. 8). Sharing this assessment, Jacobs and Liu (2007) argued that while he had played an important role in Taiwan's democratization, Lee had also contributed to the growth of "black gold" politics and vote-buying. They wrote:

> Under his [Lee's] leadership, during the first half of the 1990s, the KMT nominated many "black and gold" (that is, criminal and wealthy) figures for office and the number of criminals holding high office rose considerably. Some county leaders were murdered and others have been jailed or run away overseas to avoid prosecution. Vote-buying became rife and the old "morality" in vote-buying disappeared. (Jacobs & Liu, 2007, p. 392)

The analysis of Chen Shui-bian's corruption scandal at the outset of this chapter has shown that while he had campaigned on an anticorruption platform for the 2000 presidential election, he and his immediate family had succumbed to corruption during his two terms of office as president. Chen's arrest in November 2008 on suspicion of corruption and his subsequent trial and conviction was viewed positively by many citizens, who were heartened that corruption was being attacked and that he could stand trial like any common citizen (*Economist*, 2009a).

Ma Ying-jeou campaigned the 2008 presidential election on an anti-corruption platform and promised to (1) amend the law to punish civil servants who cannot identify the source of their assets; (2) revise the Criminal Code by adding a clause to punish government officials who cannot account for the origin of their properties and other assets; (3) amend the Public Officials Election and Recall Law to apply the penalties for vote-buying in official elections to elections held within all political parties; and (4) revise the Public Functionary Assets Disclosure Law to punish those who fail to report their assets to the Control Yuan (Wang, 2008). Ma's reputation for honesty and the corruption scandals surrounding Chen Shui-bian and the DPP enabled him and Vincent Siew to win the 2008 presidential election by capturing 58.45 percent of the votes with the DPP candidates Frank Hsieh and Su Tseng-chang obtaining 41.55 percent of the votes (Mo, Ko, & Shih, 2008, p. 1).

Ma is considered as one of the most honest politicians in Taiwan. As the Minister of Justice from 1993 to 1996, he had "frequently jailed politicians, including candidates for elective office, for vote-buying and other corrupt practices" (Copper, 2008, p. 55). He was charged with embezzling more than NT$11 million (US$340,000) from a special mayoral allowance during his tenure as the mayor of Taipei from 1998 to 2006. He denied the charges and argued that the allowance was a form of income supplement. On August 14, 2007, the Taipei District Court found Ma not guilty of embezzlement because the allowance was an official subsidy for top government officials (Ong, 2007, p. 10). This not guilty verdict was upheld by both the High Court and the Supreme Court when the prosecutors appealed. On April 24, 2008, Taiwan's Supreme Court rejected the appeal by the prosecutors and upheld the High Court's ruling that Ma was not guilty of corruption because he did not pocket any money illegally (AFP, 2008a).

While it might be premature at this stage to provide a final assessment of Ma's commitment to curbing corruption, it should be noted that he has kept his promise to fight corruption after assuming office in May 2008. First, as promised by him, the Legislative Yuan revised the Public Functionary Asset Disclosure Law and increased the number of civil servants who were required to disclose their assets to the Control Yuan from 1,800 to 9,000.

Second, the Legislative Yuan also revised the Punishment of Corruption Act in April 2009 to make it a crime for public officials to have unexplained wealth (Copper, 2009a, p. 15). Finally, as discussed earlier, as President Ma was "distressed" by the 2009 PERC corruption survey finding that Taiwan was perceived to be more corrupt than China, he urged the ACAs to enhance their anticorruption efforts (Ko, 2009, p. 1).

## ANTICORRUPTION MEASURES

Taiwan adopts the second pattern of corruption control and relies on the MJIB, the Department of Government Employee Ethics (DGEE), and the Public Prosecutors' Offices (PPOs) to combat corruption.

### *Ministry of Justice Investigation Bureau*

The MJIB is the lead ACA in Taiwan and is a law enforcement agency responsible for performing these nine functions: (1) prevention of sedition; (2) prevention of treason; (3) prevention of unauthorized disclosure of national secrets; (4) investigation of corruption, bribery, and vote-buying; (5) prevention of drug trafficking; (6) coordination in handling cases of organized crime; (7) prevention of significant economic crimes and money laundering; (8) investigation of national security matters; and (9) other investigations and prevention of matters as assigned by superior authorities concerning national security and interests (Republic of China, 2008). The fourth and ninth functions provide the MJIB with the legal basis for investigating corruption cases and enforcing preventive measures.

According to its website, the MJIB's primary mission is twofold: to protect national security and to investigate major crimes. To protect national security, the MJIB has to deal with counter-infiltration from the People's Republic of China, prevention of infiltration from other countries, counter terrorism, protection of national secrets, domestic security investigation, coordination of national internal security, and research on cross–strait relations. Second, the MJIB is also responsible for investigating these major crimes: public corruption, malfeasance and election fraud; economic crime; drug crime, money laundering, and cyber crime (http://www.mjib.gov.tw/en). In other words, the MJIB is not a dedicated ACA as the investigation of corruption, bribery, and vote-buying is only one of its nine functions.

The MJIB's origins can be traced to the establishment of the Investigation Bureau of the Ministry of Interior in Kuanchew in 1949. It was relocated together with the other government departments to Taipei in December 1949. It was renamed the Investigation Bureau of the Ministry of Judicial Administration on June 1, 1956, and assumed responsibility for major investigation and internal security issues concerning national safety and violation of national interests. With the reorganization of the judicial system on August 1, 1980, the Bureau was renamed the MJIB (http://www.mjib.gov.tw/en).

In May 1979 the Economic Crime Prevention Center (ECPC) was established to take over the anticorruption activities. The ECPC was expanded to become the Corruption and Economic Crime Prevention Center in August 1979 (Republic of China, 1995, p. 4). In February 1989, the MJIB formed the Corruption Elimination Department (CED) with a staff of 505 personnel. The CED's activities were reviewed by taking into account the experiences of the ICAC in Hong Kong and the CPIB in Singapore. Consequently, the CED was reorganized and renamed the Anti-Corruption Department (ACD) in February 1991, and its five sections were assigned new responsibilities (Republic of China, 1995, p. 8). The functions of the ACD's five sections were reviewed again in December 2007. Arising from the ACD's reorganization in 2007, its five sections are now responsible respectively for performing these functions: (1) public works abuse cases, investigation of fraudulent cases in procurement of properties and labor; (2) corruption cases in northern and eastern regions; (3) corruption cases in central and southern regions; (4) investigation of vote-buying, revisions to the MJIB's procedures and regulations, and corruption prevention education; and (5) review of anticorruption work performance, and the organization of anticorruption work consultation committee meetings and occasional review meetings (Republic of China, 2008).

### *Department of Government Employee Ethics*

Article 3 of the Act on the Establishment of the Government Employee Ethics Units and Officers identifies the MOJ as the competent authority of government ethics operations in Taiwan. The DGEE is one of the five departments in the MOJ and is responsible for the planning, supervision, and evaluation of all the government ethics units operating at all levels in the central and local government agencies and state-run enterprises. The DGEE's role is fourfold: (1) to supervise the ethics of government employees in Taiwan, (2) to execute anticorruption work, (3) to protect official secrets, and (4) to prevent "impairment to and sabotage of public agencies" (http://www.moj.gov.tw).

The work of government ethics in Taiwan is implemented by the various PPOs, the MJIB, and the government ethics units under the supervision of the DGEE. The task of eradicating corruption is performed by the PPOs and the MJIB, while the DGEE and the units under its supervision focus on preventing corruption. All public agencies in Taiwan except for elective institutions, military organizations, and public schools, have government ethics units, which are responsible for detecting corruption by advising the heads of the organizations on the establishment of built-in anticorruption mechanisms. The government ethics units also work with the PPOs and MJIB on the prevention of corruption (DGEE, 2008, p. 1).

The DGEE's role is to supervise and evaluate the performance of the personnel in all the government ethics units in the central and local government agencies in Taiwan. To prevent conflict between these personnel and the staff of the agencies when they perform their duties, the DGEE is also responsible for appointing and transferring the personnel of the government ethics units to ensure their independence and neutrality (DGEE, 2008, p. 1).

## *Public Prosecutors Offices*

Apart from the MJIB, the task of investigating corruption cases is also performed by the Supreme Prosecutors Office (SPO), the High Prosecutors Offices (HPOs), and the 21 PPOs throughout Taiwan. There are also four Special Investigation Task Forces that are located at the Taiwan HPO and its branches in Taichung, Tainan, and Kaohsiung (Republic of China, 2000b, p. 5).

All the PPOs are responsible for prosecuting crimes and supervising the execution of criminal verdicts. According to the Chief Prosecutor, these PPOs "prosecute criminals and conduct investigations to crack down on crimes and protect the public interest." Their additional functions include exercising judicative power over criminal cases, administering probation and aftercare services, increasing the legal awareness of peoples' rights and obligations, offering legal aid, and building capacity to protect victims of crime (TDPO, 2010).

Using the Taipei District Prosecutors Office (TDPO) as an example, its members perform these six functions: (1) conducting prosecutions for public offenses and investigating criminal activities; (2) implementing the government's policies on curbing organized crime and corruption, and showing its determination to crack down on "black gold" activities; (3) detecting illegal acts and protecting victims of crime; (4) deepening and broadening the scope of the judicial protective services and strengthening the community-based treatment function; (5) improving the quality of service, strengthening the commitment to a responsible and efficient office, and building a citizen-friendly image; and (6) cooperating with the police and investigation units to promote teamwork (TDPO, 2010).

Table 5.10 summarizes the preceding discussion by indicating that the function of corruption control is shared between the MJIB, DGEE, and the PPOs. Table 5.11 confirms that in terms of the sources of corruption cases in Taiwan, the MJIB is the most important ACA because it is responsible for about 40 percent of the corruption cases investigated. The government ethics units under the DGEE's supervision are second, with 20.4 percent of the corruption cases investigated. Third, the Taiwanese public is responsible for 15.1 percent of the corruption cases investigated. Fourth, the PPOs throughout Taiwan initiate 14 percent of the corruption cases investigated. The remaining 10.6 percent of corruption cases are reported by supervisory authorities, self-surrenders, and other sources.

As the MJIB is responsible for investigating 40 percent of all the investigation cases from 2004 to 2008, it is not surprising that the MJIB has more personnel and a larger budget than the DGEE. Furthermore, as mentioned earlier, the MJIB is responsible for the investigation of corruption, bribery, and vote-buying, in addition to its other eight functions. Table 5.12 shows that the MJIB's budget has increased from US$172.6 million in 2008 to US$173.4 million in 2009. However, the MJIB's budget has decreased marginally to US$171.6 million in 2010. In contrast, the DGEE, which has only 45 personnel compared to 2,498 personnel for the MJIB, has a much smaller budget of about US$1.1 million annually from 2008 to 2010. In addition to the 45 personnel in the DGEE, there are 2,583 government employee ethics officers in 573 central organizations and 487 regional organizations in Taiwan (Ministry of Justice, 2009, p. 11).

***Table 5.10.*** Anticorruption Agencies in Taiwan.

| Anticorruption Agency | Function |
|---|---|
| Ministry of Justice Investigation Bureau | Investigation of corruption cases |
| Department of Government Employee Ethics and all Government Ethics Units | Investigation and prevention of corruption |
| Public Prosecutors Offices throughout Taiwan | Investigation and prosecution of corruption cases |

*Source*: Compiled by the author.

***Table 5.11.*** Sources of Corruption Cases, 2004–2008.

| Year | MJIB | Government Ethics Units | Reports from public | Prosecutors Offices | Others[a] | Total |
|---|---|---|---|---|---|---|
| 2004 | 125 | 70 | 41 | 40 | 33 | 309 |
| 2005 | 94 | 62 | 43 | 39 | 35 | 273 |
| 2006 | 89 | 55 | 40 | 34 | 36 | 254 |
| 2007 | 185 | 68 | 58 | 51 | 33 | 395 |
| 2008 | 119 | 57 | 49 | 50 | 26 | 301 |
| Total | 612 (39.9%) | 312 (20.4%) | 231 (15.1%) | 214 (14.0%) | 163 (10.6%) | 1,532 (100%) |

*Source*: Republic of China (2009, p. 219).
[a]This category includes supervisory authorities, self-surrenders, and other sources.

***Table 5.12.*** Budget and Personnel of MJIB and DGEE, 2008–2010.

| Year | MJIB | DGEE |
|---|---|---|
| 2008 | NT$5,666,857,000 (US$172,664,740) | NT$36,406,000 (US$1,109,263) |
| 2009 | NT$5,592,435,000 (US$173,462,620) | NT$32,572,000 (US$1,010,298) |
| 2010 | NT$5,407,770,000 (US$171,620,750) | NT$37,572,000 (US$1,192,383) |
| No. of Personnel | 2,498 | 45 |

*Source*: Data provided by the MJIB and DGEE through the courtesy of Professor Yu-Ying Kuo, Chair, Department of Public Policy and Management, Shih Hsin University in Taipei, Taiwan on November 16 and December 15, 2010.
*Notes*: The conversion of NT$ into US$ is based on these exchange rates: US$1 = NT$32.82 (2008); US$1 = NT$32.24 (2009); and US$1 = NT$31.51 (2010).

As the MJIB performs eight other functions in addition to curbing corruption, its budget from 2008 to 2010, which is indicated in Table 5.12 includes the expenditure for the performance of its non-corruption-related functions too. Accordingly, Table 5.13 provides a more accurate indication of the MJIB's budget for its anticorruption activities during 2008–2010. Indeed, the MJIB's budget for anticorruption activities varies from US$4.02 million in 2008 to US$4.03 million in 2009 to US$4.31 million in 2010. These figures constitute only 2.3 percent of the MJIB's total budget in 2008 and 2009 and 2.5 percent in 2010.

***Table 5.13.*** MJIB's Budget for Anticorruption Activities, 2008–2010.

| Item | 2008 | 2009 | 2010 |
|---|---|---|---|
| Investigation of major crimes including anticorruption | NT$96,264,000 | NT$98,396,000 | NT$98,292,000 |
| Public corruption, malfeasance and election fraud | NT$35,830,000 | NT$31,696,000 | NT$37,830,000 |
| Total | NT$132,094,000 (US$4,024,801) | NT$130,092,000 (US$4,035,111) | NT$136,122,000 (US$4,319,961) |

*Source*: http://www.mjib.gov.tw/cgi-bin/mojnbi?/services/service-6.html. I thank Ms Ming-Huei Cheng, Director of Social Marketing, Transparency International Chinese Taipei, for extracting the MJIB's budget for its anticorruption activities from the MJIB's Chinese website for me.

### *AntiCorruption Laws*

The most important anticorruption law in Taiwan is the Anti-Corruption Statute, which was enacted on July 15, 1963, to "halt corruption and punish officials who engage in corrupt practices" (Article 1).[6] Article 2 states that the provisions of this statute apply to all public officials. Article 4 specifies the penalty of imprisonment from 10 years to life and a maximum fine of NT$100 million for those found guilty of any of these five offenses: (1) theft or misappropriation of public equipment or property; (2) corruptly demanding, receiving, or accepting anything of value by means of coercion, extortion, conversion, or collection; (3) falsely reporting the quantity of public equipment or goods procured, receiving an unauthorized commission on procurement or engaging in other corrupt acts relating to the construction of government projects or the procurement of government equipment or materials; (4) using government vehicles to transport contraband or to transport goods for the purpose of tax evasion; and (5) corruptly demanding, soliciting, receiving, accepting or agreeing to receive or accepting any bribe or other unjust enrichment in return for being induced to execute or fail to execute any act in violation of the official duties of such official or the commissioned duties of such person commissioned to undertake specific public affairs duties.

Table 5.14 shows that the Anti-Corruption Statute of 1963 is the most important anticorruption law in Taiwan as reflected in the fact that more than half (52.5 percent) of the corruption cases during 2004–2009 were offenses against it. Table 5.14 also indicates that the Government

***Table 5.14.*** Number of Offenses of Major AntiCorruption Laws, 2004–2009.

| Year | Anticorruption Statute | Government Procurement Act | Criminal Code | Total |
|---|---|---|---|---|
| 2004 | 269 (57.5%) | 118 (25.2%) | 81 (17.3%) | 468 (100%) |
| 2005 | 235 (59.8%) | 94 (23.9%) | 64 (16.3%) | 393 (100%) |
| 2006 | 227 (49.4%) | 155 (33.8%) | 77 (16.8%) | 459 (100%) |
| 2007 | 359 (50.3%) | 233 (32.6%) | 122 (17.1%) | 714 (100%) |
| 2008 | 289 (53.7%) | 148 (27.5%) | 101 (18.8%) | 538 (100%) |
| 2009 | 270 (47.5%) | 185 (32.6%) | 113 (19.9%) | 568 (100%) |
| Total | 1,649 (52.5%) | 933 (29.7%) | 558 (17.8%) | 3,140 (100%) |

*Sources*: Republic of China (2009, p. 226, 2010, p. 209).

Procurement Act (GPA) is the second most important anticorruption law in Taiwan from 2004 to 2009 because there were 933 cases (29.7 percent) dealing with offenses specified in the GPA.

The GPA was enacted by presidential decree on May 27, 1998, with these objectives:

> to establish a government procurement system that has fair and open procurement procedures, can promote the efficiency and effectiveness of government procurement operation, and is able to ensure the quality of procurement. (GPA, 1998, p. 1)

Article 2 of the GPA defines "procurement" as "the contracting of construction work, the purchase or lease of property, the retention or employment of services, etc." Article 3 specifies that the GPA's provisions apply to the procurement conducted by all government agencies, public schools, or government-owned enterprises (GPA, 1998, p. 1).

The GPA is divided into eight chapters and has 114 articles. After identifying the general principles in Chapter I (Articles 1–17), the subsequent chapters deal with the invitation to tender (Chapter II, Articles 18–44), the award of contracts (Chapter III, Articles 45–62), the administration of contract performance (Chapter IV, Articles 63–70), inspection and acceptance (Chapter V, Articles 71–73), dispute settlement (Chapter VI, Articles 74–86), penal provisions (Chapter VII, Articles 87–92), and supplementary provisions (Chapter VIII, Articles 93–114).

Article 87 imposes a penalty of imprisonment from one to seven years and a fine of NT$3 million for any one who commits violence, administers drugs, or hypnotizes a supplier "not to tender or to tender contrary to its real intention, or cause the winning tenderer to forego the award or to assign or subcontract after the award." However, if death results from the specified offense, the offender will be imprisoned from seven years to life imprisonment and a fine of NT$3 million. If serious bodily injury is caused by the offense, the duration of imprisonment is reduced to between three and ten years. The penalty for committing fraud or using illegal means to prevent the supplier from tendering or causing the opening of tenders to have an incorrect result is imprisonment for five years and a fine of NT$1 million. The penalty is further reduced to imprisonment from six months to five years and a fine of NT$1 million for any one who prevents the supplier from tendering or proceeding with price competition by means of "contract, agreement or other forms of meeting of minds" to "adversely affect the price of award or to gain illegal benefits." Offenders who borrow or assume another person's name or certificate to tender to adversely affect the procurement result or to gain illegal benefits will be imprisoned for three years and fined NT$1 million. Any one who allows another person to borrow or assume his name or certificate to tender will receive the same punishment (GPA, 1998, p. 22).

Table 5.15 shows that in terms of the amount of money involved, corruption cases dealing with procurement are the most important during 2004–2009 with a total of NT$42,387,276,850, followed by profiting (NT$16,314,749,002), corruption (NT$6,810,415,416), and others (NT$3,645,272,372).

Third, vote-buying is an offense according to Articles 142–148 of the Criminal Code (Republic of China, 1995, pp. 313–314), the Presidential and Vice Presidential Election and Recall Law, and the Public Officials Election and Recall Law. For example, in 2008, there were 247 indictments against voters receiving bribes according to paragraph 1 of Article 143. Similarly,

***Table 5.15.*** Amounts of Money in Corruption Cases, 2004–2009 (NT$).

| Year | Corruption | Profiting | Procurement | Others |
|---|---|---|---|---|
| 2004 | 2,306,672,761 | 2,963,781,600 | 2,573,413,272 | 142,830,780 |
| 2005 | 888,558,803 | 1,099,589,491 | 1,368,542,066 | 339,422,789 |
| 2006 | 1,400,977,341 | 1,942,485,379 | 472,386,008 | 214,166,006 |
| 2007 | 1,082,615,885 | 5,283,287,424 | 11,225,772,189 | 391,049,931 |
| 2008 | 694,848,188 | 2,582,857,582 | 8,148,494,629 | 1,495,435,818 |
| 2009 | 536,742,438 | 2,442,747,526 | 18,598,668,686 | 1,262,367,048 |
| Total | 6,810,415,416 | 16,314,749,002 | 42,387,276,850 | 3,645,272,372 |

*Sources*: Republic of China (2009, p. 247, 2010, p. 200).

***Table 5.16.*** Sources of Vote-Buying Cases, 2004–2008.

| Year | MJIB | Prosecutors Offices | Reports from public | Others | Total |
|---|---|---|---|---|---|
| 2004 | 21 | 6 | 3 | 2 | 32 |
| 2005 | 238 | 73 | 27 | 31 | 369 |
| 2006 | 360 | 108 | 26 | 3 | 497 |
| 2007 | 78 | 8 | 5 | 0 | 91 |
| 2008 | 67 | 44 | 37 | 0 | 148 |
| Total | 764 (67.2%) | 239 (21%) | 98 (8.6%) | 36 (3.2%) | 1,137 (100%) |

*Source*: Republic of China (2009, p. 254).

there are 338 indictments for bribery to voters according to paragraph 1 of Article 99 of the Public Officials Election and Recall Law and only 12 indictments for bribery to voters according to paragraph 1 of Article 86 of the Presidential and Vice Presidential Election and Recall Law in 2008 (Republic of China, 2009, p. 257).

Table 5.16 shows that more than two-thirds of the vote-buying cases investigated by the MJIB resulted from its own initiative, followed by 21 percent from the Prosecutors Offices, nearly 9 percent from the public, and 3 percent from other sources.

## EVALUATION OF ANTICORRUPTION MEASURES

These four indicators are employed to assess the perceived extent of corruption in Taiwan: (1) TI's CPI from 1995 to 2010 covering 178 countries; (2) PERC's annual survey of corruption in 16 Asia-Pacific countries from 1995 to 2010; (3) World Bank's control of corruption governance indicator from 1996 to 2009 covering 213 countries; and (4) the *Global Competitiveness Report's* indicator on the public trust of politicians in 139 countries from 1999 to 2010–2011.

Table 5.17 shows that, first, Taiwan's rank on the CPI ranges from 25th position among 41 countries in 1995 to 33rd position among 178 countries in 2010. Similarly, its CPI score varies from 4.98 in 1996 to 5.9 in 2001, 2005, and 2006. Second, Taiwan's rank on the PERC corruption surveys from 1995 to 2010 varies from 4th position in 1998, 2001, 2004, and 2005, to 9th position in 2009. As mentioned earlier, Taiwan's 9th ranking below China's 8th ranking in 2009 led to President Ma's call to the ACAs to redouble their efforts to curb corruption in Taiwan. Third, Taiwan's percentile rank for the control of

***Table 5.17.*** Taiwan's Performance on CPI, PERC, and Control of Corruption, 1995–2010.

| Year | CPI Rank & Score[a] | PERC Rank & Score[b] | Control of Corruption Percentile Rank |
|---|---|---|---|
| 1995 | 25th (5.08) | 5th (4.20) | NA |
| 1996 | 29th (4.98) | 6th (5.53) | 76.2 |
| 1997 | 31st (5.02) | 5th (5.96) | NA |
| 1998 | 29th (5.3) | 4th (5.20) | 76.7 |
| 1999 | 28th (5.6) | 5th (6.92) | NA |
| 2000 | 28th (5.5) | 5th (6.89) | 78.6 |
| 2001 | 27th (5.9) | 4th (6.00) | NA |
| 2002 | 29th (5.6) | 6th (5.83) | 75.2 |
| 2003 | 30th (5.7) | 6th (6.33) | 75.7 |
| 2004 | 35th (5.6) | 4th (6.10) | 78.6 |
| 2005 | 32nd (5.9) | 4th (6.15) | 77.2 |
| 2006 | 34th (5.9) | 6th (5.91) | 73.3 |
| 2007 | 34th (5.7) | 5th (6.23) | 72.5 |
| 2008 | 39th (5.7) | 7th (6.55) | 72 |
| 2009 | 37th (5.6) | 9th (6.47) | 72.4 |
| 2010 | 33rd (5.8) | 8th (6.28) | NA |

*Sources*: Compiled from http://www.transparency.org; PERC (2001, 2008, p. 7); Hussain (2009, p. B5); *Straits Times* (2010a); and http://info.worldbank.org/governance/wgi/sc_chart.asp
[a]The CPI score ranges from 0 (most corrupt) to 10 (least corrupt).
[b]The PERC score ranges from 0 (least corrupt) to 10 (most corrupt).

corruption varies from 72 in 2008 to 78.6 in 2000 and 2004. Furthermore, its percentile rank has declined from 76.2 in 1996 to 72.4 in 2009. Taiwan was ranked sixth after Singapore, Hong Kong, Japan, Brunei, and Bhutan among the 25 Asian countries included in the 2009 control of corruption data.

Unlike the first three indicators, the fourth indicator on the public trust of politicians provides an indirect measure of the perceived extent of corruption because a low level of public trust of politicians indicates that there is a high level of political corruption in the country. According to Table 5.18, Taiwan was ranked 24th among the 102 countries with a score of 3.6 in 2003–2004. However, in 2007–2008, Taiwan's rank dropped to 57th among the 131 countries with a score of 2.8. Since then, Taiwan was ranked 36th among 139 countries with its highest score of 3.70 in 2010–2011.

In sum, Tables 5.17 and 5.18 indicate clearly that corruption remains a serious problem in Taiwan in spite of the various anticorruption measures initiated by the different governments since December 1949. First, according to TI's CPI for 2010, Taiwan is ranked 33rd among 178 countries with a score of

***Table 5.18.*** Public Trust of Politicians in Taiwan, 1999 to 2010–2011.

| Year | Rank | Score[a] | No. of Countries |
|---|---|---|---|
| 1999 | 27th | 3.46 | 59 |
| 2000 | 35th | 2.9 | 59 |
| 2001–2002 | 29th | 3.2 | 75 |
| 2002–2003 | 30th | 3.2 | 80 |
| 2003–2004 | 24th | 3.6 | 102 |
| 2007–2008 | 57th | 2.8 | 131 |
| 2008–2009 | 54th | 3 | 134 |
| 2009–2010 | 42nd | 3.4 | 133 |
| 2010–2011 | 36th | 3.7 | 139 |
| Average | 37th | 3.25 | – |

*Sources*: Compiled from Schwab et al. (1999, p. 327), Porter et al. (2000, p. 253), Schwab et al. (2002, p. 408), Cornelius (2003, p. 619), Sala-i-Martin (2004, p. 499), Schwab and Porter (2007, p. 379), Schwab and Porter (2008, p. 367), Schwab (2009, p. 349), Schwab (2010, p. 369).
[a]The score ranges from 1 (very low) to 7 (very high) for the respondents' answers to this question: "How would you rate the level of public trust in the ethical standards of politicians in your country?"

5.8, which makes it the fourth least corrupt country in Asia. Second, Taiwan is ranked 8th among the 16th countries included in PERC's 2010 survey with a score of 6.28. Third, Taiwan is ranked sixth with a percentile rank of 72.4 among the 25 Asian countries included in the World Bank's 2009 control of corruption data. Fourth, Taiwan is ranked seventh with a score of 3.7 for the public trust of politicians among the 20 Asian countries in 2010–2011.

Finally, according to TI's Global Corruption Barometer for 2006, only 2 percent of the 1,000 Taiwanese respondents considered their government as very effective in fighting corruption, and 21 percent found their government to be effective. On the contrary, 33 percent of the respondents viewed their government as ineffective in curbing corruption, 25 percent of them said that their government did not fight corruption but actually encouraged it, and 15 percent of the respondents felt that their government did not fight corruption at all (Transparency International, 2006, p. 15).

Like India and the Philippines that rely on multiple ACAs, Taiwan also suffers from the same disadvantages of lack of coordination, overlapping of functions, competition for resources, and dilution of the country's anticorruption efforts. Sonny Lo (2008, p. 75) contends that Taiwan's "anti-corruption bodies are currently too diverse, and a single powerful agency should be vested with the necessary legal authority and status to curb graft in the private and public sectors."

The MJIB, which is the lead ACA in Taiwan, has three weaknesses. First, the MJIB is not a dedicated ACA because it is responsible for eight other functions in addition to its fourth function of investigating corruption, bribery, and vote-buying. As the MJIB's other functions include such important concerns as investigation of national security matters; prevention of drug trafficking; dealing with organized crime, economic crime, and money laundering; and prevention of sedition, treason, and unauthorized disclosure of national secrets; the function of corruption control has to compete with these functions for limited resources. A second weakness of the MJIB's performance of all these functions is that the function of combating corruption will always be given lower priority than the investigation of national security matters.

The third and most important limitation of the MJIB is that even though it is part of the MOJ, five of its functions related to national security come under the jurisdiction of the National Security Bureau (NSB). In his November 2000 interview with *Taiwan Panorama*, DPP Justice Minister Chen Ding-nan highlighted the problem of the MJIB having two bosses: the MOJ and the NSB. Describing the MOJ as the "lesser of the MJIB's two bosses" with only 20 percent of its stock if the MJIB were a company, Minister Chen's hope was "that the MJIB will fully carry out its duties as a law enforcement agency by fighting crime" (Chang, 2000, p. 38). In an earlier interview with a local radio news program in June 2000, Chen expressed his "deep frustration" with his lack of control over the MJIB, which is responsible for both intelligence gathering and criminal investigation, but "apparently prioritizes the former over the latter." He added that as long as the MJIB "continues to carry out intelligence tasks, we feel it's hopeless to talk about cracking down on corruption in the country." Indeed, the feud between Chen and the MJIB's Director General, Wang Kuang-yu, has resulted in opposition and reform groups urging the government to transfer the MJIB's intelligence role to the NSB so that the MJIB can devote its attention on investigating crimes, including corruption (Lin, 2000b, p. 1).

## CONCLUSION

Although President Chiang Kai-shek was not corrupt himself, he did not give priority to curbing corruption because he accorded more importance to promote loyalty among his supporters and the restoration of peace and unity. In contrast, his son, Chiang Ching-kuo, was committed to minimizing corruption during his term of office as vice premier and after becoming president in May 1972. On the contrary, President Lee Teng-hui, who succeeded Chiang Ching-kuo, was less committed to curbing corruption as reflected in the rapid growth of "black gold" politics during his term of office. Unfortunately, President Chen Shui-bian, who had campaigned on an anticorruption platform during the 2000 presidential election, succumbed to corruption during his eight years in power.

Unlike his predecessor, President Ma Ying-jeou appears to be more committed to curbing corruption in Taiwan. However, it is puzzling why he does not support the public demand for the establishment of an independent ACA in Taiwan. During the campaign for the March 2008 presidential election, he indicated his preference for relying on the existing government structure to curb corruption because "as long as government leaders know how to behave themselves, then we won't need to set up more agencies to do the same thing that existing agencies should be doing." Nevertheless, he qualified his decision by saying that "if corruption in the government sector still cannot be eliminated within two years, more radical measures can be considered, such as forming an independent anti-corruption commission like the one in Hong Kong or shifting the prosecution system currently under the Ministry of Justice to the oversight of the Judicial Yuan" (Wang, 2008).

On July 14, 2010, three Taiwan High Court judges and a district prosecutor were arrested for accepting bribes from a former KMT legislator, Ho Chi-hui (Chao, 2010b, p. 1). Three days later, the Judicial Yuan president, Lai In-jaw, resigned to assume responsibility for the scandal (Chang, 2010b, p. 1). President Ma Ying-jeou reacted to the scandal by reversing his earlier decision not to establish an ACA. At a press conference on July 20, 2010, Ma said that an anti-graft agency was "practical and feasible" and also "necessary in the face of public anger over the recent scandal" (Ho, 2010, p. A18). He gave three reasons for this policy reversal: to strengthen his government's efforts to fight corruption; to respond to public expectations; and to conform to international standards (Ko, 2010, p. 1).

More importantly, Ma stressed that "the new agency would not be a carbon copy" of Hong Kong's ICAC or Singapore's CPIB, and would not report directly to the head of government (Ho, 2010, p. A18). Furthermore, apart from lacking independent status, the new ACA will come under the jurisdiction of the MOJ. It will have four branches responsible for general planning, corruption prevention, graft busting, and government ethics, and three regional squads in northern, central, and southern Taiwan for investigations (*China Post*, 2010).

President Ma's decision to establish a new ACA under the MOJ is unlikely to make a significant impact in curbing corruption in Taiwan because it fails to address the problems facing the existing ACAs. Indeed, his proposal raises five questions that were not discussed at the press conference. First, how will the new ACA affect the power struggle between the MOJ and the MJIB? Second, will the new ACA replace the MJIB as the lead ACA or will it be the MJIB's poor cousin? Third, will the MJIB still be responsible for investigating corruption, bribery, and vote-buying? Fourth, contrary to Ma's claim that the new ACA would not replicate the MJIB's work (*Taiwan News*, 2010), there will be duplication unless the MJIB relinquishes its anticorruption function and focuses instead on its intelligence functions. Fifth, as discussed earlier, the MJIB has two bosses: the MOJ and the NSB. Will the new ACA suffer the same fate as the MJIB as it will also have two bosses: the MOJ (*de jure* boss) and the President (*de facto* boss) since it is not an independent body?

Finally, the most important reason why the new ACA will not be effective in curbing corruption in Taiwan is that its creation increases the number of ACAs without resolving the problems plaguing the current ACAs namely: lack of coordination, overlapping of functions, competition for limited resources, and dilution of the country's anticorruption efforts. The experience of the Philippines, which is analyzed in Chapter 4, illustrates the futility of relying on multiple ACAs to curb corruption. Unless the new ACA is set up as an independent agency outside the MOJ's purview, it will not be effective because it will be competing with the MJIB, DGEE, and PPOs to combat corruption in Taiwan. In short, instead of creating another ACA within the MOJ, President Ma Ying-jeou should learn from Singapore's and Hong Kong's success in minimizing corruption (which is analyzed respectively in Chapters 6 and 7) by establishing an independent ACA outside the MOJ's jurisdiction to replace the existing ineffective ACAs and provide it with the required legal powers, personnel and budget to enable it to perform its anticorruption functions effectively.

## NOTES

1. In addition to the main island of Taiwan, there are many islands under Taiwan's control namely: the 64 Pescadore or Penghu Islands, Orchid Island (Lan Tao), Green Island (Lu Tao), the Offshore Islands of Quemoy and Matsu, and some islands in the South China Sea (see Cooper, 2009b, p. 2).

2. Taiwan's transportation infrastructure was upgraded during the Japanese colonial period as the length of railroads increased from 30 miles in 1895 to 300 miles

in 1905. Roads and harbors were also built, and communications facilities were constructed or improved (see Cooper, 2009b, p. 39).

3. For an excellent analysis of Taiwan's evolution from martial law to democracy, see Tien (1992, pp. 3–23).

4. For details of the salaries of political leaders and senior civil servants in Japan, South Korea, Hong Kong, and Singapore, see Nakamura and Dairokuno (2003), Kim (2003), Lee (2003), and Quah (2003b).

5. The Public Officials Election and Recall Law of 1980, pp. 24–25, available at http://www.anfrel.org/resources/laws/ThePublicOfficialsElectionandRecallLaw3.pdf.

6. For details of the 20 articles of the Anti-Corruption Statute, see Lawbank, pp. 1–3 at http://db.lawbank.com.tw/Eng/FLAW/FLAWDAT0202.asp

# CHAPTER 6

# SINGAPORE

> It is easy to start off with high moral standards, strong convictions and determination to beat down corruption. But it is difficult to live up to these good intentions unless the leaders are strong and determined enough to deal with all transgressors, and without exceptions. CPIB officers must be supported without fear or favor to enforce the rules.
>
> – Lee Kuan Yew (2000, p. 189)

> More than half of those [civil servants] disciplined for corruption that year [1993] were sacked. And there lies, perhaps, the strength of Singapore's anti-corruption strategy: an unforgiving attitude towards crooked public officials.
>
> – *Straits Times* (1995, p. 4)

## TEH CHEANG WAN SCANDAL

Singapore is perceived to be the least corrupt country in Asia according to Transparency International's Corruption Perceptions Index (CPI) from 1995 to 2010. In 2010, Singapore was ranked joint first with Denmark and New Zealand among 178 countries on the CPI with a score of 9.3. However, this does not mean that corruption does not exist in Singapore, which has its share of corruption scandals too. Indeed, the scandal involving Teh Cheang Wan attracted a great deal of attention because he was the Minister for National Development in Singapore from 1979 to 1986.

Teh committed suicide on 14 December 1986, 12 days after he was interrogated for 16 hours by two senior officers of the Corrupt Practices Investigation Bureau (CPIB) regarding a complaint of corruption made against him by a building contractor (*Straits Times*, 1987a, p. 11). On 31 March 1987, the building contractor, Liu Cho Chit, was fined the maximum amount of S$10,000 for offering a bribe of S$1 million to Liaw Teck Kee, another building contractor, to persuade him to keep Teh's name out of any corruption investigation. Liaw rejected the offer and reported the bribery attempt to the CPIB (Prema, 1987, p. 1).

Chiam See Tong, the opposition MP for Potong Pasir, asked Prime Minister Lee Kuan Yew in Parliament on 4 March 1987 whether he would hold a public inquiry to "get to the bottom" of the Teh Cheang Wan affair and to recommend measures to prevent "further corruption in high places." Prime

Minister Lee replied that the government had nothing to hide and would hold a public inquiry so that there could be no question of any cover-up. Chiam agreed to Lee's request to draft the terms of reference for the public inquiry and to lead in evidence on them. Accordingly, on 26 March 1987, President Wee Kim Wee appointed a three-man Commission of Inquiry to investigate three terms of reference, two of which were drafted by Chiam.

During the first hearing of the Commission of Inquiry on 25 May 1987, Chiam requested a two-month adjournment because he needed more time to prepare the case. The Commissioners granted his request and adjourned the inquiry to 18 August 1987, when the Commission resumed hearing. Chiam complained that he was not allowed to inspect the CPIB files and also objected to the Commission's ruling that his role was that of an "accuser." When the Commissioners rejected his request for another adjournment, Chiam asked to be excused from the proceedings. However, the Commissioners ruled on the second day of the hearing that they had no power to discharge Chiam from taking part in the proceedings.

Senior State Counsel Lawrence Ang, who was assisting the Commission in conducting the investigation, proceeded with the first term of reference, namely, to ascertain whether the CPIB was thorough and comprehensive in its investigations into the acts of corruption by the late Teh Cheang Wan, to demonstrate that no one else was involved in such corruption, and to show that there was no attempt by the CPIB to cover up or conceal any information on corruption or criminal wrongdoing (*Straits Times*, 1987b, p. 10).

In his testimony to the Commission, the CPIB's Director, Evan Yeo, revealed that the CPIB had interviewed 157 persons and recorded 134 statements in its investigation against Teh Cheang Wan. He found that Teh was the only minister implicated in the two instances of graft and that no other minister, parliamentary secretary, or government official was involved (Parliament of Singapore, 1987, pp. 44–45). Liaw Teck Kee, the chief witness in the charges against Teh, admitted to the Commissioners that he acted as the middleman on two occasions and conveyed a S$500,000 bribe each time to Teh, who gave him S$200,000. The third witness was the CPIB's Senior Assistant Director, Tan Ah Leak, who told the Commissioners that Teh had offered to admit his guilt, resign as minister, and return the S$800,000, if the Prime Minister could promise not to charge him in court. Tan rejected Teh's offer because the CPIB's intention was to bring Teh to court (Parliament of Singapore, 1987, pp. 36–37).

The Commissioners ended the inquiry on 21 August 1987, when Chiam was unable to provide evidence to proceed with the other two terms of reference. They observed that "the two acts of corruption of Teh Cheang Wan might never have been uncovered but for the CPIB's commitment to investigating all leads to acts of corruption in Singapore" (Parliament of Singapore, 1987, p. 44). After considering the evidence, the Commissioners concluded that: (1) the CPIB had done all that was necessary in its investigations to uncover the acts of corruption of the late Teh Cheang Wan; (2) the CPIB was thorough in its investigations that no other minister, parliamentary secretary or government officer was involved; and (3) the CPIB had not overlooked, concealed or covered up any information concerning corruption or criminal wrongdoing (Parliament of Singapore, 1987, p. 55).

An important consequence of the Teh Cheang Wan scandal was the introduction of the Corruption (Confiscation of Benefits) Act 1989, which was enacted on 3 March 1989 to enable the court to issue a confiscation order against the estate of a defendant if he had derived his benefits from corruption. In his memoirs, former Prime Minister Lee Kuan Yew (2000, pp. 187–189) observed that Teh Cheang Wan's downfall was the "most dramatic" because

> We had established a climate of opinion which looked upon corruption in public office as a threat to society. Teh preferred to take his life rather than face disgrace and ostracism. I never understood why he took this S$800,000. He was an able and resourceful architect and could have made many millions honestly in private practice.

## AIM OF THE CHAPTER

Unlike many Asian countries, Singapore has been effective in curbing corruption as reflected in its joint first ranking and high score of 9.3 on TI's 2010 CPI. Why has Singapore succeeded in fighting corruption when other Asian countries have failed to do so? This chapter contends that Singapore's success in tackling corruption can be attributed to the People's Action Party (PAP) government's political will and the country's favorable policy context.

This chapter begins with an analysis of Singapore's favorable policy context in terms of its geography, history, economy, demography, and political system. The perceived extent of corruption is then ascertained, followed by a discussion of the major causes of corruption in Singapore during the British colonial period. The Prevention of Corruption Act (POCA) of 1960 and the CPIB, which are the two important anticorruption measures in Singapore, are then analyzed and their effectiveness evaluated.

## SINGAPORE'S POLICY CONTEXT

### *Geography*

Singapore is a city-state consisting of a main island and 63 offshore islands with a total land area of 710.3 sq km. Most Singaporeans live on the main island, which is 42 km long and 23 km wide. The rural sector is negligible as Singapore is highly urbanized, and only 1 percent of its land area is used for agricultural purposes (Department of Statistics, 2010, pp. 9, 98). This means that Singapore has no natural resources except for its strategic location, deep harbor, and resourceful people. Singapore's small land area also means that there is no large rural hinterland to permit the cultivation of crops or the mining of minerals.

Singapore's smallness and its high degree of urbanization have enhanced the policy-making process in four ways. First, as communication is not a serious problem, Singapore's diminutiveness facilitates political control by the leadership. Second, Singapore's small size improves administrative coordination and enhances the responsiveness of public officials. Third, unlike larger Asian countries such as India and Indonesia, Singapore's smallness has contributed to a highly centralized public bureaucracy, which does not face the same problems afflicting a federal civil service in its interaction with the state, provincial, or local-level bureaucracies. Fourth, the absence of a large rural sector in Singapore not only reinforces the centralized nature of its civil service but also means that Singapore is not burdened by problems arising from implementing reforms in the rural areas or provinces (Quah, 1984, pp. 109–110). In short, Singapore's small land area enables the CPIB to enforce the anticorruption laws effectively.

### *History*

Singapore was a British colony for nearly 140 years until the attainment of self-government in June 1959. The British colonial government introduced two important reforms that have strengthened the contemporary Singapore Civil Service (SCS) tremendously. First, in January 1951, meritocracy was introduced in Singapore with the establishment of the Public Service Commission (PSC) to ensure that the recruitment and promotion of civil servants was based on merit and to accelerate the pace of localization of the SCS. The PAP government has retained the PSC to attract the "best and brightest" Singaporeans to join the SCS by awarding scholarships to the best students in each cohort (Quah, 2010b, pp. 74, 91).

***Box 6.1.*** Singapore's Policy Context

| | |
|---|---|
| Land area | 710.3 sq km |
| Arable land | 1% |
| GDP | S$260,605.2 million (2009) |
| Per capita GDP | S$52,251 (US$35,924) (2009) |
| Unemployment rate | 3.2% |
| Population | 4,987,600 (2009) |
| Population density | 7,022 persons per sq km |
| Urban population | 100% |
| Adult literacy rate | 96.3% |
| Political system | Parliamentary democracy |
| Colonial rule | British colony (1819–1959) |
| 2010 CPI rank and score | 1/178 and 9.3/10 |
| 2010 PERC rank and score | 1/16 and 1.42/10 |

*Sources*: Department of Statistics (2010, pp. 2, 9, 10); http://www.transparency.org/policy_research/surveys_indices/cpi/2010/results; and *Straits Times* (2010a).

Second, the CPIB was formed in October 1952 as the first ACA in the world. As will be explained later in this chapter, the British colonial government made a serious mistake in December 1937 when it made the Anti-Corruption Branch (ACB) in the Singapore Police Force (SPF) responsible for combating corruption when police corruption was prevalent in Singapore. The British colonial government rectified their error by replacing the ACB with the CPIB after discovering that some police detectives were involved in the Opium Hijacking scandal of October 1951.

### *Economy*

Singapore was a poor country in June 1959 when it attained self-government because its per capita GDP was S$1,200 (US$400) and its unemployment rate was 14 percent. The PAP government created the Economic Development Board (EDB) in August 1961 to spearhead the industrialization program and promote economic growth by attracting foreign investment to Singapore. Its rapid economic growth during the past 51 years has transformed the economy from a purely entrepot economy to an entrepot-manufacturing economy.

Consequently, Singapore's per capita GDP has increased by 44 times to S$52,251 (US$35,924) in 2009 (Department of Statistics, 2010, p. 2).

Singapore's rapid economic growth and its transformation from a third world country to a first world country has been an asset in implementing development programs. To compensate for the lack of natural resources, the PAP government has emphasized education to improve the quality of human resources in Singapore. Hence, it is not surprising that government expenditure has increased by 137 times from S$63.39 million in 1959 to S$8,698.88 million in 2009 (Department of Statistics, 2010, p. 264).

In short, Singapore's economic affluence means that the PAP government can afford to allocate sufficient personnel and budget to the CPIB to enable it to implement the anticorruption laws effectively.

### *Demography*

In June 2009, Singapore had a total population of 4,987,600 persons with 3,733,900 (74.9 percent) of them as residents. Its multiracial resident population consists of Chinese (74.2 percent), Malays (13.4 percent), Indians (9.2 percent), and others (3.2 percent) (Department of Statistics, 2010, pp. 9, 26). There are four official languages (English, Mandarin, Malay, and Tamil), several Chinese dialects, and a few languages among the Indians. In terms of religion, the population comprises 51 percent Buddhist or Taoist in 2000, 14.9 percent Muslims, 14.8 percent with no religion, 14.6 percent Christian, 4 percent Hindu, and 0.6 percent belonging to other religions.

The population's heterogeneity in race, language, and religion imposes on the PAP government two important obligations to its citizens. First, the PAP government must promote nation building in Singapore by formulating and implementing policies to ensure racial harmony. The second obligation of the PAP government is to prevent and minimize discrimination against the minority groups by ensuring that both public and private organizations are fair and impartial in their treatment of all citizens, regardless of their ethnic origin, language, or religion. This means that anyone found guilty of corruption in multiracial Singapore is punished, regardless of his or her ethnic group, language, or religion.

### *Political System*

The PAP government assumed office in June 1959 after the PAP had won 43 of the 51 seats in the May 1959 general election. The PAP government has been in power for the past 52 years because it was reelected for 11 times after winning the general elections in 1963, 1968, 1972, 1976, 1980, 1984, 1988, 1991, 1997, 2001, and 2006 (Quah, 2010b, p. 22). Why has the PAP government remained in power for so long in Singapore?

The first reason for the PAP government's predominance in Singapore is that it had ensured Singapore's survival after separation from Malaysia in August 1965 by minimizing the economic effects of the withdrawal of the British military forces in 1971 by attracting foreign investment and by strengthening the country's armed forces through the introduction of compulsory military service in 1967 and the acquisition of military hardware. Second, the PAP government gained legitimacy among Singaporeans because of its effective response to the communist and communal threats and the problem of corruption. Third, the PAP government has delivered the economic goods as reflected in the vast improvement in living standards and per capita GDP since 1959. Finally, the PAP government has dominated Singapore politics because the other 24 registered opposition political parties are weak and ineffective and do not provide a credible alternative (Quah, 2001, pp. 301–306).

Singapore's political stability and continuity is an important asset for the PAP government because it is highly conducive for attracting foreign investment and for improving the effective implementation of public policies as the political leaders can focus on meeting the long-term goals instead of being constrained by short-term considerations. In terms of fighting corruption, the continuity of the PAP government and its commitment to curbing corruption for the past 52 years has certainly enhanced the effectiveness of its anticorruption strategy.

## PERCEIVED EXTENT OF CORRUPTION

Corruption was a way of life in Singapore during the British colonial period, but cases of corruption among civil servants were treated as "departmental" affairs and not publicized. This meant that those bureaucrats found guilty of corruption were asked to resign or were transferred to Britain to maintain the image of incorruptibility of the civil service (Quah, 1982a, p. 161).

However, cases of police corruption were reported in the local press, and 172 cases were reported in the *Straits Times* from 1845 to 1921. Table 6.1 reports that bribery was the most common form of police corruption as it constituted almost two-thirds of the cases, followed by direct criminal activities, which made up about a quarter of the cases. There was a high incidence of bribery cases among the Malay and Indian junior officers because

***Table 6.1.*** Reported Cases of Police Corruption in Singapore by Form, 1845–1921.

| Form of Police Corruption | Number | Percentage |
|---|---|---|
| Bribery | 109 | 63.4 |
| Direct criminal activities | 42 | 24.4 |
| Opportunistic theft | 10 | 5.8 |
| Corruption of authority | 9 | 5.2 |
| Protection of illegal activities | 2 | 1.2 |
| Total | 172 | 100.0 |

*Source*: *Straits Times*, 1845–1921 quoted in Quah (1979, p. 24).

they were poorly paid. In terms of rank, the police constables were the main culprits as they constituted nearly 59 percent of the bribery cases. The corrupt police officers extorted bribes from hawkers, opium shopkeepers, *rikisha*-pullers, and bullock-cart drivers. The hawkers suffered the most because they were the favorite victims of extortion by the police (Quah, 1979, p. 18).

In 1879, the SPF was in trouble because of the increase in the number of criminal cases and complaints made against its members. The British colonial government appointed a Commission of Inquiry to ascertain why the SPF was inefficient. The Commission found that while corruption existed among the European inspectors "to a greater extent than was provable in a Court of Law," it was rife among the Malay and Indian junior police officers. In April 1886, a Commission was appointed to investigate public gambling in the Straits Settlements of Malacca, Penang, and Singapore. Among the 44 witnesses that gave evidence before the Commission in Singapore, 10 testified to the prevalence of corruption in the SPF on the basis of their observations and own experiences.

A gambling informer explained to the 1886 Commission why the gambling house owners were unafraid of the police:

> These men are not afraid of the Police … . The gambling is carried on day and night …. The reason the gambling-house keepers are not afraid of the Police is because the Police are in their pay. (Straits Settlements, 1887, p. 8)

On the basis of the testimonies provided by the 10 witnesses, the Commission concluded that

> there has been a systematic arrangement, both in Singapore and Penang, for corrupting the Police Force, and that in a large degree this has been successful and has reached the Inspector class … . The system in Singapore seems to be that of two or three *kongsis* [partnerships] levying subscriptions from the gambling-houses to bribe the Police to abstain from arresting them … . (Straits Settlements, 1887, pp. i–ii)

The problem of corruption deteriorated during the Japanese Occupation (February 1942 to August 1945) because the rampant inflation made it difficult for civil servants to live on their low salaries. According to Yoong (1972, p. 55), a former CPIB Director:

> The value of the Japanese military currency was so low and the government servants were so poorly paid that if any government officer was to depend only on his salary for his livelihood, his family would have to starve for the greater part of the month. As a result, many resorted to taking bribes or doing some business on the side line to supplement their incomes.

Ronendra Karmakar recalled that his mother had to sell her jewelry in the black market to feed her family:

> If your salary was, say, $100, if you have to pay $10 for an egg, you can imagine how you are going to survive. So we used to sell our things. And the highest value was given for gold ornaments. So what my mother used to do, I remember, we survived because my mother sold her jewelry ... to buy sugar, rice and keep in the home .... (Pitt & Leong, 2009, p. 193)

Trading in the black market became a way of life because "shortages created the black market and a culture of thievery to fuel the market" (Lee, 2005, p. 205). The black market was vital for many people because it "allowed them to act as brokers between a buyer and seller and earn a commission from each transaction to supplement their wages" (Pitt & Leong, 2009, p. 194). Table 6.2 demonstrates clearly the significant differences between the black market and prewar prices of various food items. For example, the rampant inflation increased the price of pork from 30 cents to $400 for a kati, and the price of onions was also rose from 7 cents to $225.

Bribery also "worked wonders," and "nothing was impossible with the right connections." The Japanese Occupation bred corruption into Singaporean society because practices of "bribery, blackmail, and extortion grew out of the violence and fear" that the Japanese used to rule their occupied territories (Lee, 2005, p. 205). Similarly, Turnbull (1977, p. 225) contended that the Japanese Occupation's worst legacy was "the corruption of public and private integrity" because of the "flourishing gambling dens and brothels, both legalized by the Japanese, the resurgence of opium smoking, universal profiteering and bribery."

Conditions deteriorated during the postwar period, and corruption spread among civil servants as a result of their low wages, inflation, and inadequate supervision by their superior officers, thus providing them with ample opportunities for corruption with a low probability of being caught

*Table 6.2.* Prewar and Black Market Prices of Food Items in Singapore.

| Food Items | Prewar Price (British Dollar) | Black Market Price (Syonan Currency) |
|---|---|---|
| Pork (per kati) | 30 cents | $400 |
| Fish | 20 cents | $320 |
| Beef | 20 cents | $150 |
| Sugar | 4 cents | $60 |
| Kangkong (vegetable) | 1 cent | $6 |
| Eggs | 3 cents | $15 |
| Mutton | 30 cents | $125 |
| Coffee powder | 10 cents | $45 |
| Coconut oil (one bottle) | 12 cents | $120 |
| Bean curd | 1 cent | $4 |
| Prawns | 60 cents | $250 |
| Bean sprouts | 2 cents | $25 |
| Green peas | 6 cents | $90 |
| Chillies (fresh) | 14 cents | $100 |
| Dry chillies | 10 cents | $200 |
| Onions | 7 cents | $225 |
| Chinese sauce | 10 cents | $40 |
| Salt fish | 10 cents | $45 |
| Coconut | 2 cents | $12 |

*Source*: Pitt and Leong (2009, p. 197).

(Quah, 1982a, pp. 161–162). Corruption became a way of life for many people and the British Military Administration (BMA), which had taken over after the Japanese surrender in August 1945, was described pejoratively as the "Black Market Administration" because of its arbitrary requisition of private property, gross mismanagement of the distribution of rice, financial inefficiency, and "scandalous corruption" (Turnbull, 1977, p. 225).

The SPF was viewed negatively as "an ill-clad, badly equipped and poorly disciplined rabble," "undernourished, dirty, driven to corruption through necessity, and untrained" (Turnbull, 1977, p. 224). The Commissioner of Police, J P Pennefather-Evans, indicated in his 1950 Report that graft was rife in government departments. A few days later, the Chief of the ACB reported that the problem of corruption was getting worse (Quah, 1978a, p. 14). Corruption was prevalent in those government departments concerned with granting licenses, food and price control action, protection rackets connected with the smuggling of gold bars and opium, and gambling (Yoong, 1972, p. 56).

In October 1951, 1,800 pounds of opium worth S$400,000 (US$133,333) were stolen at Ponggol by a gang of robbers, which included three police detectives. The British colonial government appointed a special team led by a senior ACB officer to investigate the robbery. Investigations revealed that some senior police officers were involved in the racket with both the hijackers and the importers of the opium. However, the British colonial government was not pleased when the investigations resulted in the dismissal of an Assistant Superintendent of Police and the forced retirement of another senior officer (CPIB, 2003a, p. 0.6).

In April 1952, the British colonial government formed another special investigation team to find out what went wrong with the previous investigation conducted by the ACB. When the special team completed its investigation in September 1952, the British colonial government decided to replace the ACB with the special team, which became the CPIB one month later. Thus, the Opium Hijacking scandal of October 1951 was the triggering mechanism that catalyzed the birth of the CPIB. More importantly, the scandal also made the British colonial government realize that it had made a serious mistake in December 1937 when the ACB was entrusted with the task of curbing corruption even though police corruption was rampant in Singapore.

In the 1950s, "bribes and kickbacks were part of the way of life" in Singapore because "people had to grease palms to obtain licenses, permits, immigration papers, public housing and coveted places in schools." A retired architect, Lee Kip Lin, has described the Lim Yew Hock administration as "being corrupt from head to toe." Indeed, Singapore was viewed as "a journalist's paradise" and "a Marxist recipe for revolution" because it was afflicted by "riots, strikes, pickets, protests, demonstrations, squalor, poverty, joblessness, corruption, vice, crime, fires, floods, diseases" (Yap, Lim, & Leong, 2009, pp. 555–556).

As will be discussed in a later section, the PAP government's determination to minimize corruption was manifested in the enactment of the POCA in June 1960, which enabled the CPIB to perform its anticorruption activities effectively. The PAP government's political will and the various measures taken by the SPF to reduce opportunities for corruption have borne fruit as reflected in the reduced number of reported cases of police corruption after independence. Table 6.3 notes that the protection of illegal activities constituted about half of the 67 reported cases of police corruption from 1965 to 1977. Similarly, Table 6.4 confirms that there were 51 reported cases of police corruption in Singapore from 1996 to 2004, or an average of six cases per year during this period. When compared

***Table 6.3.*** Reported Cases of Police Corruption in Singapore by Form, 1965–1977.

| Form of Police Corruption | Number | Percentage |
|---|---|---|
| Protection of illegal activities | 33 | 49.2 |
| The fix | 14 | 20.9 |
| Bribery | 8 | 11.9 |
| Direct criminal activities | 5 | 7.5 |
| Opportunistic theft | 4 | 6.0 |
| Corruption of authority | 3 | 4.5 |
| Total | 67 | 100.0 |

*Source*: *Straits Times*, 1965–1977, cited in Quah (1979, p. 36).

***Table 6.4.*** Reported Cases of Police Corruption in Singapore, 1996–2004.

| Year | Reported Cases | No. of Cases as a Percentage of the SPF's Personnel |
|---|---|---|
| 1996 | 10 | 0.12 |
| 1997 | 3 | 0.04 |
| 1998 | 8 | 0.10 |
| 1999 | 13 | 0.16 |
| 2000 | 4 | 0.05 |
| 2001 | 5 | 0.06 |
| 2002 | NA | NA |
| 2003 | 5 | 0.03 |
| 2004 | 3 | 0.02 |
| Total | 51 | 0.58 |

*Source*: Data provided by the Manpower Department of the SPF.

to the total number of SPF's personnel, these 51 cases constituted only 0.58 percent.

In sum, while corruption is no longer a serious problem in Singapore after independence, this does not mean that it does not exist. Box 6.2 provides details of the embezzlement of the enormous sum of S$34.96 million by an employee of Singapore Airlines, which made the headlines when it was discovered in January 2000.

***Box 6.2.*** Embezzlement in Singapore Airlines

For nearly 13 years (1987–2000), Singapore Airlines (SIA) cabin crew supervisor, Teo Cheng Kiat, tweaked accounts and siphoned money from his company until he was caught on 19 January 2000. He had embezzled an enormous sum of S$34.96 million, which was the largest amount stolen by an employee in Singapore. The Judicial Commissioner, Tay Yong Kwang, sentenced Teo to 24 years imprisonment because the "gargantuan embezzlement was motivated solely by greed, greed and more greed." Teo pleaded guilty to 10 charges of misappropriating S$31 million from SIA between June 1996 and January 2000.

The Deputy Public Prosecutor, Lawrence Ang, informed the High Court that Teo had indulged in an extravagant lifestyle by splurging on properties, luxury cars, expensive watches, jewelry, and designer goods. Teo exploited the weakness in the SIA payment system because he "had the access and authority to make adjustments in the payment system, something even his superiors could not do," according to the judge. Teo was able to conceal his covert criminal activities from his superiors until he was caught.

Judicial Commissioner Tay justified the heavy sentence he imposed on Teo because "the accused was intoxicated by greed for 13 years" and the public interest demanded that "monumental crimes attract memorable sentences."

*Source*: Chong (2000, p. 3).

## CAUSES OF CORRUPTION

Why was corruption a way of life during the British colonial period in Singapore? On 17 October 1865, a reader wrote the following letter to the editor of the *Singapore Daily Times*:

> The demoralization of the Police has become so notorious a subject of conversation … . Although I am unwilling to believe that bribery is carried on to the extent which public report warrants, I unhesitatingly assert that corruption is the rule and not the exception … . It is an acknowledged fact, admitted even by the Police themselves, that the evil complained of exists to a very serious extent, and the chief causes are illicit

> gambling, the Secret Societies of the Chinese, Klings [Indians] and Malays, and the natural propensity of orientals to offer or accept bribes. (*Singapore Daily Times*, 1865)

However, the above explanation for police corruption is incorrect for two reasons. First, illicit gambling and the secret societies provide opportunities for corruption among policemen but are not causes of police corruption. Second, the assumption that "orientals" have a natural propensity for bribery is questionable and unacceptable and smacks of ethnocentricism.

### *Low Salaries*

The most important cause for police corruption during the British colonial period was the low salaries of police officers, especially those in the lower ranks of the Native Contingent. Table 6.5 provides details of the monthly salaries of the European and Native Contingents in 1887. The discrimination in monthly salary between the European and Native Contingent is reflected in the fact that the monthly salary of an European Constable was S$40 plus S$10 rations, or more than three times the monthly salary of a Native Sergeant, who earns only S$15 a month. Furthermore, all the European police officers except those who were inspectors 1st class also received monthly rations of between S$5 and S$10 (Quah, 1979, p. 28).

***Table 6.5.*** Monthly Salaries of Police Officers by Rank, 1887.

| Rank in SPF | Monthly Salary |
|---|---|
| *European contingent* | |
| Inspector 1st class | S$100 (no rations) |
| Inspector 2nd class | S$80 (S$5 rations) |
| Inspector 3rd class | S$60 (S$10 rations) |
| Sergeant | S$50 (S$10 rations) |
| Constable | S$40 (S$10 rations) |
| *Native contingent* | |
| Sergeant | S$15 |
| Corporal | S$12 |
| Constable 1st class | S$10 |
| Constable 2nd class | S$9 |
| Constable 3rd class | S$8 |
| Peon 1st class | S$5 |
| Peon 2nd class | S$4 |

*Source*: *Straits Times* (1887).

In contrast, apart from having lower salaries, the native policemen were not provided with rations, which made life more difficult for them with the increase in food prices. Furthermore, they had to pay for their uniforms, which were relatively expensive as a peon 1st class had to pay S$3.50 for his uniform from his monthly salary of S$5. The poor salaries and working conditions in the SPF led the *Straits Times* (1887) to observe that "It is at once evident that the native constables and the European police of the Inspector class are so underpaid that scandals are unavoidable."

As discussed earlier, the low salaries of the civil servants and the inflation during the Japanese Occupation exacerbated the problem of corruption. Even though the actual incomes of civil servants were increased after the World War II with the assumption of control by the BMA, their salaries remained low and made them vulnerable to corruption because many bureaucrats accepted bribes to supplement their meager wages (Yoong, 1972, p. 56).

A major factor responsible for reducing police corruption in Singapore is the improvement of salaries in the SPF since 1951, when the Police Pay Committee recommended new pay scales and allowances for police officers below the rank of inspector. Consequently, the monthly salary of recruits was increased to S$40 in contrast to the low monthly salary of S$4 for recruits in 1887 (Colony of Singapore, 1951, p. 4). In 1971, the Lee Soo Ann Salary Review Committee recommended between 20 and 25 percent pay increases for the junior police officers as well as free medical aid, free accommodation for married staff, and the reintroduction of dialect and educational allowances. The Committee's recommendations were accepted by the government and implemented in April 1972 (Quah, 2006c, p. 64).

### *Ample Opportunities for Corruption*

Apart from the low salaries, the lack of control over the SPF in areas that were most susceptible to corruption also provided many opportunities for policemen to engage in corrupt practices. The many cases of police involvement in illegal gambling resulted from the lack of control over those inspectors and constables who accepted bribes from the gambling house owners. For example, in April 1846, a European constable, Charles Cashin, was convicted of receiving bribes from illicit gambling dens and sentenced to 18 months imprisonment and a fine of S$1,000. Cashin reported that for the past three years (1843–1846), all the police constables had received S$20 monthly and that the constable who had brought the charge against him had also received bribes himself.

The Deputy Superintendent of Police, Thomas Dunman, admitted in court that the police were in the regular pay of gambling promoters and that it was difficult to rectify the situation (Buckley, 1965, pp. 446–447). Three years later, the *Straits Times* (1849) reported that the police did not take action to suppress gambling activities conducted within 50 yards of a police station in town because the policemen were paid for their silence. Even though the 1886 Commission of Inquiry had confirmed the existence of widespread police corruption in gambling activities, the SPF did nothing to prevent its members from engaging in these activities.

Furthermore, local policemen had ample opportunities for corruption during the colonial period because they sought alternative sources of income to supplement their meager salaries even though they were not legally permitted to take on second jobs. Those local policemen who owned buffalo carts and food stalls could not perform their official duties impartially as they were exposed to more opportunities for misconduct (Quah, 1979, p. 29, 31).

Corruption in Singapore during the British colonial period was not confined to the SPF only because "wet" agencies such as the customs, immigration, and internal revenue departments provided more opportunities for corruption than those "dry" public agencies that had limited contact with the public, did not issue licenses or permits, and did not collect fees or taxes. According to Yoong Siew Wah (1972, p. 57), a former CPIB Director, the granting of licenses and permits provided many opportunities for corruption because

> People were prepared to pay a little extra to obtain licenses, passports, birth certificates, citizenship papers and other kinds of documents useful to them either for their personal use or for their businesses.

Opportunities for corruption in the SCS have been reduced after the PAP government enacted the POCA in June 1960 to empower the CPIB to perform its functions more effectively. For example, the SPF and the CPIB established a joint task force in December 1976 for two reasons: (1) to curb police corruption by identifying existing corruption hazards and formulating appropriate measures to prevent them and (2) to examine those policy aspects that have an impact on corruption prevention. Corrupt police officers would be severely punished and those policemen who were living beyond their means would be watched by the task force (Quah, 2006c, p. 65).

### *Low Risk of Detection and Punishment*

As mentioned in Chapter 1, even though corruption is an illegal offense in all Asian countries, the probability of detection and punishment of corrupt offenses varies in these countries. Corruption usually thrives in those Asian countries where its citizens perceive corruption to be a "low risk, high reward" activity because corrupt offenders are unlikely to be detected and punished. In contrast, corruption is not a serious problem in those Asian countries where corruption is perceived as a "high risk, low reward" activity as those persons involved in corrupt behavior are likely to be caught and severely punished (Quah, 2003a, p. 13).

In Singapore, corruption thrived during the British colonial period when the public perceived it as a low risk, high reward activity because corrupt offenders were unlikely to be detected and punished. The British colonial government's efforts to curb corruption failed because the existing Prevention of Corruption Ordinance (POCO) was ineffective. The POCO was enacted in December 1937 to prevent "bribery and secret commissions in public and private business." Unfortunately, the POCO was ineffective for two reasons. First, its offenses were not seizable and limited the powers of arrest, search, and investigation of police officers because warrants were required before arrests could be made. Second, the penalty of imprisonment for two years and/or a S$10,000 fine for those found guilty of corruption did not deter corrupt behavior (Quah, 1978b, p. 9). A former senior CPIB officer, Muhammed Ali (2000, p. 3) revealed that the weak POCO made gathering of evidence difficult and enabled many corrupt civil servants from getting caught.

Similarly, as described in the previous section, corruption also thrived during the Japanese Occupation because it was perceived as a "low risk, high reward" activity by the public as nepotism and corruption were considered to be "perfectly acceptable" and everyone resorted to "connections, friends and relatives" to get jobs (Lee, 2005, p. 142). The POCO was only amended in 1946 to increase the penalty to a prison term of three years, thus making corrupt offenses seizable and automatically giving police officers "much wider powers of arrest, search and investigation" (Colony of Singapore, 1947, p. 4).

However, the POCO remained ineffective in spite of the 1946 amendment because corruption had become a way of life for many people in Singapore to enable them to cope with their low salaries and rising inflation during the postwar period. The situation remained unchanged until the PAP government enacted the POCA in June 1960 to replace the ineffective POCO. The enactment of the POCA was the turning point in Singapore's battle against corruption because it enabled the CPIB to curb corruption effectively, thus changing the public perception of corruption as "a low risk, high reward" activity to "a high risk, low reward" activity.

### *Cultural Factors*

Like other Asian countries, gift-giving is an important social tradition in Singapore. Among the Chinese, who constitute nearly three-quarters of the population, gift-giving is practiced during the Lunar New Year when children receive *ang pows* (small red envelopes containing money) from their parents and other married relatives. This practice was also extended during this period to civil servants such as postmen, deliverymen, and garbage collectors, who were given *ang pows* by the public in appreciation for their services.

As noted earlier, corruption thrived during the Japanese Occupation as manifested in the black market and the population's reliance on connections or *guanxi* to get things done. As *guanxi* is contextual, the giving of a gift can be considered as an accepted part of the culture of gift-giving, instrumental, or as a bribe, depending on the context (Luo, 2007, p. 11). Consequently, when Lee Kuan Yew became Prime Minister in June 1959, he received many gifts from well-wishers. However, he did not accept these gifts to set an example for his colleagues and all civil servants. Consequently, as will be elaborated later, the government introduced regulations that prohibit civil servants from accepting gifts and entertainment from members of the public to prevent gift-giving from contributing to bribery and corruption.

### *Lack of Political Will*

The British colonial government's lack of political will in curbing corruption is reflected in the delay in introducing anticorruption measures and the two policy mistakes it made after these measures were initiated. Corruption was only made illegal in 1871, 52 years after the founding of Singapore by Stamford Raffles in January 1819. The 1879 and 1886 Commissions of Inquiry confirmed that police corruption was prevalent in the SPF. However, the British colonial authorities did not introduce any measures to curb police corruption. Even though corruption was rampant, nothing was done by the British colonial government for the next 66 years until the POCO was enacted in December 1937.

In retrospect, the British colonial government's decision to make the ACB responsible for corruption control was irrational and foolish especially when the 1879 and 1886 Commissions of Inquiry had documented the prevalence of police corruption. Consequently, it was not surprising that the ACB was ineffective in curbing corruption for three reasons. First, the ACB was inadequately staffed with only 17 personnel. As the Criminal Investigation Department (CID) was mainly concerned with the detection and solving of serious crimes such as murder and kidnapping, the elimination of corruption was accordingly given much lower priority. This meant that the ACB had to compete with the other branches of the CID for limited manpower and other resources (Quah, 1978b, p. 15).

The second reason for the ACB's failure was that the CID was saddled with many functions, and the function of combating corruption was only one of the 16 duties of the Assistant Commissioner of the CID in May 1952. More specifically, apart from curbing corruption, he was also responsible for the following duties: secret societies, gambling promoters, fraud (commercial crime), anti-vice (traffickers), pawnshops, second-hand dealers, narcotics (traffickers), criminal records, banishment, naturalization, missing persons, fingerprints, photography, Police Gazette, and house-to-house and street collections (Colony of Singapore, 1952, p. 31). Thus, it was not surprising that corruption control was not the CID's top priority especially when police corruption was rampant.

The third and most important reason for the ACB's ineffectiveness was the prevalence of police corruption. The ACB officers justified their reluctance to investigate corrupt offenses committed by policemen by according lower priority to corruption control and devoting their attention instead to their other 15 duties. In her speech to the Second Legislative Council on 20 February 1952, Mrs Elizabeth Choy expressed her surprise that the ACB was understaffed and urged the government to separate the ACB from the SPF and to increase its strength (Quah, 1978b, p. 14).

The Opium Hijacking scandal of October 1951 made the British colonial government realize the folly of making the ACB responsible for curbing corruption control when police corruption was rampant in Singapore. Accordingly, it replaced the ACB with the CPIB in October 1952. Having rectified its first policy mistake of making the ACB responsible for corruption control, the British colonial government made the second policy mistake of not providing the CPIB with adequate resources or legal powers. Indeed, it is difficult to understand why the British colonial government did not provide the CPIB with more personnel and powers to enable it to perform its functions more effectively. In fact, the CPIB began its existence with only a small number of staff of 5 members, which was much smaller than the ACB's 17 personnel. The CPIB's small number of staff and lack of powers was a clear manifestation of the British colonial government's lack of political will in combating corruption.

## ANTICORRUPTION MEASURES

During its campaign for the May 1959 general election, the PAP leaders exposed the corruption scandal involving the incumbent Minister for Education, Chew Swee Kee, who had received more than S$700,000 from some American donors. Chew resigned from his position and the Legislative Assembly on 4 March. The PAP's commitment to combating corruption and its exposure of the Chew Swee Kee scandal enabled it to win 43 of the 51 seats with 54.4 percent of the votes cast in the 30 May 1959 general election.

In his memoirs, former Prime Minister Lee Kuan Yew explained clearly why he and his colleagues were determined to keep Singapore free from corruption after assuming office in June 1959:

> We were sickened by the greed, corruption and decadence of many Asian leaders .... We had a deep sense of mission to establish a clean and effective government. When we took the oath of office ... in June 1959, we all wore white shirts and white slacks to symbolize purity and honesty in our personal behavior and our public life ... . We made sure from the day we took office in June 1959 that every dollar in revenue would be properly accounted for and would reach the beneficiaries at the grass roots as one dollar, without being siphoned off along the way. So from the very beginning we gave special attention to the areas where discretionary powers had been exploited for personal gain and sharpened the instruments that could prevent, detect or deter such practices. (Lee, 2000, pp. 182–184)

As corruption was a way of life in Singapore when the PAP government assumed office in June 1959, its mission was to minimize corruption by changing the public perception of corruption as a low risk, high reward activity to a high risk, low reward activity. As the POCO was ineffective and the CPIB did not have sufficient legal powers and inadequately staffed with eight personnel in 1959, the PAP government's top priority was to strengthen both the POCO and the CPIB. In line with this objective, the PAP leaders initiated a comprehensive anticorruption strategy in June 1960 by enacting the POCA to strengthen the CPIB.

### *Prevention of Corruption Act*

On 13 February 1960, the Minister for Home Affairs, Ong Pang Boon, moved for the second reading of the Prevention of Corruption Bill in the Legislative Assembly:

> The Prevention of Corruption Bill is in keeping with the new Government's determination to stamp out bribery and corruption in the country, especially in the public services … . Therefore, this Government is determined to take all possible steps to see that all necessary legislative and administrative measures are taken *to reduce the opportunities of corruption*, to make its detection easier and to deter and punish severely those who are susceptible to it and who engage in it shamelessly. (quoted in Quah, 1978b, p. 10, emphasis added)

The POCA was enacted on 17 June 1960. It has four important features that remove the POCO's weaknesses, enhance the CPIB's legal powers, and increase its personnel. First, the POCA's scope is broader with 32 sections compared with the POCO's 12 sections.[1] Second, corruption is defined explicitly in section 2 in terms of various forms of gratification, which include the following:

(a) money or any gift, loan, fee, reward, commission, valuable security, or other property or interest in property of any description, whether movable or immovable;
(b) any office, employment, or contract;
(c) any payment, release, discharge or liquidation of any loan, obligation or other liability whatsoever, whether in whole or in part;
(d) any other service, favor, or advantage of any description whatsoever, including protection from any penalty or disability incurred or apprehended or from any action or proceedings of a disciplinary or penal nature, whether or not already instituted, and including the exercise or the forbearance from the exercise of any right or any official power or duty; and
(e) any offer, undertaking or promise of any gratification within the meaning of paragraphs (*a*), (*b*), (*c*), and (*d*).

Third, according to section 5, a person who by himself or in cooperation with another person "(a) corruptly solicit or receive, or agree to receive for himself, or for any other person; or (b) corruptly give, promise or offer to any person whether for the benefit of that person or of another person," any gratification shall be guilty of an offense and shall be liable on conviction to a fine of S$100,000 or to imprisonment for five years. To prevent corruption among civil servants in Singapore, *Instruction Manual 2* has a section on "Staff Conduct and Discipline," which includes regulations that forbid them and their families from receiving gifts or entertainment from members of the public.[2]

The fourth and most important feature of the POCA is that it gives the CPIB more powers and a new lease of life. Section 15 gives CPIB officers powers of arrest and search of arrested persons. Section 18 empowers the public prosecutor to authorize the CPIB's Director and his senior officers to investigate "any bank account, share account or purchase account" of any person suspected of having committed an offense against the POCA. Section 20 enables the CPIB officers to inspect a civil servant's banker's book and those of his wife, child, or agent, if necessary. Section 21 empowers the public prosecutor to obtain information on an individual's property, income tax, and bank accounts from the relevant government departments and banks. Police officers and CPIB officers are given powers of search and seizure by section 22, which enables them to enter any suspected place and search, seize, and detain incriminating documents under a warrant issued by a magistrate or the CPIB's Director.

Section 24 is perhaps the most important asset for the CPIB in its investigation of corruption offenses because "the fact that an accused person is in possession, for which he cannot satisfactorily account, of pecuniary resources or property disproportionate to his known sources of income" is evidence that he or she had obtained these pecuniary resources or property "corruptly as an inducement or reward." Section 27 states that those individuals required by the CPIB's Director or officers to provide information are legally bound to do so. Section 32 enables the CPIB to deal with offenders more swiftly and effectively as it specifies that all offenses under the POCA are seizable offenses. Section 35 also empowers the court to require those charged with an offense under the POCA to appear as witnesses for the prosecution. Finally, the CPIB is also assisted by section 36, which protects informers by keeping their identities confidential. In short, the POCA has given the CPIB a new lease of life by entrusting it with additional powers for performing its duties.

To ensure the POCA's continued effectiveness, the PAP government has introduced, whenever necessary, amendments (in 1963, 1966, and 1981) or new legislation (in 1989) to deal with unanticipated problems or to plug legal loopholes. For example, in 1966, the POCA was amended so that a person could be found guilty of corruption without actually receiving the bribe as long as he had shown the intention of doing so (section 9). The POCA was also amended in 1966 so that, according to section 37, Singaporeans working for their government in embassies and other government agencies abroad would be prosecuted for corrupt offenses committed outside

Singapore and would be dealt with as if such offenses had occurred within Singapore.

In 1981, the POCA was amended a third time to increase its deterrent effect by requiring those convicted of corruption to repay all the money received in addition to facing the usual court sentence (section 13). Offenders who could not make full restitution were given heavier court sentences. Eight years later, the fine for corrupt offenses was further increased by 10 times from S$10,000 to S$100,000 (US$78,511[3]) to enhance the POCA's deterrent effect. Sections 11 and 12 stipulate that MPs and members of public bodies found guilty of corrupt offenses would be fined S$100,000 and imprisoned for a term of seven years.

As discussed at the outset of this chapter, Teh Cheang Wan's suicide on 14 December 1986 led to a Commission of Inquiry and the enactment of the Corruption (Confiscation of Benefits) Act on 3 March 1989 that was designed "to provide for the confiscation of benefits derived from corruption and for purposes connected therewith." More specifically, section 4 stated that the court should issue "a confiscation order against the defendant in respect of benefits derived from him from corruption if the court is satisfied that such benefits have been so derived." If a defendant is deceased, the court would issue a confiscation order against his estate. Finally, a deceased defendant had "derived benefits from corruption" if he had owned property or interest disproportionate to his known sources of income, which cannot be explained to the court's satisfaction six years before his death (Republic of Singapore, 1989, pp. 107, 110, 129). The Corruption (Confiscation of Benefits) Act of 1989 was expanded and renamed as the Corruption, Drug Trafficking and Other Serious Crimes (Confiscation of Benefits) Act, Chapter 65A in September 1999.

### *Corrupt Practices Investigation Bureau*

In contrast to the British colonial government's lack of political will, the PAP government demonstrated its commitment to combating corruption by enacting the POCA one year after it assumed office in June 1959. The CPIB is responsible for enforcing the POCA in Singapore and performs the following three functions: (1) to receive and investigate complaints concerning corruption in the public and private sectors; (2) to investigate malpractices and misconduct by public officers; and (3) to examine the practices and procedures in the public service to minimize opportunities for corruption (CPIB, 2004, p. 3).

The Corrupt Practices Investigation Program is described in the Budget as the administration of the CPIB, the investigation of corruption and malpractices, and the review of administrative weaknesses in the public sector that "provides avenues for corruption and the screening of officers for appointment in the public service" (Republic of Singapore, 1995, p. 638). Thus, in relation to its preventive function, the CPIB also ensures that candidates selected for positions in the SCS and statutory boards in Singapore are screened to ensure that only those candidates without any taint of corruption or misconduct are actually appointed.

The CPIB has grown by nearly 19 times from a small number of staff of five officers in 1952 to its current strength of 93 officers in 2010 as noted in Table 6.6. Even though the CPIB has grown in size during its first 57 years, it is still a relatively small agency on two counts. First, the CPIB only constitutes 0.13 percent of the SCS, which had 74,201 members in 2009 (Department of Statistics, 2010, p. 52). Second, the ICAC in Hong Kong SAR is nearly 14 times larger than the CPIB because it has 1,268 personnel in 2009 (ICAC, 2010, p. 27). In spite of its workload, the CPIB does not need as much staff as the ICAC because its location within the Prime Minister's Office (PMO) and its legal powers have enabled the CPIB to obtain the necessary cooperation from both public and private organizations (Quah, 1995, p. 397).

Organizationally, the CPIB is divided into the Operations Division and the Administration and Specialist Support Division. The Operations Division is subdivided into the Operations Branch and the Operations

***Table 6.6.*** Growth of CPIB's Personnel, 1952–2010.

| Year | No of Personnel |
|---|---|
| 1952 | 5 |
| 1959 | 8 |
| 1963 | 33 |
| 1965 | 36 |
| 1970 | 50 |
| 1976 | 61 |
| 1980 | 69 |
| 1998 | 79 |
| 2000 | 84 |
| 2005 | 82 |
| 2007 | 89 |
| 2009 | 93 |
| 2010 | 93 |

*Sources*: Compiled from Quah (1978b, p. 17) and Republic of Singapore (1978–2010).

Support Branch, which includes the Intelligence Unit. The Operations Branch consists of the Special Investigation Team, which handles major and complex cases, and three other units. The Administration and Specialist Support Division has four units: Administration Unit, Prevention and Review Unit, Computer Information System Unit, and the Plans and Projects Unit (CPIB, 2004, pp. 3–4). The CPIB upgraded the Computer Information Unit in July 2004 with the formation of the Computer Forensic Unit to improve its investigative and evidence gathering capabilities (CPIB, 2008).

Table 6.7 notes that the PAP government has provided the CPIB with sufficient resources as manifested in the growth of the CPIB's budget from 1978 to 2009. The CPIB's budget has grown progressively by four times from S$1,024,370 in 1978 to S$4,147,230 in 1987. The CPIB's budget increased by almost 10 times to S$10,225,463 in 1997, by 14 times to S$14,619,718 in 2007, by 16 times to S$16,386,900 in 2009, and by about 20 times to S$20,094,000 in 2010.

For enforcement, the CPIB has adopted a "total approach" by dealing with both "big and small cases" of corruption in both the public and the private sectors, "both giver and receiver of bribes" and "other crimes uncovered in the course of [the] corruption investigation" (Soh, 2008a, pp. 1–2). In addition to its emphasis on investigation and enforcement, the CPIB employs a proactive approach to its activities on corruption prevention and education. As part of its preventive function, the CPIB reviews the procedures and practices in those government agencies where corruption has occurred and makes recommendations to remove the "loopholes and vulnerabilities." The CPIB uses this review process to "identify potential problem areas and loopholes" to minimize the opportunities for corruption (Soh, 2008b, p. 8).

***Table 6.7.*** CPIB's Budget, 1978–2010.

| Year | Budget (S$) | Percentage Increase |
|---|---|---|
| 1978 | $1,024,370 | 100 |
| 1987 | $4,147,230 | 405 |
| 1997 | $10,225,463 | 998 |
| 2007 | $14,619,718 | 1,427 |
| 2008 | $15,790,811 | 1,542 |
| 2009 | $16,386,900 | 1,600 |
| 2010 | $20,094,000 | 1,962 |

*Source*: Republic of Singapore (1978–2010).

***Table 6.8.*** Participants attending CPIB's Prevention and Education Activities, 2005–2007.

| Activity | 2005 | 2006 | 2007 |
|---|---|---|---|
| Prevention and education talks | 2,500 | 4,500 | 7,000 |
| Visits by foreign delegates | 1,000 | 1,500 | 2,000 |
| Visits by local organizations | 20 | 200 | 350 |
| Student visits | 150 | 200 | 400 |
| Total | 3,670 | 6,400 | 9,750 |

*Source*: Information provided by the CPIB on 3 July 2008.

The CPIB has an extensive outreach program that is implemented by its Public Education Group, which conducts prevention and education talks for preuniversity students, principals, and teachers; newly appointed civil servants; law enforcement agencies such as the police and immigration; and the management and staff of major organizations in key industries. Government departments and statutory boards in Singapore can book corruption prevention talks for their officers online on preferred dates and times from the CPIB's web site.

The CPIB's success has attracted worldwide attention, and it has received many visitors from other countries. The CPIB has arranged attachments for the staff of ACAs from 21 countries during 2006–2008 (Soh, 2008b, p. 5). It also conducts anticorruption training courses for civil servants at various levels in Singapore with the Civil Service College. Table 6.8 notes that the number of persons attending the CPIB's prevention and education talks has increased from 2,500 in 2005 to 7,000 in 2007. Similarly, the number of foreign visitors to the CPIB has doubled from 1,000 to 2,000 during 2005–2007. Overall, the number of persons participating in the CPIB's prevention and educational activities increased by 2.7 times from 3,670 in 2005 to 9,750 in 2007.

## EVALUATION OF ANTICORRUPTION MEASURES

How effective are the POCA and CPIB in curbing corruption in Singapore? The effectiveness of these anticorruption measures can be assessed at the national level by referring to Singapore's ranking and scores on these five indicators: TI's CPI from 1995–2010; Hong Kong's PERC annual surveys of corruption from 1995 to 2010; World Bank's control of corruption from 1996 to 2009; World Bank's *Doing Business Surveys* from 2007–2011; and the *Global Competitiveness Report's* indicator on the public trust of politicians from 1999 to 2010–2011.

Table 6.9 notes that first, Singapore has been consistently ranked as the least corrupt country in Asia from 1995 to 2009 and the least corrupt country in the world in 2010 with Denmark and New Zealand. Second, PERC's annual surveys of corruption from 1995 to 2010 also confirm Singapore's status as the least corrupt country in Asia. Third, the World Bank's control of corruption indicator from 1996 to 2009 shows that Singapore has the highest percentile rank among all the Asian countries included in the surveys.

Fourth, Table 6.10 confirms that red tape is not a problem at all because Singapore has been ranked first in terms of the ease of doing business among the 175–183 economies included in the World Bank's *Doing Business Surveys* from 2007 to 2011. The relative absence of red tape in Singapore is also an indicator that corruption is not a serious problem, as reflected in Singapore's consistently high ranking and scores on the CPI from 2007 to 2010.

***Table 6.9.*** Singapore's Performance on CPI, PERC and Control of Corruption 1995–2010.

| Year | CPI Rank & Score | PERC Rank & Score | Control of Corruption Percentile Rank |
|---|---|---|---|
| 1995 | 3rd (9.26) | 1st (1.20) | NA |
| 1996 | 7th (8.80) | 1st (1.09) | 97.6 |
| 1997 | 9th (8.66) | 1st (1.05) | NA |
| 1998 | 7th (9.1) | 1st (1.43) | 100.0 |
| 1999 | 7th (9.1) | 1st (1.55) | NA |
| 2000 | 6th (9.1) | 1st (0.71) | 99.5 |
| 2001 | 4th (9.2) | 1st (0.83) | NA |
| 2002 | 5th (9.3) | 1st (0.90) | 99.5 |
| 2003 | 5th (9.4) | 1st (0.38) | 99.0 |
| 2004 | 5th (9.3) | 1st (0.50) | 99.5 |
| 2005 | 5th (9.4) | 1st (0.65) | 99.0 |
| 2006 | 5th (9.3) | 1st (1.30) | 98.1 |
| 2007 | 4th (9.3) | 1st (1.20) | 96.1 |
| 2008 | 4th (9.2) | 1st (1.13) | 99.5 |
| 2009 | 3rd (9.2) | 1st (1.07) | 99.0 |
| 2010 | 1st (9.3) | 1st (1.42) | NA |

*Sources*: http://www.transparency.org; PERC (2001, 2008, p. 7); Hussain (2009, p. B5); *Straits Times* (2010a); and http://info.worldbank.org/governance/wgi/mc_chart.asp

*Table 6.10.* Ease of Doing Business in Singapore, 2007–2011.

| Indicator | 2007 (*N* = 175) | 2008 (*N* = 178) | 2009 (*N* = 181) | 2010 (*N* = 183) | 2011 (*N* = 183) |
|---|---|---|---|---|---|
| Ease of doing business (rank) | 1 | 1 | 1 | 1 | 1 |
| Starting a business (rank) | 11 | 9 | 10 | 4 | 4 |
| No. of procedures | 6 | 5 | 4 | 3 | 3 |
| Time (days) | 6 | 5 | 4 | 3 | 3 |
| Cost (% of income per capita) | 0.8 | 0.8 | 0.7 | 0.7 | 0.7 |
| Dealing with construction permits or licenses (rank) | 8 | 5 | 2 | 2 | 2 |
| No. of procedures | 11 | 11 | 11 | 11 | 11 |
| Time (days) | 129 | 102 | 38 | 25 | 25 |
| Cost (% of income per capita) | 22.0 | 22.9 | 21.2 | 19.9 | 19.7 |
| Registering property (rank) | 12 | 13 | 16 | 16 | 15 |
| No. of procedures | 3 | 3 | 3 | 3 | 3 |
| Time (days) | 9 | 9 | 9 | 5 | 5 |
| Cost (% of property value) | 2.8 | 2.8 | 2.8 | 2.8 | 2.8 |
| CPI rank and score | 4th (9.3) | 4th (9.2) | 3rd (9.2) | 1st (9.3) | NA |

*Sources*: World Bank (2006b, p. 140; 2007, p. 149; 2008, p. 133; 2009, p. 150; 2010a, p. 192).

Fifth, Table 6.11 confirms the high level of public trust of politicians in Singapore from 1999 to 2010–2011. Singapore has been consistently ranked first with a score ranging from 6.36 to 6.50 among the 59–139 countries surveyed in the *Global Competitiveness Reports* during this period. This finding is not surprising because it is another indication of the high level of public trust of politicians and the low level of corruption in Singapore.

### *Is the CPIB effective?*

At the agency level, the effectiveness of the CPIB in enforcing the POCA is assessed by relying on three sets of indicators: its emphasis on organizational excellence, its seven performance indicators, and its favorable public perceptions. The CPIB's commitment to organizational excellence is reflected in the many awards it has won. In 2000, the CPIB became the first agency in Singapore other than a ministry to be awarded the Public Service Award for Organizational Excellence for attaining the following three awards: ISO 9000 (awarded in December 1997 and renewed in 2000); Singapore Quality Class (awarded in July 1998 and renewed in 2000); and

***Table 6.11.*** Public Trust of Politicians in Singapore, 1999 to 2010–2011.

| Year | Rank | Score[a] | No. of Countries |
|---|---|---|---|
| 1999 | 1 | 6.36 | 59 |
| 2000 | 1 | 6.50 | 59 |
| 2001–2002 | 1 | 6.40 | 75 |
| 2002–2003 | 1 | 6.40 | 80 |
| 2003–2004 | 1 | 6.50 | 102 |
| 2007–2008 | 1 | 6.40 | 131 |
| 2008–2009 | 1 | 6.50 | 134 |
| 2009–2010 | 1 | 6.40 | 133 |
| 2010–2011 | 1 | 6.40 | 139 |
| Average | 1 | 6.43 | – |

*Sources*: Compiled from Schwab et al. (1999, p. 327), Porter et al. (2000, p. 253), Schwab et al. (2002, p. 408), Cornelius (2003, p. 619), Sala-i-Martin (2004, p. 499), Schwab and Porter (2007, p. 379), Schwab and Porter (2008, p. 367), Schwab (2009, p. 349), and Schwab (2010, p. 369).
[a]The score ranges from 1 (very low) to 7 (very high) for the respondents' answers to this question: "How would you rate the level of public trust in the ethical standards of politicians in your country?"

People Developer (awarded in March 1999 and renewed in 2002) (CPIB, 2003a, p. 15.100). Three years later, the CPIB was the first government agency to receive the People Excellence Award (CPIB, 2003b; Tan, 2003, p. 6). In 2004, the CPIB attained the Singapore Service Class and the Singapore Innovation Class. Finally, the CPIB was awarded the Distinguished Public Service Award for Organizational Excellence in 2005 because it had attained six of the eight organizational excellence awards in Singapore during 1995–2005 (*Challenge*, 2006).

Table 6.12 provides data on the CPIB's seven performance indicators that confirm its effectiveness. It shows that the CPIB has (1) exceeded its target of completing 62 percent of its investigations within 30 days by an average of 31.3 percent from 1999 to 2002; (2) exceeded its target of completing 90 percent of cases in a year from 1999 to 2002; (3) increased its prosecution rate from 47 percent to 60 percent from 2000 to 2002; (4) investigated an average of 60 percent of the reports received from 1998 to 2002; and (5) increased its conviction rate from 97 percent to 99 percent from 2000 to 2002.

The third indicator of the CPIB's effectiveness is also reflected in its favorable public perceptions in both the 2002 and 2005 surveys of 1,000 Singaporeans. According to Table 6.13, 13 percent of the respondents in the October 2002 survey gave Singapore an excellent grade for corruption control, 42 percent a very good grade, 39 percent a good grade, and only 7

***Table 6.12.*** CPIB's Performance Indicators, 1997–2002.

| Performance Indicator | Definition | Performance Data |
|---|---|---|
| 1. Cycle time | Time taken to complete an investigation | Exceeded target of completing 62% of its investigations within 30 days by an average of 31.3% during 1999–2002 |
| 2. Completion rate | Percentage of cases completed in a year | Exceeded target of completing 90% of cases in a year during 1999–2002 |
| 3. Prosecution rate | Percentage of cases resulting in prosecution | Increased from 47% in 2000 to 60% in 2002 |
| 4. Conviction rate | Percentage of cases convicted in court | Increased from 97% in 2000 to 99% in 2002 |
| 5. Attendance to visitors | Target is to attend to 80% of its visitors within five minutes | Exceeded target by 1% to 6% from 1997–2000 |
| 6. Proportion of reports investigated | Percentage of reports investigated | Average of 60% during 1998–2000 |
| 7. Number of persons charged and disciplined | Number of persons charged and the number of public officers disciplined | 680 persons were charged and 293 public officers were disciplined during 2000–2002 |

*Source*: CPIB (2003a, pp. 3.24, 3.25, 14.96, 5.36).

percent a fair grade. Similarly, 71 percent of the respondents agreed or strongly agreed that the CPIB has done well in solving corruption offenses. Furthermore, 61 percent of them trusted the CPIB to keep Singapore corruption free, and 56 percent of them agreed or strongly agreed that the CPIB was world class in curbing corruption. The respondents' positive view of the CPIB's professionalism was manifested in these survey findings: nearly 70 percent of the respondents believed that the CPIB was impartial in its investigations, 65 percent of them said that the CPIB had not abused its investigation powers, and 66 percent of them thought that the CPIB would keep the corruption reports received as confidential.

Similarly, the 2005 public perception survey commissioned by the CPIB also confirmed the public's favorable view of the CPIB's performance. First, in terms of the perceived level of corruption control, 89 percent of the respondents observed that corruption was very much under control in Singapore. Nearly half of them (48 percent) said that the level of corruption control had improved during the past three years. Furthermore, 86 percent of the respondents felt that corruption control in Singapore was better than other countries. The respondents had attributed the low level of corruption

***Table 6.13.*** Public Perceptions of CPIB's Performance in 2002.

| Survey Item | Survey Findings |
|---|---|
| 1. How would you rate corruption control in Singapore? | Excellent = 13%; very good = 42%; good = 39%; fair = 7%; poor = 0 |
| 2. CPIB has done well in solving corruption offenses | Strongly agree = 20%; agree = 51%; not sure = 28%; disagree = 2%; strongly disagree = 0 |
| 3. CPIB can be trusted to keep Singapore corruption-free | Strongly agree = 24%; agree = 37%; not sure = 32%; disagree = 2%; strongly disagree = 1% |
| 4. CPIB is world class in fighting corruption | Strongly agree = 17%; agree = 39%; not sure = 36%; disagree = 7%; strongly disagree = 1 |
| 5. Do you think the CPIB is impartial/fair in its investigations? | Yes = 69.9%; no = 5.6%; don't know/no opinion = 24.5% |
| 6. Do you think CPIB has abused its investigation powers? | No = 65%; yes = 7.2%; don't know/no opinion = 27.8% |
| 7. Do you think CPIB will keep corruption reports it receives confidential? | Yes = 66%; no = 10%; don't know/no opinion = 24% |

*Source*: CPIB (2003a, pp. 5.40, 14.97).

in Singapore to the political will to keep corruption under control, the heavy punishment for corruption offenses, and the effectiveness of the POCA (CPIB, 2006, pp. 1–2).

Second, regarding the role of the CPIB, 80 percent of the respondents knew that there was a government department responsible for investigating corruption offenses and 57 percent could identify the CPIB. Among the latter, 67 percent said that the CPIB was doing a good job and only 2 percent thought otherwise. Furthermore, 72 percent of them trusted the CPIB to be impartial in handling investigations, and 9 percent did not share this view. Similarly, 55 percent of the respondents agreed that the CPIB did not abuse its investigation powers, whereas 9 percent of them felt that it did.

Third, half of the respondents said that they would report a case of corruption, 34 percent indicated that their response depended on the situation, 12 percent would not do so, and only 4 percent had no opinion. Regarding the confidentiality of CPIB's reports, 72 percent of the respondents believed that the CPIB would keep its reports confidential, whereas the remaining 28 percent were not sure or had no opinion. Finally, 81 percent of the respondents felt that the CPIB's service targets were "just right," whereas 6 percent of them said that these targets were lenient (CPIB, 2006, pp. 2–3).

### *Is the CPIB independent?*

The CPIB's activities are reviewed by two committees: the Anti-Corruption Advisory Committee (ACAC) and the Anti-Corruption Review Committee (ACRC). The ACAC was formed in 1973 on the Prime Minister's advice to enhance the CPIB's efforts to curb corruption in the SCS. The ACAC consists of the head of the SCS and all the permanent secretaries. The ACAC was dissolved in 1975 and revived in 1996 on the ACRC's recommendation to review the CPIB's investigative and preventive measures. The ACRC was established in 1996 to review Singapore's anticorruption measures. The ACRC is also made up of senior civil servants and is chaired by the head of the SCS (Tan, 1999, p. 61).

The CPIB was originally under the Attorney General's purview when it was formed in October 1952. After being transferred to the MHA in 1959, the CPIB was under the jurisdiction of the PMO during 1963–1965, and the Attorney General from 1965 to 1968. Since 1969, the CPIB has been under the PMO's jurisdiction (CPIB, 2003a, p. 16.109). Even though the CPIB comes under the PMO's purview, it has investigated all allegations of corruption against political leaders and senior civil servants in Singapore as the PAP government is committed to curbing corruption.

The CPIB has investigated these four PAP leaders for corruption: (1) Tan Kia Gan, the Minister for National Development, in 1966 for assisting his friend in the sale of Boeing aircraft to Malaysian Airways; (2) Wee Toon Boon, Minister of State, in 1975 for accepting bribes from a property developer; (3) Phey Yew Kok, a MP and trade union leader, in 1979 for criminal breach of trust; and (4) Teh Cheang Wan, Minister for National Development, in 1986 for accepting bribes from two property developers. Tan was stripped of all his public appointments as the witnesses did not give evidence against him. Wee was found guilty and sentenced to four and a half years of imprisonment. Phey jumped bail and fled abroad and remains a fugitive. As mentioned at the beginning of this chapter, Teh committed suicide before he could be charged in court (CPIB, 2003a, pp. 6.45–6.47).

Corrupt senior civil servants have also not been spared by the CPIB. In March 1991, the Director of the Commercial Affairs Department (CAD), Glenn Knight, was investigated and sentenced to three months' jail in October 1991 for attempted cheating and giving false information to obtain a government car loan. In 1993, the Chief Executive Officer (CEO) of the Trade Development Board (TDB), Yeo Seng Teck, was investigated for cheating offenses and charged for 22 counts of forgery, cheating, and using forged invoices involving the purchases of Chinese antiques worth S$2 million. Yeo was found guilty and sentenced to four years' imprisonment. In 1995, Choy Hon Tim, the Deputy Chief Executive (Operations) of the Public Utilities Board (PUB), was investigated for receiving kickbacks from some contractors. He was convicted for receiving bribes amounting to S$13.85 million and sentenced to 14 years' imprisonment (CPIB, 2003a, pp. 6.48–6.49).

The Constitution of the Republic of Singapore was amended in 1991 to establish the elected president whose role is threefold: to protect the official foreign reserves; to maintain the integrity of the SCS and statutory boards; and to prevent the government from abusing its powers to curb subversion, religious extremism, and corruption (Quah, 1991, pp. 396–398). To prevent the government from abusing its power to curb corruption, article 22 empowers the CPIB's Director to investigate ministers and senior civil servants without the prime minister's permission if he obtains the elected president's consent. This means that the CPIB's Director can investigate the prime minister for corruption if he has the elected president's permission to do so (CPIB, 2003a, p. 2.16). In other words, the elected president was introduced to check the prime minister's power in Singapore's one-party dominant parliament because "without certain safeguards, it would be quite easy for a corrupt prime minister to squander the country's hard-earned official foreign reserves," which have increased to S$263,955.4 million (US$187,809.1 million) in December 2009 (Department of Statistics, 2010, p. 190).

There are six indicators for assessing the independence of the CPIB and other ACAs:

1. *Location*: Where is the ACA located in the government?
2. *Appointment of director*: Who appoints him/her and to whom must he/she report?
3. *Independence from police*: As the ACAs in former British colonies originated from the police, is the ACA still part of the police or an independent agency?
4. *Investigation of political leaders and senior civil servants*: Has the ACA investigated political leaders and senior civil servants if they are accused of corruption?
5. *Taking action against "big fish"*: Has the ACA taken action against corrupt prominent individuals? How many "big fish" have been prosecuted and convicted?
6. *Weapon against opposition*: Has the ACA been used by the incumbent government as a weapon against its political opponents? (Quah, 2009a, p. 786).

First, as mentioned earlier, even though the CPIB in Singapore has been under the Prime Minister's purview since 1969, it has not hesitated to investigate allegations of corruption against political leaders and senior civil servants. Second, the CPIB's Director is appointed by the President on the advice of the Prime Minister and reports to the latter. However, it should be noted that the Prime Minister does not interfere or supervise the CPIB's activities. Third, the CPIB was formed in October 1952 as an ACA that was independent of the SPF in view of the ACB's ineffectiveness to curb police corruption. Fourth, the CPIB has not hesitated to investigate political leaders and senior civil servants for corruption. Fifth, the "big fish" investigated and prosecuted by the CPIB included two ministers, a minister of state, a prominent trade union leader, the Director of the CAD, the TDB's CEO, and the PUB's Deputy Chief Executive. Sixth, the PAP government has not used the CPIB as a weapon against its political foes during the past 52 years.

Thus, the CPIB's Director can obtain the elected President's consent to investigate allegations of corruption against ministers, MPs, and senior civil servants if the Prime Minister withholds his consent. However, the fact remains that the CPIB is not immune from the Prime Minister's influence and control because it is under his jurisdiction. Nevertheless, the PAP government has remained committed to minimizing corruption and so far has not used the CPIB as a weapon against opposition political leaders. Nevertheless, the CPIB's lack of complete independence from the PMO makes it an unattractive model for those Asian countries, which are concerned with the possibility of their political leaders using a CPIB-styled agency against their political foes. In other words, the concern is whether the political leaders in other Asian countries can resist the temptation of employing a CPIB-styled agency against their political rivals (Quah, 2009a, pp. 787–788).

## CONCLUSION

The preceding discussion has shown that the CPIB is an effective and independent ACA. Singapore's success in minimizing corruption can be attributed to the PAP government's political will as manifested in the allocation of adequate legal powers, budget, and personnel to the CPIB to enable it to implement the POCA impartially and effectively. In January 1987, Prime Minister Lee Kuan Yew explained Singapore's effective anticorruption strategy in terms of these five factors:

> The effectiveness of our system to check and punish corruption rest, first, on the law against corruption contained in the Prevention of Corruption Act; second, on a vigilant public ready to give information on all suspected corruption; and third, on a CPIB which is scrupulous, thorough, and fearless in its investigations. For this to be so, the CPIB has to receive the full backing of the Prime Minister, under whose portfolio it comes. But the strongest deterrent is in a public opinion which censures and condemns corrupt persons; in other words, in attitudes which make corruption so unacceptable that the stigma of corruption cannot be washed away by serving a prison sentence. (quoted in Parliament of Singapore, 1987, p. 2)

Although the CPIB is responsible to a large extent for Singapore's effective anticorruption strategy, it should also be acknowledged that the CPIB's efforts in curbing corruption have been assisted by the PAP government's reliance on meritocracy, paying competitive salaries to ministers and senior civil servants, cutting red tape, and using e-government to reduce opportunities for corruption.

The British colonial government introduced meritocracy to Singapore with the establishment of the PSC in January 1951. The PAP government has enhanced the legacy of meritocracy by continuing to rely on the PSC to recruit and promote civil servants on the basis of merit. To attract the "best and brightest" Singaporeans into the SCS, the PSC awards scholarships to the best students in each cohort and requires them to serve for a number of years after their graduation. The PAP government reduced the PSC's heavy workload by creating the Public Service Division in 1983, the Education Service Commission and the Police and Civil Defense Services Commission in 1990, and the system of 31 personnel boards in 1995 (Quah, 2010b, pp. 76–78, 82–88).

When the PAP government assumed office in June 1959, it was forced to cut the variable allowance of senior civil servants to avoid the anticipated budgetary deficit of S$14 million. Division I officers were the hardest hit as they lost all their allowances, which constituted 35 percent of their basic salaries. The improvement of Singapore's economy in the 1970s resulted in higher salaries in the private sector and a brain drain from the SCS. In February 1972, the PAP government formed the National Wages Council, which recommended the payment of the 13th month salary in December to minimize the wage gap in the public and the private sectors. The salaries of ministers and senior civil servants were raised from 1973 to 1994 to curb the loss of talented civil servants to the private sector. However, from 1995, these salaries were benchmarked according to the average salaries of the top four earners in six private sector professions. This policy of paying competitive salaries has curbed the brain drain of ministers and permanent secretaries (but not Division I civil servants) to the private sector and reduced the temptation for senior civil servants and ministers to be corrupt (Quah, 2010b, pp. 103–116, 119–120).

To reduce red tape and minimize bureaucratic delay, the Service Improvement Unit was formed in April 1991 to improve service in the SCS by eliminating unnecessary regulations. In May 1995, Public Service for the 21st Century (PS21) was introduced to improve the quality of service and prepare civil servants to welcome and accept change. As part of PS21, the Cut Waste Panel was established in September 2003 to get public feedback on how the government can reduce waste and increase savings in the delivery of public services. Singapore's effectiveness in cutting red tape is reflected in its consistent first ranking among the 175–183 economies from 2007 to 2011 (World Bank, 2006b, p. 6, 2007, p. 6, 2008, p. 6, 2009, p. 6, 2010a, p. 4).

The PAP government has relied on e-government to enhance transparency and reduce opportunities for corruption through the simplification of the procedures for obtaining business licenses. In 2004, the On-line Applications System for Integrated Services (OASIS) was introduced to enable the public to "apply, renew or terminate 85 different types of licenses" online. Similarly, the online procurement portal known as GeBiz was launched to allow government procurement to be done through the Internet, thereby reducing the opportunities for corruption and enhancing efficiency and transparency in procurement (Soh, 2008b, p. 7). GeBiz provides a great deal of procurement information and documentation including guidelines for registration as a government supplier and details of the submitted tenders (Jones, 2002, p. 37).

Perhaps, the most important challenge facing the PAP government and the SCS is the need to maintain and preserve the tradition of honest and effective government, which has benefited Singapore and its citizens for the past 52 years. As there is no guarantee that future political leaders will remain honest and incorrupt, the current anticorruption strategy, which has been effective in curbing corruption in Singapore, should be continued and periodically reviewed and fine-tuned to ensure its continued effectiveness. In 1985, Prime Minister Lee Kuan Yew explained in Parliament that Singapore could only preserve its most precious assets by having "an administration that is absolutely corruption-free" and "a political leadership that can be subject to the closest scrutiny because it sets the highest standards" (*Straits Times*, 1985, p. 14).

In July 2005, nearly a year after assuming office, Prime Minister Lee Hsien Loong introduced revisions to the codes of conduct for ministers and MPs. The rationale for the revisions to these codes of conduct was explained by Lee thus:

> The integrity and reputation of the PAP MPs and Government is our most precious asset, which has been built up over half a century. If we lose this, we will lose the respect of voters and the confidence of investors, and Singapore will go down. (quoted in Koh & Lee, 2005, p. 113)

The PAP government has been in power for 52 years after winning the May 1959 general election. Unlike Mexico's *Partido Revolucionario Institucional*, which became corrupt after being in power for 60 years (Morris, 1991), the PAP government has succeeded in remaining incorrupt during the past five decades by relying on the CPIB to enforce the POCA impartially, regardless of a person's status or position. Thus, Singapore's success in combating corruption and maintaining the tradition of clean government are important assets that should be safeguarded for the country's long-term survival.

In sum, Singapore's successful experience in minimizing corruption shows clearly that curbing corruption is not an impossible dream if there is a strong political will and a favorable policy context.

## NOTES

1. The full text of the Prevention of Corruption Act (Chapter 241) is available at http://statutes.agc.gov.sg/non_version/cgi-bin/cgi_retrieve.pl?&actno = Reved-241& date = latest&method = part, accessed on 7 November 2010.
2. The regulations dealing with Topic 25 "Gifts and Entertainment" are specified in paragraphs 155–164 in Section L on "Staff Conduct and Discipline" in *Instruction Manual 2* (Singapore: Permanent Secretary, Prime Minister's Office, Public Service Division, 1997).
3. This conversion to US$ is based on the exchange rate of US$1 = S$1.27 on 26 February 2011.

# CHAPTER 7

# HONG KONG

> "Never stand in front of the bus" i.e., if you try to report corruption, the "bus" will knock you down and you will be injured or even killed or your business will be ruined. We will get you somehow.
>
> – Sir Alastair Blair-Kerr (1973b, p. 24)

> Qualitative accounts suggest that corruption in Hong Kong in the 1960s was as common as that found in mainland China today. In contrast to mainland China, however, modern-day Hong Kong offers an example of a successful government-coordinated "equilibrium switch" from widespread corruption to clean government. Basically, this success was achieved through the efforts of the Independent Commission Against Corruption (ICAC), created in 1974.
>
> – Melanie Manion (2004, p. 27)

## PETER F. GODBER'S ESCAPE

In late April 1973, Charles P. Sutcliffe, the Commissioner of the Royal Hong Kong Police Force (RHKPF), received confidential information that Chief Superintendent Peter F. Godber, Deputy District Police Commander for Kowloon, was remitting money abroad. This information was transmitted to James J. E. Morrin, the Director of the Anti-Corruption Office (ACO), for investigation. By the end of May 1973, investigations by the ACO officers revealed that Godber had deposited in Hong Kong banks or remitted overseas HK$650,000 (US$128,332) since 1968 (Blair-Kerr, 1973a, pp. 3–4).

As Godber had lived frugally it was not obvious that he had maintained a lifestyle that was not commensurate with his salary. Godber was informed by the Acting Attorney General that he was under investigation for an offense under section 10(1)(b) of the Prevention of Bribery Ordinance (POBO) on June 4 and was given a week to "make representations." Accordingly, the ACO officers searched his flat on the same day and found documents indicating that Godber's financial wealth far exceeded HK$1 million. The ACO requested the Immigration Authorities at Kai Tak Airport to put Godber on the Watch List and to detain him if he attempted to leave Hong Kong. By June 9, the ACO confirmed after a detailed examination of the documents seized that Godber's financial resources totaled HK$4,377,248.43 (US$864,215), which was almost six times his total net salary for the period August 10, 1952, to May 31, 1973 (Blair-Kerr, 1973a, pp. 5–6).

The police received information at 1:15 pm on June 9 that Godber and his wife were no longer in their flat. Investigations revealed that Mrs Godber left Hong Kong for Britain on June 7 and that Godber departed for Britain via Singapore a day later before he could be arrested on June 11. Godber probably managed to board his flight for Singapore on June 8 by avoiding immigration control because he had a Civil Aviation Department permit that gave him unrestricted access to all parts of Kai Tak Airport (Blair-Kerr, 1973a, pp. 6–10).

Needless to say, Godber's escape to the United Kingdom was widely publicized in the media and resulted in student protests in Hong Kong. According to an editorial in the *Hong Kong Law Journal:*

> The ordinary man in the Hong Kong street quite fairly thinks it monstrous that a senior British official should be able to commit a serious criminal offense in the Colony and then be permitted to enjoy his ill-gotten wealth in Britain, safe under the protection of British law. (quoted in Manion, 2004, p. 33)

The Governor, Sir Murray MacLehose, responded to the public outrage by appointing a one-man commission of inquiry under Sir Alastair Blair-Kerr to investigate the circumstances resulting in Godber's escape to Britain and to review the effectiveness of the POBO (Kuan, 1981, p. 39).

When Godber left Hong Kong, he knew that he could not be extradited from Britain under Section 10 of the POBO because there was no such offense in English law (Lethbridge, 1985, p. 97). The students who protested against Godber's escape to Britain petitioned the British prime minister to return him to face trial in Hong Kong (Manion, 2004, p. 33). The pressure on the Hong Kong government to extradite Godber from Britain was intense and the ICAC, which was established on February 15, 1974, focused its attention on achieving this objective (Lethbridge, 1985, p. 111).

On April 29, 1974, Godber was charged in London for accepting HK$15,000 from Superintendent Cheng Hon-kuen for appointing him as Head of the Wan Chai police division, which is a lucrative position with ample opportunities for corruption. Godber was brought back to Hong Kong on January 7, 1975, 19 months after his escape to Britain on June 8, 1973. Godber was found guilty of accepting a bribe and with conspiracy and was sentenced to four years' imprisonment on February 25, 1975 (Lethbridge, 1985, pp. 111–112). Lethbridge (1985, pp. 112, 114) commented on the significance of Godber's trial thus:

> The trial marked the completion of an investigation that had lasted over five years, and the end of an era. Corruption itself had not ceased, but the days of blatant, bare-faced, institutionalized corruption and the "firm within a firm" were over.... His conviction was meant to signify that no one was above the law and that the government was prepared to act harshly to put down corruption, wherever it appeared.

Godber was released on October 3, 1977, after being imprisoned for 31 months. He departed for Britain on the same day and later settled in the village of Porsellanes in Spain (Lethbridge, 1985, p. 115). The Godber corruption scandal was, in the view of Ian McWalters (2003, p. 23), "a watershed in the history of corruption investigation and law enforcement in Hong Kong."

## AIM OF THE CHAPTER

Hong Kong was a British colony for 156 years as it was ceded to Britain in 1841 and handed over to the People's Republic of China (PRC) on July 1, 1997. Corruption was a serious problem in Hong Kong before the advent of the ICAC in February 1974. However, as a result of the ICAC's efforts, corruption is no longer a way of life in Hong Kong, which is perceived to be the second least corrupt country in Asia after Singapore. How did the ICAC minimize corruption in Hong Kong? What are the main features of Hong Kong's anticorruption strategy? Why has Hong Kong succeeded in curbing corruption? What is the impact of the handover of Hong Kong to the PRC in July 1997 on the ICAC's performance? This chapter addresses these questions after describing the policy context, analyzing the perceived extent and causes of corruption in Hong Kong.

## HONG KONG'S POLICY CONTEXT

### *Geography*

Hong Kong has a total land area of 1,075 sq km and consists of three parts: Hong Kong Island, Kowloon peninsula, and the New Territories. Hong Kong is highly urbanized as its arable area constitutes only 5 percent of the total land area (*Economist*, 2010a, p. 154). Like Singapore, Hong Kong has no natural resources except a deep harbor and a strategic location at the southern tip of China. Its proximity to China provides a gateway to the mainland and, until June 1997, was a source of refugees and illegal immigrants.

***Box 7.1.*** Hong Kong's Policy Context

| | |
|---|---|
| Land area | 1,075 sq km |
| Arable land | 5% |
| GDP | US$215 billion (2008) |
| GDP per capita | US$30,860 (2008) |
| Population | 7.3 million (2008) |
| Population density | 6,791 persons per sq km |
| Urban population | 100% |
| Adult literacy rate | 93.5% |
| Political system | Special Administrative Region of China |
| Colonial rule | British (1841–1997) |
| 2010 CPI rank and score | 13/178 and 8.4/10 |
| 2010 PERC rank and score | 3/16 and 2.67/10 |

*Sources: Economist* (2010a, p. 154); http://www.transparency.org/policy_research/surveys_indices/cpi/2010/results; and *Straits Times* (2010a).

Unlike other small underdeveloped states, Hong Kong has not encountered the communications problems that hinder implementation because of its "heavy reliance on the values of classical bureaucracy matched by congruent Chinese values" and its allocation of more human resources to line rather than staff positions. There is effective top-down implementation because of the "strong emphasis on hierarchy, discipline, and neutrality," the clear lines of authority and communication, and the efficient implementation of orders by the junior civil servants. In short, top-down implementation is the rule and not the exception in Hong Kong (Scott, 1992, p. 111). This strength of the Hong Kong bureaucracy has assisted the ICAC in implementing the anticorruption laws effectively.

### *History*

Hong Kong was a British colony for 156 years from its cessation to Britain in 1841 until its handover to the PRC on July 1, 1997, as a Special Administrative Region (SAR). The legacy of British colonial rule in Hong Kong has been positive in three respects. First, the British introduced meritocracy in the civil service with the establishment of the Public Service Commission (PSC) in 1950. Second, the British left Hong Kong with an efficient civil service and a well-developed infrastructure. Finally, the most important legacy of British colonial rule is the commitment to clean government, which the SAR government has inherited and maintained.

However, as in the case of Singapore, the British colonial government established the Anti-Corruption Branch (ACB) within the Criminal Investigation Department (CID) of the RHKPF in 1948. It was a mistake to make the ACB responsible for curbing corruption when police corruption was rampant. As will be shown later, the ACB and its successor the ACO were ineffective in combating corruption for the next 26 years until the ICAC was formed on February 15, 1974.

### *Economy*

Hong Kong's smallness, rugged terrain, and lack of natural resources not only make it dependent on other countries for food, supplies, and raw materials but also require it to provide services to these countries. Hong Kong's status as a free port, its open economy, and political stability have enabled it to attract foreign investment and encouraged the establishment of multinational corporations (Lo, 1992, pp. 49, 63). In fact, Hong Kong's economy has been successful because of these "precious assets": "a low tax environment [15 percent flat rate], free and fair market competition, a sound legal and financial framework, a fully convertible and secure currency, a highly efficient network of transport and communication," and "a competent workforce working along with a pool of enterprising entrepreneurs" (Howlett, 1997, p. 47).

Hong Kong's GDP in 2008 was US$215 billion, and its GDP per capita was US$30,860. Its affluence is demonstrated by its consumer goods ownership in 2008: there are 99.5 color television sets per 100 households; 58.7 telephone lines per 100 population; 165.9 mobile phone subscribers per 100 population; and 69.3 computers per 100 population. Furthermore, government spending on education is 4.1 percent of the GDP (*Economist*, 2010a, pp. 154–155).

Hong Kong's economic wealth is advantageous for fighting corruption as the incumbent government can afford to pay its civil servants competitive salaries and also devote the required human and financial resources required by the ICAC to curb corruption effectively.

### *Demography*

Hong Kong's population of 7.3 million persons is homogeneous as it consists of 95 percent Chinese (*Economist*, 2010a, p. 154; Andrews, 2002, p. 69). Unlike

Singapore's multiracial population, Hong Kong's homogeneous Chinese population and its high literacy rate of 93.5 percent have proved advantageous for the ICAC's emphasis on community relations to educate Hong Kong's population on the adverse effects of corruption.

On the contrary, the fact that Hong Kong's population is mainly Chinese has also made the task of curbing corruption a challenging one for the ICAC when it was created in February 1974 for four reasons. First, as most of the population were immigrants from China, where corruption was rampant, they also expected public officials in Hong Kong to behave in the same manner as their counterparts in mainland China, who had demanded gifts for the performance of services. Without a sense of belonging or national identity, most of the population in Hong Kong view "bribes as a small price to pay for being able to get on with their lives with minimum interference from alien officialdom" (de Speville, 1997, p. 13).

Second, it should be noted that in China the terms "government" and "citizen" were unknown until the end of the Ching Dynasty. There were no civil servants, as the Emperor appointed all the officials. "Every act done by an official was regarded as a favor; and any omission a dispensation. Payment for such favor or dispensation was ... taken as a *quid pro quo*." Given this historical background, it is not surprising that "a Chinese in Hong Kong is more ready to pay a bribe ... without thinking of any moral issue. ... [as] they do not see anything wrong in buying their way out...." (de Speville, 1997, pp. 13–14). Indeed, the use of *guanxi* (connections) to get things done and for bureaucrats to accept bribes for their personal gain was accepted by the population.

Third, many middle-aged and elderly residents came to Hong Kong as refugees from China with the overthrow of the Kuomintang (KMT) government by the communists in 1949. As the KMT government was corrupt, these refugees believed that civil servants in Hong Kong were also corrupt. "This belief in itself breeds corruption because it leads to voluntary bribery by people who consider it normal practice in dealing with government" (de Speville, 1997, p. 15).

Finally, the ICAC's task of fighting corruption was made more difficult by the Chinese custom of paying "tea money" to workers as a tip in the commercial sector. For example, housewives gave tips to mechanics or repairmen to ensure good service. Junior civil servants like postmen were usually given "red packets" containing money during the Chinese Lunar New Year in appreciation for their services during the past year. In Hong

Kong those who paid tea money did not consider this practice as something wrong. Moreover, as junior civil servants were paid low salaries, the population in Hong Kong were tolerant of petty corruption and sympathetic toward those officials making some extra money (de Speville, 1997, p. 17).

### *Political System*

As mentioned earlier, Hong Kong was a British colony from 1841 to July 1, 1997, when it became an SAR of the PRC. As a British colony, power in Hong Kong was concentrated in a colonial governor appointed by the British government. Administration was conducted by career civil servants with no elected ministers to control their activities. More importantly, the positive aspects of British colonial rule in Hong Kong have helped the ICAC in its anticorruption efforts.

However, after July 1, 1997, the chief executive replaced the governor as the head of government, and he is assisted in policy-making by the Executive Council of 31 members, who are appointed by the chief executive from among the principal officials of the executive authorities, members of the Legislative Council, and public figures. The third term of the Legislative Council (2004–2008) consists of 60 members, 30 of whom are directly elected by geographical constituencies, and 30 members elected by different functional constituencies, representing different sectors of the community (Information Services Department, 2008, pp. 2–3).

## PERCEIVED EXTENT OF CORRUPTION

In his address to the Legislative Council on February 26, 1969, Governor Sir David Trench said:

> Much has been said over the years about corruption in Hong Kong. That it exists here, as everywhere else, I do not doubt; but its extent is a matter of conjecture. However, that it exists at all is intolerable, and everything possible must be done to stamp it out. (quoted in Tsang, 1995, p. 186)

Other scholars disagree with Trench's view that the extent of corruption in Hong Kong cannot be ascertained. For example, Leslie Palmier (1985,

p. 123) contended that corruption was already a way of life in Hong Kong when the British acquired it in 1841 because:

> The Chinese who formed its population had long been accustomed to a system where most of an official's income depended on what he was able to extort from the public. Not surprisingly, during the first decades of the colony's history corruption prospered at all levels of government.

Similarly, Henry J. Lethbridge (1985, pp. 51–52) observed that "syndicated corruption, the satisfied customer variant, paying for convenience, protection rackets, extortion, squeeze, kickbacks, and commissions" had existed "in a primal state" in prewar Hong Kong. Indeed, corruption "infected" all government departments that "provided any opportunity for its occurrence" and was considered "an unofficial tax levied on all those who labored or who lived exiguously on the fringes of private enterprise – factory workers, artisans, craftsmen, shop assistants and small shopkeepers, clerks and others." Corruption was rampant in the Surveyor General's Department, the Sanitary Department, the Registrar General's Department, and the Police because the Chinese "did not have immediate access to the man at the top or to his immediate European subordinates" and had to pay a small bribe or provide a gift to the clerk to "obtain speedily a license, an official form, or the transmission of a complaint" (Lethbridge, 1978, p. 225).

However, "in pre-1941 Hong Kong corruption was not in any sense a serious social problem" as it "did not give rise to great public concern, prolonged debate, uninterrupted administrative action, and the spending of large sums of public money on its control." As the scale and incidence of corruption increased after 1945, corruption began to emerge as a social problem "primarily because it is regarded as a moral problem or issue, related to the concept of social justice" (Lethbridge, 1978, pp. 229–231, 233). A 1971 survey of 1,065 household heads in the Kwun Tong District found that 29.2 percent of the respondents viewed corruption as a serious social problem and "the older or the less educated tended to be less likely to regard corruption as a social problem" (Lee, 1981b, p. 77).

In his *Second Report of a Commission of Enquiry* in 1973, Sir Alastair Blair-Kerr (1973b, p. 24) used the popular bus metaphor to describe corruption in Hong Kong:

1. "Get on the bus," that is, if you wish to accept corruption, join us;
2. "Run alongside the bus," that is, if you do not wish to accept corruption, it matters not, but do not interfere;

3. "Never stand in front of the bus," that is, if you try to report corruption, the "bus" will knock you down and you will be injured or even killed or your business will be ruined. We will get you somehow.

When the ICAC was established in February 1974, corruption had become rampant. According to Bertrand de Speville (1997, p. 11), a former ICAC commissioner:

> corruption was deeply rooted, widespread, generally tolerated and, in some sectors, highly organized. Every part of the public service was infected, especially the disciplined services, namely the police, the customs and excise service, the immigration department, the fire and ambulance services and the prison service. Certain other government departments shared the notoriety of the disciplined services: housing, public works, education and health.

In the same vein, Alan Lai, another former ICAC commissioner, described Hong Kong in the 1960s and 1970s as the "dark age" of corruption, which had reached "epidemic proportions" and affected the entire society from the poor to the business community. He highlighted these common examples of corruption:

1. Patients would have to pay "tea money," a euphemism for bribe money, for a blanket or a glass of drinking water in public hospitals;
2. A person could purchase a driving license by bribing the examiner;
3. Taxi drivers could avoid prosecution for minor traffic offenses by sticking a "procured" label on the windscreens of their vehicles;
4. By paying "protection money," street vendors could avoid having to pay penalties for not being licensed;
5. Health inspectors would turn a blind eye to unhygienic kitchens if they were given "tea money" (Lai, 2002, p. 136).

However, the corruption situation in Hong Kong improved dramatically after the establishment of the ICAC in February 1974. Table 7.1 shows that the business sector in Hong Kong is perceived to be the most corrupt sector on TI's Global Corruption Barometer from 2004 to 2010, followed by political parties and the police respectively as the second and third most corrupt sectors. This finding is not surprising as private sector corruption cases constitute the majority of corruption cases received by the ICAC in recent years.

Similarly, Table 7.2 shows that the total number of corruption reports received by the ICAC has declined from 4,390 in 2000 to 3,450 in 2009. The private sector remains as the sector that is most vulnerable to corruption in Hong Kong during this 10-year period, with the proportion of corruption reports ranging from 54.7 percent in 2000 to 66 percent in 2007. The second

***Table 7.1.*** Perceived Level of Corruption in Hong Kong by Sector, 2004–2010[a].

| Sector | 2004 | 2005 | 2006 | 2007 | 2009 | 2010 |
|---|---|---|---|---|---|---|
| Political parties | 3.0 | 3.1 | 3.5 | 3.2 | 3.3 | 3.3 |
| Parliament | 2.5 | 2.5 | 2.9 | 2.7 | 2.7 | 3.0 |
| Legal system/judiciary | 2.5 | 2.4 | 2.6 | 2.4 | 2.5 | 2.9 |
| Police | 3.0 | 2.9 | 3.4 | 3.0 | NA | 3.7 |
| Public officials/civil servants | NA | NA | NA | NA | 3.0 | 3.4 |
| Business sector | 3.2 | 3.2 | 3.9 | 3.5 | 3.9 | 3.6 |
| Tax revenue | 2.1 | 2.1 | 2.3 | 2.2 | NA | NA |
| Customs | 2.5 | 2.6 | NA | NA | NA | NA |
| Media | 3.0 | 3.0 | 3.7 | 3.4 | 3.6 | 3.2 |
| Medical services | 2.1 | 2.2 | 2.6 | 2.4 | NA | NA |
| Education | 2.2 | 2.3 | 2.6 | 2.7 | NA | 2.8 |
| Registry and permit services | 1.8 | 1.9 | 2.2 | 2.1 | NA | NA |
| Utilities | 2.0 | 2.1 | 2.4 | 2.1 | NA | NA |
| Military | 2.0 | 2.3 | 2.8 | 2.4 | NA | 2.8 |
| NGOs | 2.4 | 2.4 | 3.4 | 3.0 | NA | 2.7 |
| Religious bodies | 2.0 | 2.0 | 2.5 | 2.4 | NA | 2.6 |

*Sources*: Compiled from Transparency International (2004, p. 18, 2005, p. 18, 2006, p. 21, 2007, p. 22, 2009, p. 28, 2010, p. 43).
*Note*: NA = not available.
[a]The score ranges from 1 (not at all corrupt) to 5 (extremely corrupt).

***Table 7.2.*** Corruption Reports in Hong Kong by Sector, 2000–2009.

| Sector | 2000 | 2001 | 2002 | 2003 | 2004 | 2005 | 2006 | 2007 | 2008 | 2009 |
|---|---|---|---|---|---|---|---|---|---|---|
| Police | 602 (13.7%) | 513 (11.5%) | 565 (12.9%) | 532 (12.3%) | 435 (11.6%) | 382 (10.4%) | 298 (8.9%) | 318 (8.8%) | 268 (7.9%) | 302 (8.8%) |
| Other government departments | 1,130 (25.8%) | 1,074 (24.0%) | 1,073 (24.5%) | 1,009 (23.4%) | 851 (22.7%) | 779 (21.1%) | 770 (23.1%) | 657 (18.3%) | 692 (20.5%) | 759 22.0%) |
| Private sector | 2,402 (54.7%) | 2,542 (56.8%) | 2,403 (55.0%) | 2,472 (57.4%) | 2,176 (58.1%) | 2,247 (61.0%) | 2,037 (61.0%) | 2,376 (66.0%) | 2,188 (64.8%) | 2,183 (63.2%) |
| Public bodies | 256 (5.8%) | 347 (7.7%) | 330 (7.6%) | 297 (6.9%) | 284 (7.6%) | 277 (7.5%) | 234 (7.0%) | 249 (6.9%) | 229 (6.8%) | 206 (6.0%) |
| Total | 4,390 (100%) | 4,476 (100%) | 4,371 (100%) | 4,310 (100%) | 3,746 (100%) | 3,685 (100%) | 3,339 (100%) | 3,600 (100%) | 3,377 (100%) | 3,450 (100%) |

*Source*: ICAC (2001–2010).

most vulnerable sector is the police, with the proportion of reports of police corruption declining from 13.7 percent in 2000 to 7.9 percent in 2008. It should be noted that the proportion of police corruption reports received by the ICAC in the 1970s was 47 percent (Law, 2008, p. 91).

## CAUSES OF CORRUPTION

### *de Speville's Analysis*

Why was corruption a way of life in Hong Kong when the ICAC was created in 1974? Bertrand de Speville (1997, p. 13) has argued that Hong Kong provided "a fertile soil for corruption to flourish" for four reasons. First, the increase in population from 600,000 in 1945 to 4.3 million in 1974 severely strained the social services, government resources, and manpower. Consequently, "everything was in short supply: food, housing, water, schools, health care, services of every kind." Under such conditions of scarcity, it was not surprising that "doing business by bribing public servants and paying secret commissions to agents and employers was accepted in business circles as the way to get things done, even though such methods were deplored by senior administrators."

The second reason for the prevalence of corruption in Hong Kong was the immigrant nature of the population. As the majority of the Hong Kongers came from China, where corruption was endemic, they expected civil servants in Hong Kong to behave as their counterparts in China did and to require a gift to perform any service for them. Indeed, they were encouraged to pay bribes to the police as bribes were "a small price to pay for being able to get on with their lives with minimal interference from alien officialdom" (de Speville, 1997, p. 13).

According to Raymond Yao (1974, p. 28), Hong Kong residents believed "since early colonial days that money and expensive gifts are the best means to procure favor and to secure immunity from official interference." Corruption was widespread in Hong Kong during the postwar period and was viewed as "a long-standing cultural practice" among the refugee and migrant population (Lo, 2003, pp. 234–235).

However, Henry J. Lethbridge (1985, p. 15) cautions that "there is no simple cause and effect explanation" because the pervasive corruption in Hong Kong after 1842 among the refugees and migrants "cannot be blamed entirely on migrants or increasing Chinese settlement; nor on the folklore that *all* civil servants, especially junior officials, were always open, potentially, to business, if the price was right, the bribe big enough." Nevertheless, he acknowledges that "Chinese perceptions and attitudes must be taken into account, as an important factor" for understanding the prevalence of corruption among both locals and foreigners.

The third cause of corruption in Hong Kong was the government's control and regulation of such activities as "construction, import and export, health, hygiene, safety, prostitution, gambling, drugs, markets and stalls, immigration and emigration" (de Speville, 1997, p. 14). The government's monopoly and regulation of these activities and the discretion given to those civil servants in charge provided them with many opportunities for corruption.

The final factor identified by de Speville was the widespread police corruption, which prevented the police from resolving the problem of corruption. Palmier (1985, p. 123) had identified the police as the "most corrupt government body" in Hong Kong. Police corruption was a serious problem as "daily extensive contact with the public provided ample opportunity" (de Speville, 1997, p. 14). Despite its ineffectiveness in curbing corruption, the RHKPF refused to relinquish its responsibility for investigating corruption.

Allan Y. Jiao (2007, p. 194) has attributed the rampant police corruption during the early days of the RHKPF to three factors. First, vice activities like prostitution, gambling, and drugs flourished in the trading port of Hong Kong. Second, as the police officers were poorly paid, they relied on bribes from brothels and gambling dens to supplement their income. Third, syndicated police corruption thrived in Hong Kong because the British colonial government gave low priority to crime control and tolerated the alliance between the police and the Triads.

In his earlier and more comprehensive analysis of police corruption in Hong Kong in the 1970s, Peter N. S. Lee (1981a, pp. 173–183) identified four functional areas with "a high frequency and large magnitude" of police corruption namely: mini-bus operations; protection rackets involving taxicabs, trucks, and lorries; gambling and prostitution; and drug trafficking. Henry Lethbridge (1978, p. 226) has attributed the police's vulnerability to corruption to their control of gambling, prostitution, and opium, and the Chinese passion for gambling, which enabled "most policemen to supplement [their] meagre salaries by illegal payments from gambling dens."

### *Other Factors*

To supplement de Speville's analysis above, four additional causes must be noted. First, the British colonial government's lack of political will in curbing corruption and the population's tolerance of corruption were also responsible for the widespread corruption in Hong Kong when the ICAC was created in February 1974. As will be elaborated in the next section, the British colonial government's lack of political will is reflected in its reliance on the ACB (from 1948 to April 1971) and the ACO (from May 1971 to

January 1974) to curb corruption even though there was extensive police corruption. The location of the ACB and ACO within the RHKPF was a serious obstacle to the government's anticorruption efforts. In fact, the government rejected a recommendation by a 1968 study team that the ACB be made independent of the RHKPF following the formation of the CPIB in Singapore in October 1952.

In his analysis of the rampant police corruption in Hong Kong, de Speville did not mention the low salaries of policemen, which constituted an important cause for their corrupt behavior. Indeed, most of the policemen participated routinely and "took their weekly or monthly cut" that was "a useful supplement to [their] low official salaries" (Lethbridge, 1985, p. 120). As the salaries of junior civil servants were low during the 1960s and 1970s, senior civil servants could avoid corruption by leading a simpler life, but their junior colleagues would "suffer hardship if they were poorly paid and declined corrupt money" (Lee, 1981a, p. 190). According to the Mallaby Salaries Commission:

> It is not a question of paying sufficient salary to make a man incorruptible but rather of not paying a salary on which a man is encouraged to be corrupt in order to meet his reasonable commitments (quoted in Lee, 1981a, p. 190).

A third cause of corruption excluded from de Speville's analysis is the problem of red tape. During the 1950s when corruption was widespread in Hong Kong, the Public Works Department became the focus of attention in many government reports on corruption because of the delay in the issuing of occupation permits. There are usually three reasons for paying bribes: to show gratitude, in duress, or to buy convenience. Bribes are paid for convenience to enable an interested party to gain access to revenue or for the control over spending to be lifted after gaining access. The convenience bought by a briber may be in the expediting of the processing of documents or applications for permits, the relaxation of law enforcement, or the leakage of confidential information. The need to reduce red tape by streamlining cumbersome administrative procedures and unnecessary regulations was highlighted by many government commissions and committees on the causes of corruption in Hong Kong (Faure, 1981, pp. 133, 156, 158).

Finally, as mentioned in the previous analysis of demography in Hong Kong, the predominance of Chinese in the population and their relocation from mainland China made them tolerant of corruption as they continued their practice of paying bribes or tea money and relied on *guanxi* to obtain favors from civil servants or to expedite the approval of their applications for licenses or permits. H. J. Lethbridge has explained "why members of the public rarely spoke out about corruption" thus:

> The Chinese man in the street submitted to the practice [of corruption] as a fact of life; all those who operated without an official license, like many hawkers and all *pak pai* drivers, or who were involved in any illegal enterprise or occupation, simply accepted bribery and extortion as an additional tax or cost, a small levy or fee which allowed them to stay in business. Rich Chinese, the elite of the businessmen, industrialists, and financiers, generally accepted the utility of corruption as a means of speeding up within a sluggish bureaucracy (time is money, as the adage goes) or which allowed them to cut corners and enhance profits. If the price was right, they were always prepared to pay for convenience. (Lethbridge, 1985, p. 77)

In short, corruption was a serious problem in Hong Kong in 1974 as it was perceived as a "low risk, high reward" activity because corrupt offenders were unlikely to be detected and punished, especially if they were police officers.

## ANTICORRUPTION MEASURES

Hong Kong's anticorruption measures are analyzed in this section according to these two phases: the incremental strategy (1898–1973) and the comprehensive strategy (1974 to present).

### *Incremental Strategy (1898–1973)*

During 1842–1897, the bribery of civil servants in Hong Kong was a misdemeanor under the Common Law. The June 1897 gambling house scandal, which involved the police, "soiled the reputation of the Civil Service as a whole and it moved the legislature to enact the first local law against corruption: the Misdemeanors Punishment Ordinance [MPO]" in 1898. Section 2 of the MPO defined a bribe as "any fee, perquisite, reward or gratification, whether pecuniary or otherwise, not payable or receivable by law." Sections 3 and 4 made bribery an offense for both the person offering a bribe and the civil servant who accepts it. The MPO increased the maximum penalty to two years' imprisonment with or without hard labor or a fine not exceeding HK$500, or both. However, the MPO was ineffective because it was applicable only to civil servants and its definition was restricted to bribery only (Kuan, 1981, pp. 16–20).

To cope with the increase in corruption after the World War II, the British colonial government enacted the Prevention of Corruption Ordinance

(POCO) in 1948. The POCO was wider in scope than the MPO as it was also applicable to legislators and employees of both public and private organizations. Moreover, the POCO identified two major types of corruption: corruption in office and corrupt transactions with agents, which included civil servants and private sector employees. More importantly, the POCO authorized the Attorney General to investigate a suspect's bank account, share account, or purchase account [section 10(1)]. Another important provision dealt with the unexplained enrichment of those persons who possessed or disposed of pecuniary resources or property *disproportionate* to their known sources of income. The POCO also increased the maximum penalty for corruption to five years' imprisonment, a fine of HK$10,000 and a "possible forfeiture of the bribe to be paid to the public body or to the agent's principal" (Kuan, 1981, pp. 20, 23–24).

An ACB was established in 1948 as a special unit within the CID of the RHKPF to handle the investigation and prosecution of corruption cases (Kuan, 1981, p. 24). The ACB was separated from the CID in 1952 but it still remained within the RHKPF. The ACB had limited success as its prosecution of corruption offences resulted in between 2 to 20 court convictions per year. However, the government was criticized by the Advisory Committee for retaining the ACB within the RHKPF (Wong, 1981, pp. 45–46).

Accordingly, the ACB initiated a review of the POCO in 1968, and it recommended a scrutiny of the anticorruption legislation of Singapore and Ceylon (now known as Sri Lanka). During the same year, a study team visited these two countries to examine how their laws worked in practice. The study team was impressed with the independence of their anticorruption agencies and attributed Singapore's success in curbing corruption to the CPIB's independence from the police (Wong, 1981, p. 47). The knowledge gained from the study tour contributed to the formulation of the Prevention of Bribery Bill on October 16, 1970, and its enactment as an ordinance on May 15, 1971 (Kuan, 1981, pp. 29).

The POBO has three important features. First, it enables the government to prosecute a civil servant for corruption if he could not provide a satisfactory explanation for maintaining a standard of living or controlling excessive pecuniary resources that are not commensurate with his or her present or past official salaries. Second, the POBO provides extensive powers of investigation as the Attorney General can authorize the inspection of bank accounts, safe-deposit boxes, books, documents, or articles. He can also require the suspect or any other person to submit information and authorize the entry into and search of any premises. Third, the POBO introduces severe maximum penalties: the general maximum penalty is a fine of HK$50,000 and three years' imprisonment, or on indictment, a fine of HK$100,000 and seven years' imprisonment. The duration of imprisonment has been increased to 10 years for offenses involving contracts and tenders (Kuan, 1981, pp. 32, 38–39).

The POBO's enactment in May 1971 led to the upgrading of the ACB into an ACO, which was headed by an Assistant Commissioner of Police as its Director. The ACO's location within the RHKPF resulted from a compromise between the Attorney General's view that the ACB should remain within the RHKPF and the four Unofficial Members of the Legislative Council who believed that the ACB should be an independent body. The consequence was that the ACO was given a grace period of three years to demonstrate its worth (Lethbridge, 1985, p. 98; Wong, 1981, p. 48). The ACO was given more manpower and it worked hard and brought 152 cases to court in less than two years (Wong, 1981, p. 49).

However, as mentioned earlier, the escape of a corruption suspect, Chief Superintendent Peter F. Godber, on June 8, 1973, to Britain angered the public and undermined the ACO's credibility. The government reacted by appointing a Commission of Inquiry chaired by Sir Alastair Blair-Kerr to investigate the circumstances that enabled Godber to leave Hong Kong and to evaluate the POBO's effectiveness. The immediate consequence of Godber's escape was the amendment of the POBO to remove the safeguards in the interests of the suspect and to require a suspect to surrender all his or her travel documents (Kuan, 1981, p. 39).

In his second report, Sir Alastair dealt with the question of whether the ACA should be independent of the RHKPF by stating that "the arguments for retaining the Anti-Corruption Office in the Police Force are largely organizational and the arguments for removing it are largely political and psychological." He also advised the Governor to consider the "widespread loss of confidence in the police on the part of the public" in making his decision on the fate of the ACO (Kuan, 1981, pp. 40–41).

The governor, Sir Murray MacLehose, accepted Sir Alastair's advice of considering public opinion and made the important decision for political and psychological reasons to establish a new ACA that was independent of the RHKPF. According to Lethbridge, the governor's decision to create an independent body was influenced mainly by the exposure of Godber's corrupt activities in the RHKPF. He wrote:

> Godber's activities had thus awakened and illuminated the Governor as to the seriousness of the problem [of corruption]. Godber had fortified his resolve to create an anti-corruption organization that would be independent of the police, a force which had sheltered Godber comfortably for so many years. (Lethbridge, 1985, p. 98)

In short, the revelation of Godber's corrupt activities and the unfavorable publicity concerning his escape to Britain was the catalyst that made the governor accept the risk of breaking the RHKPF's control over the investigation of corruption. Indeed, Governor MacLehose's decision was a path-breaking one because "Governor after governor, committee after committee, had deferred to the police for a variety of reasons but principally because they feared a collapse of police morale if the control of corruption was handed over to an independent body" (Lethbridge, 1985, pp. 101–102).

On October 17, 1973, Governor MacLehose informed the Legislative Council that an independent ACA was needed for two reasons: the RHKPF should not be responsible for combating corruption but should leave this function to an independent and full-time anticorruption body; and the public would have more confidence in an independent ACA that was separate from the police (Lethbridge, 1985, p. 101). Four months later, the ICAC was formed.

### *Comprehensive Anticorruption Strategy (1974 to Present)*

On February 15, 1974, the ICAC was established with the enactment of the ICAC Ordinance and was entrusted with two tasks: "to root out corruption and to restore public confidence in the Government" (Wong, 1981, p. 45). The ICAC inherited 181 police officers and 44 civilian employees from the ACO and recruited 144 new staff members, making a combined total of 369 employees, or 54 percent of its establishment of 682 positions in 1974 (Lethbridge, 1985, p. 107). During 1974–2009, the ICAC has succeeded in recruiting more staff and has grown by more than three times to its actual strength of 1,268 officers or 92 percent of its establishment of 1,380 positions in December 2009 (ICAC, 2010, p. 27).

The ICAC is independent in terms of structure, personnel, finance, and power. Before the 1997 handover, it was directly responsible to the governor, and its commissioner reported directly to the governor and had easy access to him. Section 12 of the ICAC Ordinance describes the commissioner's duties as the investigation and prevention of corruption including the "education of the public against the evils of corruption and the enlisting and fostering of public support in combating it" (quoted in Lethbridge, 1985, p. 104). However, after July 1997, the ICAC is directly responsible to the chief executive, and its commissioner reports directly to and has easy access to him. In short, the ICAC has adopted the three-pronged approach of investigation, prevention and education to combat corruption in Hong Kong.

***Table 7.3.*** Growth of ICAC Personnel by Department, 1999–2009.

| Year | Operations Department | Community Relations Department | Corruption Prevention Department | Administration Branch | Total |
|---|---|---|---|---|---|
| 1999 | 943 (72.6%) | 212 (16.3%) | 58 (4.5%) | 86 (6.6%) | 1,299 |
| 2000 | 932 (72.5%) | 208 (16.2%) | 55 (4.3%) | 90 (7.0%) | 1,285 |
| 2001 | 943 (73.0%) | 202 (15.7%) | 57 (4.4%) | 90 (7.0%) | 1,286 |
| 2002 | 966 (74.0%) | 201 (15.3%) | 56 (4.2%) | 85 (6.5%) | 1,308 |
| 2003 | 922 (74.0%) | 191 (15.2%) | 54 (4.3%) | 82 (6.5%) | 1,249 |
| 2004 | 922 (76.0%) | 168 (13.8%) | 50 (4.1%) | 73 (6.0%) | 1,213 |
| 2005 | 904 (76.0%) | 168 (14.0%) | 50 (4.0%) | 72 (6.0%) | 1,194 |
| 2006 | 897 (75.2%) | 162 (13.6%) | 56 (4.7%) | 78 (6.5%) | 1,193 |
| 2007 | 856 (71.3%) | 169 (14.1%) | 55 (4.6%) | 120 (10.0%) | 1,200 |
| 2008 | 936 (74.0%) | 157 (12.4%) | 53 (4.2%) | 117 (9.3%) | 1,263 |
| 2009 | 941 (74.2%) | 159 (12.5%) | 51 (4.0%) | 117 (9.2%) | 1,268 |

*Source*: ICAC (2000–2010).

Table 7.3 shows that from 1999 to 2009, the Operations Department is the largest department within the ICAC with about three-quarters of the staff strength during this period. The Community Relations Department (CRD) is the second largest department, followed by the Administration Branch, and the Corruption Prevention Department (CPD), which is the smallest department with slightly more than 4 percent of the staff.

In terms of structure, the ICAC is divided into three unequal departments and the Administration Branch. Table 7.3 shows that in 2009, the Operations Department is the investigative arm of the ICAC and is the largest department with 941 staff members (74.2 percent), reflecting the importance of the ICAC's investigative function. The Deputy Commissioner is also Head of the Operations Department. He is assisted by two Directors of Investigation for the government and private sectors. There are four investigation branches, with Investigation Branches 1 and 3 under the supervision of the Director of Investigation (Government Sector) and with Investigation Branches 2 and 4 under the purview of the Director of Investigation (Private Sector) (ICAC, 2003, p. 15).

The CRD is headed by a Director and has two divisions, which deal with the mass media and the public. It is the second largest department with 159 personnel (12.5 percent). The first division consists of specialist units responsible for publicizing anti-corruption messages through the mass media and the Hong Kong Mainland Liaison Office. The second division provides in-depth, face-to-face corruption prevention education service to the public through its regional offices in the various districts (ICAC, 2007, p. 66). According to section 12 (g) and (h) of the ICAC Ordinance, this department is responsible for "educating the public against the evils of corruption and harnessing support for the ICAC." It has conducted an intensive education program for the schools, the commercial and industrial sectors, and the public sector (ICAC, 2006, p. 64).

The Hong Kong Ethics Development Center (HKEDC) was formed in 1995 under the CRD's auspices to promote business and professional ethics in Hong Kong on a long term basis. It is guided by the six major chambers of commerce in Hong Kong and also provides consultancy services on ethics programs, including the formulation of codes of conduct and ethics training. In 2009, the HKEDC provided consultancy services to 840 persons and answered enquiries from 20 countries (ICAC, 2010, p. 59).

The smallest department is the CPD as it has only 51 members (4 percent). Its role is to minimize opportunities for corruption in government departments and public agencies by reviewing and modifying those practices and procedures which are vulnerable to corruption. The CPD works with the government departments and public bodies to identify corruption prone areas for review and monitors the implementation of the recommended corruption prevention measures. It undertakes assignments from government departments to streamline their work procedures, monitors completed assignments, and provides corruption prevention advice through its consulting activities. It also provides training for civil servants in corruption prevention-related subjects. (ICAC, 1992, pp. 119–120, 2007, p. 49).

Private sector organizations may also request for free corruption prevention advice from the CPD, which provides a confidential and free internal audit service to prevent corruption and fraud (ICAC, 1991, p. 21; 2007, p. 49). The CPD has been proactive by partnering with government departments and public agencies to identify corruption prone areas for review and monitors the implementation of recommended corruption prevention measures. It also advises government departments and public agencies during the formulation of new legislation, policies or procedures to ensure that corruption prevention safeguards are provided as early as possible (ICAC, 2006, pp. 47–48).

The Administration Branch is headed by an Assistant Director and has 117 staff members (9.2 percent) and ensures that the relevant government rules and procedures are adhered by the three departments. It is responsible for managing human and financial resources, supplies, accommodation, general administration, training, staff relations and welfare matters (ICAC,

2007, p. 29). The Center of Anti-Corruption Studies (CACS) was formed in April 2009 to conduct research and analytical studies on anti-corruption issues at the local, regional and international levels. The CACS is also concerned with promoting ethics awareness and good governance to reduce malpractice in the business sector (ICAC, 2010, p. 30).

Even though Hong Kong has a small land area of 1,075 sq km, the ICAC has established seven regional offices (two each in Hong Kong island and Kowloon, and three in the New Territories) to reach out to the population by providing "in-depth, face-to-face corruption prevention education and advisory services" (Law, 2008, p. 97). These regional offices received 834 corruption reports or 24 percent of the total number of corruption reports received by the ICAC in 2009 (ICAC, 2010, p. 64).

To ensure the ICAC's integrity, its activities are scrutinized by four independent committees consisting of citizens from different sectors of the community, who are appointed by the Governor before July 1997, and the Chief Executive after July 1997. The Advisory Committee on Corruption reviews the ICAC's overall policy and the work of its three departments and the Administration Branch. The work of each department is also scrutinized by an advisory committee. Accordingly, the Operations Review Committee focuses on the Operations Department, the Corruption Prevention Advisory Committee deals with the CPD, and the Citizens Advisory Committee on Community Relations advises the CRD on its activities (ICAC, 2010, pp. 6, 72–74). In addition to the four advisory committees, there is an independent ICAC Complaints Committee, which handles all the noncriminal complaints against members of the ICAC. This committee has its own secretariat and publishes its annual report (ICAC, 2010, p. 16).

The ICAC Commissioner is appointed by the chief executive, and its staff members are recruited separately from the civil service and are outside the purview of the PSC. This means that the ICAC staff cannot be transferred to other government departments and an ICAC officer cannot be "posted later under a more senior civil servant whom he may have investigated." Finally, the ICAC has its own independent staff recruitment practices, and it processes the advertisements, examinations, screening, interviewing, appointment, and training of its officers (Wong, 1981, pp. 53–54).

The ICAC receives its resources from the government and its expenditure is charged to the general revenue. Table 7.4 shows that its budget increased by 15 times from HK$12.9 million in 1974 to HK$193 million in 1987. It was further increased to HK$698.7 million in 2000, and to HK$808.1 million in 2009 (ICAC, 1989, p. 80, 2002, p. 77, 2010, p. 75). Thus, the ICAC's budget has increased substantially by 63 times during 1974–2009. The tremendous

***Table 7.4.*** ICAC's Budget, 1974–2009.

| Year | Budget (million HK$) |
|---|---|
| 1974 | 12.9 |
| 1987 | 193.0 |
| 2000 | 698.7 |
| 2001 | 686.7 |
| 2002 | 719.8 |
| 2003 | 703.3 |
| 2004 | 677.6 |
| 2005 | 663.0 |
| 2006 | 668.5 |
| 2007 | 701.2 |
| 2008 | 756.9 |
| 2009 | 808.1 |

*Sources:* ICAC (1989, p. 80, 2002, p. 77, 2003, p. 79, 2005, p. 83, 2006, p. 85, 2008, p. 87; 2010, p. 75) and Wong (1981, p. 56).

increase in the ICAC's budget during its first 35 years is a clear indication of the government's political will and support for its activities.

The ICAC's powers are specified in the ICAC Ordinance of 1974 and the POBO of 1971. The ICAC Ordinance enables the Director of the Operations Department to authorize his officers to restrict the movement of a suspect, to examine bank accounts and safe-deposit boxes, to restrict disposal of a suspect's property and to require a suspect to provide full details of his financial situation. ICAC officers can also arrest without warrant for the offenses indicated in the two ordinances and they can search premises and seize and detain any evidence for such offenses (quoted in Kuan, 1981, p. 40).

## EVALUATION OF ANTICORRUPTION MEASURES

### *Global Indicators*

How effective are the anticorruption measures in Hong Kong? To answer this question, Hong Kong's performance on these five indicators will be assessed: (1) Transparency International's Corruption Perceptions Index (CPI) from 1995 to 2010 covering 178 countries; (2) Political Economic Risk Consultancy's annual survey of corruption in 16 Asia-Pacific countries from 1995 to 2010; (3) World Bank's control of corruption governance indicator from 1996 to 2009 covering 213 countries; (4) the ease of doing business rank in the World Bank's *Doing Business Surveys* from 2007 to 2011; and (5) the *Global Competitiveness Report's* indicator on the public trust of politicians in 139 countries from 1999 to 2010–2011.

First, according to the CPI from 1995 to 2010, Hong Kong is perceived to be the second least corrupt country in Asia after Singapore. Table 7.5 shows that Hong Kong's ranking on the CPI improved from 17th position in 1995 to 13th position in 2010. Second, Hong Kong's rank on PERC's annual survey from 1995 to 2010 has hovered between second and third positions among the 11–16 countries surveyed, with its scores ranging from 1.89 in 2009 to 4.06 in 1999. Third, Table 7.5 also confirms that Hong Kong's percentile rank on the World Bank's control of corruption indicator has improved from 87.9 in 1996 to 94.3 in 2009.

Fourth, Table 7.6 shows that red tape is not a serious problem in Hong Kong because its ease of doing business rank has improved from its fifth position in 2007 to its second position in 2011. Similarly, Hong Kong's rank

***Table 7.5.*** Hong Kong's Performance on CPI, PERC, and Control of Corruption, 1995–2010.

| Year | CPI Rank and Score[a] | PERC Rank and Score[b] | Control of Corruption Percentile Rank |
|---|---|---|---|
| 1995 | 17th (7.12) | 3rd (2.80) | NA |
| 1996 | 18th (7.01) | 3rd (2.79) | 87.9 |
| 1997 | 18th (7.28) | 2nd (3.03) | NA |
| 1998 | 16th (7.8) | 2nd (2.74) | 84.0 |
| 1999 | 15th (7.7) | 2nd (4.06) | NA |
| 2000 | 15th (7.7) | 2nd (2.49) | 84.5 |
| 2001 | 14th (7.9) | 3rd (3.77) | NA |
| 2002 | 14th (8.2) | 3rd (3.33) | 91.7 |
| 2003 | 14th (8.0) | 2nd (3.61) | 92.2 |
| 2004 | 16th (8.0) | 3rd (3.60) | 92.2 |
| 2005 | 15th (8.3) | 3rd (3.50) | 93.2 |
| 2006 | 15th (8.3) | 3rd (3.13) | 94.2 |
| 2007 | 14th (8.3) | 2nd (1.87) | 93.7 |
| 2008 | 12th (8.1) | 2nd (1.80) | 94.7 |
| 2009 | 12th (8.2) | 2nd (1.89) | 94.3 |
| 2010 | 13th (8.4) | 3rd (2.67) | NA |

*Sources:* Compiled from http://www.transparency.org; PERC (2001, 2008, p. 7); Hussain (2009, p. B5); *Straits Times* (2010a); and http://info.worldbank.org/governance/wgi/sc_chart.asp

[a]The CPI score ranges from 0 (most corrupt) to 10 (least corrupt).

[b]The PERC score ranges from 0 (least corrupt) to 10 (most corrupt).

**Table 7.6.** Ease of Doing Business in Hong Kong, 2007–2011.

| Indicator | 2007 ($N=175$) | 2008 ($N=178$) | 2009 ($N=181$) | 2010 ($N=183$) | 2011 ($N=183$) |
|---|---|---|---|---|---|
| Ease of doing business (rank) | 5 | 4 | 4 | 3 | 2 |
| Starting a business (rank) | 5 | 13 | 15 | 18 | 6 |
| No. of procedures | 5 | 5 | 5 | 3 | 3 |
| Time (days) | 11 | 11 | 11 | 6 | 6 |
| Cost (% of income per capita) | 3.3 | 3.1 | 2.0 | 1.8 | 2.0 |
| Dealing with construction permits or licenses (rank) | 64 | 60 | 20 | 1 | 1 |
| No. of procedures | 22 | 23 | 15 | 7 | 7 |
| Time (days) | 160 | 155 | 119 | 67 | 67 |
| Cost (% of income per capita) | 23.3 | 21.3 | 18.7 | 18.7 | 19.4 |
| Registering property (rank) | 60 | 58 | 74 | 75 | 56 |
| No. of procedures | 5 | 5 | 5 | 5 | 5 |
| Time (days) | 54 | 54 | 54 | 45 | 36 |
| Cost (% of property value) | 5.0 | 5.0 | 5.0 | 5.0 | 4.2 |
| CPI rank and score | 14th (8.3) | 12th (8.1) | 12th (8.2) | 13th (8.4) | NA |

*Sources*: World Bank (2006b, p. 117, 2007, p. 125, 2008, p. 109, 2009, p. 126, 2010a, p. 168) and http://www.transparency.org

**Table 7.7.** Public Trust of Politicians in Hong Kong, 1999 to 2010–2011.

| Year | Rank | Score[a] | No. of Countries |
|---|---|---|---|
| 1999 | 11th | 4.92 | 59 |
| 2000 | 7th | 5.50 | 59 |
| 2001–2002 | 10th | 4.20 | 75 |
| 2002–2003 | 5th | 5.20 | 80 |
| 2003–2004 | 13th | 4.40 | 102 |
| 2007–2008 | 11th | 5.20 | 131 |
| 2008–2009 | 12th | 5.20 | 134 |
| 2009–2010 | 15th | 4.80 | 133 |
| 2010–2011 | 16th | 4.70 | 139 |
| Average | 11th | 4.90 | – |

*Sources*: Compiled from Schwab et al. (1999, p. 327), Porter et al. (2000, p. 253), Schwab et al. (2002, p. 408), Cornelius (2003, p. 619), Sala-i-Martin (2004, p. 499), Schwab and Porter (2007, p. 379), Schwab and Porter (2008, p. 367), Schwab (2009, p. 349), and Schwab (2010, p. 369).
[a]The score ranges from 1 (very low) to 7 (very high) for the respondents' answers to this statement: "How would you rate the level of public trust in the ethical standards of politicians in your country?"

in dealing with construction permits or licenses has improved tremendously from 64th position in 2007 to first position in 2011. The relative absence of red tape in Hong Kong indicates that corruption is not a serious problem there too.

Fifth, Table 7.7 shows that the level of public trust of politicians is relatively high in Hong Kong, which has been consistently ranked behind Singapore among the 12–20 Asian countries included in the surveys from 1999 to 2010–2011. More specifically, Hong Kong's rank varies from 5th among 80 countries in 2002–2003 to 16th among 139 countries in 2010–2011. Its score ranges from 4.20 in 2001–2002 to 5.50 in 2000.

***Table 7.8.*** Productivity Ratio of ICAC's Operations Department, 1987–2009.

| Year | Number of Staff (a) | Number of Cases Investigated (b) | Productivity Ratio (b/a) |
|---|---|---|---|
| 1987 | 744 | 1,522 | 2.05 |
| 1988 | 739 | 1,699 | 2.30 |
| 1989 | 736 | 1,895 | 2.57 |
| 1990 | 791 | 2,065 | 2.61 |
| 1991 | 794 | 2,430 | 3.06 |
| 1992 | 758 | 2,502 | 3.30 |
| 1993 | 773 | 3,086 | 3.99 |
| 1994 | 814 | 3,836 | 4.71 |
| 1995 | 827 | 3,710 | 4.49 |
| 1996 | 885 | 3,257 | 3.68 |
| 1997 | 929 | 3,307 | 3.56 |
| 1998 | 925 | 3,774 | 4.08 |
| 1999 | 943 | 4,139 | 4.39 |
| 2000 | 932 | 4,748 | 5.09 |
| 2001 | 943 | 4,954 | 5.25 |
| 2002 | 966 | 4,989 | 5.16 |
| 2003 | 922 | 5,081 | 5.51 |
| 2004 | 922 | 5,130 | 5.56 |
| 2005 | 904 | 4,635 | 5.12 |
| 2006 | 897 | 4,022 | 4.48 |
| 2007 | 856 | 5,054 | 5.90 |
| 2008 | 936 | 5,594 | 5.97 |
| 2009 | 941 | 4,970 | 5.28 |

*Source*: ICAC (2003, 2006, 2009, 2010).

## ICAC's Performance Indicators

How effective is the ICAC? First, in terms of investigation, the number of cases investigated by the Operations Department has increased from 1,522 in 1987 to 4,970 in 2009, with the highest number of cases, 5,594, recorded in 2008. Table 7.8 also shows that the staff strength of the Operations Department has grown from 744 to 941 during 1987–2009. More importantly, while the Operations Department's productivity ratio has improved tremendously from 2.05 in 1987 to a peak of 5.97 in 2008, it has declined from 4.71 in 1994 to 4.39 in 1999.

Second, Table 7.9 shows that the proportion of reports considered capable of investigation, which the Operations Department describes as "pursuable reports," has increased from 71.5 percent in 2000 to a peak of 81.1 percent in 2006. The ICAC received 38,744 corruption reports during 2000–2009, and 29,332 reports (75.7 percent) were pursuable.

Third, the ICAC's output in terms of the number of persons prosecuted for corruption, its conviction rate, and the number of civil servants it recommends for disciplinary action from 2000 to 2009 is shown in Table 7.10. The ICAC's heavy workload is reflected in the fact that 4,411 persons have been prosecuted as a result of its investigations, with an average conviction rate of 83.6 percent during the same period. While the number of civil servants disciplined has decreased from 295 in 2000 to 66 in 2009, the total number of civil servants disciplined during this period is 1,657.

***Table 7.9.*** Proportion of Pursuable Reports by the ICAC, 2000–2009.

| Year | Total Corruption Reports | Pursuable Reports | Proportion of Pursuable Reports |
|---|---|---|---|
| 2000 | 4,390 | 3,140 | 71.5% |
| 2001 | 4,476 | 3,261 | 72.9% |
| 2002 | 4,371 | 3,245 | 74.2% |
| 2003 | 4,310 | 3,264 | 75.7% |
| 2004 | 3,746 | 2,856 | 76.2% |
| 2005 | 3,685 | 2,946 | 79.9% |
| 2006 | 3,339 | 2,707 | 81.1% |
| 2007 | 3,600 | 2,762 | 76.7% |
| 2008 | 3,377 | 2,621 | 77.6% |
| 2009 | 3,450 | 2,530 | 73.3% |
| Total | 38,744 | 29,332 | 75.7% |

*Source*: ICAC (2001–2010).

***Table 7.10.*** ICAC's Output: Persons Prosecuted for Corruption, Conviction Rate, and Civil Servants Disciplined, 2000–2009.

| Year | No. of Persons Prosecuted | Conviction Rate (%) | Civil Servants Disciplined |
|---|---|---|---|
| 2000 | 608 | 79 | 295 |
| 2001 | 535 | 79 | 188 |
| 2002 | 604 | 83 | 165 |
| 2003 | 421 | 85 | 234 |
| 2004 | 494 | 84 | 161 |
| 2005 | 356 | 81 | 170 |
| 2006 | 341 | 88 | 150 |
| 2007 | 353 | 85 | 123 |
| 2008 | 357 | 87 | 105 |
| 2009 | 342 | 85 | 66 |
| Total | 4,411 | 83.6% | 1,657 |

*Source*: ICAC (2001–2010).

The CRD conducts an annual survey among the population in Hong Kong to monitor its attitudes toward corruption and its perceptions of the ICAC's performance (ICAC, 2010, p. 64). Table 7.11 summarizes the major findings of the annual surveys conducted by the CRD from 2000 to 2009 and demonstrates clearly the tremendous public support for the ICAC in Hong Kong and their positive assessment of its professionalism. The ICAC's annual surveys from 2000 to 2009 show that (1) an average of 98.9 percent of the respondents indicated that the ICAC deserved to be supported; (2) an average of 95.3 percent of the respondents indicated that their confidence in the ICAC would increase or remain the same next year; (3) an average of 89.4 percent believed that the ICAC would keep its corruption reports confidential; (4) an average of 71.9 percent of the respondents trusted the ICAC because they would reveal their identity when reporting corruption to the ICAC; (5) an average of 68.4 percent of the respondents believed that the ICAC's anticorruption work was effective; and (6) an average of 75 percent of the respondents believed that the ICAC was an impartial law enforcement agency.

A final indicator of the ICAC's effectiveness is its success in transforming the population's attitudes toward corruption. Since 1977, the CRD has conduced mass surveys to decode public attitudes toward bribery and their perceptions of the prevalence of corruption in various sectors in Hong Kong (Lee, 2006, p. 225). Changes in public attitudes toward corruption in Hong

**Table 7.11.** Public Perceptions of ICAC, 2000–2009.

| Survey Item | 2000 | 2001 | 2002 | 2003 | 2004 | 2005 | 2006 | 2007 | 2008 | 2009 | Average |
|---|---|---|---|---|---|---|---|---|---|---|---|
| % indicating that ICAC deserves to be supported | 98.7 | 99.2 | 98.6 | 99.3 | 99.1 | 98.9 | 98.9 | 98.5 | 99.4 | 97.9 | 98.9 |
| % indicating that their confidence in ICAC would increase or remain same | 94.7 | 96.6 | 94.8 | 94.0 | 93.9 | 96.0 | 97.1 | 95.8 | 98.3 | 91.4 | 95.3 |
| % believing that ICAC would keep reports confidential | 86.5 | 88.1 | 88.9 | 88.9 | 89.3 | 88.6 | 92.6 | 90.4 | 92.9 | 88.1 | 89.4 |
| % indicating that they would reveal their identity when reporting corruption to ICAC | 71.7 | 71.2 | 73.3 | 75.9 | 71.8 | 70.7 | 72.0 | 71.2 | 73.8 | 67.8 | 71.9 |
| % believing that ICAC's anticorruption work is effective | 60.2 | 68.6 | 70.0 | 67.3 | 67.5 | 67.9 | 68.5 | 73.8 | 72.3 | 68.3 | 68.4 |
| % believing that ICAC is an impartial law enforcement body | 70.4 | 74.6 | 75.6 | 73.4 | 70.9 | 72.6 | 80.3 | 76.4 | 81.1 | NA | 75.0 |

*Sources*: ICAC (2001, p. 64, 2002, p. 66, 2003, pp. 69–70, 2004, p. 73, 2005, pp. 72–73, 2006, pp. 74–75, 2007, pp. 77–78, 2008, p. 76, 2009, p. 70, 2010, p. 64).

***Table 7.12.*** Public Perceptions on Prevalence of Corruption in Government Departments in Hong Kong, 1977–1980.

| Prevalence of Corruption | 1977 | 1978 | 1980 |
|---|---|---|---|
| Most departments | 38.3% | 34.8% | 16.1% |
| Number of departments or one or two departments | 45.9% | 48.3% | 31.3% |
| No corruption | 1.0% | 1.1% | 7.4% |
| No answer/don't know | 14.5% | 15.8% | 21.5% |

*Source*: Lee (2006, p. 227).

Kong could be observed by 1980, with the completion of three mass surveys by the CRD. Table 7.12 shows that the perception among the respondents of the prevalence of corruption in most government departments has decreased from 38.3 percent in 1977 to 16.1 percent in 1980. The proportion of respondents indicating that there was no corruption in government departments has increased from 1 percent to 7.4 percent during 1977–1980.

Finally, in its 1994 report, the ICAC Review Committee indicated that:

> [The ICAC] has also brought about a change in public attitudes from widespread tolerance to outright rejection of corruption. Before the advent of the ICAC, corruption was not regarded as the social evil it is seen to be today. Many members of the community are now prepared to play their part in the constant battle against corruption as shown by the continuing increase in the numbers of identifiable and pursuable complaints made to the ICAC. (quoted in de Speville, 1997, p. 61)

## CONCLUSION

In her assessment of Hong Kong's integrity system, Fanny Law, a former ICAC Commissioner from October 2006 to June 2007, concludes that Hong Kong has "a sound integrity system" with these four strengths: a strong political will to curb corruption; a common integrity framework for civil servants, politicians, judicial officers, and staff of the watchdog agencies; a vibrant civil society with independent media and nongovernment organizations; and an independent ICAC with a comprehensive anti-corruption program (Law, 2008, pp. 98–99).

The above analysis has shown that the ICAC is responsible for minimizing corruption in Hong Kong. Why has the ICAC succeeded in making corruption a fact of life in Hong Kong? Bertrand de Speville, a former ICAC Commissioner has identified five factors for the ICAC's success. The most important factor is the recognition by the government of the seriousness of the problem of corruption and the provision of adequate resources to deal with it. Second, to gain public confidence, the ICAC must be unimpeachable and its staff "must have unblemished integrity" and be "dedicated and effective graft fighters." The third factor responsible for the ICAC's success is its formulation and implementation of a carefully designed long-term three-pronged strategy, which focuses on investigation, prevention, and education. Fourth, the ICAC succeeded in gaining public confidence by ensuring that all reports of corruption, no matter how small, are investigated. Finally, the ICAC succeeded because it ensured confidentiality to those reporting corruption offenses. In sum, the ICAC succeeded because of "a combination of factors that collectively produced an advantageous environment in which to counter corruption" (de Speville, 1999, pp. 53, 55–56).

The ICAC's three-pronged strategy focusing on investigation, prevention and education has contributed to its success in curbing corruption because it has (1) inculcated fear among corrupt offenders by enforcing the anti-corruption laws impartially; (2) reduced opportunities for corruption by streamlining procedures and management processes to prevent corruption; and (3) changed the population's attitudes toward corruption through community education and publicity (Cheung, 2008, p. 106).

In short, the critical factor for the ICAC's success is the political will of the incumbent government before and after July 1997 to recognize corruption as a problem and its commitment to solve it. According to de Speville (1997, p. 71), "The decision at the highest executive level of government to tackle the problem of corruption is the *sine qua non* of effective action. That decision must be accompanied by the willingness to provide adequate funding, realizing that overcoming corruption will be expensive." This also implies that the government ensures that there is comprehensive anticorruption legislation, which is impartially enforced by a professional, independent and adequately funded ICAC. The ICAC has gained the confidence of the population in Hong Kong by investigating all reports of corruption and protecting the confidentiality of those reporting such offenses. Indeed, the proportion of complainants who identified themselves in corruption reports increased from one-third of all reports during the ICAC's early years to nearly two-thirds of all reports in the late 1990s (de Speville, 1997, p. 61).

Public opinion surveys conducted in the 1990s indicated that public confidence in the ICAC's effectiveness in curbing corruption had declined because of the "1997 syndrome" of the erosion of work ethics before and after 1997. Many respondents were afraid that the ICAC's powers would be curtailed and corruption in China would have a spill-over effect on Hong Kong. Indeed, 71 percent of the respondents in the 1996 survey believed that corruption would increase during and after the transition to July 1997 and 42 percent of them were concerned about the ICAC's ability to cope with the increase in corruption cases after the handover (Lo, 2001, pp. 26–27).

In May 1997, the Joint Standing Committee on Foreign Affairs, Defense and Trade (1997, p. 98) of the Australian Parliament indicated its concern about corruption in Hong Kong after the handover in July 1997 when it stated that "the corruption, rampant in China, if extended to Hong Kong, could prove disastrous for the territory." This concern was not original as it had been expressed earlier by Emily Lau in 1988 and by Michael Yahuda in 1996 when he referred to the "pervasive fear" of the "seepage of corruption" from mainland China to Hong Kong after July 1997 (Lau, 1988, p. 29; Yahuda, 1996, pp. 128–129).

Similarly, Wang Gungwu (1997, p. 1) identified corruption as one of the four challenges facing Tung Chee Hwa, when he became Hong Kong's new chief executive on July 1, 1997. He wrote:

> For most people, the greatest fear is of corruption as practised in China. It is not merely the question of what can prevent the infection from spreading into Hong Kong? It is also one of what can save the Hong Kong people from their own history, both from their own past brands of corruption which had taken decades to subdue, and from their own use of corrupt methods to open business doors and make quick profits in China?

While the ICAC has been effective in minimizing corruption in Hong Kong since its creation in February 1974, and its independence after July 1997 has been assured, Wang asked whether the ICAC's independence would be maintained and "not degenerate to taking action only against small-time operators and officials, and not against the rich and powerful?" He was also concerned that the new leaders in Hong Kong "will be tested to the hilt" because of the strong temptation to relax the ICAC's standards.

In 2001, the then ICAC Commissioner, Alan N. Lai, referred to the "considerable trepidation in the community concerning Hong Kong's ability to preserve its essentially corruption-free culture" and posed these questions: "Would the SAR Government have the will and determination to fight graft? Now that the territory had reintegrated with mainland China, would the irregular practices so common across the border spill over to Hong Kong?" (Lai, 2001, p. 51). His answers to these two questions were "Yes" and "No" respectively:

> Four years have passed since the 1997 sovereignty change and today, Hong Kong can say with pride that her credentials as a champion in fighting graft have remained as strong as ever. The ICAC continues to tackle the corrupt without fear or favor, and our track record of catching not only small flies, but also big tigers remains unblemished. Since July 1997, ICAC activities have regularly hit the headlines. ... Once known to the ICAC, no one can escape our scrutiny. (Lai, 2001, pp. 51–52)

After Hong Kong's handover to China in July 1997, there have been a few cases of police corruption. For example, senior superintendent Sin Kam-wah was imprisoned in 2003 for three years for accepting bribes in the form of sexual services from prostitutes. In June 2004, 20 persons were arrested for corruption by the ICAC, including five officers from the Organized Crime and Triad Bureau, who had received substantial bribes for protecting vice establishments. Even though these incidents of police corruption have adversely affected the Hong Kong police force's positive image, Sonny Lo (2009, pp. 124–125) contends that the ICAC has demonstrated "the political will to pursue corrupt police and their assets."

In short, the earlier concerns expressed by various observers above that the ICAC would not be able to sustain its antigraft credentials after July 1997 are unfounded. In fact, the ICAC's commitment in fighting corruption remains as strong as ever, almost 14 years after Hong Kong became an SAR of China. Instead of being adversely affected by the rampant corruption in mainland China, Sonny Lo (personal communication, February 13, 2011) contends that the ICAC's continued effectiveness in combating corruption provides a positive demonstration effect to the ACAs in China that corruption can be minimized if there is political will.

Jack Lo (2001, p. 28) concluded his evaluation of the ICAC by indicating that its "real challenge" was its ability "to preserve and maintain its institutional health and organizational integrity" and "to adapt to the environment without losing public support." Similarly, Alan Lai (2001, p. 54) ended his analysis by emphasizing that "building up and upholding an anti-corruption culture is never an easy task" as it requires "determination, perseverance and expertise at the government level." As new situations arise, the ICAC must remain responsive to ensure that Hong Kong "stays a leader in the world's anti-corruption efforts." In short, even though Hong Kong has succeeded in curbing corruption through the implementation of the ICAC's three-pronged strategy, it must remain vigilant as "keeping corruption at bay requires constant effort" (de Speville, 1997, p. 63).

More than three decades ago, Ambrose Y.C. King (1980, p. 133) wisely predicted that the ICAC "as a public institution will be constantly subjected to the influence of ever-changing environmental forces." Thus, the ICAC's "real challenge" is the maintenance of its institutional health or "a distinctive character of institutional integrity while at the same time being able to adapt to the environmental forces without losing public support." He also correctly predicted that the ICAC would be focusing more on prevention and public education as part of its institutional development in 10–20 years' time.

As private sector corruption cases outnumber the public sector corruption cases received by the ICAC in recent years, the ICAC's current challenge is to tackle corruption in the private sector without alienating its members. Based on its successful track record in minimizing public sector corruption in Hong Kong since its inception in February 1974, the ICAC will also be effective in curbing private sector corruption too. In short, curbing corruption in Hong Kong SAR is not an impossible dream because of the commitment of its political leaders and its favorable policy context.

# CHAPTER 8

# THAILAND

> If all corrupt persons [in Thailand] were executed, there would not be many people left. I am at my wit's end to know how to remedy it.
>
> – King Bhumibol Adulyadej (1967)[1]

> Bangkok has "the largest number of onetime financial executives selling noodles and the world's richest housewives. … [W]hen cabinet ministers were forced (in late 1998) to reveal the assets they gained while in office, former premier Chavalit Yongchaiyudh declared a figure of $620,000. Yet his wife Phamkrua, who had never held a job, was found to have accumulated $4.3 million!
>
> – *Bangkok Post* (quoted in Searle, 2000, p. 80)

## THAKSIN'S POLICY CORRUPTION

Thaksin Shinawatra became the prime minister of Thailand after his *Thai Rak Thai* (TRT) party won 248 of the 500 seats in the 6 January 2001 election. This was the first time that a single political party had won such a mandate in Thai democratic history (Pasuk & Baker, 2009, p. 8). One month earlier, the National Counter Corruption Commission (NCCC) had charged Thaksin with concealing assets worth 4.5 billion baht on three occasions during 1997–1998, accusing him of registering these assets in the names of his housekeeper, maid, driver, security guard, and business colleagues. However, the NCCC's judgment was not upheld by the Constitutional Court, which had acquitted Thaksin on a split 8–7 decision in Thaksin's favor on 3 August 2001 (Pasuk & Baker, 2004, pp. 1, 5). If Thaksin had been found guilty by the Constitutional Court, he would have to resign as prime minister and be prohibited from holding public office for five years.

Critics of Thaksin have accused him of "policy corruption" because he had formulated policies and implemented projects that favored himself and his Cabinet colleagues. The *Bangkok Post* (2004) identified three examples of such "policy corruption": the grant of a 270 billion baht port concession to a private company; a "tax exemption for a satellite operator partially owned by the Shinawatra family's Shin Corp"; and a grant of 600 million baht loan to a supplier from Shin Corp. According to Bidhya Bowornwathana (2004, p. 148), "the classic case is the accusation that the Thaksin government policies on the telecommunications industry are benefiting Thaksin's empire such as AIS (Advanced Information Services)."

Similarly, two Thai scholars contended that policy corruption was rampant during Thaksin's administration because the corruption involving 95 mega-infrastructure projects resulted in a loss of 400 million baht. They estimated that policy corruption, bid collusion, rigging of project specifications, and bribery had increased the cost of government projects by 5 percent to 30 percent. The modus operandi of the corrupt politicians, bureaucrats, and contractors depended on the amount involved. For example, for large amounts of more than 100 million baht, "they prefer to pay overseas using various methods" such as opening a letter of credit to transfer funds out of Thailand or to employ illegal money-laundering services or casinos to deposit the funds in other countries (*The Nation*, 2006).

Thaksin was reelected for a second term when his TRT party won 377 of the 500 parliamentary seats in the 6 February 2005 general election. The TRT's electoral performance exceeded Thaksin's optimistic preelection prediction of 350 seats and confirmed his "rock-solid" control over Thailand's political environment, which was "unsurpassed by any elected leader in Thailand's history" (Thitinan, 2006, pp. 286–287).

On 19 September 2006, Thaksin's government was overthrown in a bloodless coup when he was in New York to attend the United Nations General Assembly meeting. Martial law was declared, and retired army commander General Surayud Chulanont was appointed as the prime minister on 1 October. Thaksin's dominant influence as prime minister from 2001 to 2006 had eroded the positive effects of the anticorruption measures introduced by the 1997 "People's Constitution" and contributed to policy corruption as government officials were expected to "help the businesses of government politicians to make more profit."

If the coup had not occurred, it was likely that Thaksin and his TRT party would have won the October 2006 general election because of his popularity among the farmers in the north and northeastern provinces. Michael J. Montesanto (2007, p. 318) observed that "by the time of the 19 September putsch, he [Thaksin] was leading TRT towards another probable electoral victory and the formation of a new government." Critics of Thaksin were concerned that a continuation of his rule would institutionalize the policy corruption that grew during his first term in office. After 17 months in exile, Thaksin returned to Thailand on 28 February 2008, after the People's Power Party (PPP) won the postcoup elections. However, he did not return to Thailand to hear charges against him, after going to Beijing for the 2008 Summer Olympics. On 10 August 2008, Thaksin and his wife flew from Beijing to London and applied for asylum in the United Kingdom and remained there. On 21 October 2008, five members of a nine-member special bench of the Supreme Court found him guilty of a conflict of interest when he helped his wife purchase land from a state agency at a reduced price. Thaksin was sentenced to two years' imprisonment *in absentia* (MacKinnon, 2008), and his assets in Thailand were subsequently confiscated. As the British Home Office revoked the visas of Thaksin and his wife in November 2008, he has been living in exile outside Thailand and has been reported to be living in Montenegro, which has granted him citizenship, and Dubai.

## AIM OF THE CHAPTER

Corruption has been a serious problem in Thailand since the 16th century when the civil servants withheld a portion of the revenue collected for the king because they were not paid salaries for their services. However, in spite of the rampant corruption in Thailand, the first Anti-Corruption Agency (ACA), the Board of Inspection and Follow-up of Government Operations (BIFGO), was only formed in September 1972, more than 40 years after the 24 June 1932 coup that resulted in the establishment of the constitutional monarchy.

In 1995, Thailand was ranked 34th out of 41 countries with a score of 2.79 on Transparency International's Corruption Perceptions Index (CPI). It was ranked 78th out of 178 countries in 2010, with an improved score of 3.5. Why is corruption a serious problem in Thailand? What measures have been introduced by the various governments in Thailand to curb corruption? Why are these anticorruption measures ineffective? This chapter addresses these questions by describing and evaluating Thailand's anticorruption measures. However, before proceeding further, it is necessary to describe the policy context in Thailand, assess the perceived extent of corruption, and identify its causes.

## THAILAND'S POLICY CONTEXT

### *Geography*

Thailand is the eighth largest country in Asia and has a land area of 513,115 sq km (*Economist*, 2010a, p. 12). As the second largest Southeast Asian nation, it shares borders with Cambodia (in the southeast), Laos (in the northeast), Malaysia (in the south), and Myanmar (in the northwest).

Thailand has a total coastline of 2,614.4 km, 72 percent of which is along the Gulf of Thailand, with the remaining 28 percent around the Andaman Sea (Alpha Research Company, 2006, p. 29). In view of its large size, it is not surprising that Thailand is divided into Bangkok and 76 provinces.[2] Table 8.1 provides details of the number of provinces by region and indicates that the northeastern and northern regions have the most provinces.

Thailand's vast area has implications for the implementation of its anticorruption strategy. Bangkok is the capital and most densely populated province with 3,600 persons per sq km in 2004 (Alpha Research Company, 2006, p. 26). In 2010, Bangkok is the 39th largest city in the world with a population of seven million (*Economist*, 2010a, p. 20). However, with its area of 1,565.2 sq km, Bangkok is not among the 10 largest provinces of Thailand, whose size ranges from Nakhon Ratchasima (12,808,738 rai) to Lampang (7,833,726 rai) (Alpha Research Company, 2006, p. 21, 25). As Bangkok is the largest city in Thailand, it is not surprising that the population has increased substantially from the rural migration of people to the capital to enhance their livelihood.

The NCCC, which was formed on 17 November 1999, is located in Bangkok. It was renamed the National Anti-Corruption Commission (NACC) on 15 July 2008. For the NACC to perform its functions effectively throughout Thailand, it has established regional offices outside Bangkok. The NACC has launched a pilot project to establish NACC branch offices in the provinces of Sukhothai and Lamphun in the northern region, Nongkhai and Surin in the northeastern region, Chantaburi in the eastern region, Petchaburi in the western region, and Songkla and Surathani in the southern region.[3] Each NACC regional office should also be staffed with adequate

***Table 8.1.*** Number of Provinces in Thailand by Region.

| Region | Number of Provinces |
|---|---|
| Bangkok | 1 |
| Vicinity of Bangkok | 5 |
| Central region | 6 |
| Eastern region | 8 |
| Western region | 6 |
| Northeastern region | 20 |
| Northern region | 17 |
| Southern region | 14 |
| Total | 77 |

*Source*: Alpha Research Company (2006, p. 7).

***Box 8.1.*** Thailand's Policy Context

| | |
|---|---|
| Land area | 513,115 sq km |
| Arable land | 30% |
| Population | 64.3 million (2008) |
| Population density | 125.3 persons per sq km |
| Urban population | 34.0% |
| Adult literacy rate | 93.5% |
| GDP | US$272 billion (2008) |
| GDP per capita | US$4,040 (2008) |
| Unemployment Rate | 1.4% (2008) |
| Ethnic groups | Thai (54%), Lao (28%) Chinese (14%), Malay (4%) |
| Colonial heritage | Not colonized |
| Type of government | Constitutional Monarchy |
| 2010 CPI rank and score | 78/178 and 3.5/10 |
| 2010 PERC rank and score | 12/16 and 7.60/10 |

*Sources*: *Economist* (2010a, p. 226); http://www.transparency.org/policy_research/surveys_indices/cpi/2010/results; and *Straits Times* (2010a).

personnel to perform its anticorruption activities in the provinces within its purview. In other words, the NACC has been decentralized to enhance its effectiveness.

## *History*

The origins of bureaucratic corruption in Thailand can be traced to the practice by government officials in the 16th century of withholding a portion of the revenue collected for the king because they were not paid salaries for their positions (Chai-Anan, 1977, pp. 1, 4). Indeed, these officials or *khun nang* were expected under the traditional *sakdina* system of government "to remunerate themselves by retaining a reasonable portion [ranging from 10 to 30 percent] of the taxes they collected, and by exacting fees for services rendered." As there was no distinction between public and private interests, the *khun nang* used their power to serve both the king's and their own pecuniary interests. Consequently, many *khun nang* took more than the 10 to 30 percent of tax collected for their personal use (Pasuk & Sungsidh, 1996, pp. 6–7, 133).

King Chulalongkorn reformed the administrative system and established the Revenue and Audit Offices in 1873 to regularize revenue collection and separate the assets of the government from the *khun nang's* private domain. However, these reforms failed to reduce the traditional power of the *khun nang*, who continued to abuse their power and position by protecting the merchants and traders, and conducting their own privileged business enterprises, even though they were government officials (Pasuk & Sungsidh, 1996, p. 134). As the tradition of retaining part of the king's revenue by the officials was difficult to eradicate, King Chulalongkorn established a salary system and issued an order requiring that all tax collections be returned to the king regardless of the amount (Chai-Anan, 1977, p. 7).

### *Economy*

Nearly 50 years ago, David A. Wilson (1962, pp. 37–38) observed that Thailand's economy was transformed during the past century from "a system of largely self-sufficient production to a system of international trade based on rice-grain surplus, supplemented by forest products, rubber, and tin." Thailand is a resource-rich country as its top five agricultural products are rubber, rice, sugar cane, cassava, and maize (Alpha Research Company, 2006, p. 133). Agriculture constitutes 12 percent of the GDP and provides employment for 42 percent of the population. However, its major exports today are machinery and mechanical appliances, vehicle parts and accessories, integrated circuits and parts, and electrical appliances (*Economist*, 2010a, pp. 226–227).

During 1855–1949, the Thai economy stagnated as its average growth rate was 0.2 percent for two reasons. First, even though it was politically independent, Thailand was treated like a colonial economy by the colonial powers like Britain as the low import duties enabled cheap imports to replace local industrial products. Second, the Thai *Sakdina* (Thai feudalism) system did not encourage the development of the entrepreneurial class in the country (Somboon, 2007, p. 131).

Unlike the Philippines, Thailand has been one of the fastest growing economies in the world during 1955–1988 because of its sound macroeconomic policies and emphasis on foreign trade and investment (Christensen, Dollar, Ammar, & Pakorn, 1997, p. 346). However, in 1996, economic growth in Thailand had decreased by 6.8 percent, and exports declined from 20 percent to less than 2 percent. The economic decline continued in 1997, and the increase of the current account deficit to more than 8 percent of the GDP forced the Bank of Thailand to maintain high interest rates to protect the baht, which was pegged to the US dollar. On 2 July 1997, the baht was devalued and its value fell from 25.79 baht per US dollar to 30.00 baht per US dollar (Prudhisan, 1998, pp. 278–279).

The currency crisis led to the virtual collapse of the stock and property markets and forced the government to approach the International Monetary Fund (IMF) for a US$17.7 billion rescue package. Thus, the 1997 crisis not only ended Thailand's decade of rapid growth but also resulted in "considerable criticism of the Thai financial sector and its regulation" by the IMF, which blamed the Bank of Thailand for "draining" the country's resources to support the overvalued baht, thereby "undermining confidence and providing ineffective control" (Dixon, 1999, pp. 239, 245).

During 1987–1996, the decade before the 1997 crisis, the Thai economy grew at an annual average rate of 9.2 percent. Not surprisingly, it shrank by −6.1 percent during 1997–1998. However, the economy recovered from the 1997 crisis quickly as it grew by an average of 4 percent during 1999–2003. Unlike the situation in some Latin American countries, where frequent military coups had adversely affected economic growth, Thailand's political instability did not result in economic uncertainty because "the overthrown governments and the coup leaders both shared the same commitment to a market economy" and the task of managing the economy was left with the technocrats from the Ministry of Finance and the Bank of Thailand (Somboon, 2007, p. 132).

Kitti Prasirtsuk (2007, p. 882) contends that the 1997 financial crisis has encouraged prominent businessmen to "enter politics directly to seek protection for their interests" as reflected in the increase in the number of MPs with business background from 112 in the 1996 election to 148 in the 2001 election. The businesses of the "tycoon-turned-politicians" survived the 1997 crisis better than those in the financial, construction, and property sectors for two reasons. First, these businesses were less exposed to international competition because of their semi-monopoly status and protection from the government through concessions and licensing. The second reason was that the crisis had replaced the old capital with the new capital from these businesses especially those in the fields of telecommunications, media, entertainment, automobiles, and budget airlines. The linkage between politics and profits during the post-1997 period provided a "powerful incentive for big businesses to enter politics." The companies of tycoon-turned-politicians had earned more profits from government concessions than those of nonpolitical tycoons. More specifically, the 10 major tycoon families received nearly 23 percent of their income from concessions, whereas the nonpolitical tycoon families received only 2.5 percent (Kitti, 2007, pp. 883–887).

In 2008, Thailand had a GDP of US$272 billion and a GDP per capita of US$4,040 (*Economist*, 2010a, p. 226). This means that its GDP per capita is lower than those of Singapore, Japan, Hong Kong SAR, South Korea, and Taiwan, but higher than those of Indonesia, Philippines, India, and Mongolia. This factor is disadvantageous in terms of fighting corruption as the Thai government cannot afford to pay adequate salaries to junior civil servants to deter them from indulging in petty corruption or to allocate sufficient resources to the NACC to perform its functions effectively.

### *Demography*

Thailand's population of 64.3 million and its population density of 125.3 persons per sq km in 2008 make it the 20th largest population in the world and the 9th largest population in Asia (*Economist*, 2010a, pp. 14, 226). Compared to its southern neighbor Malaysia, Thailand has a more homogeneous population with 54 percent being Thai, 28 percent Lao, 14 percent Chinese, and 4 percent Malay. Indeed, the Thais regard themselves as "an ethically homogeneous society" as 95 percent of them are Buddhist and only 4 percent of the population in the south, who are ethnically Malay, are Muslim (Andrews, 2002, pp. 201–202, 205).

The Chinese constitute a significant minority group because of their involvement in business and their contribution to the economy. Although many of them have been assimilated by acquiring Thai nationality and Thai names today, the situation in the late 1940s was quite different as the activities of the first-generation immigrant Chinese (known as aliens) were restricted by legislation and they were also discriminated by the Thai officials (Coughlin, 1960, p.132).

However, the restrictions on the Chinese were ineffective as they could become Thai citizens or they could circumvent the restrictions by buying licenses or bribing officials. According to Richard J. Coughlin (1960, p. 136):

> It is commonly said that the Chinese can buy their way around almost any restriction, despite the government's warning that any alien found trying to bribe Thai nationals in order to obtain rights denied to aliens would be deported and his property confiscated, and his Thai confederate sentenced to ten years' imprisonment or subject to a fine of 20,000 baht.

Similarly, when a Chinese who had applied for Thai citizenship was selected for military service, he could avoid it by bribing a Thai army doctor to reject his selection on physical grounds. Not surprisingly, Coughlin observed that the Chinese in Thailand were often accused of corrupting government officials as they had not "hesitated to bribe officials" to protect their favored economic position (Coughlin, 1960, pp. 2, 82, 173).

### *Political System*

Thailand became a constitutional monarchy on 27 June 1932, three days after a bloodless military coup ended the royal family's absolute control on the government (Wilson, 1962, pp. 13–14). In their analysis of the Thai political system, Robert Slagter and Harold R. Kerbo (2000, pp. 58–59) identified its three basic deficiencies: political instability, a lack of policy coherence, and corruption. Political instability resulted from the competition for resources and benefits between the various factions and political parties, which viewed such competition as a zero-sum game. Consequently, "policy making becomes very ad hoc, uncoordinated, and subject to obstruction and reversal, as parties and factions compete for particular advantage." Finally, the ascendancy of provincial politicians in parliament has contributed to the "penetration of corruption into the macro decision-making agencies of government."

Thailand's chronic political instability is reflected in the fact there were 50 governments, or one government every 14 months, between the end of the absolute monarchy in June 1932 and the first rise to power of the Democrat Party in September 1992. The 1992 military coup failed because of the lack of royal support. General Chavalit's government collapsed in November 1997, and Chuan Leekpai became the prime minister. In September 1997, Parliament approved the country's 16th constitution, popularly known as the People's Constitution, which was promulgated by the King one month later (Funston, 2001, p. 339). Among other things, the 1997 Constitution introduced several anticorruption measures, the most important of which was the formation of the NCCC in 1999.

Thaksin Shinawatra's *TRT* party won the January 2001 election and Thaksin became the prime minister. He was reelected for a second term when his party won an overwhelming majority in the February 2005 election. However, as mentioned earlier, he was ousted by the 19 September

2006 military coup and remains in exile outside Thailand after he was found guilty of conflict of interest in October 2008 and sentenced to two years' imprisonment.

In his analysis of Thailand's 1997 financial crisis, John Laird (2000, pp. 102–136) focused on "cronyism, lack of transparency, and lack of disclosure" as the major deficiency of the Thai system, followed by "political and bureaucratic ineptitude," the weaknesses within the Bank of Thailand, and the Bangkok Bank of Commerce scandal. Thai-style cronyism "centred more on the relationships of extended families and their close business associates, especially where such families also owned banks or finance companies." The negative consequences of such cronyism were described by K. L. Woo, the business correspondent for *The Nation* thus:

> In their fervor to protect the moneyed interests of poorly-run finance company operators and shareholders, Thai political leaders have refused to coldly prescribe the bitter medicine necessary for righting the country's troubled financial system—letting bad financial institutions fail. Instead of forcing insolvent financial institutions to immediately cease operations during the past year [1996] government officials have poured billions of baht into a vain effort to protect their political friends who have been shoddy and sometimes dishonest caretakers of deposits from millions of this country's small savers. (quoted in Laird, 2000, p. 110)

Laird (2000, p. 120) elaborated on the second problem of "political and bureaucratic ineptitude" by highlighting these six "bureaucratic weaknesses" in Thailand: (1) promotions within government departments on the basis of seniority rather than merit, which contributes to mediocrity at executive levels in the bureaucracy as talented staff leave government service; (2) failure to pay professionally qualified staff a close equivalent to private sector salaries; (3) lack of clear responsibility in various agencies – for example, in the Bank of Thailand and the Finance and Commerce ministries, for the issues of the current account deficit, unemployment, and inflation; (4) lack of coordination among government agencies, especially regarding the country's economic management; (5) a prevailing culture of competition, rivalry, and noncommunication within agencies, rather than a conscientious atmosphere to foster a culture of cooperation and sharing of information and ideas; and (6) a politicization of certain agencies, where key officials form alliances with certain politicians in the hope of gaining security or promotions or other benefits.

## PERCEIVED EXTENT OF CORRUPTION

As mentioned earlier, bureaucratic corruption in Thailand originated in the 16th century, when the civil servants compensated for their lack of salaries by withholding between 10 and 30 percent of the taxes collected for the king for themselves. Commenting on this practice, H. G. Quaritch Wales (1934, p. 224) observed that

> The higher officials of the various *glans* [ministries], in the absence of anything in the nature of a budget system, had even greater opportunities of enriching themselves; for example by utilizing the revenues under their control for the purchase of inferior or unnecessary goods for distribution to the *brai* [clients] engaged on government service, such purchases giving them every opportunity to make large profits. In short, every conceivable species of corruption was in vogue amongst the army of officials who handled the king's revenues at one stage or another, with a result that only a comparatively small proportion of the amount collected became available for legitimate government expenditure. The endeavor to prevent this corruption, oppression, and misappropriation on the part of the officials, was naturally a fertile source of legislation ....

James Scott (1972, p. 67) identified two types of payment made to Thai civil servants engaged in corrupt behavior: (1) "speed" payments or bribes paid to expedite a decision without changing it and (2) "distortive" payments that "change the decision and contravene formal government policy." Both types of corruption are prevalent in the Thai civil service, with speed payments being more common at lower administrative levels and distortive payments being more frequent at middle and higher levels. Apart from their low salaries, the patron-client style of administration practiced by the civil servants and the absence of control structures also contributed to the prevalence of corruption in the public bureaucracy.

In October 1976, Thinapan Nakata conducted a survey of the attitudes of 300 public officials and 138 citizens toward bureaucratic corruption in Thailand. First, he found that 80 percent of the public officials and 86 percent of the citizens believed that the Thai bureaucracy was dominated by team work corruption. Second, 62.5 percent of the civil servants and 60.6 percent of the citizens indicated that corruption was most prevalent at the upper level of the Thai bureaucracy. Third, the majority of the public officials (74.3 percent) and citizens (68.4 percent) knew that there were laws restricting corruption in Thailand. However, when the respondents were asked what these laws were, 50 percent of the public officials and 82.6 percent of the citizens professed ignorance. Fourth, 52.3 percent of the civil servants and 73.9 percent of the citizens did not know what the most severe penalty for corruption was. Fifth, the respondents identified 10 causes of bureaucratic corruption in Thailand, namely, "(1) endless desires of human beings; (2) opportunities and loopholes in laws and regulations; (3) deep-rooted habits arising out of being accustomed to resorting to corruption; (4) lack of control from the superiors; (5) learning from others' experiences; (6) excessive authority and discretionary powers of public officials; (7) economic necessities; (8) need for convenience; (9) demise of morality; and (10) patron-client relationships." Finally, nearly 65 percent of the public officials and 71 percent of the citizens were pessimistic about the possibility of completely solving the problem of corruption in the Thai public bureaucracy (Thinapan, 1977, pp. 37–39, 55–56, 60, 64–65, 72–73).

On the basis of the abovementioned survey findings, Thinapan Nakata of the National Institute of Development Administration concluded that:

> Corruption is a major problem of national development, especially in Thailand. The practice is prevalent at every level, whether it is political or administrative; upper or lower level officials. Moreover, corrupt practices in the Thai bureaucracy occur in many ministries, bureaus, and departments. And yet the problem of corruption in the country is more widespread with each passing day. Urgent solutions are required to ensure the survival of the existing administrative system. (Thinapan, 1978, p. 102)

Similarly, Clark Neher (1977, pp. 482–483) observed that political corruption was pervasive in Thai politics because of the prevalence of graft, conflict of interest, and kickbacks. According to him, "Thai bureaucrats, at all levels, engage in unsanctioned use or manipulation of public office to assure financial or other resource benefits for themselves." He interviewed 50 local leaders in Asasamak Province in northern Thailand in 1974 on their views on corruption and found that most of them believed that (1) there was corruption in their province, (2) corruption was closely related to superior-subordinate relationships, (3) officials in superior and subordinate positions could and did make demands that included corrupt or potentially corrupt behavior, and (4) "they would carry out corrupt acts if convinced that it would help secure their position" (Neher, 1977, pp. 484–489). One respondent justified the corrupt practices of his colleagues thus:

> What you [the interviewer] have called corruption, I call survival. My subordinates count on me to help them in any way possible. I like my job. I am supporting a large family. There may be other ways, but I don't see them, and besides, I'm not hurting anyone. You tell me what alternatives there are. Do you know my salary? I'm not stupid. I know how to do my duty and so does everyone else. Corruption is a problem in Thailand but there's no better way now. Besides, every person in this [section] has been involved for years. (quoted in Neher, 1977, p. 489)

***Table 8.2.*** Top Three Ministries with the Most Corruption Cases in Thailand, 1970–1972, 1981–1987, and 1989–1990.

| Ministry | 1970–1972 | 1981–1987 | 1989–1990 |
|---|---|---|---|
| Interior | 857 (55.6%) | 569 (39.7%) | 710 (43.9%) |
| Education | 80 (5.2%) | 251 (17.5%) | 242 (15.0%) |
| Agriculture | – | 217 (15.2%) | 249 (15.4%) |
| Economic development | 234 (15.2%) | – | – |
| Prime Minister's Office | 182 (11.8%) | 17 (1.2%) | 23 (1.4%) |
| All ministries | 1,542 | 1,432 | 1,618 |

*Source*: Adapted from Table 1 in Pasuk and Sungsidh (1996, p. 30).

Table 8.2 identifies the top three ministries in Thailand with the most number of cases of corruption reported to the Counter Corruption Commission (CCC) and the press during 1970–1972, 1981–1987, and 1989–1990. The Ministry of Interior, which includes the Police Department, has recorded the most number of cases during the three periods, ranging from 857 cases (55.6 percent) during 1970–1972 to 569 cases (39.7 percent) during 1981–1987 and to 710 cases (43.9 percent) during 1989–1990. The Ministries of Education and Agriculture were the other two ministries with the most corruption cases during 1981–1987 and 1989–1990. During 1970–1972, the Ministry of Economic Development and the Prime Minister's Office (PMO) were the other two ministries with the most corruption cases during 1970–1972.

A 1992–1993 survey of 2,243 respondents in Bangkok and 4 regions found that the Police Department was perceived to be the most corrupt government agency by 33.7 percent, followed by the Ministry of Defense (27 percent), the Ministry of Interior (26 percent), the Department of Transport (22.5 percent), and the Land Department (10.1 percent) (Pasuk & Sungsidh, 1996, p. 156). Pasuk and Sungsidh (1996, p. 122) has estimated that more than half of the "regular policemen working in police stations are involved in syndicated corruption. Low-ranking policemen are alleged to collect money in various ways and pass it on to their seniors." Hence, it is not surprising that Victor Mallet (1999, p. 230) has described the Thai police force as being "corrupted from top to bottom," and the Thai police have been involved in "everything from massage parlors to gunrunning" (Backman, 2004, p. 30).

Table 8.3 notes that a total sum of 2,288 million baht was lost to corruption in Thailand, according to the investigation of corruption cases from 1986 to 1992 by the CCC. However, according to Pasuk and Sungsidh (1996, pp. 39, 41):

***Table 8.3.*** Amount Lost to Corruption in Thailand, 1986–1992.

| Year | Amount Lost to Corruption |
|---|---|
| 1986 | 318,000,000 baht |
| 1990 | 255,000,000 baht |
| 1991 | 470,000,000 baht |
| 1992 | 1,245,000,000 baht |
| Total | 2,288,000,000 baht |

*Source*: Preecha (2001, p. 108).

***Table 8.4.*** Reported Corruption Cases by State Officials in Local Government Organizations in Thailand, 2000–2004.

| Year | No. of Cases | No. of Persons |
|---|---|---|
| 2000 | 501 | 813 |
| 2001 | 629 | 920 |
| 2002 | 918 | 1,661 |
| 2003 | 852 | 1,504 |
| 2004[a] | 285 | 529 |
| Total | 3,185 | 5,427 |

*Source*: Connors (2005, p. 368).
[a]From January to April

> [T]he rate of corruption was highest in the Chatichai period at 633.3 million baht per year, as compared to 86.3 million for Sarit, and 60 million baht in the case of Thanom-Praphat .... When the corruption amount is expressed as a percentage of the government budget, then the Sarit period leads. Sarit's proven revenue from corruption amounted to 6.3 percent of the capital expenditure budget compared to 1.0 percent by Thanom-Praphat and 1.1 percent by Chatichai and his ministers.

During Thaksin's first term in office (2001–2005), not much was done to curb corruption among the business, political, bureaucratic, and military elite. However, the NCCC reported an alarming increase in corruption cases in local government organizations from 2000 to January–April 2004. Table 8.4 reports that there were 3,185 corruption cases involving 5,427 local government officials during this period.

More recent surveys by TI have identified the perceived level of corruption in various institutions in Thailand. More specifically,

***Table 8.5.*** Perceived Level of Corruption in Thailand by Sector, 2005–2010[a].

| Sector | 2005 | 2006 | 2007 | 2009 | 2010 |
|---|---|---|---|---|---|
| Political parties | 3.9 | 3.7 | 4.2 | 4.1 | 3.6 |
| Parliament | 2.8 | 2.9 | 3.0 | 3.1 | 3.4 |
| Legal system/judiciary | 2.8 | 2.6 | 2.9 | 2.8 | 3.0 |
| Police | 3.8 | 3.6 | 4.0 | NA | 3.6 |
| Public officials/civil servants | NA | NA | NA | 3.6 | 3.7 |
| Business sector | 2.9 | 3.2 | 3.3 | 3.2 | 3.2 |
| Tax revenue | 2.8 | 2.8 | 3.1 | NA | NA |
| Customs | 3.2 | NA | NA | NA | NA |
| Media | 2.5 | 2.8 | 2.7 | 2.8 | 2.8 |
| Medical services | 2.4 | 2.3 | 2.5 | NA | NA |
| Education | 2.8 | 2.8 | 2.9 | NA | 3.3 |
| Registry and permit services | 2.2 | 2.4 | 2.9 | NA | NA |
| Utilities | 2.6 | 2.6 | 2.8 | NA | NA |
| Military | 2.6 | 2.6 | 3.0 | NA | 3.5 |
| NGOs | 2.6 | 2.7 | 2.8 | NA | 2.5 |
| Religious Bodies | 2.2 | 2.3 | 2.2 | NA | 2.4 |

*Sources*: Compiled from Transparency International (2005, p. 18; 2006, p. 21; 2007, p. 22; 2009, p. 28; 2010, p. 43).
[a]The score ranges from 1 (not at all corrupt) to 5 (extremely corrupt). NA, not available.

Table 8.5 notes that, according to the Global Corruption Barometer from 2005 to 2007, political parties, police, and the business sector were the three most corrupt institutions in Thailand. However, in 2009, political parties were the most corrupt institution, followed by public officials and the business sector. These three sectors remained the most corrupt in 2010, but with public officials being perceived as being marginally more corrupt than political parties and the police.

## CAUSES OF CORRUPTION

The rampant corruption in Thailand can be attributed to the following five causes: low salaries, red tape, the low risk of detection and punishment, the influence of cultural factors, and the prevalence of money politics and vote-buying in elections.

### *Low Salaries*

The law regulating the *Sakdi Na* grade was implemented by King Trailok in 1454. As the *Sakdi Na* of the officials represented their pay, they were "expected to live on the produce of their land, and therefore received no salaries" (Wood, 1959, p. 85). Simon de la Loubere identified the absence of regular salaries for government officials, who lived mainly by extortion, in the Ayudhyan period as the major cause of bureaucratic corruption (Chai-Anan, 1987, p. 16). Similarly, as judges and other law officers were not paid for their services, they earned their livelihood "by levying innumerable fees on the parties to defray the cost of their services." This system encouraged corruption and "every official from the judges downwards had his price" (Wales, 1934, p. 188).

During the Ayudhyan period, the officials did not receive regular salaries and were assigned specific positions or *kin tamnaeng* (meaning "to eat the position") to enable them to control corvee labor and to raise revenue for the court. They were expected to raise their incomes from their subordinates or to retain a portion of the taxes collected or the fines imposed by them. Corruption thrived under this system because "the vast geographical area without modern communications made effective control from the center impossible" (Chai-Anan, 1987, p. 17).

Kasem Suwanagul (1962, pp. 79–80) found that the low salaries of Thai civil servants during the postwar period contributed to more bureaucratic corruption because their low salaries were inadequate to meet inflation and were below those offered in the private sector. Unfortunately, the situation today has not improved a great deal as civil service salaries are still inadequate and many civil servants resort to corruption to make ends meet.

In June 2002, Thailand's police chief, General Sant Sarutanond, admitted that Thai policemen "are undereducated and underpaid and that is the reason why they are corrupt." According to him, Thai commissioned police officers should be paid a monthly salary of 20,000 baht (US$850) to meet their expenses in large cities, but they are actually getting a starting monthly salary of 6,000 baht (US$260) (*Straits Times*, 2002b). When policemen are poorly paid, an important consequence is that corruption-prone positions are auctioned and awarded to the highest bidder. This means that junior officers who are given these positions are required to pay commissions to their senior officers to retain their positions (Backman, 2004, p. 28).

Civil servants in Thailand are poorly paid and cannot afford to buy a house or a car or other material goods. There is a substantial gap between salaries in the public and the private sectors as top executives in business firms are paid between 5 and 20 times more than senior civil servants (Amara, 1992, p. 231). Consequently, many talented civil servants leave for private sector jobs, whereas those who remain are forced to accept bribes to supplement their meager wages. Table 8.6 provides details of the monthly salaries of Thai civil servants, which range from 48,700 baht (US$1,475) to 66,480 baht (US$2,014) for executive positions, and from 25,390 baht (US$769) to 59,770 baht (US$1,811) for managerial positions. Those civil servants in general positions earn much lower monthly salaries, varying from 4,630 baht (US$140) at the lowest operational level to 59,770 baht (US$1,811) at the highest highly skilled level.

Political leaders in Thailand are also poorly paid compared to some of their Asian counterparts. For example, the Thai prime minister's annual salary of US$32,200 is much lower than that of Singapore's prime minister, whose annual salary exceeded US$1 million in 2000, or that of Hong Kong's chief executive, who earned US$800,000 annually. Similarly, Japan's prime minister, Taiwan's president, and Malaysia's prime minister earn US$307,000, US$180,000, and US$65,000, annually, respectively. On the contrary, the Indonesian president's annual salary is US$30,000, whereas the president of Vietnam earns US$1,650 annually. Backman (2004, pp. 26–28)

***Table 8.6.*** Monthly Salaries of Thai Civil Servants by Position.

| Executive Position | Primary Level | | Higher Level | |
|---|---|---|---|---|
| Highest | 64,340 baht (US$1,950) | | 66,480 baht (US$2,014) | |
| Lowest | 48,700 baht (US$1,475) | | 53,690 baht (US$1,627) | |
| Lowest (temporary) | 23,230 baht (US$704) | | 28,550 baht (US$865) | |
| **Managerial Position** | **Primary Level** | | **Higher Level** | |
| Highest | 50,550 baht (US$1,532) | | 59,770 baht (US$1,811) | |
| Lowest | 25,390 baht (US$769) | | 31,280 baht (US$948) | |
| Lowest (temporary) | 18,910 baht (US$573) | | 23,230 baht (US$704) | |
| **General Position** | **Operational** | **Experienced** | **Senior** | **Highly Skilled** |
| Highest | 18,190 baht (US$551) | 33,540 baht (US$1,016) | 47,450 baht (US$1,438) | 59,770 baht (US$1,811) |
| Lowest | 4,630 baht (US$140) | 10,190 baht (US$309) | 15,410 baht (US$467) | 48,220 baht (US$1,461) |

*Source*: Pairote (2010, p. 263).

concludes from his comparative analysis of the salaries of political leaders in several Asian countries that "all politicians in Thailand should be paid much more."

In September 2010, the National Statistical Commission reported that the average debt per household for civil servants has increased from 657,449 baht in 2006 to 872,388 baht in 2010. The proportion of indebted civil servants has risen from 81.6 percent to 84.1 percent during the same period. Civil servant households received an average monthly income of 43,650 baht, compared to their average monthly expenditure of 32,386 baht. In its editorial on 16 September 2010, *The Nation* expressed the view that "these figures are worrying" because civil servants in debt are

> more likely to seek under-the-table commissions or "tea money" for services that should be provided as part of their public duty. The financial crisis and resulting credit crunch has shown how human beings can make unwise decisions and then resort to corruption to get them out of a bind. (*The Nation*, 2010)

Furthermore, the same editorial recommended that the government should rectify the unhealthy situation as soon as possible because the "unrealistic pay structure of civil servants" would lead to a loss of talented personnel to the private sector and encourage civil servants to engage in corrupt practices. Finally, the editorial concluded that

> The government sector should be lean and effective, not a bloated bureaucracy in which officers have personal financial priorities to worry about and are subject to the temptations of graft. If the government does not address this long-standing issue, officials who are financially desperate will continue to fall into the hands of corrupt politicians who promise to spread a small share of tea money among co-conspirators. (*The Nation*, 2010)

### *Red Tape*

Red tape is the second important cause of corruption in Thailand because cumbersome administrative procedures in government agencies result in delay and provide the incentive for their clients to pay "speed money" to expedite the processing of their applications for licenses or to waive the requirements. The extent of red tape in Thailand can be assessed by referring to the ease of doing business in Thailand in the World Bank's *Doing Business Surveys* from 2007 to 2011.

Table 8.7 notes that red tape is a problem in Thailand because its ease of doing business rank has varied from 12th among 183 economies in 2010 to 19th among 183 economies in 2011 during 2007–2011. However, in terms of

***Table 8.7.*** Ease of Doing Business in Thailand, 2007–2011.

| Indicator | 2007 (*N* = 175) | 2008 (*N* = 178) | 2009 (*N* = 181) | 2010 (*N* = 183) | 2011 (*N* = 183) |
|---|---|---|---|---|---|
| Ease of doing business (rank) | 18 | 15 | 13 | 12 | 19 |
| Starting a business (rank) | 28 | 36 | 44 | 55 | 95 |
| No. of procedures | 8 | 8 | 8 | 7 | 7 |
| Time (days) | 33 | 33 | 33 | 32 | 32 |
| Cost (% of income per capita) | 5.8 | 5.6 | 4.9 | 6.3 | 5.6 |
| Dealing with construction permits or licenses (rank) | 3 | 12 | 12 | 13 | 12 |
| No. of procedures | 9 | 11 | 11 | 11 | 11 |
| Time (days) | 127 | 156 | 156 | 156 | 156 |
| Cost (% of income per capita) | 11.1 | 10.7 | 9.4 | 12.1 | 9.5 |
| Registering property (rank) | 18 | 20 | 5 | 6 | 19 |
| No. of procedures | 2 | 2 | 2 | 2 | 2 |
| Time (days) | 2 | 2 | 2 | 2 | 2 |
| Cost (% of property value) | 6.3 | 6.3 | 1.1 | 1.1 | 4.3 |
| CPI rank and score | 84th (3.3) | 80th (3.5) | 84th (3.4) | 78th (3.5) | NA |

*Sources*: World Bank (2006b, p. 146; 2007, p. 155; 2008, p. 139; 2009, p. 157; 2010a, p. 199) and http://www.transparency.org.

starting a business, Thailand's rank has fallen from 28 in 2007 to 95 in 2011. Similarly, its rank in dealing with construction permits or licenses has also declined from 3rd to 12th during the same period. Furthermore, for registering property, Thailand's rank ranges from 5th in 2009 to 20th in 2008. The prevalence of red tape in Thailand is also reflected in its ranking on the CPI from 2007 to 2010, which has varied between 78th and 84th positions, with its score ranging from 3.3 to 3.5.

### *Low Risk of Detection and Punishment*

Thirdly, the prevalence of corruption in Thailand is the result of the low risk of detecting corrupt offenses and the low probability of being punished if one is caught for corruption. During the reign of King Paramatrailokanatha (1448–1488), the senior officials were submissive before their superiors and the king, not because of their loyalty or affection but because of their "fear of punishment and the dire penalties threatened in this world and the next" (Wales, 1934, p. 43). Furthermore, section 12 of the Three Seals Law specified severe penalties for those officials who were corrupt or "*choh rat*" with the types of punishment ranging from execution to confiscation of property to probation (Chai-Anan, 1987, p. 18). In other words, corruption thrives in Thailand because the probability of detection and punishment of corrupt offenses is low as its population perceives corruption to be a low risk, high reward activity.

The Criminal Code of 1956 has 19 articles (Articles 147–166) that deal with cases involving malfeasance in office by career civil servants and 6 articles (Articles 200–205) that deal with malfeasance in judicial processes. These 26 articles cover many corrupt offenses and stipulate reasonably heavy penalties, which should have deterred public officials from committing these offenses. However, in reality, many public officials continue with their corrupt practices because of the low probability of being caught or punished. Amara Raksasataya (1992, p. 225) has explained why there is a low risk of detecting and punishing corrupt offenders in Thailand:

> Corrupt practices normally involve people who ask for illegal or immoral favors from officials. Since both parties gain, neither will report the case .... Even when corrupt practices border on extortion or demanding extra 'lubricating' money and the people feel unhappy about it, they neither have enough evidence nor time and energy to report the cases. Most of the corruption concerns petty offenses such as traffic violations. When the offenders are caught they are rather willing to pay the police officers off than going to court ... . An average citizen, or a person who could be a witness, does not want to get involved for reasons of loss of time and money. An average citizen, especially the poor and so called 'underprivileged,' is afraid of officials who can use or misuse authority to hurt him. Officials are normally willing to let their friends go free by presenting a loose case to the court.

Consequently, it is not surprising that most corruption offenses are never reported, and even if these offenses are reported, the outcome is unlikely to be successful. For example, in 1986, statistics from the Civil Service Commission in Thailand reveal that only 1,264 civil servants (or 0.5 percent) of the 276,320 civil servants were punished for various disciplinary offenses. Table 8.8 notes that the punishment meted to the guilty officials was not severe as 38.4 percent had their salaries reduced and nearly one-quarter of them were reprimanded. It should be noted that only 15.7 percent of the guilty officials were expelled and 5 percent were dismissed (Amara, 1992, pp. 226, 232).

Bonn-ua Prasertsuwan, a former Speaker of Parliament in Thailand, referred to the low probability of punishment for corrupt politicians and officials when he described how the budget process was affected by corruption:

> The Budget is like a popsicle that's passed around. Everyone gets a lick at it when it comes their way, so that by the time the one at the end of the line gets it, there's little

> left ... Most of the time corrupt politicians and officials escape punishment. In fact, most of them continue to prosper and command respect in society. (quoted in Sheridan, 1999, p. 183)

In short, as noted by the Political Risk Services Group (2010, p. 11) in its assessment of Thailand's climate for investment and trade, "convictions against public officials on corruption-related charges are rare, and the legal system offers inadequate deterrence against corruption."

## *Cultural Factors*

Corruption in Thailand can also be attributed to its culture as practices condemned as corrupt by Western norms of public service are considered as legitimate within the framework of Thai patron–client relations. Thinapan Nakata (1977, pp. 72–73) identified patron–client relations as one of the major causes of corruption in Thailand as he found that the problem of bureaucratic corruption can be traced to the incongruities between western legal codes and traditional social norms that tolerate corruption. Similarly, James Scott (1972, p. 67) argued that apart from their low salaries, the patron–client style of administration practiced by the civil servants and the absence of control structures also contributed to the prevalence of corruption in the public bureaucracy.

***Table 8.8.*** Punishment for Thai Officials Found Guilty of Disciplinary Offenses in 1986.

| Punishment | Thai Officials Punished | |
|---|---|---|
| | Number | Percentage |
| Reduction of salary | 486 | 38.4 |
| Reprimand | 315 | 24.9 |
| Expulsion | 199 | 15.7 |
| Demotion in salary step | 135 | 10.7 |
| Dismissal | 64 | 5.1 |
| Discharge | 33 | 2.6 |
| Discharge for defection in work | 32 | 2.5 |
| Total | 1,264 | 100.0 |

*Source*: Amara (1992, p. 232).

There is a high degree of public acceptance of the corrupt practices of civil servants, military leaders, and politicians. According to John Laird (2000, pp. 249–250):

> Perhaps the biggest hurdle to solving the corruption problems is the attitude of the public and of officials (including police) that accepting bribes was not corruption as long as it did not cause trouble to anyone .... By and large, Thais still see bribes given to officials as being *sin nam jai*, or gifts of goodwill, which are acceptable or tolerable. At the same time, officials rationalize that since they do not request the bribes overtly, there is no moral or social wrong incurred in receiving gifts which are "willingly" presented to them.

The population's tolerance of corruption is an important obstacle to the Thai government's anticorruption strategy. The anthropologist Niels Mulder (1996, p. 174) has observed that there is no equivalent word for corruption in the Thai language as Thais do not view corruption as harmful to the public interest. The closest Thai equivalent for corruption is *choh rat bang luang*, meaning "to defraud the state" or stealing from the King, which is risky but not perceived as an erosion of the public interest. As "nobody is hurt by corruption," Thais tolerate corruption as a way of life and "unlike Westerners, they expect their leaders to be corrupt too, and accept the fact as part of life" (Kulick & Wilson, 1992, p. 36).

The tolerant attitude of Thais toward corruption can be explained by the prevalence of the practice of gift-giving by the public to officials for services rendered. Such gifts are viewed as fees levied by the officials to supplement their low salaries. Pasuk and Sungsidh (1996, p. 166) have elaborated on the distinction between corruption and *sin nam jai* thus:

> The term *sin nam jai* or a "gift of good will" is usually applied to gifts given in return for a favor done by a friend, relative, acquaintance, or official. Such goodwill gifts are viewed positively in Thai culture. Gifts to government officials in return for a favor or service rendered may be seen as *sin nam jai* (positive) or corruption (negative) depending on the particular cultural perspective adopted. Within a modern concept of the role of bureaucracy, they constitute corruption. Within a traditional Thai context of relations between ruler and ruled, they may be assimilated into *sin nam jai*.

More specifically, as noted in Box 8.2 Thais have identified seven levels of corruption, ranging from the less severe form of misconduct, *sin nam jai* (gift of goodwill), to the most severe form of misconduct, *kan khorrapchuan* (corruption). Of these seven levels, the first three levels are viewed as acceptable practices, whereas the remaining four levels are deemed to be unacceptable practices. However, for most Thais, *sin nam jai* is not viewed as corruption as "*nam jai* or 'good will from the heart' is highly valued as a personal attribute in Thai culture" and if inexpensive gifts are given by

***Box 8.2.*** How Thais view Corruption

In his book, *The Political Economy of Telecommunications Reforms in Thailand*, Sakkarin Niyomsilpa (2000, pp. 141–142) identifies the following seven levels of corruption, which are ranked from less to more severe misconduct:

| | |
|---|---|
| 1. *Sin nam jai* (gift of goodwill)<br>2. *Khan am ron nam cha* (tea money)<br>3. *Praphuet mi chob* (improper behavior) | Acceptable practices |
| 4. *Sin bon* (bribery)<br>5. *Rith thai* (extortion)<br>6. *Thut jarit tor nathi* (dishonesty in duty)<br>7. *Kan khorrapchuan* (corruption) | Unacceptable practices |

The closest Thai word for corruption is *choh rat bang luang*, meaning "to defraud the state" or stealing from the King, which is risky, but not perceived to be an erosion of the public interest (Mulder, 1996, p. 174). In short, Thais view corruption as a way of life and is not harmful at all because nobody gets hurt.

people to show their appreciation for the service they have received (Pasuk & Sungsidh, 1996, pp. 166–167).

In his study of the promotion of Thai civil servants, Likhit Dhiravegin (1978, pp. 97–98) found that favoritism was more important than merit in determining a bureaucrat's career advancement. He wrote,

> Favoritism, if one probes deeper, is not confined just to the pleasing of the boss with gifts and servile services, but it also involves support of the boss who is engaged in "empire-building". In the Thai bureaucracy where cliques abound, internal politics and power struggles are part of the system … . Favoritism cannot be viewed as a one-way system. It is a patron-client system of "you scratch my back and I scratch yours," which involves three levels of relationships—for superiors, subordinates and equals. (Likhit, 1978, p. 101)

Likhit's observation about the importance of subordinates giving gifts to their superiors is confirmed by Clark Neher's interviews of 50 "leading figures" in Asasamak Province in 1974. One of the interviewees stated that "if a superior did not categorically state a policy of no gifts, the conclusion was that gifts were expected" as "it was Thai tradition to present gifts, and hence he expected his subordinates to be generous" (Neher, 1977, p. 491).

Finally, apart from tolerating corruption, many Thais also "cringed with embarrassment" if important people are humiliated. Thus, it is not surprising that "Thais are not used to seeing people who used to be in authority treated like dirt in that way" (Mallet, 1999, p. 229). This also explains why coup leaders are not punished but ignored if they are unsuccessful.

### *Money Politics and Vote-Buying in Elections*

The final cause of corruption in Thailand is the prevalence of money politics and the widespread practice of vote-buying in elections, which have weakened the Thai party system. Indeed, the prevalence of money politics is the result of "rural poverty, the patronage system, and feudal attitudes" (Laird, 2000, p. 231). The pervasiveness of materialism in the rural villages has increased vote-buying because rural voters prefer to exchange their votes for money to waiting for assistance from successful candidates after the election. A poor farmer in northeast Thailand explained why he sold his vote thus: "For us a general election is a time for collecting money. Democracy? I must pay off my debts first before thinking about it" (quoted in Kulick & Wilson, 1992, p. 38).

It was reported that General Kriangsak had spent US$600,000 or 40 times the legal limit on his by-election. With his huge budget, he was able to employ more canvassers than his opponents and able to pay US$3 to each voter. No one complained because almost all the candidates had exceeded the legal limit. *The Nation*, Bangkok's English language newspaper, has estimated that a MP needs US$400,000 to be reelected after the dissolution of parliament (Kulick & Wilson, 1992, pp. 38–39).

The Chart Thai Party was accused of spending US$120 million on vote-buying at the 1990 election (Kulick & Wilson, 1992, p. 39). Reports on the general elections of July 1995 and November 1996 showed that vote-buying had increased in spite of the efforts of independent agencies to monitor these elections. For example, vote-buying was rampant in northeastern Thailand, "with two major rival parties paying up to 1,000 baht for a vote" (Laird, 2000, p. 231). There was a great deal of vote-buying in the 1996 election as about 10 billion baht or US$800 million were spent on the election, with 30 million baht spent on buying votes. More recently, Thai newspapers have estimated that nearly 30 billion baht (US$75 million) were spent by the candidates in the 2001 general election.

# ANTICORRUPTION MEASURES

### *BIFGO and Anticorruption Committee*

The first ACA in Thailand was the BIFGO, which was formed in September 1972 by a Revolutionary Party Order No. 217 after the Revolutionary Party led by Field Marshal Thanom Kittikachorn had abrogated the 1968 Constitution and dissolved parliament in November 1971. The BIFGO consisted of the prime minister, who served as the chairman, and the deputy prime minister, a senior minister, the undersecretary of state for the PMO, and the secretary-general, as the other four members. It was responsible for investigating allegations of corruption against government agencies and officials (Chai-Anan, 1977, pp. 30–31).

However, the BIFGO was an ineffective ACA because its members were guilty of corruption themselves. Consequently, BIFGO was dissolved after the October 1973 Revolution, and in 1974, the Sanya government appointed a committee to probe into the wealth of Field Marshal Thanom, Prapass, and Colonel Narong, who were the Chairman, Deputy Chairman, and Deputy Secretary-General of BIFGO, respectively (Chai-Anan, 1977, pp. 36–37). The committee found that

> of the three, Prapass had been by far the richest with an aggregate of 244,871,600 baht, while Narong's wealth was figured at 22,846,700 baht and Thanom's 9,223,400 baht. Prapass was found to have owed 160 million baht in unpaid income and property taxes. Narong owed 100 million baht while his mother owed 50 million baht. (Chai-Anan, 1977, p. 37)

On 2 May 1974, Prime Minister Sanya appointed a Committee for the Prevention and Suppression of Corruption and Irregularities in the Public Service. The purpose of this Anti-Corruption Committee (ACC) was to investigate charges of corruption against public officials and to report their findings to the prime minister or the minister in charge of the ministry concerned. The ACC was merely an investigatory agency and, as such, it did not have any quasi-judicial powers. It had to rely on the CSC and the Court of Justice to take legal action against corrupt officials. By September 1974, the ACC had examined over 140 petitions (Chai-Anan, 1977, pp. 39–40).

Apart from investigating corruption cases, the ACC was also directed to prepare an anticorruption draft bill to supplement the Penal Code because the provisions of the latter were inadequate for fighting corruption. The ACC took seven months to draft the bill, which was approved by the Cabinet in December 1974 and sent to the National Legislative Assembly during the same month. The bill was passed by the Assembly and the Counter Corruption Act (CCA) was promulgated in February 1975 (Chai-Anan, 1977, p. 47).

### *Counter-Corruption Commission*

The CCA transformed the ACC into the CCC. The Counter-Corruption Office was established as part of the CCC to implement the latter's resolutions and to perform the required secretarial work. Section 4 of the CCA specified that the CCC should have between 6 and 10 members, who were appointed by the King with the approval of the Senate and House of Representatives. However, the Kukrit coalition government took nearly six months to find new commissioners to serve on the CCC. In September 1975, the government announced the appointment of the new CCC under the chairmanship of Kiat Chiwaket, acting Director General of the Public Prosecution Department (Chai-Anan, 1977, pp. 47–49, 55).

The CCC was responsible for performing these five functions: (1) submitting measures for preventing and suppressing dishonesty and corrupt practices within the government to the cabinet; (2) submitting to the cabinet for consideration proposals for directing government agencies or public enterprises to order those officials suspected of corruption to declare their assets and liabilities; (3) investigating cases of allegations regarding officials indulging in dishonest or corrupt practices in government; (4) recommending to the cabinet revision of administrative practices and devising of schemes and projects of government agencies to prevent and suppress corrupt practices; and (5) submitting a report of the CCC's performance together with remarks to the Prime Minister, the President of the Senate, and the Speaker of the House of Representatives in October of each year (quoted in Amara, 1992, pp. 238–239).

The Seni coalition government faced the same problem after the April 1976 election because it took some time to appoint new members to the CCC. However, the list of members submitted by the government was not approved by the House of Representatives on 29 July 1976 because the other three coalition parties accused the Democratic Party of monopolizing the selection process and selecting its own candidates for the CCC. The refusal to cooperate on the part of the three coalition parties indicates that these parties were not committed to the eradication of corruption (Chai-Anan, 1977, pp. 58–60).

Amara Raksasataya (1992, p. 240) contended that "despite its limited resources, the CCC has done a creditable job." However, the CCC was viewed by its critics as a "paper tiger" without real teeth because "it could only send reports to the Prime Minister and the cabinet and notify or recommend to superior officials to start disciplinary action," but it lacked "direct authority to punish public officials." Consequently, very few civil servants were punished for corruption because those who were corrupt were retired early or transferred without punishment.

The CCC's ineffectiveness resulted in the amendment of the CCA in 1987 to give it more power (Amara, 1992, pp. 240–241). In spite of this amendment, the CCC could not take action against politicians as it only had "the power to investigate a bureaucrat following a complaint." If the complaint was valid, the CCC would report it to the accused official's superior, who could order another investigation to decide whether the case should be sent to the public prosecutor for criminal charges or settled through departmental disciplinary action. Officials found "guilty" by the CCC were usually reprimanded or disciplined within the department concerned, as the public prosecutor would initiate new investigations as he would not use the evidence collected by the CCC (Pasuk & Sungsidh, 1996, pp. 180–181).

There were many changes in government after the breakup of the Seni coalition government, but the CCA and the CCC survived these changes. The CCC's membership was changed with every change of government, but the CCC itself remained intact for 24 years until it was replaced by the NCCC in November 1999. Indeed, unlike the case of the Philippines, there was no proliferation of ACAs in spite of the frequent changes in political leadership.

### *National Counter-Corruption Commission*

Unlike the previous 15 constitutions, the 1997 People's Constitution was distinctive in four ways:

> it took four years of continuous effort by civil society forces to have it drafted at all; an indirectly elected body separate from Parliament (the CDA [Constitution Drafting Assembly]) did the drafting; the public was involved to an extent unprecedented anywhere in proposing provisions and in commenting on summary drafts; and its provisions, aimed at "political reform" are markedly different from those of previous Constitutions. (Prudhisan, 1998, p. 270)

In May 1996, a Constitution Amendment Bill established the CDA, which consisted of 99 members (76 elected provincial representatives and 16 experts in public law and political science, and 7 experienced public administrators and politicians) (Ministry of Foreign Affairs, 1997, pp. 16–19). The CDA consulted and considered the views of the public through its many committees. Prudhisan (1998, p. 273) noted that "Some 122,000 people at the province level, and 4,000 people at the regional level were involved in these public hearings, and another 87,000 responded to questionnaires." The CDA completed its work within 8 months (240 days) and submitted the draft constitution to Parliament for its approval on 22 August 1997. Parliament approved the draft constitution without amendment. The new Constitution received the King's approval and came into effect on 11 October 1997 (Borwornsak, 2001, p. 178).

Thus, the raison d'etre for the 1997 People's Constitution was to reform the Thai political system by minimizing the major problem of corruption and by enhancing political participation. It has been described as the "anticorruption" Constitution by Laird (2000, pp. 163–164) because two important new institutions were established to tackle the related problems of vote-buying and corruption. First, an independent Election Commission was created to deal with the problem of money politics and vote-buying as its purpose was to organize and supervise all elections with the help of nongovernmental organizations to ensure fairness and to prevent electoral fraud by investigating complaints of electoral malpractices (Laird, 2000, p. 165). Furthermore, voting was made compulsory to ensure a high voter turn-out and to discourage vote-buying. Campaign expenditure was also limited, but the state provided assistance to the candidates and political parties to ensure fair competition (Prudhisan, 1998, p. 275). For example, the Election Commission assisted Senate candidates by providing radio and television forums to introduce them. This method has reduced electoral spending and "mud slinging" among candidates (Borwornsak, 2001, p. 182).

Second, the ineffectiveness of the CCC in curbing corruption during its 24-year existence led to its dissolution and its replacement by the NCCC in 1999. Learning from the CCC's lackluster performance, the members of the CDA enhanced the NCCC's effectiveness in combating corruption by removing those features that handicapped the CCC's performance. Thus, instead of being a toothless paper tiger like its predecessor, the NCCC has been empowered to investigate corruption complaints against both civil servants and politicians. A second important difference is that the NCCC is more independent than the CCC as it is responsible to the Senate and not to the Prime Minister. This difference is important as "removing it [the NCCC] from the supervision of the prime minister" and "making its involvement automatic when the Senate speaker receives a corruption complaint, should make it much more effective in pursuing corrupt cabinet ministers"

(Laird, 2000, pp. 165–166). A third manifestation of the NCCC's independence is its control over its staffing, budgeting, and other aspects of management. Finally, the nine members of the NCCC are nominated by the Senate and appointed by the King for a single, nonrenewable term of nine years.

The NCCC performs three functions. First, it is responsible for inspecting and verifying the declaration of the assets and liabilities submitted by the politicians and civil servants. Those officials who do not declare their assets or make false declarations are reported by the NCCC to the Constitutional Court. Those found guilty are removed from their positions and barred from holding political office for five years.

The NCCC's second function is to prevent corruption in three ways: (1) to make recommendations on preventing corruption to the Cabinet and other government agencies; (2) to enhance the integrity of the officials and public by organizing contests, meetings, and seminars on fighting corruption among the people and civil servants; and (3) to foster cooperation among the public by conducting seminars on countering corruption in Bangkok and the various provinces.

Thirdly, the NCCC is also empowered to suppress corruption by taking disciplinary action against corrupt politicians and civil servants. More specifically, it investigates complaints of corruption against politicians and civil servants and has the power to impeach them for having "unusual wealth," or for committing corruption, malfeasance, or abuse of power. Unlike Hong Kong's ICAC or Singapore's CPIB, which investigate all complaints of corruption, the NCCC only investigates those corruption complaints, which are supported by one-quarter of the House of Representatives or Senate, or if these complaints are signed by 50,000 members of the public (ONCCC, 2006a, p. 23).

Table 8.9 notes that even though the personnel of the NCCC/NACC has grown by almost three times from 332 to 965 from 1999 to 2009, it is still understaffed as its 965 members have to perform its three anticorruption functions for 2.7 million civil servants and a population of 64.3 million. When the NACC is compared with Hong Kong's ICAC, the problem of the NACC being understaffed becomes more obvious as the NCCC has only 965 members compared to the ICAC's 1,286 strong staff. Although the NCCC needs more staff to assist it in inspecting and checking the declarations of assets and liabilities of politicians and senior civil servants, this need for additional manpower must be balanced by the need to ensure the accountability of these officials. Although the ICAC has been effective in curbing corruption in Hong Kong, its large number of personnel has also given rise to the concern of whether the ICAC can monitor its staff

***Table 8.9.*** Number of NCCC/NACC Personnel, 1999–2009.

| Year | Number of Personnel |
|---|---|
| 1999 | 332 |
| 2000 | 384 |
| 2001 | 451 |
| 2002 | 532 |
| 2003 | 632 |
| 2004 | 574 |
| 2005 | 656 |
| 2006 | 645 |
| 2007 | 667 |
| 2008 | 740 |
| 2009 | 965 |

*Source:* Data provided by courtesy of Mr Akharakit Keeratithanachaiyos, Communications Specialist, Office of the NACC by e-mail on 2 February 2011. *Note*: The NCCC was renamed as the NACC on 15 July 2008.

effectively. In short, while the number of staff of the NCCC/NACC has nearly tripled during 1999–2009, it still needs more members and funding to enable it to perform its duties effectively.

The NCCC's organizational structure is divided into 11 bureaus and 4 divisions. The two Bureaus of Corruption Prevention focus, respectively, on the issuance of measures, and public relations, "ethics value," and "moral promotion." The Bureau of Corruption Suppression 1 is responsible for local government and "social," whereas the Bureau of Corruption Suppression 2 is concerned with natural resources, state enterprises, economics, and criminal justice and defense. The five Bureaus of Assets Inspection 1–5 focus, respectively, on the Cabinet, Senators and MPs, high ranking officials, local government officials, and government officials. The Bureau of Legal Affairs deals with legal affairs, procurement investigation, and partnership and share management. The Bureau of Policy and Planning takes care of research and planning, technical and foreign affairs, information technology, and the library. Finally, the four divisions deal, respectively, with personnel, NCCC affairs, finance, and reports (ONCCC, 2006b, pp. 31–37).

The NCCC's budget has increased by more than 7 times from 106.3 million baht in 1999 to 769.4 million baht in 2009. Table 8.10 also notes that its budget was progressively increased from 1999 to 2004, when 333.7 million baht were allocated to the NCCC. The amount allocated to the NCCC was nearly tripled to 935.3 million baht in 2005. However, the NCCC's budget was

***Table 8.10.*** Budget of NCCC/NACC, 1999–2009.

| Year | Budget (baht) |
|---|---|
| 1999 | 106.3 million |
| 2000 | 138.7 million |
| 2001 | 183.7 million |
| 2002 | 273.6 million |
| 2003 | 319.7 million |
| 2004 | 333.7 million |
| 2005 | 935.3 million |
| 2006 | 784.7 million |
| 2007 | 650.5 million |
| 2008 | 731.2 million |
| 2009 | 769.4 million |

*Source*: Bureau of Budget (2000–2010).

decreased to 784.7 million baht in 2006, 650.5 million baht in 2007, 731.2 million baht in 2008, and 769.4 million baht in 2009.

## EVALUATION OF ANTICORRUPTION MEASURES

How effective are the anticorruption measures in Thailand? To answer this question, Thailand's performance on these four indicators will be evaluated: (1) TI's CPI from 1995 to 2010 covering 178 countries; (2) PERC's annual survey of corruption in 16 Asia-Pacific countries from 1995 to 2010; (3) World Bank's control of corruption governance indicator from 1996 to 2009 covering 213 countries; and (4) the *Global Competitiveness Report's* indicator on the public trust of politicians in 139 countries from 1999 to 2010–2011.

Table 8.11 notes first that Thailand's CPI rank varies from 34th among 41 countries in 1995 to 78th among 178 countries in 2010. Its CPI score ranges from 2.79 in 1995 to 3.8 in 2005. Second, Thailand's best rank on PERC is 6th among 12 countries in 2000, whereas its worst rank is 15th among 16 countries in 2009. Its PERC score ranges from 5.90 in 1995 to 8.89 in 2002. Third, for the World Bank's Control of Corruption, Thailand's percentile rank has varied from 40.3 to 57.8 during 1996–1998 and fluctuated between 49.5 and 51 percentile ranks between 2000 and 2009.

***Table 8.11.*** Thailand's Performance on CPI, PERC, and Control of Corruption, 1995–2010.

| Year | CPI Rank and Score[a] | PERC Rank and Score[b] | Control of Corruption Percentile Rank |
|---|---|---|---|
| 1995 | 34th (2.79) | 7th (5.90) | NA |
| 1996 | 37th (3.33) | 7th (6.55) | 40.3 |
| 1997 | 39th (3.06) | 7th (7.49) | NA |
| 1998 | 61st (3.0) | 11th (8.29) | 57.8 |
| 1999 | 68th (3.2) | 7th (7.57) | NA |
| 2000 | 60th (3.2) | 6th (8.20) | 49.5 |
| 2001 | 61st (3.2) | 8th (8.55) | NA |
| 2002 | 64th (3.2) | 10th (8.89) | 46.6 |
| 2003 | 70th (3.3) | 9th (8.75) | 51.0 |
| 2004 | 64th (3.6) | 8th (7.80) | 50.0 |
| 2005 | 59th (3.8) | 8th (7.20) | 54.9 |
| 2006 | 63rd (3.6) | 10th (7.64) | 50.5 |
| 2007 | 84th (3.3) | 11th (8.03) | 48.3 |
| 2008 | 80th (3.5) | 12th (8.00) | 43.5 |
| 2009 | 84th (3.4) | 15th (7.63) | 51.0 |
| 2010 | 78th (3.5) | 12th (7.60) | NA |

*Sources:* Compiled from http://www.transparency.org; PERC (2001, 2008, p. 7); Hussain (2009, p. B5); *Straits Times* (2010a); and http://info.worldbank.org/governance/wgi/sc_chart.asp.
[a]The CPI score ranges from 0(most corrupt) to 10 (least corrupt).
[b]The PERC score ranges from 0 (least corrupt) to 10 (most corrupt).

As corruption is a serious problem in Thailand, it is not surprising that the level of public trust of politicians is also low. Table 8.12 notes that Thailand's rank on the *Global Competitiveness Report*'s indicator on public trust in politicians ranges from 36th among 80 countries with a score of 2.60 in 2002–2003 to 83rd among 139 countries with a score of 2.50 in 2010–2011. Thailand's lowest score was 2.10 in 2000 and its highest score was 2.90 in 2003–2004.

If effectiveness is defined as the "degree of goal achievement" (Price, 1968, p. 3), the effectiveness of the NCCC can be ascertained in terms of whether it has attained its three objectives of (1) inspecting and verifying the declaration of assets and liabilities of the politicians and senior civil servants; (2) preventing corruption; and (3) suppressing corruption by investigating complaints of corruption and taking action against those found guilty of corruption.

***Table 8.12.*** Public Trust of Politicians in Thailand, 1999 to 2010–2011.

| Year | Rank | Score[a] | No. of Countries |
|---|---|---|---|
| 1999 | 45th | 2.22 | 59 |
| 2000 | 47th | 2.10 | 59 |
| 2001–2002 | 37th | 2.80 | 75 |
| 2002–2003 | 36th | 2.60 | 80 |
| 2003–2004 | 40th | 2.90 | 102 |
| 2007–2008 | 60th | 2.70 | 131 |
| 2008–2009 | 64th | 2.70 | 134 |
| 2009–2010 | 71st | 2.70 | 133 |
| 2010–2011 | 83rd | 2.50 | 139 |
| Average | 54th | 2.58 | – |

*Sources*: Compiled from Schwab et al. (1999, p. 327), Porter et al. (2000, p. 253), Schwab et al. (2002, p. 408), Cornelius (2003, p. 619), Sala-i-Martin (2004, p. 499), Schwab and Porter (2007, p. 379), Schwab and Porter (2008, p. 367), Schwab (2009, p. 349), and Schwab (2010, p. 369).
[a]The score ranges from 1 (very low) to 7 (very high) for the respondents' answers to this statement: "How would you rate the level of public trust in the ethical standards of politicians in your country."

Of these three objectives, it must first be acknowledged that the second objective is difficult to measure as the impact of the NCCC's recommendations and its various activities on the prevention of corruption cannot be ascertained. Accordingly, we are left with determining the NCCC's output in terms of the first and third objectives and its impact on minimizing corruption in Thailand.

In his analysis of the NCCC's staffing situation in 1999, when it took over from the CCC, Borwornsak (2001, p. 199) indicated that it did not have enough staff to handle its heavy workload of investigating "5,741 asset and liability declarations of politicians and high-ranking officials; 530 accusations launched against holders of public office; 1,967 cases of corruption transferred from the now defunct CCMC [CCC]; 19 criminal cases transferred from investigation and prosecution police in the Supreme Court's Criminal Division for Persons Holding Political Positions; 73 cases of unusual wealth; and 48 urgent cases."

Similarly, Nualnoi Treerat (2004, p. 195) observed that the NCCC could "barely keep up with the increasing number of cases" from 1,646 corruption cases in 2000 to 2,179 cases in 2001. Furthermore, almost all these cases involved civil servants as only 30 politicians were accused of dishonesty or corruption, and another 45 politicians were investigated for unusual wealth. In her assessment of the NCCC's effectiveness, Nualnoi found that the

NCCC's performance was "slower than expected" because of its "limited resources and weak governance environment." Accordingly, she recommended that (1) the NCCC's resources should be increased, (2) training programs should be provided for NCCC staff, and (3) skilled staff should be recruited by the NCCC (Nualnoi, 2004, p. 202).

Thus, while the 1997 People's Constitution led to the formation of the NCCC, which is not handicapped by the CCC's weaknesses, many observers have stressed the importance to the government of providing adequate financial and human resources to support the new anticorruption institutions as "such resource constraints would naturally limit the ability of these organizations" (Nualnoi, 2004, p. 193). Referring to the NCCC's plight, Borwornsak (2001, pp. 198–199) warned:

> Staff and funding are critical factors in agency performance because control agencies cannot operate effectively without qualified personnel and adequate resources … . Without adequate funding for new staff and an appropriate pay scale, it is difficult to imagine how the NCCC is to operate effectively. If the situation is not improved the NCCC risks being labeled a "paper tiger"—an appellation often assigned to the CCMC [or CCC]. In such a case the blame rests squarely on the shoulders of the government.

A NCCC official, who declined to be identified, had informed a *Straits Times* correspondent based in Bangkok in May 2000 that the NCCC needed an additional 200 personnel as its staff was overworked. Furthermore, budget constraints had forced the NCCC to limit its expenditure in 2000 to 100 million baht, which was "hardly enough to cover operational costs" (Tang, 2000, p. 27).

However, in spite of its resource constraints, the NCCC has done a creditable job so far as, unlike its predecessor, it has investigated corruption cases involving politicians and senior bureaucrats. For example, as mentioned earlier, it charged Thaksin Shinawatra in December 2000 for concealing assets worth 4.5 billion bahts by registering these assets in the names of his employees and business colleagues. Thaksin's *TRT* party won the January 2001 general election and he became the prime minister. However, Thaksin was later acquitted by the Constitutional Court as "the judges decided in Thaksin's favor by an 8–7 split decision" (Pasuk & Baker, 2004, pp. 1, 5).

Apart from strengthening the NCCC, the 1997 People's Constitution was also concerned with reducing the potential conflicts of interest of public officials by prohibiting Cabinet members from holding partnerships or owning shares of more than 5 percent in business companies and participating in commercial transactions with state agencies (Nualnoi, 2004, p. 185). However, critics of Thaksin accused him of "policy corruption" because he had formulated policies and implemented projects that favored himself and his Cabinet colleagues.

Initially, the NCCC was viewed favorably by the public in Thailand especially when Deputy Prime Minister Sanan Kachornprasart had resigned in March 2000 after the NCCC had charged him for fabricating documents to conceal assets worth 45 million baht. Two months later, the NCCC's investigations led to the firing of the Deputy Finance Permanent Secretary, Nibhat Bhukkanasut, for accepting a 30 million baht bribe (Tang, 2000, p. 27). However, the NCCC's "most memorable ruling occurred in January 2001, when it convicted Thaksin of concealing his assets," and the NCCC received "widespread accolades and public trust for its handling of alleged corruption cases" (Mutebi, 2006, p. 309).

The NCCC's efforts in curbing corruption suffered a serious setback when its nine commissioners resigned in May 2005. They were found guilty by the Supreme Court of Thailand of abusing their powers in August 2004, when they issued an executive decree to increase their monthly salaries by 45,000 baht (US$1,125). This episode shows that the NCCC members are not above the law and are accountable for the abuse of their powers (Quah, 2007a, p. 14). Consequently, the NCCC's work "came to a grinding halt" after the Supreme Court's historic ruling led to the resignations of its nine commissioners. As the NCCC had about 7,000 pending corruption cases, including 20 against powerful political leaders, the delay in appointing new commissioners had resulted in the lapsing of some of these cases under Thailand's statute of limitations (Mutebi, 2006, pp. 309–310).

The NCCC was expected to be more independent than the CCC because it came under the jurisdiction of the Senate and not the PMO. However, this expectation was unrealistic during Thaksin's tenure of office as the Senate was controlled by his political party, the *TRT* party. Consequently, the NCCC and the other watchdog agencies were "mired in seemingly endless leadership and operations struggles" because of the "differences between the legislature, the judiciary, and the executive on the qualifications and legal process of appointing Commissioners" (Mutebi, 2006, p. 306).

Alex M. Mutebi (2009, p. 116) contends that the anticorruption institutions created by the 1997 People's Constitution are "woefully inadequate" to deal with the type and levels of corruption under Thaksin's leadership because he "expertly exploited loopholes" in the constitution. Distinguishing between administrative corruption and state capture, Mutebi (2009, pp. 119, 129) argues that the 1997 anticorruption measures are designed to deal with administrative corruption but not equipped to handle the state capture under Thaksin's leadership. In other words, these measures are ineffective because "the extent of state capture that ensued during the Thaksin era simply overwhelmed them."

## CONCLUSION

The preceding analysis has shown that corruption remains a serious problem in Thailand in spite of the many anticorruption measures introduced by various governments in Thailand since the establishment of the BIFGO in September 1972. The ineffective and corrupt BIFGO survived for a year and was replaced by the ACC, which was transformed by the CCA into the CCC in February 1975.

The CCC survived for nearly 25 years even though it was ineffective and could not punish corrupt officials. Indeed, its relatively long existence is a reflection of the lack of political will of the various coalition governments to curb corruption from 1975 to 1999. The NCCC, which replaced the CCC in November 1999, was the product of the 1997 People's Constitution. The NCCC was renamed the NACC in July 2008. Bidhya Bowornwathana (2005, p. 1) has aptly used the analogy of a tiger to describe the evolution of ACAs in Thailand from the CCC as a "paper tiger" to the creation of the NCCC as a "ferocious tiger" in November 1999. However, after Thaksin became prime minister in 2001, the NCCC was transformed into a "circus tiger" with Thaksin as the ring master. Finally, with the suspension of the nine commissioners in October 2004 and their resignation in May 2005, the NCCC has become a "sick tiger."

The Council for Democratic Reform under Constitutional Monarchy (CDRM) justified the 19 September 2006 coup to the "deep social divisions, corruption and the undue politicization of state institutions, and the Thaksin regime's disrespect for the monarchy" (Montesanto, 2007, p. 322). The CDRM abrogated the 1997 Constitution, restricted political activity, declared martial law, and promised to hold elections within a year. Has the 19 September 2006 coup reduced corruption as promised by the coup leaders?

The People's Power Party (PPP) won the December 2007 general election, and its leader, Samak Sundaravej, formed a coalition government with five smaller parties on 29 January 2008. However, on 9 September 2008, the Constitutional Court found Samak guilty of conflict of interest because he was employed and paid for hosting two shows for a television cooking program after becoming prime minister. His deputy, Somchai Wongsawat, succeeded him as prime minister on 17 September, but he was rejected by the

People's Alliance for Democracy (PAD) because he was Thaksin's brother-in-law. After weeks of protests led by the opposition PAD (or "yellow shirts"), the Constitutional Court found the ruling PPP and two coalition member parties guilty of electoral fraud on 2 December and banned their leaders, including Prime Minister Somchai, from politics for five years.

Somsak was succeeded by Abhisit Vejjajiva, leader of the Democrat Party, who became Thailand's 27th prime minister on 17 December 2008. At the forum of the Foreign Correspondents Club of Thailand on 15 January 2009, Abhisit stated that his government would perform its duties transparently and "without corruption and without violation of human rights." However, according to Chairat Charoensin-o-larn (2010, p. 314), Abhisit's government was mired in many corruption scandals related to the government's economic stimulus package, "Thailand Strength" (or *Thai Kem Kaeng*), since its inception.

These scandals involved ministers and politicians from the ruling Democrat Party, and those who controlled the funds in various schemes had demanded "an overly high corruption cut of 20 to 25 percent" when the "going rate was generally 5 to 10 percent." The corruption scams linked to the "Thailand Strength" project involved the following programs:

> The school milk program, in which the milk was spoilt, to the purchase of new flagpoles at inflated prices of 49,500 baht each under the nationwide patriotic campaign to sing the national anthem, the procurement at extremely high prices of medical equipment that was unsuitable for use in community hospitals, and corruption in the twenty-six billion baht community sufficiency project, which involved the purchase of drinking water machines that communities did not need and the extortion of money in exchange for placing these products in the community sufficiency stores. (Chairat, 2010, p. 314)

Corruption was also widespread among the coalition parties, especially the Bhumjaithai Party, which was implicated in the 60 billion baht bus-leasing project by the Transport Minister of 4,000 Natural Gas Vehicle public buses (Chairat, 2010, p. 315).

As mentioned earlier, the 19 September 2006 coup leaders had used corruption as their excuse for overthrowing the Thaksin government. However, instead of minimizing corruption, the military-backed Abhisit government is itself plagued with corruption, with the PAD leader, Sondhi Limthongkul, claiming that corruption under the Abhisit government was "worse than Thaksin." On 4 October 2009, the *Bangkok Post* reported that 50 percent of the respondents in a survey believed that the "Thailand Strength" project lacked transparency (quoted in Chairat, 2010, p. 316).

In sum, the 1997 People's Constitution, which was designed to combat corruption and promote good governance in Thailand, failed to prevent

Thaksin Shinawatra from exploiting its loopholes and enhancing his personal wealth from policy corruption. In lamenting the demise of the 1997 constitution, Thitinan Pongsudhirak (2009, p. 36) blames Thaksin and his supporters for "being so brilliant and shrewd in undermining, politicizing and capturing the constitution" as well as his opponents for "violating the spirit of the constitution in Thaksin's 2001 court case, and allowing Thaksin to get away with other violations for several years."

Unfortunately, the 19 September 2006 coup, which ousted Thaksin from power, has not eliminated corruption but has perpetuated it because the incumbent Abhisit government is also chronically afflicted with corruption after assuming office in December 2008. Thus, curbing corruption in Thailand remains an impossible dream because the various governments that assumed power after the establishment of the constitutional monarchy in June 1932 have not demonstrated the necessary political will to minimize corruption.

## NOTES

1. *Far Eastern Economic Review*, 28 December 1967, quoted in Kulick and Wilson (1992, p. 36).
2. This includes the latest province of Bueng Karn in the Northeast, which was approved by the Thai Cabinet on 3 August 2010.
3. Information provided by Mr. Piyachat Niamsaeng, NACC Officer, Bureau of International Affairs, on 20 February 2009 by e-mail.

# CHAPTER 9

# SOUTH KOREA

> Korea has been called a "ROTC" (Republic of Total Corruption) by the people and the media. The efforts of the Government of Korea have resulted in failure to minimize corruption.
>
> – Young Jong Kim (1994, p. 215)

> Each new administration in Korea has sought to curry popular support and legitimize its rule by exposing the corruption of its predecessor. But it has continued. The higher the position, the bigger the amounts. From the top, corruption has flowed downstream, like a lazy river of filth, leaving its scum lines everywhere.
>
> – Michael Breen (1998, p. 238)

## THE HANBO SCANDAL

The Hanbo (meaning Korean treasure) scandal or "Hanbogate" occurred on January 23, 1997, with the bankruptcy of Hanbo Iron and Steel Company, the second largest steel company and 14th largest conglomerate in South Korea, as its debt had accumulated to US$5.6 billion. Hanbo's bankruptcy triggered an investigation by the Public Prosecutor's Office that resulted in the imprisonment for 15 years of Hanbo's founder, Chung Tae-Soo, for bribing politicians and bankers to pressure banks to extend hugh bank loans to Hanbo. Nine other persons were also convicted including Chung's son, who was jailed for three years for bribery and embezzlement, and Kim Hyun-Chol, the second son of President Kim Young-Sam, who was sentenced to three years jail and fined US$1.5 million (*New York Times*, 1997).

The Hanbo scandal not only contributed to the Korean currency crisis in November 1997, it also "destroyed a myth in [South] Korea that a large conglomerate could never be brought down" because "financial institutions were in fact hostages to their large loan commitments." Indeed, Hanbo's bankruptcy was soon followed by the bankruptcy of another 10 conglomerates with the most serious being the bankruptcy of Kia, the seventh largest conglomerate, in July 1997. Perhaps, the "most damaging aspect" of the Hanbo scandal was that it exposed these four weaknesses of South Korea's economy to the international financial community: "excessive reliance on bank borrowing by conglomerates, political collusion between conglomerates and politicians, lack of transparency in business accounts, and an ineffective bank supervisory mechanism" (Suh, 1998, pp. 11–12).

The traditional model of corruption in South Korea was characterized by the flow of money from big business to the politicians and senior bureaucrats to projects related to urban planning and government procurement but not to projects in the manufacturing sectors. Indeed, the Hanbo scandal is the "first revelation that there had been a fundamental transformation in the state-business relationship in Korea, which meant that the major manufacturing sectors were now not as insulated from corrupt political exchanges as before" (Chang, 1998, p. 1557).

Politically, the Hanbo scandal undermined the credibility and legitimacy of President Kim Young-Sam's anticorruption campaign, which he launched after assuming office in February 1993. The Hanbo scandal not only made a mockery of President Kim's "much trumpeted" anticorruption campaign but also "discredited his earlier promises to sever the ties between big business and politics" (Economist, 1997). Indeed, Kim's image as an incorrupt politician was eroded by the arrest and conviction of his second son, Kim Hyun-Chol, because in South Korea's Confucian culture, "the father is the source of moral authority of the family and his son's illicit acts caused Kim Young-Sam to lose face and moral authority as a political leader" (Kihl, 2005, p. 134).

However, to his credit, President Kim did not prevent the arrest of his son in May 1997 for his involvement in the Hanbo scandal and his conviction and imprisonment five months later. Kim Hyun-Chol did not complete his three-year term of imprisonment as he was released in August 2000 as part of an amnesty granted by President Kim Dae-Jung. Thus, the Hanbo scandal also "destroyed the illusion" among South Koreans that "the end of authoritarian rule also meant an end to corruption and related practices." Furthermore, the involvement of the President's son in influence-peddling and corruption also showed the tremendous importance of "personal ties and family or clan membership in Korean politics" (Blechinger, 2000, p. 7).

In short, the Hanbo scandal not only demonstrated "the fundamental corruption that runs through [South] Korea's system" but also exposed "a banking system that continues to rely on political connections more than hard-headed credit analysis" (Clifford, 1998, p. 330).

## AIM OF THE CHAPTER

Corruption has been a serious problem in South Korea since the 16th century, when the participation of the King's family in politics led to "increasing nepotism and corruption in administration" (Rahman, 1986, p. 118). As a result of the spate of corruption scandals in South Korea in recent years, Young Jong Kim (1994, p. 215), a leading Korean scholar of corruption studies, contends that his country has been described as "a ROTC" or "Republic of Total Corruption by the people and mass media."

Why is corruption such a serious problem in South Korea? When did the fight against corruption begin? What are the various measures employed to combat corruption in South Korea? How effective are these measures? This chapter addresses these questions by describing the salient features of its policy context, assessing the extent and causes of corruption in South Korea, and describing and evaluating the anticorruption measures introduced.

## SOUTH KOREA'S POLICY CONTEXT

### *Geography*

South Korea has a total area of 99,274 sq km and is the 26th largest country in Asia (Andrews, 2002, pp. 14, 172). It is a mountainous country as rugged

***Box 9.1.*** South Korea's Policy Context

| | |
|---|---|
| Land area | 99,274 sq km |
| Arable land | 16% |
| Population | 48.4 million (2008) |
| Population density | 487.5 persons per sq km |
| Urban population | 83.0% |
| GDP | US$929 billion (2008) |
| GDP per capita | US$19,120 (2008) |
| Unemployment rate | 3.2% (2008) |
| Ethnic groups | Korean (99%)<br>Chinese (50,000) |
| Colonial heritage | Mongols (1259–1392)<br>Japanese (1905–1945) |
| Type of government | Presidential Democracy |
| 2010 CPI rank and score | 39/178 and 5.4/10 |
| 2010 PERC rank and score | 7/16 and 5.98/10 |

*Sources: Economist* (2010a, p. 216); *Straits Times* (2010a); and http://www.transparency.org/policy_research/surveys_indices/cpi/2010/results

mountains constitute between 70 percent and 80 percent of the land area (Saccone, 1994, p. 4). According to Donald Stone Macdonald (1996, p. 6), "the Koreans themselves speak of their 'three thousand *ri* [about 0.5 kilometer] of beautiful rivers and mountains' in song and often go to the mountains for meditation or enjoyment." With its "restricted valleys and lack of major river systems," there was no need to mobilize labor and develop administrative mechanisms for flood control and management of irrigation in South Korea (Steinberg, 1989, p. 12).

While the Korean peninsula is moderately endowed with natural resources, South Korea has been less endowed than North Korea with only tungsten, graphite, and limestone. However, it has 16 percent of arable area and is the "traditional rice bowl of Korea, with somewhat greater rainfall, [and] warmer climate" (Economist, 2010a, p. 216; Macdonald, 1996, pp. 8–9). South Korea is also resource-poor like Hong Kong and Singapore, but it is better endowed with mineral resources and has a higher proportion of arable land than the two city-states. South Korea's ample reserves of limestone for producing cement have enabled it to expand its construction industry domestically and to the Middle East in the 1970s (Song, 1997, p. 13).

On the contrary, regional cleavages have developed in response to "wide regional economic disparities, the continued political dominance of one region (Kyongsang) over others until recently, and political manipulation and amplification of regional conflicts by political elites." Regional cleavages affect many aspects of South Korean society viz., "choice of marriage partner, recruitment and promotion of employees in firms, support for specific political leaders and political parties, formation and fragmentation of the political parties, and much more" (Seong, 2000, pp. 98–99). Regionalism was suppressed during the Japanese colonial period, the U.S. military administration, and the pre-1987 era of authoritarian rule (Steinberg, 2000, p. 225). However, with the transition to democracy in 1987, regional ties "fully surfaced and became the pre-eminent line of cleavage in party politics" (Kim, 2000a, p. 79). Political parties became more regionally focused in the 1990s, and the origins of their leaders determined the location of their strength. For example, Kim Dae-Jung's stronghold was in the Cholla provinces and Seoul; Kim Young-Sam's strength was in Pusan and South Kyongsang Province; and Kim Jong-Pil came from the Chungchong provinces (Steinberg, 2000, pp. 225–226).

Regionalism is an important factor affecting South Korea's anticorruption strategy as regional cleavages can undermine the incumbent government's commitment to fighting corruption as "reliance on regionalism undercuts effective national debate on national public policy issues essential to democratic governance" (Steinberg, 2000, p. 226).

## History

Korea's history can be traced to Tangun, who was made the first king in 2333 BC. However, political unity was only attained in 668 AD, with the establishment of the Silla dynasty. Korea was colonized twice, first by the Mongols, and later, by the Japanese. The Mongols ruled Korea for 113 years from 1259 until 1392, when Yi Song-gye, a former Koryo general, created the Yi or Chosun dynasty. In contrast, the Japanese colonized Korea for 40 years from 1905 to 1945. While "Japanese colonialism improved Korea's agriculture and gave it the infrastructure for its subsequent economic success," such improvements, however, only benefited Japan's own settlers at the expense of the Koreans, who lost their land (Andrews, 2002, p. 172).

The origins of corruption in Korea can be traced to the Yi Dynasty (1392–1910) that had introduced various anticorruption measures. The most important measure was the King's Secret Mission or *Amhaing-osa*, whose duty was to investigate the corruption of government officials and to report their investigations secretly to the King. There were also other criminal, personnel, and financial regulations that were designed to prevent the abuse of power by the officials and to protect the population from their corrupt behavior. The various anticorruption measures were effective until the beginning of the 16th century (Rahman, 1986, pp. 117–118).

However, corruption became a serious problem from the 16th century onwards for three reasons. First, the participation of the King's relatives in politics and governmental affairs and their acquisition of farm land from independent farmers contributed to nepotism and bureaucratic corruption. Second, the officials abandoned their rectitude and thrifty behavior for a luxurious lifestyle, which was supported by their involvement in corrupt activities. Finally, the many anticorruption measures were no longer effective and their ineffectiveness aggravated the problem of corruption (Rahman, 1986, pp. 118–119).

## Economy

In 2008, South Korea's GDP was US$929 billion, and its GDP per capita was US$19,120. Its average annual growth in GDP during 2003–2008 was 4.2 percent. Given its lack of natural resources, it is not surprising that South Korea has allocated 4.9 percent of its GDP to education, and 6.3 percent of its GDP to health. The relatively high standard of living in South

Korea is reflected in the high consumer goods ownership per 100 households or the population. More specifically, there are 99.4 color television sets per 100 households, 44.3 telephone lines per 100 population, 94.7 mobile telephone subscribers per 100 population, 57.6 computers per 100 population, and 6.1 Internet hosts per 1,000 population (*Economist*, 2010a, pp. 216–217).

The growth of South Korea's economy since independence has been remarkable as its GDP per capita has grown by 68 times from US$50 in 1948 to US$3,396 in 1990 (Steinberg, 1989, p. 123). During 1990–2008, its GDP per capita increased by nearly six times to US$19,120. Steinberg (1989, p. 157) has attributed South Korea's success in the economic development to these factors: "political will, sound economic policies, effective implementation, mass mobilization, a skilled but often exploited labor force, a vigorous private sector under the guidance and control of an interventionist centralizing government, a strong subsidization program to induce exports and rural growth and to open new sectors for expansion, and an international scene conducive to Korean exports."

South Korea's economy today is the fourth largest in Asia after China, Japan, and India. Its GDP per capita is ranked sixth after Macao SAR, Japan, Singapore, Brunei, and Hong Kong (*Economist*, 2010a, pp. 24, 26). In short, South Korea is rich enough to devote sufficient resources for fighting corruption and for its incumbent government to raise the salaries of civil servants.

### *Demography*

South Korea has a population of 48.4 million persons in 2008 and a population density of 487.5 persons per square kilometre (Economist, 2010a, p. 216). Its population is homogeneous with 99 percent being Korean and 50,000 Chinese as the only minority group. In terms of religion, 47 percent of the population are Buddhist and 49 percent are Christian. The adult literacy rate of South Koreans is 97.8 percent (Andrews, 2002, p. 181). With a homogeneous population, common language, and the tremendous importance given to education, the incumbent government in South Korea can spread its anticorruption messages easily throughout the country. Steinberg (1989, p. 188) has argued that "the cultural, ethnic, and linguistic homogeneity of the Korean people" gave South Korea "a developmental edge" as it provided "an easier milieu in which a powerful regime could mobilize for developmental (or political) purposes."

On the contrary, Sung Chul Yang (1995, pp. 11–12) has argued that some aspects of Korean culture or "traditional mores" have contributed to the spread of corruption in South Korea:

> A reciprocal giving and receiving common in a traditional setting, for example, may lose its original virtue and become the root cause of corrupt practices in urban and industrial life. Corruption, which permeates contemporary Korean society, may also have originated from some transplantation of rural and traditional values and behaviors to urban and industrial living. Like cancer, it has spread through the entire community – schools and academe, business, commercial and labor establishments, civil services, mass media and political parties. Few individuals or organizations are, in fact, free of, or immune from, such a nexus of corruption and bribery. Two scandals of the Roh administration, the Suso real estate development project irregularities and the Ministry of Defense land scam ... are only conspicuous symptoms of a much deeper socio-political disease rooted in agrarian belief systems and traditional behavior transplanted into a rapidly urbanizing milieu.

In his analysis of Korean political culture, Woon-Tai Kim (2001, pp. 25–29) identified four distinctive features: communitarian identity, authoritarian values, factionalism, and formalism. More specifically, he argued that the negative effects of factionalism outweighed the positive aspects as "rent-seeking, corruption, irrational pattern of recruitment, and the politics of exclusion, all of which are closely associated with factionalism, have undermined political development and economic efficiency."

## *Political System*

On May 10, 1948, Korea was divided into two at the 38th parallel: the Republic of Korea under Syngman Rhee in the south, and the Democratic People's Republic of Korea under Kim Il-Sung in the north. On June 25, 1950, the North attacked the South, and this led to the Korean War, which claimed four million lives and ended on July 27, 1953, and confirming the division of the Korean peninsula along the 38th parallel (Andrews, 2002, p. 173). Since then, Korea has remained divided and the United States has maintained 40,000 troops in South Korea to protect it from invasion by North Korea.

South Korea became independent on August 15, 1948. After 26 years of authoritarian rule under President Park Chung-Hee (1961–1979) and President Chun Doo-Hwan (1980–1988), South Korea became democratic when President Roh Tae-Woo assumed power in 1988.[1] South Korea is a parliamentary democracy with a National Assembly consisting of 299 members who are elected for four years. The president is elected for a five-year term. Kim Young-Sam became the first civilian president in February

1993. He was succeeded by Kim Dae-Jung in February 1998, by Roh Moo-Hyun in February 2003, and by Lee Myung-Bak in February 2008.

While economic growth and democratization in South Korea have increased the opportunities for corruption, the transformation of its political system from authoritarianism to democracy has also assisted the governments of Kim Young-Sam, Kim Dae-Jung, Roh Moo-Hyun, and Lee Myung-Bak in curbing corruption because the holding of periodic elections enables the citizens to punish governments that fail to control corruption.

## PERCEIVED EXTENT OF CORRUPTION

From January 1894 to March 1897, Isabella L. Bird, a British travel writer made four visits to Korea and recorded her impressions in her book, *Korea and Her Neighbors*, which was published in two volumes in 1898. In her last chapter on "Last Words on Korea" in volume 2 of her book, Bird referred to the problem of corruption by observing that there were two classes in Korea: "the Robbers and the Robbed, – the official class recruited from the *yang-bans*, the licensed vampires of the country, and the *Ha-in*, literally 'low men,' a residuum of fully four-fifths of the population, whose *raison d'etre* is to supply the blood for the vampires to suck." The Treasury Department was "in a more chaotic and corrupt condition, and the ramifications of its corruption were spread all through the Provinces" as earlier attempts to reform it were thwarted by "the rapacity of the King's male and female favorites, and the measureless cunning and craft of corrupt officials." However, after one year of "firm and capable foreign supervision," the Treasury Department was "cleansed" as the accounts were "kept on a uniform system, and with the utmost exactitude." Consequently, Korea closed the financial year in April 1897, "with every account paid and a million and a half in the Treasury, out of which she has repaid one million of the Japanese loan of three millions" (Bird, 1986, pp. 281–282).

Bureaucratic corruption increased during the postindependence period and the government introduced the criminal code and administrative restrictions to curb it. According to Myoung-Soo Kim (1997, pp. 253–254):

> Corruption has been recognized since the early days of the first Republic, which began in 1948, as one of the most serious social ills facing Korea and, therefore, is a problem to be tackled by all the means at the country's disposal.... After the early 1960s, all new administrations in Korea waged anti-corruption drives because it was recognized that corruption was widespread in the public, as well as in the private, sectors and was one of the major concerns of the time.... Corruption has survived and outlived administrations that campaign against it and has proven to be indestructible.

The anticorruption measures introduced in the 1950s and 1960s were formal and ineffective. During the 1960s and 1970s, the United States Army in South Korea "could not procure local goods and services without encountering collusion and corruption." While "bribery and corruption were not applauded in Korean culture," "collusion and kickbacks were also facilitated by certain 'cultural traits'" such as the custom of gift-giving. The Korean suppliers subverted the U.S. army's policy of competitive bidding by colluding to over-charging the army by 30 percent or more above competitive prices. They also gave gifts (including money) to the Korean accountants and contract specialists working for the army to induce them to provide higher cost estimates, as their low salaries made them vulnerable to corruption. If the gifts did not work, the Korean accountants would be threatened by the suppliers (Klitgaard, 1988, pp. 134–135, 138–139, 149). Furthermore, no other legal or administrative anticorruption measures were initiated until 1974 when major corruption scandals involving civil servants were exposed and there was increasing public dissatisfaction with bureaucratic corruption (Rahman, 1986, p. 119).

Corruption was also manifested in the 1987 presidential election and the April 1988 legislative election. As the ruling Democratic Justice Party (DJP) had a great deal of money to spend, many observers believed that it spent between US$300 million and US$1 billion in the 1987 presidential election. Vote-buying was rampant as both the DJP and opposition parties were corrupt in handling their campaigns. However, as the DJP had more resources than the opposition parties, it gave US$30 to US$60 to junior civil servants and rice to low-income families. The DJP threatened to dismiss the civil servants if either of the two opposition candidates won the election (Lee, 1990, pp. 73–74).

Unlike previous legislative elections where corruption, vote-buying, and mobilization of civil servants to campaign for the ruling party were conducted discreetly, the DJP performed these activities openly in the April 1988 legislative election, which was considered by many observers to be "the most corrupt in the nation's history" as "money, violence, corruption, mudslinging, fraud, and every other conceivable means were permitted to determine" its outcome. As the average DJP candidate spent about US$1.5 million (the cost of 50,000 votes) to get elected, each vote costs between US$25 to US$30. However, some candidates spent nearly US$3.5 million and "several spent over US$7 million to gain a legislative seat" (Lee, 1990, pp. 101–102).

A 1990 survey on the Korean people's belief system regarding the 21st century conducted by Seoul National University's Social Science Research

Center found that 40.7 percent of the respondents identified the corruption of politicians as the most important obstacle to South Korea's democratization (Yang, 1995, p. 29). More importantly, as shown in Table 9.1, politicians were considered by 70.1 percent of the same respondents to be the most corrupt in South Korea, followed by businessmen (10.9 percent), government officials (9.3 percent), journalists (3.3 percent), military (2.5 percent), and educators (2.1 percent).

Similarly, the Korea Survey (Gallup) Polls conducted a public opinion survey on the government's anticorruption activities since 1993 in August–September 1993 and found that the respondents believed that "South Korean society seriously suffers from corruption of politicians (85.3 percent), public employees (52.9 percent), lawyers (34.3 percent), and the military (30.2 percent), and that the two most contributing factors to current corruption are selfishness and mammonism of each individual member of society." Another important finding was that 78.5 percent of the respondents wanted more punishment and a stricter control system for those found guilty of corrupt practices (Hwang, 1996, p. 161).

An analysis of the 237 reported cases of corruption by public employees in *HanKuk-Ilbo*, a major newspaper in South Korea, in 1993–1994 by Kee-Chul Hwang (1996, pp. 180–181) found that bribery (53.6 percent) was the most common form of corruption, followed by fraud (21.1 percent), forgery of official documents (8 percent), embezzlement of public money (7.2 percent), misappropriation of public money (4.6 percent), and other (5.5 percent). Another important finding was that the amount of the average bribe exceeded two million won (or US$2,000) or more than a month's salary for a lower-level civil servant. Furthermore, Hwang found that 22.4 percent of the

***Table 9.1.*** Corruption in South Korea by Group or Profession, 1990.

| Group or Profession | Number of Responses | Percentage of Responses |
|---|---|---|
| Politicians | 1071 | 70.1 |
| Businessmen | 167 | 10.9 |
| Government officials | 141 | 9.3 |
| Journalists | 50 | 3.3 |
| Military | 38 | 2.5 |
| Educators | 31 | 2.1 |
| Others | 20 | 1.3 |
| No answer | 85 | 5.6 |
| Total | 1526 | 100.0 |

*Source*: Yang (1995, p. 29).

237 cases involved the police, 19.4 percent dealt with licensing, 15.6 percent involved registration, 13.9 percent concerned taxation, and 7.2 percent focused on health. Hwang attributed the higher proportion of cases of police corruption to the 36 years of Japanese colonial rule when the police was employed as the primary tool of control over the Korean population. In his 1995 survey of 957 public employees and 925 members of the public, Hwang (1996, pp. 158–159) found that while 81.3 percent of the public viewed public employees as corrupt, but only 47.3 percent of public employees considered themselves to be corrupt.

In their analysis of Korean public administration, Jong S. Jun and Myung S. Park (2001, pp. 8–9) argued that "deeply rooted corruption" was a major reason for the incapability of Korean public administrators and the 1997 financial crisis. They wrote:

> Corruption is the cancer of Korean society, and it is found at every level of Korean society, from top officials down to minor civil servants....Corruption at high-level is widespread, but scandals involving bureaucrats, particularly those who collect taxes and enforce customs regulations, are often reported in newspapers as well.

They substantiated their argument by referring to three scandals: the scandal involving the development of the *Soosuh Area* suburb in Seoul, the Hanbo scandal, and the procurement of fighter planes by the Ministry of Defense. They concluded that "corruption will not go away until high-level government officials and politicians live morally and ethically and become models of honesty" (Jun & Park, 2001, p. 9).

Surveys conducted by the Korea Independent Commission Against Corruption (KICAC) from 2003 to 2007 and by its successor, the Anti-Corruption and Civil Rights Commission (ACRC) in 2008 have identified the nine public service areas which are perceived by citizens to be vulnerable to corruption. Table 9.2 shows that construction, housing, and land is perceived by Korean citizens as the most corrupted area, followed by taxation, legal affairs, police, military affairs, education, public health, procurement, and environment. While the overall perception has improved from 64.6 percent in 2003 to 57.1 percent in 2008, Lee and Jung (2010, p. 410) have expressed concern that corruption has worsened in the three areas of construction, housing, and land; education; and procurement.

TI's Global Corruption Barometer from 2004 to 2010 have identified political parties and parliament as the two most corrupt sectors in South Korea. They are closely followed by the police, judiciary, and business sector. A close analysis of Table 9.3 shows that the perceived extent of corruption in these five sectors has remained consistently at the same levels from 2004 to 2010.

***Table 9.2.*** Citizens' Perceptions of Corrupt Public Service Areas in South Korea, 2003–2008.

| Public Service Area | 2003 | 2004 | 2005 | 2006 | 2007 | 2008 | Average |
|---|---|---|---|---|---|---|---|
| Construction, housing & land (%) | 72.6 | 71.3 | 73.9 | 71.7 | 70.8 | 76.9 | 72.9 |
| Taxation (%) | 58.1 | 59.4 | 54.0 | 49.9 | 53.4 | 53.6 | 54.7 |
| Legal affairs (%) | 57.0 | 46.0 | 52.3 | 53.6 | 52.8 | 52.7 | 52.4 |
| Police (%) | 51.3 | 54.9 | 48.0 | 44.9 | 48.0 | 53.4 | 50.1 |
| Military affairs (%) | 54.6 | 51.9 | 52.6 | 42.4 | 47.5 | 44.9 | 49.0 |
| Education (%) | 45.1 | 45.1 | 48.9 | 40.4 | 40.7 | 48.4 | 44.8 |
| Public health (%) | 32.3 | 47.3 | 33.4 | 29.2 | 36.3 | 32.8 | 35.2 |
| Procurement (%) | 27.4 | 36.1 | 26.0 | 23.1 | 34.2 | 47.9 | 32.5 |
| Environment (%) | 32.0 | 37.9 | 32.7 | 28.1 | 30.3 | 29.7 | 31.8 |
| Overall perception (%) | 64.6 | 60.9 | 60.8 | 57.1 | 56.5 | 57.1 | 59.5 |

*Source*: Lee and Jung (2010, p. 411).

***Table 9.3.*** Perceived Level of Corruption in South Korea by Sector, 2004–2010[a].

| Sector | 2004 | 2005 | 2006 | 2007 | 2009 | 2010 |
|---|---|---|---|---|---|---|
| Political parties | 4.4 | 4.4 | 4.3 | 4.2 | 4.3 | 4.0 |
| Parliament | 4.5 | 4.4 | 4.2 | 4.1 | 4.2 | 4.0 |
| Legal system/judiciary | 3.6 | 3.7 | 3.5 | 3.5 | 3.6 | 3.6 |
| Police | 3.8 | 3.7 | 3.3 | 3.5 | NA | 3.7 |
| Public officials/civil servants | NA | NA | NA | NA | 3.7 | 3.6 |
| Business sector | 3.4 | 3.5 | 3.7 | 3.5 | 3.8 | 3.4 |
| Tax revenue | 3.4 | 3.5 | 3.3 | 3.3 | NA | NA |
| Customs | 3.7 | 3.6 | NA | NA | NA | NA |
| Media | 3.6 | 3.5 | 3.5 | 3.4 | 3.6 | 3.4 |
| Medical services | 3.4 | 3.3 | 3.1 | 3.3 | NA | NA |
| Education | 3.5 | 3.6 | 3.3 | 3.2 | NA | 3.5 |
| Registry and permit services | 2.5 | 2.4 | 2.4 | 2.4 | NA | NA |
| Utilities | 2.5 | 2.4 | 2.4 | 2.4 | NA | NA |
| Military | 3.4 | 3.4 | 3.2 | 3.2 | NA | 3.3 |
| NGOs | 2.8 | 2.9 | 2.9 | 2.9 | NA | 2.7 |
| Religious bodies | 3.1 | 3.0 | 3.1 | 3.1 | NA | 3.0 |

*Sources*: Compiled from Transparency International (2004, p. 18, 2005, p. 18, 2006, p. 21, 2007, p. 22, 2009, p. 28, 2010, p. 43).
*Note*: NA = not available.
[a]The score ranges from 1 (not at all corrupt) to 5 (extremely corrupt).

## CAUSES OF CORRUPTION

### *Low Salaries*

In addition to the historical reasons for the emergence of corruption in South Korea in the 16th century, the low salaries of civil servants constitute an important reason for the pervasive corruption in contemporary South Korea. During the First, Second, and Third Republics, corruption was rampant because the salaries of civil servants were inadequate for them to support their families. During the First Republic under Syngman Rhee, the poorly paid civil servants succumbed to bribes provided by those requiring government positions or favors (Oh, 1999, p. 165). Jong S. Jun and Jae Poong Yoon (1996, p. 107) have argued that it is difficult to expect Korean civil servants to be dedicated in their work "without providing adequate remuneration and changing the administrative culture." Similarly, Yun-sik Kim (2009b) contends that it is unrealistic to "expect bureaucrats to serve well without solving their own economic problems, since they could not support their families via their salaries alone."

In 1988, the wages of civil servants were estimated to be about 80 percent of those of their counterparts in the public enterprises (Park, 1997, p. 55). In 1994, Young Jong Kim (1994, p. 222) argued that as the salaries of civil servants are about 70–80 percent of the salaries of their counterparts in the private sector, the "low salary structure of public officials forces them not only [to] tolerate corruption, but also initiate corruption." The problem of corruption was aggravated during the 1997 financial crisis as civil service salaries were further reduced by 30 percent. Apart from being lower than private-sector salaries, the wage level of South Korean civil servants is lower than the salaries of their counterparts in Japan, Singapore, and Hong Kong (Kim, 2003, p. 125). In 2008, the average pay level of civil servants in South Korea was 89 percent of the average salary of their private sector counterparts. Although the salaries of junior civil servants are not bad, it should be noted that the salaries of senior civil servants are low (Kim, 2010, p. 367).

In 2001, the government froze the salaries of political appointees and agency heads at the Grade 1 level in the central government but increased the salaries of the other civil servants by a 5.5 percent increase in base salary and 6.7 percent increase in total pay (Kim, 2003, p. 125). Consequently, the vertical compression ratio of the Korean civil service (highest to lowest level, in terms of base pay) was lower than that of Japan's in 1990 as the "top public officeholders in Korea were only paid about three times what entry-level graduates obtained" compared to "eight or nine times in Japan." In contrast, "Singapore's top earners were paid 17 times what the entry-level graduates were paid (and nearly 80 times what the lowest ranks in the civil service were paid)" (Hood & Askim, 2003, pp. 36–37).

President Lee Myung-Bak's annual salary was increased in 2011 by 6.1 percent to 179 million won (US$160,000) or 219 million won (US$195,754) if the allowances and benefits are included (*Yonhap News*, 2011). Although this salary is higher than those of the political leaders in Malaysia, Thailand, Philippines, Indonesia, Vietnam, and Cambodia, it pales in comparison with the annual salaries of Singapore's president (S$3.14 million or US$2.22 million) or prime minister (S$3.04 million or US$2.15 million) (PSD, 2008, pp. 1–2).

The low salaries of Korean civil servants can be illustrated by referring to the monthly salaries of junior soldiers in June 2010. Table 9.4 shows that the monthly salaries of sergeants, corporals, private first class, and private second class are inadequate to meet their average monthly expenditures, with the largest difference of US$31 recorded for corporals, US$24 for sergeants, US$21 for privates first class, and US$9 for privates second class.

### *Gift-Giving Tradition*

According to John Kie-Chiang Oh (1999, p. 165), there is "a culture of corruption in Korea." The Koreans have a long tradition of gift-giving that causes corruption because "when the gift was an expensive item presented to a powerful individual with the expectation of receiving a favor it was akin to a bribe." Gift-giving is an honored tradition in all Asian countries, but in

***Table 9.4.*** Monthly Salaries and Average Monthly Expenditures of Soldiers in South Korea, June 2010.

| Rank | Monthly Salary (*a*) | Average Monthly Expenditure (*b*) | Difference (*a–b*) |
|---|---|---|---|
| Sergeant | 97,500 won (US$82) | 126,097 won (US$106) | –US$24 |
| Corporal | 88,000 won (US$74) | 125,214 won (US$105) | –US$31 |
| Private first class | 79,500 won (US$67) | 104,403 won (US$88) | –US$21 |
| Private second class | 73,500 won (US$62) | 84,478 won (US$71) | –US$9 |

*Source:* "Statistical Office and Civil Service pay provisions" quoted in *Joong Ang Daily* (2010).

"Korea the tradition has [been] transformed into what can only be called bribery." Indeed, gift-giving has evolved from "a means of showing respect and confirming reciprocal relationships" to "a means of obtaining business, political election, [or] favors" and "degenerating into bribery and graft" (Genzberger, 1994, p. 144, 23).

*Chonji* or "bribe money" is a way of life in South Korea as rich persons and large companies are expected to pay *chonji* for the services and cooperation provided by civil servants. This "deeply entrenched custom" is also practised by government ministries and agencies that pay *chonji* to journalists and editors for favorable coverage of their activities. According to Boye Lafayette de Mente (1994, p. 30):

> In effect the *chonji* system makes the various government offices hostage to the reporters who cover them. If officials fail to hand over acceptable amounts, reporters write critical articles about them. Press coverage of scandalous behavior by government officials is frequently linked to the failure of officials to hand over enough *chonji* to ensure a cover-up. Officials also regularly pay off reporters when they want to place a story in a newspaper or magazine.

Similarly, senior executives of major corporations also pay *chonji* to reporters for favorable press coverage. These executives usually pay *chonji* of one million won for a favorable interview (de Mente, 1994, p. 30).

Finally, the practice of *chonji* is widespread in South Korean society as illustrated by these examples:

> mothers hand them out to ensure their kids get good marks at school; young lecturers to get jobs at colleges; and drivers to avoid speeding tickets. Small businesses constantly give *chonji* to public servants seeking money in exchange for every stage of administrative action related to their trade. (Kim, 1998, p. 53)

## *Red Tape*

The plethora of government regulations in South Korea has given rise to ample opportunities for corruption. For example, to obtain a permit for building a factory, a company must prepare an average of 44.2 documents. These complex procedures requiring many documents resulted in delays, which increased the costs in time and money for the clients, private persons, or business firms. Thus, the latter are "tempted into collusion with the bureaucrats who have control over the matter to seek other, easier ways to get what they need, even by illegitimate means" (Kim, 1997, pp. 261–262).

Boye Lafayette de Mente (1994, p. 42) has described red tape as a "formidable" problem in South Korea and provided this example of the "red tape syndrome":

> In one application for a joint venture involving pharmaceuticals, the various government ministries and agencies required 312 documents covering sixty-two administrative procedures, and taking two years and nine months to prepare.... Among the documents needed in Korea: a description of the investment plan, evidence of proxy authority, a certificate of nationality, specifications of foreign capital to be introduced, the joint-venture agreement, and documentation showing that the applicants will subscribe to stocks and shares.

The existence of red tape in South Korea is confirmed by the World Bank's *Doing Business Surveys* from 2007 to 2011. Table 9.5 shows that South Korea's ease of doing business rank has improved from 30th among 178 economies in 2008 to 16th among 183 economies in 2011. However, in terms of starting a business, South Korea's ranking has declined from 116th among 175 economies in 2007 to 126th among 181 economies in 2009. Its ranking in starting a business improved to 53rd and 60th positions among the 183 economies in 2010 and 2011. For construction permits or licenses, South Korea's ranking has improved from 28th among 175 economies in

***Table 9.5.*** Ease of Doing Business in South Korea, 2007–2011.

| Indicator | 2007 ($N=175$) | 2008 ($N=178$) | 2009 ($N=181$) | 2010 ($N=183$) | 2011 ($N=183$) |
|---|---|---|---|---|---|
| Ease of doing business (rank) | 23 | 30 | 23 | 19 | 16 |
| Starting a business (rank) | 116 | 110 | 126 | 53 | 60 |
| No. of procedures | 12 | 10 | 10 | 8 | 8 |
| Time (days) | 22 | 17 | 17 | 14 | 14 |
| Cost (% of income per capita) | 15.2 | 16.9 | 16.9 | 14.7 | 14.7 |
| Dealing with construction permits or licenses (rank) | 28 | 22 | 23 | 23 | 22 |
| No. of procedures | 14 | 13 | 13 | 13 | 13 |
| Time (days) | 52 | 34 | 34 | 34 | 34 |
| Cost (% of income per capita) | 175.9 | 170.2 | 154.6 | 135.6 | 131.2 |
| Registering property (rank) | 67 | 68 | 67 | 71 | 74 |
| No. of procedures | 7 | 7 | 7 | 7 | 7 |
| Time (days) | 11 | 11 | 11 | 11 | 11 |
| Cost (% of property value) | 6.3 | 6.3 | 5.1 | 5.1 | 5.1 |
| CPI rank and score | 43rd (5.1) | 40th (5.6) | 39th (5.5) | 39th (5.4) | NA |

*Sources*: World Bank (2006b, p. 122, 2007, p. 130, 2008, p. 114, 2009, p. 131, 2010a, p. 173) and http://www.transparency.org

2007 to 22nd among 183 economies in 2011. On the contrary, for the registration of property, South Korea's ranking ranges from 67th position among 175 economies in 2007 to 74th position among 183 economies in 2011. In sum, while South Korea has made some progress in reducing red tape, its performance on the World Bank's *Doing Business Surveys* from 2007 to 2011 shows that much more needs to be done by the Lee Myung-Bak's government to reduce red tape in the civil service.

### *Low Probability of Punishment for Corrupt Officials*

Another important cause of corruption in South Korea is the low probability of punishment for corrupt officials. Table 9.6 provides details of the court judgments and punishment for corruption-related offenses during 1993–2004. From 1981 to 1988, of the 64 public officials found guilty of corruption-related offenses, only 22 had served actual prison sentences, while 42 (or 65.63 percent) received suspended sentences (Kim, 2009, p. 146). However, Table 9.6 shows that the percentage of suspended sentences for public officials for corruption offenses and all aggravated crimes (grand corruption) was more than 3 percent higher at 68.7 percent and 69 percent, respectively. It should be noted that for aggravated crimes under 50 million won, 49 (or 79 percent) of the 62 guilty public officials were given suspended sentences.

Even though South Korea has a specific law which stipulates aggravated punishment for certain corruption-related offenses, Joongi Kim (2009, p. 148) laments that "not only were stiffer sentences not rendered, but they also became futile due to suspensions." According to the law, those found

***Table 9.6.*** Punishment of Public Officials for Corruption-Related Offenses, 1993–2004.

| Type of Case | Guilty Judgment | Served Actual Prison Sentence | Suspended Sentence | % of Suspended Sentences |
|---|---|---|---|---|
| Corruption cases | 131 | 41 | 90 | 68.7 |
| Aggravated crimes under 50 million won | 62 | 13 | 49 | 79.0 |
| Aggravated crimes over 50 million won | 35 | 17 | 18 | 51.4 |
| Aggravated crimes total | 97 | 30 | 67 | 69.0 |

*Source*: Kim (2009, p. 147).

guilty of accepting bribes greater than 50 million won (US$50,000) would be imprisoned for longer than 10 years, while those who had accepted bribes between 10 million won and 50 million won (US$10,000 to US$50,000) would receive sentences of more than five years. However, in reality, the courts "have been unusually lenient" as they have not imposed the stricter sentences as required by the law. Indeed, Table 9.6 shows that for the 35 public officials convicted for accepting bribes exceeding 50 million won, only 17 (or 48.6 percent) were imprisoned, while 18 (or 51.4 percent) received suspended sentences. Thus, more than half of the public officials found guilty of grand corruption are not punished at all for their misconduct.

Former President Chun Doo-Hwan was sentenced by the Seoul district court on August 26, 1996, to death for mutiny, treason, and corruption. His successor, former President Roh Tae-Woo, was sentenced to 22.5 years imprisonment on similar charges. Both Chun and Roh were convicted of amassing huge sums of illegal political funds during their terms of office and were fined US$270 million and US$350 million, respectively. The trial and guilty verdict on the two former presidents was an important step toward the establishment of the rule of law in South Korea and strengthened President Kim Young-Sam's anticorruption reforms. However, on December 26, 1997, President Kim Young-Sam, after consulting President-Elect, Kim Dae-Jung, granted amnesty to both Chun and Roh (Kihl, 2005, pp. 132–133, 136). In other words, while former presidents Chun and Roh were punished for their corruption offenses, their punishment was reduced considerably as they were granted amnesty after serving only 16 months in jail.

In short, corruption in South Korea can be attributed to the combined influence of these four factors: low salaries of public officials, the tradition of gift-giving, red tape, and the low probability of punishment for corrupt public officials.

## ANTICORRUPTION MEASURES

### *Park Chung-Hee's Anticorruption Campaign*

In 1509 during the Chosun Dynasty secret royal inspectors were appointed by the king from those who passed the state-administered examination to investigate administrative practices and "any possible corruption within local governments" (BAI, 1999, p. 4). However, the fight against corruption in South Korea began with President Park Chung-Hee, who assumed office in May 1961 after ousting the government of Chang Myon because of its involvement in corruption, its inability to defend the country from communism, and its incompetence in initiating economic and social change (Han, 1989, p. 273).

As "a thrifty, clean and unusually able officer," Park had "built an indisputable reputation as a stubborn and incorruptible general." Hence, it was not surprising that President Park promised to "do away with the 'evil legacies' of Korean history, end corruption, rebuild national pride, and spur economic development" (Kim, 2007, pp. 94, 99). He formed the Board of Audit and Inspection (BAI) in 1963 by merging the Board of Audit and the Commission of Inspection, which were established in 1948, to act as a direct check on the economic bureaucracy (BAI, 1999, p. 5; Hart-Landberg, 1993, p. 54). The BAI is the first *de facto* anticorruption agency (ACA) in South Korea.

In March 1975, Park introduced the *Seojungshaeshin Undong* (general administration reform) to curb corruption in the civil service, beginning with the elimination of corruption in those public services that directly affected the public and the correction of illegal and unnecessary execution of budgetary regulations. To eliminate bureaucratic corruption, the government identified these four targets: (1) corrupt and troublesome personnel; (2) inefficient and wasteful tasks; (3) improprieties in the administrative system; and (4) the environment of both public and private life (Oh, 1982, pp. 325, 329). As punishment was stressed by the *Seojungshaeshin* movement, it was not surprising that the number of civil servants prosecuted increased from 21,919 in 1975 to 51,468 in 1976 (Rahman, 1986, p. 122).

Even though the *Seojungshaeshin's* anticorruption measures were unsatisfactory, Suek Hong Oh (1982, pp. 343–344) has contended that their impact was better than all the previous anticorruption campaigns for four reasons. First, the *Seojungshaeshin* was strongly supported by Park. Second, their scope was much wider than the previous campaigns. Third, unlike previous efforts, the intensive remedial measures proposed were long term rather than short term. Fourth, the government established various channels of feedback for confirming, evaluating, and correcting the results of the *Seojungshaeshin's* anticorruption activities.

### *AntiCorruption Campaigns of Chun Doo-Hwan and Roh Tae-Woo*

Park's assassination on October 26, 1979, led to the assumption of power on August 27, 1980, by his successor, Chun Doo-Hwan, who re-affirmed his government's anticorruption stance by purging corrupt public officials and introducing ethics laws to reward honest officials and to enhance the structures for civil service reforms (Jun, 1985, p. 63). In 1981, he initiated several anticorruption measures in the form of a *Sahoejungwha Undong* (social purification movement) (Caiden & Kim, 1993, p. 137). Furthermore, high-ranking officials were required to register their assets as an institutional device to prevent them from gaining illegal wealth by taking advantage of their positions. President Chun also initiated programs to improve government efficiency including the elimination of red tape to reduce corruption (Kim, 2007, pp. 170, 173).

However, Chun's government lacked legitimacy because of opposition by rival political parties, student leaders, intellectuals, and progressive Christians (Han, 1989, pp. 282–284). The "Lady Chang loan scandal" in spring 1982 "dealt a blow to the moral authority of the Chun regime" as Chang Young-ja, was a relative of the first lady, Lee Soon-ja. The scandal led to the bankruptcy of two major companies and several medium-sized companies. The investigation of the scandal, which was ordered by Chun, resulted in the arrest of 32 persons, including the main culprits, Chang and her husband, and several bank executives (Kim, 2007, pp. 174–175).

In July 1982, the Chun government introduced a financial reform measure known as the "7.3 Measure" to restructure the financial structure by promoting the "regularity in financial transactions by establishing the practice of using real names." Accordingly, in December 1983, the National Assembly enacted the Act on Real Name Financial Transactions, which was "a significantly watered-down version of the 7.3 Measure," because it indicated that the "implementation of the real-name system would begin at a time to be determined by presidential decree after January 1, 1986" (Kim, 2007, p. 175; Lee, 1995, pp. 109–110). Chun's unpopularity led to his retirement in February 1988, at the end of his seven-year term.

The peaceful transfer of power to President Roh Tae-Woo enabled him to investigate the abuses and corruption during his predecessor's regime. Although Chun was strict with others, he was not stern with himself and his relatives as he could not control their activities (Kim, 2007, p. 212). During the parliamentary hearings in November and December 1988, Chun, his two brothers, and his wife's family were accused of massive corruption. On November 23, 1988, Chun and his wife apologized for their misbehavior and returned 13.9 billion won (US$20 million) to the government. In his statement of apology to the country, Chun said:

> When I was inaugurated as president, most relatives of mine, including close relatives were not so well-off. They were proud and surprised at first, but then they started to be disturbed by the temptations around them. They began to cause various problems. I

> asked them many times to be prudent and sometimes I controlled them. I really am sorry that many relatives of mine have been involved in irregularities and made you very angry. I sincerely apologize and beg your pardon. (quoted in Lee, 1990, p. 156)

In July 1989, Chun's brothers were convicted for corruption and sentenced to between four and seven years imprisonment. Mark L. Clifford (1998, p. 287) has commented on the consequences of the corruption of Chun and his family thus:

> What became apparent after Chun left office was the depth of corruption and the degree to which it had been quietly tolerated, even expected. The pervasive corruption is another of the ugly legacies bequeathed by the Fifth Republic. Corruption had long been part of the Korean system, but *Chun did the country a tremendous disservice by allowing his relatives to prosper*. For all his faults, Park had never allowed his family to profit personally from his position. Unfortunately, the Chun and Lee families set an example of egregiously corrupt behavior that still undermines the Korean social contract. (emphasis added)

Indeed, Chun's "image as an effective leader was seriously tarnished" by his own "slush fund" scandal and the corruption scandals involving his relatives (Kim, 2007, pp. 212–213).

While President Roh remained committed to the establishment of democracy during his term of office, he was nevertheless plagued by the long-festering problem of political corruption, as six legislators were found guilty of extorting funds from the business community. On February 15, 1991, the chairman of the Hanbo Group, Chung Tae-Soo, was arrested for bribery because the Hanbo Construction Company was accused of paying off politicians and officials to rezone land in Seoul's green belt for commercial use. This scandal dealt a "severe blow" to the Roh administration's moral authority (Kim, 2007, p. 248). However, Roh himself was not immune as it was discovered in October 1995 that the major business conglomerates and numerous individuals had contributed almost US$600 million to his private political fund, which he had used to reward supporters and kept for himself and his family (Macdonald, 1996, pp. 159–160).

### *Kim Young-Sam's Anticorruption Campaign*

When Kim Young-Sam became the first civilian president in February 1993, he launched an intensive anticorruption campaign to curb the Korean disease namely corruption. He began with the voluntary disclosure of his personal assets and those of his extended family amounting to 1.77 billion won (US$2 million) (Oh, 1999, p. 139). President Kim encouraged his cabinet colleagues and ruling party members to follow suit. In June 1993, the Public Officials' Ethics Law was revised to institutionalize the disclosure of public officials' assets, and all senior officials were required to periodically register and disclose their assets (Kim, 1997, p. 255). He gave up golf, which had become a symbol of corporate-government cronyism and the exchange of corrupt gifts (Sheridan, 1994, p. 15). In August 1993, President Kim issued an emergency presidential decree to establish the Real-Name Financial Transaction System, which prohibited the use of anonymous financial accounts and required individuals to use their own names for operating bank accounts, as the anonymous or false-name account had been the backbone of the black economy and massive fraud, corruption and tax evasion schemes (Sheridan, 1994, p. 15; Kim, 1997, p. 255). The use of fake or borrowed accounts enabled individuals to avoid paying tax and conceal the trail of recipients of illicit incomes (Guerrero, 1999, p. 77).

In March 1994, the Election for Public Office and Election Malpractice Prevention Act was introduced to reduce corruption in politics by ensuring transparency in campaign financing, limiting campaign expenditures, preventing electoral irregularities, and imposing heavy penalties for offenders (Kim, 1997, p. 255). However, the most important reforms introduced by President Kim were the strengthening of the BAI, and the creation of the Commission for the Prevention of Corruption (CPC), which is an advisory body of private citizens formed to assist the BAI's chairman in the task of fighting corruption.

The BAI performs three functions: to confirm the closing accounts of the state's revenues and expenditures; to audit the accounts of the central government agencies, provincial governments and other local autonomous bodies, and government-invested organizations to ensure proper and fair accounting; and to inspect the work done by government agencies and the duties of public officials to improve the operation and quality of government services (BAI, 1999, pp. 7–8).

The BAI's chairman is appointed by the president for four years with the consent of the National Assembly. The BAI's commissioner is also appointed by the president for four years on the recommendation of the chairman (Kim, 1994, p. 218). In March 1993, government formed a team of 100 special inspectors within the BAI to implement President Kim's anti-corruption campaign by focusing on officials handling taxes, government contracts, procurement, military conscription, and licenses, who were suspected of being corrupt (*Straits Times*, 1993). In August 1993, the BAI had 776 officials involved in audit and administrative inspection. The number of BAI staff was increased to 849 officials by July 1998 (BAI, 1999, p. 12). Article 24 of the BAI Act enabled the BAI to conduct anticorruption activities by scrutinizing the behavior of civil servants (Kim, 1994, p. 219).

### *Kim Dae-Jung's Comprehensive Anticorruption Campaign*

Kim Dae-Jung won the December 1997 presidential election and was inaugurated as president on February 25, 1998. He demonstrated his concern in combating corruption through the implementation of a comprehensive anticorruption strategy with the objectives of ensuring clean and upright public office, transparent, and reliable government, and a just and fair society to become a transparent state and to improve its ranking on TI's CPI from 43rd position in 1998 to 20th position by 2003 (Republic of Korea, 1999, p. 6).

President Kim's comprehensive anticorruption strategy had six major components in response to the various causes of corruption in South Korea (Republic of Korea, 1999, pp. 9–22). The first component was the improvement of the existing system of corruption control through the implementation of these measures: the creation of an AntiCorruption Committee for the coordination of anticorruption programs and activities; and the formulation of the Anti-Corruption Law to provide protection for whistle-blowers, to strengthen citizen watch and participation in anticorruption movements, and to reinforce detection and punishment for corrupt practices.

The second component of President Kim's anticorruption campaign involved the reform of the attitudes and consciousness of civil servants by enforcing codes of conduct and education and revising the salaries of medium to low level bureaucrats to match their counterparts in the private sector within five years. Third, public awareness of corruption was promoted by means of education in school and other social and cultural education centers, the use of mass media to publicize anticorruption materials, a national movement against corruption, and strengthening of international cooperation in fighting corruption.

The fourth aspect was the creation of a social and cultural environment against corruption through the scrutiny and strict control of former government officials, enhancing the transparency of private industries, and eroding the collusion between politicians, government officials, and businessmen. Fifth, detection and punishment for corruption was reinforced by improving the reward/protection system for informers, activating citizen watch and report against corruption, creating a special inspection office to focus on the corruption of senior government officials, and increasing the financial penalty for corrupt officials by retrieving personal gains and government losses, and confiscating the bribes.

Finally, administrative reforms were introduced in the six corruption-prone areas of tax administration, construction, housing, food and entertainment, environmental management, and police work. In 1998, President Kim formed the Regulatory Reform Committee to make the country more business friendly by eliminating unnecessary or irrational economic and social regulations that hindered business activities or interfered in people's lives. For example, as mentioned earlier, to obtain a permit to build a factory, a company has to prepare an average of 44.2 documents and wait for several months for approval. These excessive regulations encourage corruption as businessmen are prepared to bribe the relevant officials to bypass the cumbersome and tedious procedures for obtaining a factory permit (Kim, 1997, pp. 261–262). In April 1999, the Seoul Metropolitan Government launched an "Online Procedure Enhancement for Civil Applications (OPEN)" system to improve civil applications covering 54 common procedures, which could be filed through the Internet.[2]

### *Korea Independent Commission against Corruption*

The Anti-Corruption Act of July 2001 was originally proposed for legislation in 1996 by the People's Solidarity for Participatory Democracy (PSPD) and supported by TI Korea, the Citizens' Coalition for Economic Justice and the Citizens' Association for Anti-Corruption. These civil society organizations participated in public hearings, legislation requests, national assembly person signature drives, campaigning, rallies and television broadcast discussions during 2000–2001 to advocate the passing of the bill. The introduction of an investigative authority for the Anti-Corruption Act was an important item in the original proposal of the civil society organizations. However, as the original bill met with stiff resistance in the National Assembly, the Anti-Corruption Act that was enacted on July 24, 2001, did not include that important provision and other provisions proposed by the civil society organizations (Kim, 2006, p. 53).

Article 10 of the Anti-Corruption Act provided for the establishment of an Anti-Corruption Commission under the President's jurisdiction "to revamp Acts and subordinate statutes, institutions" and "to formulate and implement policies" to prevent corruption (Republic of Korea, 2001, p. 7). Accordingly, the KICAC was formed six months later on January 25, 2002. As its name implies, the KICAC was based on Hong Kong's ICAC. However, the KICAC's formation was opposed by the Public Prosecutor's Office (PPO) and the National Police Agency (NPA) because both agencies wanted to perform the anticorruption function themselves. Furthermore, many lawyers from the National Assembly and the legal policy community did not support the creation of the KICAC in view of the different sectoral group interests (Kim, 2008, p. 159). Consequently, the KICAC that was established in January 2002 was a "poor cousin" of the ICAC because it cannot investigate corruption cases (Quah, 2010a, pp. 41–42).

Articles 10–24 of the Anti-Corruption Act of 2001 specify the establishment, functions, and composition of the KICAC. Article 11 describes the KICAC's original eight functions, but only the following six functions are identified in the KICAC's *Annual Report 2005:*

1. Policy-maker: to formulate and coordinate anticorruption policies by organizing on a regular basis the Inter-Agency Meeting on Corruption.
2. Evaluator: to evaluate the levels of integrity and anticorruption practices of public-sector organizations.
3. Observer: to monitor corruption and protect whistle-blowers by handling reports on alleged corrupt conduct and protecting and offering rewards for whistle-blowers.
4. Partner: to promote cooperation for the fight against corruption by encouraging civil society involvement and public–private partnership against corruption, and engaging in the global fight against corruption.
5. Legal-reformer: to improve the legal and institutional frameworks to remove laws and practices that encourage corruption.
6. Ethics-leader: to inculcate ethical values in society by promoting public awareness on the risks of corruption, and by enforcing the code of conduct for public sector employees (KICAC, 2006, pp. 4, 7).

The KICAC was not a full-fledged ACA like the ACAs in the other countries analyzed in this book because it could not investigate corruption cases itself as it had to rely on the BAI and the PPO to do so. According to article 29, section 3, the KICAC had to refer the investigation of a whistle-blowing case involving a public official to the BAI, an investigative agency, or an agency in charge of supervising the relevant public agency. The investigative agency would inform the KICAC of the results of its investigation within 60 days. The KICAC would then notify the whistle-blower of the results of the investigation. However, the KICAC could request for a re-investigation if the results of the earlier investigation were incomplete (Republic of Korea, 2001, pp. 18–21). In short, unlike other Asian ACAs, the KICAC performed the functions of preventing corruption and community education, but not the critical role of investigating corruption cases, which was delegated to other investigative agencies.

The KICAC was merged with the Ombudsman and the Administrative Appeals Commission to form the ACRC on February 29, 2008. From its inception in January 2002 until December 2008, the KICAC/ACRC received a total of 1,258 corruption reports and 12,523 general complaints. Table 9.7 shows that of the 562 corruption reports transferred by the KICAC/ACRC to other investigative agencies from 2002 to 2008, there were 359 disclosed corruption cases, 150 cases resulting in no charges, and the remaining 53 cases still under investigation. This means that the investigative agencies achieved a corruption detection rate of 70.5 percent during 2002–2008 (ACRC, 2009, p. 33).

In terms of organizational structure, the KICAC was divided into the Policy Planning Office (PPO), the Corrupt Practices Inspection Unit (CPIU), the Report Inspection Bureau (RIB), and the Public Relations and Cooperation Bureau (PRCB). The PPO had two director-generals and officers concerned with innovation and personnel, policy planning and coordination, evaluation and surveys, and institution and practices improvement. The CPIU consisted of a legal adviser and four inspection teams. The RIB was composed of the Corruption Report Center, the Inspection Coordination Division, Protection and Reward Division, and the Code of Conduct Division. The PRCB was subdivided into the Education and Public Relations Division, International Cooperation Division, and Nongovernmental Organizations and Business Cooperation Division. Finally, the General Services Division and Legal Affairs Management Officer provided support and assistance to the PPO, CPIU, RIB, and PRCB (KICAC, 2006).

***Table 9.7.*** Status of Corruption Reports Transferred by the KICAC to Investigative Agencies, 2002–2008.

| Classification | Total | Transfer to Investigative Agencies | | | | Corruption Detection Rate (2/1) |
|---|---|---|---|---|---|---|
| | | Notice of Investigation Results | | | Under investigation | |
| | | Subtotal (1) | Disclosed corruption (2) | No charge | | |
| 2002 | 74 | 74 | 47 | 27 | – | 63.5% |
| 2003 | 100 | 100 | 67 | 33 | – | 67.0% |
| 2004 | 66 | 66 | 48 | 18 | – | 72.7% |
| 2005 | 82 | 82 | 53 | 29 | – | 64.6% |
| 2006 | 83 | 82 | 63 | 19 | 1 | 76.8% |
| 2007 | 92 | 85 | 66 | 19 | 7 | 77.6% |
| 2008 | 65 | 20 | 15 | 5 | 45 | 75.0% |
| Total | 562 | 509 | 359 | 150 | 53 | 70.5% |

*Source*: ACRC (2009, p. 33).

*Table 9.8.* Personnel and Budget of the KICAC/ACRC, 2004–2009.

| Year | Personnel | Budget |
|---|---|---|
| 2004 | 139 | US$13.7 million |
| 2005 | 205 | US$17.8 million |
| 2006 | 205 | US$20.0 million |
| 2009 | 466 | US$61 million |

*Sources*: Choi (2005, p. 28, 2011, p. 39) and Kim (2008, p. 160).

Table 9.8 shows that the KICAC's personnel increased from 139 in 2004 to 205 in 2006. Similarly, its budget rose from US$13.7 million to US$20 million during 2004–2006. The budget of the ACRC, which was formed from the merger of the KICAC, the Ombudsman and the Administrative Appeals Commission in February 2008, has been increased to US$61 million in 2009. However, the number of personnel in the KICAC was reduced from 542 in 2007 to 466 after its merger to form the ACRC in February 2008 (ACRC, 2010b, p. 6).

### *Roh Moo-Hyun's Anticorruption Campaign*

When President Roh Moo-Hyun assumed office in February 2003, he distanced himself from the scandals surrounding President Kim Dae-Jung's family and aides. He also followed former President Kim Young-Sam's example by promising to disclose his assets and those of his family members (Kihl, 2005, p. 300). His administration revised the Public Office Election Act to reduce corruption in public office elections and introduced these three approaches to reduce corruption systematically:

1. Strengthening direct democratic values by means of the residents' lawsuit system, the local referendum system, and the citizen recall system;
2. Using e-government such as the online public engagement system; and
3. Expanding the disclosure of administrative information and enhancing access to it (Lee & Jung, 2010, p. 414).

President Roh had campaigned and was known for his strong anti-corruption rhetoric. He and his family were not accused of any serious corruption scandal during his presidency. However, after leaving office in 2008, they became the target of an influencing peddling scandal. About a year after Roh left office, he was suspected by the prosecutors to have accepted US$6 million in bribes from Pak Yeon-Cha, a close business associate of President Kim Dae-Jung. He committed suicide in May 2009 (Lee & Jung, 2010, pp. 414–415).

### *Lee Myung-Bak's Anticorruption Campaign*

Soon after assuming office, President Lee Myung-Bak merged the KICAC with the Ombudsman and the Administrative Appeals Commission on February 29, 2008, to form the ACRC, which performs these three functions:

1. Handle and address public complaints and improve related unreasonable systems;
2. Build a clean society by preventing and deterring corruption in the public sector; and
3. Protect people's rights from illegal and unfair administrative practices through the administrative appeals systems (ACRC, 2010a).

Unlike the KICAC, which focused solely on curbing corruption, the ACRC is concerned not only with combating corruption but also with dealing with public complaints and protecting citizens' rights. More importantly, the organizational integration in February 2008 resulted in the reduction of employees in the ACRC from 542 to 466 (ACRC, 2010b, p. 6).

While it might be premature to pass judgment on President Lee Myung-Bak's anticorruption campaign, the unintended (or intended?) consequence of the KICAC's merger with the Ombudsman and the Administrative Appeals Commission is the dilution of the emphasis given by previous governments to combating corruption by according lower priority to this objective. In other words, the ACRC's formation by President Lee Myung-Bak's government is a reflection of the lower priority given to curbing corruption (Quah, 2010a, p. 42). In the same vein, Lee and Jung (2010, p. 415) have observed that "the current government's will to fight against corruption seemed to weaken after the institutional merger." According to Jin-Wook Choi (2009, p. 209), the ACRC's creation, which resulted from a merger of three agencies with "weak functional relevancy and coherence," may blur its anticorruption role.

## EVALUATION OF ANTICORRUPTION MEASURES

How effective are the anticorruption measures introduced by various presidents in South Korea? Caiden and Kim (1993, pp. 137–139) have criticized the anticorruption campaigns of Presidents Park and Chun for being "sporadic, periodic, episodic, incidental and improvisatory ... too cosmetic and lip-serving" and for being implemented quickly and without careful preparation. The results of Park's *Seojungshaeshin Undong* and Chun's *Sahoejungwha Undong* were "disappointing" because they were based on the misconception that corruption was "a personalized or individual phenomenon rather than as an institutional or systemic problem." Consequently, both campaigns employed punitive measures to weed out the "rotten apples" instead of reforming the "rotten barrels" or system. However, the punishment of hundreds of public officials in both campaigns without making appropriate changes in existing structures and practices, means that the "same old routines of wrongdoing were repeated and will continue."

President Kim Young-Sam's anticorruption campaign confirmed that corruption is a way of life in South Korea and exposed its pervasiveness in the country. As he turned the spotlight on corrupt practices, "it exposed more dirt than the Korean people had ever imagined or are comfortable with" (Genzberger, 1994, p. 25). Young Jong Kim (1994, p. 207) has lamented the lack of political will in South Korea's efforts to curb corruption, especially under the regimes of Presidents Rhee, Park and Chun. Although Kim's anticorruption drive was hindered by the May 17, 1997, arrest of his son for bribery and tax evasion in the Hanbo loan scandal and his sentencing to three years' imprisonment five months later, President Kim had clearly demonstrated his commitment to eliminating corruption by not obstructing the legal arrest and sentencing of his son to three years' imprisonment. However, his son was released in August 2000 because of a presidential amnesty to celebrate the Korean national holiday (Blechinger, 2000, p. 7). Nevertheless, the Hanbo scandal and his son's arrest and imprisonment had seriously undermined Kim's legitimacy and jeopardized the continued success of his anticorruption campaign. Moreover, despite all these efforts made against corruption, there is no evidence that corruption has been contained during President Kim Young-Sam's administration (Kim, 1997, p. 255).

How effective was President Kim Young-Sam's anticorruption strategy in curbing the endemic corruption in South Korea that has been fuelled by 30 years of authoritarian rule? How effective was his moral crusade against illicit and unethical behavior in transforming the primordial and particularistic standards of behavior among the Korean people? The 1996 Korean Democratization Survey found that 71 percent of the respondents experienced some degree of decrease in political corruption and only 4 percent reported having experienced an increase in corruption. However, the 1997 Korean Democratization Survey reported that 49 percent and 36 percent of the respondents perceived the level of corruption of Kim Young-Sam's government to be high and very high respectively. Doh C. Shin (1999, pp. 212–214) contends that this finding illustrates the fact that for all the important steps President Kim Young-Sam took during 1993–1997, the age-old custom of corruption was not dying at all in the South Korean political marketplace; instead the informal norms were still overpowering the formal rules of the newly implanted democratic political game. Myoung-Soo Kim (2000b, pp. 2–3) contends that corruption remains a serious problem in South Korea because of the lack of effective anti-corruption measures, the lack of independence of ACAs, and the lack of consistent and fair enforcement of the anticorruption laws.

A similar negative assessment has been provided by Jon Moran (1999, pp. 575–576), who has argued that President Kim Young-Sam's anti-corruption reforms were initially successful but floundered later because of three problems. First, these reforms were viewed as part of Kim's strategy of removing past opponents to secure his position. Second, the economic crisis and the need for economic growth compelled Kim to abandon by 1995 his attempts to reform *chaebol* structures in production and finance. Finally, Kim's anticorruption reforms rebounded on himself as the real name system flushed into the open massive secret accounts held by Chun and Roh and exposed the full extent of informal network politics and the links between the state elite, the *chaebol* and the politicized financial system. On the contrary, Kim's anticorruption reforms were successful because they inaugurated important legislative initiatives, laid the groundwork for future reforms and provided a further legitimation for the oppositional activities of civil society activities.

Indeed, the adoption of the real name system in August 1993 was Kim's "most potent antidote to the 'Korean disease'" of corruption as it "dealt a major blow to the prevalent practice of amassing unearned income, and soliciting bribes or political funds through fake or borrowed accounts." Credit should be given to Kim for implementing a policy that was deferred in 1982 and 1987 because of "fears of its negative impact on growth." The implementation of the real name system has "proved reform seekers correct" because "billions stashed in fake and borrowed accounts had to be transferred to real-name accounts" (Guerrero, 1999, p. 77).

In contrast, President Kim Dae-Jung's comprehensive anticorruption strategy was much more effective for three reasons. First, after its first year of operations, Table 9.9 shows that the Regulatory Reform Committee formed by President Kim had abolished 5,326 or 48 percent of 11,125 administrative regulations. As red tape is one of the four causes of corruption in South Korea, the elimination of nearly half of the administrative regulations has strengthened President Kim's anticorruption strategy.

Second, the OPEN system has also enhanced the transparency of civil procedures and reduced the opportunities for corruption by "preventing unfairness and delays in administrative procedures." By May 2000, the OPEN system had handled 28,000 cases of civil applications and over 648,000 visitors had visited its website. Thus, the OPEN system has improved "customer-oriented delivery of public services" and "transparency of city administration" as those officials responsible for permit or approval procedures (usually perceived to be corruption-prone) are "required to upload their work reports and documents to the Internet" to enable citizens to monitor the progress of their applications (Moon, 2001, p. 41).

Finally, and most importantly, the arrests of President Kim Dae-Jung's two sons for corruption have shown his commitment to curbing corruption as he did not prevent the arrests. President Kim admitted that the arrests of his two sons were "heartbreaking" but he said that he would not interfere and let the court decide on their fate (Shin, 2002, p. 1). On the contrary, Young Whan Kihl (2005, p. 297) contends that President Kim's legacy remains tainted because his accomplishments have been compromised by the conviction of his two sons and close aides on bribery charges.

***Table 9.9.*** Government Regulations Abolished in South Korea in 1998.

| Ministries | No. of Regulations | No. of Regulations Eliminated | Percentage of Elimination |
|---|---|---|---|
| Economy-related | 6,433 | 3,293 | 51.2 |
| Society-related | 3,967 | 1,788 | 45.1 |
| General administration | 715 | 245 | 34.3 |
| Total | 11,125 | 5,326 | 47.9 |

*Source*: Quoted in Cho (1999, p. 3).

## CONCLUSION

This chapter has shown that corruption is a serious problem in South Korea despite the attempts by various governments to curb it. First, Table 9.10 shows that South Korea's performance on TI's CPI from 1995–2010 has improved from a ranking of 27th among 41 countries with a score of 4.29 in 1995 to 39th position among 178 countries and a score of 5.4 in 2010. South Korea's CPI scores ranges from 3.8 in 1999 to 5.6 in 2008. It should be noted here that the objective of President Kim Dae-Jung's comprehensive anti-corruption strategy of improving South Korea's CPI ranking to 20th position by 2003 was not attained because its actual ranking was 50th position among the 133 countries surveyed. Second, South Korea's rank on PERC's annual surveys from 1995 to 2010 has fluctuated between fourth and eighth positions among the 11–16 countries surveyed. Its PERC score has declined from 4.00 in 1995 to 8.33 in 2000. Third, South Korea's

***Table 9.10.*** South Korea's Performance on CPI, PERC, and Control of Corruption, 1995–2010.

| Year | CPI Rank and Score[a] | PERC Rank and Score[b] | Control of Corruption Percentile Rank |
|---|---|---|---|
| 1995 | 27th (4.29) | 4th (4.00) | NA |
| 1996 | 27th (5.02) | 5th (5.16) | 68.4 |
| 1997 | 34th (4.29) | 8th (7.71) | NA |
| 1998 | 43rd (4.2) | 7th (7.12) | 64.6 |
| 1999 | 50th (3.8) | 8th (8.20) | NA |
| 2000 | 48th (4.0) | 7th (8.33) | 63.6 |
| 2001 | 42nd (4.2) | 6th (7.55) | NA |
| 2002 | 40th (4.5) | 5th (5.75) | 69.9 |
| 2003 | 50th (4.3) | 4th (5.50) | 67.5 |
| 2004 | 47th (4.5) | 5th (6.67) | 68.9 |
| 2005 | 40th (5.0) | 6th (6.50) | 71.8 |
| 2006 | 42nd (5.1) | 5th (5.44) | 68.4 |
| 2007 | 43rd (5.1) | 8th (6.30) | 72.9 |
| 2008 | 40th (5.6) | 5th (5.65) | 69.1 |
| 2009 | 39th (5.5) | 6th (4.64) | 71.4 |
| 2010 | 39th (5.4) | 7th (5.98) | NA |

*Sources*: Compiled from http://www.transparency.org; PERC (2001, 2008, p. 7); Hussain (2009, p. B5); *Straits Times* (2010a); and http://info.worldbank.org/governance/wgi/sc_chart.asp

[a]The CPI score ranges from 0 (most corrupt) to 10 (least corrupt).

[b]The PERC score ranges from 0 (least corrupt) to 10 (most corrupt).

percentile rank on the World Bank's control of corruption indicator varies from 68.4 in 1996 to 71.4 in 2009. In sum, while South Korea's performance on these three indicators has improved during 1995–2010, its CPI and PERC scores in 2010 and its 2009 control of corruption percentile rank confirm that corruption remains a serious problem in the country.

Since corruption is still a serious problem in South Korea, it is not surprising that the level of public trust in politicians is also low. Table 9.11 shows that its score on this indicator has remained at 2.10 in 1999 and 2010–2011. Its best performance was attained in 2008–2009 with a rank of 25th among the 134 countries surveyed and a score of 4.30. However, its score declined again to 2.80 in 2009–2010 and 2.10 in 2010–2011. Similarly, its ranking has also deteriorated from 48th among 59 countries to 105th among 139 countries during 1999 to 2010–2011.

These findings on the low level of public trust in politicians are not surprising as Jun and Kim (2002, p. 6) have attributed the endemic distrust in Korean society to "the abuse of political power, the abuse of personal connections, the lack of social responsibility, and corruption at the higher level." According to them, South Korea's presidents, from Syngman Rhee to Kim Dae-Jung, "did not establish trusting relationships with the people." Furthermore, the decline in the South Korean citizens' trust in government

***Table 9.11.*** Public Trust of Politicians in South Korea, 1999 to 2010–2011.

| Year | Rank | Score[a] | No. of Countries |
|---|---|---|---|
| 1999 | 48 | 2.10 | 59 |
| 2000 | 44 | 2.30 | 59 |
| 2001–2002 | 51 | 2.10 | 75 |
| 2002–2003 | 39 | 2.30 | 80 |
| 2003–2004 | 42 | 2.90 | 102 |
| 2007–2008 | 22 | 4.00 | 131 |
| 2008–2009 | 25 | 4.30 | 134 |
| 2009–2010 | 67 | 2.80 | 133 |
| 2010–2011 | 105 | 2.10 | 139 |
| Average | 49 | 2.77 | – |

*Sources*: Compiled from Schwab et al. (1999, p. 327), Porter et al. (2000, p. 253), Schwab et al. (2002, p. 408), Cornelius (2003, p. 619), Sala-i-Martin (2004, p. 499), Schwab and Porter (2007, p. 379), Schwab and Porter (2008, p. 367), Schwab (2009, p. 349), Schwab (2010, p. 369).

[a]The score ranges from 1 (very low) to 7 (very high) for the respondents' answers to this statement: "How would you rate the level of public trust in the ethical standards of politicians in your country."

and institutions was the result of the decline in respect for authority (because of the "increase in political freedom and openness in society") and the improvement of the economic condition of most of the population (Jun & Kim, 2002, pp. 6, 10).

South Korea has shifted from Pattern 1 to Pattern 3 with the implementation of Kim Dae-Jung's comprehensive anticorruption strategy that resulted in the enactment of the Anti-Corruption Act on July 24, 2001, and the establishment of the KICAC in January 2002. Unlike the ACAs in the other Asian countries, the KICAC and its successor, the ACRC, cannot investigate corruption cases. This weakness was highlighted by Seong Youn Kim (2005, pp. 130–131), the Chief Deputy Director of the Korean Civil Service Commission, in his evaluation of South Korea's anticorruption measures:

> The Government [of South Korea] adopted a check-and-balance system with the creation of the KICAC. But considering that [the] KICAC is not given investigative power, the check-and-balance system would not work as effectively as the Government originally intended.

In sum, South Korea's experience in combating corruption demonstrates clearly that an ACA will not be able to perform its functions effectively if it lacks investigative powers. Indeed, the KICAC's and ACRC's Achilles' heel is that both agencies have to rely on other agencies to investigate corruption cases instead of doing so themselves. Thus, the establishment of the KICAC and ACRC as "toothless" ACAs without the ability to investigate corruption cases is a manifestation of the lack of political will to curb corruption among the various governments in South Korea, which are responsible for creating and maintaining these flawed agencies. In other words, curbing corruption in South Korea remains an impossible dream as long as their political leaders continue to rely on an ineffective ACA that cannot investigate corruption cases.

## NOTES

1. For an analysis of South Korea's political development under these three presidents, see Steinberg (1989, pp. 55–68).
2. For more details on the OPEN system, see *Online Procedures Enhancement for Civil Applications* (Seoul: Seoul Metropolitan Government, July 2001), pp. 6–13. See also: http://open.metro.seoul.kr.

# CHAPTER 10

# INDONESIA

> Corruption, in short, has now become so institutionalized in Indonesia that its eradication, if that were conceivable, might mean the critical dislocation of the whole shaky national structure.... Korupsi, people conclude, must be eradicated – but no one seriously thinks that it will be or even that it will soon be much reduced.
>
> – Willard A. Hanna (1971, pp. 1, 7)

> The civil servants, and particularly the police [in Indonesia], refer to their duties as either wet or dry. Wet means you have access to the fee-paying public. Dry means you don't. Being posted to a dry position is about the worst fate any official could fear.
>
> – Keith Loveard (1999, p. 111)

## THE FAMILY BUSINESS

Willard A. Hanna's astute observation above about the institutionalization of corruption in Indonesia was published in August 1971, five years after President Soeharto assumed power. The origins of corruption in Indonesia can be traced to the Dutch colonial period as bribery was rife among the lowly paid personnel of the Dutch East India Company (Day, 1966, pp. 100–103). However, corruption became institutionalized during President Soeharto's 32-year reign as his cronies and family "made an art form of creaming off many of Indonesia's most profitable ventures ... while being protected by monopoly regulations and their relationship to the president" (Kingsbury, 1998, p. 202). Raymond Bonner (1988, p. 80) has used the euphemism "the family business" to describe "the corruption surrounding members of the Suharto family," which was "a public secret" in 1988.

A former cabinet minister has described President Soeharto's children as his Achilles' heel:

> As long as his children are not involved, the president makes very rational economic decisions. But when the kids get involved, rationality loses. Then it is the father that speaks, not the president. (quoted in Schwarz, 2004, p. 146)

More importantly, Soeharto did not consider his children to be corrupt as they had "as much right as any to be in business." Indeed, he believed that they deserved special treatment because they were his children (Schwarz, 2004, p. 146).

The "family business" involving President Soeharto's children and grandchildren grew rapidly during the 1980s and 1990s. His late wife, Siti Tien Hartinah, was called "Madame Ten Percent" for the commission she obtained from business deals or even "Fifi" for 50 percent (Glickman, 1991, p. 25). The extent of the Soeharto business empire or "President Soeharto Inc." becomes obvious to visitors within an hour after their arrival in Jakarta because:

> The management of the airport was undertaken by Humpuss Group – which was owned by Soeharto's son Tommy. The airport ground handling services were undertaken by the Bimantara Group – which was owned by another Soeharto son, Bambang. Outside the airport, they might have hired a Citra taxi – owned by daughter Tutut Soeharto. As they took the 30-kilometer drive to the center of Jakarta, they drove along a toll-road owned by Tutut. Along the way, they would pass billboards owned by Tommy Soeharto, managed by another of his companies, and which usually displayed advertising for other Soeharto-owned companies. On the way to their hotel, they would drive past Plaza Senayan, a massive shopping center in which another daughter had a share. And eventually they would pull up at their hotel, often the Grand Hyatt, which is owned partly by another Soeharto son. (Backman, 1999, pp. 260–261)

According to Michael Backman (1999, p. 263), the Soeharto clan consisted of these 17 members: his six children, their spouses, two grandchildren, a brother of a son-in-law, a cousin, and a half-brother. All of them were actively involved in business and prospered during Soeharto's 32 years in office because they were given monopolies or near-monopolies for the import, manufacture, and distribution of various products.

Soeharto and his wife established seven charity foundations (or *yayasan*) from the 1970s to raise funds for sociocultural and political purposes. These foundations were managed by members of his family and provided Soeharto with a great deal of funding for his personal and political activities (Suryadinata, 1997, p. 275). Reuters reported in February 1997 that Soeharto's family was the nine richest in Asia with an estimated fortune of US$6.3 billion (Saeki, 1997). In May 1999, one year after Soeharto's resignation, *Time* magazine published a special report on "The Family Firm" accusing Soeharto and his family of accumulating a US$15 billion fortune in "cash, property, art, jewelry and jets" (Colmey & Liebhold, 1999, pp. 15–29). In the *Global Corruption Report 2004*, TI identified President Soeharto as the world's most corrupt political leader during 1984–2004 as he had allegedly embezzled between US$15 and US$35 billion during his 32 years in office (Hodess et al., 2004, p. 13).

However, Soeharto was not prosecuted after his resignation on May 21, 1998. He was placed on house arrest in May 2000 when he was being investigated for corruption during his term of office. In August 2000, Soeharto was formally charged with siphoning 5.1 trillion rupiahs (US$570 million) from the charity foundations operated by his family. However, the corruption case against Soeharto was dismissed in May 2006 because of his poor health (*Global Integrity Report*, 2009, pp. 1–4). He died on January 27, 2008, at the age of 86 years, without being prosecuted or punished for corruption.

## AIM OF THE CHAPTER

Indonesia is perceived to be the most corrupt of the Asian countries participating in Transparency International's Corruption Perceptions Index (CPI) from 1995 to 2000. From 2001 to 2010, its CPI rank declined from 88th to 110th, but its CPI score increased from 1.9 to 2.8. Why is corruption a way of life in Indonesia? What are its causes? How effective are the various anticorruption measures adopted in Indonesia? Can corruption in Indonesia be minimized or is the situation hopeless? The purpose of this chapter is to answer these questions by relying on the published literature[1] and two surveys on bureaucratic corruption in Indonesia conducted by the World Bank in 2000 and the Partnership for Governance Reform in 2001.

This chapter is divided into five sections. The first section describes the policy context in Indonesia in terms of its geography, history, economy, demography, and political system. The second section provides the empirical data on the perceived extent of corruption in Indonesia by referring to the relevant findings from two national surveys. The third section identifies the major causes of corruption in Indonesia. The fourth section assesses whether the various anticorruption measures adopted in Indonesia are effective. The final section concludes the chapter by suggesting that corruption in Indonesia can only be minimized if the political leaders demonstrate the political will required to minimize or eliminate the major causes of corruption and to impartially implement a comprehensive anti-corruption strategy.

## INDONESIA'S POLICY CONTEXT

### *Geography*

Indonesia is the largest archipelago in the world as it consists of 18,108 islands with a land area of 1,904,443 sq km (Cribb & Ford, 2009, p. 1; *Economist*, 2010a, p. 160). However, only 6,000 of these islands are inhabited, and there are five major islands namely: Java, Sumatra, Sulawesi, Kalimantan, and Irian Jaya. In terms of terrain, Indonesia is mainly mountainous and two-thirds of the country is covered by forest and jungle (Dunung, 1998, p. 189).

Among the 10 countries discussed in this book, Indonesia faces the most difficult challenges in implementing the incumbent government's anti-corruption laws across its vast domain, which stretches for 5,120 km from east to west and for nearly 2,000 km from north to south (Sidik, 2007, p. 23). According to James Clad (1989, p. 75), "Indonesia's size is often forgotten" even though "its reach exceeds the distance from California to Florida or from Ireland to eastern Turkey." Herbert Feith (1964, p. 183) has astutely observed that "Indonesia as a unit must do battle with geography to maintain itself." Compared to the Philippines, which has 7,107 islands, Indonesia is more than six times larger and has a much longer coastline.

***Box 10.1.*** Indonesia's Policy Context

| | |
|---|---|
| Land area | 1,904,443 sq km |
| GDP | US$ 511 billion (2008) |
| GDP per capita | US$ 2,250 (2008) |
| Population | 234.3 million (2008) |
| Population density | 122.9 persons per sq km |
| Urban population | 44.3% |
| Adult literacy rate | 92.0% |
| Political system | Presidential Democracy |
| Colonial rule | Dutch colonial rule (1619–1942) |
| 2010 CPI rank and score | 111/178 and 2.8/10.0 |
| 2010 PERC rank and score | 16/16 and 9.27/10.0 |

*Sources*: *Economist* (2010a, p. 160); http://www.transparency.org/policy_research/surveys_indices/cpi/2010/results; and *Straits Times* (2010a).

Indonesia has 33 provinces, two special autonomous regions, the Jakarta special metropolitan district, and the special region of Yogyakarta. The 33 provinces are further subdivided into 440 districts and cities, 5,263 subdistricts, 62,806 villages, and 7,123 urban-villages (Sidik, 2007, p. 38). Thus, in terms of fighting corruption, the incumbent government in Indonesia has a much more difficult task than its counterparts in the other nine Asian countries discussed in this book in enforcing the anticorruption laws especially in the rural provinces and outer reaches of the vast archipelago. Nicola Frost (2002, p. 16) observes that this "system of top-down, uniform government" from Jakarta has "facilitated the endemic corruption that plagues the Indonesian bureaucracy" because the poorly paid civil servants rely on bribes to supplement their incomes.

Another important aspect of Indonesia's geographical location is that "most of the world's worst disasters tend to occur in the areas between the Tropic of Cancer and the Tropic of Capricorn" (Frost, 2002, p. 25). The major disasters that have frequently afflicted Indonesia include earthquakes, tsunamis, tropical cyclones, and floods. Apart from causing serious economic and physical damage and casualties, the frequency of such disasters also provide ample opportunities for corruption especially in the distribution of the humanitarian aid received from other countries for the disaster victims.

The massive humanitarian response to the December 2004 Indian Ocean tsunami that wrecked havoc in South and Southeast Asia caused concern among many quarters and resulted in the hosting of an Expert Meeting on Corruption Prevention in Tsunami Relief by the Asian Development Bank, the Organization for Economic Co-operation and Development, TI, and the Indonesian Government jointly in Jakarta on April 7–8, 2005. Indeed, humanitarian relief operations after natural disasters are vulnerable to corruption because

> Sudden flows of large amounts of money, goods and services, pressure to deliver aid quickly, as well as the substantial economic opportunities that arise from large-scale reconstruction, all contribute to increasing the risk of corruption, waste and mismanagement. (ADB, 2005, p. 1)

More specifically, Peter Walker (2005, p. 91) contends that a "geographically massive disaster and an equally massive rapid build up of funding" enhance existing inequalities and provide ample opportunities for corruption. According to him:

> disasters often exacerbate existing disparities in wealth and power, thus increasing the likelihood of corruption.... This major influx of resources ... provides an additional

> opportunity for corruption for those willing to exploit it.... Errors of exclusion happen when individuals, households, or communities who should have been targeted are left out.... Errors of inclusion happen when people are targeted with assistance when they actually do not need it.... Both errors may create opportunities for corruption, particularly exclusion errors, which may force desperate households and communities into illegal and unsustainable survival strategies. (Walker, 2005, pp. 93, 95–96)

In short, Indonesia's vast archipelago and its vulnerability to natural disasters have increased the opportunities for corruption and hindered the impartial enforcement of the anticorruption laws by the *Komisi Pemberantasan Korupsi* (KPK or the Corruption Eradication Commission). Given the archipelagic nature of the country and the size of the civil service, curbing corruption among the 4.7 million civil servants (Haryanto, 2010) is certainly an arduous task.

### *History*

Donald P. Warwick (1978, p. 3) has argued that the civil service's "present difficulties are a direct consequence of the country's unique historical experience." The origins of bureaucratic corruption in Indonesia can be traced to the Dutch colonial period because "bribery and corruption were rife among the [Dutch East India] Company's personnel as their salaries were quite low," and they were not properly monitored (Quah, 1982a, p. 154). Corruption was introduced to Indonesia during the Dutch colonial period, contrary to Furnivall's argument that it was "practically unknown" in Java.

Furnivall (1948, p. 269) attributed the "absence of judicial corruption" to the "trivial penalties" for corruption that meant it was "cheaper to be punished than to bribe a policeman or magistrate to escape punishment." Furthermore, "it would be difficult and dangerous to bribe the whole bench," which consisted of "three judicial officers as well as laymen of good standing." He gave two reasons for the absence of corruption in general administration in Java: the tradition of encouraging the people to complain of "any oppressive act" including corruption; and the permanence of the Regent, whose "position and his high pay protect him against the temptation to accept petty bribes, and concern for his own authority and prestige makes him jealous of the influence of corrupt subordinates" (Furnivall, 1948, pp. 270–271).

The conventional view is that the Japanese Occupation was responsible for introducing corruption on a wide scale in Indonesia. However, Theodore

M. Smith (1971, p. 23) rejects this view and contends that the Dutch East India Company (1602–1798) "offered Indonesians flagrant examples of corrupt behavior." Indeed, even Furnivall in his earlier book had referred to the corruption in the Dutch East India Company that "reached such lengths that shortly before the fall of the Company officers were taxed on their illicit gains." Not surprisingly, the Company's fall was blamed on corruption and "its initials, V.O.C. (*Vereenigle Oost-indische Compagnie)* were interpreted as *Vergaan onder Corruptie* (perished by corruption)" (Furnivall, 1939, p. 49).

## *Economy*

Indonesia's GDP of US$511 billion in 2008 makes it the fifth largest economy in Asia after Japan, China, India, and South Korea. However, its GDP per capita in 2008 of US$2,250 is lower than those of Japan, Singapore, Hong Kong, South Korea, Taiwan, and Thailand, but exceeds those of India, Mongolia, and the Philippines (*Economist*, 2010a, p. 160).

More than four decades ago, Indonesia was considered by the World Bank as the poorest country in Asia, and among the poorest economies in the world as its GDP per capita in 1966 was only US$50 (Prawiro, 1998, p. xxiv; Sidik, 2007, p. 29). More specifically, Indonesia's GDP per capita declined by 3.7 percent during 1961–1965, and many Indonesians were living at a subsistence level (Prawiro, 1998, p. 7). President Sukarno's mismanagement of the economy resulted in hyperinflation of 1,000 percent by 1965 and the dwindling of foreign exchange reserves. Consequently, economic growth stagnated and exacerbated the poverty level (Bhattacharya & Pangestu, 2000, p. 393).

In contrast to the economic chaos under Sukarno's leadership, President Soeharto restored macroeconomic stability and introduced market-oriented reforms after assuming office in 1967. He succeeded in reducing inflation to less than 20 percent in 1969 (Bhattacharya & Pangestu, 2000, pp. 393–394) and the economy grew as a result of foreign aid and investment and the increased revenue from the oil and gas exports in the 1970s (Dunung, 1998, p. 198). Despite the fall in oil prices in the early 1980s, Indonesia's GDP grew by 95 percent with an annual inflation rate of below 10 percent during 1985–1995. The July 1997 Asian financial crisis resulted in the decline of the GDP by 13.2 percent in 1998 and in the resignation of Soeharto in May 1998 (Sidik, 2007, pp. 36–37).

Indonesia is rich in natural resources and has huge deposits of oil and natural gas, tin, bauxite, copper, nickel, and coal. It also has smaller amounts of silver, gold, diamonds, and rubies (Sidik, 2007, p. 28). Indonesia is the world's second largest producer of palm oil and is a leading producer of rubber, pepper, cloves, nutmeg, tobacco, tea, coffee, and timber (Andrews, 2002, p. 84). Its major exports are petroleum products, natural gas, textiles, and timber. Agriculture contributes to 14 percent of the GDP and provides employment for 45 percent of the labor force. The unemployment rate in Indonesia in 2008 was 8.4 percent (*Economist*, 2010a, p. 160).

Thus, despite its abundant natural resources and Soeharto's economic policies, Indonesia remains a relatively poor country. Indeed, the poverty rate in Indonesia decreased from 17.7 percent to 15.9 percent during 1997–2000 (Strauss et al., 2004, p. 47). In sum, Indonesia's low GDP per capita and relative poverty account for the low wages of civil servants and the resulting rampant corruption in the country.

### *Demography*

In 2008, Indonesia has the world's fourth largest population with 234.3 million and a population density of 122.9 persons per sq km. The literacy rate of the adult population is 92 percent and the percentage of the urban population is 44.3 percent (*Economist*, 2010a, pp. 14, 160). Apart from having the largest population among the 10 countries discussed in this book, Indonesia also has the most heterogeneous population in terms of ethnic group, language, and religion.

There are more than 1,000 ethnic or subethnic groups in Indonesia, but only 15 groups have more than 1 million members. According to the 2000 population census, Indonesia had a total population of 205,843,196 with the largest group being the Javanese (41.71 percent), followed by the Sundanese (15.41 percent), Malays (3.45 percent), Madurese (3.37 percent), Batak (3.02 percent), Minangkabau (2.72 percent), Betawi (2.51 percent), Buginese (2.49 percent), Bantenese (2.05 percent), Banjarese (1.74 percent), Balinese (1.51 percent), and Sasak (1.3 percent) (Suryadinata, Arifin, & Ananta, 2003, pp. 6–7).

There is also a great deal of linguistic diversity as nearly 300 languages and dialects are spoken in Indonesia. While Bahasa Indonesia is the official and most widely spoken language, the other major languages are Javanese, Sundanese, Achehnese, Batak, Minangkabau, Malay, Minahasan, Buginese, Makassarese, Balinese, Sasak, and Sumbawan (Sidik, 2007, p. 34). Finally, Indonesia has the largest Muslim population in the world with 87 percent, followed by 9 percent of Christians, and the rest consisting of those Chinese who are Buddhists or Confucianists, and the Balinese who are Hindus (Sidik, 2007, pp. 34–35).

There are three important aspects of Indonesia's population that should be emphasized in analyzing the causes of corruption in Indonesia. First, as the Chinese minority control about 80 percent of the private business in Indonesia, the rich Chinese tycoons or *cukongs* rely on the patronage of the top political leaders to minimize obstacles or discrimination in conducting their business enterprises (Sawarjuwono & Goodfellow, 1997, pp. 78–80). The nature of the "Soeharto-Business Symbiosis" was described thus by Ross H. McLeod (2000, pp. 148, 157):

> An important feature of the business sector is that it is heavily dominated by firms owned by Chinese Indonesians. ... The manner in which Soeharto and those around him promoted the interests of a few prominent Chinese Indonesian families served to deepen resentment against this whole minority community. ... The legal system did little to protect their interests, and it suited Soeharto and his franchisees to maintain this state of affairs. Given the Chinese Indonesian minority's vulnerability to outbreaks of mob violence and to extortion by neighborhood thugs, they could always be expected to pay in various ways for protection.

Second, as in other Asian countries, the family plays an important role in Indonesia. Indeed, during his 32 years in power, "Soeharto and his family enriched themselves on a scale never before seen" (Backman, 1999, p. 261). The growth and extent of the "family business" or the corruption involving the Soeharto clan during the 1980s and 1990s led to public criticism during his last decade in power.

Third, like other Asian countries, gift-giving is a traditional part of Indonesian culture. When a family member travels abroad, he or she is expected to return with small gifts or *oleh-oleh* for the family. More importantly, as exchanging gifts is important for concluding business negotiations, "gifts are presented after negotiation begins and well before the signing of the final agreement" (Da Gama Pinto, 1997, p. 202). The importance of gift-giving among Indonesians may encourage them to bribe civil servants especially if they expect their gifts to be reciprocated with preferential treatment of their requests for services.

### *Political System*

Indonesia was proclaimed to be independent on August 17, 1945, by Sukarno and Hatta after 300 years of Dutch colonial rule and the brief period of occupation by the Japanese (1942–1945). However, the refusal of the Netherlands to accept an independent Indonesia led to more than four years of revolutionary conflict between the Dutch government and the Indonesian nationalist leaders (Feith, 1964, pp. 199–204). Independence was attained in Indonesia on December 27, 1949, and Sukarno was appointed as its first president.

The first eight years of President Sukarno's government have been described as the period of "liberal democracy" as political power was shared among the major political parties, parliament, and the army. However, the increasing power of President Sukarno and the army led to a period of "guided democracy" as "there was little left of parliamentary government from the second half of 1958" (Feith, 1964, pp. 204, 213). The rapidly declining economy and increasing political instability contributed to the loss of control of the economy by Sukarno's government in 1965 as inflation rose to 500 percent, the price of rice escalated by 900 percent, and the budget deficit increased to 300 percent of government revenue (Kingsbury, 2005, pp. 52–53).

The September 30, 1965, coup resulted in the killing of six senior generals, and the replacement of President Sukarno by General Soeharto, who assumed *de facto* power from March 1966 until he was formally endorsed by the *Majelis Permusyawaratan Rakyat* (MPR or People's Consultative Assembly) as president in 1968 (Kingsbury, 2005, pp. 54–61). President Soeharto's 32 years in power were characterized by rapid economic growth and rampant corruption. However, the 1997 Asian financial crisis forced him to resign in May 1998.

President Soeharto was succeeded by Vice-President B. J. Habibie, who served as president until he was replaced by Abdurrahman Wahid, when he won the October 1999 presidential election. President Wahid in turn was succeeded by his Vice-President, Megawati Sukarnoputri, on July 23, 2001. On October 4, 2004, the team of Susilo Bambang Yudhoyono-Jusuf Kalla won the first direct presidential elections in Indonesia and were inaugurated as president and vice-president respectively on October 20, 2004 (Sidik, 2007, pp. 46–47). President Yudhoyono was re-elected for a second term after winning the presidential elections in October 2009.

Indonesia's current political system is a constitutional republic with an elected president, an elected parliament, and an appointed judiciary. The president is both head of government and head of state. He is elected for five years by the MPR, which includes a legislative House of Representatives (*Dewan Perwakilan Rakyat* or DPR), with 462 elected members and 38 army nominations, 135 members from the regions and 65 members appointed by the National Election Commission (Andrews, 2002, p. 87).

There are two important aspects of the political system in Indonesia that should be highlighted. First, after more than 300 years of Dutch colonial rule, the post-independence period has been characterized by political instability after the first two presidents: Sukarno (1949–1966) and Soeharto (1966–1998). Soeharto was succeeded in turn by Habibie (1998–1999), Wahid (1999–2001), Megawati (2001–2004) and Yudhoyono (2004 to present). This political instability has hindered the efforts of the incumbent government in curbing corruption because of the lack of political continuity after the resignation of Soeharto in May 1998.

In addition to political instability, Indonesia's political system has become more democratic after the resignation of President Soeharto in May 1998.[2] Except for the first eight years of "liberal democracy," the remaining years of President Sukarno's administration was described as a "guided democracy," which was a euphemism for authoritarian rule. Similarly, President Soeharto relied on the military to maintain his authoritarian rule in Indonesia for 32 years. Thus, the democratization of Indonesia's political system during the past 13 years has strengthened the national anticorruption strategy by enabling civil society to enhance the accountability of the incumbent government.

## PERCEIVED EXTENT OF CORRUPTION

Dutch colonial rule ended with the Japanese occupation of Indonesia from 1942 to 1945. Nationalism and the attainment of independence on August 17, 1945, eroded the traditional tolerance for corrupt behavior as "claims to state resources increasingly became public claims and the private use of what were now 'public' funds became 'corruption.'" In other words, corruption, which was condoned during the colonial era, was viewed more critically during the postwar period. Indeed, corruption became endemic during President Sukarno's rule because his "disastrously inflationary budgets eroded civil service salaries to the point where people simply could not live on them and where financial accountability virtually collapsed because of administrative deterioration" (Mackie, 1970, pp. 87–88).

President Soeharto was succeeded in turn by B. J. Habibie, Abdurrahman Wahid, Megawati Sukarnoputri, and Susilo Bambang Yudhoyono. As the system of corruption became so deeply entrenched during Soeharto's 32-year rule, his successors have found it difficult to eradicate corruption. Indeed, instead of improving, corruption in contemporary Indonesia, in the view of some observers, "has got worse, not better" because the "bureaucrats sense that the game is up and this is the last chance for them to gouge all the money they can out of the system" (Loveard, 1999, p. 378).

Moreover, the breakdown of central authority during the post-Soeharto period has contributed to the decentralization of power and the creation of "300 Soehartos" (Shari, 2002, p. 21).

Law No. 22/1999 on regional governance has devolved the functions of health, education, environmental, and infrastructure services to the local governments. The Governance and Decentralization Survey (GDS) was conducted during February to May 2002 to ascertain the impact of decentralization on various aspects of governance, including corruption. The GDS found that KKN (*Korupsi, Kolusi dan Nepotisme* or corruption, collusion and nepotism) was "rampant in every sector of government activity and on every level." Furthermore, KKN was increasing rather than decreasing as a result of decentralization (Hofman, Kaiser, & Schulze, 2009, p.104).

According to the representatives of nongovernmental organizations, KKN was prevalent in the local legislative assembly (47 percent of the respondents), followed by the district head (45 percent), the district education office (36 percent), district health office (30 percent), subdistrict (23 percent), and village (22 percent). Furthermore, corruption was also rampant in government procurements in the tender procedure for public works or projects, and in the recruitment of civil servants in all areas (Hofman et al., 2009, pp. 104–105).

From May 1999 to March 2000, the Institute for Policy and Community Development Studies conducted a survey of 692 public officials (52 heads and 640 general officials) from 15 agencies in Indonesia for the World Bank. This survey focused on the performance orientation of Indonesian public officials, including bureaucratic corruption as one of the aspects discussed (Manning, Mukherjee, Gokcekus, & Hofman, 2000, pp. 7–8). In contrast, the Partnership for Governance Reform (2001, pp. 7–8) and the World Bank conducted a national survey of 2,300 respondents (comprising 650 public officials from 19 agencies, 1,250 households in 14 provinces, and 400 business enterprises in seven industry sectors and eight cities) between October 2000 and March 2001 to ascertain their views on corruption. As these two surveys are not comparable because of the different emphasis, only their major findings concerning bureaucratic corruption will be discussed with emphasis on the 2001 survey because of its more comprehensive scope. For convenience, these surveys will be referred to as the 2000 and 2001 surveys.

The public officials in both surveys viewed corruption as a serious problem as indicated by 94 percent of them in the 2000 survey and 71.1 percent of public officials in the 2001 survey viewed corruption as "a disease against which we should all combat, denouncing every case that we know of." This view was shared by 70.8 percent of the business firms and 67.5 percent of households interviewed in 2001. On the contrary, 2.3 percent of the public officials, 4 percent of the business enterprises, and 3.2 percent of the households felt that corruption was a "natural occurrence and part of our daily life, so denouncing it is unnecessary" (Manning et al., 2000, p. 16; Partnership for Governance Reform, 2001, p. 30).

### *Most Corrupt Agencies and Types of Corruption*

The public officials in the 2000 survey identified regulatory agencies (70 percent), government purchasing agencies (69 percent), and service delivery agencies (63 percent) as the most corruption-prone agencies. Moreover, the most common types of corruption practised in these agencies were payments for service speed, petty bribery for jobs, and purchase of preferential treatment in procurement (Manning et al., 2000, p.18). It is interesting to note that the Directorate General of Land Transport, which was the least successful of the 15 agencies in implementing performance standards, had also the largest proportion of officials who did not perceive corruption in government as a serious problem. In contrast, the National Savings Bank, which was the most effective of the 15 agencies, was also the agency with the highest percentage of officials perceiving corruption in government to be a serious problem (Manning et al., 2000, pp. 17, 20).

Table 10.1 shows that the public officials, business enterprises and households in the 2001 survey agreed with the choice of the three least corrupt and the three most corrupt public institutions in Indonesia when they were asked to rank a list of 35 public institutions in terms of their integrity. However, when the 650 public officials were asked to identify those public institutions where corruption was the most prevalent, 24 percent identified the National Land Agency, 22.9 percent the Industry and Trade Department, 20 percent the Forestry Department, and 18.5 percent the Interior Department (Partnership for Governance Reform, 2001, pp. 10–12).

Finally, as shown in Table 10.2, the public officials identified 15 public agencies where they were perceived to be receiving unofficial payments, ranging from the Housing Department with the highest proportion of 70 percent to the Education Department's 24 percent. Surprisingly, the proportions reported for the police (48 percent) and the National Land Agency (56 percent) were lower.

***Table 10.1.*** Most Corrupt and Least Corrupt Public Institutions in Indonesia Perceived by 2,300 Respondents in 2001.

| Public Institution | Integrity Score[a] | | |
|---|---|---|---|
| | Public Official | Business | Household |
| *Least corrupt* | | | |
| Mosque, Church, Temple | 4.6 | 4.2 | 4.3 |
| Post Office | 4.1 | 3.6 | 3.6 |
| News Media | 3.6 | 3.5 | 3.5 |
| *Most Corrupt* | | | |
| Judiciary | 2.8 | 2.3 | 2.3 |
| Customs Authority | 2.8 | 2.2 | 2.3 |
| Traffic Police | 2.6 | 2.1 | 2.2 |

*Source*: Partnership for Governance Reform (2001, p. 11, Figure D1).
[a]The integrity score ranges from 1 (very corrupt) to 5 (very honest).

***Table 10.2.*** Proportion of Public Officials Perceived by Themselves to be Receiving Unofficial Payments in 2001.

| Public Institution | % Officials with Unofficial Payments |
|---|---|
| Housing Department | 70 |
| Industry and Trade Department | 66 |
| Interior Department | 59 |
| National Land Agency | 56 |
| Forestry Department | 56 |
| Local Government | 56 |
| Finance Department | 54 |
| Police Department | 48 |
| Law Department | 46 |
| Transportation Department | 45 |
| Health Department | 42 |
| Public Service Provider | 42 |
| Public Works Department | 40 |
| Mining and Energy Department | 37 |
| Education Department | 24 |

*Source*: Partnership for Governance Reform (2001, p. 13, Figure D3).

### *Bribery: Frequency and Amount Paid*

In the 2000 survey, both the heads of organizations (87 percent) and the general officials (68 percent) agreed that the most important reason for taking bribes was for faster service. Furthermore, 97 percent of the heads and 70 percent of the general officials indicated that bribes were usually paid to officials in regulatory agencies (Manning et al., 2000, p.19). However, unlike the 2001 survey, data on the frequency and amount of bribes paid were not collected.

Table 10.3 shows that (1) the households paid fewer bribes than business firms; and (2) the average amount of bribes paid by business firms to the Customs, Trade and Industry, and Tax were higher than those paid by households to District/Village Administration, Civil Registry, Land Registry and Immigration; and (3) only the average amount of bribes paid by the households to Police was more than three times the amount paid by business firms to the Traffic Police (Partnership for Governance Reform, 2001, p. 15).

Even though 70 percent of the 2001 survey respondents viewed corruption as a serious social problem, their responses to three hypothetical situations involving the payment of bribes indicated that many of them considered corruption as normal and paid bribes themselves. Table 10.4 shows that

***Table 10.3.*** Average Amount of Bribes Paid by Households and Business Firms in 2001.

| Public Agency | Average No. of Bribes | Minimum Amount (Rp) | Maximum Amount (Rp) | Average Amount (Rp) |
|---|---|---|---|---|
| *Households* | | | | |
| District/village administration | 2.08 | 500 | 2,500,000 | 9,778 |
| Civil Registry (birth/marriage certificates) | 1.70 | 1,500 | 500,000 | 38,602 |
| Land Registry | 1.72 | 10,000 | 3,000,000 | 192,717 |
| Immigration (passport) | 1.48 | 2,000 | 1,000,000 | 131,222 |
| Police (crimes) | 1.27 | 1,000 | 2,000,000 | 203,464 |
| *Business firms* | | | | |
| Customs | 9.6 | 5,000 | 30,000,000 | 1,184,571 |
| Trade & Industry (licensing) | 3.3 | 7,000 | 5,000,000 | 475,634 |
| Tax | 3.8 | 2,500 | 500,000,000 | 9,726,949 |
| Traffic Police | 4.6 | 5,000 | 2,000,000 | 63,860 |

*Source*: Partnership for Governance Reform (2001, p. 15, Tables D (iii) and D (iv)).

***Table 10.4.*** Payment of Bribe to Village Chief (*Lurah*).

| Bribe *Lurah* | Normal | Not Normal | Pay Up | Do Not Pay | Don't Know |
|---|---|---|---|---|---|
| Households | 64.4% | 34.5% | 72.7% | 26.2% | 1.1% |
| Businesses | 62.8% | 36.8% | 82.0% | 17.5% | 0.5% |
| Public officials | 58.6% | 40.9% | 70.6% | 28.9% | 0.5% |
| Average | 61.9% | 37.4% | 75.1% | 24.2% | 0.7% |

*Source*: Partnership for Governance Reform (2001, p. 31, Table F (i)).

64.4 percent of the households said that it was normal to pay a bribe to the village chief (*lurah*) to accelerate the issuance of identity cards, and 72.7 percent of them would pay the bribe for this service. Similarly, 82 percent of the business firms would pay a bribe to expedite the provision of identity cards as 62.8 percent of them viewed corruption as normal. Finally, while 58.6 percent of public officials considered corruption as normal, 70.6 percent of them would pay a bribe to obtain their identity cards faster.

Table 10.5 shows that 50.7 percent of the public officials viewed bribing a police officer to avoid a traffic ticket was normal and 54.9 percent of them would pay such a bribe. While the proportion of businesses (45 percent) and the households (44.1 percent) considered such behavior to be normal, 61 percent and 60.3 percent of them respectively said that they would pay a bribe to a police officer. In contrast, as shown in Table 10.6, 80.8 percent of businesses viewed bribing a judge as abnormal and only 27 percent of them would do so. While 69.3 percent of the households did not consider bribing a judge as normal, 34.8 percent of them said that they would so.

### *Public Reporting and Not Reporting of Corruption Cases*

The household respondents were the least informed as 87 percent did not know the reporting procedure for corruption cases, 98 percent did not report corruption cases and 65 percent had not observed corruption cases. In contrast, 42 percent of the public officials knew the reporting procedure for corruption cases, 23 percent of them had reported corruption cases, and 41 percent of them had observed corruption cases. Table 10.7 shows that 45 percent of the business enterprises had observed corruption cases, 22 percent had reported corruption cases, and 32 percent knew how to report corruption cases.

***Table 10.5.*** Payment of Bribe to a Police Officer.

| Bribe Police | Normal | Not Normal | Pay Up | Do Not Pay | Don't Know |
|---|---|---|---|---|---|
| Households | 44.1% | 53.2% | 60.3% | 37.1% | 2.6% |
| Businesses | 45.0% | 55.0% | 61.0% | 39.0% | 0.0% |
| Public officials | 50.7% | 47.9% | 54.9% | 43.8% | 1.4% |
| Average | 46.6% | 52.0% | 58.7% | 40.0% | 1.3% |

*Source*: Partnership for Governance Reform (2001, p. 31, Table F (ii)).

***Table 10.6.*** Payment of Bribe to a Judge.

| Bribe Judge | Normal | Not Normal | Pay Up | Do Not Pay | Don't Know |
|---|---|---|---|---|---|
| Households | 26.3% | 69.3% | 34.8% | 60.8% | 4.4% |
| Businesses | 17.3% | 80.8% | 27.0% | 71.0% | 2.0% |
| Public officials | 23.1% | 74.0% | 18.5% | 78.6% | 2.9% |
| Average | 22.2% | 74.7% | 26.8% | 70.1% | 3.1% |

*Source*: Partnership for Governance Reform (2001, p. 32, Table F (iii)).

***Table 10.7.*** Reporting of Corruption Cases.

| Activity | Households | Business Enterprises | Public Officials |
|---|---|---|---|
| Observing corruption cases | 35% | 45% | 41% |
| Reporting corruption cases | 2% | 22% | 23% |
| Knowing reporting procedure for corruption cases | 13% | 32% | 42% |

*Source*: Partnership for Governance (2001, p. 34, Table F (vii)).

The reasons for not reporting corruption cases varied among the households, the business enterprises, and the public officials as shown in Table 10.8. More specifically, 51.6 percent of the households did not know where to report, 27.3 percent of them believed that the process was too complex and long, and 30.4 percent of them were concerned about potential harassment and reprisal. The business enterprises did not report corruption cases because 27.3 percent did not know where to report, 22.3 percent said that the process was too complex and long, and 25.2 percent of them were concerned about potential harassment and reprisal. Finally, the public

***Table 10.8.*** Reasons for Not Reporting Corruption.

| Reason | Household | Business Enterprises | Public Officials |
|---|---|---|---|
| First | No knowledge (51.6%) | No knowledge (27.3%) | Case could not be proven (34%) |
| Second | Complex and long process (27.3%) | Complex and long process (22.3%) | No investigation of report (20.8%) |
| Third | Fear of harassment & reprisal (30.4%) | Fear of harassment & reprisal (25.2%) | No enforcement of decision (25.6%) |

*Source*: Partnership for Governance Reform (2001, p. 35, Figure F2).

officials did not report corruption cases because of their belief that the case could not be proven (34 percent), that investigation would not be made about the report (20.8 percent), and no enforcement even if the decision was made (25.6 percent).

### *Desired Outcome for Convicted Corruptors*

When asked about their preference for the desired outcome for convicted corruptors, Table 10.9 shows that 64.9 percent of the public officials, 50.8 percent of the business enterprises, and 50.6 percent of the households wanted convicted corruptors to be jailed and their assets seized. Furthermore, 37.8 percent of the business enterprises, 36.4 percent of the households, and 15.7 percent of the public officials wanted convicted corruptors to be shamed publicly in addition to imprisonment and seizure of their assets. Finally, the death penalty was not favored as only 1.5 percent of the public officials, 0.8 percent of the business enterprises, and 0.6 percent of the households wanted convicted corruptors to be sentenced to death.

### *Transparency International's Global Corruption Barometer*

The above major survey findings provide useful empirical data on corruption in Indonesia which should be considered in any effort to minimize corruption in the country. Table 10.10 provides details of TI's Global Corruption Barometer from 2004 to 2010, which identifies parliament as the most corrupt sector in Indonesia during this period, followed by political parties, police, and the judiciary.

***Table 10.9.*** Desired Outcomes for Convicted Corruptors.

| Desired Outcome | Public Officials | Business Enterprises | Households |
|---|---|---|---|
| Jail and seize assets | 64.9% | 50.8% | 50.6% |
| Jail, seize assets and shame publicly | 15.7% | 37.8% | 36.4% |
| Death sentence | 1.5% | 0.8% | 0.6% |

*Source*: Partnership for Governance Reform (2001, p. 37, Figure F4).

***Table 10.10.*** Perceived Level of Corruption in Indonesia by Sector, 2004–2010[a].

| Sector | 2004 | 2005 | 2006 | 2007 | 2009 | 2010 |
|---|---|---|---|---|---|---|
| Political Parties | 4.4 | 4.2 | 4.1 | 4.0 | 4.0 | 3.5 |
| Parliament | 4.4 | 4.0 | 4.2 | 4.1 | 4.4 | 3.6 |
| Legal System/Judiciary | 4.2 | 3.8 | 4.2 | 4.1 | 4.1 | 3.3 |
| Police | 4.2 | 4.0 | 4.2 | 4.2 | NA | 3.5 |
| Public officials/civil servants | NA | NA | NA | NA | 4.0 | 3.2 |
| Business sector | 3.7 | 3.5 | 3.6 | 3.1 | 3.2 | 2.8 |
| Tax revenue | 4.0 | 3.8 | 3.4 | 3.6 | NA | NA |
| Customs | 4.3 | 4.0 | NA | NA | NA | NA |
| Media | 2.6 | 2.4 | 2.8 | 2.5 | 2.3 | 2.8 |
| Medical services | 3.0 | 2.7 | 3.0 | 2.8 | NA | NA |
| Education | 3.2 | 3.0 | 3.3 | 3.0 | NA | 3.0 |
| Registry and permit services | 3.7 | 3.5 | 3.6 | 3.8 | NA | NA |
| Utilities | 3.1 | 3.0 | 2.9 | 3.1 | NA | NA |
| Military | 3.3 | 2.9 | 3.3 | 3.0 | NA | 2.8 |
| NGOs | 2.4 | 2.4 | 2.9 | 2.8 | NA | 2.5 |
| Religious bodies | 1.8 | 2.1 | 2.3 | 2.2 | NA | 3.0 |

*Sources*: Compiled from Transparency International (2004, p. 18, 2005, p. 18, 2006, p. 21, 2007, p. 22, 2009, p. 28, 2010, p. 43).
NA = not available.
[a]The score ranges from 1 (not at all corrupt) to 5 (extremely corrupt).

## CAUSES OF CORRUPTION

The rapid increase in the tasks of the civil service during the postindependence period expanded the government's role in society and also increased the opportunities for corruption among civil servants. In 1978, Bruce Glassburner (1978, p. 163) observed that the deep historical roots of corruption "have been more deeply implanted by the policies of governments of Indonesia over the last quarter-century [1953–1978]." The civil service in Indonesia has five major defects that not only make its members vulnerable to corrupt behavior but also render the task of curbing corruption a much more difficult one viz., lack of meritocracy, low salaries, red tape and inefficiency, weak disciplinary control and ineffective policing, and reliance on incremental and institutional reform.

### *No Tradition of Meritocracy*

Unlike Singapore and Hong Kong, which benefited from the tradition of meritocracy introduced by the British colonial government, the Dutch did not introduce a similar tradition during their more than three centuries years of colonial rule (1619–1942) in Indonesia. When Stamford Raffles was governor of Java from 1811 to 1816, he tried "to rid the service of administrative malpractices which had been detrimental to the people." However, "his stay was too short, the available funds to finance his reforms were scanty, while the personnel involved was generally accustomed to corruption, and gave no enthusiastic support to the reforms which were to limit their accustomed gains" (Hadisumarto, 1974, p. 120).

The Dutch colonial government adopted a system of dual administration with a European Civil Service concerned with direction and inspection, and a Native Civil Service, "in which hereditary officials, governing on 'oriental lines' enforced the policy of government." In 1825, a Royal Ordinance was introduced to ensure that "no one should be appointed to the civil service in the East Indies who had not obtained from the Crown a diploma, to be issued only upon certain conditions designed to secure a good standard of capacity and morality." However, these provisions were not implemented and failed to prevent unqualified candidates from joining the civil service (Hadisumarto, 1974, pp. 123, 129).

For the European civil servants, the Royal Ordinance of 1864 stipulated that only candidates with a degree or diploma and who were knowledgeable in the history, geography, and ethnology of the Netherlands Indies, the public institutions of the Dutch Indies, and Javanese or Malay would be eligible for an administrative position in the civil service. In contrast, the native civil servants were not selected by means of examinations. For example, the regents were recruited by "a hereditary succession, tempered by fitness, while the lesser officials were selected freely, a good deal of attention being paid to social influence over the other natives as well as to intellectual capacity" (Hadisumarto, 1974, pp. 131–132, 134). Thus, the

Dutch did not rely on merit to recruit the local civil servants, who were instead selected by hereditary succession.

In short, as Warwick (1978, p. 3) had astutely observed, "the Dutch left behind no workable model of public administration, and had done little to train Indonesians for responsible positions." The lack of meritocracy was further reinforced during the Japanese Occupation as "many of the new heads of the bureaucracies had achieved their high position in the colonial days because they were loyal to the colonial government." During the postindependence period, the appointment of senior positions in the civil service was not based on merit but on their personal background especially whether the candidates had participated in the revolution (Hadisumarto, 1974, pp. 161, 164). Indeed, the civil service faced the problem of scarcity of trained personnel after independence because of the exodus of many Dutch and Eurasian civil servants. The revolutionary war of 1945–1949 prevented the Indonesian government from solving the lack of trained personnel immediately. Consequently, the problem was aggravated after the war by the abundance of untrained civil servants who were recruited into the civil service as a reward for their services in the war (Siagian, 1965, p. 71).

Moreover, "political party patronage through the civil service became a common feature during that time, especially during the first Ali Sastroamidjojo's cabinet." Indeed, the criterion of party loyalty was more important than the criterion of performance of work in the selection of officials. In other words, "personal relations appear to govern personnel advancement, and the civil service is constantly criticized for *bapakisme*, fatherism" (Hadisumarto, 1974, p. 165). Hence it was not surprising that "the principles of merit system in hiring, promoting and firing of personnel were completely disregarded, while political and ascriptive considerations became criteria for appointment to key positions in the bureaucracy" during President Sukarno's regime (Siagian, 1970, p. 100).

Warwick (1978, p. 19) had noted that "many departments recruit substantial numbers of new employees from their own training academies." He was critical of this arrangement because it fostered parochialism and in-breeding and also resulted in "lost opportunities to hire staff with a wider range of skills." Unfortunately, the situation has not changed very much since then as the civil service still relies on a decentralized system of recruitment, with new civil servants being recruited by the individual central government agencies or the regional governments. While recruitment decisions are usually based on written tests and interviews, there are no "system-wide criteria and standards" (Rohdewohld, 1995, p. 103). The absence of general standards for recruitment and the absence of a central personnel agency to enforce such standards for the civil service do not ensure that civil servants are recruited on the basis of merit.

In this connection, an Indonesian civil servant interviewed by Hilton L. Root observed that recruitment in the civil service:

> is often [done] with no standards of needs.... It is easy to recruit and I would say we can cut more than half of our civil servants and the work is still going on in Indonesia... . [For promotion] ... many other political factors come in ... whether you are belonging to one group or you are friends or you are relatives of the higher ranking positions is necessary to get promoted, so there is not an incentive for the civil servants to prove themselves to perform well to get to a higher ranking. (quoted in Root, 1996a, p. 99)

Warwick's assessment of the civil service's promotions policy and performance evaluation system was also extremely negative:

> The existing policy on promotions is probably the strongest disincentive to professionalism, and the area with the greatest potential for improvement. ...The existing performance evaluation system is a waste of the government's time and money. For over 90 percent of the civil service, performance appraisals make absolutely no difference for either promotions or salary increases, and yet they consume substantial amounts of time, money, and storage space. The most basic problem is that these appraisals are not taken seriously by most supervisors. Such a reaction is understandable, *since performance itself is not a major criterion for promotion in the great majority of cases.* Aggravating this situation is the widespread tendency, which some attribute to Javanese culture, to avoid making negative comments about employees, even when their work has been abysmal. (Warwick, 1978, pp. 32, 34–35, emphasis added)

Similarly, not much progress has been made as promotion in the civil service today is based on four criteria: "personal merit (work performance), seniority, work experience, and the fulfilment of certain training requirements in the case of structural and functional positions" (Rohdewohld, 1995, p. 104). The promotion of senior administrators (those in echelon I) is decided by the President. However, the performance criteria for evaluating civil servants are not specified and performance is not measured against agreed targets and objectives. The UNDP has identified the following weaknesses in the performance evaluation of Indonesian civil servants:

> There is usually no appraisal interview, no discussion of individuals' aims and ambitions, and no development plan. ... the system has minimal influence on performance, allocation of staff, training plans, promotion or individual development. (quoted in Rohdewohld, 1995, p. 105)

During 1972–1995, 368,135 persons applied to join the Armed Forces Academy but only 13,443 of them (or 3.65 percent) actually graduated. Not surprisingly, this "tight selection process" led to cases of bribery and reliance on "inside connections" by applicants to ensure their selection (Kristiadi, 2001, p. 100). From 1966–1980, "military officers were placed in almost all government departments" and almost all the provincial governors had military backgrounds. However, the number of military appointments declined during the 1980s and 1990s as half of the provincial governors and 40 percent of the *bupati* were military officers. By the late 1990s, there were 6,000 military officers serving in civilian positions (Crouch, 1999, p. 141). As President Abdurrahman Wahid did not make any major changes, the military still occupied some important positions during his regime as 119 (36 percent) of the 329 *bupati* and mayors had a military background (Suryadinata, 2002, pp. 164–165).

Moreover, President Soeharto by-passed the established mechanisms for evaluating senior officers and promoted those politically ambitious officers who had built a good relationship with him and his family. According to Kristiadi, the selection process was designed to produce officers who were loyal to the president. He wrote:

> After serving for three to five years at Cendana, the presidential residence in Jakarta, as an adjutant to the president or in the presidential guard, an officer could expect a soaring career with promotions to strategic positions in the military as well as the civilian bureaucracy. The president increasingly promoted officers who acted as loyal guardians of his power. Professionalism was replaced by favoritism. The results were evident: in the 1990s, all the top officers were from Suharto's inner circle, cynically known as graduates of the "University of Cendana." (Kristiadi, 2001, p. 102)

In sum, the lack of a meritocratic tradition in the civil service is reflected in the importance of patronage and nonmerit criteria on the one hand and the neglect of merit on the other hand in the recruitment and promotion of its civil servants. The absence or lack of importance attached to meritocracy in the civil service increases the vulnerability of its members to corruption.

### *Low Salaries*

The low salaries of the Indonesian civil servants can also be traced to the Dutch colonial period, when the native officials were paid parsimonious salaries which

> were not only insufficient to guarantee good service on the part of the subordinate native officials; they were not sufficient even to support life on the standard to which natives of the official class were used. The officials as a matter of course made up the deficit by exactions imposed on the natives, and the government, forced to recognize the necessity of such exactions, had no ability to hold them within bounds. (Day, 1966, pp. 299–300)

Clive Day (1966, pp. 100–104) explained that the personnel of the Dutch East India Company were corrupt because they

> were underpaid and exposed to every temptation that was offered by the combination of a weak native organization, extraordinary opportunities in trade, and an almost complete absence of checks from home or in Java. Under these circumstances corruption was inevitable. ...Officials were holding a plurality of offices or were drawing the Company's pay and using their time to build up their private fortunes; they were selling goods to the Company at advanced prices; they were leading a luxurious life and conniving at all kinds of corruption.... The second way in which officials became rich was by stealing from the Company. ...Finally, officials used the tremendous power that their position in the Company gave them to extort money from the few Europeans who were settled in Java and from the many natives.

The low salaries paid to the Company's personnel had adverse consequences. The Company was unable to attract competent and honest candidates to join it. Consequently, the standards of administration were low, especially financial administration as "large dividends were regularly paid out whether earned or not." More importantly, the poorly paid officials were tempted to "supplement their meager salaries by dishonest practices" such as smuggling in the Company's own ships (Hadisumarto, 1974, p. 115).

Unfortunately, the above description by Clive Day of the low salaries of the local civil servants during the Dutch colonial period still applies to their counterparts today because the situation has not improved dramatically. Apart from being paid lower salaries than the Dutch civil servants, the gap between the salaries of the Dutch and local civil servants was justified thus:

> On the surface the differences in salary scale and fringe benefits were quite understandable – Dutch personnel needed more days of leave in order to spend their vacations in Holland; they needed more money to make their tropical homes comfortable; and they needed more compensation if they planned to retire in their home country. The native personnel had no such needs. (Hadisumarto, 1974, pp. 138–139)

In 1798, the Company was liquidated and the Netherlands government appointed Lieutenant-General William Daendels as the Governor-General of the Netherlands Indies. Daendels introduced several drastic measures to curb corruption among the Company's personnel. He divided Java into administrative units resembling the French *prefects*. He also reorganized the personnel system by abolishing the previous ranks and replacing them with five classes of civil servants. Furthermore, salary scales were standardized, detailed job descriptions were provided, and civil servants were expected to be competent and honest in performing their duties (Hadisumarto, 1974,

p. 116). Thus, Daendels succeeded in transforming "a commercial and loose organization into a centralized state authority supported by a disciplined Dutch and Javanese administrative body" (de Kat Angelino, 1931, pp. 2–3). In doing so, Daendels was responsible for the emergence of the civil service in the Netherlands Indies, which is the precursor of the contemporary civil service (Hadisumarto, 1974, pp. 116–118).

In 1955, "the volume of corruption among civilian politicians and bureaucrats had grown as inflation reduced the civil servant's real income and as the government parties' machine politics practices undermined civil service norms and morale" (Hadisumarto, 1974, p. 175). In his open letter to President Sukarno, Dr A. Halim wrote:

> In general the wages of government servants are only sufficient for subsistence for two weeks or, at the most, twenty days. ...The majority ... eventually fall into the chasm of dishonor and start to indulge in minor corruption ... there has been a general trend towards petty theft – once or twice a week ... to increase their income. (quoted in Hadisumarto, 1974, pp. 175–176)

Under President Sukarno's regime, the economy was dominated by state enterprises and "tied up in bureaucratic red-tape, providing ample opportunities for corruption." Furthermore, his economic policies hindered development, increased inflation and the opportunities for corruption. Consequently, senior civil servants and political leaders "were impoverished by the rising inflation, and low-level officials were simply not paid enough to live on." By the early 1960s, Sukarno's disastrous economic policies had aggravated the problem of low salaries so that "it was impossible for an honest civil servant to subsist on his salary alone" which lasted "little more than a week." The poor compensation of junior civil servants encouraged them to "charge an unofficial fee to facilitate the processing of documents" to supplement their low wages (Robertson-Snape, 1999, pp. 592–593).

In his 1969–1970 survey of regional civil servants in Indonesia, Theodore M. Smith (1971) found that there was a significant gap between their minimal monthly salary needs and their official monthly income. Table 10.11 shows that the official monthly incomes of the economic planners and higher level officials constituted only 56 percent of their minimal monthly salary needs. The situation was worse for the lower level officials and subdistrict officers as the income–needs gap was 43 percent and 46 percent respectively. Smith (1971, pp. 28–29) concluded that "there is not a single official who can live by his government income alone" as the "official income amounts to approximately half of [his] essential monthly needs."

***Table 10.11.*** Comparison of the Minimal Monthly Salary Needs and Official Monthly Income of Regional Civil Servants in Indonesia, 1969–1970.

| Type of Regional Official | Stated Minimal Monthly Needs (a) | Official Monthly Income (b) | Percentage of Income-Needs Gap (b/a) |
|---|---|---|---|
| Economic Planners | Rp. 15,132 | Rp. 8,514 | 56 |
| Higher Level | Rp. 20,028 | Rp. 11,268 | 56 |
| Lower Level | Rp. 16,434 | Rp. 7,050 | 43 |
| Subdistrict Officers | Rp. 15,361 | Rp. 7,050 | 46 |

*Source*: Adapted from Smith (1971, p. 28, Table III (a)).

The civil service salary structure is complicated and "lacks transparency and simplicity." The Indonesian civil servant's salary consists of three main components: (1) basic salary, which is based on his rank and grade; (2) standardized allowances, including rice and family allowances, structural allowances, functional allowances, and special allowances for civil servants working in remote areas; and (3) salary supplements in cash or kind: project honoraria, bonuses, housing allowances, transport allowances, daily subsistence allowance, and medical care (Rohdewohld, 1995, pp. 101–102). Warwick (1978, p. 7) has described Indonesia's system of civil service compensation as "among the most complicated in the world" because "not even the Department of Finance knows exactly how much an official at a certain rank earns in a given year" because of the plethora of allowances and benefits.

As mentioned in the other chapters, scholars like Palmier (1985, p. 2) and Mauro (1997, p. 5) have highlighted low salaries as an important cause of corruption in Asian countries. Apart from encouraging corruption, a second consequence of the low salaries of the Indonesian civil servants is "moonlighting" as many, if not all of them, have a second job to make ends meet. A 1988 survey of lecturers in four Indonesian public universities found that they did not earn enough to live on from their combined civil service salary and academic allowance as their income was less than one-third of what they needed. The survey also found that while most of the lecturers of lower rank had another job, the number of additional jobs increased with rank, with those who were deputy heads (*Golongan* IVD) holding between four to five additional jobs (Clark & Oey-Gardiner, 1991, pp. 134–136).

Another important consequence of the low base salaries of Indonesian civil servants is "projectism" or their neglect or reformulation of routine activities, which do not attract a bonus or allowance, into projects. Rainer Rohdewohld (1995, p. 102) has highlighted the negative consequences of "projectism" thus:

> This "projectism" [or] the habit to formulate everything possible as a *proyek* [project] which is eligible [for] bonuses, jeopardizes the continuity of activities and the completion of work already started, it leads to a rather erratic, incremental and spontaneous way of work which is dictated by the supply of domestic or foreign project funds. [Often] ... activities come to a standstill as soon as project funds (and project bonuses) have been exhausted.

As the government could not afford to raise the salaries of civil servants for many years, the working hours of civil servants were adjusted to allow them to work elsewhere after their office hours. For example, for civil servants based in Jakarta, their working hours are: Monday to Thursday, from 8 am to 3 pm; Friday, 8 am to 11:30 am; and Saturday, 8 am to 2 pm. Thus, during each week they are required to spend 37.5 hours on their first job (Zainun, 1982, p. 453). However, the necessity of holding more than one job by the Indonesian civil servants means that their time and energies must be divided between their various jobs. This might lower their productivity and even commitment to their primary jobs, especially when their secondary jobs pay better. According to Clive Gray (1979, p. 92), many Indonesian civil servants "hold two or more jobs, but those who put in the contractual time on each of one or more public sector appointments constitute a minority of dedicated souls."

The oil boom in the 1970s enabled the government to "raise the salaries of a discouraged and over-staffed civil service and encourage improvements in productivity" in 1977, when wages were doubled, and substantial increases were made again in 1980 and 1981. Thus, from 1976 to 1981, "nominal basic salaries of lower level civil servants rose more than fourfold, and real basic salaries by over 100 percent." However, with the slower economic growth from 1985 to 1988, nominal civil service wages stayed constant but real wages declined. The annual increases in civil service salaries during 1972–1991 were positively correlated with rises in wages in Bandung textiles and to a lesser extent with construction, estate and rice wages (Manning, 1994, pp. 88–90).

In 1984, there was parity between public and private sector compensation for unskilled and lower rank workers, but there was a "growing differential in favor of the private sector at higher skill levels" (Wirutomo, 1991, pp. 113–134). Similarly, the World Bank found that the gap between public and private sector salaries was wider at the highest ranks as junior civil servants earned about half the salary of their private sector counterparts, but director-generals only made one-tenth to one-fifteenth of the salary of CEOs in the private sector (Filmer & Lindauer, 2001, pp. 189–190).

More recently, Filmer and Lindauer (2001, p. 191) analyzed wage data from the 1998 labor force survey and the 1999 household expenditure survey in Indonesia and found that:

> On average, government earnings at Rp 414,000/month *exceed* the national non-government average of Rp 274,000/month. ... When data are disaggregated by education level, a government pay premium remains at lower education levels; close to pay parity is achieved for graduates of senior high school; and a private sector premium emerges for those with some tertiary education ... or a university degree.

Arising from their comparison of wages in the public and private sectors in Indonesia, Filmer and Lindauer (2001, p. 192) concluded that (1) almost 75 percent of civil servants with a high school diploma or less were paid comparable or higher salaries than their private sector counterparts; (2) civil servants with post-secondary education in 1998 earned less than their private sector counterparts with the pay ratio between the private and public sectors of 1.2: 1 for those with some tertiary education, and 1.5:1 for university graduates; and (3) "the pattern of government pay exceeding private compensation for less educated workers and private pay exceeding government compensation for more educated workers" was not unique to the Indonesian civil service as it was common to other civil services also.

After rejecting the long accepted assumption that Indonesian civil servants are not poorly paid compared to their private sector counterparts, Filmer and Lindauer (2001, p. 201) also reject the simplistic linkage between pay and corruption by asking "How can we explain the prevalence of petty corruption by lower ranking government workers, if they earn a premium over the private sector?" Viewing corruption as a response to opportunity, they contend that "if the risks of getting caught are low and punishment minimal, corruption is apt to flourish." If corrupt officials are not punished, salary increases alone will not change the cost-benefit calculation, and corruption will not be reduced. In other words, salary increase is a necessary but insufficient condition for curbing corruption.

Moreover, even if the salaries of junior civil servants are higher than those of their counterparts in the private sector, the fact remains that these civil servants consider their salaries to be low and inadequate for satisfying the monthly needs of their families. In short, for most civil servants in Indonesia, especially those in senior positions, their monthly salaries and allowances are clearly inadequate for their monthly needs, and this inadequacy serves to justify their reliance on corrupt practices to "make ends meet." Indeed, in a recent interview with *Tempo*, the Minister for Justice and Human Rights, Dr Yusril Ihza Mahendra, complained that his monthly salary of Rp 19 million was "nothing" and "too little for a cabinet minister" as, in his opinion, a cabinet minister should be paid a salary of between Rp 50 million to Rp 100 million (*Tempo*, 2003, pp. 30–31).

Indeed, this is confirmed by the 2001 survey respondents when they were asked to rank the major causes of corruption from a list of 12 causes.[3] More than half (51.4 percent) of the public officials, 36.5 percent of the business enterprises, and 35.5 percent of the households identified low salaries as the most important cause of corruption. There was no consensus regarding the second cause of corruption as 28.5 percent of the public officials and 22 percent of the business firms identified poor law enforcement/punishment and 19.9 percent of the households mentioned the lack of controls and accountability. Regarding the third cause of corruption, 20.5 percent of the public officials emphasised poor law enforcement/punishment, while 18.3 percent of the business firms and 19.4 percent of the households identified lack of morals. Table 10.12 provides details of the three most important causes of corruption identified by the public officials, the business firms, and the households.

Needless to say, the above list of causes of corruption is not exhaustive. Instead of providing a list of 12 causes and asking the respondents to rank the three major causes, the respondents should have been asked an open-ended question like: "In your opinion, what do you think are the three major causes of corruption?" In other words, instead of providing the respondents with a list of causes and influencing their views, the respondents should have been asked to identify the three main causes of corruption.

***Table 10.12.*** The Three Most Important Causes of Corruption.

| Causes | Public Officials | Business Firms | Households |
|---|---|---|---|
| First | Low salaries (51.4%) | Low salaries (36.5%) | Low salaries (35.5%) |
| Second | Poor law enforcement/ punishment (28.5%) | Poor law enforcement/ punishment (22.0%) | Lack of controls and accountability (19.9%) |
| Third | Poor law enforcement/ punishment (20.5%) | Lack of morals (18.3%) | Lack of morals (19.4%) |

*Source*: Adapted from Partnership for Governance Reform (2001, p. 39, Figure G1).

### *Red Tape and Inefficiency*

Max Weber believed that a bureaucracy was technically the most efficient form of organization possible because its features demonstrated "the existence of a system of control based on rational rules, rules which try to regulate the whole organizational structure and process on the basis of technical knowledge and with the aim of maximum efficiency" (Mouzelis, 1967, p. 39). One of the hallmarks of a bureaucracy is the existence of rules that regulate the performance of official functions. Apart from being labor-saving devices (by increasing efficiency through removing the need to formulate a new solution for every problem), such rules (or standard operating procedures) ensure that the clientele of a bureaucracy receive uniform and impartial treatment from its officials as "they facilitate standardization and equality in the treatment of many cases" (Etzioni, 1964, p. 53). In short, the rationale for establishing a bureaucracy is twofold: to promote efficiency and ensure equal treatment for its clients, regardless of their social status, ethnic group, gender, education level, or religion.

However, as pointed out by Robert K. Merton (1952, pp. 364–366), Weber's analysis of bureaucracy ignored the "imperfections of bureaucracy" or such bureaucratic dysfunctions as goal displacement, excessive rigidity, red tape, impersonal treatment of clients and unreasonable resistance to change. The Indonesian civil service has demonstrated these dysfunctions as Warwick (1978, p. 2) described it as "cumbersome, uncoordinated, inefficient and, in some cases, a barrier to effective action on development." Red tape is a serious problem in Indonesia as Table 10.13 shows that its ease of doing business rank ranges from 135th position among 175 economies in 2007 to 121st position among 183 economies in 2011. Furthermore, even though Indonesia's rank in starting a business has improved from 161st position to 155th position, red tape remains a problem because it requires nine procedures and 47 days to start a business in 2011. Similarly, the 2011 survey shows that 14 procedures and 160 days are required to obtain a construction permit.

In Indonesia, civil servants distinguish between "wet" and "dry" agencies according to their access to resources and the fee-paying public. According to Warwick (1987, p. 43):

> "Wet" agencies ... are generous with honoraria, allowances, service on committees, boards, and development projects, and, recently, opportunities for foreign training. They are departments that deal in money, planning, banking, or public enterprises. "Dry" agencies are those doing traditional administrative work. Perceptions of unfairness about benefits not only reduce staff morale, but lead to the feeling that illegal compensation is a fair way to even out staff benefits across agencies.

***Table 10.13.*** Ease of Doing Business in Indonesia, 2007–2011.

| Indicator | 2007 ($N=175$) | 2008 ($N=178$) | 2009 ($N=181$) | 2010 ($N=183$) | 2011 ($N=183$) |
|---|---|---|---|---|---|
| Ease of doing business (rank) | 135 | 123 | 129 | 122 | 121 |
| Starting a business (rank) | 161 | 168 | 171 | 161 | 155 |
| No. of procedures | 12 | 12 | 11 | 9 | 9 |
| Time (days) | 97 | 105 | 76 | 60 | 47 |
| Cost (% of income per capita) | 86.7 | 80.0 | 74.2 | 26.0 | 22.3 |
| Dealing with construction permits or licenses (rank) | 131 | 99 | 80 | 61 | 60 |
| No. of procedures | 19 | 19 | 18 | 14 | 14 |
| Time (days) | 224 | 196 | 176 | 160 | 160 |
| Cost (% of income per capita) | 311.0 | 286.8 | 221.1 | 194.8 | 173.3 |
| Registering property (rank) | 120 | 121 | 107 | 95 | 98 |
| No. of procedures | 7 | 7 | 6 | 6 | 6 |
| Time (days) | 42 | 42 | 39 | 22 | 22 |
| Cost (% of property value) | 10.5 | 10.5 | 10.7 | 10.7 | 10.9 |
| CPI Rank and Score | 143rd (2.3) | 126th (2.6) | 111th (2.8) | 110th (2.8) | NA |

*Sources*: World Bank (2006b, p. 118, 2007, p. 126, 2008, p. 110, 2009, p. 127, 2010a, p.169) and http://www.transparency.org

Similarly, Young (1990, p. 154) has observed that "some positions in the state are more desirable than others – everyone in Indonesia knows what is meant by *jabatan basah* ('wet jobs'). These glistening prizes could make a man … rich." It should be noted that the "wet-dry" dichotomy also applies to journalism because "journalists might debate the wetness of particular desks, but few would deny that the business desk is relatively well-drenched. … While business reporters are stereotyped as the wettest, many dry desks, such as city hall, crime or courts, have considerable potential for reporters who seek personal benefit" (Romano, 2003, p. 154). In short, civil servants working in "wet" agencies will have more opportunities to engage in corrupt activities because of their access to more resources and their contact with the public.

Radius Prawiro (1998, pp. 230–231, 264), Co-ordinating Economics Minister in 1989–1993, identified the tax office and the customs service as the most lucrative of the "wet" government agencies. Before the implementation of the 1983 Income Tax Law, there were 48 tax rates for individuals and ten for corporations. As the pre-1983 tax system was "entirely inaccessible to modern accounting practices," Prawiro observed that "the only way for taxpayers to determine their tax obligations was by visiting the tax office and reviewing their financial data with a tax officer." As the taxpayer could negotiate his tax assessment with the tax officer, it was not surprising that "a job as a tax collector was one of the surest roads to riches in the government bureaucracy." Similarly, customs officers had abundant opportunities for "supplemental income" since "Indonesia's customs service had become a law unto itself according to which the entire trade process was readily manipulated to serve the interests of a retinue of customs officials."

Nick Manning (2000, pp. 71–72) has refined the wet–dry dichotomy for agencies into a threefold distinction with the inclusion of a third category of "moderate" agencies. To ascertain whether an agency was wet, moderate, or dry, they calculated the average of these four indicators of the degree of "wetness" of an agency: share of the routine budget, share of the developmental budget, the proportion of total regional offices, and the proportion of total attached state-owned enterprises. An agency was deemed to be "wet" if its average exceeds 2.5 percent, "moderate" if its average ranges between 1 percent and 2.5 percent, and "dry" if its average is below 1 percent. On the basis of these criteria, they identified 11 "wet" agencies, 13 "moderate" agencies, and 29 "dry" agencies. The 11 "wet" agencies are Defense, Education and Culture, Mining and Energy, Public Works, Forestry, Finance, Home Affairs, Religious Affairs, Health, National Development Planning Agency (BAPENAS), and Transmigration.

In sum, the inefficiency of the civil service has increased the opportunities for corruption, especially among the "wet" agencies identified earlier. Conversely, as such opportunities decline significantly in "dry" agencies, "being posted to a dry position is about the worst fate any official could fear" (Loveard, 1999, p. 111). Consequently, Palmier (1985, pp. 272–274) has contended that an important element of an effective anticorruption strategy would include the reduction of opportunities for corruption by removing officials from controlling commercial activities, by ensuring that laws and regulation do not lead to abuse, and by encouraging public vigilance. Clearly, the opportunities for corruption in the many "wet" public agencies in Indonesia can be reduced by increasing their efficiency through the streamlining of cumbersome procedures and eliminating red tape.

### *Weak Disciplinary Control and Ineffective Policing*

Discipline refers to "the moulding of employee behavior through punishment," that is, by taking action against an employee to reduce or eliminate an unwanted behavior, or by withholding a reward from an employee to reduce or eliminate an undesirable behavior (McAfee & Poffenberger, 1982, p. 45). Thus, disciplinary action is "the application of penalties that lead to an inhibition of undesired behavior" (Flippo, 1984, p. 473). Civil servants are usually disciplined or punished for two reasons: for breaking the organization's rules (misconduct) and for low productivity. While most civil servants conform to the rules of their organization, the minority that violate these rules must be disciplined to prevent the former from misbehaving too. Thus, disciplinary control is the process of enforcing an organization's rules and punishing those employees for violating these rules.

In the Indonesian civil service, Government Regulation No. 30 of Year 1980 identified 26 obligations and 17 prohibitions for civil servants to observe. Those civil servants who have infringed these obligations and prohibitions are punished according to the severity of the offence. Table 10.14 shows that there are three levels and 10 types of penalties, ranging from light, medium to severe disciplinary measures. A civil servant who has been accused of poor discipline can submit a written appeal to an Appeals Committee for a review of his case. In 1970, Theodore M. Smith (1970, p. 9) observed that the lack of discipline was a serious problem in the Indonesian civil service.

***Table 10.14.*** Disciplinary Measures in Indonesian Civil Service by Level and Type.

| Light Disciplinary Measures |
|---|
| 1. Oral reminder<br>2. Written reminder<br>3. Written statement of dissatisfaction |
| **Medium Disciplinary Measures** |
| 1. Postponement of salary increase for a maximum of one year<br>2. Reduction of one year's salary increase for a maximum of one year<br>3. Postponement of promotion for a maximum of one year |
| **Severe Disciplinary Measures** |
| 1. Demotion to one lower level for a maximum of one year<br>2. Release from position<br>3. Dismissal with honor but not at the request of the civil servant<br>4. Dismissal without honor as a civil servant |

*Source*: Reksosoedirdjo (1985, pp. 131–132).

The Indonesian civil service's poor record in disciplinary control is reflected in the difficulty in detecting corrupt behavior among its members and the absence or light penalty for such behavior. The Commission of Four recommended, among other things, that civil servants should submit an annual return of their personal assets. President Soeharto accepted this recommendation and published an Instruction in 1970 requiring all public officials to conform to this recommendation. However, the civil servants ignored this requirement for nine years as it was only in 1979 that 90 percent of the officials submitted their annual returns (Palmier, 1985, pp. 257–258).

In his 1969 survey of regional economic planners in Indonesia, Theodore M. Smith (1971, p. 30) found that apart from the lack of incentives for correct behavior, sanctions were also absent or rarely applied to those officials who were under-performing as "cultural norms effectively preclude punitive denial of the perquisites, however minor, that attend each position." It can be seen from Table 10.15 that nearly three-quarters of the 120 higher regional officials who responded to the question on the action to be taken against poor performers said that they did not dismiss their ineffective subordinates. Only about 16 percent of them had dismissed such subordinates and about 11 percent of them had taken similar action sometimes. Smith concluded (1971, p. 30) that: "The responses require no interpretation except to point out that the common procedure for dealing with officials whose corrupt practices became open knowledge is to transfer them to new jobs before their activities gain wide attention." Similarly, when a senior Indonesian civil servant was advised to dismiss his indolent and corrupt subordinates, he replied that he could not do so because they "had large families to support and needed these jobs. Besides, they didn't earn enough anyhow" (quoted in Palmier, 1985, p. 210).

***Table 10.15.*** Responses of 120 Higher Regional Officials to the Question: "If the Performance of Your Subordinates is Poor or Not Good in Any Way, Can You Relieve Them of Their Jobs?" (1969).

| Response | Number | Percentage |
|---|---|---|
| It is possible according to the regulations, but I have never done it | 88 | 73.3 |
| Sometimes | 13 | 10.8 |
| Usually | 19 | 15.8 |
| Total | 120 | 99.9 |

*Source*: Smith (1971, p. 30, Table IV).

In addition to low salaries and ample opportunities, Leslie Palmier argued that ineffective policing or the low probability of detecting and punishing corrupt behavior was also an important cause of corruption. Indeed, the weak disciplinary control in the Indonesian civil service is clearly manifested in the ineffective policing of the corrupt civil servants. According to a senior official:

> The just law applying sanction to corruptors is not consistently enforced, with the consequence that corruption is rife ... a substantial portion of the officers, especially those in the upper echelons, have been dishonest, thus facilitating corruption.... (quoted in Palmier, 1985, p. 207)

Palmier (1985, pp 241–244, 276, 280) found that corruption was rampant in Indonesia because it was tolerated as corrupt officials were seldom punished. He further noted that "*Opstib* [*Operasi Tertib*] was created because the Departments were simply not controlling corruption, but rather indulging in it themselves." He concluded that while there was strong policing against corruption in Hong Kong, "policing is very poor in Indonesia, and insufficient in India."

Finally, those found guilty of corrupt offenses can bribe the prison officials to make their life in prison more comfortable with special privileges and lavishly furnished cells. Indeed, the recent revelation that Gayus Tambunan was able to leave and return to jail at will on 68 occasions by bribing the prison officials shows that imprisonment for rich corrupt officials does not impose any hardship for them. Details of Gayus Tambunan's exploits during his imprisonment are provided in Box 10.2

### *Reliance on Incremental and Institutional Reform*

Administrative reform refers to "a deliberate attempt to change both (a) the structure and procedures of the public bureaucracy (i.e., reorganization or the institutional aspect) and (b) the attitudes and behavior of the public bureaucrats involved (i.e., the attitudinal aspect), in order to promote organizational effectiveness and attain national development goals" (Quah, 1976, p. 58). Thus, there are two components of administrative reform: institutional reform and attitudinal reform. Furthermore, the choice between a comprehensive or incremental strategy to reform depends on whether the timing, leadership, and risk acceptability are favorable. The comprehensive strategy is employed when these three variables are favorable. Conversely, the incremental strategy is used when one or more of these variables are unfavorable (Quah, 1976, pp. 62–63).

***Box 10.2.*** Gayus Tambunan's Corruption Scandal

Gayus Tambunan, 31, was a junior tax official in Jakarta earning a monthly salary of US$1,300 until 2009, when he was charged with accepting US$2.7 million in bribes from 44 companies to evade taxes by falsifying their tax documents. It has been estimated that the Indonesian government has lost more than US$700 million in revenue from the tax evasion by these companies.

On January 19, 2011, Gayus was found guilty on four counts of corruption and was sentenced to seven years' imprisonment and fined 300 million rupiah (US$30,000) by Judge Albertina Ho even though the prosecutors had demanded a 20-year jail sentence. During the trial, Gayus admitted that apart from helping many companies to evade taxes, he had also bribed judges, prosecutors and police and immigration officers to enable him to leave jail 68 times to travel on false passports with his wife to Bali (to reduce his stress by watching an international tennis tournament there), Guangzhou, Kuala Lumpur, Macao and Singapore.

According to Emerson Yuntho, from Indonesian Corruption Watch, the Gayus case highlights the problems of tax evasion and the judicial mafia. More importantly, it has shone the spotlight on government corruption in Indonesia and damaged President Yudhoyono's reputation as an anticorruption reformer.

While Gayus' ability to leave his prison cell with impunity for trips abroad makes a mockery of Indonesia's prison system, it should be noted that influential or rich inmates have received special treatment in lavishly furnished cells during their imprisonment. For example, businesswoman Artalyta Suryani, who was imprisoned in 2009 for bribing prosecutors, was living in a 690 square foot air-conditioned cell furnished with a double bed, flat-screen television, refrigerator, private kitchen and bathroom, and a playpen for children. When the members of the Task Force for Legal Mafia Eradication visited the prison on an unscheduled inspection, they found that she was undergoing laser beauty treatment in her cell.

Finally, the most recent prison scandal involved Kasiem, a 55-year-old woman, who was convicted of selling government-subsidized fertiliser and sentenced to seven months' imprisonment. As she did not want to serve her sentence, she paid 10 million rupiah (US$1,100) to Kami, a 50-year-old widow, to take her place in jail. One of Kasiem's neighbors visited her in jail and discovered that Kami was an imposter.

*Sources*: Budisatrijo (2011); Najiah (2011); Rondonuwu (2011) and Soedarjo (2011).

During the colonial period, administrative reform was neglected as the *raison d'etre* of the Dutch authorities was the economic exploitation of the natural resources of Indonesia for the benefit of the home government in the Netherlands. Similarly, not much was done by President Soekarno as he was not receptive to administrative reform. For example, the Commission for the Retooling of State Apparatus initiated a general reform of the civil service involving senior officials in 1958, but it could not implement the program because of the lack of support from President Sukarno and the strong influence of political parties within the civil service (Quah, 1989b, p. 249).

The Soeharto administration inherited an inefficient and ineffective public bureaucracy from the Sukarno regime. Indeed, the civil service in 1966 was "plagued by corruption, non-adherence to [the] merit system in personnel management, absenteeism, indiscipline, low salaries, and excessive red tape." In late 1966, President Soeharto formed an Advisory Committee to the President on Administrative Reform. In June 1968, President Soeharto created the post of Minister of State for Administrative Reform with the aim of implementing administrative reform in a more systematic and coordinated manner. In 1969, the government launched a Five-Year Development Plan, better known as *Repelita I*, which included a chapter on the administrative reform of the government apparatus (Quah, 1989b, pp. 249–250).

*Repelita I* identified the following areas of administrative reform for action: (1) improvement of organizational structures, (2) procedural improvement, (3) improvement in the quality of civil servants, (4) improvement in financial administration, (5) improvement in logistical administrations, (6) improvement in statistical administration, (7) improvement in the administration of state enterprises, and (8) improvement in research and development of public administration. However, unlike *Repelita I*, *Repelita II* and *Repelita III* did not focus on administrative reform per se since the impetus for such reform were set in motion by *Repelita I*. Instead, *Repelita II* (1974–1978) emphasized infrastructural investment, but there was inadequate accountability of government and quasi-government organizations. Similarly, in spite of the continuing need for administrative reform, *Repelita III* emphasized instead on banking and tax reforms during 1979–1983 (Quah, 1989b, pp. 250–251).

During *Repelita IV* (1984–1988), the government introduced a coordinating system to integrate the various functional controls into a single line of command (Legowo, 1999, p. 91). Finally, for *Repelita V* (1989–1993), eight priority areas for administrative reform were identified by the State Minister for Administrative Reform to improve the quality of services provided to the public. These areas were: (1) improved built-in or internal management,

(2) application of job analysis, (3) development of functional positions, (4) improved leadership quality, (5) simplification of civil service procedures, (6) improved management of public services, (7) design of management information systems, and (8) emphasis on autonomy in local government level II (Kristiadi, 1992, pp. 97–98).

What are the main features of the Indonesian approach to administrative reform? First, in terms of the content of administrative reform, the Indonesian approach during both the Sukarno and the Soeharto periods focused only on the institutional aspect at the expense of the attitudinal dimension. Indeed, administrative reform took the form of reorganization with little emphasis on attitudinal change. Second, the Soeharto government's reform strategy was designed, among other things, to improve organizational efficiency and effectiveness of the governmental apparatus, enabling it to perform developmental tasks (Quah, 1989b, p. 251).

Third, regarding the choice between a comprehensive and an incremental reform strategy, Hadisumarto (1974, pp. 291–292) contended that an incremental approach was more appropriate for Indonesia in the 1970s. He found that selective procedural reforms concerned with economic development or which promoted better services to the public had received more popular support. On the contrary, Donald P. Warwick (1978) from the Harvard Institute for International Development contended that the problems of the Indonesian civil service could not be solved by the incremental approach to administrative reform.

Finally, the Indonesian case illustrates the importance of the political leadership in ensuring the successful implementation of administrative reform through its sponsorship and support of the reform effort. While President Soeharto was more supportive of administrative reform than his predecessor, civil service reforms were incremental rather than comprehensive and emphasized institutional rather than attitudinal aspects (Quah, 1989b, p. 253). In sum, reform efforts in the Indonesian civil service have failed because of the lack of political support, their emphasis on institutional reform and the incremental strategy, their neglect of attitudinal reform and the avoidance of the comprehensive strategy.

## ANTICORRUPTION MEASURES

The fight against corruption in Indonesia began after the 1955 election as corruption was rife especially in the area of import licenses. This led to the first attempt by the government to curb corruption and resulted in the arrests of those involved, including civil servants and a minister. Following this, a bill for special anticorruption tribunals was drafted but never became law because President Sukarno refused to sign it. However, in September 1959, President Sukarno tried to weaken the army by appointing a new Attorney General who was instructed to investigate several senior army officers for corruption. In 1964, *Operasi Budhi* was initiated to examine the management, organization, and inventory of all state enterprises, including the wealth of its directors. However, only 11,000 million rupiahs were retrieved and one-seventh of the reports received within the first three months when the operation was dissolved by President Soeharto (Palmier, 1985, pp. 200, 203, 205).

### *President Soeharto's Anticorruption Measures*

After assuming power, President Soeharto initiated measures to improve the government apparatus. However, the task of dealing with corruption cases was entrusted in December 1967 to the *Team Pemberantasan Korupsi* (corruption eradication team or CET), which was established for this purpose within the Attorney General's Office (AGO). However, the CET was ineffective because its efforts were blocked by influential men in the regime. A CET official said that the "big fish" who were corrupt were protected by powerful men. Consequently, "wherever we went, we found stone walls" (Palmier, 1985, pp. 214–215).

In January 1970, students in Jakarta protested against corruption in their government by staging "the strongest anti-corruption outburst" in Indonesia since independence (Smith, 1971, p. 21). The press also joined the students in criticizing the government and this resulted in the appointment of a special Commission of Four (*Komisi IV*) elder statesmen by President Soeharto to review the problem of corruption within the Indonesian civil service and to suggest recommendations for improvement on January 31, 1970. The Commission presented seven reports to President Soeharto from February 27 to June 30, 1970. It focused attention on the state oil enterprise (*Pertamina*), the rice procurement agency (*Bulog*), and the state forestry enterprise (*Perhutani*). The Commission also identified areas where large sums of money had been lost as a result of inefficiency, poor accounting, or corruption. It recommended, inter alia, that the "Attorney-General's Department must be more energetic in dealing with corruption" and urged the "immediate completion of a bill proposed by the

Minister of Justice on the investigation, examination, and prosecution of corruption cases" (Mackie, 1970, pp. 87–101).

Although the Commission confirmed much of what everyone in Indonesia knew about the operation of government offices and state enterprises, its most important consequence was the passing of the Prevention Against Corrupt Criminal Acts Bill in 1971. Before the enactment of this law, corruption was dealt with as a crime in accordance with the Penal Code. In short, there was no specific anticorruption law in Indonesia before 1971.

The Commission of Four also recommended that civil servants should submit an annual return of their personal assets. President Soeharto accepted this recommendation and published an Instruction in 1970 requiring all civil servants to conform to this recommendation. However, as mentioned earlier, they ignored this requirement for nine years as it was only in 1979 that 90 percent of them submitted their annual returns. This example clearly illustrates that laws in Indonesia are not always implemented, especially those concerning corruption as the implementation of such laws would prevent the corrupt civil servants from continuing their corrupt practices (Quah, 1982a, p. 171).

Despite the vigorous public discussion on corruption generated by the reports of the Commission of Four and the resulting enactment of the 1971 anticorruption law, the problem of corruption has not been solved in Indonesia. Indeed, corruption appears to be a more serious problem today than during the pre-1971 period because of the non-enforcement of the 1971 law. To reinforce the Law No. 3 of Year 1971 on Prevention Against Corrupt Criminal Acts, President Soeharto issued a Decree No. 9 of Year 1974 on Organization, Fundamentals, and Procedures of the Operation Command for Restoration of Security and Order, and Presidential Instruction No. 9 of 84 of Year 1977 on Operation for Order. Hadisumarto (1974, pp. 266, 282, n. 108) has described President Soeharto's response to the corruption problem as "a low cost strategy" because "the psychic costs of direct interpersonal conflicts and the dangers involved in levelling charges of corruption appear too high to encourage much aggressive behavior that is a *sine qua non* for successful anti-corruption drives."

The 1977 Presidential Instruction transferred the task of combating corruption to the National Security Agency (*Kopkamtib*) in June 1977. *Kopkamtib* was formed on October 10, 1965, by Major General Soeharto, the Commander of the Army Strategic Reserve, to "restore order and security" as a result of the instability and disorder created by the abortive 30 September *coup d'etat* attempt (Thoolen, 1987, p. 67). *Kopkamtib* was instructed to take action against "unofficial levies," which included forced discounts, extortion, and bribes. It initiated Operation Orderliness *(Operasi Tertib* or *Opstib*) by making "lightning visits" to those "wet" government departments which were prone to corruption, and dismissing those civil servants caught red-handed on the spot. Consequently, some officials were arrested and charged in court, including the heads of the state enterprise for tin and the rice procurement agency. However, the major handicap of *Kopkamtib* was its inability to take action against those generals and senior civil servants involved in corrupt practices (Quah, 1982a, p. 171).

For the next 21 years until President Soeharto stepped down in May 1998, nothing was done by him to curb corruption among his family, ministers and cronies. For example, when one of his ministers was exposed for being involved in corruption, the matter was not handled by the courts or the civil service but by Soeharto himself, who would make his decision after a few days. The minister concerned would not be dismissed or imprisoned but asked to "engage in a period of 'introspection'" (McLeod, 2000, pp. 150–151). Similarly, President Soeharto was also "most reluctant" to control the excessive behavior of his children and grandchildren. According to Ross H. McLeod (2000, p. 161):

> His [Soeharto's] late wife Tien had been known as "Madame Ten Percent" because of her alleged propensity for skimming 10 percent of the value of government projects with which she had some connection, but this "tax rate" was reasonable .... Several of the Soeharto offspring appear to have taken the view that 10 per cent was far too modest and by all appearances seem to have grabbed lustily for everything they could, without any concern for the longer-term consequences for the franchise their father had built.

### *Anticorruption Measures during the Post-Soeharto Era*

Since the phrase *korupsi, kolusi dan nepotisme* symbolizes the "social costs, inequities and abuses of the Soeharto regime," it is not surprising that President Suharto's successors have "espoused the goal of combating corruption" (Hamilton-Hart, 2001, p. 66) to accommodate the widespread public demand to eradicate KKN. Accordingly, President B. J. Habibie's administration was concerned with reform and "the eradication of KKN" became "the rallying cry" (Assegaf, Ahmad, Damayana, & Cahyadi, 2002, p. 149). More specifically, he introduced many laws, including the passing of the Law on the State Organization Clean and Free from KKN (Law No. 28 of Year 1999) and the Anti-Corruption Law (Law No. 31 of Year 1999), which increased the penalty for corruption to a maximum of 20 years imprisonment or one billion Rupiahs in fines and created the Anti-Corruption Commission, chaired by former Supreme Court Justice Adi Andojo Soetjipto, and which included police officials, Bank Indonesia officers and civil society activists. Law No. 28 of Year 1999 also provided for the establishment of the State Commission for Audit of Public Officials' Wealth and its members were approved by Parliament in July 2000 (Hamilton-Hart, 2001, p. 72).

The Habibie administration exposed the problem of KKN and made its eradication a top priority. However, its anti-corruption efforts were ineffective for two reasons. First, there was no serious effort made to "bring offenders to justice" during Habibie's presidency as KKN was instead "sidelined as a legislative problem" to be resolved by introducing new laws. Second, the various institutions created by President Habibie to eradicate KKN "failed to perform, and no significant progress was made" (Assegaf et al., 2002, p. 150). In other words, the introduction of new laws and institutions was ineffective in curbing corruption. This negative view of Habibie's efforts to curb corruption is shared by Damien Kingsbury (2002, p. 213), who argued that "little happened to address corruption" during Habibie's presidency because he was "himself a beneficiary of corruption and nepotism, while his party, Golkar, was able to function only as a result of its various and usually illegal money-gathering schemes."

Eradicating KKN was "a monumental challenge to the Wahid administration" because it inherited "a substandard legal system" and "a murky taxation system" which provided ample opportunities for corruption (Smith, 2001, p. 11). President Wahid inherited the new anticorruption laws and the Joint Team for the Eradication of Corruption (TGPTPK) was formed in June 2000 according to Article 27 of Law No. 31 of 1999 to deal with "criminal acts of corruption that are difficult to prove." However, the TGPTPK team was ineffective because of the poor work commitment of its members, the lack of financing that resulted in the nonpayment of its members' salaries for several months, and its lack of authority to investigate corruption cases which occurred before 1999 (Assegaf et al., 2002, pp. 168–169).

More importantly, the major problem undermining President Wahid's efforts in curbing corruption was that "his own rule was not without an increasingly strong stench of 'KKN'" because he was personally implicated in three corruption scandals (Kingsbury, 2002, p. 214). First, in May 2000 Wahid was involved in the "Buloggate" scandal that resulted from his private masseur, Suwondo, borrowing Rp 35 billion (US$4 million) from the State Logistics Agency (*Bulog* or *Badan Urusan Logistik*) and distributing this amount among several persons and an airline company in which Wahid and Suwondo were connected. The second scandal, known as "Bruneigate" occurred because of Wahid's failure to declare to the state treasury a personal gift of US$2 million from the Sultan of Brunei. The third scandal was "Borobudurgate," which arose from Wahid's meeting with Tommy Soeharto to arrange a presidential pardon for his jail sentence for corruption (Budiman, 2001, p. 149). Needless to say, all these scandals damaged Wahid's image and undermined his credibility in curbing KKN.[4]

In their evaluation of the pattern of corruption management under Presidents Soeharto, Habibie and Wahid, Assegaf et al. (2002, p. 188) concluded that:

> From the three periods of administration, it is apparent that corruption has not been handled seriously. The problem of corruption is merely articulated as a matter of shortcomings of the people or the government's apparatus in putting into practice the general principles of good governance. Hence, it has been considered sufficient to supervise and detect them. Things have not reached a stage where a firm and repressive sanction is provided for the criminal act of corruption, Even if it has reached the repressive dimension, such matters will only seem artificial and far from the sense of legal justice.

When Megawati Sukarnoputri became president in July 2001, she inherited "a severely weakened presidency" (Sen, 2002, p. 17) and the unresolved problem of KKN. Accordingly, in her first state of the nation speech on August 16, 2001, she promised that her anticorruption campaign would begin with her family and that corruption must be eliminated to strengthen Indonesia's democratization. She revealed that:

> I have privately gathered all members of my immediate family requesting them to solemnly pledge not to open the slightest window of opportunity for the recurrence of KKN in my family. They have given me their solemn pledge, and I hope that they will be able to resist the many temptations around them. (quoted in Sen, 2002, p. 22)

Furthermore, she directed her cabinet ministers and senior civil servants to declare their assets to the state auditors. She also indicated that her ministers would be held responsible if they were found to have given unlawful benefits to her relatives. She added: "If later it is found that any of the children have benefited from any project, or anything else, it will be the minister who will bear the blame" (*BBC News*, 2001b, pp. 1–2). However, it is particularly significant that she has made no reference to her husband, who is a prominent businessman.

Six months after she assumed office, the head of the State Auditing Agency (BPK), Satrio "Billy" Joedono, criticized President Megawati for not doing enough to curb corruption in her government. In an interview with the *Straits Times* on January 21, 2002, he said:

> There is yet no indication of stronger commitment to fighting corruption in this government. The number of graft cases in the government that have made it to court is

> still small and the level of successful prosecution of the cases remains low. ... BPK cannot do much to help. We're like a medical laboratory, we tell people if they have high blood pressure or high cholesterol level, but it is up to them to change their lifestyle to be healthy. The current government will not be able to fight graft without a major overhaul of the bureaucracy, which comprises largely of corrupt officials.... The country needed a groundbreaking move to cleanse the bureaucracy of officials with dubious integrity and poor capability. There should be a re-screening process for existing bureaucrats, and a new recruitment system with fit and proper integrity tests. It will take a while to complete the overhaul, perhaps five to six years, but at least we make a start. (quoted in Asmarani, 2002, p. A5)

On February 11, 2002, President Megawati likened her government to "a trash can" and criticized civil servants for being desk-bound and not pro-active and only concerned with good news and paying inadequate attention to negative reports (*Straits Times*, 2002a, p. A5). On March 17, 2002, she reaffirmed her commitment to curbing corruption in Indonesia. Expressing concern over PERC's survey that had identified Indonesia as one of the most corrupt Asian countries, she said: "Whether the survey is valid or not, still the report concerns me and makes me sick. We have to end the [corrupt] condition and uphold the law" (Unidjaja, 2002).

Unfortunately, President Megawati's initial interest in fighting corruption waned and she demonstrated her lack of political will by delaying the establishment of the KPK by her refusal to sign the authorizing legislation for more than two years (Quah, 2006b, p. 178).

### *Komisi Pemberantasan Korupsi*

The KPK was formed on December 29, 2003, according to Law No. 30 of 2002, which was passed in December 2002 (KPK, 2009, p. 14). The KPK consists of five commissioners, with a chairman and four vice-chairmen, who serve for a maximum of two four-year terms. There is also an advisory team consisting of four advisors. The KPK has 652 employees and its investigators and prosecutors are seconded from the AGO and the police (KPK, 2010, p. 84; Davidsen, Juwono, & Timberman, 2006, p. 47).

According to Law No. 30 of 2002, the KPK is responsible for these five functions:

1. Coordination with other state institutions to eradicate corruption.
2. Supervision of other state institutions authorized to eradicate corruption.
3. Performing investigations, indictments and prosecutions of corruption cases.

4. Preventing corruption by examining wealth and gratification reports, conducting anticorruption education and socialization programmes, and engaging in bilateral and multilateral cooperation to eradicate corruption.
5. Monitoring the administration of state institutions and making recommendations for making them more corruption-resistant (Davidsen et al., 2006, pp. 48).

Furthermore, the KPK is also empowered by the same law to (1) conduct surveillance of other state institutions that are involved in fighting corruption; (2) carry out wire taps, record conversations, and access bank and tax records; and (3) take over investigations or prosecutions performed by the police or AGO (Davidsen et al., 2006, p. 48).

Organizationally, the KPK is divided into these five divisions:

1. The *Office of the Deputy for Prevention*, which consists of the Directorate of Registering and Examining of Public Officials' Wealth Reports, the Directorate of Gratuity, the Directorate of Education and Public Services, and the Directorate of Research and Development.
2. The *Office of the Deputy for Repression*, which is made up of the Directorate of Preliminary Investigations, the Directorate of Investigations, and the Directorate of Prosecutions.
3. The *Office of the Deputy for Information and Data*, which consists of the Directorate of Information and Data Processing, the Directorate of Fostering Networks between Commissions and Institutions, and the Directorate of Monitoring.
4. The *Office of the Deputy for Internal Monitoring and Public Complaints*, which is made up of the Directorate of Internal Monitoring and the Directorate of Public Complaints.
5. The *Secretariat General*, which consists of these five bureaus: Bureau of Human Resources; Bureau of Planning and Finance; Bureau of General Affairs; the Legal Bureau; and Bureau of Public Relations (KPK, 2009, pp. 5–6).

The KPK's personnel has more than doubled from 305 in 2005 to 652 in 2009, as indicated in Table 10.16. The most substantial increase occurred in 2007 with the addition of 135 staff. There were further increases in staff in 2008 (91 persons) and in 2009 (112 persons).

Table 10.17 shows that the Office of the Deputy for Repression is the largest division in the KPK with almost 29 percent of its total personnel. The Office of the Deputy for Information and Data is the second largest division, followed by the Secretariat General, the Office of the Deputy for

***Table 10.16.*** KPK Personnel, 2005–2009.

| Year | Number of Personnel | Percentage Increase |
|---|---|---|
| 2005 | 305 | 100 |
| 2006 | 314 | 103 |
| 2007 | 449 | 147 |
| 2008 | 540 | 177 |
| 2009 | 652 | 214 |

*Sources:* Davidsen et al. (2006, p. 52) and KPK (2007, p. 3.6, 2008, p. 21, 2009, p. 100, 2010, p. 84).

Prevention, and the Office of the Deputy for Internal Monitoring and Public Complaints. Table 10.18 shows that the KPK's budget has also increased by more than four times from Rp 109 billion (US$11 million) in 2004 to Rp 461.7 billion (US$51.3 million) in 2009. Except for 2007–2008 when the budget allocated to the KPK was the same, the KPK's budget has been increasing, with the highest increase in 2009.

## EVALUATION OF ANTICORRUPTION MEASURES

The effectiveness of the anticorruption measures in Indonesia can be evaluated by ascertaining Indonesia's performance on these four indicators: (1) TI's CPI from 1995–2010 covering 178 countries; (2) PERC's annual survey of corruption in 16 Asia-Pacific countries from 1995–2010; (3) World Bank's control of corruption governance indicator from 1996 to 2009 covering 213 countries; and (4) the *Global Competitiveness Report's* indicator on the public trust of politicians in 139 countries from 1999 to 2010–2011.

Table 10.19 provides details of Indonesia's performance on the first three indicators. First, Indonesia was ranked last among the 41 countries in the 1995 CPI with a score of 1.94. Even though its CPI rank has improved to 110th position among the 178 countries surveyed in 2010 with a score of 2.8, corruption is still perceived to be a serious problem in Indonesia. Second, Indonesia's rank on the PERC survey ranges between 10th position in 1996 and 16th position in 2009 and 2010. Third, in terms of control of corruption, Indonesia's percentile rank varies from 13.1 in 1998 to 33.3 in 2007 and 2008. Fourth, as corruption is perceived as a serious problem in Indonesia, it is not surprising that the level of public trust in politicians is low. It can be seen in Table 10.20 that Indonesia's rank on this indicator varies from 41st

***Table 10.17.*** KPK Personnel by Division, 2009.

| Division | Number | Percentage |
|---|---|---|
| Board of Commissioners | 7 | 1.07 |
| Advisory Team | 2 | 0.31 |
| Office of the Deputy for Prevention | 122 | 18.71 |
| Office of the Deputy for Repression | 187 | 28.68 |
| Office of the Deputy for Information and Data | 131 | 20.09 |
| Office of the Deputy for Internal Monitoring and Public Complaints | 74 | 11.35 |
| Secretariat General | 129 | 19.79 |
| Total | 652 | 100.00 |

*Source*: KPK (2010, p.84).

***Table 10.18.*** KPK's Budget, 2004–2009.

| Year | Budget | Percentage Increase |
|---|---|---|
| 2004 | Rp 109 billion (US$11 million) | 100 |
| 2005 | Rp 170 billion (US$18 million) | 156 |
| 2006 | Rp 248.5 billion (US$27.6 million) | 228 |
| 2007 | Rp 346.2 billion (US$36.8 million) | 318 |
| 2008 | Rp 346.8 billion (US$31.7 million) | 318 |
| 2009 | Rp 461.7 billion (US$51.3 million) | 424 |

*Sources*: Davidsen et al. (2006, p. 52) and KPK (2007, p. 3.8, 2008, p. 28, 2009, p. 106, 2010, p. 88).

position among the 59 countries in 1999 to 51st position among the 139 countries in 2010–2011. Furthermore, its score ranges from 1.70 in 2002–2003 to its best score of 3.30 in 2010–2011. In short, Indonesia's poor performance on these four indicators is a reflection of the ineffectiveness of its anticorruption measures.

President Susilo Bambang Yudhoyono became the first directly elected president of Indonesia in October 2004. Unlike his predecessors, he has been more committed to combating corruption and has emphasized the importance of clean government. However, he had unwittingly undermined the KPK's effectiveness in May 2005 when he formed an anticorruption task force, consisting of prosecutors, police, and auditors. This task force has not only diluted the KPK's efforts but also competes with the KPK instead of cooperating with it (Quah, 2006b, pp. 178–179).

The conflict and competition between the KPK and the police and the AGO erupted in the arrest in November 2009 of two senior KPK officials by

***Table 10.19.*** Indonesia's Performance on CPI, PERC, and Control of Corruption, 1995–2010.

| Year | CPI Rank and Score[a] | PERC Rank and Score[b] | Control of Corruption Percentile Rank |
|---|---|---|---|
| 1995 | 41st (1.94) | 12th (7.30) | NA |
| 1996 | 45th (2.65) | 10th (7.69) | 32.0 |
| 1997 | 46th (2.72) | 12th (8.67) | NA |
| 1998 | 80th (2.0) | 12th (8.95) | 13.1 |
| 1999 | 96th (1.7) | 12th (9.91) | NA |
| 2000 | 85th (1.7) | 12th (9.88) | 16.0 |
| 2001 | 88th (1.9) | 11th (9.67) | NA |
| 2002 | 96th (1.9) | 12th (9.92) | 10.2 |
| 2003 | 122nd (1.9) | 12th (9.33) | 15.5 |
| 2004 | 133rd (2.0) | 12th (9.25) | 19.9 |
| 2005 | 137th (2.2) | 13th (9.10) | 20.9 |
| 2006 | 130th (2.4) | 13th (8.16) | 25.2 |
| 2007 | 143rd (2.3) | 11th (8.03) | 33.3 |
| 2008 | 126th (2.6) | 11th (7.98) | 33.3 |
| 2009 | 111th (2.8) | 16th (8.32) | 28.1 |
| 2010 | 110th (2.8) | 16th (9.27) | NA |

*Sources*: Compiled from http://www.transparency.org; PERC (2001, 2008, p. 7); Hussain (2009, p. B5); *Straits Times* (2010a); and http://info.worldbank.org/governance/wgi/sc_chart.asp
[a]The CPI score ranges from 0 (most corrupt) to 10 (least corrupt).
[b]The PERC score ranges from 0 (least corrupt) to 10 (most corrupt).

***Table 10.20.*** Public Trust of Politicians in Indonesia, 1999 to 2010–2011.

| Year | Rank | Score[a] | No. of Countries |
|---|---|---|---|
| 1999 | 41st | 2.26 | 59 |
| 2000 | 40th | 2.50 | 59 |
| 2001–2002 | 53rd | 2.00 | 75 |
| 2002–2003 | 61st | 1.70 | 80 |
| 2003–2004 | 38th | 3.10 | 102 |
| 2007–2008 | 63rd | 2.60 | 131 |
| 2008–2009 | 59th | 3.00 | 134 |
| 2009–2010 | 52nd | 3.20 | 133 |
| 2010–2011 | 51st | 3.30 | 139 |
| Average | 51st | 2.63 | – |

*Sources*: Compiled from Schwab et al. (1999, p. 327), Porter et al. (2000, p. 253), Schwab et al. (2002, p. 408), Cornelius (2003, p. 619), Sala-i-Martin (2004, p. 499), Schwab and Porter (2007, p. 379), Schwab and Porter (2008, p. 367), Schwab (2009, p. 349) and Schwab (2010, p.369).
[a]The score ranges from 1 (very low) to 7 (very high) for the respondents' answers to this statement: "How would you rate the level of public trust in the ethical standards of politicians in your country."

the police allegedly for bribery. The arrest of these officials in the wake of the arrest of the KPK Chairman Antasari Azhar for murder in May 2009 was widely viewed as "an apparent high-level conspiracy" by the police and AGO to weaken the KPK (Osman, 2009, p. A9; Onishi, 2009, p. A10). Nevertheless, Azhar's arrest was "a huge blow to the KPK" because it changed public opinion and gave the impression that the KPK was "doing business as usual" like the police, prosecutors, judges and prison guards (Harsono, 2009).

Emil P. Bolongaita (2010, p. 9) has compared the performance of the KPK with the Ombudsman in the Philippines and concludes that "the KPK's achievements are especially remarkable given its relatively brief existence in a corruption-hardened environment" in contrast to the Ombudsman's "paucity in performance" even though it was established in July 1979 and has more personnel. He attributes the KPK's effectiveness to its wider jurisdiction, investigative powers, consultation between investigators and prosecutors in preparing cases for prosecution, selective recruitment of qualified and experienced investigators and prosecutors, and the support provided by President Yudhoyono and the public (Bolongaita, 2010, pp. 13–20).

Similarly, Emily Hartwell (2009, pp. 32–33) contends that "the KPK's record is strong" because "it has won all 32 cases" it has prosecuted since 2006. The KPK's effectiveness is reflected in Indonesia's improved rating on the World Bank's control of corruption indicator from 2004 onwards. However, despite its "strong start in addressing impunity for corruption," the KPK has four weaknesses. First, the KPK has not compelled civil servants to submit asset disclosures or made these disclosures widely accessible to citizens. Second, in view of its mandate and limited resources, the KPK has been selective in "pursuing corruptors in high levels of government in the executive and legislative branches" at the expense of seeking indictments in the police and judiciary, where corruption is most rampant. While some government officials have been convicted and imprisoned, the KPK has not prosecuted any "big fish" in the business community. Third, as the KPK "faces a delicate problem of backlash from those powerful figures who come under its scrutiny," it has to gather evidence and wait for the "right moment" before prosecuting such "big fish" or presidential allies to avoid endangering its own survival. Fourth, the KPK has also faced tremendous resistance in its anticorruption efforts from those being investigated. For example, a successful challenge by a person accused by the KPK that the Anti-Corruption Court, where the KPK tries its cases, was unconstitutional had weakened both institutions

(Hartwell, 2009, pp. 33–35). More recently, the KPK has been "a target of criticism" from politicians after it had named 25 senior politicians as graft suspects in 2010 and detained 19 of them on January 28, 2011 (Saragih, 2011).

Marcus Mietzner (2009, p. 149) contends that President Yudhoyono has "failed to take an unambiguous stance toward the anti-corruption campaign hailed by many as the hallmark and principal achievement of his government." Even though there were high-profile arrests of parliamentarians, bureaucrats, and investigators (which included his brother-in-law), Yudhoyono supported politicians' complaints about the KPK's intrusive methods of relying on sting operations and scrutiny of their private bank accounts. Anticorruption activists were upset with Yudhoyono in April 2008 when he advised the KPK to help corrupt politicians understand the law better instead of "trapping" them. Meitzner concludes that Yudhoyono's "reluctance to openly defend his government's most popular policy was the ultimate confirmation" of his inability to be tough and decisive to many Indonesians.

Hartwell (2009, pp. 36–37) acknowledges that the KPK "does not have the resources or the mandate to take on all corruption cases and cannot root out impunity for corruption on its own." Accordingly, she recommends that the KPK's catalytic role can only be realized by systematically tackling corruption in the police and judiciary. More specifically, "the police, AGO [Attorney-General's Office], and judiciary are all in need of corruption accountability measures themselves before they can effectively take on the bulk of corruption cases that the KPK cannot." She further recommends that the KPK should devote its limited capacity and resources to eradicating corruption and transfer the functions of corruption education and prevention to another agency.

Tables 10.21 and 10.22 confirm that the KPK has insufficient budget and personnel to perform all its functions effectively. Table 10.21 shows that while the KPK's per capita expenditure is low, it has increased from US$0.08 in 2005 to US$0.21 in 2009. Similarly, Table 10.22 confirms the KPK's unfavorable staff-population ratio, which has improved from 1:730,491 to 1:368,404 during 2005–2009.

In sum, President Yudhoyono has to demonstrate unequivocally his commitment to fighting corruption by allocating more budget and personnel to the KPK to increase its per capita expenditure and improve its staff-population ratio. He should enhance the KPK's capacity instead of weakening it by creating taskforces or other agencies to compete with it.

***Table 10.21.*** Per Capita Expenditure of KPK, 2005–2009.

| Year | Budget | Population | Per Capita Expenditure |
|---|---|---|---|
| 2005 | US$18 million | 222.8 million | US$0.08 |
| 2006 | US$27.6 million | 225.5 million | US$0.12 |
| 2007 | US$36.8 million | 228.1 million | US$0.16 |
| 2008 | US$31.7 million | 234.3 million | US$0.14 |
| 2009 | US$51.3 million | 240.2 million | US$0.21 |

*Sources*: Davidsen, Juwono, and Timberman (2006, p. 52); KPK (2007–2010); *Economist* 2007b–2010; CIA (2011a).

***Table 10.22.*** Staff-Population Ratio of KPK, 2005–2009.

| Year | Personnel | Population | Staff–Population Ratio |
|---|---|---|---|
| 2005 | 305 | 222.8 million | 1:730,491 |
| 2006 | 314 | 225.5 million | 1:718,152 |
| 2007 | 449 | 228.1 million | 1:508,017 |
| 2008 | 540 | 234.3 million | 1:433,888 |
| 2009 | 652 | 240.2 million | 1:368,404 |

*Sources*: Davidsen, Juwono, and Timberman (2006, p. 52); KPK (2007–2010); *Economist* (2007b–2010); CIA (2011a).

## CONCLUSION

The preceding analysis of anticorruption measures in Indonesia since the 1950s shows that these measures are ineffective mainly because of the lack of political will of the various political leaders such as President Sukarno, President Soeharto, President Habibie, President Wahid, President Megawati, and, to a lesser extent, President Yudhoyono.

That bureaucratic corruption is a serious problem in Indonesia has been acknowledged not only by the respondents in the 2000 and 2001 surveys but also by Indonesia's consistently poor ranking in the CPI and PERC's annual surveys from 1995 to 2010. Is the situation in Indonesia "hopeless" as far as minimizing bureaucratic corruption is concerned? Needless to say, to minimize corruption in the Indonesian civil service is a gargantuan task, which cannot be done overnight. However, to do nothing and maintain the status quo is also not a desirable option for the current political leadership in Indonesia. What can be realistically done by President Yudhoyono's government to ensure success and avoid the same road to failure of previous anti-corruption efforts?

First, to minimize corruption in the Indonesian civil service, its five major weaknesses must be minimized if not eliminated. In other words, the absence of a tradition of meritocracy in the civil service must be rectified to ensure that recruitment and promotion of civil servants are based on merit and not patronage or other ascriptive criteria. In this connection, the "re-screening" process recommended by the State Auditing Agency Head, Joedono, for existing civil servants is a useful suggestion for re-instating the tradition of meritocracy. The performance evaluation system in the civil service must also be improved to ensure that promotion is based on merit and a civil servant's actual performance and not on patronage and other ascriptive criteria.

The second defect of inadequate compensation has been identified by public officials, business enterprises, and households in the 2001 survey as the most important cause of corruption. Even though the salaries of junior civil servants are higher than their counterparts in the private sector, what they earn is still inadequate to meet all their monthly needs. In contrast, the situation for senior civil servants is more difficult as they earn much less than their counterparts in the private sector. As both petty and grand corruption are rampant in the civil service, raising civil service salaries alone, as was done by President Wahid in April 2000, is a necessary but insufficient precondition for curbing corruption effectively.

It is unrealistic to expect poorly-paid civil servants and political leaders to perform their jobs effectively and honestly especially when the probability of being detected and punished is also not high. Singapore's experience in curbing corruption, which is analyzed in Chapter 6, shows that it has succeeded in minimizing corruption by relying on the CPIB to implement impartially the POCA from 1960 to 1971. The salaries of civil servants and political leaders were only raised in 1972 to prevent the brain drain of civil servants to the private sector and not to curb corruption, which had been minimized by then. In short, Singapore succeeded in curbing corruption by enforcing the POCA impartially and not by raising the salaries of the civil servants and political leaders. Thus, as Mark Baird, the World Bank's Country Director for Indonesia, correctly pointed out, "To reduce corruption in the [Indonesian] bureaucracy, there was a need for fundamental reforms in the civil service. But higher salaries alone, without accountability, would not suffice to root out corruption" (Jakarta Post, 2000).

As red tape and inefficiency breed corruption in the civil service, the elimination of this third weakness will help to reduce the opportunities for corruption. Businessmen are prepared to pay bribes to civil servants to expedite the processing of their applications for permits as delay would reduce their profits. Given their low salaries, Indonesian civil servants would not want to jeopardize their source of extra income by reducing red tape and improving efficiency by streamlining their procedures. South Korea's success in eliminating unnecessary regulations during President Kim Dae-Jung's administration, which is dealt with in Chapter 9, shows that red tape can be reduced to minimize the opportunities for corruption if the political will exists to do so. Thus, the Indonesian civil service can learn from South Korea's example to minimize opportunities for corruption by reducing red tape and relying on information technology to improve transparency.

The fourth defect of weak disciplinary control is clearly manifested in the lack of punishment for corrupt civil servants in Indonesia. The 2001 survey shows that 64.9 percent of the public officials, 50.8 percent of the business enterprises, and 50.6 percent of the households in the sample were in favor of punishing convicted corruptors with imprisonment and seizure of their assets. Needless to say, the clearest manifestation of the ineffective policing of Indonesia's anticorruption strategy was the freedom and lack of punishment of former President Soeharto before his death and his family for their misdeeds. As mentioned earlier, Soeharto was protected from prosecution because of his "ill health." Since the "big fish" are protected from prosecution for corruption, and only the "small fry" (ordinary people) are caught, Indonesia's anticorruption strategy has been ineffective and lacked credibility during the last 56 years. The Indonesian civil service must strengthen its disciplinary control and punish those civil servants who are unproductive or violate the organizational rules, including misconduct and involvement in corrupt practices.

The KPK must be supported by President Yudhoyono in its investigations against the corrupt practices of political leaders and senior civil servants. It was reported that the Indonesian government had lost more than 80 percent of the 400 lawsuits during 1999–2002 because of corrupt judges and prosecutors (Go, 2002, p. A4). In short, unless the Yudhoyono's government enhances the policing of corrupt activities by increasing the probability of detection and punishment of corrupt civil servants and political leaders, corruption will remain a way of life in Indonesia.

The final weakness of the Indonesian civil service is its reliance on institutional and incremental reform. This defect is a major reason why it has not succeeded in curbing corruption so far. In his 1974 analysis of administrative reforms in the civil service, Djunaedi Hadisumarto had recommended incremental civil service reforms in the 1970s. However, the ineffectiveness of these reforms lends credence to Donald P. Warwick's preference for comprehensive reforms to resolve the problems of the Indonesian civil service. He highlighted the weaknesses of the incremental approach and recommended its replacement by a more comprehensive approach thus:

> The great drawback to this [incremental] approach is that it does not attack the underlying problems of the [Indonesian] civil service, especially the lack of an overall system based on a clear vision of what Indonesia's civil service should be. *The incremental strategy does what the government has done since 1949: apply dressings to surface infections without examining the source of those infections.* It is no exaggeration to say that the dressings of an earlier day have now become part of the disease which they were intended to cure.... More specifically the incremental strategy runs the great risk of *changing form but not substance*.... The incremental approach has been tried and failed. The time seems ripe and the need urgent for deeper analysis and comprehensive reform of the Indonesian civil service system. (Warwick, 1978, pp. 14–15, emphasis added)

However, Warwick (1978, pp.16–18) was realistic to acknowledge that comprehensive reform of the Indonesian civil service would only be successful if these preconditions were satisfied: (1) strong political support for the reform at the top, (2) careful analysis of alternatives with those most affected by the changes, and (3) pilot-testing of reforms and follow-up. Unfortunately, Warwick's 1978 recommendation went unheeded by the Indonesian government. The situation in Indonesia today, 33 years later, is slightly better as the cumulative research done and survey data collected on the civil service and corruption show that we know the source of the infections.

Thus, instead of "muddling through" using the incremental approach and not resolving the problem, President Yudhoyono's government should seize the opportunity to introduce comprehensive reforms in the civil service, beginning with the elimination of its five weaknesses, as the timing, leadership, and risk acceptability are favorable. The timing and leadership are favorable as President Yudhuyono was re-elected for a second term in October 2009. The failure of Presidents Habibie, Wahid, and Megawati to eradicate KKN presents President Yudhoyono with a golden opportunity to demonstrate his political will in combating corruption by introducing comprehensive reforms in the civil service to deal with the three major causes of corruption: low salaries, ample opportunities, and low probability of detection and punishment for corrupt behavior. The risk acceptability is also favorable because if President Yudhoyono follows the example of his predecessors, nothing will be accomplished during the remaining three years of his second term of office.

Finally, is it an impossible dream to minimize corruption in Indonesia? So far, Indonesia's record in combating corruption during the past 56 years has not been an impressive one, to say the least. Minimizing corruption in Indonesia is not an impossible dream if President Yudhoyono or his successor is prepared to implement impartially a comprehensive anti-corruption strategy and if the Indonesian people are prepared to give their support by avoiding corrupt practices themselves and reporting such practices to the KPK. Indeed, as shown in Chapters 6 and 7, Singapore and Hong Kong SAR have succeeded in curbing corruption because of the commitment of their political leaders to implement impartially a comprehensive anti-corruption strategy, which was supported by their civil servants and population.

## NOTES

1. There is an extensive literature on corruption in Indonesia as can be seen from the references cited in this chapter.
2. For a detailed analysis of the consolidation of democratization in Indonesia after May 1998, see Abdulbaki (2008).
3. The 12 causes listed were: low salaries of public officials, lack of controls and accountability of public officials, lack of independent and ineffective judiciary, lack of effective and independent media, lack of democracy, lack of effective corruption reporting system, poor law enforcement/punishment of corrupters, cultural reasons, lack of effective civil society, legacy of the New Order regime, lack of moral [*sic*], and complex government regulations. See Partnership for Governance Reform (2001, p. 52, endnote 1).
4. For another assessment of President Wahid's presidency, see Kingsbury (2001).

# CHAPTER 11

# MONGOLIA

> There is corruption in every country, but in Mongolia it is everywhere, from the lowest levels all the way up to the [Cabinet] ministers.
>
> – Garigtsatsralt Chuluunkhuu[1] (quoted in Jones, 2009)

> In the countryside, one out of three judges does not have an apartment. Consequently, some judges live in their office, which is clearly not desirable and does not enhance the status of the judiciary.
>
> – Stephanie McPhail (1995, p. 45)

## JUDICIAL CORRUPTION IN MONGOLIA

Stephanie McPhail's description above of the difficult living conditions of the judges in Mongolia in 1995 underscores their vulnerability to corrupt practices and their negative perception by the public. Judicial salaries during that year were comparable to those of civil servants but lower than those of lawyers in private practice and ranged from US$33 to US$51 per month (Quah, 2003a, p. 43). More importantly, the living conditions of judges were difficult, especially in the countryside, where one-third of the judges did not own an apartment, and were forced to live in their offices. Consequently, McPhail (1995, p. 45) concluded that the "relatively low salaries and mediocre working conditions" of the judges were "an impediment to attracting highly qualified candidates to the profession."

Although judges' monthly salaries have increased to US$200 in 2007, their salaries constitute "only half the average in the private legal sector." Furthermore, the Chief Justice S. Batdelger of the Supreme Court has revealed that more 70 percent of judges have to pay rent for their apartments (TI Mongolia, 2007, p. 230). Even though judicial monthly salaries have improved further to US$300 to US$400 for lower court judges and US$700 for Supreme Court judges in 2009, Brent T. White (2010, p. 323) contends that "such salaries are, at best, barely sufficient for judges to secure basic necessities such as food and housing for their families." Needless to say, their low salaries and unsatisfactory living conditions make judges vulnerable to corruption.

Apart from a lack of transparency in Mongolian courts, many experts interviewed have observed that senior government officials, especially the President, have exerted "considerable influence over Supreme Court and Constitutional Court decisions." More than three-quarters of the experts have agreed that court decisions are influenced by improper payments, gifts, or favors from litigants or other interested parties and the judges' own personal interests. The experts' negative perception of the Mongolian courts is shared by the general public. A national survey of public attitudes toward the Mongolian courts in 2007 has shown that 85 percent of the respondents believed that they would not be treated fairly in the courts, which favor the wealthy, public officials, relatives and friends of court personnel, and corporations. Similarly, 75 percent of them believed that judicial decisions are influenced by political considerations, the judges' own personal interests, and government officials (White, 2010, pp. 323–324).

However, the judges themselves have denied that court decisions are influenced by improper payments, their own personal interests, and government officials. Instead, they attribute the public perception of a corrupt judiciary to an irresponsible press and incompetent lawyers who have accused judges of accepting bribes to hide their own inadequacies as lawyers. Regardless of the real or perceived extent of corruption among judges in Mongolia, White (2010, p. 325) contends that the Mongolian courts are facing "a crisis of confidence," which constitutes a serious threat to the goal of "developing a judiciary that the public trusts to render fair, just, and consistent decisions."

Of the 456 criminal investigations of abuse of authority by judges and police during 2000–2001, only 250 cases were taken to court because the other 206 cases were dismissed. During the same period, disciplinary cases were filed against 37 judges, and 9 of them had their salaries reduced, 20 judges received formal warnings, and 8 judges were dismissed (La Mont, 2002, p. 1, n. 3). However, the number of cases heard by the judicial disciplinary committee has decreased from 25 in 2003 to 21 in 2004, 19 in 2005, and 6 until May 2006 (TI Mongolia, 2007, p. 230).

The existence of a vague and weak judicial code of ethics also contributes to corruption among the judges because it "only vaguely prohibits judges from deciding cases in which they have an interest." Consequently, many judges preside over cases where "there is an appearance of impropriety" because of their family, business, or other relationships. Furthermore, judges who accept bribes are seldom held accountable as most of the complaints against them are usually "dismissed without action or explanation" (White, 2010, p. 326).

As judges are widely perceived to be corrupt, it is not surprising that they are ranked in public opinion surveys after customs officials as the second most corrupt officials in Mongolia. Accordingly, White (2010, p. 327) cautions that if corruption within the Mongolian judiciary is not addressed, the provision of "refurbished courtrooms and buildings, a modern legal training center, automated computer systems and nice new furniture (with USAID stickers) risks doing little more than legitimizing a corrupt regime."

## AIM OF THE CHAPTER

Mongolia became the first communist state in Asia in July 1921 (Haggard, 1965) and was dependent on the former Soviet Union for foreign aid, technical assistance, and a large market for her exports for 70 years until the departure of the Soviet advisers in 1991. Corruption existed in Mongolia during its seven decades under communist rule. However, the transition from a Soviet style command economy to a market economy in Mongolia since 1991 has increased the opportunities for corruption and made the environment conducive for corruption for the following three reasons: the poverty of the population, the low salaries of public officials, and the nonenforcement of the anticorruption laws.

How serious is the problem of corruption in Mongolia today? What measures have been employed by the Mongolian government to combat corruption? How effective are its anticorruption measures? What problems have been encountered in fighting corruption and what are the prospects of minimizing corruption in Mongolia? Before addressing these questions, it is necessary to provide a brief description of Mongolia's policy context to understand the problem of corruption.

## MONGOLIA'S POLICY CONTEXT

### *Geography*

Mongolia is the 5th largest country in Asia and the 19th largest in the world with a total area of 1,565,000 sq km (*Economist*, 2010a, p. 12). It is also landlocked by Russia to the north and the People's Republic of China (PRC) to the south, east, and west. Indeed, there is a Mongolian saying that "Mongolia exists because Russia and China exist" (Boone, Tarvaa, Tsend,

Tsendjav, & Unenburen, 1997, p. 106). Edward Cody (2006, p. A27) has accurately described how Mongolians view their neighbors thus:

> When Mongolians look north, they see the Russian colossus that controlled them for most of the 20th century. When they look south, they see 1.3 billion Chinese, hereditary adversaries whose booming growth and insatiable appetite for raw materials touch almost everything that happens in the Mongolian economy.

In fact, Mongolia is the largest land-locked state in Africa and Asia (McLachlan, 1998, p. 2). With a small population of 2.7 million persons dispersed over a vast area, Mongolia is sparsely populated with a population density in 2008 of only 1.7 persons per sq km (*Economist*, 2010a, p. 252).

Mongolia is divided into the following three zones: the mountains in the north and west; the intermountain basins; and the steppe, which includes the Gobi Desert, constitutes three-quarters of the land. It has a high altitude, with an average elevation of 1,580 meters above sea level. Mongolia has also an extreme climate as there is no sea to moderate its semiarid continental climate, which has been exacerbated by its high altitude. Indeed, its harsh winters (from October to March) and its vulnerability to earthquakes "add substantial costs to the development of socioeconomic structure" (Milne, Leimone, Rozwadowski, & Sukachevin, 1991, p. 2). Mongolia's harsh climate and remoteness from sea transport and markets constitute a serious constraint to economic growth. Indeed, Mongolia faces many obstacles to international trade and growth as there is only one railway traversing the country from north to south, without access to ports, deteriorating road conditions, and payment of heavy transit fees through Russia and China (Brun & Odgaard, 1996, p. 24). Mongolia's poorly developed infrastructure is reflected in the fact that it has only 1,748 km of railways and 47,600 km of roads even though it measures 2,368 km east to west and 1,260 km north to south. Its telecommunications system is also congested and outdated (Kim, 1996, p. 297). The lack of all-weather roads and useful waterways means that 90 percent of the national freight is carried by the railway system (McLachlan, 1998, p. 8).

Mongolia's geographical context has made the task of fighting corruption much harder for two reasons. First, as Mongolia is divided into 21 provinces and the municipality of Ulaanbataar, its large size is not advantageous for policy formulation and implementation as there are problems of communication and enforcing the anticorruption measures, especially in the more remote provinces. Second, Mongolia's proximity to the PRC and Russia, where corruption in rampant, constitutes an obstacle to its government's anticorruption drive as these countries were role models during the nearly seven decades of communist rule and the two centuries of Chinese rule. In

***Box 11.1.*** Mongolia's Policy Context

| | |
|---|---|
| Land area | 1,565,000 sq km |
| Arable land | 1.0% |
| GDP | US$ 4.2 billion (2009) |
| GDP per capita | US$1,551 (2009) |
| Unemployment rate | 2.8% (2008) |
| Population | 2.7 million (2008) |
| Population density | 1.7 persons per sq km |
| Urban population | 57% |
| Adult literacy rate | 97.8% |
| Political system | Presidential democracy |
| Colonial rule | China (1691–1911)<br>Soviet Union (1921–1991) |
| 2010 CPI rank and score | 116/178 and 2.7/10 |

*Sources*: *Economist* (2010a, p. 252); CIA (2011b); United States Department of State (2010); and http://www.transparency.org/policy_research/surveys_indices/cpi/2010/results

other words, Mongolia is located in a "bad neighborhood" as far as fighting corruption is concerned.

## *History*

Mongolia was a province of China for 220 years under the Ching dynasty from 1691 to 1911 (Sanders, 1998, p. 134). It asserted its autonomy from 1911 to 1919, when a Chinese army occupied the capital, Urga (known today as Ulaanbaatar). In January 1920, two groups of revolutionaries united to form the Mongolian People's Party (MPP), which was later renamed the Mongolian People's Revolutionary Party (MPRP) in 1922. In February 1921, Mongolia was occupied by an army led by a White Russian, the Baron von Ungern-Sternberg, who provided the Bolsheviks with an excuse to invade and "liberate" it. The Bolsheviks had assisted some Mongols to organize the MPP, a provisional government in exile, and an army. The small Mongolian army and the provisional government appealed to the Soviets for military assistance to liberate their country. The Soviet forces defeated Ungern and a new government was formed in July 1921 (Hammond, 1975a, p. 9).

The many Soviet advisers who were placed in important government departments and the MPP became the real rulers of the country from 1921, and they gradually changed Mongolia into "a capsular imitation of the Soviet Union" (Hammond, 1975a, pp. 9–10). For example, the MPRP was organized in the manner of its Soviet counterpart, and the supreme organ of government was the Great Khuraldan (now known as the State Great Hural), which resembled the Congress of Soviets, and the Small Khuraldan, which was similar to the Central Executive Committee in the U.S.S.R. According to Hammond (1975b, p. 139), "the chief objective of Soviet economic policy in Mongolia was not the establishment of a socialist system, but rather the exploitation of Mongolia for the benefit of Russia." Indeed, this policy of exploitation was implemented through the control of Mongolian foreign trade. Consequently, Mongolia's exports to the U.S.S.R. rose from 24.1 percent to 99.2 percent during 1925–1931.

### *Economy*

As large-scale agriculture is not possible in Mongolia because of its harsh climate and high altitude, its economy is "based primarily upon herding and secondarily upon hunting, both of which were supplemented by trade and raiding." However, the herding economy did not expand because of internecine warfare, the payment of tribute to the Manchu rulers in Peking, and the conversion of the population to Lamaist Buddhism and the consequent growth of the monasteries. In addition to the climate and geography, which do not make the Mongolian steppe suitable for agriculture, "Mongolian nomads have been psychologically conditioned for centuries to feel that toiling in the soil is not a proper way for humans to make a living." Consequently, they prefer "to work on horseback and look after one's animals than to dig in the dirt" (Jachid & Hyer, 1979, pp. 297–299, 310).

Manufacturing and industry developed very late in Mongolia because of "the non-development of urban life, the far-flung migrations of the Mongolian people, and the recruitment of all able-bodied males for military service" and the "high incidence of warlike activity in Mongol history." Moreover, during the Ching dynasty, the free flow of Chinese goods into the steppe areas and the settling of Chinese artisans in the monasteries hindered the growth of an indigenous class of Mongol artisans. Indeed, manufacturing activity and artisans were only developed in Mongolia in the 1930s and 1940s as a result of the efforts of its nationalist leaders (Jachid & Hyer, 1979, pp. 316–317).

With its extensive pasture land and limited arable land, animal husbandry is important in Mongolia as "livestock production using pastoral grazing management strategies has dominated Mongolian agriculture for centuries" (Sheehy, 1996, p. 42). Mongolia is a poor country with a weak industrial base and animal husbandry as the major source of livelihood for its nomadic population. Although its livestock population has increased from 23.6 million to 28 million during 1930–2004 (Sheehy, 1996, p. 46; World Bank, 2006a, p. 4), Mongolia has imported wheat, butter, and other dairy products from other countries to feed its livestock and population even though the agricultural sector has grown during the past 30 years.

Mongolia is rich in mineral resources as "600 mineral deposits bearing over 80 minerals have been discovered including coal, iron, tin, copper, molybdenum, gold, silver, tungsten, zinc, lead, phosphates, wolfram, fluorspar, uranium, oil shale, and semiprecious stones (agate, lapis, lazuli, garnet)." The country also has over 170 deposits of construction materials such as marble and granite. Copper is the major mineral as 400,000 tons are produced annually at the copper plant in Erdenet (ADB, 1992, p. 176). Martha Brill Olcott's (2002, p. 10) description of Kazakhstan as being "blessed with resources but cursed by geography" also applies to Mongolia.

Mongolia's economic history can be divided into five periods: the feudal period; the postrevolutionary period (1921–1948); the development of the command economy (1948–1984); the period of Mongolian *Perestroika* (1984–1989) (Kaser, 1992, pp. 167–171); and the transition to a market economy (1991–1998). What is important for our analysis is the fact that Mongolia was under communist rule and Soviet influence for seven decades, from July 1921 until January 1991, when the Soviet advisers left the country (Brun & Odgaard, 1996, p. 23). In fact, Mongolia was the second longest communist-ruled country after the former Soviet Union (Boone et al., 1997, p. 103). This meant the development of a command economy, based on central planning and the Soviet system of economic management, in Mongolia from 1948 until 1984. In 1946, Mongolia signed a Friendship and Mutual Assistance Treaty with the Soviet Union, and it joined the Council for Mutual Economic Assistance (CMEA), the Soviet trade bloc, in 1962.

The former Soviet Union provided Mongolia with foreign aid, technical assistance, and "a large market for her exports, a secure supply of required imports and exceptionally favorable terms of trade." Furthermore, Mongolia's trade with the CMEA constituted 93 percent of its total trade in 1988 (Griffin, 1995, p. 1). Until 1990, the Soviet Union had provided Mongolia with US$800 million annually in grants and loans, 40 percent of its consumer goods, 80 percent of its supplies for the economy, and 90 percent of its technical equipment (Scalapino, 1992, pp. 37–38).

Economic reforms were introduced during 1984–1989 within the context of a planned economy. However, in 1991, the Mongolian economy was exposed to the following three external shocks: "an aid shock, a trade shock and a macroeconomic management shock" (Griffin, 1995, p. 3). First, the reduction of Soviet aid in 1989 and its cessation in 1991 deprived the Mongolian economy of the concessions needed for financing the investment program. Second, the collapse of the CMEA in 1991 affected Mongolia adversely because its total exports decreased from US$739.1 million to US$348 million during 1988–1991. Finally, the departure of the Soviet technical advisers in 1991 also left Mongolia with few experienced people to run the economy. The combined effect of these three shocks was devastating because "Mongolia suffered the most serious peacetime economic collapse any nation has faced during this century" (Brun & Odgaard, 1996, p. 23). Indeed, Mongolia's economic collapse "was possibly the greatest of all the (peaceful) formerly socialist countries" as "the decline in domestic absorption equalled approximately 62 percent of GNP, much more than the decline experienced in Eastern European countries or during wartime destruction" (Boone et al., 1997, p. 103). The Mongolian government responded to the economic crisis by rejecting the former Soviet style command economy and introducing reforms to transform it into a market economy (Pomfret, 1996, pp. 75–90). According to Nixson and Walters (2000, p. 217), the basic aim of the reform program was to transform the "centrally planned economy into a free market economy in the shortest possible time."

Official statistics during 1985–1990 revealed that Mongolia's per capita GDP was between US$600 and US$2,100. However, the dismantling of the command economy led to the reduction of the per capita GDP from 5,400 tugriks to 3,700 tugriks during 1989–1993. Even though Mongolia's per capita GDP rose from US$224 in 1993 to US$260 in 1994 (Odgaard, 1996, pp. 105–107), its status as a poor country is confirmed by two surveys on poverty, which found that poverty had increased from 14.5 percent to 19.2 percent of the population during 1991–1996, and 36 percent of the population was estimated by the World Bank to be poor in 1995 (UNDP, 1997). However, more recently, the World Bank found that the incidence of poverty in Mongolia had declined from 43 percent in 1998 to 36 percent in 2002 (World Bank, 2006a, p. 12).

During 1990 to 1993, the economy "contracted by over 20 percent of GDP, and annual inflation rate peaked at 325.5 percent in 1992," and unemployment increased to 20 percent. Consequently, Mongolia's per capita GDP decreased from US$511 in 1989 to US$371 in 1993. However, with economic recovery, the per capita GDP has increased to US$457 in 2003 and US$1,551 in 2009 (World Bank, 2006a, pp. 5–6; United States

Department of State, 2010). Nevertheless, Mongolia's economic growth has not resulted in poverty reduction because 36 percent of its population was still living below the poverty line in 2004. To compound the problem of poverty, thousands of Mongolians from the countryside have migrated to the cities in search of economic opportunities (Tuya, 2005, p. 69). In 2005, the poverty level increased to 43 percent in the rural areas and the government admitted that it would not be able to attain the Millennium Development Goal of reducing poverty by half by 2015 (Tuya, 2006, p. 82).

The challenges faced by Mongolia today result from its attempt to "reform simultaneously the political and economic structure, without attendant traditions, experiences, and a necessary material base." Its economic challenges are threefold and involve balancing growth with social protection, continuing with privatization, and encouraging industry to develop technology (Noerper, 2007, pp. 75–76, 78). Verena Fritz (2007, pp. 198–200) has identified the following three major sources of potential rents in Mongolia in recent years: foreign aid, privatization, and natural resources. Mongolia has received substantial foreign aid from the World Bank and Asian Development Bank and bilateral assistance from Germany, Japan, and the United States after the departure of the Soviet advisers in 1991. The privatization of land and large enterprises in Mongolia from the early 1990s has increased the opportunities for corruption as many valuable assets have been privatized to relatives of state officials. The importance of natural resource extraction in Mongolia in recent years is reflected in the replacement of the Ministry of Industry and Trade by a new Ministry of Minerals and Energy in 2008 (Bulag, 2009, p. 132). The increasing importance of Mongolia as a location for exploration by international mining companies has increased the opportunities for corruption in the allocation of exploration licenses with the emergence of a "gray" market for trading licenses among these companies (Fritz, 2007, p. 199).

The transition of the Mongolian economy from a centrally planned one to a market economy has three important implications for curbing corruption in the country. First, as the former Soviet Union had exerted tremendous influence on Mongolia for 70 years, it is not surprising that the Soviet forms of corruption were also prevalent in Mongolia during the socialist period. Second, the experiences of other transitional economies have shown that the transition from a command economy to a market economy has also increased the opportunities for corruption. Finally, the Mongolian government's efforts to curb corruption are handicapped by its inability to increase the low salaries of its civil servants because of the country's low GDP per capita.

### *Demography*

Mongolia's small population of 2.7 million people consists of 94.9 percent Khalkha Mongol, 5 percent Turkic (mostly Kazakh), and 0.1 percent other groups (including Chinese and Russians). The population has an average life expectancy of 68 years and a high literacy rate of 97.8 percent among those over 15 years old in 2000. Mongolia's population is young as those under 14 years of age constitute 28 percent of the total population. In terms of religion, 50 percent of Mongolians are Lamaist Buddhists, 6 percent are Shamanist and Christian, 4 percent are Muslim, with the remaining 40 percent with no religion (CIA, 2011b).

What are the values of the Mongolian population which are relevant for curbing corruption in the country? First, the tradition of gift-giving exists and the taboo of returning or presenting "an empty container to a person who has brought a gift" without placing a small token in it (Jachid & Hyer, 1979, p. 159) encourages reciprocity in human relations and could possibly contribute to extensive bribery of civil servants in the form of "gifts" provided by those citizens who wish to "cut red tape" or to obtain licenses improperly. Second, the national currency, the tugrik, was established in 1925 by the communist government to pay the civil service and "to benefit the small urban proletariat" (Campi, 1996, p. 97).

In 1994, the average income for city families was 27,900 tugriks compared to 32,900 tugriks for rural families. However, according to Campi (1996, pp. 97–98), money was unimportant for the Mongols for two reasons: the limited functions of currency in a nomadic economy; and the low salaries and limited salary range of workers during the communist era as "the most highly rewarded Mongols received only three times the pay of the least skilled workers." Today, the salaries of civil servants are among the lowest in Asia and constitute an important factor contributing to corruption in Mongolia.

### *Political System*

In 1989, two years after the advent of *perestroika* in the Soviet Union, the Mongolian Democratic Union (MDU) was formed in Ulaanbaatar with the aim of overthrowing the MPRP. However, the MPRP responded to the wave of demonstrations in the capital by launching extensive political reforms. President Batmonh was replaced by Ochirbat, the Central Committee was reorganized, and the government indicated that the

Constitution would be amended. The reformed MPRP called for immediate elections to give the urban-based opposition minimal time for organization.

The first democratic election was held in July 1990, and the MPRP won 62 percent of the votes and obtained a secure majority of deputies in the new bicameral legislature. In 1991, the MPRP passed a law banning political parties from operating in government organs and required all government officials to drop their party affiliation, thus eroding the relevance of communism. A constitutional drafting committee was formed and the new constitution was passed in1992 (Brun & Odgaard, 1996, pp. 28–29).

During the second election in July 1992, the MPRP won 71 of the 76 parliamentary seats and secured 56 percent of the popular vote. The MPRP was the only party that was able to field candidates for every seat, and it succeeded in promoting "itself as a reformed party aiming at a more gradual-and socially acceptable-transition towards a market economy." In contrast, the Democratic Coalition was divided and lost its credibility when a banking scandal was revealed implicating central bankers (associated with the opposition), who had squandered the country's entire gold reserves through currency speculation. In October 1992, the four major opposition parties united to form the National Democratic Party (NDP). The Social Democratic Party (SDP) was the second major opposition party and in January 1993, the NDP and the SDP agreed to field a single candidate in the presidential election. The MPRP nominated L. Tudev, the editor of the party newspaper, as its presidential candidate and rejected Ochirbat, who accepted the opposition's offer to be their candidate. The opposition won in 14 of the 18 provinces in the June 1993 first presidential election, which resulted in "a new era of divided government between parliament and presidency" (Brun & Odgaard, 1996, pp. 29–31).

The opposition won a landslide victory in the June 1996 parliamentary election as the Democratic Union coalition captured 50 of the 76 seats in the Hural. The NDP won 34 seats, whereas the MPRP won 25 seats (Brun & Odgaard, 1996, p. 32). The opposition's victory signaled not only the end of more than 70 years of the MPRP's dominance but also the establishment of a democratic government in Mongolia. However, the May 1997 second presidential election resulted in the election of the MPRP's candidate, Natsagin Bagabandi, as president. There was a split between the communist-led presidency and the democratic, pro-reform legislature, which was dominated by the ruling Democratic Coalition (EIU, 1997b, p. 47). Indeed, in mid-October 1998, President Bagabandi rejected Davaadoriin Ganbold, the Democratic Coalition's candidate for prime minister, for the seventh time (Kohn, 1998, p. 1). However, the Democratic

Coalition was ineffective because of political infighting, a corruption scandal, and the MPRP's efforts to obstruct its reform agenda. Consequently, it was not surprising that the MPRP won 72 of the 76 seats in the 2000 parliamentary election and took over power from the Democratic Coalition.

The MPRP consolidated its political power and showed its commitment to keep the market economic reforms on track in 2001. Accordingly, it was not surprising that incumbent President N. Bagabandi won the May 20 presidential election with 58 percent of the vote. Bagabandi's victory not only "enhanced the MPRP's political dominance" but also demonstrated "the democrats' difficulties in rebuilding public confidence after their four tumultuous years in power" (Finch, 2002, p. 39–40). However, the June 2004 parliamentary election did not result in victory for either the MPRP or the Homeland-Democracy Coalition because each party won 36 seats in the 76-seat parliament. Consequently, both parties agreed to form a "grand coalition" to govern the country (Tuya, 2005, pp. 67–68). The MPRP won 46 seats in the June 2008 parliamentary election, but the DP leader, Tsakhiagiin Elbegdorj, "refused to concede defeat, protesting that the elections were rigged." On 1 July 2008, five persons were killed and hundreds of civilians and police were injured and hospitalized in riots in Ulaanbaatar in the wake of the election. After a stalemate of almost two months, a MPRP-DP coalition government assumed office in mid-September (Bulag, 2009, pp. 129–131).

The transformation of Mongolia's political system from seven decades of communism under the control of the MPRP to a new democracy that has adopted a market economy poses two important challenges for the incumbent government in terms of combating corruption. First, like the former Soviet Union, Mongolia has been afflicted by corruption during its 70 years of communist rule. Second, and more importantly, the task of fighting corruption has been made more difficult as the Mongolian government has to deal with both the legacy of corruption and the many opportunities for corruption arising from the democratization process and the transition to a market economy.

## PERCEIVED EXTENT OF CORRUPTION

There is limited information on the perceived extent of corruption in Mongolia during its 70 years of communist rule (1921–1991). One of the earliest observations about the existence of corruption in Mongolia was made by Robert A. Rupen (1966, p. 23) 45 years ago:

> Most members of the Mongolian elite were patriotic, and they differed genuinely in their opinions as to the policies that would be best for their country. *They took bribes, however, and allowed personal concerns to influence their political opinions. In this respect the Church [Buddhist monasteries] also was generally corrupt.* (emphasis added)

However, Rupen did not provide any empirical evidence for his generalization about the practice of bribery among the Mongolian elite and the Buddhist monks.

In her study of communist societies, Maria Hirszowicz (1986, pp. 127–128) found that "under Stalinist rule, the Communist bureaucracies enjoyed many privileges, ranging from better food in their canteens, higher salaries, and special shops, to better flats, chauffeur-driven cars and luxurious holidays in the best health resorts." Although corruption among party and state officials was quite common under Stalinist regimes, "there were many disincentives which prevented malpractices from spreading." First, there was "a general feeling of insecurity and fear" among these officials and "constant purges, trials, and witch-hunts" made them cautious. Second, these officials had to work long hours and observe the official "disapproval of 'petty bourgeois' desires for material luxuries." Third, "the range of goods available in the post-war decades was rather limited." Furthermore, overseas trips were restricted to "a narrow circle of functionaries who usually did their best to show their contempt for the decadent West." Fourth, as accommodation and some "consumer durables" could be used but not owned, "flats were nationalized, private cars were rare, chauffeur-driven limousines belonged to state enterprises and offices, and land could not be acquired by private individuals." Fifth, as "officials were subject to tight control by security and party organs both in their official and private lives," they could not spend their money "without attracting the attention of the security apparatus" and "party comrades were alert for any sign of improper conduct in their friends and even in members of their families."

The quality of life of party and state officials was not based on their ownership of material assets but on the various perks associated with their positions. In her study of *blat*, networking and informal exchange in Russia, Alena V. Ledeneva (1998, p. 127) observed that cadres were "the most adept *blat* practitioners" as they "had at their disposal decision-making and resource-allocation powers" which "made them frequent recipients of *blat* overtures." Thus, "the system protected itself against the excessive greed of state functionaries" by providing them with the privileges gained from their official positions and not "with the individual ownership of valuable material assets" (Hirszowicz, 1986, p. 128). As Mongolia was a communist state under the Soviet Union's influence for seven decades, it also exhibited the same pattern of "restrained" corruption during this period.

In 1981, General Secretary Tsedenbal had called for "a clampdown on corruption and promised to root out 'weeds of all kinds' from the party" at the 18th MPRP Congress. In January 1982, Professor B. Shirendev, who was president of the Mongolian Academy of Sciences for 22 years, a member of the MPRP's Central Committee, and a deputy chairperson of Parliament, was accused by the MPRP's Central Committee of embezzling "hundreds of thousands" of dollars, which were used for hosting lavish parties and acquiring luxury items for his personal use (Holmes, 1993, pp. 114–115).

O. Adiya (1998, p. 3) has observed that corruption was "not an entirely new phenomenon in Mongolian society" because "it existed under the previous regime, in which a few people made decisions and everyone else was held accountable for those decisions." However, "the level of corrupted officials in the former Politburo had far less magnitude and scale than today's wide-ranging, all-encompassing abuses of power. *Today, corruption is everywhere*" (emphasis added). However, what is more important is the public perception by Mongolians that they had to bribe officials to get things done. This view was clearly expressed by Adiya (1998, p. 3) thus:

> The most unfortunate thing with regard to corruption [in Mongolia] is how commonly it is accepted as necessary to ensure the smooth running of one's affairs. We take for granted the giving of a bottle of vodka to a teacher, small presents to a doctor or nurse, incentives to traffic police, hospitality to a tax officer, "sharing" your goods with a customs inspector, bribing an official to get a business license, whether for gold mining or vodka-making. *It is just all around you.* It has to be. "Well, let me see. Who's next on my target list for bribing?". (emphasis added)

In similar vein, B. Batchuluun (2004), a Mongolian doctor, has provided several examples to illustrate his argument that Mongolians usually encounter some form of corruption in their daily lives:

> The bus conductor will charge you the bus fare, but not her or his acquaintance. Go to shop, and you will get the bad, while the shop assistant's acquaintance will get the best. Provided, you supply your kid's teacher with sweets and chocolates, your child is assured of good marks. Your child graduates from the tenth grade and it's time for her or him to go for university admission examinations, and there you'll see the classical form of corruption. Get hospitalized, you will have to give the best to the doctors and nurses to get the appropriate treatment and medicines. Go to the higher official and you have to bribe the secretary with souvenirs or perfume to ensure the access to that person. These are the everyday, in a way, accepted forms of corruption. The higher the official you have to meet, the graver the issue you are dealing with, the bigger and more hidden the bribe.

In April 1994, a group that included some opposition Members of Parliament (MPs) launched a hunger strike in front of the government buildings in Ulaanbaatar to protest against corruption, which "was rife among the parliament and government" (Brun & Odgaard, 1996, p. 31). Four months later, the press published the results of an opinion poll of 830 persons conducted in 8 provinces and 2 cities by the Academy of Sciences and the Konrad Adenauer Foundation of Germany (EIU, 1994, p. 37). The findings showed that the Mongolian respondents were very concerned about bribery and corruption at all levels of administration.[2]

First, 68 percent of the respondents strongly agreed with the "strong social perception that without giving incentives to officials one's matter cannot be processed." Second, regarding the forms of corruption, 75.5 percent of the respondents gave cash, 55.2 percent gave gifts, and 43 percent participated in mutual exchange of services and assistance. Third, 46.6 percent of the respondents felt that all those who try to process matters would offer bribes to public officials, and 38.6 percent of them identified businessmen, entrepreneurs, and vendors as bribe-givers. Fourth, the most corrupt agencies in Mongolia according to the respondents were the customs office (55.7 percent); the banking and financial sector (51.2 percent); the police and prosecutors (46.5 percent); the immigration office responsible for foreign and national passports (28.05 percent); the taxation office (15.3 percent); and local government (13.4 percent). Fifth, 54 percent of the respondents viewed the middle-level officials as the most corrupt; 25.5 percent believed that the senior government officials were the most corrupt; and 18.3 percent said that the junior officials were the most corrupt. Sixth, Table 11.1 notes that the banking sector and the customs office were the most corrupt sectors in Ulaanbaatar, the provinces, and the counties. Seventh, 44 percent of the respondents from Ulaanbaatar, 44 percent of the respondents from the provinces, and 38.4 percent of the respondents from the counties strongly agreed with the view that corruption was everywhere. Finally, 47.2 percent of the respondents felt that the government did not

***Table 11.1.*** Most Corrupt Sectors in Mongolia by Location in 1994.

| Corrupt Sector | Ulaanbaatar | Provinces | Counties |
|---|---|---|---|
| 1st | Banking sector | Customs office | Customs office |
| 2nd | Customs office | Banking sector | Courts |
| 3rd | Immigration office | Immigration office | Banking sector |

*Source*: Erdenebileg (1994, p. 2).

take any action to fight corruption, and 37.1 percent believed that the anticorruption measures taken were ineffective (Erdenebileg, 1994).

In October 1996, an inspection of a military unit at Nalaikh at the request of the Minister of Defense, Dambiin Dorligjav, revealed a corruption scandal involving senior military officers who sold 8 million tugriks (US$17,500) worth of military hardware for less than its real value and without permission to China through a third party. Among those implicated were the former Minister of Defense, Lieutenant General Shagalyn Jadambaa, who had died recently, and the former chief-of-staff, R. Davaa (EIU, 1996, p. 47). After conducting its investigations, the Ministry of Defense sacked three generals for misappropriating 87 million tugriks (US$124,000) of assets belonging to military unit 137 (EIU, 1997a, p. 49).

During the same month, another corruption scandal involving the transfer of funds from the Erdenet ore-dressing plant to private business and abroad was uncovered by the State Property Committee, which "revealed corruption, misconduct, neglect of duty and mismanagement of funds by the hierarchy of the State-owned Erdenet Ore Dressing Plant" (*Mongol Messenger*, 1996, p. 1). The plant's commercial director, Sh. Otgonbileg, was accused of misappropriating more than US$23 million and transferring this amount from the joint venture to the privately owned Erdenet Concern. In late October, the police charged the director, Ch. Zorig, with cheating the state of US$4.6 million because he paid this sum to the Russian Neman company of Novosibirsk in advance for petroleum products that were not delivered (EIU, 1996, p. 51). The State Property Committee closed Erdenet Concern at the end of November 1996 after an audit of its finances revealed that it had violated the privatization law by using its status as a state-owned enterprise to obtain foreign loans. However, President Ochirbat allowed the director, Sh. Otgonbileg, to remain in his position even though the public had called for his dismissal (EIU, 1997a, p. 56). Otgonbileg's term of office ended on 1 January 1998, but he was allowed to remain as an interim director. He disappeared on 7 August 1998, when he was supposed to hand over his duties to the new director (Indra, 1998).

In his review of Mongolian society, Tom Ginsburg (1998, p. 67) observed that "there is also a perception that government corruption is rising as well" Indeed, the director of the General Customs Board, D. Tsend, who was appointed in July 1996, said in early 1997 that the customs service was "riddled with bribery and corruption and suitable candidates for over 100 vacancies were hard to find. Out of 300 recent applicants only ten were deemed suitable" (EIU, 1997a, p. 59). The morale in the education sector was low in recent years, and there were several strikes for better wages and conditions. More importantly, this sector was also not free of corruption as it was reported that "some head teachers and others have been forging secondary-level examination certificates for considerable sums of money" (EIU, 1997c, p. 41). Finally, a civil service audit during the first half of 1998 found that 1.14 billion tugriks were misappropriated by officials by mismanaging foreign aid in some cases and only 248 million tugriks were returned to the Treasury (EIU, 1998b, p. 43).

Transparency International's Global Corruption Barometer has identified the judiciary as the most corrupt sector in Mongolia in 2009, followed by political parties and parliament. However, as noted in Table 11.2, the most corrupt sectors in 2010 were political parties and parliament, followed by the judiciary, and the police. It should be noted here that in the 10 corruption benchmarking surveys conducted by the Asia Foundation and the Sant Maral Foundation from March 2006 to September 2010, the five most corrupt sectors were the land authority, mining sector, judiciary, customs, and political parties (Asia Foundation, 2010, pp. 7–8).

Another important finding of the 10 corruption benchmarking surveys is that the actual incidence of corruption has declined during 2006–2010. In March 2006, 26 percent of the 1,030 respondents indicated that they or someone else in their household had paid a bribe in the past three months. Although this percentage increased to 28 percent in the September 2006 survey, the proportion of respondents paying bribes has gradually decreased to 13 percent in the September 2010 survey. However, Table 11.3 notes that

***Table 11.2.*** Perceived Level of Corruption in Mongolia by Sector, 2009–2010.

| Sector | 2009 | 2010 |
|---|---|---|
| Political parties | 3.9 | 4.2 |
| Parliament/legislature | 3.9 | 4.2 |
| Judiciary | 4.1 | 4.1 |
| Police | NA | 4.0 |
| Public officials/civil servants | 3.6 | 3.6 |
| Business/private sector | 3.3 | 3.0 |
| Media | 3.0 | 2.9 |
| NGOs | NA | 2.5 |
| Religious bodies | NA | 2.1 |
| Military | NA | 2.9 |
| Education system | NA | 3.7 |

*Source:* Transparency International (2009, p. 29, 2010, p. 44).

***Table 11.3.*** Amount Spent by Mongolian Households on Bribes, 2006–2010.

| Item | March 2006 | September 2006 | March 2007 | September 2007 | March 2008 | September 2008 | March 2009 | September 2009 | March 2010 | September 2010 |
|---|---|---|---|---|---|---|---|---|---|---|
| Average bribe (in 1,000 MNT) | 181 | 136 | 102 | 187 | 180 | 298 | 397 | 308 | 195 | 416 |
| Households giving bribes (%) | 26 | 28 | 23 | 22 | 19 | 21 | 15 | 20 | 16 | 13 |
| Total amount paid (in billion MNT) in 3 months | 28.8 | 23.3 | 14.8 | 26 | 23.2 | 42.4 | 40.3 | 41.7 | 21.2 | 38.8 |

*Source*: Asia Foundation (2010, p. 19).

***Table 11.4.*** Impact of Bribes Paid on Family Budgets in Mongolia, 2008–2010.

| Date | Percentage of Households Whose Family Budget was "Seriously" Damaged by Payment of Bribes (%) |
|---|---|
| March 2008 | 16.5 |
| September 2008 | 24.8 |
| March 2009 | 42.5 |
| September 2009 | 29.4 |
| March 2010 | 28.5 |
| September 2010 | 33.6 |

*Source*: Asia Foundation (2010, p. 20).

the amount of the average bribe paid by a household has increased from 181,000 tugriks in March 2006 to 416,000 tugriks in September 2010. Similarly, the total amount spent by households on bribes in three months grew from 28.8 billion tugriks to 38.8 billion tugriks during the same period. Needless to say, as noted in Table 11.4, the percentage of those households whose family budgets were "seriously" damaged increased from 16.5 percent in March 2008 to a peak of 42.5 percent in March 2009, before declining to 33.6 percent in September 2010 (Asia Foundation, 2010, pp. 18–20).

***Table 11.5.*** Bribe Recipients in Mongolia, 2006–2010.

| Category | March 2006 (%) | September 2006 (%) | March 2007 (%) | September 2007 (%) | March 2008 (%) | September 2008 (%) | March 2009 (%) | September 2009 (%) | March 2010 (%) | September 2010 (%) |
|---|---|---|---|---|---|---|---|---|---|---|
| Doctor | 38.4 | 37.6 | 32.1 | 32.5 | 35.1 | 29.3 | 42.8 | 42.7 | 41.4 | 34.6 |
| Teacher | 29.1 | 39.3 | 22.1 | 36.6 | 21.1 | 34.1 | 17.1 | 23.1 | 23.6 | 31.5 |
| Clerk | 35.3 | 34.1 | 39.7 | 33.3 | 39.5 | 35.0 | 29.6 | 29.9 | 24.8 | 27.7 |
| Police | 21.7 | 22.7 | 25.2 | 13.8 | 18.4 | 13.8 | 17.8 | 20.5 | 22.9 | 20.8 |
| Customs | 10.9 | 9.6 | 10.7 | 6.5 | 8.8 | 8.1 | 5.9 | 10.3 | 5.1 | 6.2 |
| Lawyer | 4.3 | 3.1 | 3.8 | 3.3 | 2.6 | 1.6 | 2.0 | 3.4 | 5.1 | 5.4 |
| Prosecutor | 3.1 | 1.7 | 0.8 | 1.6 | 4.4 | 1.6 | 2.0 | 0.9 | 3.2 | 3.1 |
| Judge | 5.8 | 7.0 | 3.1 | 3.3 | 5.3 | 3.3 | 3.3 | 6.8 | 4.5 | 2.3 |
| Tax officer | 9.3 | 8.3 | 6.1 | 0.8 | 6.1 | 6.5 | 8.6 | 6.0 | 1.9 | 2.3 |
| Other | 3.9 | 7.0 | 6.9 | 3.3 | 2.6 | 4.1 | 6.6 | 5.1 | 1.9 | 1.5 |
| Press | 1.2 | 0.9 | 0.0 | 1.6 | 0.9 | 0.0 | 0.7 | 1.7 | 0.6 | 0.8 |

*Source*: Asia Foundation (2010, p. 21).

Furthermore, the respondents who paid bribes during the previous three months also identified doctors, teachers, clerks, and policemen as the most frequent bribe recipients. Table 11.5 notes that, apart from these four groups, the other bribe recipients were, in descending order of importance, customs officials, lawyers, prosecutors, judges, tax officers, others, and the press.

In sum, the various surveys mentioned earlier confirm that corruption is a serious problem in Mongolia affecting various sectors with the most vulnerable sectors being the land authority, mining sector, judiciary, customs, and political parties. However, doctors, teachers, clerks, and policemen were identified as the most frequent bribe recipients by those households that had paid bribes during the past three months from March 2006 to September 2010.

## CAUSES OF CORRUPTION

### *Low Salaries*

An important cause of corruption in Mongolia is the extremely low salaries of its civil servants and politicians. In the 2002 national survey conducted by the Mongolian Chamber of Commerce and Industry, 74.5 percent of the 1,386 respondents identified low salaries as the most important cause of corruption in Mongolia (ADB, 2004, p. 52). In 1998, the highest monthly salary of top officers of the Presidency, Parliament, Supreme Court, General Prosecutor, and Constitutional Court was 60,113 tugriks (US$71), whereas the monthly salary for the lowest position was 29,297 tugriks (US$35). Similarly, the monthly salaries of government administrative employees in Mongolia varied from 23,377 tugriks (US$28) for the lowest position to 57,836 tugriks (US$68) for the highest position. Finally, the monthly salaries of the Mongolian government special service employees were also low, ranging from 21,556 tugriks (US$25) to 57,836 tugriks (US$68).[3]

The low salaries in the Mongolian civil service relative to the wages in the private sector constitute an important source of corruption because when civil servants are poorly paid, they are tempted to accept bribes to make ends meet. Given their low salaries, it is not surprising that teachers had gone on strike for higher wages. For example, on 17 April 1995, teachers went on strike to demand a threefold increase in their salaries. During 1993–1995, 2,000 teachers resigned in Ulaanbaatar. As the average teacher's monthly salary was 12,000–14,000 tugriks (US$28 to US$32), this amount was inadequate to support a family. By June 1995, the number of teachers on strike increased to 6,000 because the strikers in Ulaanbataar were joined by other teachers from five provinces (EIU, 1995a, p. 45).

The State Statistical Board reported that data on family incomes for August 1995 showed that some families were spending more than they earned, especially those living in the aimag centers, as their average monthly expenditure per family of 40,117.3 tugriks exceeded their average cash income per family of 39,705.6 tugriks. Furthermore, data for September 1995 revealed that the average family in Ulaanbaatar obtained 38 percent of their monthly cash income from salaries. The percentage increased to 49 percent for families living in the aimag centers and declined to 9 percent for rural families (EIU, 1995b, p. 45).

On 28 February 1997, nearly half of Mongolia's 32,000 doctors and nurses went on strike to demand higher wages. In April 1997, the teachers complained that they could not survive on their monthly salary of 26,000 tugriks (US$33) because of inflation. Public sector salaries were raised on 1 May 1997, but the teachers were dissatisfied because not everyone was eligible for the pay increase (EIU, 1997b, p. 51). When the government did not pay the increases in public sector pay and pensions promised on 1 April 1998, there were demonstrations outside the parliament. On 15 April, the government agreed to pay a 10 percent increase in salaries and raised the minimum monthly pension from 9,200 tugriks (US$11) to 12,000 tugriks (US$14). Arising from this, the government had to raise an additional seven billion tugriks to cover the increase in wages and pensions (EIU, 1998a, pp. 47–48).

However, those teachers and health service staff who were not paid for two or three months in 1998 were dissatisfied. Consequently, between 10,000 and 20,000 people participated in a demonstration in Ulaanbaatar on 2 November 1998. The Mongolian Association of Trades Unions issued an ultimatum to the government and demanded the implementation of a 20,000 tugriks (US$23) minimum monthly wage, a 10 percent increase on pensions and salaries, and payment of overdue salaries and benefits (EIU, 1998c, pp. 47–48).

In 2001, the basic salary scale for parliamentary or working group officials consisted of 11 ranks with the base monthly salary ranging from 42,784 tugriks (US$38.89) to 85,155 tugriks (US$77.13). In 2002, the basic monthly salary for a minister was 100,000 tugriks (US$84). The monthly salary of Chief Justice of the Supreme Court was 165,553 tugriks (US$139), which consisted of a basic salary of 98,544 tugriks (US$83) and a 70 percent supplementary allowance. The prime minister and president received between 170,000 tugriks (US$142) and 200,000 tugriks (US$168) per month including salary supplements. The salaries for the administrative service were slightly lower than those of the parliamentary service and ranged over 13 ranks from 35,144 tugriks (US$29) to 82,025 tugriks (US$69) per month (ADB, 2004, p. 46).

Table 11.6 notes that the monthly salaries of such high-ranking state officials as the President, Prime Minister, Supreme Court judges, MPs, Ministers, Prosecutor General, and IAAC's Commissioner General (CG) have increased from April 2004 to October 2010. For example, the President's monthly salary has risen by more than four times from US$214 in April 2004 to US$937 in January 2008. Although his monthly salary has remained at 1,095,720 tugriks in October 2010, its value has declined to US$761 because of the reduction in the exchange rate of the US dollar. Similarly, the monthly salary of the Prime Minister has also increased by the same proportion from US$162 to US$745 for the same period. It should be noted that the monthly salary of the IAAC's CG, who assumed office in December 2006, has also risen from US$203 in February 2007 to US$550 in October 2010.

Table 11.7 provides details of the increases in monthly salaries of judges in Mongolia from April 2004 to October 2010. For example, the monthly salary of the Chief Judge of the Capital has risen by nearly five times from US$106 to US$491 for the same period. Similarly, the monthly salary of the judges of Soum and Inter Soum of the Aimag has also increased from US$92 in April 2004 to US$421 in October 2010. Two important points should be noted here. First, in spite of the fivefold increase in monthly salaries of Mongolian judges during 2004–2010, their salaries are still very low by international standards and barely adequate for them to cope with

**Table 11.6.** Monthly Salaries in Tugriks of High-Ranking State Officials in Mongolia, 2004–2010.

| Official Position | April 2004 | June 2005 | April 2006 | February 2007 | November 2007 | January 2008 | October 2010 |
|---|---|---|---|---|---|---|---|
| President | 254,200<br>US$214 | 273,300<br>US$227 | 355,290<br>US$301 | 426,348<br>US$364 | 852,700<br>US$729 | 1,095,720<br>US$937 | 1,095,720<br>US$761 |
| Prime Minister | 191,600<br>US$162 | 206,000<br>US$171 | 267,800<br>US$227 | 321,360<br>US$275 | 642,700<br>US$549 | 825,870<br>US$706 | 1,073,630<br>US$745 |
| Chief Justice | 147,500<br>US$124 | 158,600<br>US$132 | 206,180<br>US$175 | 247,416<br>US$211 | 494,800<br>US$423 | 635,818<br>US$544 | 826,563<br>US$574 |
| MPs, Ministers, Prosecutor General, IAAC CG | 141,500<br>US$119 | 152,100<br>US$126 | 197,730<br>US$168 | 237,276<br>US$203 | 474,600<br>US$405 | 609,861<br>US$522 | 792,819<br>US$550 |
| Supreme Court Judge IAAC DCG | 131,100<br>US$111 | 140,900<br>US$117 | 183,170<br>US$155 | 219,804<br>US$188 | 439,600<br>US$376 | 564,886<br>US$483 | 734,352<br>US$510 |
| Deputy Ministers | 125,000<br>US$105 | 134,400<br>US$112 | 174,720<br>US$148 | 209,664<br>US$179 | 419,300<br>US$358 | 538,801<br>US$461 | 700,441<br>US$486 |
| Average exchange rate for US$ | 1,185.19 | 1,205.27 | 1,179.55 | 1,170.43 | 1,170.43 | 1,169.26 | 1,440.76 |

*Source:* Data provided by courtesy of Mr Batzorig Badam, Head of the Research and Analysis Division of IAAC, in e-mail correspondence on 17 February 2011.

***Table 11.7.*** Monthly Salaries in Tugriks of Judges in Mongolia, 2004–2010.

| Official Position | April 2004 | June 2005 | April 2006 | February 2007 | November 2007 | January 2008 | October 2010 |
|---|---|---|---|---|---|---|---|
| Chief Judge of the Capital | 126,100<br>US$106 | 135,600<br>US$113 | 176,280<br>US$149 | 211,536<br>US$181 | 423,100<br>US$361 | 543,684<br>US$465 | 706,789<br>US$491 |
| Judge of the Capital | 115,900<br>US$98 | 124,600<br>US$103 | 161,980<br>US$137 | 194,376<br>US$166 | 388,800<br>US$332 | 499,608<br>US$427 | 649,490<br>US$451 |
| Chief Judge of Aimag | 121,000<br>US$102 | 130,100<br>US$108 | 169,130<br>US$143 | 202,956<br>US$173 | 405,900<br>US$347 | 521,582<br>US$446 | 678,057<br>US$471 |
| Judge of Aimag | 112,200<br>US$95 | 120,600<br>US$100 | 156,780<br>US$133 | 188,136<br>US$161 | 376,300<br>US$322 | 483,546<br>US$414 | 628,610<br>US$436 |
| Chief Judge of District of Capital | 113,600<br>US$96 | 122,100<br>US$101 | 158,730<br>US$135 | 190,476<br>US$163 | 381,000<br>US$326 | 489,585<br>US$419 | 636,461<br>US$442 |
| Judge of District of Capital | 108,400<br>US$92 | 116,500<br>US$97 | 151,450<br>US$128 | 181,740<br>US$155 | 363,500<br>US$311 | 467,098<br>US$399 | 607,227<br>US$421 |
| Chief Judge of Soum and Inter Soum of Aimag | 113,600<br>US$96 | 122,100<br>US$101 | 158,730<br>US$135 | 190,476<br>US$163 | 381,000<br>US$326 | 489,585<br>US$419 | 636,461<br>US$442 |
| Judge of Soum and Inter Soum of Aimag | 108,400<br>US$92 | 116,500<br>US$97 | 151,450<br>US$128 | 181,740<br>US$155 | 363,500<br>US$311 | 467,098<br>US$399 | 607,227<br>US$421 |
| Average exchange rate for US$ | 1,185.19 | 1,205.27 | 1,179.55 | 1,170.43 | 1,170.43 | 1,169.26 | 1,440.76 |

*Source*: Data provided by courtesy of Mr Batzorig Badam, Head of the Research and Analysis Division of IAAC, in e-mail correspondence on 17 February 2011.

the rising cost of living in Mongolia. Second, the vertical compression or difference between the monthly salaries of the Chief Judge of the Capital and the Judge of Soum and Inter Soum of the Aimag is only US$70 (US$491–US$421) or a ratio of 1.16:1.00 in October 2010.

### *Red Tape*

Red tape is a serious problem that has contributed to corruption in Mongolia. According to the World Bank's *Doing Business Surveys* from 2007 to 2011, Mongolia's ease of doing business rank has steadily declined from 45th position among 175 economies in 2007 to 73rd position among 183 economies in 2011. More specifically, Table 11.8 notes that Mongolia's rank in starting a business has deteriorated from 55th position to 86th position during 2007–2011. Indeed, it is difficult to obtain construction permits or licenses in Mongolia because its rank has worsened from 34th position in 2007 to 104th position in 2011 as the time required has increased from 96 to 215 days during the same period. Similarly, Mongolia's rank in registering property has also declined from 17th position in 2007 to 27th position in 2011.

***Table 11.8.*** Ease of Doing Business in Mongolia, 2007–2011.

| Indicator | 2007 (*N*=175) | 2008 (*N*=178) | 2009 (*N*=181) | 2010 (*N*=183) | 2011 (*N*=183) |
|---|---|---|---|---|---|
| Ease of doing business (rank) | 45 | 52 | 58 | 60 | 73 |
| Starting a business (rank) | 55 | 62 | 59 | 78 | 86 |
| No. of procedures | 8 | 8 | 7 | 7 | 7 |
| Time (days) | 20 | 20 | 13 | 13 | 13 |
| Cost (% of income per capita) | 5.1 | 4.3 | 4.0 | 3.0 | 3.2 |
| Dealing with construction permits or licenses (rank) | 34 | 43 | 103 | 103 | 104 |
| No. of procedures | 18 | 21 | 21 | 21 | 21 |
| Time (days) | 96 | 126 | 215 | 215 | 215 |
| Cost (% of income per capita) | 48.4 | 15.7 | 81.3 | 61.2 | 65.1 |
| Registering property (rank) | 17 | 18 | 20 | 25 | 27 |
| No. of procedures | 5 | 5 | 5 | 5 | 5 |
| Time (days) | 11 | 11 | 11 | 11 | 11 |
| Cost (% of property value) | 2.2 | 2.2 | 2.1 | 2.1 | 2.2 |
| CPI rank and score | 99th (3.0) | 102nd (3.0) | 120th (2.7) | 116th (2.7) | NA |

*Sources*: World Bank (2006b, p. 129, 2007, p. 138, 2008, p. 121, 2009, p. 139, 2010a, p. 181).

According to the IAAC's Mongolian Corruption Index for 2009, there was a strong correlation between red tape and nepotism (correlation level of 0.91) and between red tape and bribed decision-making (correlation level of 0.89). As red tape is an important cause of corruption in Mongolia, it is hoped that enhanced transparency in the provision of information on public services and their rules and procedures to the public will reduce red tape and corruption (IAAC, 2010, p. 9). Thus, the existence of red tape and cumbersome administrative procedures in Mongolia's civil service creates ample opportunities for corruption because the poorly paid civil servants succumb easily to temptation by accepting bribes from those who wish to expedite the processing of their applications for permits or to gain unfair access to services or benefits.

### *Cultural Factors*

Cultural factors are also responsible for corruption in Mongolia because family and kinship ties among a small nomadic population as well as the tradition of gift-giving "often blur the lines between malicious graft and benevolent custom." The notion of *ariin khaalga* or "back door" refers to "an unwritten system of long-term barters, favors, relationships, and IOUs that have governed commerce for centuries, in which money may or may not exchange hands." Instead of navigating through the "complex maze" of regulations and procedures, many Mongolians rely on *ariin khaalga* by looking for friends, family members, or acquaintances (*tanidag hun* or those persons who can get you through the back door) to assist them to bypass the formal rules. These "back door" solutions usually result in favoritism, cronyism, and nepotism and apply to both petty and grand corruption. Indeed, decisions involving recruitment for management positions, procurement, electoral processes, licenses, and permits for lucrative mining operations are "made along networks of families, friends, and associates" (Casals & Associates, 2005, pp. 19–20).

Traditional Mongolian culture has undermined the rule of law in Mongolia because of its emphasis on obligation and reciprocity among an individual's friends and relatives. However, in Mongolia, the reciprocal obligation to assist close friends and relatives extends beyond them to distant relatives, colleagues, neighbors or *net nutgiinkhan* (those from the same birth place), and acquaintances (Byambajav, 2010, p. 93). These informal circles of connected individuals are described as *tanil tal* or exchange networks, which are important because they enable individuals to gain access to assistance, goods, and services in Mongolia. Mongolian judges belong to *tanil tal* too and respond accordingly to their social obligations. For example, a judge will be lenient toward an official or his relative if he receives help in getting medical treatment for his family (White, 2010, pp. 328–330).

Mongolians rely increasingly on their *tanil tal* to cope with the pressures of daily life. Apart from securing health care, Mongolians use their connections and reciprocal favors to "cope and grab" what they need to improve their lives. Consequently, searching for ties, whether strong or weak, within one's *tanil tal* is usually the first tactic in getting things done in Mongolia. Whether an individual can mobilize his *tanil tal* also depends on the perception of his ability to offer reciprocal assistance in the future. However, the poor and disenfranchised are unable to mobilize their *tanil tal* effectively, and this unequal access to *tanil tal* has legitimized the paying of bribes and other inducements. In other words, those Mongolians who cannot mobilize their *tanil tal* to get things done will resort to bribery if they can afford to do so. Indeed, 60 percent of Mongolians have paid bribes in the absence of *tanil tal* to "get something done" (White, 2010, pp. 330–331).

### *Low Probability of Punishment*

The low probability of punishment for corrupt offenses is another important cause of corruption in Mongolia. Few public officials have been punished in Mongolia. In 1997, three MPs were found guilty of corruption and jailed for taking bribes for approving a casino tender. In 2001, 43 persons in the Customs General Administration (CGA) were dismissed after audits of their work, but none of them were fired because of corruption even though the 1999 UNDP survey had identified the CGA as one of the most corrupt departments in Mongolia (ADB, 2004, p. 52).

During the seven decades of communist rule, corruption in Mongolia was suppressed by "the threat of severe punishments for embezzlers, disapproval of bourgeois materialism, the impossibility of owning land, apartments, and vehicles, the fear of arousing suspicion by high living, and the paucity of consumer goods." However, these constraints disappeared after 1990 with the emergence of these factors, which contributed to the spread of corruption: a weak government; the growing importance of private property in the form of factories, vehicles, and herds; and the erosion of the ideal of economic equality (Rossabi, 2005, pp. 59–60).

As mentioned in the introductory section on "Judicial Corruption in Mongolia," judges are perceived by the public to be corrupt as they readily accept bribes or gifts to influence their decisions. Indeed, in the corruption benchmarking surveys conducted by the Asia Foundation and Sant Maral

Foundation in 2010, the percentage of respondents who agreed with the statement: "The court system has a role to play, but it is too corrupt to deal with corruption cases" has increased from 58.6 percent in March 2010 to 59.4 percent in September 2010 (Asia Foundation, 2010, p. 16). Hence it is not surprising that there are very few convictions for corruption offenses in Mongolia. The Special Investigative Unit of the Prosecutor General investigated 20 bribery investigations from September 2002 to June 2005 but these investigations resulted in only four convictions because the other 16 cases were dismissed at the prosecutor's request (Casals & Associates, 2005, p. 28).

### *Lack of Political Will*

The lack of political will or commitment of the political leaders is the most important cause of corruption in Mongolia. In their assessment of corruption in Mongolia, Casals & Associates (2005, p. 17) noted that "the current state of corruption in Mongolia demands clear and decisive political will to minimize the growing risks of corruption entrenchment, but it seems to be missing at the highest level of government." Using David Brinkerhoff's five indicators of political will, they observed that the Mongolian government's political will to curb corruption was "relatively weak."

Among the Mongolian political leaders, the leaders of the Democratic Party were concerned about fighting corruption when they held the parliamentary majority from 1996 to 2000. In 1998, the democratic leader, Sanjaasurengiin Zorig, was murdered probably because of his efforts to curb corruption. In 2002, Mongolia's Parliament approved the National Program for Combating Corruption and the creation of the National Council for coordinating and monitoring its implementation. However, it did not implement or pass legislation to prevent corruption. Indeed, anticorruption initiatives have not received consistent or strong support from the political leaders. Some MPs concerned about combating corruption have formed a Parliamentary Anticorruption Working Group, but their efforts are not supported by most of their colleagues, who favor the maintenance of the status quo instead. In short, political will in curbing corruption in Mongolia is "weak and dispersed" (Casals & Associates, 2005, pp. 17–18).

As the lead consultant for the United Nations Development Programme (UNDP) mission to Mongolia, I visited Ulaanbataar in September and October 1998 to assess the legal and institutional framework for addressing corruption and integrity-related issues and to formulate a National Action Plan for preventing and combating corruption in Mongolia. I proposed a

National Anticorruption Plan consisting of four components: the improvement of the implementation of existing laws, conducting a national survey to assess the extent of corruption; a study tour of Singapore and Hong Kong to observe the operations of the Corrupt Practices Investigation Bureau (CPIB) and the Independent Commission Against Corruption (ICAC) and the implementation of the anticorruption laws to ascertain the suitability of establishing an independent ACA in Mongolia; and the convening of a national workshop for senior public officials, MPs, mass media representatives, and leaders of nongovernmental organizations in Mongolia (Quah, 1998, pp. 27–30).

When I presented my preliminary report to some senior public officials and MPs during my second visit to Ulaanbataar in October 1998, an opposition MP voiced his concern about introducing a CPIB or ICAC-styled ACA in Mongolia because of his fear that the President would use this agency against his political foes. Hence, I was not surprised that even though the National Anticorruption Plan was accepted by the Government of Mongolia and UNDP, it took more than eight years before the IAAC was established in December 2006, more than a year after Mongolia's ratification of the United Nations Convention Against Corruption (UNCAC) in October 2005.

The creation of the IAAC in December 2006, more than 10 years after Mongolia began its campaign against corruption with the enactment of the Law on Anti-Corruption (LAC) in April 1996 is an indication of enhanced political will in curbing corruption in Mongolia. However, as will be analyzed in the section on evaluating the anticorruption measures later, whether such political will in combating corruption can be sustained on a long-term basis by the government depends on the allocation of adequate budget and personnel to the IAAC and its impartial enforcement of the Anti-Corruption Law (ACL) of July 2006.

## ANTICORRUPTION MEASURES

Mongolia began its fight against corruption with the enactment of the LAC on 5 April 1996. As there was no independent ACA, the task of implementing the LAC and other relevant legislation was shared among the police, the General Prosecutor's Office (GPO), and the aimag courts, the Capital City Court, and the Supreme Court. However, the pattern of corruption control was changed from Pattern 1 to Pattern 3 with the establishment of the IAAC in December 2006, six months after the enactment of the ACL in July 2006.

## *Pattern 1 (April 1996–October 2006)*

### *Law on Anticorruption of April 1996*

The LAC consisted of three chapters and 18 articles. It defined bribery as "a process of giving incentives, compensation or advantage by the subject to the subject referred to in Article 4, who abuses his/her position and possibility to do so to receive a bribe, materialistic or other types of incentives or compensation" (Article 2). According to Article 3, the anticorruption legislation not only consisted of the LAC but also included the Criminal Code, and the Law on Government Service. Article 4 was very important because it identified the six categories of civil servants who were subject to the LAC: (1) the political, administrative, and special service civil servants identified in the Law on Government Service; (2) the chief and secretary of the province, capital city, soumon, district citizens representatives' hurals; (3) those civil servants in charge of licensing, authorizing, distributing, and registering of aid; (4) those civil servants in management and administrative positions of the state property; (5) managers and executives of nongovernmental organizations; and (6) senior rank civil servants.

Furthermore, all state organizations were required by Article 5 to perform the following four duties to prevent corruption: (1) to publicize the procedures of "licensing, authorizing, registering, monitoring and selecting in accordance with the function of the specific organization"; (2) to "define clearly the responsibility distribution"; (3) to define the procedure for a meeting between a civil servant and a citizen; and (4) to "supervise income declaration of civil servants" and to "audit and resolve claims and complaints." All senior officials of state organizations at all levels were expected "to disclose, to stop, to undertake measures to eliminate consequences of corruption."

To prevent corruption, Article 7 prohibited the officials identified in Article 4 from the following nine activities: travelling within the country or abroad at the expense of business firms, citizens, foreign organizations, and individuals, except for officially authorized missions; receiving "gifts, money honorarium, compensation from other organizations, economic entities and citizens"; abusing "for non-official purposes the state organization's assets, facilities, financial and information resources, and official information"; being involved in business activities and serving as a mediator; possession of "securities, assets by credit and an advantageous right abusing the position"; influencing the "activity of other organizations on matters unrelated to his duties"; offering advantage to individuals and legal bodies and obstructing the legitimate decision-making process; attempting to "illegally influence on the actions of the same rank or supervised officials";

and undertaking activities that involve the possession of illegal income, incentives, and advantage abusing the position.

Perhaps the key measure for preventing corruption was the declaration of income and assets of public officials stipulated in Article 8. More specifically, these officials were required to indicate in the "asset, income declaration the sources of income, real estate, securities, bank savings, animals, and other assets, total income, its sources for himself and family members." Furthermore, they were required to submit their income and asset declarations within 30 days of assuming their positions and thereafter to submit their annual declarations during 1–15 February of each year.

Article 14 stated that those committing bribery and corruption-related crimes were liable for prosecution according to the relevant provisions of the Criminal Code. Officials who failed to submit their declarations of income and assets could be fined between 5,000 and 25,000 tugriks (US$6 and US$29). Those officials who did not perform their duty of monitoring the declarations would be fined between 20,000 and 30,000 tugriks (US$24 to US$35). Officials who did not declare gifts or their foreign bank accounts were required to pay between 30,000 and 40,000 tugriks (US$35 to US$47) in fines. Finally, officials found guilty of corruption would be discharged or displaced according to the procedure provided in the law.

*The Criminal Code*

The Criminal Code contains several articles that deal with bribery and related offenses. For example, Articles 195–197 focus on bribery. According to Article 195, an official who receives bribes directly or through a mediator can be suspended from his position or sentenced to six years of imprisonment without suspension of power. If an official is a repeat offender or accepts a large bribe, or if bribery is committed by an organized group, or a senior civil servant, the guilty official will be suspended from his position and jailed from 10 to 25 years. Article 196 focuses on the bribe-givers, who can be imprisoned for four years or required to perform public work for 18 months. Recalcitrant bribe-givers can be sentenced for periods ranging from 3 to 10 years imprisonment. Finally, Article 197 punishes those who mediate in bribe-taking and giving with either a jail sentence of up to four years or 18 months of public work.

Articles 192 and 193 prescribe punishment for those officials who abuse their power or position. The punishment for officials who abuse their power is a three-year jail sentence without suspension or being required to perform public work up to 18 months. Repeat offenders will be suspended and imprisoned for eight years. For excessive abuse of power, the guilty officials will be suspended or jailed for up to four years without suspension or be compelled to perform 18 months of public work. If officials abuse their power by using violence, weapons, or torturing victims, or are repeat offenders, they will be suspended and imprisoned for up to 10 years.

*Procedure for Dealing with Corrupt Offenses*

Reports of crime, including corruption offenses, were received by the Criminal Police Department (CPD), which investigated these reports and referred them to the Investigation Department (ID) for the next stage of the investigation, which could last from 2 to 26 months. The CPD had 10 divisions, with 2 divisions dealing with corruption. The Organized Crime Division (OCD) was concerned with corruption, money-laundering, casino-related crime, environmental crime, crime involving foreigners, terrorism, and trafficking in firearms. The second division was the Economic Crime Division (ECD), which dealt with the suppression of financial crime. The ID had two similar divisions that would continue the work initiated by the OCD and the ECD (UNODC & CPCICP, 1997, pp. 12–14).

The CPD and ID investigated complaints of corruption against public officials, and if there was evidence to verify these complaints, the cases were handed over to the GPO, which supervised "inquiries by the police in both criminal and civil cases" and represented "the state in both civil and criminal proceedings." From the GPO, the cases were processed by the aimag courts and the Capital City Court (for serious crimes where the amount exceeded 10 million tugriks or US$22,000) and the Supreme Court (for those cases outside the jurisdiction of other courts and appeals from decisions of the aimag courts and the Capital City Court) (McPhail, 1995, pp. 49–50, 38).

### *Pattern 3 (November 2006 to Present)*

As mentioned earlier, the government ratified the UNCAC in October 2005 and adopted the ACL in July 2006, more than six years after it was first introduced in parliament. The most important consequence of the enactment of the ACL, which came into force on 1 November 2006, was the formation of the IAAC in December 2006.[4]

*Anticorruption Law of July 2006*

The ACL has 6 chapters and 35 articles. Article 1 identifies its purpose as the definition of the legal basis for anticorruption activities and IAAC and the regulations governing it. Chapter 2 focuses on the need for increasing public awareness of anticorruption education and corruption prevention. Article 6.9 stipulates that any official who fails to prevent and combat corruption will be fined between 150,000 tugriks (US$120) and 200,000 tugriks (US$160). Article 8.1 requires judges, prosecutors, police or intelligence officers, public audit and professional control agents, and central and local administrative officials to report to the IAAC any corruption-related activities detected by them in performing their official duties. They will be fined between 200,000 tugriks (US$160) and 250,000 tugriks (US$200) for violating Article 8.1.

Chapter 3 describes the registering and storing of the assets and income declarations of all appointed or elected, permanent or temporary officials in Mongolia holding political, administrative, or special office of the State. Table 11.9 reports the responsibilities of the four organizations identified in Article 11.1, which handle the registering and storing of the assets and income declarations of all government officials. Article 13 makes the IAAC responsible for reviewing and inspecting the assets and income declarations. Officials who fail to submit their assets and income declarations are dismissed or suspended from their duties (Article 13.5). Article 13.7 specifies that the failure of officials to register the assets and income declarations, to perform the review, and to submit the documents within a specified time period will be fined between 100,000 tugriks (US$80) and 150,000 tugriks (US$120). The public disclosure of the assets and income declarations of all officials is described in Article 14.1, which states that these declarations will

***Table 11.9.*** Registration and Storage of Assets and Income Declarations of Officials by Organization.

| Organization | Responsible For |
|---|---|
| Independent Authority Against Corruption | High-level government officials |
| General Election Committee | Candidates in presidential election, members of district election committee of candidates in parliamentary elections and in the elections of aimag, the capital city, and soumon citizens' representatives |
| General Council of Courts | All judges except those of the Supreme Court |
| Government Service Council | Officials appointed by the government |

*Source:* Anticorruption Law of 2006, Article 11.1.

be published online in the Government News Magazine during the second quarter of each year. Citizens may also request information on these declarations in writing, orally, or from the Internet, and the IAAC is required to inform the public annually on how the officials have followed the required procedures for submitting their assets and income declarations (Articles 14.4 and 14.5).

*Independent Authority Against Corruption*

Chapter 4 of the ACL is devoted to the IAAC's mandate and describes its basic principles of operation, its organizational structure, its functions, requirements for selecting its staff, the criteria for appointing its CG and Deputy Commissioner General (DCG), their terms of office, and the circumstances under which they can be suspended from their duties or dismissed.

The IAAC performs three important functions. First, according to Article 18.1, the IAAC is responsible for educating and improving the public awareness regarding the adverse effects of corruption and for preventing corruption. Apart from organizing national programs on anticorruption education and corruption prevention, the IAAC has to conduct a biannual survey on the scope, forms, and causes of corruption in Mongolia and to develop a corruption index.

Second, the IAAC is empowered by Article 18.2 to investigate the assets and income declarations submitted by all officials holding political, administrative, or special office of the State in Mongolia. More specifically, this means that the IAAC has to conduct training, issue manuals, and instructions regarding the correct and accurate declaration of assets and income. It has to respond to oral or written requests for advice on the completion, amendment, registration, or transfer of such declarations.

The third and perhaps most important function performed by the IAAC is the investigation of corruption cases under its jurisdiction (Article 18.4.7). Related to this function is the acceptance and inspection by the IAAC of corruption-related requests and complaints. It also conducts undercover operations and work with other relevant government agencies in its investigations for detecting corruption offenses.

The IAAC is headed by a CG, who is assisted by a DCG. It consists of the Research and Analysis Service, Intelligence Service, Internal Affairs Service, and Finance and Logistic Service, and the following four departments: Administration Department, Investigation Department, Inspection and Analysis Department, and Corruption Prevention and Public Awareness Department. Since its establishment in December 2006, the IAAC has a total staff of 90 officers.[5]

Article 19.1 specifies that IAAC officers should be Mongolian citizens without a criminal record, a record of violating the code of ethics, or of disciplinary penalties during their service in the government, and a bachelor's degree. The CG and DCG are appointed for six years by Parliament based on the nomination of the President of Mongolia. The requirements for the CG's position are 15 years of government service; at least 55 years old; a lawyer by profession; relevant managerial and professional experience; and not occupying a political position for the past five years. Similarly, the DCG must also be a lawyer with at least 10 years of government service and experience in undercover and investigative work (Articles 21.2.1 and 21.2.2). Both the CG and the DCG can be relieved of their duties for health reasons and will be dismissed if they are convicted of a crime.

IAAC officers are prohibited by Article 25 from joining political parties, trade unions, or religious organizations. They cannot disclose State, organizational, or personal secrets revealed to them in the course of performing their duties. They are also not allowed to inform members of the public about their official duties without special permission from their superiors. They are required to seek approval from the CG for travel abroad for official or private purposes. To maintain their integrity, IAAC officers are not allowed to travel at the expense of domestic or foreign economic entities, organizations, or individuals or accept any gifts or souvenirs from anyone.

The IAAC is required by Article 26.1 to submit an annual report on the implementation of the ACL and the general condition and status of corruption in Mongolia. Article 26.2 specifies that the IAAC's implementation of the Law on Undercover Operations is monitored by the Special Supervisory Sub-Committee of Parliament. Furthermore, the IAAC's undercover operations, investigative work, and case registration are supervised by the Prosecutor General. An ad hoc Public Council of 15 members is established by Article 27 to enhance public involvement in combating corruption by allowing its members to voice their opinions and provide advice on the condition and implementation of the ACL. Career government officers and political appointees are not eligible for membership of the Public Council.

To ensure its independence, Article 29 guarantees that the IAAC's activities are financed from the State budget. Article 29.2 states that the IAAC will be provided with a budget to enable it to operate independently. More importantly, Article 29.3 specifies that the IAAC's budget for a given year cannot be less than its budget for the previous year. The remuneration for the CG, DCG, and all IAAC officers consists of their basic salaries, special conditions allowances, and bonuses for seniority and academic qualifications. Table 11.10 reports that the IAAC budget has increased from

***Table 11.10.*** IAAC's Budget, 2007–2011.

| Year | Tugriks | US$ | Percentage Increase |
|---|---|---|---|
| 2007 | 2,367,426,600 | 2,007,059 | 100 |
| 2008 | 3,720,166,600 | 3,138,461 | 156 |
| 2009 | 2,837,185,400 | 2,097,993 | 105 |
| 2010 | 2,923,100,000 | 2,028,860 | 101 |
| 2011 | 2,980,000,000 | 2,197,754 | 110 |

*Source:* Data provided by Mr. Batzorig Badam, the IAAC's Head of the Research and Analysis Division, through e-mail correspondence on 11 February 2011.

2,367,426,600 tugriks (US$2,007,059) in 2007 to 2,980,000,000 tugriks (US$2,197,754) in 2011. The 156 percent increase in the 2008 budget can be attributed to the additional allocation of 1.1 billion tugriks (US$939,825) for the maintenance work at the IAAC Headquarters.

## EVALUATION OF ANTICORRUPTION MEASURES

How effective are the anticorruption measures in Mongolia? Three indicators are used to assess the effectiveness of the anticorruption measures in Mongolia: (1) Transparency International's Corruption Perceptions Index (CPI) in 1999 and from 2004 to 2010; (2) World Bank's control of corruption indicator in 1996, 1998, 2000, and from 2002 to 2009; and (3) the *Global Competitiveness Report's* indicator on public trust of politicians from 2007 to 2011.

First, as three independent surveys must be conducted in a country before it can be included in the CPI, Mongolia has only been included for eight years: in 1999 and from 2004 to 2010. In 1999, Mongolia was ranked 43rd among 99 countries with a score of 4.3. As it was excluded from the CPI from 2000 to 2003, Table 11.11 notes that its rank has gradually declined to 85th among 146 countries in 2004, 85th among 159 countries in 2005, 99th among 163 countries in 2006, 99th among 180 countries in 2007, 102nd among 180 countries in 2008, 120th among 180 countries in 2009, and 116th among 178 countries in 2010. More importantly, Mongolia's CPI score has decreased from 4.3 in 1999 to 3.0 in 2004, 2005, 2007, and 2008, to 2.8 in 2006, and to 2.7 in 2009 and 2010.

Second, the pattern of decline can also be observed in Mongolia's percentile rank on the World Bank's control of corruption governance

***Table 11.11.*** Mongolia's Performance on the CPI and Control of Corruption, 1995–2010.

| Year | CPI Rank and Score[a] | Control of Corruption Percentile Rank |
|---|---|---|
| 1995 | NA | NA |
| 1996 | NA | 64.1 |
| 1997 | NA | NA |
| 1998 | NA | 46.6 |
| 1999 | 43rd (4.3) | NA |
| 2000 | NA | 44.7 |
| 2001 | NA | NA |
| 2002 | NA | 57.8 |
| 2003 | NA | 51.9 |
| 2004 | 85th (3.0) | 47.1 |
| 2005 | 85th (3.0) | 39.3 |
| 2006 | 99th (2.8) | 37.9 |
| 2007 | 99th (3.0) | 28.5 |
| 2008 | 102nd (3.0) | 31.4 |
| 2009 | 120th (2.7) | 23.8 |
| 2010 | 116th (2.7) | NA |

*Sources*: http://www.transparency.org and http://info.worldbank.org/governance/wgi/sc_chart.asp
[a]The CPI score ranges from 0 (most corrupt) to 10 (least corrupt).

indicator from 1996 to 2009. Table 11.11 also notes that, from its peak of 64.1 percentile rank in 1996, Mongolia's control of corruption has deteriorated to 23.8 in 2009. Although Mongolia's CPI score increased to 3.0 during the first two years of the IAAC (2007–2008), it declined to 2.7 in 2009 and 2010. Furthermore, its percentile rank in control of corruption decreased to 28.5 in 2007, 31.4 in 2008, and 23.8 in 2009. In short, contrary to expectations, the establishment of the IAAC in December 2006 has not resulted in any substantial improvement in the perceived extent of corruption in Mongolia.

Third, as can be seen in Table 11.12, the level of public trust of politicians in Mongolia is very low but has increased marginally from 1.6 in 2007–2008 to 1.9 in 2010–2011. The low level of public trust of politicians in Mongolia is not surprising and is consistent with Mongolia's poor performance on the CPI and the World Bank's control of corruption indicator. In other words, it is unrealistic to expect Mongolians to trust their politicians if they are widely perceived by the public to be corrupt.

The LAC was the major anticorruption law in Mongolia from April 1996 to June 2006. During Mongolia's first major corruption trial on 21 October

***Table 11.12.*** Public Trust of Politicians in Mongolia, 2007–2008 to 2010–2011.

| Year | Rank | Score[a] | No. of Countries |
|---|---|---|---|
| 2007–2008 | 122nd | 1.6 | 131 |
| 2008–2009 | 120th | 1.6 | 134 |
| 2009–2010 | 119th | 1.8 | 133 |
| 2010–2011 | 118th | 1.9 | 139 |
| Average | 120th | 1.7 | – |

*Sources:* Compiled from Schwab et al. (1999, p. 327), Porter et al. (2000, p. 253), Schwab et al. (2002, p. 408), Cornelius (2003, p. 619), Sala-i-Martin (2004, p. 499), Schwab and Porter (2007, p. 379), Schwab and Porter (2008, p. 367), Schwab (2009, p. 349), and Schwab (2010, p. 369).
[a]The score ranges from 1 (very low) to 7 (very high) for the respondents' answers to this statement: "How would you rate the level of public trust in the ethical standards of politicians in your country."

1999, three MPs from the ruling Democratic Union coalition were jailed from three to five and a half years for receiving bribes amounting to US$210,000 from a casino official in connection with a casino tender in 1998 (*Straits Times*, 1999, p. 23). The fact that only three MPs were convicted of corruption and that only two cases involving cashiers and accountants were settled in court (Naruntuya, 1998, p. 3) even though the LAC was in existence since April 1996 is a reflection of the LAC's ineffectiveness. The major problem was the difficulty in obtaining evidence for prosecuting those suspected of corruption offenses. Indeed, many public officials were not punished for bribery even though the public perception was that they were corrupt as these officials cannot be convicted because of the lack of evidence. Similarly, the public perceived the Mongolian police to be corrupt, but it was rare for police officers to be found guilty of bribery in the absence of evidence.

The LAC had two major weaknesses. First, the responsibility for implementing the LAC was not clearly stated as Article 5 indicated that all State organizations were required to perform four common duties to prevent corruption. Furthermore, Article 10 identified the agencies and officials responsible for registering and storing the declarations of assets and incomes of all public officials. The experiences of the CPIB in Singapore (which is analyzed in Chapter 6) and the ICAC in Hong Kong (dealt with in Chapter 7) demonstrate the effectiveness of a single ACA in implementing the anticorruption laws in both countries.

The second weakness of the LAC was that the penalties for those public officials who did not submit and monitor their income and assets declarations specified in Article 15 were not effective deterrents because the fines ranged from 5,000 tugriks (US$6) to 40,000 tugriks (US$47) and there was no imprisonment. As these fines could easily be paid by those officials who were corrupt, the punishment for corrupt officials should be enhanced by confiscating their properties or cars and dismissing them from the civil service.

The procedure for dealing with corrupt offenses in Mongolia was ineffective because it provided opportunities for corruption among the officials concerned as they could interpret the law differently. For example, a case considered to be bribery by the police was viewed as a smuggling offense by the GPO and as illegal crossing of borders by the courts.[6] Furthermore, the courts were perceived by the public to be corrupt as individuals could pay the poorly paid judges to make decisions in their favor. As the Mongolian public perceived police officers to be corrupt without providing relevant evidence, few police officers were convicted for corrupt offenses because complaints of police corruption were investigated by the CPD and the ID. Under such circumstances, it was very difficult for the CPD and ID to be objective in the investigation of cases of police corruption, especially if their colleagues were involved.

How effective is the IAAC in minimizing corruption in Mongolia? As the IAAC was formed in December 2006, it might be premature to provide a comprehensive evaluation of its effectiveness in curbing corruption after only four years. Nevertheless, it is possible to provide an interim evaluation on the basis of the views expressed by the respondents on the IAAC's effectiveness in the corruption benchmarking surveys conducted by the Asia Foundation and the Sant Maral Foundation. First, in terms of the IAAC's performance, Table 11.13 notes that the proportion of respondents who rated the IAAC's performance as "bad" has increased from 20 percent in March 2007 to 29.5 percent in March 2009. Similarly, the percentage of those respondents with a "very bad" assessment of the IAAC's performance has grown from 9.2 percent to 10.5 percent. On the contrary, only 8.7 percent of the respondents said that the IAAC's performance was "very good" or "good" in March 2007. This proportion of respondents increased to 14.5 percent in March 2009.

In view of the respondents' negative assessment of the IAAC's performance, it is not surprising that about one-third of them have also indicated that they were "rather not confident" in the IAAC while another third expressed their confidence in the IAAC as can be seen in Table 11.14.

***Table 11.13.*** IAAC's Performance, 2007–2009.

| Performance Category | March 2007 (%) | September 2007 (%) | March 2008 (%) | September 2008 (%) | March 2009 (%) |
|---|---|---|---|---|---|
| Very good | 0.7 | 1.7 | 3.6 | 1.5 | 1.8 |
| Good | 8.0 | 11.7 | 11.1 | 8.7 | 12.7 |
| Average | 22.3 | 27.2 | 28.4 | 30.2 | 27.4 |
| Bad | 20 | 25.5 | 21.0 | 27.3 | 29.5 |
| Very bad | 9.2 | 8.0 | 10.5 | 13.7 | 10.5 |
| Don't know/no answer | 39.9 | 26.0 | 25.4 | 18.7 | 18.1 |

*Source*: Asia Foundation (2009, p. 15, Table 22).

***Table 11.14.*** Confidence in the IAAC, 2007–2009.

| Confidence Level | March 2007 (%) | September 2007 (%) | March 2008 (%) | September 2008 (%) | March 2009 (%) |
|---|---|---|---|---|---|
| Very confident | 7.8 | 7.3 | 7.7 | 5.5 | 5.6 |
| Confident | 32.0 | 34.0 | 30.5 | 26.8 | 31.5 |
| Rather not confident | 31.3 | 26.0 | 32.3 | 30.8 | 33.8 |
| Not confident | 10.2 | 9.7 | 9.0 | 16.2 | 11.8 |
| Don't know/no answer | 20.5 | 23.0 | 20.5 | 20.7 | 17.5 |

*Source*: Asia Foundation (2009, p. 15, Table 23).

***Table 11.15.*** Preference for IAAC to Lead Anticorruption Fight, 2006–2009.

| Date | Percentage Favoring IAAC as Anticorruption Leader |
|---|---|
| March 2006 | 40.7 |
| September 2006 | 42.4 |
| March 2007 | 51.5 |
| September 2007 | 52.3 |
| March 2008 | 53.2 |
| September 2008 | 56.6 |
| March 2009 | 54.1 |

*Source*: Asia Foundation (2009, p. 14, Table 21).

The proportion of respondents who were "very confident" in the IAAC has declined from 7.8 percent to 5.6 percent from March 2007 to March 2009.

Even though the respondents had given the IAAC a negative assessment and not clearly confident toward it, many of them felt that the IAAC should lead the fight against corruption in Mongolia rather than the government or citizens. According to Table 11.15, the proportion of respondents expressing the view that the IAAC should lead the fight against corruption has increased from 40.7 percent in March 2006 to 54.1 percent in March 2009.

## CONCLUSION

The creation of the IAAC in December 2006 has transformed the pattern of corruption control in Mongolia from Pattern 1 (anticorruption laws without a single ACA) to Pattern 3 (anticorruption laws with a single ACA). From April 1996 to June 2006, Mongolia relied on the LAC and the police to combat corruption. As the LAC and police were ineffective in curbing corruption, Mongolia was ranked 43rd among 99 countries with a score of 4.3 on the 1999 CPI. Table 11.11 reports that when Mongolia was included again in the CPI five years later, its rank and score declined further to 85th position and score of 3.0 in 2004 and 2005, and to 99th position and score of 2.8 in 2006.

Contrary to expectations, the establishment of the IAAC in December 2006 has not resulted in any significant improvement in Mongolia's performance in fighting corruption as reflected in TI's CPI, the World Bank's control of corruption indicator, and the *Global Competitiveness Report's* public trust of politicians indicator. The CPI score improved marginally to 3.0 for 2007 and 2008 but dropped again to 2.7 in 2009 and 2010. Mongolia's percentile rank in controlling corruption declined from 37.9 in 2006 to 28.5 in 2007, 31.4 in 2008, and 23.8 in 2009. As Mongolia was not included in the earlier surveys of the *Global Competitiveness Report's* indicator on public trust of politicians, it is not possible to ascertain the impact of the setting up of the IAAC on this indicator. However, Table 11.12 shows clearly that the level of public trust of politicians in Mongolia is extremely low and ranges from 1.6 to 1.9 from 2007 to 2010.

The findings of the 10 Asia Foundation's corruption benchmarking surveys from March 2006 to September 2010 also confirm that corruption is still a serious problem in Mongolia and that the respondents are not impressed so far with the IAAC's performance even though many of them have expressed their preference for the IAAC to lead the fight against corruption in Mongolia. The findings of the latest September 2010 corruption benchmarking survey identify the three serious challenges faced by the IAAC in combating corruption.

First, while 59.4 percent of the respondents are confident that the ICAC is an impartial law enforcement body, 16.7 percent of them do not share this opinion, and 23.9 percent do not know or have no opinion. A second challenge is reflected in the high proportion of the respondents who do not believe that the IAAC would keep the reports on corruption cases confidential. Indeed, the percentage of respondents who do not believe that the IAAC would keep its corruption reports confidential is 53.8 percent in March 2010 and 52.5 percent in September 2010. The third related challenge is the public's lack of trust in the IAAC as manifested in the finding that 63 percent of the respondents would not reveal their identity when reporting to the IAAC in the March 2010 survey. The percentage of these respondents has dropped slightly to 59.7 percent in the September 2010 survey (Asia Foundation, 2010, pp. 13–15, Tables 12, 15, 16).

To gain the trust and confidence of the citizens in Mongolia, the IAAC needs to enforce the ACL impartially by investigating all cases of corruption, regardless of the status or position of the suspects. Anyone found guilty of corruption offenses, whether petty or grand in nature, must be punished according to the law. If the "big fish" (rich and powerful) are protected from investigation and prosecution and only the "small fish" (powerless individuals) are investigated and punished, it will be difficult for the IAAC to gain the respect and trust of the citizens. However, the IAAC needs the continued support of the government to provide sufficient budget and personnel to enable it to perform its functions effectively. In the final analysis, strong political will is the most important prerequisite for ensuring Mongolia's long-term success in curbing corruption. As the IAAC is still a young organization with only four years in existence, it needs to be given more time and resources to enable it to ensure sustained success in making corruption a fact of life rather than a way of life in Mongolia.

## NOTES

1. Mr. Garigtsatsralt Chuluunkhuu is 26 years old and Head of the Marketing Research Department at the Transportation and Development Bank of Mongolia.
2. I am very grateful to Mr. Tumur-Ochiryn Erdenebileg, MP in Mongolia, for providing me with his paper on "Public Opinion on Corruption in Mongolia" and to Mr. Oyungerel Adiya for translating the paper into English.

3. Information on these monthly salaries was provided by courtesy of the Cabinet Secretariat, Government of Mongolia. The exchange rate was US$1 = 850 tugriks during September–November 1998.

4. According to Mr. Batzorig Badam, Head of the IAAC's Research and Analysis Division, the Parliament of Mongolia appointed Mr. Baasai Dangaasuren as the IAAC's CG on 28 December 2006 and approved its organizational structure on 11 January 2007. Mr. Dorj Sunduisuren was appointed by Parliament as the DCG on 6 February, 2007. E-mail correspondence on 17 February 2011.

5. Information on the IAAC's organizational structure and personnel was provided by Mr. Batzorig Badam, through e-mail correspondence on 11 February 2011.

6. Interview with an officer of the General Council of Courts in Ulaanbataar on 19 October 1998.

# CHAPTER 12

# CURBING CORRUPTION: AN IMPOSSIBLE DREAM?

> While the rhetoric about the evils of corruption remains strong, corruption is alive and well.
>
> – Steve Berkman (2008, p. 5)

> Anti-corruption reform is a marathon, not a sprint, and even MCA [Millennium Challenge Account]-eligible countries have a long way to go in terms of curbing corruption.
>
> – Millennium Challenge Corporation (2007, p. 8)

The preceding 10 chapters analyze respectively how Japan, India, the Philippines, Taiwan, Singapore, Hong Kong SAR, Thailand, South Korea, Indonesia, and Mongolia are combating corruption. These 10 Asian countries demonstrate between them the three patterns of controlling corruption. Chapters 6 and 7 have shown that the third pattern of corruption control practised by Singapore and Hong Kong SAR is more effective than Japan's pattern 1 and pattern 2 in the cases of India, Philippines, and Taiwan. However, Chapters 8–11 show that the adoption of pattern 3 by Thailand, South Korea, Indonesia, and Mongolia has not been effective because of the lack of political will and their unfavorable policy contexts.

The purpose of this concluding chapter is fivefold: (1) to demonstrate the relationship between corruption and governance; (2) to compare the effectiveness of the 10 Asian countries in curbing corruption according to five indicators; (3) to explain why pattern 3 is more effective than the other two patterns of corruption control if there is political will and a favorable policy context; (4) to identify the key ingredients for an effective anti-corruption strategy; and (5) to ascertain whether curbing corruption in Asian countries is an impossible dream.

## CORRUPTION AND GOVERNANCE

The negative consequences of corruption for a country's development have been identified in Chapter 1. Corruption is ubiquitous and is found in "all political systems, at every level of government, and in the delivery of all scarce public goods and services" (Caiden, 1988, p. 6). Corruption is a universal problem, and governments all over the world have introduced measures to tackle this "social pandemic" which has "many faces" and is "the most challenging obstacle to economic development" (Campos & Bhargava, 2007, pp. 1–2).

What is the relationship between corruption and governance? The answer to this question depends on whether corruption is viewed as the independent variable or the dependable variable. If corruption is the independent variable, it is only one factor determining the governance of a country, which is the dependent variable. This means that curbing corruption is a necessary but insufficient prerequisite for good governance. On the contrary, if corruption is the dependent variable, poor governance will be one of the major independent variables, with the other causes being low salaries of civil servants, ample opportunities and red tape, ineffective policing, cultural factors, and the lack of political will, as explained in Chapter 1. Viewed from this perspective, corruption is a serious consequence of poor governance in a country.

If a country is well governed, it is less likely to suffer from corruption if the government implements impartially the various anticorruption measures. Conversely, if a country is poorly governed, it is more likely to be afflicted by rampant corruption because the government lacks the political will to implement impartially the anti-corruption measures. This is clearly seen in "failed states" that are "consumed by internal violence and cease delivering positive political goods to their inhabitants" (Rotberg, 2004, p. 1). More importantly, Robert Rotberg (2004, p. 8) contends that corruption "thrives on an usually destructive scale" in failed states because there is widespread "petty or lubricating corruption" as well as "escalating levels of venal corruption."

The correlation between poor governance and rampant corruption is demonstrated clearly by the low percentile ranks of the seven failed states of Myanmar (0.0), Somalia (0.5), Afghanistan (1.4), Zimbabwe (1.9), Democratic Republic of Congo (2.9), Iraq (4.8), and Sudan (6.2) on the 2009 World Bank's control of corruption indicator. These seven countries also score poorly on Transparency International's 2010 Corruption Perceptions Index (CPI) and the World Bank's *Doing Business 2010 Survey*, as indicated in Table 12.1.

***Table 12.1.*** Corruption Indicators of Seven Failed States, 2009–2010.

| Country | Control of Corruption 2009 Percentile Rank | Corruption Perceptions Index 2010 Score | Doing Business Survey 2010 Rank ($N = 183$) |
|---|---|---|---|
| Myanmar | 0.0 | 1.4 | NA |
| Somalia | 0.5 | 1.1 | NA |
| Afghanistan | 1.4 | 1.4 | 160th |
| Zimbabwe | 1.9 | 2.4 | 159th |
| Democratic Republic of Congo | 2.9 | 2.0 | 182nd |
| Iraq | 4.8 | 1.5 | 153rd |
| Sudan | 6.2 | 1.6 | 154th |

*Sources:* Compiled from http://info.worldbank.org/governance/wgi/mc_chart.asp; http://www.transparency.org/policy_research/surveys_indices/cpi/2010/results; and World Bank (2009, p. 4).

In their *Index of State Weakness in the Developing World*, Susan E. Rice and Stewart Patrick (2008, p. 10) have identified 141 weakest states with the eight weakest states as Somalia (0.52), Afghanistan (1.65), Democratic Republic of Congo (1.67), Iraq (3.11), Burundi (3.21), Sudan (3.29), Central African Republic (3.33), and Zimbabwe (3.44). Somalia, Afghanistan and the Democratic Republic of Congo are defined as "failed states" because they are the three weakest states in the world and are unable to perform these four critical functions of government:

> fostering an environment conducive to sustainable and equitable economic growth; establishing and maintaining legitimate, transparent, and accountable political institutions; securing their populations from violent conflict and controlling their territory; and meeting the basic human needs of their population. (Rice & Patrick, 2008, p. 8)

In my analysis of the challenges of building an inclusive, responsive, and capable state in 42 Asia-Pacific countries, I found that 20 of these countries have exhibited varying degrees of state weakness, according to Rice and Stewart's Index of State Weakness. These 20 countries are: Afghanistan, the only "failed state," the three "critically weak states" of North Korea, Myanmar and Nepal, the eight "weak states" of Pakistan, Cambodia, Papua New Guinea, Timor-Leste, Laos, Bangladesh, Solomon Islands, and Sri Lanka, and these eight "states to watch" namely: the Philippines, Iran, India, China, Fiji, Indonesia, Thailand, and Vietnam (Quah, 2010c, pp. 74–78).

The current crisis in the failed state of Afghanistan illustrates clearly the linkage between poor governance and rampant corruption. Nashreen Ghufran (2008, p. 157) has highlighted the corruption and inefficiency of the Afghan National Police, which has developed slowly because of corruption, incompetence and factional politics. Similarly, Jaap de Hoop Scheffer (2009, p. B07), NATO Secretary-General, has attributed Afghanistan's instability to corruption and bad governance thus:

> The basic problem in Afghanistan is ... too little good governance. Afghans need a government that deserves their loyalty and trust.... But we have paid enough in blood and treasure, to demand that the Afghan government take more concrete and vigorous action to root out corruption and increase efficiency, even where that means difficult political choices.

Another journalist, Dexter Filkins (2009) reported that "the government of Afghanistan is shot through with corruption and graft" because "everything seems to be for sale: public offices, access to government services, even a person's freedom" and people pay bribes to "get electricity for their homes, to get out of jail, even to enter the airport." The Social Audit Committees (SACs) formed by the Aga Khan Development Network in hundreds of villages in northern Afghanistan have also exposed many cases of corruption by examining the books and records of the *shuras* or elected councils. The most blatant example of corruption was the discovery by the SAC of a village that its *shura* had spent nearly US$1,000 for a kebab (Gopal, 2009).

Ashraf Ghani, a former World Bank official, said that "the entire economy has been criminalized" and there is "a crisis of governance" in Afghanistan because the tremendous increase in corruption has been accompanied by massive poverty (Constable, 2009, p. A06). A recent Congressional Committee Report urged the national security components of the United States government to "systematically track and analyze the effects of U.S., NATO, and other international donor funds on corruption in Afghanistan" because corruption is "smothering the nascent efforts at Afghan governance" (Tierney, 2010, p. 68).

In sum, the critical situation in Afghanistan and other failed states shows how corruption and poor governance are closely intertwined. Corruption must be curbed to ensure good governance in Asian countries because poor governance breeds corruption and makes the fight against corruption much more difficult in these countries. Unfortunately, failed states like Somalia and Afghanistan, lack the procedures for blocking the advancement of bad leaders who are kleptocrats, psychopaths, and tyrants. The greatest fear, according to Paul Collier (2010, p. 88), occurs when "politically ambitious crooks do not just fritter away the money they make from corruption; they invest it in future power." The plunder of the Philippines by the late President Ferdinand Marcos, and the pillage of Indonesia by the late President Mohammad Soeharto, and their families and cronies, have undermined the rule of law and left a legacy of entrenched corruption in both countries today.

## COMPARATIVE ANALYSIS OF EFFECTIVENESS OF 10 ASIAN COUNTRIES IN CURBING CORRUPTION

### *Corruption Perceptions Index, 1995–2010*

Of the 10 Asian countries discussed in this book, Singapore is the most effective and Indonesia the least effective, judging from their CPI scores from 1995 to 2010. Table 12.2 provides details of the average CPI scores for these 10 countries

***Table 12.2.*** CPI Scores[a] of 10 Asian Countries, 1995–2010.

| Year | SG | HK | JAP | TAI | KOR | THA | MON | IND | PHP | INDO |
|---|---|---|---|---|---|---|---|---|---|---|
| 1995 | 9.26 | 7.12 | 6.72 | 5.08 | 4.29 | 2.79 | NA | 2.78 | 2.77 | 1.94 |
| 1996 | 8.80 | 7.01 | 7.05 | 4.98 | 5.02 | 3.33 | NA | 2.63 | 2.69 | 2.65 |
| 1997 | 8.66 | 7.28 | 6.57 | 5.02 | 4.29 | 3.06 | NA | 2.75 | 3.05 | 2.72 |
| 1998 | 9.1 | 7.8 | 5.8 | 5.3 | 4.2 | 3.0 | NA | 2.9 | 3.3 | 2.0 |
| 1999 | 9.1 | 7.7 | 6.0 | 5.6 | 3.8 | 3.2 | 4.3 | 2.9 | 3.6 | 1.72 |
| 2000 | 9.1 | 7.7 | 6.4 | 5.5 | 4.0 | 3.2 | NA | 2.8 | 2.8 | 1.72 |
| 2001 | 9.2 | 7.9 | 7.1 | 5.9 | 4.2 | 3.2 | NA | 2.7 | 2.9 | 1.9 |
| 2002 | 9.3 | 8.2 | 7.1 | 5.6 | 4.5 | 3.2 | NA | 2.7 | 2.6 | 1.9 |
| 2003 | 9.4 | 8.0 | 7.0 | 5.7 | 4.3 | 3.3 | NA | 2.8 | 2.5 | 1.9 |
| 2004 | 9.3 | 8.0 | 6.9 | 5.6 | 4.5 | 3.6 | 3.0 | 2.8 | 2.6 | 2.0 |
| 2005 | 9.4 | 8.3 | 7.3 | 5.9 | 5.0 | 3.8 | 3.0 | 2.9 | 2.5 | 2.2 |
| 2006 | 9.4 | 8.3 | 7.6 | 5.9 | 5.1 | 3.6 | 2.8 | 3.3 | 2.5 | 2.4 |
| 2007 | 9.3 | 8.3 | 7.5 | 5.7 | 5.1 | 3.3 | 3.0 | 3.5 | 2.5 | 2.3 |
| 2008 | 9.2 | 8.1 | 7.3 | 5.7 | 5.6 | 3.5 | 3.0 | 3.4 | 2.3 | 2.6 |
| 2009 | 9.2 | 8.2 | 7.7 | 5.6 | 5.5 | 3.4 | 2.7 | 3.4 | 2.4 | 2.8 |
| 2010 | 9.3 | 8.4 | 7.8 | 5.8 | 5.4 | 3.5 | 2.7 | 3.3 | 2.4 | 2.8 |
| Mean | 9.2 | 7.9 | 7.0 | 5.6 | 4.7 | 3.3 | 3.1 | 3.0 | 2.7 | 2.2 |
| Rank | 1 | 2 | 3 | 4 | 5 | 6 | 7 | 8 | 9 | 10 |

*Source*: Compiled from the CPI from 1995–2010 at http://www.transparency.org.
*Note*: NA refers to not available as Mongolia was not included in the CPI from 1995–1998 and 2000–2003.
[a]The score ranges from 0 (most corrupt) to 10 (least corrupt).

***Table 12.3.*** PERC's Scores of Nine Asian Countries, 1995–2010[a].

| Year | SIN | HK | JAP | TAI | KOR | THA | PHP | IND | INDO |
|---|---|---|---|---|---|---|---|---|---|
| 1995 | 1.20 | 2.80 | 2.00 | 4.20 | 4.00 | 5.90 | 6.60 | 7.00 | 7.30 |
| 1996 | 1.09 | 2.79 | 1.93 | 5.53 | 5.16 | 6.55 | 6.95 | 6.86 | 7.69 |
| 1997 | 1.05 | 3.03 | 4.60 | 5.96 | 7.71 | 7.49 | 6.50 | 8.20 | 8.67 |
| 1998 | 1.43 | 2.74 | 5.00 | 5.20 | 7.12 | 8.29 | 7.17 | 7.40 | 8.95 |
| 1999 | 1.55 | 4.06 | 4.25 | 6.92 | 8.20 | 7.57 | 6.71 | 9.17 | 9.91 |
| 2000 | 0.71 | 2.49 | 3.90 | 6.89 | 8.33 | 8.20 | 8.67 | 9.50 | 9.88 |
| 2001 | 0.83 | 3.77 | 2.50 | 6.00 | 7.00 | 8.55 | 9.00 | 9.67 | 9.67 |
| 2002 | 0.90 | 3.33 | 3.25 | 5.83 | 5.75 | 8.89 | 8.00 | 9.17 | 9.92 |
| 2003 | 0.38 | 3.61 | 4.50 | 6.33 | 5.50 | 8.75 | 7.67 | 9.30 | 9.33 |
| 2004 | 0.50 | 3.60 | 3.00 | 6.10 | 6.67 | 7.80 | 8.33 | 8.90 | 9.25 |
| 2005 | 0.65 | 3.50 | 3.46 | 6.15 | 6.50 | 7.20 | 8.80 | 8.63 | 9.10 |
| 2006 | 1.30 | 3.13 | 3.01 | 5.91 | 5.44 | 7.64 | 7.80 | 6.76 | 8.16 |
| 2007 | 1.20 | 1.87 | 2.10 | 6.23 | 6.30 | 8.03 | 9.40 | 6.67 | 8.03 |
| 2008 | 1.13 | 1.80 | 2.25 | 6.55 | 5.65 | 8.00 | 9.00 | 7.25 | 7.98 |
| 2009 | 1.07 | 1.89 | 3.99 | 6.47 | 4.64 | 7.63 | 7.00 | 7.21 | 8.32 |
| 2010 | 1.42 | 2.67 | 3.49 | 6.28 | 5.98 | 7.60 | 8.06 | 7.18 | 9.27 |
| Mean | 1.02 | 2.94 | 3.32 | 6.03 | 6.24 | 7.75 | 7.85 | 8.05 | 8.83 |
| Rank | 1 | 2 | 3 | 4 | 5 | 6 | 7 | 8 | 9 |

*Sources*: Compiled from PERC (2001, 2008, p. 7); Hussain (2009, p. B5); and *Straits Times* (2010a).

[a]The score ranges from 0 (least corrupt) to 10 (most corrupt).

from 1995 to 2010. Singapore's average CPI score is 9.2, followed by Hong Kong SAR (7.9), Japan (7.0), Taiwan (5.6), South Korea (4.7), Thailand (3.3), Mongolia (3.1), India (3.0), Philippines (2.7), and Indonesia (2.2).

### *PERC's Annual Surveys on Corruption, 1995–2010*

As Mongolia has been excluded from PERC's annual surveys on corruption, Table 12.3 shows that the ranking for the nine countries is similar to that of the 2010 CPI, except that the Philippines has been ranked higher than India.

### *Control of Corruption, 1996–2009*

Table 12.4 shows the World Bank's control of corruption data for the 10 Asian countries from 1996 to 2009. It confirms the same rank order for these countries except that India is ranked 7th with an average percentile rank of

***Table 12.4.*** Control of Corruption Percentile Rank of 10 Asian Countries, 1996–2009.

| Year | SG | HK | JAP | TAI | KOR | THA | IND | MON | PHP | INDO |
|---|---|---|---|---|---|---|---|---|---|---|
| 1996 | 96.6 | 87.9 | 80.1 | 76.2 | 68.4 | 40.3 | 36.4 | 64.1 | 52.9 | 32.0 |
| 1998 | 96.1 | 84.0 | 85.4 | 76.7 | 64.6 | 57.8 | 43.7 | 46.6 | 48.1 | 13.1 |
| 2000 | 96.6 | 84.5 | 86.9 | 78.6 | 63.6 | 49.5 | 41.3 | 44.7 | 39.3 | 16.0 |
| 2002 | 98.5 | 91.7 | 82.5 | 75.2 | 69.9 | 46.6 | 39.3 | 57.8 | 41.3 | 10.2 |
| 2003 | 98.5 | 92.2 | 85.9 | 75.7 | 67.5 | 51.0 | 44.7 | 51.9 | 41.3 | 15.5 |
| 2004 | 98.5 | 92.2 | 86.9 | 78.6 | 68.9 | 50.0 | 45.1 | 47.1 | 36.4 | 19.9 |
| 2005 | 98.1 | 93.2 | 85.0 | 77.2 | 71.8 | 54.9 | 43.2 | 39.3 | 36.9 | 20.9 |
| 2006 | 97.6 | 94.2 | 90.3 | 73.3 | 68.4 | 50.5 | 50.0 | 37.9 | 26.2 | 25.2 |
| 2007 | 98.1 | 93.7 | 85.5 | 72.5 | 72.9 | 48.3 | 44.4 | 28.5 | 29.0 | 33.3 |
| 2008 | 98.6 | 94.7 | 85.5 | 72.0 | 69.1 | 43.5 | 44.4 | 31.4 | 30.9 | 33.3 |
| 2009 | 99.0 | 94.3 | 87.1 | 72.4 | 71.4 | 51.0 | 46.7 | 23.8 | 27.1 | 28.1 |
| Mean | 97.8 | 91.1 | 85.6 | 75.3 | 68.8 | 49.4 | 43.6 | 43.0 | 37.2 | 22.5 |
| Rank | 1 | 2 | 3 | 4 | 5 | 6 | 7 | 8 | 9 | 10 |

*Source*: Compiled from http://info.worldbank.org/governance/wgi/mc_chart.asp

43.6 and Mongolia is ranked 8th with an average percentile rank of 43.0. Singapore retains its first ranking with an average percentile rank of 97.8 and Indonesia remains last with an average percentile rank of 22.5.

### *Ease of Doing Business, 2007–2011*

In addition to the CPI, PERC's annual surveys on corruption, and the World Bank's control of corruption indicator, we can also analyze how the 10 Asian countries perform on these two indirect indicators of corruption: the World Bank's *Doing Business Surveys* from 2007–2011; and the *Global Competitiveness Report's* indicator on public trust of politicians from 1999 to 2010–2011. Table 12.5 shows, in terms of the ease of doing business, Singapore ranks first, followed by Hong Kong SAR, Japan, Thailand, South Korea, Taiwan, Mongolia, Indonesia, India, and the Philippines.

### *Public Trust of Politicians, 1999–2010*

For the public trust of politicians from 1999 to 2010–2011, Table 12.6 shows that Singapore has the highest average score (6.43) for this period, followed

***Table 12.5.*** Ease of Doing Business in 10 Asian Countries, 2007–2011.

| Country | 2007 (*N* = 175) | 2008 (*N* = 178) | 2009 (*N* = 181) | 2010 (N = 183) | 2011 (*N* = 183) | Average Rank |
|---|---|---|---|---|---|---|
| Singapore | 1st | 1st | 1st | 1st | 1st | 1st |
| Hong Kong SAR | 5th | 4th | 4th | 3rd | 2nd | 4th |
| Japan | 11th | 12th | 12th | 15th | 18th | 14th |
| Thailand | 18th | 15th | 13th | 12th | 19th | 15th |
| South Korea | 23rd | 30th | 23rd | 19th | 16th | 22nd |
| Taiwan | 47th | 50th | 61st | 46th | 33rd | 47th |
| Mongolia | 45th | 52nd | 58th | 60th | 73rd | 58th |
| Indonesia | 135th | 123rd | 129th | 122nd | 121st | 126th |
| India | 134th | 120th | 122nd | 133rd | 134th | 129th |
| Philippines | 126th | 133rd | 140th | 144th | 148th | 138th |

*Sources*: World Bank (2006b, p. 6, 2007, p. 6, 2008, p. 6, 2009, p. 4, 2010a, p. 4).

***Table 12.6.*** Public Trust of Politicians in 10 Asian Countries, 1999 to 2010–2011.

| Country | Average Score[a] | Rank | 2010 CPI Score |
|---|---|---|---|
| Singapore | 6.43 | 1st | 9.3 |
| Hong Kong SAR | 4.90 | 2nd | 8.4 |
| Taiwan | 3.25 | 3rd | 5.8 |
| Japan | 2.84 | 4th | 7.8 |
| South Korea | 2.77 | 5th | 5.4 |
| Indonesia | 2.63 | 6th | 2.8 |
| Thailand | 2.58 | 7th | 3.5 |
| India | 2.07 | 8th | 3.3 |
| Philippines | 1.71 | 9th | 2.4 |
| Mongolia[b] | 1.70 | 10th | 2.7 |

*Sources*: Compiled from Schwab et al. (1999, p. 327), Porter et al. (2000, p. 253), Schwab et al. (2002, p. 408), Cornelius (2003, p. 619), Sala-i-Martin (2004, p. 499), Schwab and Porter (2007, p. 379), Schwab and Porter (2008, p. 367), Schwab (2009, p. 349) and Schwab (2010, p. 369).
[a]The score ranges from 1 (very low) to 7 (very high) for the respondents' answers to this statement: "How would you rate the level of public trust in the ethical standards of politicians in your country."
[b]Mongolia's average score is based on the 2007–2008, 2008–2009, 2009–2010 and 2010–2011 surveys because it was not included in the previous surveys.

***Table 12.7.*** Effectiveness of Curbing Corruption in 10 Asian Countries by Indicators.

| Country | CPI Rank & Score 2010 | PERC Rank & 2010 | Control of Corruption 2009 | Doing Business Rank 2011 | Public Trust of Politicians Rank & Score 2010 |
|---|---|---|---|---|---|
| Singapore | 1st (9.3) | 1st (1.42) | 99.0 | 1st | 1st (6.4) |
| Hong Kong | 13th (8.4) | 3rd (2.67) | 94.3 | 2nd | 16th (4.7) |
| Japan | 17th (7.8) | 5th (3.49) | 87.1 | 18th | 58th (3.1) |
| Taiwan | 33rd (5.8) | 8th (6.28) | 72.4 | 33rd | 36th (3.7) |
| South Korea | 39th (5.4) | 7th (5.98) | 71.4 | 16th | 105th (2.1) |
| Thailand | 78th (3.5) | 12th(7.60) | 51.0 | 19th | 83rd (2.5) |
| India | 87th (3.3) | 11th(7.18) | 46.7 | 134th | 88th (2.3) |
| Indonesia | 110th (2.8) | 16th(9.27) | 28.1 | 121st | 51st (3.3) |
| Mongolia | 116th (2.7) | NA | 23.8 | 73rd | 118th (1.9) |
| Philippines | 134th (2.4) | 13th(8.06) | 27.1 | 148th | 134th (1.6) |
| Sample size | 178 | 16 | 213 | 183 | 139 |

*Sources*: http://www.transparency.org/policy_research/surveys_indices/cpi/2010/results; *Straits Times* (2010a); http://info.worldbank.org/governance/wgi/sc_chart.asp; World Bank (2010a) and Schwab (2010, p. 369).

by Hong Kong SAR (4.90), and Taiwan (3.25). The average scores for the other seven countries are much lower, ranging from 2.84 for Japan to 1.71 for the Philippines, and 1.70 for Mongolia. The level of public trust of Japanese politicians is lower than the level of public trust of Taiwanese politicians even though Japan's 2010 CPI score is higher than that of Taiwan's.

### *Comparative Analysis*

The effectiveness of the 10 Asian countries in curbing corruption is compared according to the five indicators mentioned in Table 12.7, which confirms Singapore's consistent first ranking on all five indicators on the one hand, and the poor performance of Mongolia and Philippines on the other hand.

Similarly, Table 12.8 ranks the 10 Asian countries according to the five indicators, with Singapore occupying the top position, followed by Hong Kong SAR, Japan, Taiwan, South Korea, Thailand, India, Indonesia, Mongolia, and Philippines.

***Table 12.8.*** Ranking of 10 Asian Countries in Curbing Corruption by Indicators.

| Country | CPI 2010 | PERC 2010 | Control of Corruption 2009 | Doing Business 2011 | Public Trust of Politicians 2010 | Overall Rank |
|---|---|---|---|---|---|---|
| Singapore | 1 | 1 | 1 | 1 | 1 | 1st |
| Hong Kong | 2 | 2 | 2 | 2 | 2 | 2nd |
| Japan | 3 | 3 | 3 | 4 | 5 | 3rd |
| Taiwan | 4 | 5 | 4 | 6 | 3 | 4th |
| South Korea | 5 | 4 | 5 | 3 | 8 | 5th |
| Thailand | 6 | 7 | 6 | 5 | 6 | 6th |
| India | 7 | 6 | 7 | 9 | 7 | 7th |
| Indonesia | 8 | 9 | 8 | 8 | 4 | 8th |
| Mongolia | 9 | NA | 10 | 7 | 9 | 9th |
| Philippines | 10 | 8 | 9 | 10 | 10 | 10th |

*Source*: Compiled from Table 12.7.

## PATTERNS OF CORRUPTION CONTROL IN ASIAN COUNTRIES

### *Singapore's CPIB and POCA*

Corruption was first made an offense in Singapore in 1871, but it was only in December 1937 that the first anticorruption law, the Prevention of Corruption Ordinance (POCO), was enacted. However, as shown in Chapter 6, the POCO was ineffective in curbing corruption because of its limited powers and penalties and its implementation by the Anti-Corruption Branch (ACB) of the Criminal Investigation Department of the Singapore Police Force (SPF). The ACB failed to curb corruption because of its limited manpower and resources, its priority in fighting serious crimes like homicide instead of corruption, and the prevalence of police corruption. The incident that triggered the British colonial government's decision to transfer the task of controlling corruption from the SPF to an independent anticorruption agency (ACA) was the revelation that senior police officers and detectives were involved in the robbery of S$400,000 worth of opium in October 1951. The Corrupt Practices Investigation Bureau (CPIB) was established as the world's first independent ACA in October 1952.

However, the POCO and CPIB were ineffective in curbing corruption because of their limited powers and resources. Accordingly, the PAP government, which assumed power in June 1959 after winning the May 1959 general election, demonstrated its commitment to fighting corruption by replacing the weak POCO in June 1960 with the Prevention of Corruption Act (POCA), which enhanced the penalties for corrupt offenses and strengthened the CPIB's powers. The CPIB's ability to enforce the POCA impartially against all those found guilty of corrupt offenses, including the rich and famous, is responsible for Singapore's success in minimizing corruption because corruption is now perceived as a "low-reward, high-risk" activity.

### *Hong Kong's ICAC*

Singapore's innovative approach in fighting corruption by relying on an ACA independent of the police was adopted by Hong Kong on 15 February 1974, when the Independent Commission Against Corruption (ICAC) was formed. A study team of Hong Kong civil servants, who visited Singapore and Sri Lanka in 1968 to examine their anticorruption laws, had recommended, inter alia, that the task of curbing corruption should be transferred from the Royal Hong Kong Police Force (RHKPF) to another independent agency. However, this recommendation was rejected by the RHKPF and was only accepted by Governor MacLehose after the June 1973 escape of a corruption suspect, Chief Superintendent Peter Godber, to the United Kingdom.

Unlike the CPIB, which focuses mainly on investigating corruption cases and enforcing the POCA, the ICAC initiated a three-pronged strategy of emphasizing investigation, education, and prevention. Accordingly, it is not surprising that the ICAC has almost 14 times more staff than the CPIB, and is organized in terms of the Operations Department, the Community Relations Department (CRD), and the Corruption Prevention Department (CPD), to take care of its three main functions.

In short, Singapore and Hong Kong SAR have adopted the third pattern of corruption control by relying on the CPIB and ICAC respectively to enforce impartially their comprehensive anticorruption laws.

### *Thailand, South Korea, Indonesia, and Mongolia*

Following Singapore and Hong Kong SAR, Thailand, South Korea, Indonesia, and Mongolia have also adopted pattern 3 by relying on an independent ACA to implement the anti-corruption laws. Chapter 8 on Thailand shows that the National Counter Corruption Commission was formed in November 1999 to replace the ineffective Counter Corruption Commission, which was established in February 1975.

South Korea's anticorruption measures are analyzed in Chapter 9, beginning in 1963, when President Park Chung-Hee formed the Board of Audit and Inspection (BAI) as a *de facto* ACA by merging the Board of Audit and the Commission on Inspection. However, the BAI is not a specialized ACA as it is more concerned with its auditing and inspection duties. The BAI was strengthened under President Kim Young-Sam's administration (1993–1998) when he introduced new laws to reduce corruption and increased the BAI's staff. President Kim Dae-Jung should be credited for initiating comprehensive anticorruption reforms that resulted in the enactment of the Anti-Corruption Act in July 2001 and the establishment of the Korea Independent Commission Against Corruption (KICAC) in January 2002. The creation of the KICAC to implement the Anti-Corruption Act is a clear demonstration that South Korea has adopted the third pattern of corruption control. However, unlike other ACAs, the KICAC could not investigate corruption cases and had to rely on the BAI and other agencies to do so. The KICAC's successor, the Anti-Corruption Civil Rights Commission (ACRC) suffers from the same limitation.

In Indonesia's case, the *Komisi Pemberantasan Korupsi* (KPK) was established in December 2003, almost five decades after Indonesia began its battle against corruption in 1955. Chapter 10 shows that while the KPK has achieved some success in curbing corruption in Indonesia, it is still under-staffed and not provided with adequate resources by the government to enable it to perform its anti-corruption functions effectively.

Chapter 11 focuses on Mongolia, which is the only country among the 10 countries analyzed in this book that was under communist rule for 70 years (1921–1991). The legacy of communist rule was not positive as the transition from a command economy to a market economy not only increased the opportunities for corruption, but also added new forms of corruption to those cultivated under communist rule. After holding democratic elections in 1992, the Law on Anti-Corruption was enacted by the government in April 1996. The absence of an independent ACA in Mongolia meant that it had to rely on the police to investigate corrupt offenses. This method was ineffective as the low salaries of civil servants and political leaders contributed to corruption in many government departments, including the police. However, Mongolia's first pattern of corruption control (anticorruption laws without an independent ACA) was transformed to the third pattern with the enactment of the Anti-Corruption Law in July 2006, and the establishment of the Independent Authority Against Corruption (IAAC) six months later.

### *India, Philippines, and Taiwan*

The experiences of India, the Philippines, and Taiwan in fighting corruption are analyzed respectively in Chapters 3, 4, and 5. These three countries adopt pattern 2 because of their reliance on multiple agencies to combat corruption. India began her fight against corruption in 1941 with the creation of the Delhi Special Police Establishment. The enactment of the Prevention of Corruption Act in 1947 was followed by the establishment of the Central Bureau of Investigation (CBI) in April 1963 and the Central Vigilance Commission (CVC) in February 1964. In addition to the CBI and CVC, there are also Anti-Corruption Bureaus (ACBs) at the state level for handling vigilance and anti-corruption work. As the CBI is a police organization and the ACBs derive their investigation powers from the Police Act, India has not learnt the lesson from Singapore's and Hong Kong's success in curbing corruption namely: "do not rely on the police to curb corruption" especially when the police are corrupt because this "would be like giving candy to a child, expecting that it would not be eaten" (Quah, 2004, pp. 1–2).

The Philippines has the most number of anticorruption laws and agencies in Asia. As indicated in Chapter 4, it has relied on seven anticorruption laws and 19 presidential ACAs since its battle against corruption began in the 1950s. Despite the record number of anticorruption measures, the Philippines has not implemented these measures impartially. The lack of policing in the Philippines is reflected in a comparative analysis of those arrested for corruption offenses, which shows that an individual is 35 times more likely to be arrested for a corrupt offense in Hong Kong than in the Philippines.

The analysis of anticorruption measures in Taiwan in Chapter 5 shows that the three ACAs are the Ministry of Justice Investigation Bureau (MJIB), the Department of Government Employee Ethics, which supervises all the government ethics units, and the Public Prosecutors Offices throughout the country. However, the MJIB, which is the lead ACA, is not concerned with fighting corruption only because it is also responsible for performing such important functions as national security matters, prevention of drug trafficking, and dealing with organized crime.

Unfortunately, the multiple ACAs in India, the Philippines, and Taiwan are ineffective in curbing corruption because of their limited powers and resources, their competition for scarce resources, their lack of coordination, and their inability to enforce impartially the anticorruption laws. In other words, the critical factor for success is not the number of anticorruption measures but whether these measures are impartially implemented.

### *Japan as an Anomaly*

The anomalous case of Japan, which is analyzed in Chapter 2, shows that, unlike the other nine countries, there is a high level of grand corruption coexisting with a low level of petty corruption. The high level of grand corruption in Japan can be attributed to the high cost of getting elected and being a politician as well as the practice of *amakudari* (descent from heaven).

Japan's political system is the most expensive in the world as Bouissou (1997, pp. 133–134) had estimated in 1997 that Japanese politicians had spent an average annual expenditure of ¥900 billion (£6.5 billion). As the official salaries of Diet members are inadequate for meeting their social obligations, they are compelled to raise funds from business firms, associations, and individuals. Elections in Japan are expensive because the electoral system, which provides voters with a single nontransferable vote, encourages vote-buying. Furthermore, Diet members must build and maintain their own political machines by employing staff in their districts and also in Tokyo to deal with their constituents' requests and to raise funds.

Japanese politicians rely on two main sources for political funds: the business community and the construction industry. While "big business" provides the lion's share of funds for politicians, the construction industry is also an important source of funding for their electoral campaigns. Similarly, the practice of *amakudari* is a mechanism for re-employing retired senior civil servants in high-level positions in private corporations or public enterprises. *Amakudari* has been criticized because strong ministry-business ties have resulted in bureaucratic corruption in the construction industry in the form of the *dango* (secret bid-rigging) system, which is illegal. Consequently, the Ministry of Construction has many *amakudari* positions for its retired senior bureaucrats in the construction and real estate industries.

The low level of petty corruption in Japan can be explained by the important social tradition of gift-giving, which makes it difficult for prosecutors to distinguish between a gift and a bribe. Japanese give gifts during midsummer and end of the year, on their return from trips, and at weddings and funerals to strengthen mutual ties and obligations between givers and recipients. The regulations prohibiting gift-giving in government and private organizations are ineffective because they contradict all the traditional norms as those violating these regulations are not ostracized. It is difficult for a prosecutor to convict a civil servant for bribery if he receives a gift-envelope containing clean money bills as a gift from his friend. Consequently, the number of Japanese civil servants convicted of bribery is very low.

As corruption is a structural problem in Japan, the reliance on the first pattern of corruption control reflects the lack of political will of the government to curb corruption. Instead of relying on an independent ACA to combat corruption, all the post-war governments in Japan have adopted a reactive approach by only requesting the SIDs of the Public Prosecutors' Offices in Tokyo, Osaka and Nagoya to investigate the 52 corruption scandals during 1948–2008 after their public exposure.

As noted in Chapter 2, this emphasis on *post hoc* investigation of corruption scandals without any concern for educating the population on the importance of corruption prevention and education confirms the government's disinterest in curbing corruption effectively and does not augur well for the future. Indeed, curbing corruption in Japan remains an impossible dream until the "rotten triangle" of politicians, bureaucrats and businessmen, which nurtures the existing system of structural corruption, is destroyed.

## THE IMPORTANCE OF POLITICAL WILL

Which of the three patterns of corruption control is the most effective and why? To answer these questions, it is necessary to explain why the third pattern is more effective than the first two patterns.

The experiences of Singapore and Hong Kong SAR described in Chapters 6 and 7 have demonstrated clearly the critical importance of political will in curbing corruption. If political will is defined as "the demonstrated credible intent of political actors (elected or appointed leaders, civil society watchdogs, stakeholder groups, etc.) to attack perceived causes or effects of corruption at a systemic level," Sahr J. Kpundeh (1998, p. 92) contends that it is "a critical starting point for sustainable and effective programs" as "without it, governments' statements to reform civil service, strengthen transparency and accountability and reinvent the relationship between government and private industry remain mere rhetoric."

The political leadership in other Asian countries must be sincerely committed to the eradication of corruption by demonstrating exemplary conduct and adopting a modest life-style themselves. Those found guilty of corruption must be punished, regardless of their position or status in society. Political will is absent or lacking when the "big fish" (rich and famous) are protected from prosecution for corruption, and only the "small fish" (ordinary people) are caught. Under these circumstances, the anti-corruption strategy lacks credibility and will be doomed to failure.

Political will is the most important prerequisite as a comprehensive anticorruption strategy will fail if it is not supported by the political leadership in a country. For example, as shown in Chapter 4, the Philippines has the most anticorruption laws and agencies in Asia, but it has been ineffective in curbing corruption because of the absence of political will among the political leaders. Indeed, even though President Corazon Aquino was more honest than her predecessor, President Ferdinand Marcos, she lacked the political will to punish her corrupt relatives. In short, the commitment of the political leaders in fighting corruption ensures the allocation of adequate personnel and resources to the anticorruption effort, and the impartial enforcement of the anticorruption laws by the ACAs.

Japan's continued reliance on the ineffective first pattern of corruption control reflects the government's lack of political will in combating corruption during the past 63 years. Japan's lack of political will in curbing corruption is understandable because the existing system of structural corruption favors the "rotten triangle" of politicians, bureaucrats and businessmen. There is thus no incentive to undermine the status quo by replacing the ineffective anti-corruption laws and the reactive strategy of relying on the three inadequately staffed Special Investigation Departments in Tokyo, Nagoya, and Osaka to investigate corruption scandals after their exposure.

The analysis of Taiwan's anticorruption measures in Chapter 5 shows that the lack of political will is the critical factor responsible the country's failure to curb corruption effectively. Unlike his father, President Chiang Ching-kuo was committed to curbing corruption during his term of office and the government and provincial bureaucracy did not tolerate corruption and punished the corrupt officials. In contrast, his successor, Lee Teng-hui, tolerated corruption because of his personal friendships with business tycoons. Consequently, the scale and cost of vote-buying increased, and *heijin* or "black gold" politics blossomed.

In addition to the impartial enforcement of the anticorruption laws by the ACA, there are two manifestations of a government's political will in curbing corruption. First, there must be comprehensive anticorruption legislation to prevent loopholes and periodic review of such legislation to introduce amendments whenever necessary. Second, the ACA must be provided with sufficient legal powers, personnel, and budget to perform its functions effectively. Richard Rose (2005, p. 103) has stressed the critical importance of resources in lesson-drawing as the application of a policy lesson requires "a multiplicity of resources involving legislation, money, personnel, and organizations."

More specifically, there are two indicators for assessing the political will of a government: (1) the per capita expenditure of the lead ACA (if there are multiple ACAs) that is calculated by dividing its budget for a selected year by the population in the country for the same year; and (2) the staff-population ratio for the same ACA by calculating the ratio of the population in the country for the selected year that are served by the number of personnel in the ACA for the same year (Quah, 2009c, pp. 181–182).

According to Table 12.9, Hong Kong's ICAC has the highest per capita expenditure of US$13.40 in 2008, followed by Singapore's CPIB (US$2.32), South Korea's ACRC (US$1.26), Mongolia's IAAC (US$1.15), Thailand's National Anti-Corruption Commission (NACC) (US$0.33), the Philippines' Office of the Ombudsman (OMB) (US$0.22), Taiwan's MJIB (US$0.18), Indonesia's KPK (US$0.14) and India's CBI (US$0.04). Among these nine ACAs, it should be noted that the MJIB, ACRC, OMB, and CBI are not dedicated ACAs because they are also responsible for performing other functions that are not related to fighting corruption. As the MJIB's budget for its anticorruption activities is indicated in Table 12.9, this means that the per capita expenditure for the ACRC, OMB, and CBI includes their expenditure on the non-corruption-related functions too.

Table 12.10 shows that in terms of staff-population ratio, Hong Kong's ICAC retains its first position with a staff-population ratio of 1: 5,780. Taiwan's MJIB is second with a staff-population of 1: 27,262, followed by Mongolia's IAAC (1: 30,000), Singapore's CPIB (1: 56,163), Thailand's NACC (1: 86,892), Philippines' OMB (1: 89,076), South Korea's ACRC (1: 103,863), India's CBI (1: 243,373), and Indonesia's KPK, which has the worst staff-population ratio of 1: 433,888.

***Table 12.9.*** Per Capita Expenditure of Nine Asian ACAs in 2008[a].

| ACA | Budget | Population | Per Capita Expenditure | Rank |
|---|---|---|---|---|
| ICAC | US$97.7 million | 7.3 million | US$13.40 | 1 |
| CPIB | US$11.2 million | 4.83 million | US$2.32 | 2 |
| ACRC | US$61 million[b] | 48.4 million | US$1.26 | 3 |
| IAAC | US$3.1 million | 2.7 million | US$1.15 | 4 |
| NACC | US$21.3 million | 64.3 million | US$0.33 | 5 |
| OMB | US19.6 million | 89.7 million | US$0.22 | 6 |
| MJIB | US$4.02 million | 22.9 million | US$0.18 | 7 |
| KPK | US$31.8 million | 234.3 million | US$0.14 | 8 |
| CBI | US$52.1 million | 1,186.2 million | US$0.04 | 9 |

*Sources:* Compiled from ICAC (2009, p. 28); MJIB (2010); Republic of Singapore (2010, p. 382); Republic of the Philippines (2010, p. 183); OMB (2009, p. 10); Bureau of the Budget (2009, pp. 81); KPK (2009, p. 106); CBI (2009, pp. 56, 65); and Choi (2011, p. 39).

[a]Japan is excluded because it does not have an ACA.

[b]2009 figure.

***Table 12.10.*** Staff-Population Ratio of Nine Asian ACAs in 2008.

| ACA | Personnel | Population | Staff-Population Ratio | Rank |
|---|---|---|---|---|
| ICAC | 1,263 | 7.3 million | 1: 5,780 | 1 |
| MJIB | 840[a] | 22.9 million | 1: 27,262 | 2 |
| IAAC | 90 | 2.7 million | 1: 30,000 | 3 |
| CPIB | 86 | 4.83 million | 1: 56,163 | 4 |
| NACC | 740 | 64.3 million | 1: 86,892 | 5 |
| OMB | 1,007 | 89.7 million | 1: 89,076 | 6 |
| ACRC | 466[b] | 48.4 million | 1: 103,863 | 7 |
| CBI | 4,874 | 1,186.2 million | 1: 243,373 | 8 |
| KPK | 540 | 234.3 million | 1: 433,888 | 9 |

*Sources*: As in Table 12.7.
[a]This figure consists of the 40 personnel in the Anti-Corruption Division in the MJIB's Headquarters and the 800 personnel in the field offices across Taiwan.
[b]2009 figure.

Pattern 3 is also more effective because the ACA is a specialized agency concerned solely with minimizing corruption. The agency's specific focus on combating corruption is an advantage as it is not distracted by other priorities (Quah, 2009b, pp. 173–174). Thus, the CPIB in Singapore and the ICAC in Hong Kong focus their energies and resources on curbing corruption unlike India's CBI, which is concerned also with tackling terrorism and organized crime in addition to corruption, or Taiwan's MJIB, which is also responsible for national security matters, preventing drug trafficking, and curbing organized crime.

In sum, pattern 3 is the most effective pattern in combating corruption because of the presence of political will, which ensures the impartial enforcement of the anticorruption laws by an independent ACA. In contrast, patterns 1 and 2 are ineffective in curbing corruption because of the absence of political will. For India, the Philippines, and Taiwan, which have adopted pattern 2, there are many ACAs and laws to combat corruption. However, the political leaders in these three countries lacked the political will to implement these measures effectively. Pattern 1 is also ineffective as both political will and an independent ACA are absent in the case of Japan.

## THE IMPORTANCE OF POLICY CONTEXT

The effectiveness of Singapore's CPIB and Hong Kong's ICAC in curbing corruption has been publicized widely as "best practices" at various

***Table 12.11.*** Anti-Corruption Agencies in Asian Countries.

| Country | Anticorruption Agency | Date Established |
|---|---|---|
| Singapore | Corrupt Practices Investigation Bureau | October 1952 |
| Malaysia | Anti-Corruption Agency | October 1967 |
| | Malaysian Anti-Corruption Commission | January 2009 (reorganized) |
| Hong Kong SAR | Independent Commission Against Corruption | February 1974 |
| Brunei Darussalam | Anti-Corruption Bureau | February 1982 |
| Nepal | Commission for the Investigation of Abuse of Authority | 1990 |
| Sri Lanka | Commission to Investigate Allegations of Bribery or Corruption | November 1994 |
| Pakistan | National Accountability Bureau | November 1999 |
| Thailand | National Counter Corruption Commission | November 1999 |
| | National Anti-Corruption Commission | July 2008 (renamed) |
| Macao SAR | Commission Against Corruption | November 1999 |
| South Korea | Korea Independent Commission Against Corruption | January 2002 |
| | Anti-Corruption and Civil Rights Commission | February 2008 (reorganized) |
| Indonesia | *Komisi Pemberantasan Korupsi* (Corruption Eradication Commission) | December 2003 |
| Bangladesh | Anti-Corruption Commission | May 2004 |
| Bhutan | Office of the Anti-Corruption Commission | January 2006 |
| Mongolia | Independent Authority Against Corruption | December 2006 |

*Source*: Compiled by the author.

international conferences and workshops. This explains why pattern 3 has been adopted by many Asian countries, as can be seen in Table 12.11, following the examples of Singapore and Hong Kong. However, as explained in the previous section, the adoption of pattern 3 and a single ACA has not automatically resulted in a significant reduction in corruption in these countries for two reasons: the absence of political will in these countries to implement the necessary anti-corruption reforms and their unfavorable policy contexts.

Table 12.12 shows the differences in policy context among 21 Asian countries. The first contextual difference is that Singapore and Hong Kong, which are city-states, are among the smallest of the 21 Asian countries as only Macao SAR is smaller in land area. Thus, except for Macao SAR, the other 18 countries are much larger, with China, India, Indonesia, and Mongolia being the four largest countries.

Second, in terms of population, China and India have the two largest populations in the world with 1,345.8 million and 1,198 million, respectively. Indonesia is next with 230 million, followed by Pakistan (180.8 million), Bangladesh (162.2 million), Japan (127.2 million), Philippines (92 million), Vietnam (88.1 million), Thailand (67.8 million), South Korea (48.3 million), Nepal (29.3 million), Malaysia (27.5 million), Taiwan (23.1 million), Sri Lanka (20.2 million), and Cambodia (14.8 million). Only Brunei Darussalam (400,000), Macao SAR (542,200), Bhutan (691,141), and Mongolia (2.7 million) have smaller populations than Hong Kong (7 million) or Singapore (4.98 million).

Third, the variations in GDP per capita are wide, with Japan leading the pack, followed by Macao SAR, Singapore, Hong Kong SAR, Brunei Darussalam, South Korea, Taiwan, Malaysia, Thailand, China, Indonesia, and Sri Lanka. The GDP per capita of the remaining nine countries are below US$2,000 namely: the Philippines (US$1,746), Mongolia (US$1,560), Bhutan (US$1,410), Vietnam (US$1,060), India (US$1,031), Pakistan (US$1,017), Cambodia (US$775), Bangladesh (US$574), and Nepal (US$452).

The final difference in policy context is the nature of the political system. China and Vietnam are communist states while Mongolia, which was communist for 70 years, became democratic in 1991. India is the world's largest democracy with the second largest population, a GDP per capita of US$1,031, and ranked 87th with a score of 3.3 in the 2010 CPI. Hong Kong was a British colony until July 1997 when it became a SAR of China. Similarly, Macao was a Portuguese colony and became a SAR of China in November 1999. Of the remaining 15 countries, six are constitutional monarchies namely: Bhutan, Brunei Darussalam, Cambodia, Japan, Malaysia, and Thailand. The other nine countries have democratic political systems, with three parliamentary democracies (Bangladesh, Nepal, and Singapore) and six presidential democracies (Indonesia, Pakistan, the Philippines, South Korea, Sri Lanka, and Taiwan).

In short, both Singapore and Hong Kong SAR have more favorable policy contexts than most of the other 19 Asian countries because both are politically stable city states with smaller territories to govern, with higher GDP per capita and relatively small populations. Except for Japan and

***Table 12.12.*** Policy Contexts of 21 Asian Countries.

| Country | Land Area (sq km) | Population (2009) | GDP per capita (2009) | Political System | 2010 CPI Ranking |
|---|---|---|---|---|---|
| Singapore | 710 | 4.98 million | US$37,293 | Parliamentary democracy | 1st (9.3) |
| Hong Kong SAR | 1,075 | 7 million | US$29,826 | SAR of China | 13th (8.4) |
| Japan | 377,727 | 127.2 million | US$39,731 | Constitutional monarchy | 17th (7.8) |
| Taiwan | 36,179 | 23.1 million | US$16,392 | Presidential democracy | 33rd (5.8) |
| Bhutan[a] | 47,000 | 691,141 | US$1,410 | Constitutional monarchy | 36th (5.7) |
| Brunei Darussalam | 6,000 | 400,000 | US$26,325 | Constitutional monarchy | 38th (5.5) |
| South Korea | 99,274 | 48.3 million | US$17,074 | Presidential democracy | 39th (5.4) |
| Macao SAR | 29.5 | 542,200 | US$38,964 | SAR of China | 46th (5.0) |
| Malaysia | 332,665 | 27.5 million | US$6,897 | Constitutional monarchy | 56th (4.4) |
| China | 9,560,900 | 1,345.8 million | US$2,430 | Communist state | 78th (3.5) |
| Thailand | 513,115 | 67.8 million | US$3,940 | Constitutional monarchy | 78th (3.5) |
| India | 3,287,263 | 1,198 million | US$1,031 | Parliamentary democracy | 87th (3.3) |
| Sri Lanka | 66,000 | 20.2 million | US$2,041 | Presidential democracy | 91st (3.2) |
| Indonesia | 1,904,443 | 230 million | US$2,329 | Presidential democracy | 110th (2.8) |
| Mongolia | 1,565,000 | 2.7 million | US$1,560 | Presidential democracy | 116th (2.7) |
| Vietnam | 331,114 | 88.1 million | US$1,060 | Communist state | 116th (2.7) |
| Bangladesh | 143,998 | 162.2 million | US$574 | Parliamentary democracy | 134th (2.4) |
| Philippines | 300,000 | 92 million | US$1,746 | Presidential democracy | 134th (2.4) |
| Pakistan | 803,940 | 180.8 million | US$1,017 | Presidential democracy | 143rd (2.3) |
| Nepal | 147,000 | 29.3 million | US$452 | Federal Parliamentary Democracy | 146th (2.2) |
| Cambodia | 181,000 | 14.8 million | US$775 | Constitutional Monarchy | 154th (2.1) |

*Sources*: *Economist* (2010a), Schwab (2010, pp. 361–362), Statistics & Census Service (2011, pp. 1, 5, 7).
[a]Bhutan's population and GDP per capita in 2008 are taken from Schwab (2009, pp. 341–342) as the 2009 data are not available.

Macao SAR, which have higher GDP per capita, Singapore and Hong Kong SAR are richer and smaller in terms of land area and population. These two assets of their policy context and the political will of their governments enable the CPIB and ICAC to curb corruption more effectively than the other Asian countries.

In contrast to Singapore's and Hong Kong's favorable policy contexts, the policy contexts in India, Indonesia and the Philippines are less favorable because of their larger land area, population and lower GDP per capita. India is the seven largest country in the world, followed by Indonesia, which is the 16th largest, and the Philippines, which has a land area of 300,000 sq km. India is a subcontinent and Indonesia and the Philippines are large archipelagos. All three countries have GDP per capita ranging from US$1,031 for India, to US$1,746 for the Philippines, and to US$2,239 for Indonesia. The policy contexts in these three countries are unfavorable for implementing the anticorruption laws because of their large territories and populations. Furthermore, their low GDP per capita means that their governments cannot afford to allocate adequate budgets and personnel for the CBI, KPK, and OMB, as shown in Tables 12.9 and 12.10.

## KEY INGREDIENTS FOR AN EFFECTIVE ANTICORRUPTION STRATEGY

In addition to the critical factor of political will, there are four other ingredients for an effective anticorruption strategy namely: (1) the ACA must be incorruptible and independent; (2) corrupt offenders must be punished; (3) opportunities for corruption in vulnerable government departments must be reduced; and (4) political leaders and civil servants should be paid adequate salaries to prevent them from succumbing to the temptation to accept bribes if they are poorly paid.

### *An Incorruptible and Independent ACA*

As shown in Chapters 6 and 7, Singapore and Hong Kong are effective in minimizing corruption because of their reliance on a single ACA solely dedicated to the task of corruption control. In contrast, the task of combating corruption in India and the Philippines is shared among many ACAs. The CBI is the most important ACA in India but it is not concerned mainly with fighting corruption because it is also responsible for dealing with terrorism and organized crime. Unlike the other former British colonies like Singapore, Hong Kong, and Malaysia, which have rejected the inherited British method of employing the police to curb corruption, India has continued to rely on the CBI and the state ACBs, which are all police units.

The ACA must be incorruptible for two reasons. First, if its personnel are corrupt, its legitimacy and public image will be eroded as its officers have broken the law by being corrupt. Second, corruption among its staff prevents them from performing their tasks impartially and effectively. For example, as shown in Chapter 4, President Aquino's creation of the Presidential Commission on Good Government (PCGG) to retrieve the money stolen by the Marcos family and his cronies was viewed critically by the public as two of her Cabinet members and her relatives were accused of corruption. In June 1988, five PCGG agents were accused of graft and 13 more were under investigation.

To ensure its incorruptibility, the ACA must be controlled or supervised by honest and incorruptible political leaders. In Singapore, the CPIB comes under the jurisdiction of the Prime Minister's Office (PMO) and its director reports directly to the Prime Minister. For example, on November 21, 1986, the CPIB's Director informed Prime Minister Lee Kuan Yew that a complaint of corruption had been made against the Minister for National Development, Teh Cheang Wan. Lee authorized the CPIB's Director to pursue the case. Teh was interviewed by a senior CPIB officer on December 2, 1986, for 16 hours. Three days later, Teh was required by the Attorney General's Office to provide the CPIB within two weeks with a sworn statement of assets belonging to him and his family and details of money or property sent out of Singapore during 1979–1986. On December 14, Teh committed suicide without furnishing the CPIB with a list of his assets. During the hearings held by the Commission of Inquiry, Prime Minister Lee Kuan Yew, stressed that: "there is no way a Minister can avoid investigations, and a trial if there is evidence to support one. Teh Cheang Wan chose death rather than face a trial on the charges of corruption which the Attorney-General had yet to settle" (Parliament of Singapore, 1987, pp. 27–30).

The CPIB will continue to investigate allegations of political corruption in Singapore as long as the incumbent government remains committed to minimizing corruption. However, if the CPIB's director does not have the prime minister's consent to investigate complaints of corruption against a minister, article 22G of the Constitution of the Republic of Singapore empowers him to continue his investigations if he obtains the support of the elected president (Thio, 1997, p. 114).

Hong Kong's ICAC is scrutinized by several independent committees made up of citizens from different sectors of the community, who were appointed by the Governor before July 1997 and by the Chief Executive after that date. As mentioned in Chapter 7, the Advisory Committee on Corruption reviews the ICAC's overall policy and reviews the work of the Operations Department, the CRD, the CPD, and the Administration Branch. The work of each department is also examined by an advisory committee. The Operations Review Committee focuses on the Operations Department, the Corruption Prevention Advisory Committee examines the work of the CPD, and the Citizens Advisory Committee on Community Relations deals with the CRD.

The ACA must be staffed by honest and competent personnel. Overstaffing should be avoided, and any staff member found guilty of corruption must be punished and dismissed. Details of such punishment must be widely publicized in the mass media to deter others and to demonstrate the ACA's integrity and credibility to the public. In contrast to the CPIB's 93 staff members, the ICAC is much larger and has 1,268 staff members.

### *Minimize Corruption by Punishing the Guilty*

As corruption is an illegal activity, corrupt individuals should be punished. However, the probability of detecting and punishing corrupt offenders varies in Asian countries. Corruption thrives in those countries where the public perceives it to be a "low-risk, high-reward" activity because the probability of detecting and punishing corrupt offenders is low. In contrast, corruption can only be minimized when it is perceived by the population to be a "high-risk, low-reward" activity, that is, when corrupt individuals are likely to be caught and severely punished for their offenses.

A comparison of successful prosecution of corrupt offenders in Hong Kong and the Philippines in Chapter 4 has shown that a person involved in corrupt behavior in Hong Kong is 35 times more likely to be detected and punished than his or her counterpart in the Philippines. In his memoirs, Senior Minister Lee Kuan Yew blamed the "soft, forgiving culture" of the Philippines for the lack of punishment meted to Marcos and his family and cronies for their corrupt activities (Lee, 2000, p. 342).

In his comparative analysis of how bureaucratic corruption is curbed in three Asian countries, Palmier (1985, p. 280) found that corruption was rampant in Indonesia because it was tolerated as corrupt officials were seldom punished. As noted in Chapter 10, Theodore M. Smith's 1969 survey of regional economic planners in Indonesia reported that three-quarters of the respondents admitted that they did not dismiss their ineffective subordinates. Indeed, the most common procedure for dealing with corrupt officials was to transfer them to other positions. Palmier concluded that while there was strong policing against corruption in Hong Kong, "policing is very poor in Indonesia, and insufficient in India."

The analysis of the causes of corruption in South Korea in Chapter 9 shows that of the 131 persons found guilty of corruption offenses from 1993 to 2004, only 41 persons (31.3 percent) served their prison sentences while 90 persons (68.7 percent) received suspended sentences. The courts in South Korea are lenient and do not impose the stricter sentences required by law. For example, among the 35 public officials convicted for accepting bribes exceeding 50 million won, only 17 (48.6 percent) were imprisoned, while 18 (51.4 percent) received suspended sentences. Similarly, former presidents Chun Doo-Hwan and Roh Tae-Woo were found guilty of corruption and were fined and imprisoned. However, their punishment was reduced considerably by President Kim Young-Sam when he granted both ex-presidents amnesty after serving only 16 months in jail.

For corruption to be perceived as a high-risk, low-reward activity, the governments in Asian countries must publicize through the mass media the detection of corrupt behavior among civil servants and political leaders, and their punishment according to the law if they are guilty. The mass media reduces corruption by exposing it, as corruption "thrives in secrecy, and withers in the light" (Palmier, 1985, p. 279). In short, negative publicity is an effective deterrent against corruption.

The experiences of Singapore and Hong Kong SAR demonstrate the importance of punishing corrupt offenders, regardless of their status or position, to deter others from being involved in corruption. The other Asian countries can learn from their experiences by minimizing corruption and deterring those who are not involved in corrupt practices from doing so by recognizing and rewarding civil servants and political leaders for being honest and incorruptible instead of punishing them. Indeed, the lack of punishment of corrupt civil servants and political leaders in these Asian countries sends the wrong message to their honest counterparts and the population at large because it makes a mockery of the anticorruption laws and encourages others to become corrupt as the probability of being caught and punished is low.

In other words, the political systems in those Asian countries plagued with corruption reward those who are corrupt and punish those who are honest. Consequently, in order to curb corruption effectively, these countries must reverse their system of reward and punishment by punishing the corrupt offenders and rewarding those who have abstained from being corrupt.

### *Reducing Opportunities for Corruption in "Wet" Government Departments*

The expanding role of the civil service in Asian countries has increased the opportunities for administrative discretion and corruption. For example, as mentioned in Chapter 6, the regulation, control and prohibition of certain activities by the government in Hong Kong provided ample opportunities for corruption in construction, import and export, health, prostitution, gambling, drugs, and immigration.

As noted in Chapter 10, Indonesian civil servants distinguish between "wet" and "dry" agencies in terms of the opportunities for corruption. "Wet" agencies are preferred by them as civil servants in such agencies have larger budgets and access to the fee-paying public while those in "dry" agencies are denied such access. According to Indonesia's coordinating minister from 1989 to 1993, Radius Prawiro, the tax office and customs service are the most lucrative of the "wet" government agencies because of the abundant opportunities for corruption in these agencies.

In the Philippines, which is analyzed in Chapter 4, the Bureau of Customs, Bureau of Immigration, Bureau of Internal Revenue, Department of Education, Culture and Sports (DECS), Department of Public Works and Highways (DPWH), Land Transportation Office, and the Philippine National Police are "wet" agencies because of their large budgets and access to the public. For example, the DECS was a "fertile ground for corruption because it is oozing with money." Congress provided the DECS with a budget of 86.9 billion pesos or 18.9 percent of the Philippines' national budget in 1998 (Chua, 1999, p. 6). According to Yvonne T. Chua (1999, p. 7):

> There is so much money at DECS that it drives officials into a spending frenzy. The funds also draw a swarm of suppliers and contractors, many of them unscrupulous. There is so much available that even those outside DECS, especially politicians and other officials, demand a piece of the action.

Similarly, the DPWH, which deals with huge infrastructure projects involving vast sums of expenditure, has been described as "a bastion of graft" and "a den of corrupt practices" because of the ample opportunities for corruption among its employees and external vested interests (Vitug, 1998, p. 188).

In Thailand's case, which is described in Chapter 8, the Ministry of Interior is the most corruption-prone ministry because it includes the Police Department, which is the most corrupt government agency. The other four ministries with the most corruption cases are the Ministry of Education, the Ministry of Agriculture, the Ministry of Economic Development, and the PMO. The 1992–1993 survey of 2,243 respondents in Bangkok and four regions identified these five "wet" and corrupt public agencies: Police Department (33.7 percent); Ministry of Defense (27 percent); Ministry of Interior (26 percent); Department of Transport (22.5 percent); and the Land Department (10.1 percent).

In sum, those Asian countries with vulnerable or "wet" government agencies must review their procedures periodically to reduce opportunities for corruption. Unnecessary regulations and excessive red tape should be reduced and cumbersome administrative procedures streamlined in order to minimize the opportunities for corruption.

### *Reducing Temptation by Paying Adequate Salaries*

An important cause for corruption in India, Indonesia, Mongolia, the Philippines, South Korea, Taiwan, and Thailand is the low salaries of its civil servants and political leaders. Low salaries in these Asian countries contribute to corruption as poorly paid bureaucrats and politicians will be tempted to resort to corruption.

Chapter 11 shows that the major cause of corruption in Mongolia is the extremely low wages of its civil servants and politicians. The highest monthly salary is that of the President, who earns US$761 per month in October 2010. Table 12.13 confirms that the Prime Minister of India is the poorest paid political leader among the ten Asian countries as his annual basic salary in 2010 is US$4,106. In the Philippines, civil servants describe their salaries as "starvation wages" that are inadequate to meet the needs of their families. As civil service salaries in South Korea are equivalent to 70 percent of private sector wages, some scholars have suggested that bureaucratic corruption can be reduced by improving the salaries of the civil servants.

The salaries of civil servants and political leaders in Singapore and Hong Kong are among the highest in the world, and certainly higher than those in Japan, Taiwan, South Korea, Indonesia, Thailand, the Philippines, Mongolia, and India. The low salaries of police officers in Singapore during the British colonial period were a major cause of police corruption. However, Singapore did not solve the problem of corruption by increasing civil service salaries as it could not afford to do so when it attained self-government in 1959. Indeed, the salaries of civil servants were only raised in 1972 to minimize the brain drain from the civil service and only after corruption had been minimized through the impartial implementation of the POCA by the CPIB.

***Table 12.13.*** Salaries of Political Leaders in 10 Asian Countries, 2010.

| Country | Annual Basic Salary | Rank |
|---|---|---|
| Singapore | US$2,183,516 | 1 |
| Hong Kong SAR | US$513,245 | 2 |
| Japan | US$273,676 | 3 |
| Taiwan | US$184,200 | 4 |
| South Korea | US$136,669 | 5 |
| Indonesia | US$124,171 | 6 |
| Thailand | US$32,200 | 7 |
| Philippines | US$24,000 | 8 |
| Mongolia | US$9,132 | 9 |
| India | US$4,106 | 10 |

*Sources: Economist* (2010b). The salaries for Thailand and the Philippines are taken from Backman (2004, p. 27), and the Mongolian President's annual basic salary is provided by the IAAC.

Robert S. Leiken (1996–97, p. 68) has recommended that "when the people pay government functionaries decent salaries, they are buying a layer of insulation against patronage and bribery." Singapore's experience, as recounted in Chapter 6, demonstrates "the importance of reducing the incentive for corruption by keeping the salaries of civil servants and political leaders competitive with the private sector" for they will be more vulnerable to corruption if their salaries are low (Quah, 1989a, p. 850).

However, this strategy of reducing corruption through salary increase is expensive and many governments in Asian countries cannot afford to raise salaries. More importantly, raising salaries alone will not solve the problem of corruption if the government does not have the political will to minimize corruption and ensure the incorruptibility of the ACA, and if it does not punish corrupt officials or reduce opportunities for corruption in the vulnerable agencies. In short, raising salaries of civil servants and political leaders is a necessary but insufficient prerequisite for an effective anti-corruption strategy.

## CURBING CORRUPTION IS NOT AN IMPOSSIBLE DREAM

Is it possible for Asian countries to curb corruption or is corruption an unbeatable foe? The successful experiences of Singapore and Hong Kong SAR in minimizing corruption demonstrate that curbing corruption in

Asian countries is not an impossible dream if there is political will. Both city-states have adopted the effective third pattern of corruption control of relying on an independent ACA to implement the anticorruption laws. Corruption was a way of life in these two city-states during the British colonial period. However, the establishment of the CPIB as an independent ACA in October 1952 and the enactment of the POCA in June 1960 strengthened the CPIB's powers and enhanced its effectiveness in minimizing corruption. Similarly, the fight against corruption in Hong Kong only made progress after the creation of the ICAC in February 1974.

Of the 10 countries discussed in this book, Singapore and Hong Kong are among the smallest in terms of land area and population, but also the richest in terms of GDP per capita. In contrast, the other eight countries are larger with bigger populations with the exception of Mongolia, which has a small population of 2.7 million. India is a subcontinent with a federal system, while Indonesia and the Philippines are archipelagos. Mongolia is also much larger than Singapore and Hong Kong, but has fewer people and a much lower population density. As former British colonies, Singapore, and Hong Kong have also benefited from the legacy of meritocracy and clean government on the one hand, but suffered from relying on the British method of relying on the police to curb corruption.

The policy contexts of the other 19 Asian countries listed in Table 12.12 are quite different from the more favorable policy contexts of Singapore and Hong Kong. Apart from being city-states with smaller populations, Singapore and Hong Kong are also richer than the other Asian countries except Japan and Macao SAR, and can therefore devote the required resources for the CPIB and ICAC and to pay competitive salaries to their civil servants and political leaders. In the final analysis, whether the effective anti-corruption measures of Singapore and Hong Kong can be successfully transplanted to the other Asian countries depends on two important factors: the nature of their policy context, and whether their political leaders have the political will to implement the required reforms.

Given the contextual differences between the two city-states and the other Asian countries, and the absence of political will, it is unlikely that many Asian countries can successfully transplant the effective anticorruption strategies of Singapore and Hong Kong. Indeed, according to Michael Johnston (1999, p. 225), while Independent Commissions Against Corruption "are unlikely to be right for every country," they do demonstrate that "permanent, independent agencies addressing corruption as a deep-rooted problem, making society a partner in reform, and developing careful strategies for prevention may be a promising way to confront serious corruption."

Nevertheless, in view of the different policy contexts, other Asian countries can emulate and adapt some features of Singapore's and Hong Kong's anticorruption strategy to suit their own needs, provided that their political leaders, civil servants, and the population are prepared to support and implement the required reforms.

Finally, as noted in Chapter 3 on India, the $64,000 question is: If political will is the critical factor responsible for ensuring the effectiveness of an anti-corruption strategy, how can it be nurtured in those countries where there is no political will to fight corruption? As suggested in Chapter 3, to enhance the political will to minimize corruption in other Asian countries like Mongolia, India, Indonesia, Japan, the Philippines, South Korea, Taiwan, and Thailand, the citizens in these eight countries must elect to public office honest and incorrupt political leaders who will strengthen or improve the existing anticorruption measures and enforce these measures impartially. This is the critical first step as the role of the political leaders is to serve as a catalyst to change the population's tolerant attitude toward corruption by introducing more effective anti-corruption measures and enforcing such measures fairly.

The UNDP's Asia-Pacific Human Development Report on *Tackling Corruption, Transforming Lives*, has recommended a comprehensive seven-point agenda for action by governments, international organizations, civil society, media, and private sector organizations to fight corruption. Its most important recommendation is the adoption of a pragmatic two-pronged approach (combining top-down efforts by governments and bottom-up initiatives by civil society and media organizations), which gives top priority to curbing corruption in the police, health and education services, and natural resources because of the critical impact of these three sectors on the poor and human development (UNDP, 2008, pp. 12–13, 151–155).

Robert Klitgaard (1997, p. 502) has suggested three "almost psychological steps" for generating the political will to fight corruption. First, "leaders must see that improvements are possible without political suicide." Second, "leaders must develop a strategy that recognizes that not everything can be done at once." Third, "leaders need political insulation." All three steps can be provided by international collaboration with other countries and international agencies like the Asian Development Bank, the Inter-American Development Bank, the Organization for Economic Cooperation and Development, the UNDP, and the World Bank.

Singapore's and Hong Kong's success in curbing corruption not only indicates that curbing corruption is not an impossible dream but also shows how corruption can be defeated. Indeed, both city-states can assist other

Asian countries interested in improving the effectiveness of their anti-corruption measures by sharing their experience and "best practices" at international conferences, seminars and workshops and on-site visits to the CPIB and ICAC.

As rampant corruption in many Asian countries cannot be reduced overnight, it might be more realistic for these countries to adopt the sectoral approach that provides a road map for tracking and addressing the vulnerabilities to corruption in those critical sectors that require reform urgently (Campos & Bhargava, 2007, p. 8). Bertram I. Spector (2005, p. 6) contends that "corruption needs to be addressed by demands for reform on a *sector-by-sector basis*" because programs focusing on vulnerable sectors "can take hold and be sustained over the longer term." In concluding his synthesis of the corruption vulnerabilities and their remedies in nine sectors, Stephen Schwenke (2005, p. 177) astutely observes that "significant advances can be made in the fight against public sector corruption provided there is the requisite political will, competent and well-trained public sector staff, and effective and civic-minded leadership."

In the final analysis, whether corruption remains a fact of life or a way of life in Asian countries depends mainly on whether their political leaders, civil servants and citizens are committed to minimizing it by addressing its causes through the implementation of a policy of zero-tolerance towards corruption. As the "journey of a thousand miles begins with a single step," the critical first step that must be taken by those Asian countries afflicted with widespread corruption is for their political leaders to demonstrate their political will to curbing corruption. Without such political will, curbing corruption in these Asian countries will remain an impossible dream.

# REFERENCES


Abdulbaki, L. (2008). Democratization in Indonesia: From transition to consolidation. *Asian Journal of Political Science, 16*(2), 151–172.

Abidi, S. H. S. (1998). *Seth and Capoor's commentaries on Prevention of Corruption Act with a treatise on anti-corruption laws*. Allahabad: Law Publishers, India.

*ABS-CBN News*. (2009a). RP ranking improves in Asian corruption survey. *ABS-CBN News*, April 8. Available at http://www.abs-cbnnews.com/print/49430.

*ABS-CBN News*. (2009b). PAGC chief denies nepotism rap. *ABS-CBN News*, November 17. Available at http://www.abs-cbnnews.com/nation/11/17/09/pagc-chief-denies-nepotism-rap. Retrieved on November 25, 2010.

*ABS-CBN News*. (2010). Investors rank Philippines 4th most corrupt in AsiaPac. *ABS-CBN News*, March 9. Available at http://www.abs-cbnnews.com/business/03/09/10/investors-rank-philippines-4th-most-corrupt-asiapac. Retrieved on November 6, 2010.

ACRC (Anti-Corruption and Civil Rights Commission). (2009). *Korea anti-corruption annual report 2008*. Seoul. Available at http://www.acrc.go.kr/eng_index.html. Retrieved on January 14, 2011.

ACRC. (2010a). *About us: Functions*. Available at http://www.acrc.go.kr/eng_index.html. Retrieved on January 14, 2011.

ACRC. (2010b). *Annual Report 2009*. Seoul. Available at http://www.acrc.go.kr/eng_index.html. Retrieved on January 14, 2011.

Acuna, M. (2009). Corruption in RP has become family-based, says bishop. *CBCP News*, March 16. Available at http://www.cbcpnews.com/?q=node/7874

ADB (Asian Development Bank). (1992). *Mongolia: A centrally planned economy in transition*. Hong Kong: Oxford University Press.

ADB. (2000). *Combating corruption in Asian and Pacific economies*. Manila: ADB.

ADB. (2004). *Governance: Progress and challenges in Mongolia*. Manila: ADB.

ADB. (2005). Meeting conclusions and framework of action. In: *Curbing corruption in Tsunami relief operations* (pp. 1–6). Manila: ADB.

Adiya, O. (1998). A beginner's guide to corruption. *UB Post*, September 15, p. 3.

*AFP (Agence France-Presse)*. (2008a). Taiwan's top court clears president-elect of corruption. *AFP*, April 25.

*AFP*. (2008b). Taiwan former first lady absent from trial again. *AFP*, September 20.

*AFP*. (2009). Taiwan's ex-leader's wife admits money laundering. *AFP*, February 11.

Agrawal, P. (2010). Corruption: India's growth industry. *Wall Street Journal*, November 18. Available at http://blogs.wsj.com/indiarealtime/2010/11/18/corruption-indias-growth-industry. Retrieved on November 20, 2010.

Ahmad, M. (2009). Corruption could eat up all development funds. *The News*, February 1. Available at http://www.thenews.com.pk/print1.asp?id=160121. Retrieved on February 3, 2009.

Ahmad, N., & Brookins, O. T. (2004). On corruption and countervailing actions in three South Asian nations. *Journal of Economic Policy Reform, 7*(1), 21–30.

AISS (Asian Institute of Strategic Studies). (2003). *Grappling with graft and corruption*. Quezon City: AISS.

Akio, K. (2010). Public service ethics and corruption in Japan. In: E. M. Berman, M. J. Moon & H. Choi (Eds), *Public administration in East Asia: Mainland China, Japan, South Korea, and Taiwan* (pp. 251–271). Boca Raton: CRC Press, chap. 12.

Alatas, S. H. (1991). *Corruption: Its nature, causes and functions*. Kuala Lumpur: S. Abdul Majeed.

Alexander, P. C. (1995). *The perils of democracy*. Bombay: Somaiya Publications.

Alfiler, M. C. P. (1979). Administrative measures against bureaucratic corruption: The Philippine experience. *Philippine Journal of Public Administration, 23*(3–4), 321–349.

Ali, M. (2000). Eradicating corruption – The Singapore experience. Paper presented at the Seminar on International Experiences on Good Governance and Fighting Corruption in Bangkok, Thailand, February 17.

Allen, L. (1990). Kakuei Tanaka/Lockheed affair (1976–1986). In: *Political scandals and causes celebres since 1945: An international reference compendium* (pp. 153–161). Harlow: Longman Group UK.

Alpha Research Company. (2006). *Pocket Thailand in Figures 2006* (9th ed.). Muang.

Amara, R. (1992). Bureaucracy vs. bureaucracy: Anti-corrupt practice measures in Thailand. In: R. K. Arora (Ed.), *Politics and administration in changing societies: Essays in honor of Professor Fred W. Riggs* (pp. 220–244). New Delhi: Associated Publishing House, chap. 15.

Ambraseys, N., & Bilham, R. (2011). Corruption kills. *Nature, 469*(7329), 153–155.

Amundsen, I. (1999). *Political corruption: An introduction to the issues*. Working Paper No. 7. Chr. Michelsen Institute, Bergen.

Andrews, J. (2001). *Pocket Asia* (6th ed.). London: Profile Books.

Andrews, J. (2002). *Pocket Asia* (7th ed.). London: Profile Books.

Appleby, P. A. (1953). *Public administration in India: Report of a survey*. New Delhi: Cabinet Secretariat, Organization and Methods Division, Government of India.

Aquino, B. A. (1999). *Politics of plunder: The Philippines under Marcos* (2nd ed.). Quezon City: National College of Public Administration and Governance, University of the Philippines.

Asia Foundation. (2009). *Mongolia corruption benchmarking survey April 2009*. San Francisco. Available at http://www.asiafoundation.com/publication/pdf/522

Asia Foundation. (2010). *Mongolia corruption benchmarking survey X: The tenth semi-annual corruption benchmarking survey in Mongolia*. San Francisco. Available at http://www.asiafoundation.org/publications/pdf/817

Asmarani, D. (2002). Audit chief slams Mega's battle on graft. *Straits Times*, January 23, p. A5.

Assegaf, I. S., Ahmad, R. G., Damayana, G. P., & Cahyadi, A. (2002). A gloomy picture of the attempts to eradicate corruption: Reflection of the policies, laws and institutions of corruption management in Indonesia, 1969–2001. In: R. Holloway (Ed.), *Stealing from the people: 16 studies on corruption in Indonesia, Book 1 Corruption – from top to bottom* (pp. 143–200). Jakarta: Aksara Foundation.

*Associated Press*. (2008). Taiwan ex-leader indicted for graft: Ex-president Chen denies bribery, money-laundering allegations. *Associated Press*, December 12.

Averech, H. A., Koehler, J. E., & Denton, F. H. (1971). *The matrix of policy in the Philippines*. Princeton: Princeton University Press.

Azfar, O., & Murrell, P. (2007). Identifying reticent respondents in Romanian corruption surveys. In: D. Rodriguez & L. Ehrichs (Eds), *Global corruption report 2007* (pp. 352–353). Cambridge: Cambridge University Press.

Babb, J. (2000). *Tanaka: The making of postwar Japan*. Harlow: Pearson Education.

Babb, J. (2005). Corruption and governance in Japan. In: G. D. Hook (Ed.), *Contested governance in Japan: Sites and issues* (pp. 174–191). London: RoutledgeCurzon.

Backman, M. (1999). *Asian eclipse: Exposing the dark side of business in Asia*. Singapore: Wiley.

Backman, M. (2004). *The Asian insider: Unconventional wisdom for Asian business*. (chap. 4, Paying peanuts: Politicians' pay in Asia, pp. 25–29). Basingstoke: Palgrave Macmillan.

Balakrishnan, K. G. (2009). Address at the National Seminar on Fighting Crimes related to Corruption organized by the Central Bureau of Investigation in New Delhi, India on September 12. Available at http://www.cbi.gov.in/speech/nsfcr_120909_cji.php. Retrieved on November 16, 2010.

Balgos, C. C. A. (1998). Ombudsman. In: S. S. Coronel (Ed.), *Pork and other perks: Corruption and governance in the Philippines* (pp. 244–271). Quezon City: Philippine Center for Investigative Journalism.

Banerjee, A. (1996). Can anything be done about corruption? In: M. G. Quilbria & J. M. Dowling (Eds), *Current issues in economic development: An Asian perspective* (pp. 107–131). Hong Kong: Oxford University Press, chap. 4.

Banfield, E. C. (1958). *The moral basis of a backward society*. New York: Free Press.

*Bangkok Post*. (2004). Corruption now 'Worst in Century.' *Bangkok Post*, December 10.

Bankoff, G. (2005). Profiting from disasters: Corruption, hazard, and society in the Philippines. In: N. Tarling (Ed.), *Corruption and good governance in Asia* (pp. 165–185). London: Routledge, chap. 8.

Bannister, M. (2003). Corruption in development – A killing virus. In: *29th WEDC International Conference: Towards the Millennium Development Goals*. Abuja, Nigeria.

Batalla, E. C. (2001). De-institutionalizing corruption in the Philippines. In: A. C. Pedro, Jr. (Ed.), *Combating corruption in East Asia* (pp. 41–78). Manila: Yuchengco Center, De La Salle University.

Batchuluun, B. (2004). Reflections on corruption and anti-corruption legal framework. January 7. Available at http://www.forum.mn/en/index.php?sel=news&obj_id=156

Baum, J. (1996). Hard guys get hit: Public outrage spurs crackdown on gangs. *Far Eastern Economic Review*, February 19, pp. 18–20.

Bayley, D. H. (1969). *The police and political development in India*. Princeton: Princeton University Press.

*BBC News*. (2001a). Heads roll in India bribery scandal. *BBC News*, March 14. Available at http://news.bbc.co.uk/2/hi/south_asia/1219434.stm. Retrieved on November 10, 2010.

*BBC News*. (2001b). Megawati says 'no' to kickbacks. *BBC News*, August 16, pp. 1–2. Available at http://news.bbc.uk/hi/english/business/newsid_1493000/1493709.stm

Bearak, B. (2009). Desperate children flee Zimbabwe, for lives just as desolate. *New York Times*, January 24.

Becker, J. (2008). Tackling corruption at its source: The national corruption prevention bureau. *Journal of Chinese Political Science*, *13*(3), 287–303.

Beeson, M. (2003). Japan's reluctant reformers and the legacy of the development state. In: A. B. L. Cheung & I. Scott (Eds), *Governance and public sector reform in Asia: Paradigm shifts or business as usual?* (pp. 25–43). London: RoutledgeCurzon, chap. 2.

Befu, H. (1971). Bribery in Japan: When law tangles with culture. Paper presented at the Colloquium, Center for Japanese and Korean Studies, University of California, Berkeley, April 21.

Berkman, S. (2008). *The World Bank and the gods of lending*. Sterling: Kumarian Press.

Beschel, R. P., Jr. (1999). *Corruption, transparency and accountability in the Philippines*. Manila: Asian Development Bank.

Bhargava, V. (1999). *Combating corruption in the Philippines*. Manila: Philippine Country Management Unit, World Bank.

Bhattacharya, A., & Pangestu, M. (2000). Indonesia: Development transformation and the role of public policy. In: D. M. Leipziger (Ed.), *Lessons from East Asia* (pp. 387–442). Ann Arbor: University of Michigan Press, chap. 7.

Bidhya, B. (2004). Thaksin's model of government reform in Thailand: Prime ministerialization through 'A country is my company' approach. *Asian Journal of Political Science, 12*(1), 135–153.

Bidhya, B. (2005). Dynamics and effectiveness of the NCCC and the new counter corruption network in Thailand: The story of the struggling tiger. Paper presented at the International Conference on Asian Horizons: Cities, States and Society, Singapore, August 1–3.

Bird, I. L. (1986). *Korea and her neighbors: A narrative of travel, with an account of the recent vicissitudes and present position of the country* (Vol. 2). Tokyo: Charles E. Tuttle Co. Publishers.

Black, W. K. (2007). Corruption kills. In: H. N. Pontell & G. Geis (Eds), *International handbook of white-collar and corporate crime* (pp. 439–455). New York: Springer Science and Business MediaPart 8, chap. 1.

Blair-Kerr, Sir A. (1973a). *First report of a commission of enquiry* (July). Hong Kong: Government Printer.

Blair-Kerr, Sir A. (1973b). *Second report of a commission of enquiry* (September). Hong Kong: Government Printer.

Blechinger, V. (2000). Report on recent bribery scandals, 1996–2000. Paper presented at a Transparency International Workshop on "Corruption and Political Party Funding" at La Pietra, Italy, in October. Available at http://www.transparency.org/documents/work-papers/s_korea_paper.html

Board of Audit and Inspection (BAI). (1999). *Annual Report 1998*. Seoul.

Bolongaita, E. P. (2010). An exception to the rule? Why Indonesia's Anti-Corruption Commission succeeds where others don't – A comparison with the Philippines' Ombudsman. *U4 Issue*, No. 4, August. Bergen: Christian Michelsen Institute.

Bonner, R. (1988). The new order – II. *New Yorker Magazine*, June 13, pp. 73–91.

Boone, P., Tarvaa, B., Tsend, A., Tsendjav, E., & Unenburen, N. (1997). Mongolia's transition to a democratic market system. In: W. T. Woo, S. Parker & J. D. Sachs (Eds), *Economies in transition: Comparing Asia and Eastern Europe* (pp. 103–130). Cambridge: The MIT Press, chap. 4.

Borwornsak, U. (2001). Depoliticizing key institutions for combating corruption: The new Thai constitution. In: P. Larmour & N. Wolanin (Eds), *Corruption and anti-corruption* (pp. 177–203). Canberra: Asia Pacific Press, chap. 11.

Bosco, J. (1992). Taiwan's factions: *Guanxi*, patronage, and the state in local politics. *Ethnology, 31*(2), 157–183.

Bouissou, J.-M. (1997). Gifts, networks and clienteles: Corruption in Japan as a redistributive system. In: D. D. Porta & Y. Meny (Eds), *Democracy and corruption in Europe* (pp. 132–147). London: Pinter, chap. 9.

Bowen, R. W. (2003). *Japan's dysfunctional democracy: The Liberal Democratic Party and structural corruption*. Armonk: M.E. Sharpe.

Bowie, A., & Unger, D. (1997). *The Politics of open economies: Indonesia, Malaysia, the Philippines and Thailand*. Cambridge: Cambridge University Press.

Breen, M. (1998). *The Koreans: Who they are, what they want, where their future lies*. London: Orion Books.

Brillantes, A. B., Jr., & Sonco, J. O. T. (2010). Civil service reforms in the Philippines: Its many faces, leadership and politics. In: P. S. Kim (Ed.), *Civil service system and civil service reform in ASEAN member countries and Korea* (pp. 210–252). Seoul: Daeyoung Moonhwasa Publishing Company, chap. 8.

Brun, O., & Odgaard, O. (1996). A society and economy in transition. In: O. Brun & O. Odgaard (Eds), *Mongolia in transition: Old patterns, new challenges* (pp. 23–41). Richmond: Curzon Press.

Buckley, C. B. (1965). *An anecdotal history of old times in Singapore*. Kuala Lumpur: University of Malaya Press.

Budiman, A. (2001). Indonesia: The trials of President Wahid. In: D. Singh & A. Smith (Eds), *Southeast Asian affairs 2001* (pp. 145–158). Singapore: Institute of Southeast Asian Studies.

Budisatrijo, A. (2011). Indonesian taxman Gayus Tambunan jailed for corruption. *BBC News*, January 19. Available at http://www.bbc.co.uk/news/world-asia-pacific-12224782. Retrieved on February 4, 2011.

Bulag, U. E. (2009). Mongolia in 2008: From Mongolia to mine-golia. *Asian Survey*, *49*(1), 129–134.

Bull, M. J., & Newell, J. L. (Eds). (2003). *Corruption in contemporary politics*. Basingstoke: Palgrave Macmillan.

Bureau of the Budget. (2000–2010). *Thailand's budget in brief fiscal years 1999–2009*. Bangkok.

Bureau of the Budget. (2009). *Thailand's budget in brief fiscal year 2008*. Bangkok.

Burke, J. (2010). Does this look ready to you? Chaos in run-up to Commonwealth Games. *The Guardian*, 22 September.

Burns, J. P. (1994). Civil service reform in China. *Asian Journal of Political Science*, *2*(2), 44–72.

Byambajav, D. (2010). Informal and formal networks in post-socialism: A synthetic analysis of access to networks in Mongolia. *Journal of the Graduate School of Letters, Hokkaido University*, *5*(March), 89–98.

Caiden, G. E. (1971). *The dynamics of public administration: Guidelines to current transformations in theory and practice*. Hinsdale: Dryden Press.

Caiden, G. E. (1981). Public maladministration and bureaucratic corruption. *Hong Kong Journal of Public Administration*, *3*(1), 58–62.

Caiden, G. E. (1988). Toward a general theory of official corruption. *Asian Journal of Public Administration*, *10*(1), 3–26.

Caiden, G. E. (1997). Undermining good governance: Corruption and democracy. *Asian Journal of Political Science*, *5*(2), 1–22.

Caiden, G. E. (2001). Dealing with administrative corruption. In: T. L. Cooper (Ed.), *Handbook of administrative ethics* (2nd ed., pp. 429–455). New York: Marcel Dekker.

Caiden, G. E., & Caiden, N. J. (1977). Administrative corruption. *Public Administration Review*, *37*(3), 301–309.

Caiden, G. E., Dwivedi, O. P., & Jabbra, J. (Eds). (2001). *Where corruption lives*. Bloomfield: Kumarian Press.

Caiden, G. E., & Kim, J. H. (1993). A new anti-corruption strategy for Korea. *Asian Journal of Political Science*, *1*(1), 133–151.

Campi, A. J. (1996). Nomadic cultural values and their influence on modernization. In: O. Bruun & O. Odgaard (Eds), *Mongolia in transition: Old patterns and new challenges* (pp. 90–102). Richmond: Curzon Press.

Campos, J. E., & Bhargava, V. (2007). Introduction: Tackling a social pandemic. In: J.E. Campos & S. Pradhan (Eds), *The many faces of corruption: Tracking vulnerabilities at the sector level* (pp. 1–25). Washington, DC: World Bank.

Caoili, R. (2005). Reflections on democracy and development in Southeast Asia: Why do the Philippines and Singapore differ? *Culture Mandala: The Bulletin of the Center for East-West Cultural and Economic Studies*, *6*(2), 1–28.

Carino, L. V. (1986a). Tonic or toxic: The effects of graft and corruption. In: L. V. Carino (Ed.), *Bureaucratic corruption in Asia: Causes, consequences and controls* (pp. 163–194). Quezon City: JMC Press and College of Public Administration, University of the Philippines, chap. 5.

Carino, L. V. (Ed.) (1986b). *Bureaucratic corruption in Asia: Causes, consequences and controls*. Quezon City: JMC Press and College of Public Administration, University of the Philippines.

Carino, L. V. (1988). The land and the people. In: R. P. de Guzman & M. A. Reforma (Eds), *Government and politics of the Philippines* (pp. 3–17). Singapore: Oxford University Press, chap. 1.

Carino, L. V. (1994). Enhancing accountability in the Philippines: The continuing quest. In: J.P. Burns (Ed.), *Asian civil service systems: Improving efficiency and productivity* (pp. 106–125). Singapore: Times Academic Press, chap. 5.

Casals & Associates. (2005). *Assessment of corruption in Mongolia: Final report*. Alexandria: Casals & Associates, August 31. Available at http://www.usaid.gov.mn/library/documents/MongoliaCorruptionAssessmentFinalReport.pdf

Cawthorne, N. (1999). *The world's greatest political scandals* (chap. 24, Imelda Marcos and the scandal of the shoes, pp. 125–135). London: Chancellor Press.

*CBC News*. (2008). Imelda Marcos acquitted after 17-year trial. *CBC News*, March 10. Available at http://www.cbc.ca/world/story/2008/03/10/marcos-trial.html. Retrieved on November 9, 2010.

CBI (Central Bureau of Investigation). (2005). *Annual report 2004*. New Delhi. Available at http://www.cbi.gov.in

CBI. (2006). *Annual report 2005*. New Delhi. Available at http://www.cbi.gov.in

CBI. (2008). *Annual report 2007*. New Delhi. Available at http://www.cbi.gov.in/annualreport/cbi_annual_report_2007.pdf. Retrieved on November 19, 2010.

CBI. (2009). *Annual report 2008*. New Delhi. Available at http://www.cbi.gov.in/annualreport/cbi_annual_report_2008.pdf. Retrieved on November 19, 2010.

CBI. (2010a). *Annual report 2009*. New Delhi. Available at http://www.cbi.gov.in/annualreport/cbi_annual_report_2009_3.pdf. Retrieved on November 16, 2010.

CBI. (2010b). Overall vacancy position of CBI as on 1 November 2010. Available at http://www.cbi.gov.in/rt_infoact/cbi_vac20101101.pdf. Retrieved on November 16, 2010.

Cerojano, T. (2009). UN official says Philippine poverty 'unacceptable'. *Taiwan News Online*, October 20. Available at http://www.etaiwannews.com/etn/php. Retrieved on October 23, 2009.

Chai-Anan, S. (1977). Problems of bureaucratic corruption in Thailand: A study of legal codes, administrative and institutional arrangements. Paper presented at the Bureaucratic Behavior in Asia Project, Pattaya, January 18–23.

Chai-Anan, S. (1987). Political history. In: X. Somsakdi (Ed.), *Government and politics of Thailand* (pp. 1–40). Singapore: Oxford University Press, chap. 1.

Chaikin, D., & Sharman, J. C. (2009). *Corruption and money laundering: A symbiotic relationship* (chap. 6, The Marcos kleptocracy, pp. 153–186). New York: Palgave Macmillan.

Chairat, C. (2010). Thailand in 2009: Unusual politics becomes usual. In: D. Singh (Ed.), *Southeast Asian affairs 2010* (pp. 303–331). Singapore: Institute of Southeast Asian Studies.

Chakraborty, S. (2010). Will hiking MP pay reduce corruption? *Wall Street Journal*, August 23.

*Challenge*. (2006). CPIB on the fast track. *Challenge*, November. Available at http://www.ps21.gov.sg/Challenge/2006_11/system.html. Retrieved on July 27, 2009.

Chan, K. M. (1999). Corruption in China: A principal-agent perspective. In: H. K. Wong & H. S. Chan (Eds), *Handbook of public administration in the Asia-Pacific basin* (pp. 299–324). New York: Marcel Dekker, chap. 14.

Chandler, R. C., & Plano, J. C. (1988). *The public administration dictionary* (2nd ed.). Santa Barbara: ABC-Clio Inc.

Chang, C. J. (2000). An interview with justice minister Chen Ding-nan. *Taiwan Panorama*, November, p. 38. Available at http://www.sino.gov.tw/en/show_issue.php?id=200011 8911038e.txt&table=2

Chang, H. J. (1998). Korea: The misunderstood crisis. *World Development*, *26*(8), 1555–1561.

Chang, R. (2010a). Chen acquitted on graft charge. *Taipei Times*, June 9, p. 1.

Chang, R. (2010b). Judicial Yuan chief quits. *Taipei Times*, July 18, p. 1.

*Channel News Asia* (Singapore). (2003). Arroyo launches anti-corruption drive on anniversary of popular uprising. *Channel News Asia*, February 8.

Chao, V. Y. (2010a). Chen's sentence cut to 20 years. *Taipei Times*, June 12, p. 1.

Chao, V. Y. (2010b). Three judges, prosecutor held on graft charges. *Taipei Times*, July 15, p. 1.

Chao, V. Y. (2010c). Court sets Chen's prison term at 17-and-a-half-years. *Taipei Times*, December 7, p. 1.

Chapman, W. (1991). *Inventing Japan: The making of a postwar civilization*. New York: Prentice-Hall.

Chen, S. B. (1999). *The son of Taiwan: Chen Shui-bian and his dreams for Taiwan*. Taipei: Taiwan Publishing Company.

Cheng, A. T. (2000). The Curse of 'Black Gold': Lee Teng-hui's darker legacy may be a political culture riddled with corruption and gangsters. *Asiaweek*, *26*(10), 24–25.

Cheng, W. (2010). Aquino abolishes anti-graft body. *ABS-CBN News*, November 24. Available at http://www.abs-cbnnews.com/nation/11/24/10/aquino-abolishes-anti-graft-body. Retrieved on November 25, 2010.

Cheung, A. B. L. (2008). Evaluation of the Hong Kong integrity system. In: L. Huberts, F. Anechiarico & F. Six (Eds), *Local integrity systems: World cities fighting corruption and safeguarding integrity* (pp. 105–115). The Hague: BJu Legal Publishers, chap. 7.

Chew, D. C. E. (1992). *Civil service pay in South Asia*. Geneva: International Labor Office.

Ch'i, H. S. (1982). *Nationalist China at war: Military defeats and political collapse, 1937–1945*. Ann Arbor: University of Michigan Press.

Chin, K. L. (2003). *Heijin: Organized crime, business, and politics in Taiwan*. Armonk: M. E. Sharpe.

*China Post*. (2006). First lady Wu Su-chen indicted for corruption. *China Post*, November 4.

*China Post*. (2010). Anti-corruption agency to be created: Ma. *China Post*, July 21.

Cho, Y. H. (1999). *Regulatory reform in Korea. Seoul: Graduate school of international studies*. Unpublished paper, Sogang University, June 23, pp. 1–18.

Choi, J. W. (2005). The effectiveness of anti-corruption agencies: A comparative analysis of Hong Kong's ICAC and South Korea's KICAC. Paper presented at the International Conference on "Asian Horizons: Cities, States and Society", Singapore, 1–3 August.

Choi, J. W. (2007). Governance structure and administrative corruption in Japan: An organizational network approach. *Public Administration Review*, *67*(5), 930–942.

Choi, J. W. (2009). Institutional structures and effectiveness of anti-corruption agencies: A comparative analysis of South Korea and Hong Kong. *Asian Journal of Political Science*, *17*(2), 195–214.

Choi, J. W. (2011). Anti-corruption and governance. In: A. Widaningrum & J. Park (Eds), *Governance reform in Indonesia and Korea: A comparative perspective* (pp. 32–48). Yogyakarta: Gadjah Mada University Press, chap. 2.

Chong, E. (2000). Greed, greed and more greed. *Straits Times*, July 1, p. 3.

Christensen, S., Dollar, D., Ammar, S., & Pakorn, V. (1997). Thailand: The institutional and political underpinnings of growth. In: D. M. Leipziger (Ed.), *Lessons from East Asia* (pp. 345–385). Ann Arbor: University of Michigan Press, chap. 6.

Chua, Y. T. (1999). *Robbed: An investigation of corruption in Philippine education*. Quezon City: Philippine Center for Investigative Journalism.

Chua, Y. T., & Rimban, L. (1998). Gatekeeper. In: S. S. Coronel (Ed.), *Pork and other perks: Corruption and governance in the Philippines* (pp. 150–185). Quezon City: Philippine Center for Investigative Journalism.

Chuang, J. (2001). Minister says the anti-vote-buying effort is successful. *Taipei Times*, December 1, p. 1.

CIA (Central Intelligence Agency). (2011a). Indonesia population. In: *World Factbook*. Washington, DC: CIA. Available at http://www.indexmundi.com/indonesia/population.html

CIA. (2011b). Mongolia. In: *World Factbook*. Washington, DC: CIA. Available at https://www.cia.gov/library/publications/the-world-factbook/geos/mg.html

Clad, J. (1989). *Behind the myth: Business, money and power in Southeast Asia*. London: Unwin Hyman.

Clark, C. (2002). Democratization and the evolving nature of parties, issues, and constituencies in the ROC. In: P. C. Y. Chow (Ed.), *Taiwan's modernization in global perspective* (pp. 135–159). Westport: Praeger Publishers, chap. 7.

Clark, D. H., & Oey-Gardiner, M. (1991). How Indonesian lecturers have adjusted to civil service compensation. *Bulletin of Indonesian Economic Studies*, *27*(3), 129–141.

Clifford, M. L. (1998). *Troubled tiger: Businessmen, bureaucrats, and generals in South Korea* (Rev. Ed.). Armonk: M.E. Sharpe.

*CNN.com*. (2008a). Court orders detention of Taiwan's ex-president. *CNN.com*, November 12.

*CNN.com*. (2008b). Taiwan's ex-president released on bail. *CNN.com*, December13.

*CNN.com*. (2008c). Taiwan's ex-president jailed. *CNN.com*, December 30.

Co, E. E. A., Lim, M., Lao, M. E. J., & Juan, L. J. (2007). *Minimizing corruption: Philippine democracy assessment*. Pasig City: Friedrich Ebert Stiftung Philippine Office.

Cody, E. (2006). Feeling the squeeze of China and Russia, Mongolia courts U.S. *Washington Post*, February 12, p. A27.

Colignon, R. A., & Usui, C. (2003). *Amakudari: The hidden fabric of Japan's economy*. Ithaca: Cornell University Press.

Collier, P. (2010). Bad guys matter: They put the failed in failed states. *Foreign Policy* (July/August), 88.

Colmey, J., & Liebhold, D. (1999). The family firm. *Time*, May 24, pp. 15–29.

Colony of Singapore. (1947). *Twentieth meeting of the advisory council*. Singapore: Government Printing Office.

Colony of Singapore. (1951). *Police pay committee*. Singapore: Government Printer.

Colony of Singapore. (1952). *Distribution of work 1st May, 1952*. Singapore: Government Printing Office.

Conde, C. H. (2005). A Hong Kong outsider aids a troubled Manila. *International Herald Tribune*, May 20.

Conde, C. H. (2007). Pardoning Estrada could benefit Arroyo. *International Herald Tribune*, September 25, p. 3.

Connors, M. K. (2005). Thailand: The facts and f(r)ictions of ruling. In: K. W. Chin & D. Singh (Eds), *Southeast Asian affairs 2005* (pp. 365–384). Singapore: Institute of Southeast Asian Studies.

Constable, P. (2009). Inexplicable wealth of Afghan elite sows bitterness: in one of the world's poorest nations, myriad tales of official corruption. *Washington Post*, January 12, p. A06.

Copper, J. F. (2006). *Taiwan's 2006 metropolitan mayoral and city council elections and the politics of corruption*. Baltimore, MD: School of Law, University of Maryland.

Copper, J. F. (2008). *Taiwan's 2008 presidential and vice presidential election: Maturing democracy*. Baltimore, MD: School of Law, University of Maryland.

Copper, J. F. (2009a). Transitioning from the Chen Shui-bian to the Ma Ying-jeou presidency: The state of democratization in Taiwan. In: S. Brown, C. Clark, H. Takeuchi & A. Tan (Eds), *Taiwan at a turning point* (pp. 4–21). Baltimore, MD: School of Law, University of Maryland, chap. 1.

Cooper, J. F. (2009b). *Taiwan: Nation-state or province?* (5th ed.). Boulder: Westview Press.

Cornelius, P. K. (Ed.) (2003). *The global competitiveness report, 2002–2003*. New York: Oxford University Press.

Corpuz, O. D. (1957). *The bureaucracy in the Philippines*. Manila: Institute of Public Administration, University of the Philippines.

Coughlin, R. J. (1960). *Double identity: The Chinese in modern Thailand*. Hong Kong: Hong Kong University Press.

CPIB (Corrupt Practices Investigation Bureau). (2003a). *Swift and sure action: Four decades of anti-corruption work*. Singapore: CPIB.

CPIB. (2003b). *Transforming business through people excellence: Corrupt Practices Investigation Bureau 2003 people excellence award winner*. Singapore: CPIB.

CPIB. (2004). *Corrupt Practices Investigation Bureau*. Singapore: CPIB.

CPIB. (2006). *CPIB's public perceptions survey 2005*. Singapore: Press Release.

CPIB. (2008). Interview with CPIB senior officers on June 27.

Cribb, R., & Ford, M. (2009). Indonesia as an archipelago: Managing islands, managing the seas. In: R. Cribb & M. Ford (Eds), *Indonesia beyond the water's edge: Managing an archipelagic state* (pp. 1–27). Singapore: Institute of Southeast Asian Studies, chap. 1.

Crouch, H. (1999). Wiranto and Habibie: Military-civilian relations since May 1998. In: A. Budiman, B. Hatley & D. Kingsbury (Eds), *Reformasi: Crisis and change in Indonesia* (pp. 127–148). Clayton: Monash Asia Institute, Monash University.

Curtis, G. L. (1988). *The Japanese way of politics.* New York: Columbia University Press.

Curtis, G. L. (1999). *The logic of Japanese politics: Leaders, institutions, and the limits of change.* New York: Columbia University Press.

CVC (Central Vigilance Commission). (2005). *Annual report 2004.* New Delhi. Available at http://cvc.nic.in/ar2004.pdf. Retrieved on April 11, 2006.

CVC. (2009). *Annual report 2008.* New Delhi. Available at http://cvc.nic.in/AR2008.pdf. Retrieved on November 26, 2010.

Da Gama Pinto, C. (1997). Indonesian business almanac. In: R. Goodfellow (Ed.), *Indonesian business culture: An insider's guide* (pp. 175–207). Singapore: Butterworth-Heinemann Asia, chap. 9.

*Daily Tribune.* (2009). DepEd noodles found 'fortified' with corruption. *Daily Tribune*, May 13. Available at http://www.tribune.net.ph/headlines/20090513hed6.html. Retrieved on May 15, 2009.

Dairokuno, K. (2000). Corruption and rewards for high public offices: A Japanese experience. *Asian Review of Public Administration, 13*(1), 102–117(January–June).

Dalpino, C. E. (1991). Thailand's search for accountability. *Journal of Democracy, 2*(4), 61–71(Fall).

Das, S. K. (2001). *Public office, private interest: Bureaucracy and corruption in India.* New Delhi: Oxford University Press.

Davidsen, S., Juwono, V., & Timberman, D. G. (2006). *Curbing corruption in Indonesia (2004–2006): A survey of national policies and approaches.* Washington, D.C. and Jakarta: United States-Indonesia Society and Center for Strategic and International Studies.

Davies, R. J., & Ikeno, O. (2002). In: *The Japanese mind: Understanding contemporary Japanese culture* (p. 235). Boston, MA: Tuttle Publishing.

Day, C. (1966). *The Dutch in Java.* Kuala Lumpur: Oxford University Press.

de Guzman, R. P. (1986). Foreword. In: L. V. Carino (Ed.), *Bureaucratic corruption in Asia: Causes, consequences and controls* (pp. iii–v). Quezon City: JMC Press and College of Public Administration, University of the Philippines.

de Guzman, R. P., Brillantes, A. B., Jr., & Pacho, A. G. (1988). The bureaucracy. In: R. P. de Guzman & M. A. Reforma (Eds), *Government and politics of the Philippines* (pp. 180–206). Singapore: Oxford University Press, chap. 7.

de Kat Angelino, A. D. A. (1931). *Colonial policy* (G. J. Renier, Trans.) (Vol. 2). The Hague: Martinus Nijhoff.

de Mente, B. L. (1994). *Korean etiquette and ethics in business* (2nd ed.). Lincolnwood: NTC Business Books.

de Mente, B. L. (1997). *The Japanese have a word for it: The complete guide to Japanese thought and culture* (chap. 19, Ama Kudari, pp. 33–34). Chicago: Passport Books.

Department of Statistics. (2010). *Yearbook of statistics Singapore, 2010.* Singapore: Department of Statistics. Available at http://www.singstat.gov.sg/pubn/reference/yos10/yos2010.pdf

de Speville, B. (1997). *Hong Kong: Policy initiatives against corruption.* Paris: Organization for Economic Co-operation and Development.

de Speville, B. E. D. (1999). The experience of Hong Kong, China, in combating corruption. In: R. Stapenhurst & S. J. Kpundeh (Eds), *Curbing corruption: Toward a model for building national integrity* (pp. 51–58). Washington, DC: World Bank, chap. 3.

Desai, R. (1999). *Indian business culture.* Oxford: Butterworth-Heinemann.

*Deutsche Presse-Agentur.* (2007). Philippine leader grants clemency to Estrada. *Deutsche Presse-Agentur*, October 25.

DGEE (Department of Government Employee Ethics). (2008). *Anticorruption strategies in Taiwan*. Taipei: Ministry of Justice, December 15.

Diamond, L. (2000). What the election signifies for democracy. *Taipei Times*, March 15, p. 10.

Diamond, L. (2001). How democratic is Taiwan? Five key challenges for democratic development and consolidation. Paper presented at the Symposium on The Transition from One-Party Rule: Taiwan's New Government and Cross-Straits Relations at Columbia University, New York, USA, April 6–7.

Diaz-Briquets, S., & Perez-Lopez, J. (2006). *Corruption in Cuba: Castro and beyond*. Austin: University of Texas Press.

Dickson, B. J. (2001). Taiwan's democratization: What lessons for China? In: M. Alagappa (Ed.), *Taiwan's presidential politics: Democratization and cross strait relations in the twenty-first century* (pp. 115–132). Armonk: M.E. Sharpe, chap. 3.

Dimock, M. E. (1968). *The Japanese technocracy: Management and government in Japan*. New York: Walker/Weatherhill.

Dixon, C. (1999). *The Thai economy: Uneven development and internationalization*. London: Routledge.

Dixon, K. (1977). Japan's Lockheed Scandal: 'Structural Corruption'. *Pacific Community*, *8*(January), 340–362.

Dizon, D. (2010). Corruption was Gloria's biggest mistake: Survey. *ABS-CBN News*, August 4. Available at http://www.abs-cbnnews.com/nation/08/04/10/corruption-was-glorias-biggest-mistake-survey. Retrieved on November 25, 2010.

Dizon, Fr. J. (2007). The Philippine anti-corruption drive: A critique. In: B. M. Tuazon (Ed.), *Dissecting corruption: Philippine perspectives* (pp. 115–119). Quezon City: CenPEG Books.

Dunung, S. P. (1998). *Doing business in Asia: The complete guide* (2nd ed.). San Francisco: Jossey-Bass Publishers.

*Economist*. (1997). Next, please: South Korea. *Economist*, March 6.

*Economist*. (2006). *Pocket world in figures 2007 edition*. London: Profile Books.

*Economist*. (2007a). Pardon in the Philippines: The current president controversially pardons a former one. *Economist*, October 30. Available at http://www.economist.com.cfm?story_id=10052413. Retrieved on August 22, 2008.

*Economist*. (2007b). *Pocket world in figures 2008 edition*. London: Profile Books.

*Economist*. (2008). *Pocket world in figures 2009 edition*. London: Profile Books.

*Economist*. (2009a). Trial and error. *Economist*, January 22.

*Economist*. (2009b). Cold medicine. *Economist*, February 19.

*Economist*. (2009c). *Pocket world in figures 2010 edition*. London: Profile Books.

*Economist*. (2010a) *Pocket world in figures 2011 edition*. London: Profile Books.

*Economist*. (2010b). Politicians' salaries, Leaders of the fee world: How much a country's leader is paid compared to GDP per person. *Economist*, July 5. Available at http://www.economist.com/node/16525240/?story_id=16525240. Retrieved on February 4, 2011.

EIU (Economist Intelligence Unit). (1994). *Country Report: China, Mongolia Fourth Quarter 1994*. London: EIU.

EIU. (1995a). *Country Report: China, Mongolia Third Quarter 1995*. London: EIU.

EIU. (1995b). *Country Report: China, Mongolia Fourth Quarter 1995*. London: EIU.

EIU. (1996). *Country Report: China, Mongolia Fourth Quarter 1996*. London: EIU.

EIU. (1997a). *Country Report: China, Mongolia First Quarter 1997*. London: EIU.

EIU. (1997b). *Country Report: China, Mongolia Second Quarter 1997*. London: EIU.

EIU. (1997c). *Country Report: China, Mongolia Third Quarter 1997*. London: EIU.

EIU. (1998a). *Country Report: China, Mongolia Second Quarter 1998*. London: EIU.

EIU. (1998b). *Country Report: China, Mongolia Third Quarter 1998*. London: EIU.

EIU. (1998c). *Country Report: China, Mongolia Fourth Quarter 1998*. London: EIU.

Eldersveld, S. J., Jagannadham, V., & Barnabas, A. P. (1968). *The citizen and the administrator in a developing democracy*. Glenview: Scott, Foresman and Company.

Elliot, K. A. (Ed.) (1997). *Corruption and the global economy*. Washington, DC: Institute for International Economics.

Endriga, J. N. (1979). Historical notes on graft and corruption in the Philippines. *Philippine Journal of Public Administration*, *23*(3–4), 241–254.

Erdenebileg, T. O. (1994). Public opinion on corruption in Mongolia. Ulaanbataar.

Etzioni, A. (1964). *Modern organizations*. Englewood Cliffs: Prentice-Hall.

Executive Yuan. (2009). CPA dismisses salary cut proposal. *Taiwan Headlines*, June 18. Available at http://www.ey.gov.tw/ct.asp?xItem=55437&ctNode=1335&mp=11

Faul, M. (2009). Physicians: Corruption killing people in Zimbabwe. *Associated Press*, January 13.

Faure, D. (1981). Paying for convenience: An aspect of corruption that arises from revenue spending. In: R. P. L. Lee (Ed.), *Control and its control in Hong Kong: Situations up to the late seventies* (pp. 133–165). Hong Kong: Chinese University Press, chap. 5.

Feith, H. (1964). Indonesia. In: G. M. Kahin (Ed.), *Government and politics of Southeast Asia* (2nd ed., Chaps. 9–12, pp. 183–278). Ithaca: Cornell University Press.

Fernandez, F. U., Jr. (1980). The civil service system in the Philippines. In: Amara R. & H. Siedentopf (Eds), *Asian civil services* (pp. 363–430). Kuala Lumpur: Asian Pacific Development Administration Center.

Filkins, D. (2009). Bribes corrode Afghans' trust in government. *New York Times*, January 2.

Filmer, D., & Lindauer, D. L. (2001). Does Indonesia have a 'low pay' civil service? *Bulletin of Indonesian Economic Studies*, *37*(2), 189–205.

Finch, C. M. (2002). Mongolia in 2001: Political consolidation and continued economic reform. *Asian Survey*, *42*(10), 39–45.

Flippo, E. B. (1984). *Personnel management* (6th ed.). New York: McGraw-Hill Book Company.

Freedman, C. (2007). Japan. In: A. Chowdhury & I. Islam (Eds), *Handbook on the northeast and southeast Asian economies*. Cheltenham: Edward Elgar.

Friedrich, C. J. (1989). Corruption concepts in historical perspective. In: A. J. Heidenheimer, M. Johnston & V. T. LeVine (Eds), *Political corruption: A handbook* (pp. 15–24). New Brunswick: Transaction Publishers, chap. 1.

Fritz, V. (2007). Democratization and corruption in Mongolia. *Public Administration and Development*, *27*, 191–203.

Frost, N. (2002). *Indonesia*. Oxford: Oxfam Publishing.

Funston, J. (2001). Thailand: Reform politics. In: J. Funston (Ed.), *Government and politics in Southeast Asia* (pp. 328–371). Singapore: Institute of Southeast Asian Studies, chap. 9.

Furnivall, J. S. (1939). *Netherlands India: A study of plural economy*. Cambridge: Cambridge University Press.

Furnivall, J. S. (1948). *Colonial policy and practice: A comparative study of Burma and Netherlands India*. Cambridge: Cambridge University Press.

Galtung, F. (2006). Measuring the immeasurable: Boundaries and functions of (macro) corruption indices. In: C. Sampford, A. Shacklock, C. Connors & F. Galtung (Eds), *Measuring corruption* (pp. 101–130). Aldershot: Ashgate, chap. 6.

Garg, S. P. (2006). *The Indian enigma: A plea for good governance*. New Delhi: Commonwealth Publishers.

Gaus, J. M. (1947). *Reflections on public administration*. University: University of Alabama Press.

Genzberger, C. A. (1994). *Korea business: The portable encyclopedia for doing business with Korea*. San Rafael: World Trade Press.

Ghosh, A. (1997). Corruption: Reform's dark side. *Far Eastern Economic Review*, *20*(March), 18–20.

Ghufran, N. (2008). Afghanistan in 2007: A bleeding wound. *Asian Survey*, *48*(1), 154–163.

Gill, S. S. (1998). *The pathology of corruption*. New Delhi: HarperCollins Publishers India.

Ginsburg, T. (1998). Mongolia in 1997: Deepening democracy. *Asian Survey*, *38*(1), 64–68.

Glassburner, B. (1978). Indonesia's new economic policy and its socio-political implications. In: K. D. Jackson & L. W. Pye (Eds), *Political power and communications in Indonesia* (pp. 137–170). Berkeley: University of California Press, chap. 5.

Gleeck, L. E. (1998). *The American half-century (1898–1946)*. Quezon City: New Day Publishers.

Glickman, P. (1991). *Off limits: Censorship and corruption* (Indonesia, pp. 25–34). New York: Fund for Free Expression.

*Global Integrity Report*. (2009). *Indonesia: Corruption timeline*. Washington, DC: Global Integrity. Available at http://report.globalintegrity.org/Indonesia/2009/timeline

Glynn, P., Kobrin, S. J., & Naim, M. (1997). The globalization of corruption. In: K. A. Elliott (Ed.), *Corruption and the global economy* (pp. 7–27). Washington, DC: Institute for International Economics, chap. 1.

*GMA News.TV* (Philippines). (2007). Survey: Arroyo most corrupt, Aquino cleanest of 5 Prexies. December 11. Available at http://www.gmanews.tv/print/72457.

Go, R. (2002). Jakarta lost 400 lawsuits because of graft. *Straits Times*, July 1, p. A4.

Godbole, M. (1997). Corruption, political interference and the civil service. In: S. Guhan & S. Paul (Eds), *Corruption in India: Agenda for action* (pp. 60–87). New Delhi: Vision Books, chap. 3.

Godbole, M. (2000). *The changing times: A commentary on current affairs*. New Delhi: Orient Longman.

Gopal, A. (2009). $1,000 for a kebab? Afghan villages fight corruption. *Christian Science Monitor*, March 25.

Gould, D. J., Amaro-Reyes, J. A. (1983). *The effects of corruption on administrative performance: Illustrations from developing countries*. World Bank Staff Working Papers No. 580. Washington, D.C.

Government Information Office (GIO). (2010). *The Republic of China yearbook 2009*. Taipei: GIO (chap. 1, Geography; chap. 2, People and language; chap. 9, Economy; chap. 21, Religion).

Government of Japan. (1999). National Public Service Ethics Act (Act No. 129 of 1999). Available at http://www.jinji.go.jp/rinri/eng/index.htm. Retrieved on December 14, 2010.

Government Procurement Act (GPA). (1998). Taipei: Public Construction Commission, Executive Yuan. Available at http://erp.pcc.gov.tw/pccap2/BIZSfront/Eng/MenuContent.do?site = 004&bid = BIZS_C00000022#

Gray, C. (1979). Civil service compensation in Indonesia. *Bulletin of Indonesian Economic Studies*, *15*(1), 85–113.

Griffin, K. (1995). Economic strategy during the transition. In: K. Griffin (Ed.), *Poverty and the transition to a market economy in Mongolia* (pp. 1–26). Basingstoke: Macmillan Press, chap. 1.

Grossholz, J. (1964). *Politics in the Philippines*. Boston, MA: Little Brown and Company.

Grudgings, S. (2003). Corruption remains Philippines' public ticket to personal wealth. *Taipei Times*, September 29. Available at http://www.taipeitimes.com/News/edit/archives/2003/09/29/2003069760. Retrieved on September 4, 2004.

Guerrero, D. M. (1999). A tiger changing stripes: Post-development, transitions and democracy in South Korea. In: K. N. Gaerlan (Ed.), *Transitions to democracy in east and southeast Asia* (pp. 61–103). Quezon City: Institute for Popular Democracy, chap. 3.

Guerrero, L. L. B., Mangahas, M., & Laroza, L. R. S. (2007). *The 2006–2007 SWS surveys of enterprises on corruption*. Quezon City: Social Weather Stations.

Guerrero, L. L. B., Mangahas, M., & Laroza, L. R. S. (2010). *The 2009 SWS surveys of enterprises on corruption*. Quezon City: Social Weather Stations.

Guhan, S. (1997). Introduction. In: S. Guhan & S. Paul (Eds), *Corruption in India: Agenda for action* (pp. 9–28). New Delhi: Vision Books, chap. 1.

Gulati, M., & Rao, M. Y. (2007). Corruption in the electricity sector: A pervasive scourge. In: J. E. Campos & S. Pradhan (Eds), *The many faces of corruption: Tracking vulnerabilities at the sector level* (pp. 115–157). Washington, DC: World Bank, chap. 4.

Hadisumarto, D. (1974). *The Indonesian civil service and its reform movements*. D. P. A. dissertation, University of Southern California.

Hager, L. M. (1973). Bureaucratic corruption in India: Legal control of maladministration. *Comparative Political Studies*, *6*(2), 197–219.

Haggard, M. T. (1965). Mongolia: The first communist state in Asia. In: R. A. Scalapino (Ed.), *The communist revolution in Asia: Tactics, goals, and achievements* (pp. 82–113). Englewood Cliffs: Prentice-Hall.

Hamilton-Hart, N. (2001). Anti-corruption strategies in Indonesia. *Bulletin of Indonesian Economic Studies*, *37*(1), 65–82.

Hammond, T. T. (1975a). The history of communist takeovers. In: T. T. Hammond (Ed.), *The anatomy of communist takeovers* (pp. 1–45). New Haven: Yale University Press.

Hammond, T. T. (1975b). The communist takeover of Outer Mongolia: Model for Eastern Europe? In: T. T. Hammond (Ed.), *The anatomy of communist takeovers* (pp. 107–144). New Haven: Yale University Press.

Han, S. J. (1989). South Korea: Politics in transition. In: L. Diamond, J. J. Linz & S. M. Lipset (Eds), *Democracy in developing countries: Asia* (Vol. 3, pp. 267–303). Boulder: Lynne Rienner Publishers, chap. 7.

Hanna, W. A. (1971). A primer of *Korupsi*. *AUFS Southeast Asia Series*, *19*(8), 1–8.

Haq, K. (1999). *Human development in South Asia 1999: The crisis of governance*. Karachi: Oxford University Press.

Harden, B. (2008). In rural Philippines, a dearth of doctors: Thousands of physicians, retrained as nurses, take jobs abroad. Available at http://washingtonpost.com, September 20, pp. A13–A14.

Harding, L. (2003). Website pays price for Indian bribery expose. *The Guardian*, 6 January. Available at http://www.guardian.co.uk/ technology/2003/jan/06/newmedia.india.

Hariharan, A. (1974). A common goal: Get-rich-quick. *Far Eastern Economic Review*, *85*(35), September 6, p. 25.

Harris, P. B. (1987). Review of *The control of bureaucratic corruption* by Leslie H. Palmier. *Corruption and Reform*, *2*(1), 89–91.

Harsono, A. (2009). The gecko vs. the crocodile. In: *Global Integrity Report: Indonesia 2009*. Washington, DC: Global Integrity. Available at http://report.globalintegrity.org/Indonesia/2009/notebook/

Hart-Landberg, M. (1993). *The rush to development: Economic change and political struggle in South Korea*. New York: Monthly Review Press.

Hartwell, E. (2009). *"Wild money": The human rights consequences of illegal logging and corruption in Indonesia's forestry sector*. New York: Human Rights Watch.

Haryanto, U. (2010). Indonesia civil service by the numbers: What governs the bureaucrats? *Jakarta Globe*, November 23.

Hasegawa, T. (2000). Investigation of corruption in Japan. *Resource Materials Series No. 56* (pp. 469–475). Tokyo: UNAFEI.

Heidenheimer, A. J., Johnston, M., & LeVine, V. T. (Eds). (1989). *Political corruption: A handbook*. New Brunswick: Transaction Publishers.

Heller, N. (2009). Defining and measuring corruption: Where have we come from, where are we now, and what matters for the future? In: R. I. Rotberg (Ed.), *Corruption, global security, and world order* (pp. 47–65). Washington, D.C.: Brookings Institution Press, chap. 3.

Hess, D., & Dunfee, T. W. (2000). Fighting corruption: A principled approach, the $C^2$ Principles (Combating Corruption). Available at http://knowledge.emory.edu/papers/947.pdf. Retrieved on July 26, 2009.

Hilton, R. (2000). The Philippines: Catholicism, poverty and corruption. Available at http://wais.stanford.edu/Philippines/philippines_cathpovcorr110500.html.

Hirszowicz, M. (1986). *Coercion and control in communist society: The visible hand of bureaucracy*. Brighton: Wheatsheaf Books.

Ho, A. L. (2010). Taiwan to set up agency to fight graft. *Straits Times*, July 21, p. A18.

Hodess, R., Inowlocki, T., Rodriguez, D., & Wolfe, T. (Eds). (2004). *Global corruption report 2004*. London: Pluto Press and Transparency International.

Hodge, A. (2010). India rules out probe into Games graft. *The Australian*, August 6.

Hofman, B., Kaiser, K., & Schulze, G. G. (2009). Corruption and decentralization. In: C. J. G. Holtzappel & M. Ramstedt (Eds), *Decentralization and regional autonomy in Indonesia: Implementation and challenges* (pp. 99–113). Singapore: Institute of Southeast Asian Studies, chap. 3.

Holmes, L. (1993). *The end of communist power: Anti-corruption campaigns and legitimation crisis*. New York: Oxford University Press.

Holmes, R. D. (2007). Combating corruption in the Philippines: The difficulty and danger of organizational reform/human resource development initiatives. In: M. C. P. Alfiler & E. E. Nicolas (Eds), *Public administration plus governance: Assessing the past, addressing the future* (pp. 173–197). Quezon City: National College of Public Administration and Governance, University of the Philippines.

Hood, C., & Askim, J. (2003). Alike at the summit. In: C. Hood, B. G. Peters & G. O. M. Lee (Eds), *Reward for high public office: Asian and Pacific rim states* (pp. 22–46). London: Routledge, chap. 2.

Howlett, B. (Ed.) (1997). *Hong Kong 1997: A review of 1996*. Hong Kong: Information Services Department.

Hrebenar, R. J. (2000). *Japan's new party system*. Boulder: Westview Press.

Hsieh, J. F. S. (1996). The SNTV system and its political implications. In: H. M. Tien (Ed.), *Taiwan's electoral politics and democratic transition: Riding the third wave* (pp. 193–212). Armonk: M.E. Sharpe, chap. 8.

Huang, S. (2009). Chen Shui-bian gets life. *Taipei Times*, September 12, p. 1.

Hussain, Z. (2009). S'pore remains Asia's least corrupt country. *Straits Times*, April 8, p. B5.

Hwang, K. C. (1996). *Administrative corruption in the Republic of Korea*. Ph.D. dissertation, University of Southern California, Los Angeles, USA.

IAAC (Independent Authority Against Corruption). (2010). *The Result of the Mongolian Corruption Index 2009 (Summary)*. Ulaanbataar. Available at http://www.iaac.mn/pdf/ssha/Abstract_Corruption%20Index_eng.pdf. Retrieved on February 1, 2011.

ICAC (Independent Commission Against Corruption). (1989). *1988 Annual report*. Hong Kong.

ICAC. (1992). *1991 Annual report*. Hong Kong.

ICAC. (2002). *2001 Annual report*. Hong Kong.

ICAC. (2003). *2002 Annual report*. Hong Kong.

ICAC. (2005). *2004 Annual report*. Hong Kong.

ICAC. (2006). *2005 Annual report*. Hong Kong.

ICAC. (2007). *2006 Annual report*. Hong Kong.

ICAC. (2008). *2007 Annual report*. Hong Kong.

ICAC. (2009). *2008 Annual report*. Hong Kong.

ICAC. (2010). *2009 Annual report*. Hong Kong.

Iglesias, G. U. (1963). The passage of the anti-graft law. In: R. P. de Guzman (Ed.), *Patterns in decision-making: Case studies in Philippine public administration* (pp. 15–68). Manila: College of Public Administration, University of the Philippines.

Indra, B. (1998). Otgonbileg gives gov[ernmen]t the slip. *Mongol Messenger*, August 12, pp. 1, 3, 5.

Information Services Department. (2008). *Hong Kong 2007*. Hong Kong.

Ito, M. (2007). Funds law no match for wily politicians. *Japan Times*, September 11.

Jachid, S., & Hyer, P. (1979). *Mongolia's culture and society*. Boulder: Westview Press.

Jacobs, J. B. (2008). *Local politics in rural Taiwan under dictatorship and democracy*. Norwalk: EastBridge.

Jacobs, J. B., & Liu, I. B. (2007). Lee Teng-hui and the idea of "Taiwan". *China Quarterly*, *190*, 375–393 (June).

Jain, N. K. (2000). The Corruption Act of 1988 and the role and treatment of victims and witnesses in corruption case. *Honorable Justice N.K. Jain*, February 24. Available at http://justicenagendrakjain.com/Corruption.aspx. Retrieved on November 22, 2010.

*Jakarta Post*. (2000). World Bank wants good governance, anti-corruption. *Jakarta Post*, May 12.

*Japan Press Weekly*. (2009). Political funds control law is full of loopholes. *Japan Press Weekly*, March 5. Available at http://www.japan-press.co.jp/2009/2613/scandal_5.html. Retrieved on December 18, 2010.

*Japan Times*. (2010). 1,757 got jobs via 'amakudari' from '07 to '09. *Japan Times*, August 24.

*Japan Today*. (2001). Corruption cases at local governments rise. *Japan Today*, September 3. Available at http://www.japantoday.com/gidx/news188274.html.

*Japan Today*. (2004). Japan: Postal service rife with corruption. *Japan Today*, August 23.

Jenkins, G. P., Kuo, C. Y., & Sun, K. N. (2003). *Taxation and economic development in Taiwan*. Cambridge: John F. Kennedy School of Government, Harvard University and Chung-Hua Institution for Economic Research.

Jiao, A. Y. (2007). *The police in Hong Kong: A contemporary view*. Lanham: University Press of America.

Johnson, C. (1995). *Japan: who governs? The rise of the developmental state* (chap. 7, The reemployment of retired government bureaucrats in Japanese big business, pp. 141–156;

chap. 9, Tanaka Kakuei, structural corruption, and the advent of machine politics in Japan, pp. 183–211). New York: W.W. Norton.

Johnson, D. (2003a). A tale of two systems: Prosecuting corruption in Japan and Italy. In: F. J. Schwartz & S. J. Pharr (Eds), *The state of civil society in Japan* (pp. 257–277). Cambridge: Cambridge University Press, chap. 12.

Johnson, D. T. (2003b). Above the law? Police integrity in Japan. *Social Science Japan Journal*, *6*(1), 19–37.

Johnston, M. (1982). *Political corruption and public policy in America*. Monterey: Brooks Cole Publishing.

Johnston, M. (1991). Historical conflict and the rise of standards. *Journal of Democracy*, *2*(4), 48–60.

Johnston, M. (1996). The search for definitions: The vitality of politics and the issue of corruption. *International Social Science Journal*, *149*(September), 321–335.

Johnston, M. (1999). A brief history of anti-corruption agencies. In: A. Schedler, L. Diamond & M. F. Plattner (Eds), *The self-restraining state: Power and accountability in new democracies* (pp. 217–226). Boulder: Lynne Rienner, chap. 13.

Johnston, M. (Ed.) (2005a). *Civil society and corruption: Mobilizing for reform*. Lanham: University Press of America.

Johnston, M. (2005b). *Syndromes of corruption: Wealth, power and democracy*. New York: Cambridge University Press.

Johnston, M. (2010a). *Political and social foundations for reform: Anti-corruption strategies for the Philippines*. Manila: Asian Institute of Management.

Johnston, M. (Ed.) (2010b). *Public sector corruption* (Vols. 1–4). London: Sage Publications.

Joint Standing Committee on Foreign Affairs, Defense and Trade. (1997). *Hong Kong: The transfer of sovereignty* (May). Canberra: Parliament of the Commonwealth of Australia.

Jones, D. S. (2002). Procurement practices in the Singapore civil service: Balancing control and delegation. *Journal of Public Procurement*, *2*(1), 29–53.

Jones, D. W. (2009). Mongolia sitting on a gold mine. *Washington Times*, August 2.

*Joong Ang Daily*. (2010). A soldier's pay. *Joong Ang Daily*, June 3.

Joshi, G. P. (2003). *The story of the Central Vigilance Commission Bill, 2003*. New Delhi: Commonwealth Human Rights Initiative. Available at http://www.humanrightsinitiative.org/programs/aj/police/india/initiatives/story_of_the_central_vigilance_commission_story_2003.pdf. Retrieved on November 26, 2010.

Jun, J. S. (1985). The paradoxes of development: Problems of Korea's transformation. In: B. W. Kim, D. S., Bell, Jr. & C. B. Lee (Eds), *Administrative dynamics and development: The Korean experience* (pp. 56–75). Seoul: Kyobo Publishing.

Jun, J. S., & Kim, T. Y. (2002). Distrust as a hindrance to democratic governance in South Korea. *Asian Journal of Political Science*, *10*(1), 1–16.

Jun, J. S., & Park, M. S. (2001). Crisis and organizational paralysis: The lingering problem of Korean public administration. *Journal of Contingencies and Crisis Management*, *9*(1), 3–13.

Jun, J. S., & Yoon, J. P. (1996). Korean public administration at a crossroads: Culture, development and change. In: A. S. Huque, J. T. M. Lam & J. C. Y. Lee (Eds), *Public administration in the NICs: Challenges and accomplishments* (pp. 90–113). Basingstoke: Macmillan Press, chap. 4.

Kaplan, D. E., & Dubro, A. (2003). *Yakuza: Japan's criminal underworld*. Berkeley: University of California Press.

Kasem, S. (1962). *The civil service of Thailand.* Ph.D. dissertation, New York University.

Kaser, M. (1992). Mongolia. In: I. Jeffries (Ed.), *Industrial reform in socialist countries: From restructuring to revolution* (pp. 166–176). Aldershot: Edward Elgar, chap. 9.

Kau, M. Y. M. (1996). The power structure in Taiwan's political economy. *Asian Survey*, *36*(3), 287–305.

Kauffman, D. (2008). Governance, crisis, and the longer view: Unorthodox reflections on the new reality. Farewell presentation at the World Bank, Washington, DC, December 9. The PowerPoint presentation is available at http://www.thekaufmannpost.net

Kaufman, H. (1977). *Red tape: Its origins, uses and abuses.* Washington, DC: Brookings Institution.

Kearns, I. (1990). The Recruit scandal and corruption in Japanese political life. *Corruption and Reform*, *5*(1), 63–70.

Kennedy, B. (2000). Corruption, not China is the main challenge. *Taipei Times*, March 15, p. 8.

Khan, M. M. (1998). *Administrative reforms in Bangladesh.* New Delhi: South Asian Publishers.

Kharas, H. J. (1997). The Philippines: Three decades of lost opportunities. In: D. M. Leipziger (Ed.), *Lessons from East Asia* (pp. 443–479). Ann Arbor: University of Michigan Press, chap. 8.

Kihl, Y. W. (2005). *Transforming Korean politics: Democracy, reform, and culture.* Armonk: M.E. Sharpe.

Kilman, L. (2005). The role of the press in fighting corruption. Paper presented at the Fourth Global Forum on Fighting Corruption in Brasilia, Brazil on June 8, pp. 1–8. Available at https://bvc.cgu.gov.br/bitstream/123456789/3428/1/the-role-of-the.pdf

Kim, B. K. (2000a). Party politics in South Korea's democracy: The crisis of success. In: L. Diamond & B. K. Kim (Eds), *Consolidating democracy in South Korea* (pp. 53–86). Boulder: Lynne Rienner Publishers, chap. 3.

Kim, B. S. (1998). Corruption and anti-corruption policies in Korea. *Korea Journal*, *38*(1), 46–69.

Kim, C. N. (2007). *The Korean presidents: Leadership for nation building.* Norwalk: Eastbridge.

Kim, J. (2006). *National integrity systems Transparency International country study report Republic of Korea 2006.* Berlin: Transparency International.

Kim, J. (2009a). The judiciary's role in good governance in Korea. In: M. Ramesh & S. Fritzen (Eds), *Transforming Asian governance: Rethinking assumptions, challenging practices* (pp. 135–153). London: Routledge, chap. 8.

Kim, M. S. (1997). Regulation and corruption. In: Y. H. Cho & H. G. Frederickson (Eds), *The White House and the Blue House: Government reform in the United States and Korea* (pp. 253–269). Lanham: University Press of America, chap. 12.

Kim, M. S. (2000b). Causes of corruption and irregularities. *Korea Focus*, *8*(1) (January–February):2–3. Available at: http://www.kf.or.kr/koreafocus/focus_detail.asp?no = 143&title=VOL0801&category=ess

Kim, P. S. (2003). The politics of rewards for high public office in Korea. In: C. Hood, B.G. Peters & G. O. M. Lee (Eds), *Reward for high public office: Asian and Pacific rim states* (pp. 119–129). London: Routledge, chap. 7.

Kim, P. S. (2008). Building national integrity through corruption eradication in South Korea. In: B. Bidhya & C. Wescott (Eds), *Comparative governance reform in Asia: Democracy, corruption, and government trust* (pp. 155–178). Bingley: Emerald Group Publishing.

Kim, P. S. (2010). Korean civil service system and civil service reform. In: P. S. Kim (Ed.), *Civil service system and civil service reform in ASEAN member countries and Korea* (pp. 357–393). Seoul: Daeyoung Moonhwasa Publishing Company, chap. 12.

Kim, S. Y. (2005). Review on assessing effectiveness of integrity and anti-corruption measures in the Korean public service. In: J. Bertok & E. Beth (Eds), *Public sector integrity: A framework for assessment* (pp. 125–160). Paris: Organization for Economic Cooperation and Development.

Kim, W. T. (2001). Korean politics: Setting and political culture. In: S. H. Kil & C. I. Moon (Eds), *Understanding Korean politics: An introduction* (pp. 9–32). Albany: State University of New York, chap. 2.

Kim, Y. C. (1996). Mongolia: Background and history. In: P. B. Rana & N. Hamid (Eds), *From centrally planned to market economics: The Asian approach, Vol. 2 People's Republic of China and Mongolia* (pp. 295–312). Hong Kong: Oxford University Press, chap. 12.

Kim, Y. J. (1994). *Bureaucratic corruption: The case of Korea* (4th ed.). Seoul: Chomyung Press.

Kim, Y. S. (2009b). Corruption in Korea. *Korea Times*, July 16.

King, A. Y. C. (1980). An institutional response to corruption: The ICAC of Hong Kong. In: C.K. Leung, J. W. Cushman & G. Wang (Eds), *Hong Kong: Dilemmas of growth* (pp. 115–142). Canberra: Research School of Pacific Studies, Australian National University.

Kingsbury, D. (1998). *The politics of Indonesia*. Melbourne: Oxford University Press.

Kingsbury, D. (Ed.) (2001). *The presidency of Abdurrahman Wahid: An assessment after the first year*. Clayton: Monash Asia Institute, Monash University.

Kingsbury, D. (2002). *The politics of Indonesia* (2nd ed.). Melbourne: Oxford University Press.

Kingsbury, D. (2005). *The politics of Indonesia* (3rd ed.). South Melbourne: Oxford University Press.

Kitti, P. (2007). From political reform and economic crisis to coup d'etat in Thailand. *Asian Survey*, *47*(6), 872–893.

Klitgaard, R. (1988). *Controlling corruption*. Berkeley: University of California Press.

Klitgaard, R. (1997). Cleaning up and invigorating the civil service. *Public Administration and Development*, *17*(5), 487–509.

Kluckhohn, C. (1951). The study of culture. In: D. Lerner & H. D. Lasswell (Eds), *The policy sciences: Recent developments in scope and method* (pp. 86–101). Stanford: Stanford University Press, chap. 5.

Knapp, W. (1972). *The Knapp commission report on police corruption*. New York: George Braziller.

Ko, S. L. (2009). Ma 'distressed' by corruption rankings. *Taipei Times*, April 9, p. 1.

Ko, S. L. (2010). Ma calls [for] anti-corruption unit. *Taipei Times*, July 21, p. 1.

Koh, B. C. (1989). *Japan's administrative elite*. Berkeley: University of California Press.

Koh, L., & Lee, L. (2005). Board seats: Code updated for MPs. *Straits Times*, July 6, p. H3.

Kohli, C. (1975). In cinema. In: S. Kohli (Ed.), *Corruption in India* (pp. 67–71). New Delhi: Chetana Publications, chap. 9.

Kohn, M. (1998). Bagabandi keeps tough line against Dem[cratic] Union. *The Mongol Messenger*, October 21, p. 1.

Kohno, M. (1997). *Japan's postwar party politics*. Princeton: Princeton University Press.

Korea Independent Commission Against Corruption (KICAC). (2006). *Annual report 2005*. Seoul.

KPK (*Komisi Pemberantasan Korupsi*). (2007). *Annual Report 2006*. Jakarta.

KPK. (2008). *Annual Report 2007*. Jakarta.

KPK. (2009). *Annual Report 2008*. Jakarta.

KPK. (2010). *Annual Report 2009*. Jakarta.

Kpundeh, S. J. (1998). Political will in fighting corruption. In: S. Kpundeh & I. Hors (Eds), *Corruption and integrity improvement initiatives in developing countries* (pp. 91–110). New York: United Nations Development Programme, chap. 6.

Kpundeh, S. J., & Hors, I. (Eds). (1998). *Corruption and integrity improvement initiatives in developing countries*. New York: United Nations Development Programme.

Krastev, I. (2000). The strange (re) discovery of corruption. In: L. Dahrendorf, Y. Elkana, A. Neier, W. Newton-Smith & I. Rev (Eds), *The paradoxes of unintended consequences* (pp. 23–41). Budapest: Central European University Press, chap. 4.

Kristiadi, J. (2001). Indonesia: Redefining military professionalism. In: M. Alagappa (Ed.), *Military professionalism in Asia: Conceptual and empirical perspectives* (pp. 93–110). Honolulu: East-West Center, chap. 7.

Kristiadi, J. B. (1992). Administrative reform in Indonesia: Streamlining and professionalizing the bureaucracy. In: Z. Zhang, R. P. de Guzman & M. A. Reforma (Eds), *Administrative reform towards promoting productivity in bureaucratic performance* (Vol. 1, pp. 97–106). Manila: EROPA Secretariat General, chap. 9.

Kuan, H. K. (1981). Anti-corruption legislation in Hong Kong – A history. In: R. P. L. Lee (Ed.), *Control and its control in Hong Kong: Situations up to the late seventies* (pp. 15–43). Hong Kong: Chinese University Press, chap. 1.

Kulick, E., & Wilson, D. (1992). *Thailand's turn: Profile of a new dragon*. New York: St. Martin's Press.

Kumar, P. (2001). Small corruption can be ugly and costly too. *The Tribune*, April 1. Available at http://www.tribuneindia.com/2001/20010401 /edit.htm#3. Retrieved on November 10, 2010.

Kuo, C. T. (2000). Taiwan's distorted democracy in comparative perspective. *Journal of Asian and African Studies*, *34*(1), 85–111.

*Kyodo News Service*. (2003). 42 police officers punished for corruption. December 5.

La Mont, R. (2002). Some means of addressing judicial corruption in Mongolia. Unpublished paper, August 1, pp. 1–8. Available at http://pdc.ceu.hu/archive/00002274/01/Judicial_Corruption_in_Mongolia.pdf. Retrieved on October 31, 2008.

Lai, A. (2002). Building public confidence in anti-corruption efforts: The approach of the Hong Kong special administrative region of China. *Forum on Crime and Society*, *2*(1), 135–146.

Lai, A. N. (2001). Keeping Hong Kong clean: Experiences of fighting corruption post 1997. *Harvard Asia Pacific Review*, *5*(2), 51–54.

Laird, J. (2000). *Money politics, globalization, and crisis*. Singapore: Graham Brash.

Lall, B. R. (2007). *Who owns CBI: The naked truth*. New Delhi: Manas Publications.

Lambsdorff, J. G. (2008). *The methodology of the corruption perceptions index 2008*. Berlin: Transparency International and University of Passau.

Lande, C. H. (2001). The return of 'people power' in the Philippines. *Journal of Democracy*, *12*(2), 88–102.

Langston, R. L. (1991). *Bribery and the Bible: Applied to the Philippines*. Singapore: Campus Crusade Asia Limited.

Laskar, R. H. (2002). Tehelka scandal: Much ado but few lessons learnt. *Indo-Asian News Service*, March 12. Available at http://india. indymedia.org/en/2002/03/917.shtml

Lau, E. (1988). Graft-busters and 1997: Concern arises over anti-corruption commission's future. *Far Eastern Economic Review*, December 8, p. 29.

Law, F. (2008). The Hong Kong integrity system. In: L. Huberts, F. Anechiarico & F. Six (Eds), *Local integrity systems: World cities fighting corruption and safeguarding integrity* (pp. 79–101). The Hague: BJu Legal Publishers, chap. 6.

Ledeneva, A. V. (1998). *Russia's economy of favors: Blat, networking and informal exchange*. Cambridge: Cambridge University Press.

Lee, A. (2006). The public as our partner in the fight against corruption. In: C. Sampford, A. Shacklock, C. Connors, & F. Galtung (Eds), *Measuring corruption* (pp. 221–232). Aldershot: Ashgate, chap. 11.

Lee, G. B. (2005). *The Syonan years: Singapore under Japanese rule 1942–1945*. Singapore: National Archives of Singapore and Epigram.

Lee, G. O. M. (2003). Hong Kong – Institutional inheritance from colony to special administrative region. In: C. Hood, B. G. Peters & G. O. M. Lee (Eds), *Reward for high public office: Asian and Pacific rim states* (pp. 130–144). London: Routledge, chap. 8.

Lee, J. (1995). The real name financial system and the politics of economic reform in the Republic of Korea. *Pacific Focus, 10*(1), 109–110.

Lee, K. Y. (2000). *From third world to first, The Singapore story: 1965–2000*. Singapore: Times Media.

Lee, M. (1990). *The odyssey of Korean democracy: Korean politics 1987–1990*. New York: Praeger Publishers.

Lee, P. N. S. (1981a). The causes and effects of police corruption: A case in political modernization. In: R. P. L. Lee (Ed.), *Control and its control in Hong Kong: Situations up to the late seventies* (pp. 167–198). Hong Kong: Chinese University Press, chap. 6.

Lee, R. P. L. (1981b). Incongruence of legal codes and folk norms. In: R. P. L. Lee (Ed.), *Control and its control in Hong Kong: Situations up to the late seventies* (pp. 75–104). Hong Kong: Chinese University Press, chap. 3.

Lee, S. Y., & Jung, K. (2010). Public service ethics and anti-corruption efforts in South Korea. In: E. M. Berman, M. J. Moon & H. Choi (Eds), *Public administration in East Asia: Mainland China, Japan, South Korea, and Taiwan* (pp. 401–425). Boca Raton: CRC Press, chap. 19.

Leff, N. H. (1964). Economic development through bureaucratic corruption. *American Behavioral Scientist, 8*(3), 8–14.

Legowo, T. A. (1999). The bureaucracy and reform. In: R. W. Baker, M. H. Soesastro, J. Kristiadi & D. E. Ramage (Eds), *Indonesia: The challenge of change* (pp. 81–98). Singapore: Institute of Southeast Asian Studies, chap. 4.

Leichter, H. M. (1979). *A comparative approach to policy analysis: Health care policy in four nations*. Cambridge: Cambridge University Press.

Leiken, R. S. (1996/1997). Controlling the global corruption epidemic. *Foreign Policy, 105* (Winter), 55–73.

Lethbridge, H. J. (1978). The emergence of bureaucratic corruption as a social problem in Hong Kong. In: H. J. Lethbridge (Ed.), *Hong Kong: Stability and change* (pp. 214–237). Hong Kong: Oxford University Press, chap. 9.

Lethbridge, H. J. (1985). *Hard graft in Hong Kong: Scandal, corruption, the ICAC*. Hong Kong: Oxford University Press.

Levitt, S. D., & Dubner, S. J. (2010). *Superfreakonomics: Global cooling, patriotic prostitutes, and why suicide bombers should buy life insurance*. London: Penguin Books.

Leys, C. (1989). What is the problem about corruption? In: A. J. Heidenheimer, M. Johnston & V. T. LeVine (Eds), *Political corruption: A handbook* (pp. 51–66). New Brunswick: Transaction Publishers, chap. 5.

Likhit, D. (1978). The Thai bureaucratic elite: A study of their promotion and career advancement patterns. In: P. S. J. Chen & H. D. Evers (Eds), *Studies in ASEAN sociology: Urban society and social change* (pp. 96–114). Singapore: Chopmen Enterprises, chap. 8.

Lin, I. (2000a). Anti-corruption drive renewed. *Taipei Times*, January 24, p. 4.

Lin, I. (2000b). MJIB, Chen lock horns over role. *Taipei Times*, June 8, p. 1.

Lipset, S. M., & Lenz, G. S. (2000). Corruption, culture, and markets. In: L. E. Harrison & S. P. Huntington (Eds), *Culture matters: How values shape human progress* (pp. 112–124). New York: Basic Books, chap. 9.

Lo, C. P. (1992). *Hong Kong*. London: Bedhaven Press.

Lo, J. M. K. (2001). Controlling corruption in Hong Kong: From colony to special administrative region. *Journal of Contingencies and Crisis Management*, *9*(1), 21–28.

Lo, S. S. H. (2008). The politics of controlling *Heidao* and corruption in Taiwan. *Asian Affairs: An American Review*, *35*(2), 59–79.

Lo, S. S. H. (2009). *The politics of cross-border crime in greater China: Case studies of mainland China, Hong Kong, and Macao*. Armonk: M. E. Sharpe.

Lo, T. W. (2003). Minimizing crime and corruption in Hong Kong. In: R. Godson (Ed.), *Menace to society: Political-criminal collaboration around the world* (pp. 231–256). New Brunswick: Transaction Publisers, chap. 8.

Los, M. (1988). *Communist ideology, law and crime: A comparative view of the USSR and Poland*. Basingstoke: Macmillan Press.

Loveard, K. (1999). *Suharto: Indonesia's last sultan*. Singapore: Horizon Books.

Lovell, D. W. (2005). Corruption as a transitional phenomenon: Understanding endemic corruption in post-communist states. In: D. Haller & C. Shore (Eds), *Corruption: Anthropological perspectives* (pp. 65–82). London: Pluto, chap. 4.

Low, Y. F. (2009). President reaffirms resolve to fight corruption. *Central News Agency*, April 8. Available at http://www.etaiwannews.com/etn/print.php.

Lu, Y. L. (2002). Lee Teng-hui's role in Taiwan's democratization: A preliminary assessment. In: B. J. Dickson & C. M. Chao (Eds), *Assessing the Lee Teng-hui legacy in Taiwan's politics: Democratic consolidation and external relations* (pp. 51–72). Armonk: M.E. Sharpe, chap. 3.

Luo, J., Miao, C., & Guo, H. (Eds.). (n.d.). *The work against embezzlement and bribery in the People's Procuratorates of the People's Republic of China*. Beijing: Procuratorial Department for Embezzlement and Bribery, Supreme People's Procuratorate.

Luo, Y. (2007). *Guanxi and business* (2nd ed.). Singapore: World Scientific Publishing.

Ma, Y. J. (1995). War on election bribery. Taipei: Ministry of Justice.

Mabrey, D. (2007). Lockheed bribing scandal. In: J. Gerber & E. L. Jensen (Eds), *Encyclopedia of white-collar crime* (pp. 175–177). Westport: Greenwood Press.

Macdonald, D. S. (1996). *The Koreans: Contemporary politics and society* (D. N. Clark, Ed. & Rev. Ed.) (3rd ed.). Boulder: Westview Press.

Macdougall, T. (1988). The Lockheed scandal and the high costs of politics in Japan. In: A.S. Markovits & M. Silverstein (Eds), *The politics of scandal: Power and process in liberal democracies* (pp. 193–229). New York: Holmes & Meier Publishers, chap. 8.

Mackie, J. A. C. (1970). The Commission of Four report on corruption. *Bulletin of Indonesian Economic Studies*, *6*(3), 87–101.

MacKinnon, I. (2008). Former Thai PM Thaksin found guilty of corruption. *guardian.co.uk*, October 21, 2008. Available at http://www.guardian.co.uk/world/2008/oct/21/thaksin-thailand-corruption/print. Retrieved on January 21, 2009.

Maejima, I. (1980). Seasonal and regional aspects of Japan's weather and climate. In: The Association of Japanese Geographers (Ed.), *Geography of Japan* (pp. 54–72). Tokyo: Teikoku-Shoin Company, chap. 3.

Magno, A. R. (2001). Philippines: Trauma of a failed presidency. *Southeast Asian Affairs 2001* (pp. 251–262). Singapore: Institute of Southeast Asian Studies.

Maguire, K. (1997). Modernization and clean government: Tackling crime, corruption and organized crime in modern Taiwan. *Crime, Law and Social Change*, *28*(1), 73–88.

Maguire, K. (1998). *The rise of modern Taiwan*. Aldershot: Ashgate.

Maheshwari, S. R. (2005). *Public administration in India: The higher civil service*. New Delhi: Oxford University Press.

*Mainichi Daily News*. (1989). Politicians living high off the hog. *Mainichi Daily News*, September 9, p. 12.

Mallet, V. (1999). *The trouble with tigers: The rise and fall of Southeast Asia*. London: HarperCollins Publishers.

Manion, M. (2004). *Corruption by design: Building clean government in mainland China and Hong Kong*. Cambridge: Harvard University Press.

Manning, C. (1994). What has happened to wages in the New Order? *Bulletin of Indonesian Economic Studies*, *30*(3), 73–114.

Manning, N. (2000). *Pay and patronage in the core civil service in Indonesia*. Washington, DC: World Bank.

Manning, N., Mukherjee, R., Gokcekus, O., & Hofman, B. (2000). *Performance orientation among public officials in Indonesia: Report on a survey of public officials*. Washington, DC: World Bank.

Marcelo, S. V. (2004). Combating corruption in the Philippines. In: *Controlling Corruption in Asia and the Pacific* (pp. 37–43). Manila: Asian Development Bank.

Marcelo, S. V. (2005). Combating corruption in the Philippines: Status, challenges and prospects. In: *Combating corruption in the Philippines: Are we plundering our chances or doing it better?* (pp. 1–26). Quezon City: National College of Public Administration and Governance, University of the Philippines, Working Paper Series No. 2, July.

Marican, Y. M. (1979). Combating corruption: The Malaysian experience. *Asian Survey*, *19*(6), 597–610.

Mauro, P. (1997). *Why worry about corruption?* Washington, DC: International Monetary Fund.

Mauro, P. (2007). World Bank researchers and the study of corruption. *Brown Journal of World Affairs*, *13*(2), 68.

McAfee, R. B., & Poffenberger, W. (1982). *Productivity strategies: Enhancing employee job performance*. Englewood Cliffs: Prentice-Hall.

McBeath, G. A. (1998). *Wealth and freedom: Taiwan's new political economy*. Aldershot: Ashgate.

McCoy, A. W. (1994). 'An anarchy of families': The historiography of state and family in the Philippines. In: A. W. McCoy (Ed.), *An anarchy of families: State and family in the Philippines* (pp. 1–32). Quezon City: Ateneo de Manila University Press.

McLachlan, K. (1998). Introduction. In: D. Hodder, S. J. Lloyd & K. McLachlan (Eds), *Land-locked states of Africa and Asia* (pp. 1–11). London: Frank Cass.

McLeod, R. H. (2000). Government-business relations in Soeharto's Indonesia. In: P. Drysdale (Ed.), *Reform and recovery in East Asia: The role of the state and economic enterprise* (pp. 146–168). London: Routledge, chap. 7.

McPhail, S. (1995). *Developing Mongolia's legal framework: A needs analysis*. Manila: Asian Development Bank.

McWalters, I. (2003). *Bribery and corruption law in Hong Kong*. Hong Kong: LexisNexis Butterworths.

Meagher, P. (2005). Anti-corruption agencies: Rhetoric versus reality. *Journal of Policy Reform*, *8*(1), 69–103.

Menon, V. (2006). Anti-corruption in India: Issues and strategies. In: V. K. Chand (Ed.), *Reinventing public service delivery in India: Selected case studies* (pp. 333–362). New Delhi: Sage Publications, chap. 10.

Merton, R. K. (1952). Bureaucratic structure and personality. In: R. K. Merton, A. P. Gray, B. Hockey & H. C. Selvin (Eds), *Reader in bureaucracy* (pp. 361–371). New York: Free Press.

Meyer, J. C., Jr. (1973). A descriptive study of police corruption. *The Police Chief*, *60*(8), 38–41.

Mietzner, M. (2009). Indonesia in 2008: Yudhoyono's struggle for reelection. *Asian Survey*, *49*(1), 146–155.

Millennium Challenge Corporation. (2007). Building public integrity through positive incentives: MCC's role in the fight against corruption. Working Paper, 24 pages, Washington, DC. Available at http://www.mcc.gov/documents/reports/mcc-workingpaper-corruption.pdf

Milne, E., Leimone, J., Rozwadowski, F., & Sukachevin, P. (1991). *The Mongolian People's Republic: Toward a market economy*. Washington, DC: International Monetary Fund.

Ministry of Foreign Affairs. (1997). *Political reform in Thailand: From representative democracy towards participatory democracy*. Bangkok: News Division, Information Department.

Ministry of Justice. (2009). *Government employee ethics White Paper 2009*. Taipei.

Mitchell, R. H. (1996). *Political bribery in Japan*. Honolulu: University of Hawaii Press.

Mitchell, R. H. (2002). *Justice in Japan: The notorious Teijin scandal*. Honolulu: University of Hawaii Press.

MJIB (Ministry of Justice Investigation Bureau). (2010). Chinese website. Available at http://www.mjib.gov.tw/cgi-bin/mojnbi?/services/service-6.html

Mo Y. C, Ko, S. L., & Shih, H. C. (2008). Decisive victory for Ma Ying-jeou. *Taipei Times*, March 23, p. 1.

Mogato, M. (2010). Aquino needs to deliver in graft fight. *ABS-CBN News*, September 29. Available at http://www.abs-cbnnews.com/-depth/09/29/10/aquino-needs-deliver-graft-fight. Retrieved on November 25, 2010.

*Mongol Messenger*. (1996). Copper giant caught in corruption web. *Mongol Messenger*, October 9, p. 1.

Montesanto, M. J. (2007). Thailand: A reckoning with history begins. In: D. Singh & L. C. Salazar (Eds), *Southeast Asian affairs 2007* (pp. 311–339). Singapore: Institute of Southeast Asian Studies.

Moody, P. R., Jr. (2002). Some problems in Taiwan's democratic consolidation. In: B. J. Dickson & C. M. Chao (Eds), *Assessing the Lee Teng-hui legacy in Taiwan's politics: Democratic consolidation and external relations* (pp. 27–50). Armonk: M. E. Sharpe, chap. 2.

Moody-Stuart, G. (1997). *Grand corruption: How business bribes damage developing countries*. Oxford: WorldView Publishing.

Moon, S. Y. (2001). The utilization of the internet technology in the public services of Korea. *Asian Review of Public Administration*, *13*(1), 30–45.

Moran, J. (1999). Patterns of corruption and development in East Asia. *Third World Quarterly*, *20*(3), 569–589.

Moreau, R., & Mazumdar, S. (2003). New tales of graft and greed: corrupt politicians are fuelling a deep cynicism. *Newsweek*, November 25.

Morris, S. D. (1991). *Corruption and politics in contemporary Mexico*. Tuscaloosa: University of Alabama Press.

Mouzelis, N. P. (1967). *Organization and bureaucracy: An analysis of modern theories*. Chicago: Aldine.

Mulder, N. (1996). *Inside Thai society: Interpretation of everyday life*. Amsterdam: Pepin Press.

Munro, M. (2011). Corrupt societies have greater death tolls from quakes: Report. *Montreal Gazette*, January 12.

Mutebi, A. M. (2006). Thailand's independent agencies under Thaksin: Relentless gridlock and uncertainty. In: D. Singh & L. C. Salazar (Eds), *Southeast Asian affairs 2006* (pp. 303–321). Singapore: Institute of Southeast Asian Studies.

Mutebi, A. M. (2009). "Good governance" and the constraints of local conditions: Thaksin and the breakdown of Thailand's public integrity system. In: M. Ramesh & S. Fritzen (Eds), *Transforming Asian governance: Rethinking assumptions, challenging practices* (pp. 116–134). London: Routledge, chap. 7.

Myers, R. H., Chao, L., & Kuo, T. C. (2002). Consolidating democracy in the Republic of China on Taiwan, 1996–2000. In: B. J. Dickson & C. M. Chao (Eds), *Assessing the Lee Teng-hui legacy in Taiwan's politics: Democratic consolidation and external relations* (pp. 73–90). Armonk: M.E. Sharpe, chap. 4.

Myrdal, G. (1968). *Asian drama: An enquiry into the poverty of nations*, Vol. 2 (chap. 20, Corruption – Its causes and effects. pp. 937–960). New York: Twentieth Century.

Najiah. (2011). Gayus Tambunan in jail again. *Malay Mail Online*, January 20.

Nakamura, A., & Dairokuno, K. (2003). Japan's pattern of rewards for high public office: A cultural perspective. In: C. Hood, B. G. Peters & G. O. M. Lee (Eds), *Reward for high public office: Asian and Pacific rim states* (pp. 105–118). London: Routledge, chap. 6.

Narasimhan, C. V. (1997). Prevention of corruption: Towards effective enforcement. In: S. Guhan & S. Paul (Eds), *Corruption in India: Agenda for action* (pp. 251–285). New Delhi: Vision Books, chap. 10.

Naruntuya, D. (1998). Top officials slam door on corruption. *Mongol Messenger*, October 21, p. 3.

National Statistical Coordination Board (NSCB). (2008). Poverty worsens between 2003 and 2006. Manila: Press Release, March 7. Available at http://www.nscb.gov.ph/pressreleases/2008/PR-200803-SS2-02_pov.asp. Retrieved on October 31, 2010.

Neher, C. D. (1977). Political corruption in a Thai province. *Journal of Developing Areas, 11*(4), 479–492.

*New York Times*. (1997). Hanbo steel founder given 15 years in Korean scandal. *New York Times*, June 2.

*Newsbreak Online*. (2006). The street ombudsman. *Newsbreak Online*, November 21. Available at http://newsbreak.com.ph/index2.php?option=com_content&task=view&id=1338&Itemid=88889005

Nixson, F. I., & Walters, B. (2000). Administrative reform and economic development in Mongolia, 1990–1997: A critical perspective. In: K. T. Liou (Ed.), *Administrative reform and national economic development* (pp. 213–239). Aldershot: Ashgate, chap. 10.

Noerper, S. (2007). Mongolia in 2006: Land of the rising khan. *Asian Survey, 47*(1), 74–79.

Nualnoi, T. (2004). Controlling corruption in Thailand: Transforming the problems and paradoxes. In: V. Bhargava & E. Bolongaita (Eds), *Challenging corruption in Asia: Case studies and a framework for action* (pp. 171–207). Washington, DC: World Bank, chap. 5.

Nye, J. S. (1967). Corruption and political development. *American Political Science Review, 56*(2), 417–427.

Obejas, J. D. R. (2009). Wiping away the footprints of corruption in the Philippines. *Resource Material Series*. No.77, 138th International Senior Seminar Participants' Papers (pp. 97–122). Fuchu: UNAFEI.

Odgaard, O. (1996). Living standards and poverty. In: O. Brun & O. Odgaard (Eds), *Mongolia in transition: Old patterns, new challenges* (pp. 103–134). Richmond: Curzon Press.

OECD (Organization for Economic Cooperation and Development). (2000). *Trust in government: Ethics measures in OECD countries* (Japan, pp. 205–211). Paris.

Oh, J. K. C. (1999). *Korean politics: The quest for democratization and economic development*. Ithaca: Cornell University Press.

Oh, S. H. (1982). The counter-corruption campaign of the Korean government (1975-1977): Administrative anti-corruption measures of the *Seojungshaeshin*. In: B. W. Kim & W. J. Rho (Eds), *Korean public bureaucracy* (pp. 322–344). Seoul: Kyobo Publishing, chap. 14.

Olaguer, R. J. A. (2006). *Fighting corruption*. Manila: University of Santo Tomas Publishing House.

Olcott, M. B. (2002). *Kazakhstan: Unfulfilled promise*. Washington, DC: Carnegie Endowment for International Peace.

OMB (Office of the Ombudsman). (2009). *Annual Report 2008*. Manila. Available at http://www.ombudsman.gov.ph/docs/statistics/Annual%20Report%202008.pdf

ONCCC (Office of the National Counter Corruption Commission). (2006a). *Anti-corruption laws and regulations*. Bangkok.

ONCCC. (2006b). *The National Counter Corruption Commission (NCCC) Thailand*. Bangkok.

Ong, H. H. (2007). Taiwan opposition leader cleared of graft. *Straits Times*, August 15, p. 10.

Onishi, N. (2009). Indonesia officials resign in graft scandal. *New York Times*, November 6, p. A10.

Osman, S. (2009). KPK scandal captivates Indonesians: Wide media coverage fuelling anger over alleged plot against graft busters. *Straits Times*, November 6, p. A9.

O'uchi, M., Ishii, Y., Konishi, A., Kuroda, T., Sugawara, S., Umeda, T., & Yamazaki, K. (2006). *National integrity systems Transparency International country study report Japan 2006*. Berlin: Transparency International.

Oyamada, E. (2005). President Gloria Macapagal-Arroyo's anti-corruption strategy in the Philippines: An evaluation. *Asian Journal of Political Science*, *13*(1), 81–107.

Padilla, P. L. (1995). Low salary grades, income-augmentation schemes and the merit principle. In: P. D. Tapales & N. N. Pilar (Eds), *Public administration by the year 2000: Looking back into the future* (pp. 186–214). Quezon City: College of Public Administration, University of the Philippines.

Pagulayan, R. (2007). The government's lifestyle check as an anti-corruption program: Selective and ineffective. In: B. M. Tuazon (Ed.), *Dissecting corruption: Philippine perspectives* (pp. 111–114). Quezon City: CenPEG Books.

Painter, M. (2001). *Building institutional capacity in Asia report 2001: Public sector challenges and government reforms in South East Asia*. Sydney: Research Institute for Asia and the Pacific, University of Sydney.

Pairote, P. (2010). Civil service reform in Thailand: A perspective in transition. In: P. S. Kim (Ed.), *Civil service system and civil service reform in ASEAN member countries and Korea* (pp. 253–285). Seoul: Daeyoung Moonhwasa Publishing Company, chap. 9.

Palmier, L. (1985). *The control of bureaucratic corruption: Case studies in Asia*. New Delhi: Allied Publishers.

Park, Y. B. (1997). Wages policy and inter-sectoral pay differentials in the Republic of Korea, 1975–91. In: C. Colclough (Ed.), *Public-sector pay and adjustment: Lessons from five countries* (pp. 46–67). London: Routledge, chap. 3.

Parliament of Singapore. (1987). *Report of the commission of inquiry on investigations concerning the late Teh Cheang Wan*. Cmd. 18 of 1987. Singapore: Singapore National Printers.

Parry, R. (1998). Why so many gifts? In: J. Mak, S. Sunder, S. Abe & K. Igawa (Eds), *Japan: Why it works, why it doesn't: Economics in everyday life* (pp. 27–32). Honolulu: University of Hawaii Press.

Partnership for Governance Reform. (2001). *A national survey of corruption in Indonesia*. Final Report, December, Jakarta.

Pasuk, P., & Baker, C. (2004). *Thaksin: The business of politics in Thailand*. Chiang Mai: Silkworm Books.

Pasuk, P., & Baker, C. (2009). *Thaksin* (2nd ed.). Chiang Mai: Silkworm Books.

Pasuk, P., & Sungsidh, P. (1996). *Corruption and democracy in Thailand* (2nd ed.). Chiang Mai: Silkworm Books.

Paul, S. (2002). *Holding the State to account: Citizen monitoring in action*. Bangalore: Books for Change.

Paul, S., & Shah, M. (1997). Corruption in public service delivery. In: S. Guhan & S. Paul (Eds), *Corruption in India: Agenda for action* (pp. 144–163). New Delhi: Vision Books, chap. 6.

Pedrosa, C. N. (1987). *Imelda Marcos: The rise and fall of the world's most powerful woman*. New York: St. Martin's Press.

PERC (Political Economic Risk Consultancy). (2001). Corruption in Asia in 2001. *Asian Intelligence*. No. 579, March 7. Available at http://www.asiarisk.com/lib10.html

PERC. (2008). Corruption as a force destabilizing the business environment. *Asian Intelligence*. No. 750, March 12.

Pharr, S. J. (2000). Officials' misconduct and public distrust: Japan and the trilateral democracies. In: S. J. Pharr & R. D. Putnam (Eds), *Disaffected democracies: What's troubling the trilateral countries?* (pp. 173–201). Princeton: Princeton University Press, chap. 8.

*Philippine Daily Inquirer*. (2008). Editorial: Uncontrolled corruption. *Philippine Daily Inquirer*, October 21. Available at http://services.inquirer.net.php?article_id=20081021-167698. Retrieved on July 26, 2009.

Pitt, K. W., & Leong, W. K. (Eds). (2009). *Syonan years 1942–1945: Living beneath the Rising Sun*. Singapore: National Archives of Singapore.

Political Risk Services Group. (2010). Thailand country conditions. In: B. F. McTernan (Ed.), *Political Risk Yearbook 2010, Vol. 5 East Asia and the Pacific* (pp. 1–21). East Syracuse: PRS Group Inc.

Pomfret, R. (1996). *Asian economies in transition: Reforming centrally planned economies* (chap. 6, Mongolia's economic reforms, pp. 75–90). Cheltenham: Edward Elgar.

Pope, J. (2000). *Confronting corruption: The elements of a national integrity system*. Berlin: Transparency International.

Porter, M. E., Sachs, J. D., Warner, A. M., Cornelius, P. K., Levinson, M., & Schwab, K. (2000). *The global competitiveness report 2000*. New York: Oxford University Press.

Potter, D. M. (2000). Controlling state crime in Japan: A case study of political corruption. In: J. I. Ross (Ed.), *Varieties of state crime and its control* (pp. 181–198). Monsey: Criminal Justice Press, chap. 8.

Prasad, K. (2006). *Indian administration: Politics, policies and prospects* (chap. 12, Administrative corruption and public integrity, pp. 301–337). Delhi: Dorling Kindersley (India).

Prawiro, R. (1998). *Indonesia's struggle for economic development: Pragmatism in action*. Kuala Lumpur: Oxford University Press.

Preecha, L. (2001). Institutionalizing strategies to combat corruption in Thailand. In: A.C., Pedro, Jr. (Ed.), *Combating corruption in East Asia* (pp. 105–119). Manila: Yuchengco Center for East Asia, De La Salle University.

Prema, L. E. (1987). Teh affair: builder fined. *Straits Times*, April 1, p. 1.

Price, J. L. (1968). *Organizational effectiveness*. Homewood: Richard D. Irwin.

Prins, H. (1982). *Criminal behavior: An introduction to criminology and the penal system* (2nd ed.). London: Tavistock Publications.

Prudhisan, J. (1998). Thailand: Constitutional reform amidst economic crisis. In: D. da Cunha & J. Funston (Eds), *Southeast Asian affairs 1998* (pp. 265–291). Singapore: Institute of Southeast Asian Studies.

PSD (Public Service Division). (2008). Civil servants' annual pay to fall. Singapore, November 24, pp. 1–2.

Quah, J. S. T. (1976). Administrative reform: A conceptual analysis. *Philippine Journal of Public Administration*, *20*(1), 50–67.

Quah, J. S. T. (1978a). The origins of the public bureaucracies in the ASEAN Countries. *Indian Journal of Public Administration*, *24*(2), 400–429.

Quah, J. S. T. (1978b). *Administrative and legal measures for combating bureaucratic corruption in Singapore*. Singapore: Department of Political Science, University of Singapore, Occasional Paper No. 34.

Quah, J. S. T. (1979). Police corruption in Singapore: An analysis of its forms, extent and causes. *Singapore Police Journal*, *10*(1), 7–43.

Quah, J. S. T. (1982a). Bureaucratic corruption in the ASEAN countries: A comparative analysis of their anti-corruption strategies. *Journal of Southeast Asian Studies*, *13*(1), 153–177.

Quah, J. S. T. (1982b). Tackling bureaucratic corruption: The ASEAN experience. In: G.E. Caiden & H. Siedentopf (Eds), *Strategies for administrative reform* (pp. 109–121). Lexington: Lexington Books, chap. 9.

Quah, J. S. T. (1984). The public policy-making process in Singapore. *Asian Journal of Public Administration*, *6*(2), 108–126.

Quah, J. S. T. (1989a). Singapore's experience in curbing corruption. In: A. J. Heidenheimer, M. Johnston & V. T. LeVine (Eds), *Political corruption: A handbook* (pp. 841–853). New Brunswick: Transaction Publishers, chap. 48.

Quah, J. S. T. (1989b). Bureaucracy and administrative reform in the ASEAN countries: A comparative analysis. In: R. B. Jain (Ed.), *Bureaucratic politics in the third world* (pp. 247–275). New Delhi: Gitanjali Publishing House, chap. 11.

Quah, J. S. T. (1991). The 1980s: A review of significant political developments. In: E. C. T. Chew & E. Lee (Eds), *A history of Singapore* (pp. 385–400). Singapore: Oxford University Press, chap. 18.

Quah, J. S. T. (1995). Controlling corruption in city-states: A comparative study of Hong Kong and Singapore. *Crime, Law and Social Change*, *22*, 391–414.

Quah, J. S. T. (1997). Combating corruption in Asia: Comparing anti-corruption agencies in South Korea, Taiwan and Thailand. Paper presented at the Conference on "Institutionalizing Horizontal Accountability: How Democracies can fight Corruption and Abuse of Power" organized by the Institute of Advanced Studies and the International Forum for Democratic Studies in Vienna, Austria on June 26–29, 1997, 35 p.

Quah, J. S. T. (1998). *National anti-corruption plan for Mongolia*. Confidential report prepared for the UNDP and the Mongolian Government, November, 41 p.

Quah, J. S. T. (1999a). *Combating corruption in Mongolia: Problems and prospects*. Singapore: Department of Political Science, National University of Singapore, Working Paper No. 22, July, 35 p.

Quah, J. S. T. (1999b). Combating Corruption in South Korea and Thailand. In: A. Schedler, L. Diamond & M. F. Plattner (Eds), *The self-restraining state: Power and accountability in new democracies* (pp. 245–256). Boulder: Lynne Rienner, chap. 15.

Quah, J. S. T. (1999c). Comparing anti-corruption measures in Asian countries: Lessons to be learnt. *Asian Review of Public Administration, 11*(2), 71–90.

Quah, J. S. T. (1999d). Singapore's anti-corruption strategy: Some lessons for South Korea. *Korean Corruption Studies Review, 4*(December), 173–193.

Quah, J. S. T. (2001). Singapore: Meritocratic city-state. In: J. Funston (Ed.), *Government and politics in Southeast Asia* (pp. 291–327). Singapore: Institute of Southeast Asian Studies, chap. 8.

Quah, J. S. T. (2002). *Bureaucratic corruption in Indonesia: Some suggestions for reform*. Background report prepared for the World Bank Office in Jakarta, Indonesia, June, 42 p.

Quah, J. S. T. (2003a). *Curbing corruption in Asia: A comparative study of six countries*. Singapore: Eastern Universities Press. The six countries analyzed in this book are: Hong Kong, India, Mongolia, Philippines, Singapore, and South Korea.

Quah, J. S. T. (2003b). Paying for the 'best and brightest': Rewards for high public office in Singapore. In: C. Hood, B. G. Peters & G. O. M. Lee (Eds), *Reward for high public office: Asian and Pacific rim states* (pp. 145–162). London: Routledge, chap. 9.

Quah, J. S. T. (2003c). Combating corruption in India: Some lessons from Asian experiences. In: S. Howes, A. Lahiri & N. Stern (Eds), *State-level reforms in India: Towards more effective government* (pp. 84–97). New Delhi: Macmillan India, chap. 9.

Quah, J. S. T. (2003d). Causes and consequences of corruption in Southeast Asia: A comparative analysis of Indonesia, the Philippines and Thailand. *Asian Journal of Public Administration, 25*(2), 235–266.

Quah, J. S. T. (2004). Best practices for curbing corruption in Asia. *The Governance Brief 11*, 1–4. Available at http://www.adb.org/Documents/Periodicals/GB/GovernanceBrief11.pdf

Quah, J. S. T. (2006a). Analyzing the formulation and implementation of anti-corruption measures in Asian countries: Some relevant questions. Paper presented at the Workshop on "Research on Corruption and Its Control: The State of the Art" at the Zicklin Center for Business Ethics, Wharton School, University of Pennsylvania, Philadelphia on March 3–4.

Quah, J. S. T. (2006b). Curbing Asian corruption: An impossible dream? *Current History, 105*(690), 176–179.

Quah, J. S. T. (2006c). Preventing police corruption in Singapore: The role of recruitment, training and socialization. *Asia Pacific Journal of Public Administration, 28*(1), 59–75.

Quah, J. S. T. (2007a). *National integrity systems Transparency International regional overview report East and Southeast Asia 2006* (Available at http://www.transparency.org/policy_research/nis/nis_reports_by_country/asia_pacific). Berlin: Transparency International.

Quah, J. S. T. (2007b). *Combating corruption Singapore-style: Lessons for other Asian countries*. Baltimore, MD: School of Law, University of Maryland.

Quah, J. S. T. (2008). Curbing corruption in India: An impossible dream? *Asian Journal of Political Science, 16*(3), 240–259.

Quah, J. S. T. (2009a). Benchmarking the performance of anti-corruption agencies in the Asia-Pacific countries. In: A. Rajivan & R. Gampat (Eds), *Perspectives on corruption and human development* (Vol. 2), pp. 763–805). Delhi: Macmillan Publishers India, chap. 18.

Quah, J. S. T. (2009b). Civil service and corruption. In: A. K. Rajivan & R. Gampat (Eds), *Perspectives on corruption and human development* (Vol. 2, pp. 802–838). Delhi: Macmillan Publishers India, chap. 19.

Quah, J. S. T. (2009c). Benchmarking for excellence: A comparative analysis of seven Asian anti-corruption agencies. *Asia Pacific Journal of Public Administration, 31*(2), 171–195.

Quah, J. S. T. (2010a). Defying institutional failure: Learning from the experiences of anti-corruption agencies in four Asian countries. *Crime, Law and Social Change, 53*(1), 23–54.

Quah, J. S. T. (2010b). *Public administration Singapore-style*. Bingley: Emerald Group Publishing.

Quah, J. S. T. (2010c). Asia-Pacific states: Building an inclusive, responsive and capable state. In: B. Forde (Ed.), *Building an inclusive, responsive and capable state: Background papers* (pp. 61–85). Oslo: UNDP Oslo Governance Center.

Quah, J. S. T. (2010d). *Taiwan's anti-corruption strategy: Suggestions for reform*. Baltimore, MD: School of Law, University of Maryland.

Quimson, G. (2006). *National integrity systems Transparency International country study report Philippines 2006*. Berlin: Transparency International.

Raghunathan, V. (2006). *Games Indians play: Why we are the way we are*. New Delhi: Penguin Books India.

Rahman, A. T. R. (1986). Legal and administrative measures against bureaucratic corruption in Asia. In: L. V. Carino (Ed.), *Bureaucratic corruption in Asia: Causes, consequences and control* (pp. 109–162). Quezon City: JMC Press and College of Public Administration, chap. 4.

Ramseyer, J. M., & Rosenbluth, F. M. (1997). *Japan's political marketplace* (2nd ed.). Cambridge: Harvard University Press.

Rebullida, M. L. G. G. (2006). The executive: Martial law, constitutional authoritarianism, and the Marcos administration. In: N. M. Morada & T. S. E. Tadem (Eds), *Philippine politics and governance: An introduction* (pp. 153–178). Quezon City: Department of Political Science, University of the Philippines, chap. 8.

Reed, S. R. (1996). Political corruption in Japan. *International Social Science Journal, 149* (September), 395–405.

Reiber, B., & Spencer, J. (1996). *Japan* (3rd ed.). New York: Macmillan Travel.

Reid, R. H., & Guerrero, E. (1995). *Corazon Aquino and the brushfire revolution*. Baton Rouge: Louisiana State University Press.

Reischauer, E. O. (1988). *The Japanese today: Change and continuity*. Cambridge: Belknap Press.

Reksosoedirdjo, W. (1985). Civil service system in Indonesia. In: *Trends in civil service reforms in ASEAN countries* (pp. 91–155). Bangkok: Office of the Civil Service Commission.

Republic of China. (1995–2003). *Anti-corruption yearbook 1993–2002*. Taipei: Ministry of Justice Investigation Bureau.

Republic of China. (1996). *Anti-corruption yearbook 1995*. Taipei: Ministry of Justice Investigation Bureau.

Republic of China. (2000a). *Anti-corruption yearbook 1999*. Taipei: Ministry of Justice Investigation Bureau.

Republic of China. (2000b). *Eradicating organized crime and corruption in Taiwan*. Taipei: Government Information Office, November 6. Available at http://www.gio.gov.tw/ct.asp?xItem=18703&ctNode=2501

Republic of China. (2002). *Anti-corruption yearbook 2001*. Taipei: Ministry of Justice Investigation Bureau.

Republic of China. (2003). *Anti-corruption yearbook 2002*. Taipei: Ministry of Justice Investigation Bureau.

Republic of China. (2008). *Anti-corruption yearbook 2007* (Available at http://www.mjib.gov.tw/newworkitem/crime/event/96event/index.htm). Taipei: Ministry of Justice Investigation Bureau.

Republic of China. (2009). *Anti-corruption yearbook 2008* (Available at http://www.mjib.gov.tw/newworkitem/crime/event/97event/fscommand/english.pdf). Taipei: Ministry of Justice Investigation Bureau.

Republic of China. (2010). *Anti-corruption yearbook 2009*. Taipei: Ministry of Justice Investigation Bureau.

Republic of Korea. (1999). *Korea's comprehensive anti-corruption programs*. Seoul: Office of the Prime Minister.

Republic of Korea. (2001). *Anti-corruption Act*. Seoul: Office for Government Policy Coordination.

Republic of the Philippines. (2010). *Year 2010: National Government Expenditures*. Manila: Department of Budget and Management, Table B.10. Available at http://www.dbm.gov.ph/data/Image/TableB.10.pdf. Retrieved on February 5, 2011.

Republic of Singapore. (1978–2010). *The Budget for the Financial Years 1978/1979 to 2010–2011*. Singapore: Budget Division, Ministry of Finance.

Republic of Singapore. (1989). The Corruption (Confiscation of Benefits) Act 1989 (No. 16 of 1989). *Government gazette: Acts supplement*, No. 13, Friday, March 31: pp. 105–130. Singapore: Singapore National Printers.

Republic of Singapore. (1995). *The Budget for the Financial Year 1994/1995, Command 2 of 1994*. Singapore: Budget Division, Ministry of Finance.

Republic of Singapore. (2010). *The Budget for the Financial Year 2010/2011. Annex to the Expenditure Estimates*. Singapore: Budget Division, Ministry of Finance.

*Reuters India*. (2009). Economists say graft weakens Philippine bureaucracy. May 20. Available at http://in.reuters.com/article?articleId=INIndia-39753220090520. Retrieved on May 23, 2009.

Reyes, V. C., Jr. (2007). Corruption and policy implementation in the Philippines: A comparative analysis of the teacher training and textbook delivery programs. *Asian Journal of Political Science*, *15*(1), 97–125.

Reyes, V. C., Jr. (2009). *Corruption and implementation: Case studies in Philippine public administration*. Quezon City: National College of Public Administration and Governance, University of the Philippines.

Rice, S. E., & Patrick, S. (2008). *Index of state weakness in the developing world* (Available at http://www.brookings.edu/reports/2008/~/media/Files/rc/reports/2008/02_weak_index/02_weak_states_index.pdf). Washington, DC: Brookings Institution.

Richardson, B. M., & Flanagan, S. C. (1984). *Politics in Japan*. Boston, MA: Little, Brown and Company.

Richter, L. K. (1987). Public bureaucracy in post-Marcos Philippines. *Southeast Asian Journal of Social Science*, *15*(2), 57–76.

Rigger, S. (1999). *Politics in Taiwan: Voting for democracy*. London: Routledge.

Robertson-Snape, F. (1999). Corruption, collusion and nepotism in Indonesia. *Third World Quarterly, 20*(3), 589–602.

Rocamora, J. (1998). Corruption in the Philippines: A beginner's guide. In: S. S. Coronel (Ed.), *Pork and other perks: Corruption and governance in the Philippines* (pp. 8–31). Quezon City: Philippine Center for Investigative Journalism.

Rohdewohld, R. (1995). *Public administration in Indonesia*. Melbourne: Montech.

Romano, A. (2003). *Politics and the press in Indonesia: Understanding an evolving political culture* (chap. 11, The envelope please, pp. 150–163). London: RoutledgeCurzon.

Rondonuwu, O. (2011). Game over for corrupt, wig-wearing Indonesian tax official. *Reuters*, January 19.

Root, H. L. (1996a). *Small countries, big lessons: Governance and the rise of East Asia*. Hong Kong: Oxford University Press.

Root, H. (1996b). Corruption in China: Has it become systemic? *Asian Survey, 36*(8), 741–757.

Rose, R. (2005). *Learning from comparative public policy: A practical guide*. London: Routledge.

Rosenbluth, F. M., & Thies, M. F. (2010). *Japan transformed: Political change and economic restructuring*. Princeton: Princeton University Press.

Rossabi, M. (2005). *Modern Mongolia: From khans to commisars to capitalists*. Berkeley: University of California Press.

Rotberg, R. I. (2004). The failure and collapse of nation states: Breakdown, prevention, and repair. In: R. I. Rotberg (Ed.), *When states fail: causes and consequences* (pp. 1–49). Princeton: Princeton University Press, chap. 1.

Rothacher, A. (2003). Political corruption in Japan. In: M. J. Bull & J. L. Newell (Eds), *Corruption in contemporary politics* (pp. 106–119). Basingstoke: Palgrave Macmillan, chap. 9.

Roy, W. T. (1967). The steel frame: The legend of the Indian civil service. *New Zealand Journal of Public Administration, 30*(1), 39–51, September.

Rupen, R. A. (1966). *The Mongolian People's Republic*. Stanford: Hoover Institution Studies, No. 12, Stanford University.

Saccone, R. (1994). *The business of Korean culture*. Seoul: Hollym Corporation Publishers.

Saeki, N. (1997). The Soeharto family business. *AMPO, 27*(1), 1–4.

Sakaguchi, Y. (1980). Characteristics of the physical nature of Japan with special reference to landform. In: The Association of Japanese Geographers (Ed.), *Geography of Japan* (pp. 3–28). Tokyo: Teikoku-Shoin Company, chap. 1.

Sakkarin, N. (2000). *The political economy of telecommunications reforms in Thailand*. London: Pinter.

Sala-i-Martin, X. (Ed.) (2004). *The global competitiveness report 2003–2004*. New York: Oxford University Press.

Sampson, S. (2009). Corruption and anti-corruption in Southeast Europe. In: L. de Sousa, P. Larmour & B. Hindess (Eds), *Governments, NGOs and anti-corruption: The new integrity warriors* (pp. 168–185). London: Routledge.

Sanders, A. (1998). Mongolia: Looking to the sea. In: D. Hodder, S. J. Lloyd & K. McLachlan (Eds), *Land-locked states of Africa and Asia* (pp. 134–152). London: Frank Cass.

Sanghvi, V. (2004). The paradoxes of Tehelka. Available at http://www.india-seminar.com/2004/533/533%20vir%20sanghvi.htm. Retrieved on November 10, 2010.

Santhanam, K. (1964). *Report of the committee on prevention of corruption*. New Delhi: Government of India Press.

Saragih, B. B. (2011). KPK vows to defy political pressure. *Jakarta Post*, January 30.

Sawarjuwono, T., & Goodfellow, Rob. (1997). The Chinese Indonesians and business. In: R. Goodfellow (Ed.), *Indonesian business culture: An insider's guide* (pp. 77–93). Singapore: Butterworth-Heinemann Asia, chap. 4.

Scalapino, R. A. (1992). *The last Leninists: The uncertain future of Asia's communist states*. Washington, DC: Center for Strategic and International Studies.

Schaffer, F. C. (2004). Vote buying in East Asia. In: R. Hodess, T. Inowlocki, D. Rodriguez & T. Wolfe (Eds), *Global corruption report 2004* (pp. 83–87). Berlin: Transparency International.

Scheffer, J. d. H. (2009). Afghanistan: We can do better. *Washington Post*, January 18, p. B07.

Schlesinger, J. M. (1999). *Shadow shoguns: The rise and fall of Japan's postwar political machine*. Stanford: Stanford University Press.

Schwab, K. (Ed.) (2009). *The global competitiveness report 2009–2010*. Geneva: World Economic Forum.

Schwab, K. (Ed.) (2010). *The global competitiveness report 2010–2011*. Geneva: World Economic Forum.

Schwab, K., & Porter, M. E. (2007). *The global competitiveness report 2007–2008*. Basingstoke: Palgrave Macmillan.

Schwab, K., & Porter, M. E. (2008). *The global competitiveness report 2008–2009*. Geneva: World Economic Forum.

Schwab, K., Porter, M. E., Sachs, J. D., Cornelius, P. K., & McArthur, J. W. (2002). *The global competitiveness report 2001–2002*. New York: Oxford University Press.

Schwab, K., Porter, M. E., Sachs, J. D., Warner, A. M., & Levinson, M. (1999). *The global competitiveness report 1999*. New York: Oxford University Press.

Schwarz, A. (2004). *A nation in waiting: Indonesia's search for stability*. Singapore: Talisman Publishing.

Schwenke, S. (2005). Sectoral synthesis. In: B. I. Spector (Ed.), *Fighting corruption in developing countries* (pp. 153–178). Bloomfield: Kumarian Press, chap. 11.

Scott, I. (1992). Administration in a small capitalist state: The Hong Kong experience. In: R. Baker (Ed.), *Public administration in small and island states* (pp. 99–115). West Hartford: Kumarian Press, chap. 7.

Scott, J. C. (1972). *Comparative political corruption*. Englewood Cliffs: Prentice-Hall.

Searle, P. (2000). Coping with corruption and cronyism. In: G. Segal & D. S. G. Goodman (Eds), *Towards recovery in pacific Asia* (pp. 69–84). London: Routledge, chap. 6.

Sen, K. (2002). The Mega factor in Indonesian politics: A new president or a new kind of presidency? In: K. Robinson & S. Bessell (Eds), *Women in Indonesia: Gender, equity and development* (pp. 13–27). Singapore: Institute of Southeast Asian Studies, chap. 2.

Senior, I. (2006). *Corruption – The world's big C: Cases, causes, consequences, cures*. London: Institute of Economic Affairs.

Seong, K. R. (2000). Civil society and democratic consolidation in South Korea: Great achievements and remaining problems. In: L. Diamond & B. K. Kim (Eds), *Consolidating Democracy in South Korea* (pp. 87–110). Boulder: Lynne Rienner Publishers, chap. 4.

Shari, M. (2002). Indonesia: In the post-Suharto era, everyone wants a piece of the action. Result: An investor nightmare. *BusinessWeek*, May 20, pp. 21–24.

Sharma, P. D., & Sharma, B. M. (2009). *Indian administration: Retrospect and prospect*. Jaipur: Rawat Publications.

Sheehan, D. (2001). More power to the powerful. *Far Eastern Economic Review*, February 1, p. 17.

Sheehy, D. P. (1996). Sustainable livestock use of pastoral resources. In: O. Brun & O. Odgaard (Eds), *Mongolia in transition: Old patterns, new challenges* (pp. 42–64). Richmond: Curzon Press.

Sheng, A. (2009). *From Asian to global financial crisis: An Asian regulator's view of unfettered finance in the 1990s and 2000s*. Cambridge: Cambridge University Press.

Sheridan, G. (1994). *Tigers: Leaders of the new Asia-Pacific* (chap. 1, Kim Young-sam and the crucible of Korean politics, pp. 1–36). St. Leonards: Allen and Unwin.

Sheridan, G. (1999). *Asian values western dreams: Understanding the new Asia*. St. Leonards: Allen and Unwin.

Shih, J. N. (2007). Government reform experience in Taiwan (1990–2006): A critical assessment. In: G. E. Caiden & T. T. Su (Eds), *The repositioning of public governance: Global experience and challenges* (pp. 291–320). Taipei: Taiwan Public Affairs Center, chap. 10.

Shin, D. C. (1999). *Mass politics and culture in democratizing Korea*. Cambridge: Cambridge University Press.

Shin, P. (2002). South Korean president laments corruption scandals involving his sons. *Yahoo!News*, July 15, p. 1. Available at http://story.news.yahoo.com/new?tmpl=story&u = /ap/20020715/ap_wo_en_po/skorea

Shiratori, R. (1994). Political finance and scandal in Japan. In: H. E. Alexander & R. Shiratori (Eds), *Comparative political finance among the democracies* (pp. 187–205). Boulder: Westview Press, chap. 14.

Shunglu, V. K. (2000). India's anti-corruption strategy. In: *Combating corruption in Asian and Pacific economies* (pp. 13–18). Manila: Asian Development Bank.

Siagian, S. P. (1965). *The development and problems of indigenous bureaucratic leadership in Indonesia*. Ph.D. dissertation, Indiana University.

Siagian, S. P. (1970). Improving Indonesia's administrative infrastructure: A case study. In: H.B. Lee & A. G. Samonte (Eds), *Administrative reforms in Asia* (pp. 95–124). Manila: Eastern Regional Organization for Public Administration, chap. 5.

Sidik, M. (2007). *A new perspective of intergovernmental fiscal relations: Lessons from Indonesia's experience*. Jakarta: Ripelge.

*Singapore Daily Times*. (1865). October 17.

Singh, G. (1997). Understanding political corruption in contemporary Indian politics. In: P. Heywood (Ed.), *Political corruption* (pp. 210–222). Oxford: Blackwell Publishers.

Singh, N. K. (1999). *The politics of crime and corruption: A former CBI officer speaks*. New Delhi: HarperCollins Publishers India.

Slagter, R., & Kerbo, H. R. (2000). *Modern Thailand*. Boston, MA: McGraw-Hill.

Smith, A. L. (2001). Introduction: Abdurrahman Wahid's economic agenda: The views of leading decision-makers and commentators. In: A. L. Smith (Ed.), *Gus Dur and the Indonesian economy* (pp. 1–22). Singapore: Institute of Southeast Asian Studies, chap. 1.

Smith, H. (1976). *The Russians*. New York: Ballantine Books.

Smith, H. (2008). Japan. In: H. Smith (Ed.), *Guide to anti-corruption regulation in Asia 2008/2009* (pp. 19–23). Hong Kong: Herbert Smith.

Smith, T. M. (1970). *A tentative report concerning Indonesia's administrative system, its capacity and problems in connection with economic development*. Jakarta, unpublished report, January.

Smith, T. M. (1971). Corruption, tradition and change. *Indonesia*, *11*(April), 21–40.

Soedarjo, A. D. (2011). Fake Indonesian inmate exposes prison corruption. *Agence France Presse*, January 7.

Soh, K. H. (2008a). Corruption enforcement. Paper presented at the Second Seminar of the International Association of Anti-Corruption Associations in Chongqing, China, May 17–18.

Soh, K. H. (2008b). Role of awareness and education in the fight against corruption. Paper presented at the Asia Anti-Corruption Conference in Qatar, June, 9–11.

Somboon, S. (2007). Thailand. In: A. Chowdhury & I. Islam (Eds), *Handbook on the Northeast and Southeast Asian Economies* (pp. 129–148). Cheltenham: Edward Elgar, chap. 7.

Song, B. N. (1997). *The rise of the Korean economy* (2nd ed.). Hong Kong: Oxford University Press.

Sosmena, G. C., Jr. (1995). *Breaking the cocoon: Bureaucracy reborn*. Manila: Local Government Development Foundation.

*South China Morning Post*. (2007). A job for Estrada would help Arroyo keep hers. *South China Morning Post*, October 29, p. 14.

Spector, B. I. (2005). Fighting corruption. In: B. I. Spector (Ed.), *Fighting corruption in developing countries* (pp. 1–9). Bloomfield: Kumarian Press, chap. 1.

Spector, R. H. (2007). *In the ruins of empire: The Japanese surrender and the battle for postwar Asia*. New York: Random House.

Srivastava, C. P. (2001). *Corruption: India's enemy within*. Delhi: Macmillan India.

Stapenhurst, R., & Kpundeh, S. J. (Eds). (1999). *Curbing corruption: Toward a model for building national integrity*. Washington, DC: World Bank.

Statistics and Census Service. (2011). Principal Statistical Indicators of Macao, 3rd Quarter 2010, No. 3 (pp. 1–8). Macao. Available at http://www.dsec.gov.mo/statistic.aspx

Statistics Bureau of Japan. (2008). *Statistical handbook of Japan 2008*. Tokyo. Available at http://www.stat.go.jp/english/data/handbook/c01cont.pdf

Steinberg, D. I. (1989). *The republic of Korea: Economic transformation and social change*. Boulder: Westview Press.

Steinberg, D. I. (2000). Continuing democratic reform: The unfinished symphony. In: L. Diamond & B. K. Kim (Eds), *Consolidating democracy in South Korea* (pp. 203–238). Boulder: Lynne Rienner Publishers, chap. 8.

Steinberg, D. J. (1982). *The Philippines: A singular and a plural place*. Boulder: Westview Press.

Stockwin, J. A. A. (1983). *Why Japan matters*. An inaugural lecture delivered at the University of Oxford on January 27. Oxford: Clarendon Press.

Stockwin, J. A. A. (2003). *A dictionary of the modern politics of Japan*. London: RoutledgeCurzon, pp. 9–10.

Straits Settlements. (1887). *Report of commission appointed to enquire into the question of public gambling in the Straits Settlements*. Singapore: Colonial Secretary's Office.

*Straits Times*. (1849). June 13.

*Straits Times*. (1887). October 4.

*Straits Times*. (1985). PM: Pay well or we pay for it. *Straits Times*, March 23, pp. 1, 14–16.

*Straits Times*. (1987a). January 27, p. 11.

*Straits Times*. (1987b). August 20, p. 10.

*Straits Times*. (1987c). Govt files graft charges against Aquino's uncle. *Straits Times*, November 7, p. 44.

*Straits Times*. (1993). Special team to root out graft among top South Korean officials. *Straits Times*, March 12.

*Straits Times*. (1995). How Singapore combats graft. *Straits Times*, October 8, p. 4.

*Straits Times*. (1998). August 1, p. 14.

*Straits Times*. (1999). Corrupt Mongolia MPs jailed. *Straits Times*, October 22, p. 23.

*Straits Times*. (2000a). March 6, p. 23.

*Straits Times*. (2000b). March 9, p. 30.

*Straits Times*. (2000c). April 24, p. 2.

*Straits Times*. (2002a). Megawati lambasts her own govt for being a 'trash can'. *Straits Times*, February 14, p. A5.

*Straits Times*. (2002b). Police chief admits: Yes, Thai cops are corrupt, what do you expect? *Straits Times*, June 5.

*Straits Times*. (2003). Coalition of the suspicious to catch govt crooks. *Straits Times*, March 22, p. A15.

*Straits Times*. (2010a). S'pore least corrupt nation. *Straits Times*, March 9.

*Straits Times*. (2010b). A third of Indians utterly corrupt. *Straits Times*, September 9, p. A19.

Strauss, J., Beegle, K., Dwiyanto, A., Herawati, Y., Pattinasarany, D., Satriawan, E., Sikoki, B., Sukamdi, B., & Witoelar, F. (2004). *Indonesian living standards: Before and after the financial crisis*. Singapore: Institute of Southeast Asian Studies.

Sugita, K. (1999). Looking into Japanese police corruption. Available at http://tokyoprogressive.org/~tpgn/japan/japanesepolice.html. Retrieved on 18 December 2010.

Suh, S. M. (1998). *The Korean currency crisis: What can we learn from it?* Stanford: Asia-Pacific Research Center, Stanford University.

Suryadinata, L. (1997). Democratization and political succession in Suharto's Indonesia. *Asian Survey*, *37*(3), 269–280.

Suryadinata, L. (2002). *Elections and politics in Indonesia*. Singapore: Institute of Southeast Asian Studies.

Suryadinata, L., Arifin, E. N., & Ananta, A. (2003). *Indonesia's population: Ethnicity and religion in a changing political landscape*. Singapore: Institute of Southeast Asian Studies.

Suwanagul, K. (1962). *The civil service of Thailand*. Ph.D. dissertation, New York University, New York, USA.

Tachi, Y. (2001). An overview of the Japanese criminal justice legislation against corruption. Paper presented at the Third annual conference of the ADB/OECD anti-corruption initiative for Asia-Pacific in Tokyo, Japan, November 28–30.

Tachi, Y. (2002). Role of public prosecutors in Japan. In: *Taking action against corruption in Asia and the Pacific* (pp. 119–126). Manila: Asian Development Bank, chap. 11.

*Taipei Times*. (2000). Editorial: What is really the 'Lee way'? *Taipei Times*, March 15, p. 8.

*Taipei Times*. (2001). Editorial: Corruption still rampant. *Taipei Times*, April 5, p. 8.

*Taipei Times*. (2009). Civil servant pay won't be cut. *Taipei Times*, February 21, p. 3.

*Taiwan News*. (2010). Taiwan President announces plan for anti-corruption administration. *Taiwan News*, July 20.

Takeshi, T. (2000). Light and shadow in Japan's police system. *Japan Quarterly*, *47*(2), 41–49.

Tan, A. L. (1999). The experience of Singapore in combating corruption. In: R. Stapenhurst & S. J. Kpundeh (Eds), *Curbing corruption: Toward a model for building national integrity* (pp. 59–66). Washington, DC: World Bank, chap. 4.

Tan, M. (2003). Incorruptible excellence. In: Special Feature on Celebrating Excellence 2003. *Today*, November 27, p. 6.

Tandon, S. (2010). Corruption – The main games in India. *ABC News*, October 1.

Tang, E. (2000). Thai graft busters mean business. *Straits Times*, May 24, p. 27.

Taub, R. P. (1969). *Bureaucrats under stress: Administrators and administration in an Indian state*. Berkeley: University of California Press.

Taylor, J. (2000). *The generalissimo's son: Chiang Ching-Kuo and the revolutions in China and Taiwan*. Cambridge: Harvard University Press.

Taylor, J. (2009). *The generalissimo: Chiang Kai-shek and the struggle for modern China*. Cambridge: Belknap Press of Harvard University Press.

TDPO (Taipei District Prosecutors Office). (2010). About the chief prosecutor. Available at http://www.tpc.moj.gov.tw/ct.asp?xItem=75273&CtNode=18307&mp=103. Retrieved on December 6, 2010.

*Tempo*. (2003). Interview with Yusril Ihza Mahendra: I am not happy. *Tempo*, December 15, pp. 30–31.

Thampi, G. K. (2002). *Corruption in South Asia: Insights and benchmarks from citizen feedback surveys in five countries*. Berlin: Transparency International.

*The Nation*. (2006). Thaksin-era corruption 'cost state Bt400 bn.' *The Nation*, October 1. Available at http://www.nationmultimedia.com/option/print.php?newsid=30015092. Retrieved on January 22, 2009.

*The Nation*. (2010). Editorial: Fair pay is one way to root out corruption. *The Nation*, September 16.

Thinapan, N. (1977). *Bureaucratic corruption in Thailand: Incongruities between legal codes and social norms*. Bangkok: School of Public Administration, National Institute of Development Administration.

Thinapan, N. (1978). Corruption in the Thai bureaucracy: Who gets what, how and why in its public expenditures. *Thai Journal of Development Administration, 18*(1), 102–128.

Thio, L. A. (1997). The elected president and the legal control of government: *Quis custodes ipsos custodes*? In: K. Y. L. Tan & P. E. Lam (Eds), *Managing political change in Singapore: The elected presidency* (pp. 100–143). London: Routledge, chap. 5.

Thitinan, P. (2006). Thaksin's political zenith and nadir. In: D. Singh & L. C. Salazar (Eds), *Southeast Asian affairs 2006* (pp. 285–302). Singapore: Institute of Southeast Asian Studies.

Thitinan, P. (2009). The tragedy of the 1997 constitution. In: J. Funston (Ed.), *Divided over Thaksin: Thailand's coup and problematic transition* (pp. 27–37). Singapore: Institute of Southeast Asian Studies, chap. 2.

Thompson, M. R. (1998). The Marcos regime in the Philippines. In: H. E. Chehabi & J. J. Linz (Eds), *Sultanistic regimes* (pp. 206–229). Baltimore, MD: John Hopkins University Press, chap. 9.

Thoolen, H. (Ed.) (1987). *Indonesia and the rule of law: Twenty years of 'New Order' government*. London: Frances Pinter Publishers.

Thoppil, D. A., & Sharma, A. (2010). Indian telecom minister resigns. *Wall Street Journal*, November 16. Available at http://online.wsj.com/article/SB10001424052748704584504575616003755644076.html. Retrieved on November 20, 2010.

Tien, H. M. (1992). Taiwan's evolution toward democracy: A historical perspective. In: D. F. Simon & M. Y. M. Kau (Eds), *Taiwan: Beyond the economic miracle* (pp. 3–23). Armonk: M.E. Sharpe, chap. 1.

Tierney, J. F. (2010). *Warlord, Inc.: Extortion and corruption along the U.S. supply chain in Afghanistan*. Washington, DC: Report of the Majority Staff, Subcommittee on National

Security and Foreign Affairs, Committee on Oversight and Government Reform, U.S. House of Representatives, June.

Timberman, D. G. (1991). *A changeless land: Continuity and change in Philippine politics*. Singapore: Institute of Southeast Asian Studies.

Todaro, M. P., & Smith, S. C. (2003). *Economic development* (8th ed.). Harlow: Pearson Edition.

Transparency and Accountability Network (TAN). (2009). *The office of the Ombudsman: Is there institutional weakness*? (pp. 1–5). Quezon City: PHDR Issue 2008/2009, No. 2.

Transparency International. (2004). *Report on the Transparency International global corruption barometer 2004*. Berlin, December 9.

Transparency International. (2005). *Report on the Transparency International global corruption barometer 2005*. Berlin, December 9.

Transparency International. (2006). *Report on the Transparency International global corruption barometer 2006*. Berlin, December 7.

Transparency International. (2007). *Report on the Transparency International global corruption barometer 2007*. Berlin, December 6.

Transparency International. (2009). *Global corruption barometer 2009*. Berlin.

Transparency International. (2010). *Global corruption barometer 2010*. Berlin.

Transparency International India. (2002). Corruption in India: An empirical study. Available at http://unpan1.un.org/intradoc/groups/public/documents/APCITY/UNPAN019888.pdf. Retrieved on November 17, 2010.

Transparency International Mongolia. (2007). Corruption within Mongolia's legal profession. In: D. Rodriguez & L. Ehrichs (Eds), *Global corruption report 2007* (pp. 228–232). Cambridge: Cambridge University Press.

Trehan, M. (2009). *Tehelka as metaphor: Prism me a lie, tell me a truth*. New Delhi: Roli Books.

Trimnell, E. (2008). *Japanese culture from A to Z: Business, history, politics, sex, and more*. Cincinnati: Beechmont Crest Publishing.

Tsang, S. (Ed.) (1995). *Government and politics: A documentary history of Hong Kong* (chap. 4, The civil service, pp. 141–194). Hong Kong: Hong Kong University Press.

Tummala, K. K. (2002). Corruption in India: Control measures and consequences. *Asian Journal of Political Science*, *10*(2), 43–69 (December).

Tummala, K. K. (2004). Paul H. Appleby and India's administration. In: P. L. S. Reddy, J. Singh & R. K. Tiwari (Eds), *Democracy, governance and globalization: Essays in honor of Paul H. Appleby* (pp. 209–228). New Delhi: Indian Institute of Public Administration, chap. 11.

Tummala, K. K. (2010). Political corruption in India: Coalition Dharma? *International Public Management Review*, *11*(2), 78–94.

Turnbull, C. M. (1977). *A history of Singapore: 1819–1975*. Kuala Lumpur: Oxford University Press.

Tuya, N. (2005). Mongolia in 2004: Testing politics and economics. *Asian Survey*, *45*(1), 67–70.

Tuya, N. (2006). Mongolia in 2005: Sharing power, dealing with corruption. *Asian Survey*, *46*(1), 79–84.

Umeda, T. (2004). Japan: Integrity Assessment. *Global Integrity – 2004 Country Report*. Washington, DC: Global Integrity. Available at http://www.globalintegrity.org/reports/2004/2004/country20b3.html?cc=jp&act=ia. Retrieved on December 14, 2010.

Umeda, T., Yamazahi, K., & O'uchi, M. (2008). "Japan". In: D. Zinnbauer & R. Dobson (Eds), *Global corruption report 2008: Corruption in the water sector* (pp. 200–201). Cambridge: Cambridge University Press.

Underkuffler, L. S. (2009). Defining corruption: Implications for action. In: R. I. Rotberg (Ed.), *Corruption, global security, and world order* (pp. 27–46). Washington, DC: Brookings Institution Press, chap. 2.

UNDP (United Nations Development Programme). (1997). *Human development report Mongolia 1997*. Ulaanbaatar.

UNDP. (1999). *Fighting corruption to improve governance*. New York.

UNDP. (2008). *Tackling corruption, transforming lives: Accelerating human development in Asia and the Pacific*. Delhi: Macmillan India.

UNICEF. (2010). India: Statistics, economic indicators. March 2. Available at http://www.unicef.org/infobycountry/india_statistics.html. Retrieved on November 25, 2010.

Unidjaja, F. D. (2002). Megawati renews call to combat graft, uphold law. *Jakarta Post*, March 18.

United States Department of State. (2010). Background Note: Mongolia. August 26. Available at http://www.state.gov/r/pa/ei/bgn/2779.htm

UNODC (United Nations Office for Drug Control) and Crime Prevention Center for International Crime Prevention (CPCICP). (1997). Restructuring the police in Mongolia. Vienna.

Ursal, S. B. (2006). *Anti-graft guidebook*. Quezon City: Good Governance Books.

van Klaveren, J. (1989). The concept of corruption. In: A. J. Heidenheimer, M. Johnston & V.T. LeVine (Eds), *Political corruption: A handbook* (pp. 25–28). New Brunswick: Transaction Publishers, chap. 2.

van Wolferen, K. (1993). *The enigma of Japanese power: People and politics in a stateless nation*. Tokyo: Charles E. Tuttle Company.

Vanzi, S. J. (2005). Hong Kong graft buster seeks to clean up Philippines. *Philippine Headline News Online*. August 25. Available at http://www.newsflash.org/2004/02/hl/hl102676.htm

Varela, A. P. (1995). Different faces of Filipino administrative culture. In: P. D. Tapales & N.N. Pilar (Eds), *Public administration by the year 2000: Looking back into the future* (pp. 161–177). Quezon City: College of Public Administration, University of the Philippines.

Vittal, N., & Mahalingam, S. (2000). *Fighting corruption and restructuring government*. New Delhi: Manas Publications.

Vitug, M. D. (1998). Highway robbery. In: S. S. Coronel (Ed.), *Pork and other perks: Corruption and governance in the Philippines* (pp. 186–215). Quezon City: Philippine Center for Investigative Journalism.

*VOA News*. (2010). India orders probe into Commonwealth games corruption. *VOA News*, October 16.

Volcker, P. A., Gaviria, G., Githongo, J., Heineman, B. W., Van Gerven, W., & Vereker, J. (2007). *Independent panel review of the World Bank Group Department of Institutional Integrity*. Washington, DC: World Bank, September 13.

Wade, R. (1985). The market for public office: Why the Indian state is not better at development. *World Development*, *13*(4), 467–495.

Wade, R. (1990). *Governing the market: Economic theory and the role of government in East Asian industrialization*. Princeton: Princeton University Press.

Wales, H. G. Q. (1934). *Ancient Siamese government and administration*. London: Bernard Quaritch.

Walker, P. (2005). Opportunities for corruption in a celebrity disaster. In *Curbing corruption in tsunami relief operations* (Appendix 1: Background paper, pp. 89–103). Manila: Asian Development Bank.

Wang, F. (2008). KMT candidate proposes stiffer anti-corruption law. *Central News Agency*, January 18.

Wang, F. Y. (1995). Civil service, uncivil image? *Taiwan Review*, March 1, pp. 6–7. Available at http://taiwanreview.nat.gov.tw/site/Tr/fp.asp?xItem=74&CtNode=128

Wang, G. (1997). The new politics in Hong Kong. *ISEAS Trends*, No. 81, in *Business Times*, Weekend Edition, 31 May–1 June, p. 1.

Wang, T. S. (2000). *Legal reform in Taiwan under Japanese colonial rule, 1895–1945: The reception of Western law*. Seattle: University of Washington Press.

Warwick, D. P. (1978). Civil service reform in Indonesia: Problems and possibilities. Cambridge: Harvard Institute for International Development, unpublished confidential report, October.

Warwick, D. P. (1979). Cultural values and population policies: Cases and contexts. In: J.D. Montgomery, H. D. Lasswell & J. S. Migdal (Eds), *Patterns of policy: Comparative and longitudinal studies of population events* (pp. 295–337). New Brunswick: Transaction Books, chap. 11.

Warwick, D. P. (1987). The effectiveness of the Indonesian civil service. *Southeast Asian Journal of Social Science*, *15*(2), 40–56.

Watson, R. (1986). How to spend a billion: Imelda Marcos squandered her country's money and her own reputation. *Newsweek*, March 24, pp. 14–17.

Weng Y. J. (1996). An exploration of judicial and prosecution differences regarding corruption and malfeasance cases ruled not guilty. In: Republic of China. *Anti-corruption yearbook 1995* (pp. 387–400). Taipei: Ministry of Justice Investigation Bureau.

White, B. T. (2010). Putting aside the rule of law myth: Corruption and the case for juries in emerging democracies. *Cornell International Law Journal*, *43*, 307–363.

White, L. T. (2009). *Political booms: Local money and power in Taiwan, East China, Thailand, and the Philippines*. Singapore: World Scientific Publishing.

Wilkinson, J. (1993). Lords of corruption. *AMPO*, *24*(4), 4–6.

Williamson, R. C. (2006). *Latin America: Cultures in conflict*. Basingstoke: Palgrave Macmillan.

Wilson, D. A. (1962). *Politics in Thailand*. Ithaca: Cornell University Press.

Wirutomo, P. (1991). Labor in the Indonesian public service. In: W. van Ginneken (Ed.), *Government and its employees* (pp. 113–134). Aldershot: Avebury and International Labor Organization, chap. 4.

Wolff, C. (1990). A world class shopper: Imelda Marcos's New York trial. *New York Times*, April 20.

Wong, J. K. H. (1981). The ICAC and its anti-corruption measures. In: R. P. L. Lee (Ed.), *Control and its control in Hong Kong: Situations up to the late seventies* (pp. 45–72). Hong Kong: Chinese University Press, chap. 2.

Woodall, B. (1996). *Japan under construction: Corruption, politics, and public works*. Berkeley: University of California Press.

Wood, W. A. R. (1959). *A history of Siam*. Bangkok: Chalermnit Bookshop.

Woods, D. L. (2006). *The Philippines: A global studies handbook*. Santa Barbara: ABC-CLIO, Inc.

World Bank. (2004). *Combating corruption in Indonesia: Enhancing accountability for development*. Jakarta: World Bank Office.

World Bank. (2006a). *Mongolia poverty assessment*. Washington, DC.

World Bank. (2006b). *Doing business 2007*. Washington, DC.

World Bank. (2007). *Doing business 2008*. Washington, DC.

World Bank. (2008). *Doing business 2009*. Washington, DC.
World Bank. (2009). *Doing business 2010*. Washington, DC.
World Bank. (2010a). *Doing business 2011*. Washington, DC.
World Bank. (2010b). Worldwide Governance Indicators: Philippines. Available at http://info.worldbank.org/governance/wgi/sc_chart.asp
Woronoff, J. (1986). *Politics: The Japanese way*. Tokyo: Yohan Publications.
Wraith, R., & Simpkins, E. (1963). *Corruption in developing countries*. London: George Allen & Unwin.
Wu, C. L., & Huang, C. (2004). Politics and judiciary verdicts on vote-buying litigation in Taiwan. *Asian Survey*, *44*(5), 755–770.
Wurfel, D. (1988). *Filipino politics: Development and decay*. Ithaca: Cornell University Press.
Yahuda, M. (1996). *Hong Kong: China's challenge*. London: Routledge.
Yanaga, C. (1956). *Japanese people and politics*. New York: Wiley.
Yanaga, C. (1968). *Big business in Japanese politics*. New Haven: Yale University Press.
Yang, S. C. (1995). An analysis of South Korea's political process and party politics. In: J. Cotton (Ed.), *Politics and policy in the new Korean state: From Roh Tae-Woo to Kim Young-Sam* (pp. 6–34). Melbourne: Longman Australia Pty Ltd, chap. 2.
Yao, R. (1974). The emergence of a new order. *Far Eastern Economic Review*, *85*(35), 28.
Yap, S., Lim, R., & Leong, W. K. (2009). *Men in white: The untold story of Singapore's ruling political party*. Singapore: Singapore Press Holdings.
Yayama, T. (1990). The Recruit scandal: Learning from the causes of corruption. *Journal of Japanese Studies*, *16*(Winter), 93–114.
*Yonhap News*. (2011). January 5.
Yoong, S. W. (1972). Some aspects of corruption. *National Youth Leadership Training Institute Journal* (January), 54–59.
Young, K. R. (1990). Middle bureaucrats, middle peasants, middle class? The extra-urban dimension. In: R. Tanter & K. Young (Eds), *The politics of middle class Indonesia* (pp. 147–166). Clayton: Centre of Southeast Asian Studies, Monash University, chap. 15.
Zainun, B. (1982). Effective and efficient utilization of civil service working time: Indonesian case. *Indian Journal of Public Administration*, *28*(3), 452–460.
Ziemba, W. T., & Schwartz, S. L. (1992). *Power Japan: How and why the Japanese economy works*. Chicago: Probus Publishing Company.

# AUTHOR INDEX

# SUBJECT INDEX

RECEIVED
AUG 2 2 2011
Golden Gate University, Univ. Library
536 Mission St., San Francisco, CA 94105